943.053092

Frederick the Great

WATERFORD CITY AND COUNTY WITHDRAWN LIBRARIES

TIM BLANNING

Frederick the Great
King of Prussia

ALLEN LANE
an imprint of
PENGUIN BOOKS

ALLEN LANE

UK | USA | Canada | Ireland | Australia
India | New Zealand | South Africa

Allen Lane is part of the Penguin Random House group of companies
whose addresses can be found at global.penguinrandomhouse.com.

First published 2015
001

Copyright © Tim Blanning, 2015

The moral right of the author has been asserted

Set in 10.5/14 pt Sabon LT Std
Typeset by Jouve (UK), Milton Keynes
Printed in Great Britain by Clays Ltd, St Ives plc

A CIP catalogue record for this book is available from the British Library

ISBN: 978–1–846–14182–9

www.greenpenguin.co.uk

MIX
Paper from
responsible sources
FSC
www.fsc.org FSC® C018179

Penguin Random House is committed to a
sustainable future for our business, our readers
and our planet. This book is made from Forest
Stewardship Council® certified paper.

For Nicky, Tom, Lucy and Harry

Contents

List of Illustrations

1. Frederick William I, *Self-portrait*, 1737. Stiftung Preußische Schlösser und Gärten, Berlin-Brandenburg. Photo: © SPSG / Fotothek (Roland Handrick)
2. Wusterhausen Hunting Lodge, Brandenburg. Photo: Clemensfranz
3. Francesco Carlo Rusca *or* Georg Lisiewski, *Crown Prince Frederick with his brothers Ferdinand, August Wilhelm and Henry*, 1737. Stiftung Preußische Schlösser und Gärten, Berlin-Brandenburg. Photo: © SPSG / Fotothek (Klaus G. Bergmann)
4. The château at Rheinsberg, 1740. Engraving from Friedrich Ekel, *Plans et Vues du Château, du Jardin et de la Ville de Reinsberg* (Berlin: 1773)
5. The château at Schönhausen. Engraving by Schwarz, 1787. Photo: © ullsteinbild / TopFoto
6. Jean-Étienne Liotard, *Francesco Algarotti*, 1745. Photo: © Rijksmuseum, Amsterdam
7. Carl Friedrich Fecheim's set for Act III of Frederick's opera *Montezuma*, 1755. Stiftung Preußische Schlösser und Gärten, Berlin-Brandenburg. Photo: © SPSG / Fotothek (Wolfgang Pfauder)
8. *The Berlin Dessert Service*, manufactured by the Royal Porcelain Factory and presented by Frederick to Catherine the Great of Russia in 1772. The State Hermitage Museum, St Petersburg. Photo: © The State Hermitage Museum / Vladimir Terebenin
9. The 'Golden Gallery' in the Charlottenburg Palace. Stiftung Preußische Schlösser und Gärten, Berlin-Brandenburg. Photo: © SPSG / Fotothek (Leo Seidel)

22. E. Henne after Daniel Chodowiecki, *The Dispatch of Dr Aprill when he notified the Prussian ambassador Baron von Plotho of the Imperial declaration of outlawry*, 1780. From Gustav Berthold Volz, *Friedrich der Große im Spiegel seiner Zeit*, vol. 2 (Berlin: 1926)

23. Bernhard Rode, *Allegory on the Foundation of the League of Princes by Frederick the Great*, 1786. Gemäldegalerie, Staatliche Museen zu Berlin. Photo: © 2015 Scala, Florence/bpk, Bildagentur für Kunst, Kultur und Geschichte, Berlin (Jörg P. Anders)

24. Vivat ribbons, made in celebration of Frederick's birthday, 1759. Photo: akg-images

25. Heinrich Franke, *Frederick the Great*, 1764. Stiftung Preußische Schlösser und Gärten, Berlin-Brandenburg. Photo: © SPSG / Fotothek (Jörg P. Anders)

26. Johann Friedrich Bolt after Johann Gottfried Schadow, *Frederick the Great Victorious at the Battle of Rossbach*, 1801. Handschriftenabteilung, Staatsbibliothek, Berlin SMPK

27. Christian Daniel Rauch, Equestrian statue of Frederick the Great on Unter den Linden, Berlin, unveiled 1851. Photo: Maximilian Weinzierl / Alamy

28. Bartolomeo Verona, *The Interior of the Cathedral of St Hedwig, Berlin*, c. 1780. Kunstbibliothek, Staatliche Museen zu Berlin. Photo: © 2015 Scala, Florence/bpk, Bildagentur für Kunst, Kultur und Geschichte, Berlin

29. Vincenzo Vangelisti, *The Scales of Frederick*, 1780. Kupferstichkabinett, Berlin SMPK

30. Olaf Thiede, *Reconstruction of the Pisang House at Sanssouci*, 2011. Stiftung Preußische Schlösser und Gärten, Berlin-Brandenburg. Photo: © SPSG

31. E. Henne after Daniel Chodowiecki, *Frederick the Great in his last illness on the Terrace of Sanssouci*. From Gustav Berthold Volz, *Friedrich der Große im Spiegel seiner Zeit*, vol. 3 (Berlin: 1926)

32. Frederick's death-mask, taken on the day of his death by Johann Eckstein, photographed in 1913. Formerly Monbijou Palace, Berlin. Photo: akg-images.

List of Maps

The Holy Roman Empire

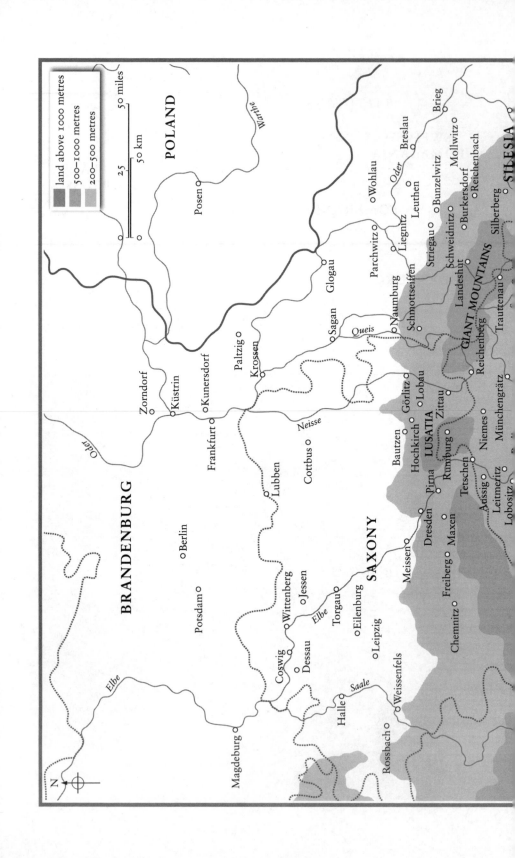

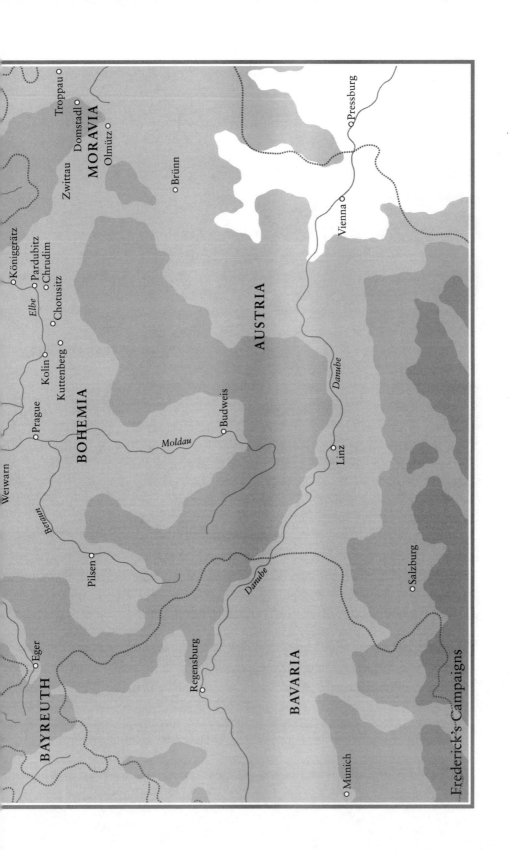
Frederick's Campaigns

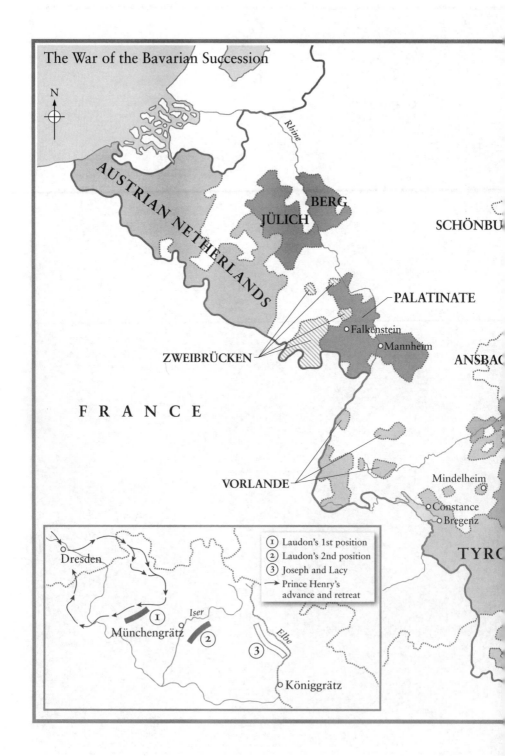

The War of the Bavarian Succession

N

AUSTRIAN NETHERLANDS

Rhine

BERG

JÜLICH

SCHÖNBU

PALATINATE

oFalkenstein

oMannheim

ANSBAC

ZWEIBRÜCKEN

FRANCE

VORLANDE

Mindelheim

oConstance

oBregenz

TYRO

Dresden

① Laudon's 1st position
② Laudon's 2nd position
③ Joseph and Lacy
→ Prince Henry's
   advance and retreat

Iser

Münchengrätz

①

②

③

Elbe

oKöniggrätz

Territories of the Monarchy
The Palatinate
Bavaria
Zweibrücken
Austrian gain from Bavaria 1779

PRUSSIA

oBerlin

POLAND

SAXONY

Elbe

oDresden

Münchengrätz

Königgrätz o

YREUTH

Prague

Neustadt o

GALICIA

UPPER
PALATINATE

BOHEMIA

MORAVIA

Teschen

Regensburg

PASSAU

OWER BAVARIA

AVARIA

ER BAVARIA

AUSTRIA

INNVIERTEL

Vienna o

Munich

Danube

Reichenhall o

SALZBURG

STYRIA

HUNGARY

ENICE

Introduction

In his winter quarters at Freiberg in Saxony on 28 January 1760 Frederick II, King in Prussia since 1740 and already enjoying the sobriquet 'the Great', had a nightmare, which he recounted to his Swiss secretary, Henri de Catt, when he awoke. He had dreamed that he had been arrested on the orders of his father, King Frederick William I, and was about to be carried off to the grim fortress of Magdeburg on the river Elbe. When he asked his sister what he had done to deserve it, she replied that it was because he did not love their father enough. Although he tried to protest that this was not true, he was taken away in a tumbril.[1] As we shall see, this was an understandable shriek from the subconscious mind at what was probably his darkest hour.* During the previous campaign he had come within a whisker of total defeat at the hands of his enemies at the battle of Kunersdorf (12 August 1759) on the river Oder, a disaster compounded by his own obstinate folly in allowing the Austrians to force the capitulation of a substantial Prussian corps at Maxen in Saxony three months later. Ill, exhausted, depressed and despairing, Frederick could not even find solace in an untroubled night's sleep.

That the ghost who came to haunt him was paternal was no accident. So deep was the imprint bludgeoned into Frederick by his terrifying father that it could never be erased. One episode, from the summer of 1730, when Frederick was eighteen, will illustrate their relationship. He had spent the morning, as usual, on the parade ground, his body encased in a tight uniform and tight boots, his hair crimped close to his scalp and gathered in a pigtail. Released after

* See below, pp. 41–4.

lunch, he could retire to his private apartment in the royal palace, where the virtuoso flautist Johann Joachim Quantz was waiting. Frederick had made his acquaintance at Dresden two years earlier on a visit to the sybaritic court of Augustus 'the Strong', King of Poland and Elector of Saxony. Frederick's doting mother, Queen Sophia Dorothea, had then provided the necessary funds to bring Quantz to Prussia twice a year to give him tuition. This all had to be kept strictly secret from the king, however, for he regarded anything smacking of high culture as 'effeminate'. Out of the royal gaze Frederick could shed the military uniform he found so distasteful and slip into something more comfortable – a sumptuous red silk dressing-gown covered in gold brocade – could let his hair down both literally and metaphorically and turn to music-making. This agreeable *après-midi d'une flûte* was rudely interrupted when Frederick's intimate friend Lieutenant Hans Hermann von Katte burst in with the warning that the king, suspecting that something effeminate was going on, was on his way upstairs and on the warpath. Quantz was bundled into a closet together with the instruments and the sheet music, the dressing-gown was discarded, the uniform pulled on again. When he arrived puffing and panting, the short and stout Frederick William was not deceived, especially as Frederick had had no time to remove the modish chignon in which his hair was arranged. Although the hiding-place of Quantz and Katte was missed, the offending clothes were soon located and thrown straight on the fire. A cache of French-language books was confiscated and sent off to be sold.[2]

Although this was only one of many humiliations inflicted on the crown prince, it may have been the last straw, for almost immediately afterwards he tried to run away from Prussia to England, taking advantage of a journey with his father to the Rhineland.* That ended in disaster. Although Frederick William did not carry out his threat to have his son and heir executed for desertion, he did make him witness the beheading of his accomplice, friend and possible lover Lieutenant von Katte. A long and very arduous process of rehabilitation followed, punctuated by further acts of brutal degradation. Relief was obtained only when Frederick performed what he saw as the ultimate

* See below, pp. 39–40.

act of submission – marriage. Not to love a bride in an age of arranged marriages was normal; to make a secret vow to put her aside as soon as the parental match-maker died was more unusual. Frederick objected to his wife because she was unintellectual, a devout Christian and his father's choice. It is also likely that a more fundamental objection was her sex.

Partial relief was upgraded to total release when Frederick William I died in 1740. At the age of twenty-eight, Frederick could now set about his psychological rehabilitation. This he did in three ways. Firstly, he deployed the very considerable financial assets inherited from his father to create for himself a comfortable, not to say luxurious, material environment. He built an opera house, enlarged two palaces and commissioned a new one; expanded his musical establishment; bought clothes, pictures, books, porcelain, snuff-boxes and other *objets d'art*, many of which he lavished on his male friends; and generally turned his father's Sparta into Athens (or even Babylon).* Secondly, he gathered around him a French-speaking intelligentsia to provide him with intellectual stimulation and to serve as an audience for his wit, philosophical disquisitions, literary creations and musical performances. The ambience of this *cercle intime* was both homosocial and homoerotic and, for Frederick himself, probably homosexual too. This aspect of his life should not be seen as something peripheral. As he himself made plain,† this cultural self-fashioning was central to his identity, aspiration and achievement.

It was also intimately related to his third route to repairing the damage inflicted by his father: to do what the latter desired most, but *to do it better*. This should not be seen as a separate category: the cultural and the power-political advanced not so much in tandem as dialectically, the one feeding off the other. It meant the assertion of the rights of the Hohenzollern family against the rival Wettins of Saxony, Wittelsbachs of Bavaria or Habsburgs of Austria, and the elevation of Prussia to great-power status. Frederick William I had forged the weapons but had been too timid to make use of them. His son would

---

* Had he lived to witness it, Frederick William would probably have called it 'Sodom and Gomorrah'.
† See below, p. 351.

prove he was more of a man than his father by supplying the missing audacity, resolution and endurance. If only Frederick William could have been present when he invaded Silesia in 1740 or routed the French at Rossbach and the Austrians at Leuthen in 1757! In a sense he was, even if only in Frederick's subconscious mind. Six months after the nightmare recounted to de Catt in January 1760, he dreamed of his father again. By this time, the desperate military situation had been stabilized. When the dream began, Frederick was at Strassburg with the Austrian Field Marshal Daun. He was then suddenly transported to the palace of Charlottenburg near Berlin where his father was waiting for him, together with his most trusted general, Prince Leopold of Anhalt-Dessau. 'Have I done well?' asked Frederick. 'Yes,' said Frederick William. 'Then I am content,' replied Frederick. 'Your approval is worth more to me than that of everyone else in the universe.'[3]

Frederick was on the throne for forty-six years and was exceptionally active in all spheres, at home and abroad. To view his reign as a prolonged exercise in therapy would of course be absurdly reductionist. Many and powerful were the constraints and influences operating on him. Indeed, his life could be said to be a perfect illustration of Marx's dictum that 'Men make their own history, but they do not make it as they please.' Obviously we shall never know how Frederick might have turned out if his father had been understanding, loving and supportive. On the other hand, there was no even trajectory from 1740 to 1786. This was not a steady-state universe; rather there was one big bang, the explosion occurring less than a year after his accession when he took the decision to seize the Austrian province of Silesia. To put it simply, he began by robbing an apparently defensive woman and spent the rest of his life trying to hang on to his booty, a herculean effort which coloured all his foreign and domestic policies and actions. So much flowed from that primal act that his state of mind following the prolonged trauma of adolescence and early manhood is a legitimate, not to say essential, dimension to an understanding of his amazing life.

PART I

The Sufferings and Greatness of Frederick

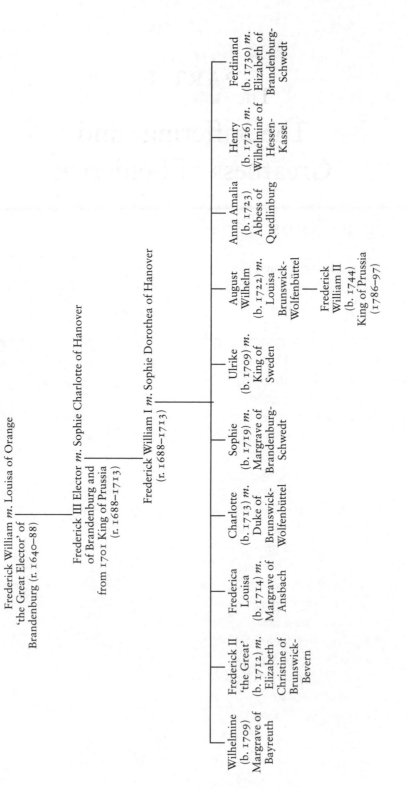

Frederick's Family Tree

Frederick William *m.* Louisa of Orange
'the Great Elector' of
Brandenburg (r. 1640–88)

Frederick III Elector *m.* Sophie Charlotte of Hanover
of Brandenburg and
from 1701 King of Prussia
(r. 1688–1713)

Frederick William I *m.* Sophie Dorothea of Hanover
(r. 1688–1713)

Wilhelmine
(b. 1709)
Margrave of
Bayreuth

Frederick II
'the Great'
(b. 1712) *m.*
Elizabeth
Christine of
Brunswick-
Bevern

Frederica
Louisa
(b. 1714) *m.*
Margrave of
Ansbach

Charlotte
(b. 1713) *m.*
Duke of
Brunswick-
Wolfenbüttel

Sophie
(b. 1719) *m.*
Margrave of
Brandenburg-
Schwedt

Ulrike
(b. 1709) *m.*
King of
Sweden

August
Wilhelm
(b. 1722) *m.*
Louisa
Brunswick-
Wolfenbüttel

Anna Amalia
(b. 1723)
Abbess of
Quedlinburg

Henry
(b. 1726) *m.*
Wilhelmine of
Hessen-
Kassel

Ferdinand
(b. 1730) *m.*
Elizabeth of
Brandenburg-
Schwedt

Frederick
William II
(b. 1744)
King of Prussia
(1786–97)

I

The Inheritance

THE LANDS OF THE HOHENZOLLERNS

'Apart from Libya, there are few states that can equal ours when it comes to sand,' wrote Frederick to Voltaire early in 1776, adding later the same year in his *Account of the Prussian Government* that it was 'poor and with scarcely any resources'.[1] Not for nothing was Frederick's core territory Brandenburg known as the 'sandbox of the Holy Roman Empire'. This was a land of thin soil thinly populated, where lakes alternated with heaths, bogs with moors. Frederick told d'Alembert that the good people of Aachen had come to believe that their foul-tasting mineral water represented the summit of God's creation, in the same way that the Jews worshipped the mud of Jerusalem, but as for himself, he could never work up the same sort of enthusiasm for the Prussian equivalent: sand.[2]

This repeated denigration was, of course, fishing for compliments. 'If I could do all this with so little, what might I have done if I had had the population of France or the riches of England?' was his unspoken question. It was all greatly overdone. Much of the soil of Brandenburg may have been infertile, but at least it was not mountainous. Across its featureless landscape wound rivers wide and slow-flowing, well suited for transportation in an age when roads were dust bowls when the sun shone and glutinous pits when the rains came. This was a natural gift to which Frederick's predecessors had given a generous helping hand. During the 1660s, for example, his great-grandfather, Frederick William 'The Great Elector', had completed the 'Müllrose canal', begun back in 1558, to allow shipping to cross from the Oder to the Spree and Berlin, and from there via the Havel to the Elbe and the North Sea.[3] As his Austrian enemies slogged their way up hill and down dale, how they must have envied the Prussians the waterways that allowed them to move men and matériel so easily.

In any case, the Hohenzollern possessions were much more than just Brandenburg. In the far west, on the Dutch frontier, was the duchy of Cleves, sitting astride the Rhine, together with the adjacent county of Mörs. The latter included the town of Krefeld, home to a large community of Mennonites and their flourishing textile manufactories. On the right (eastern) bank of the Rhine was the county of Mark, bisected by the river Ruhr, which eventually gave its name to the most industrialized region of continental Europe. Also in fertile Westphalia were the counties of Ravensberg, Tecklenburg and Lingen and the principality of Minden. Further east, immediately to the south of Brandenburg, were the principality of Halberstadt and the duchy of Magdeburg. The city of Magdeburg on the river Elbe boasted one of Germany's biggest cathedrals and strongest fortifications.[4] This was a famously rich and fertile province and any sand to be found there was used for building. Attending a peasant wedding outside the town just before the end of the Seven Years War, Count Lehndorff and the 300-odd other guests sat down to a feast of 42 boiled capons, 2 steers, 14 calves, carp worth 150 talers, all washed down with wine and brandy to the value of another 150 talers.[5]

Away to the north-east of Brandenburg was the duchy of Pomerania, with its long Baltic coastline and the excellent port of Stettin at the mouth of the river Oder. In the opinion of Frederick's demanding father, Frederick William I, this was 'a good fertile province'.[6] Further east still, separated by a broad stretch of territory ruled by Poland, was East Prussia, outside the Holy Roman Empire and on the very edge of German-speaking Europe. Although decimated by plague between 1708 and 1710, which killed around a third of the population, and fought over repeatedly during the Great Northern War of 1700–1721, the province had then enjoyed a sustained revival. Waves of refugee immigrants from oppressed or overpopulated parts of southern and western Germany, including the 17,000 Protestants expelled by the Archbishop of Salzburg in 1732, increased the population by 160,000 to reach 600,000 by 1740.[7] Thanks partly to the need to offer new settlers favourable terms, there was a surprisingly high proportion of completely free peasant holdings, comprising around a fifth of the total.[8]

THE ROYAL DOMAINS

These bits and pieces of territory strung out across a thousand miles of the North European Plain had been acquired at different times and in different circumstances.[9] They were held together by four threads of varying thickness: dynasty, religion, language and membership of the Holy Roman Empire of the German Nation (with the exception of East Prussia, which had been a fief of the Polish crown until 1660). Of these, the most material link was spiritual, for the secularization of Church property following the reception of the Reformation had given the Electors of Brandenburg a colossal domain far in excess of that enjoyed by any other European ruler. Unlike the spendthrift Tudor and Stuart monarchs of England, the Hohenzollerns had held on to their windfall and had even increased it. Frederick William I issued a standing order to his officials to purchase at regular intervals any large estate in the duchy of Magdeburg worth between 100,000 and 150,000 talers that came on the market.[10] In the course of his reign (1713–40) he spent 8,000,000 talers on new acquisitions and had doubled domain income to c. 3,500,000 talers a year.[11]

To say that the king was the largest landowner in his state gives only a weak impression of his ascendancy. These domains covered no less than a quarter of his territory, including about a third of the cultivable area, providing some 50 per cent of the total revenue in 1740.[12] Only about a dozen estates, most of them studs, were administered directly. Most were leased by auction to about 1,100 to 1,500 tenants for periods of six to twelve years in units of about 2,000 acres. The tenant-in-chief, who not only had to make the highest bid but also provide evidence of financial security, retained at most two or three farms, subletting the remainder, along with the mills, breweries, distilleries, brickworks and other royal property he had leased.[13] Perhaps surprisingly, these officials, known as *Beamte*, were all commoners, indeed nobles were expressly excluded from the bidding process.[14]

THE JUNKERS

In an agrarian world, land is status, land is power. As we shall see, it was this degree of control which allowed Frederick to direct agricultural development with a precision denied less well-endowed sovereigns.* It also elevated the Hohenzollerns to a lofty eminence from which they towered over even their biggest magnates. There were very few of the latter anyway and certainly no equivalents of the French or English grandees who lived in palaces like the princes they were. In Brandenburg and Pomerania there were no magnates at all.[15] Only in East Prussia did the Dohnas, Finckensteins and Schliebens live in some style on large estates, but even there the average size of the 420 noble estates in the province was only 667.5 acres.[16] The origin of the word used to designate a Prussian noble – 'Junker' – is revealing, deriving as it does from '*junk herr*' or 'young lord', the younger son sent off from the German interior in the Middle Ages to seek his fortune in the wild lands of the east.[17]

Fame and fortune often proved elusive for the migrants. Over the centuries, however, they became the beneficiaries of a distinctive institution based on land ownership which became established in the lands to the east of the river Elbe. This was the manorial estate, combining both social control and economic domination. Over the peasants on his estate the Junker not only exercised judicial authority and police powers but also conscripted their labour to till his soil, milk his cows, tend his flocks, transport his goods, work in his breweries or mills and even serve in his household. He was also in charge of the community's religious, social and educational facilities (where they existed). His permission was required – and usually had to be purchased – when the peasant wished to marry, choose a different profession or leave the estate. In return, the Junker provided the peasant with a plot of land and was obliged to provide assistance in the event of sickness or old age.[18] Needless to say, not all of these conditions existed in equal measure in all places all of the time. In some places there were peasants who were completely free and independent landowners, or enjoyed heredi-

* See below, pp. 412–15.

tary tenure, or were paid wages for additional services.[19] Nevertheless, this manorial system gave the Prussian Junkers a distinctive identity and control of local government.

In common with many parts of the Holy Roman Empire, and indeed Europe, they also enjoyed representation at a provincial level through their control of the assemblies confusingly known as 'Estates' (*Landstände*). Aided by their superior creditworthiness, the Estates had achieved considerable influence on both financial and judicial affairs. During the long reign of the energetic Frederick William the Great Elector (1640–88), however, their role had been reduced. The creation of a standing army, a central authority – the Privy Council – independent of the Estates, and an effective fiscal system combined to relocate sovereignty in the Hohenzollern territories.[20] Whether this represented the establishment of an 'absolutist' system is neither here nor there. What it did mean was that decision-making at a national level was now firmly in the hands of one man and a relatively high degree of integration had been achieved in both civil and military administration.[21] A crucial date was 1653 and the agreement between the Elector and the Estates of Brandenburg known as the '*Rezess*'. This used to be presented as a shameful deal between ruler and nobles, with the former being given control of the centre in return for ceding the landowners control of their peasants. The current view is that the Junkers gained little or nothing they did not have already, whereas the Elector achieved everything he wanted.[22]

Even if 'compromise' is not quite the appropriate label for the *Rezess* of 1653, relations between the Elector and his nobles were always more cooperative than confrontational. Every now and again the stick had to be brandished, as in 1672 when the recalcitrant East Prussian noble Christian Ludwig von Kalckstein was abducted from Warsaw and executed.[23] Even more brutal was Frederick William I's treatment of another East Prussian Junker, Councillor von Schlubhut, accused of misappropriating money intended for the relief of the Salzburg refugees. Interrogated by the king in person when on a visit to Königsberg in 1731, von Schlubhut made light of the offence, condescendingly promising to pay the money back. His further observation, when told that he deserved to be hanged – 'It is not the done thing to execute a Prussian nobleman' – showed how little he knew his sovereign. Frederick William had a gallows erected outside Schlubhut's office the same night and hanged him from it the next day, but not before first attending church and listening attentively to a sermon on mercy ('Blessed are the merciful: for they shall obtain mercy' – *Matthew* 5:7).[24]

Frederick William had a generally low opinion of his nobles. In the 'political testament' he wrote for his son in 1722, he denounced those of East Prussia as 'false and sly', those of the Altmark, Magdeburg and Halberstadt as 'very bad and disobedient' (especially the Schulenburgs, Alvenslebens and Bismarcks) and those of Cleves and Mark as 'stupid oxen, as malicious as the Devil and very attached to their privileges'. On the other hand, he thoroughly approved of the Pomeranian Junkers ('as good as gold, a bit argumentative but obedient if spoken to properly') and those of the Neumark, Uckermark and Mittelmark regions of Brandenburg.[25] The acid test was their willingness to send their sons for army training. In the past, they had shown little enthusiasm for a military career and, when they did, they preferred Dutch, Danish or Polish service. Frederick William soon put a stop to that, having registers compiled of all young nobles between the ages of twelve and eighteen. If they were backward in coming forward, as they often were in East Prussia, he despatched armed posses to round them up. By 1722 his new academy at Berlin had more than 300 cadets.[26] As he freely admitted, his motive was aimed as much at social disciplining as at military efficiency.[27]

Life at a Prussian cadet school probably compared unfavourably even with life at English boarding schools, but it did have its compensations, including – as in the latter institutions – a good education. Frederick William promised reluctant parents that their sons would be taught reading, writing, mathematics, the French language, geography, history, fencing, dancing and riding, would be well housed and well fed and – most important of all, in his view – would be brought up to be God-fearing Christians.[28] They were also, of course, guaranteed employment in the Prussian army. This was very welcome, given the relative poverty of most Junker families. Only very few could afford to allow even the eldest son to live on the estate in a manner befitting a nobleman. Denied access to ecclesiastical benefices by their Protestantism, they found an austere but welcome substitute in the officer corps. Frederick William I more than doubled the size of the army, increasing the officer corps to 3,000.[29]

The early years for the young Junkers were undeniably difficult. No matter how ancient their pedigree, they had to start as ill-paid ensigns and could barely survive without assistance from their families. But promotion to the rank of captain and control of a company's finances brought relative comfort; further promotion to a colonelcy and a regiment brought relative riches.[30] Of the 1,600 Junker boys who attended the Berlin cadet school between 1717 and 1740, more than 90 per cent were commissioned and forty became generals during Frederick the Great's reign.[31] No wonder that Frederick William I admired the Pomeranians so much: as early as 1724 the nobility there consisted almost entirely of serving or retired officers and there was not one family in the province without at least one serving member.[32]

A Junker leaving military service could find alternative employment in the civilian administration, most notably as a *Landrat* (district councillor). This was the most important post in the Prussian system because the eighty-odd *Landräte* formed the vital interface between central government and local landowners. It was they who directed all the important business, supervising the collection of taxes, providing for troops moving through their districts, regulating relations between peasants and their lords, promoting agricultural improvement, preventing or mitigating natural disasters, collecting information and publicizing government decrees.[33] They represented both their fellow-Junkers and the ruler, for they were appointed by the latter but were proposed by the former. Even if Frederick William I often ignored their recommendation, this was always a system founded on cooperation. That goes a long way in explaining the effectiveness of the Prussian administration: what the centre directed was often actually put into practice. It was no accident that the most efficient local government in Europe was to be found in England and Prussia, for in both it was based on partnership between the sovereign at the centre and the notables in the localities. If the English Justices of the Peace were 'partners in oligarchy',[34] the Prussian *Landräte* were 'partners in autocracy'.

AUTOCRACY

'Autocracy', not 'oligarchy' or 'aristocracy', for Frederick William I was far more imperious than his Hanoverian relations. Neither of the first two English Georges would have written: 'I am going to ruin the Junkers' authority, I shall achieve my objective and anchor my sovereignty like a rock of bronze.'[35] Frederick William scribbled those words in the margin of a decree enforcing taxation on the nobles of East Prussia. This was his preferred way of doing business. Not for him discussions with a cabinet of ministers or a panel of experts: what he liked was a written report to which he alone added the decision.

This highly personalized form of decision-making was combined with a hierarchical and bureaucratized form of implementation. Above the *Landrat* were the provincial War and Domains Chambers, which in turn answered to the General Directory in Berlin, all staffed by professionals. Unlike their equivalents in most other European countries, the Prussian officials could neither buy nor inherit their positions. The same applied to the urban equivalent of the *Landrat*, the *Steuerrat* (fiscal councillor), who exercised similar powers in groups of six to twelve towns.[36] For both offices Frederick William introduced a system of in-service training for probationers attached to the provincial chambers, complete with examinations to weed out the unfit. Also surprisingly forward-looking was the establishment of chairs of 'cameralism' (applied political science) at the universities of Halle and Frankfurt an der Oder in 1727, with specific instructions that their main task was the training of officials.[37] It was during his reign that something approximating to a modern civil service emerged: mixed in terms of social origin, meritocratic, non-venal, salaried, hierarchical, academically trained, and appointed, directed and monitored by the central authorities. Many are the qualifications that need to be made about how this system worked in practice, for nepotism, corruption, obstruction, incompetence – and all the other vices inseparable from public employment in any age – were certainly to be found.[38] Nevertheless, in 1740 Frederick inherited from his father an administrative system more efficient than anything possessed by his rivals. In the land of the blind, the one-eyed man is king, as Erasmus put it.

THE ARMY

The test that really mattered was its ability to sustain a standing army. Prussia not only had a big one, it came to be synonymous with militarism. In the eighteenth century, however, this status was of recent origin. In 1610, when the Elector Johann Sigismund instructed his militia to conduct training exercises, the timorous soldiers declined on the ground that firing their guns might frighten their women.[39] Alas, this pleasing sense of priorities did not serve Brandenburg well when the Thirty Years War erupted eight years later. For a state stretched out across the North German Plain with no natural frontiers, security could only come from a strong army. The attempt by the Elector Georg Wilhelm (r. 1619–40) to stay out of the conflict ended in disaster. In 1630 he sent an emissary to his brother-in-law, King Gustavus Adolphus of Sweden, who had just landed in Pomerania, asking him to respect Brandenburg's neutrality. Gustavus Adolphus replied tartly that in an existential struggle between good and evil (Protestant and Catholic), non-commitment was not an option.[40] Georg Wilhelm's great-great-grandson, Frederick, provided a withering account of this episode in his *Memoirs of the House of Brandenburg*, as he described how the Elector's ministers bleated pathetically 'What can we do? They've got all the big guns' as they counselled surrender to the Swedes.[41] During the last two decades of the war, Brandenburg was repeatedly fought over by the various combatants, losing between 40 and 50 per cent of its entire population.[42]

Georg Wilhelm's son, Frederick William, who succeeded him in 1640 at the age of twenty, had learned the lesson that it was better to be predator than prey.* Later in his reign he observed to his chief minister Otto von Schwerin: 'I have experienced neutrality before; even under the most favourable conditions, you are treated badly. I have

---

* The limited range of first names employed by the Hohenzollerns – either Frederick or Frederick William – has naturally led to confusion. Frederick William 'the Great Elector' (1620–88) must not be confused with his grandson King Frederick William I (1688–1740). Even more miserly in their allocation of first names were the princes of Reuss of Thuringia, all of whose numerous sons were christened Henry.

vowed never to be neutral again as long as I live.'[43] By 1646 he had managed to scrape together an army of 8,000, which allowed him some sort of scope for independent action in the dog-days of the Thirty Years War.[44] His reward came in the final peace settlement. Although bitterly disappointed not to make good his claim to western Pomerania and the all-important mouth of the Oder, he did secure the impoverished eastern part, together with three secularized prince-bishoprics (Kammin, Halberstadt and Minden) and the reversion of the wealthy and strategically important archbishopric of Magdeburg, of which he eventually took possession in 1680.[45] Frederick William was now in a self-sustaining spiral: the more troops he had at his disposal, the more easily he could extract money from the Estates, and the more money he was able to extract, the more troops he was able to recruit. He was assisted by the decision of the Holy Roman Empire in 1654 that princes could raise taxes to maintain essential garrisons and fortifications.[46] By the time he died in 1688 he had a standing army of 31,000 at his disposal.[47]

It was also more securely under his command. Until late in his reign he had been obliged to rely on private warlords to supply him with troops. In 1672 General Georg von Derfflinger, who had been born in Austria and had served in several different armies, including the Swedish, declined an order from the Elector because his contract had not specified unconditional obedience.[48] Three years later, on 18 June 1675, Derfflinger was second-in-command to Frederick William at the battle of Fehrbellin, the first major victory won by a Brandenburg army solely through its own efforts. Although the numbers involved on each side were modest – 12,000–15,000 – its significance was recognized by contemporaries when they awarded Frederick William the sobriquet 'The Great Elector'. His great-grandson observed: 'He was praised by his enemies, blessed by his subjects; and posterity dates from that famous day the subsequent elevation of the house of Brandenburg.'[49]

Although during the next three years the Great Elector's army pushed the Swedes out of Germany, it brought him scant reward when peace was made. Real power rested in the hands of the big battalions, and they were commanded by the French King Louis XIV, who intervened at the negotiating table to rescue his Swedish allies. All that

Frederick William had to show for five years of successful campaigning was a modest frontier adjustment and the cession by the Swedes of their right to a share in the tolls of the Brandenburg part of Pomerania. All the conquered territory had to be handed back. On a medal struck to mark the peace, the disappointed Great Elector had inscribed Dido's lines from Virgil's *Aeneid* addressed to the as-yet-unborn Hannibal – *exoriare aliquis nostris ex ossibus ultor* (may you arise from my bones, you unknown avenger).[50] Rather oddly, Frederick the Great, who was to play Hannibal to Frederick William's Dido, did not mention this in his account of the episode.

For all the importance assigned to the Great Elector by his successors, Brandenburg was still only a second- or third-rate power when he died in 1688. It was only towards the very end that he managed to assert sole control of his army and he was still dependent on foreign subsidies to wage war.[51] His observation that 'alliances are good but one's own forces are better' referred to an aspiration not an achievement.[52] The same could be said of his son Frederick III (who dropped two digits to become Frederick I when he gained the royal title of 'King in Prussia' in 1701). It used to be thought that the Hohenzollern rulers of Brandenburg-Prussia could be divided into two types – the exceptionally gifted, and the dim and/or unstable. It was Frederick III/I's misfortune to be sandwiched between two high-achievers (Frederick William the Great Elector and Frederick William I) and also to become the target of some of his grandson Frederick the Great's most scathing comments. Yet he steered his state safely through the very choppy waters stirred up by the Nine Years War (1688–97), the Great Northern War (1700–1721) and the War of the Spanish Succession (1701–14). On occasions his army intervened effectively, not least at the battle of Blenheim in 1704, where it played an important role in helping the Duke of Marlborough and Prince Eugene win a crushing victory over the French. By 1709 Frederick had increased his army to 44,000, the largest in the Holy Roman Empire after Austria's.[53]

In that year it was also present in strength at the battle of Malplaquet when Marlborough and Eugene again defeated the French in the bloodiest engagement of the War of the Spanish Succession. Leading the Prussian contingent were two men who were to make a decisive contribution to Prussia's military elevation: the Crown Prince Frederick

William and General Prince Leopold of Anhalt-Dessau. Despite, or perhaps because of, the carnage, which inflicted 25 per cent casualties on the victors, the former always maintained that the day of the battle – 11 September 1709 – had been the happiest of his life and he always celebrated the anniversary.[54] When he succeeded to the throne in 1713, he and Prince Leopold at once set about increasing the quantity and improving the quality of the army. By a combination of ferocious discipline and incessant drilling, it was turned into a responsive killing machine that could move rapidly across country and then deploy on the battlefield with unprecedented speed. Their innovations included: a metal ramrod, which allowed more rapid rates of fire; an improved bayonet, which was constantly at the ready; and quick-marching in step.[55] In his *History of My Own Times*, the main beneficiary of these reforms commented on his father's achievement: 'a Prussian battalion became a walking battery whose speed in reloading tripled its fire-power and so gave the Prussians an advantage of three to one'.[56] Their grasp of cavalry was much less sure. Frederick William's notorious obsession with very large soldiers meant that very large – and slow – horses had to be found for them: 'giants on elephants' was his son's dismissive comment.[57] This was based on first-hand experience, for when Frederick first took them to war in 1740, the Austrian cavalry found it all too easy to immobilize their opponents' gigantic but ponderous horses with one sabre slash to the head.[58] Also of dubious military value was Frederick William's obsession with recruiting giant soldiers for his Guards, which cost four times as much as any other regiment but never saw action.[59]

Overall the quality may have been impressive, the width was much less so. When he came to the throne in 1713, Frederick William could recruit from a total population of only around 1,600,000.[60] At once he abolished the notoriously inefficient militia system and resorted to a mixture of impressment at home and voluntary enlistment from abroad. The unpopularity of the former and the expense of the latter led to a major reform in 1733 by which the Prussian lands were divided into cantons of some 5,000 households, each assigned to a regiment for recruiting. All male children were inscribed on the regimental rolls at the age of ten. Although it was stated firmly that 'all inhabitants are born into the service of the country', numerous groups were exempted: peasant farmers and their eldest sons, immigrants, merchants, manufacturers, craftsmen and those in certain 'reserved occupations' such as seafaring.[61] Even so, a good quarter of the total population was inscribed on the cantonal lists and two thirds of the army could be raised from native resources.[62]

Combined with the relative efficiency of the fiscal and administrative system, this cantonal organization worked well enough to promote Prussia to something approaching the premier league of European military powers. In 1713 the peacetime strength of around 30,000 put the country on a par with Piedmont or Saxony; by 1740 the equivalent figure was 80,000, which outstripped Spain, the Dutch Republic or Sweden and brought it within striking distance of Austria. Frederick the Great commented in his *Political Testament* of 1768: 'these cantons are the pure substance of the state'.[63] Flattering sincerely by imitation, the Austrians followed their enemies' example, albeit with a long delay, and introduced cantonal recruiting in 1777.[64]

PIETISM

Not only did successive Electors and kings of Prussia learn to make the most of the modest human resources allocated by nature, they also contrived to enhance their quality. However fanciful it may sound, they both encouraged and benefited from a Prussian ethos of duty. At its heart was 'Pietism', a reform movement within Lutheranism which developed a tremendous impetus during the second half of the seventeenth century. Reacting against what they believed to be the ossification and formalism of the official Lutheran Church, the Pietists stressed the priesthood of all believers, the need for a born-again conversion experience and the priority of the 'inner light'. Dr Serenus Zeitblom in Thomas Mann's *Dr Faustus* summed up the Pietist outlook very well when he described the movement as 'a revolution of pious feelings and heavenly joy against a petrified orthodoxy from which not even a beggar would any longer want to accept a piece of bread'. Of all the German Protestant states, Brandenburg was the most receptive to Pietism. Since converting to Calvinism at the beginning of the seventeenth century, its rulers had had a vested interest in promoting harmony, at least between the various brands of Protestantism. Frederick William the Great Elector had instructed his son in his *Political Testament*: 'You must love the subjects entrusted to your care by God, and seek to further their welfare and interests, without regard to their form of religion.'[65] This tolerant attitude was fostered not only by tradition and conviction, but also by political interest. The need to repopulate territories devastated by the Thirty Years War dictated a relaxed attitude to the confessional affiliation of immigrants. So did the attachment of Brandenburg's chief rival for the leadership of Protestant Germany – Saxony – to Lutheran Orthodoxy. It was probably this latter consideration that prompted the creation of a new university at Halle in the recently acquired province of Magdeburg in 1694, to serve as a rival to the two adjacent Saxon universities of Wittenberg and Leipzig, both renowned for their adherence to strict orthodoxy.[66]

The dominant figure at Halle was August Hermann Francke (1663–1727), who had fallen foul of Orthodox Lutherans in Saxony. A remarkable combination of prophet and bureaucrat, he turned Pietism from a devotional pattern into an organized movement. On the one hand, he had personal experience of a desperate struggle for repentance, complete with all the fears of eternal damnation, culminating in an intense conversion, and brought to his mission all the enthusiasm born of certain conviction. On the other hand, he was an organizer of genius. King Frederick William I paid him the ultimate compliment (in his eyes) when he observed 'he carries God's blessing, for he can do more with two talers than I can with ten'.[67] Within a few years of taking up his position as pastor to the Halle suburb of Glaucha, Francke had created an extraordinary complex of institutions. For all their introspection and mysticism, the Pietists had a strong practical bent. Work was seen in a positive light, not just as a means of atonement but as a good in its own right. It was made a sacred duty for all believers, for constructive activity was the best means of overcoming sinful temptations, while practical charity was the best external sign of Christian virtue. In Francke's view, the idle and lazy were destined for hell-fire. In the Pietist canon, the poor did not deserve the kingdom of heaven.

Francke quickly put these principles into action. At the school attached to the orphanage he established with an anonymous wind-fall, his pupils were taught practical skills to equip them for a practical contribution to the community. The same orientation was given to the other educational establishments which were soon added, including an academy for young nobles, where the promotion of manufacturing and mining was high on the agenda, and a school for aspiring diplomats, where the emphasis was on modern languages. Of the numerous commercial enterprises founded, the most successful was a bookshop, which sent Pietist publications across the world in many different languages, and a pharmacy, 'the first producer of standardised branded medicaments on a commercial scale, able and anxious to sell a complete public-health kit for a city or province and marketing its wares by brochures in Latin, French, English, Dutch and Greek'.[68] By the time Francke died, he was presiding over one of the biggest building complexes in Europe, housing 2,200 children and a teaching staff of 167. His fame and faith had reached the four corners of the continent, if not the earth. He had arrived in Halle with nothing.

He would soon have left with nothing too, had not successive kings of Prussia come to his aid. The orthodox Lutherans of Brandenburg were just as much opposed to the Pietists as were their brethren in Saxony. Moreover, this hostility came not just from the clergy but also from the provincial Estates of the province of Magdeburg, whose representatives heartily disliked the levelling implications of the Pietist project. At all the moments that mattered, Francke and his successors were able to persuade their sovereigns that, far from posing a threat, the Pietists had a great deal to offer. It was a persuasive argument because it was true. They did help the Prussian state to solve one of its most pressing social problems, namely the poverty of soldiers' wives and dependants. They did provide an excellent practical education to thousands of Prussians. And they did inculcate ideals of duty, obedience and industry, to both nobles and commoners, soldiers and civilians. As Francke told Frederick William when the latter was still crown prince, a Pietist education produced for the state honest and obedient subjects in every class and walk of life.[69]

Although initially sceptical, Frederick William I was soon won over. A crucial influence was the Pietist General Dubislav Gneomar von Natzmer, who was appointed commander of the royal life-guards in

1713 and so saw his king on a daily basis.[70] When Francke succeeded in converting Prince Leopold of Anhalt-Dessau, the Pietist infiltration of the centre of power was complete.[71] In the course of his reign, Frederick William made sure that his army chaplains were Pietists, allowed the Pietists to take control of the University of Königsberg, and from 1717 made it obligatory for candidates for the (Lutheran) ministry to have studied theology for two years at Halle. In effect, he made Pietism the state religion.[72] Of course it would be absurd to suggest that Prussian soldiers were all clean-living, pure-speaking, God-fearing paragons, but there was more than a touch of Cromwell's Ironsides about them all the same, not least when they launched into psalms and chorales before and after battle.*

SAXONY

To be Protestant but tolerant was a sensible combination at a time when militant Catholicism was in the ascendant. The Austrian reconquest of Hungary after the failure of the Turkish siege of Vienna in 1683, followed swiftly by Louis XIV's forcible conversion or expulsion of the Huguenots, created intense alarm among German Protestants. They were already fearful because of the numerous apostasies of their rulers: between 1650 and 1750 there were at least thirty-one princely conversions to Catholicism.[73] The most spectacular occurred in 1697 in Saxony, the very heartland of the Lutheran Reformation, when the Elector Frederick Augustus (better known as 'Augustus the Strong') sought to facilitate his election as King of Poland by apostasy. His success in the ensuing contest appeared to pose a serious threat to Brandenburg-Prussia, for it matched quality with quantity: Saxony was economically and culturally the most advanced state in Central Europe, while the Polish-Lithuanian Commonwealth, now joined to it, covered around a million square kilometres and stretched from the Baltic almost to the Black Sea. In reality, Warsaw did not prove to be worth a Mass. Although the Electorate retained the nominal presidency of the Protestant members of

* See below, p. 224.

the Imperial Diet (the *corpus evangelicorum*), effective leadership now moved north to Berlin. It was a transfer made permanent when Augustus's son and successor also converted and married a Habsburg archduchess into the bargain.

There was much more to this than a confessional change. Nervously aware that they owed their Polish crown to a combination of bribery and diplomatic pressure enforced by Austria and Russia, both Augustus II (1697–1733) and Augustus III (1733–63) felt obliged to present themselves as every inch a king. What they lacked in military muscle they made up for in extravagant display. The result was the unfolding of 'the most dazzling court in Europe', the authoritative verdict of the peripatetic Baron Pöllnitz in 1729.[74] It boasted the best balls, pageants, opera and hunting to be found anywhere in the Empire outside Vienna. Augustus's ambition to make Dresden the Venice of the North, both the playground of choice for the elites and the economic entrepôt between East and West, went a long way to fulfilment. Some idea of the city's fabled beauty can be gained from Bernardo Bellotto's justly celebrated painting, with the dome of the Frauenkirche strongly reminiscent of Santa Maria della Salute in Venice.

This cultural climbing did pay dividends. The clearest sign that Augustus the Strong had thrust his way into the premier league of European sovereigns came in 1719 when his son and heir was married to the Habsburg Archduchess Maria Josepha, daughter of the late Emperor Joseph I. To celebrate the occasion, Augustus unleashed the full panoply of his court. Two years of preparations, which involved among other things the extension of the 'Zwinger', as the great representational arena next to the Electoral palace was known, and the construction of the largest opera house north of the Alps, reached a climax with a full month of festivities to greet the bride and bridegroom on their return from Vienna. The ceremonies can be followed with some precision, for Augustus was careful to have each one recorded in word and image and then broadcast to the world by brochure and engraving. Moreover, the marriage paid a recurring dividend for succeeding generations of the dynasty. His son succeeded him as King of Poland and, of his grandchildren, Maria Amalia married Charles III of Spain; Maria Anna married Maximilian III Joseph,

Elector of Bavaria; Maria Josepha married the Dauphin of France, and thus was the mother of Louis XVI; Albert married Maria Christina, daughter of the Empress Maria Theresa, and later became Governor of the Austrian Netherlands; Clemens Wenzeslaus became Prince-Bishop of Freising, Regensburg and Augsburg and Archbishop-Elector of Trier; and Kunigunde became Princess-Abbess of Thorn and Essen (where she could seek spiritual consolation for having been jilted by Joseph II). This list alone should be sufficient to remind us that dynastic politics supported by representational court culture could bring substantial benefits.[75]

Saxony-Poland was not exceptional. Augustus II's elevation to a royal throne was part of a 'wave of regalization'[76] that swept across the Holy Roman Empire in the second half of the seventeenth century. Partly this was due to the acquisition of imperial territory by foreign sovereigns – of part of Pomerania by Sweden or Holstein by Denmark, for example. Partly it was due to German princes succeeding to foreign thrones – the Duke of Zweibrücken to Sweden, for example. By far the most important, from the Prussian point of view, was the royalist ambition of the House of Brunswick-Lüneburg. Deftly exploiting Emperor Leopold's need for military assistance in his war against France, in 1692 Duke Ernst August had secured the dignity and title of 'Elector of Hanover'.[77] Simultaneously an even greater prize began to appear on the horizon, for his wife Sophia was a granddaughter of James I of England and thus the best claimant should the Protestant Stuart line fail. The death of Princess Anne's only surviving child, the Duke of Gloucester, in 1700, made this virtually certain, although it was not until 1714 that Sophia's son succeeded to the British throne as George I.

FROM ELECTORATE TO KINGDOM

What did a royal title matter? For contemporaries, the answer was: a very great deal. In an age when the representation of power was not carapace but core, regality was power. A king was sovereign, a status exemplified by his ability to make and unmake nobles. For a prince of the Holy Roman Empire, it was also a step towards complete independence. As the structure of the Holy Roman Empire often seems mysterious, especially to British or American readers, whose respective countries have been unified states since time out of mind, some account of its structure is now essential. It is best thought of as a 'composite state', comprising some 300 territories whose rulers enjoyed most but not all of the powers usually associated with a sovereign. They were bound together by the allegiance they owed to the emperor; their subjection to imperial law administered by the two imperial courts; and through representation in the *Reichstag* (Imperial Diet) at Regensburg. This Diet was divided into three colleges, the first comprising the nine Electors (Mainz, Trier, Cologne, Bohemia, Saxony, the Palatinate, Brandenburg, Bavaria and, after 1692, Hanover). The second and largest college was that of the princes, comprising thirty-four ecclesiastical princes, plus two collective votes shared by about forty monasteries and abbeys, and sixty secular princes, plus four collective votes shared by 100-odd imperial counts. The third college consisted of fifty-one 'Free Imperial Cities', the self-governing republics subject only to the authority of the emperor. The institutional structures had been fixed around 1500 but the world had moved on since then, divorcing power from appearance.[78] In the second half of the seventeenth century, it was the more important secular princes who proved the most dynamic, as the acquisition of royal titles demonstrated. Just staying still meant falling behind. If the Elector of Brandenburg had sat idly by as his Hanoverian and Saxon neighbours moved from the well of the hall to the top table, he would soon have found himself being jostled by lesser fry. It was well known that other princes, notably the Electors of Bavaria and the Palatinate, were also on the hunt for royal or even imperial titles. It was to avoid being overtaken that in the 1690s the Elector of Brandenburg Frederick III embarked on his own campaign. A sharp reminder of his subordinate status had been delivered by the peace negotiations at Rijswijk in 1697 when the Brandenburg envoy was excluded from the inner circle.[79]

As usual, it was the emperor's pressing need for men and money that gave him his chance. In November 1700 the promise of a contingent of 8,000 Brandenburg soldiers for the war about to get underway over the Spanish succession, plus promises of support in imperial politics, extracted the necessary approval. On 18 January 1701 the Elector Frederick III announced that henceforth he would be 'Frederick I King in Prussia': 'in Prussia' rather than 'of Prussia' because West Prussia remained under Polish suzerainty.[80] Prussia rather than Brandenburg was chosen for the title because it lay outside the Holy Roman Empire and was unquestionably a sovereign possession.

To assist credibility, Frederick went out of his way to ensure that the festivities attending his coronation in Königsberg, the capital of East Prussia, were worthy of the greatest sovereign. Thirty thousand horses were needed to pull the cavalcade of 1,800 carriages that took the court from Berlin to the coronation. His scarlet coronation robes were studded with diamond buttons costing 3,000 ducats each, while just the crowns created for himself and his queen exceeded the event's total budget. Anticipating Napoleon by more than a century, Frederick did the crowning himself, indeed it was only after the coronation ceremony had been performed in a room in Königsberg castle that the royal couple proceeded to the cathedral to be anointed by two bishops (one Calvinist, one Lutheran) specially appointed for the occasion.[81] On the day of his coronation the new king created the Order of the Black Eagle, to symbolize the unity of all the Hohenzollern territories.[82]

The profligacy of the coronation was both anticipated and followed by extravagant representational display, whose very excess revealed the *parvenu* quality of the Prussian crown. In the space of little more than twenty years, Frederick I turned Berlin from provincial backwater into a capital fit for a king. His father's cultural preferences had been austere, orientated towards the practicality of the Dutch Republic where he had spent several years as a young man. The new style looked further south, to the court culture exemplified by Versailles. Two great new palaces were erected, a gargantuan winter residence in the centre of Berlin and a summer retreat to the north-west, built on a green-field site and named Charlottenburg. Also influenced by Louis XIV was the promotion of cultural projects, most notably the foundation of the new university at Halle; an Academy of Art founded in 1697, which was to be 'a high school of art or university of art like the academies in Rome and Paris'; and an Academy of Sciences in 1700, whose first president was no less a figure than Leibniz.[83]

Frederick III/I has been treated roughly by historians, not least because he was criticized so severely by his grandson in his *Memoirs of the House of Brandenburg*. The indictment to be found there can be summarized as follows: the new king compensated for his inability to assert himself against his neighbours with an inflation of titles. Small and deformed, he was greedy for grandeur, mistaking the trappings of royalty for the substance. His capricious extravagance served no useful purpose, being merely dissipation born of vanity and stupidity. He sacrificed the lives of his soldiers to his allies without reward and exploited his poor to benefit the rich. He allowed the eastern provinces of his kingdom to succumb to famine and plague. His court drained off the wealth of his kingdom to form a great cesspit in which the corrupt courtiers could wallow. Feeble-minded and superstitious, he was so attached to his Calvinist faith that he would have resorted to persecution if only his clergy had devised a suitably gorgeous ceremonial to accompany it. All that could be said in his favour was that he had secured the royal title, which at least delivered Brandenburg from the yoke of Austrian sovereignty. But even this was just an empty shell thrown to posterity with the message: 'I have won a title for you, now show you are worthy of it by giving it some substance.'[84]

What Frederick II should have conceded was that the creation of a magnificent court was considered *de rigueur* for any self-respecting prince, let alone a king. Frederick I considered his palace-building to be 'a necessity'.[85] The rest of Germany is still covered with great palaces dating from around 1700 – Nymphenburg and Schleissheim in Bavaria, Dresden and Moritzburg in Saxony, Herrenhausen in Hanover, Mannheim in the Palatinate, Wilhelmshöhe in Hessen-Kassel, Ludwigsburg in Württemberg, Würzburg, Brühl (Cologne), Bruchsal (Speyer), Mainz, Bamberg and Würzburg, just to name a few.[86] The odd king out was not Frederick I but his son, Frederick William. The culture shock brought by the latter's accession in 1713 could not have been more shattering. From boasting one of the most glamorous courts in the Holy Roman Empire, Prussia plunged to the opposite extreme, for Frederick William was convinced that theatre, opera, concerts, balls and all the other court activities were 'the work of Satan'.[87] The court budget was drastically reduced; the court painter, Antoine Pesne, was put on half-pay; the orchestra was disbanded.[88]

The royal library's purchasing grant was cut to a contemptuous four talers per annum and the post of librarian made honorary.[89] The pleasure gardens were levelled and turned into parade grounds.[90] Huge amounts of silverware were gathered in from palaces and hunting lodges, melted down regardless of aesthetic merit into bars, stamped with the army's mark and stored away in barrels in the cellars of the Potsdam palace.[91] And that would prove to be Frederick William's most concrete legacy: by 1740 this great hoard had swollen to 8,700,000 talers in hard cash, as his son gratefully acknowledged.[92] It might have been even greater, had Frederick William not increased expenditure on his court and his palaces as his reign progressed.[93]

A large, well-equipped and well-trained army; a loyal nobility accustomed to serve; an efficient administration; a war-chest big enough to allow a war to be waged without additional taxation or loans – such was Frederick's inheritance when his father died on 31 May 1740. Had any other crown prince or princess ever succeeded under such favourable circumstances? When the Habsburg Emperor Charles VI died later in the year (20 October), he bequeathed to his daughter Maria Theresa an empty treasury, mountainous debts, a faction-ridden ministry of old men and an army less than half its notional strength and still licking its wounds after a disastrous war against the Turks. The Habsburg Monarchy was well endowed only with tradition. As Frederick acidly commented, 'its pride supplied its want of strength, and its past glory screened its present humiliation'.[94] Unfortunately, Frederick William's dazzling material legacy to his son was accompanied by a psychological burden of corresponding magnitude.

2

The Breaking of Frederick

FREDERICK AND HIS FATHER

It is a wise father who does not try to turn his son into a miniature version of himself. If the old block is hit hard enough, the chip is liable to spin off in quite unexpected directions. So it was with Frederick William and his eldest son, Frederick, born on 24 January 1712. This was third time lucky, for two previous sons had died in infancy, in 1708 and 1711. Another was to go the same way in 1719. It was not until Frederick was ten years old that the badly needed spare heir appeared in the vigorous shape of August Wilhelm, joined later by Henry in 1726 and August Ferdinand in 1730. In addition, six out of seven daughters survived childhood to make an impressive total of ten adult offspring.

By its very nature, the relationship between sovereigns and their waiting heirs is bound to be problematic. The early eighteenth century was marked by some spectacular generational conflicts, most famously that which ended in the death in 1718 of Peter the Great's eldest son, Alexei, who cheated the executioner only by succumbing first to the torture and beatings ordered by his father. Less lethal but more frequent were the family rows of the Hanoverians, to whom the Hohenzollerns were closely related. Frederick William was the son of the Hanoverian duchess Sophia Charlotte and was married to his Hanoverian first cousin Sophia Dorothea, daughter of George I, Elector of Hanover and – from 1714 – King of England.

Keeping it in the family was, of course, normal for the ruling families of Europe, but a shallow gene pool could have unfortunate consequences. There was a strain of mental instability in the family

which was to reappear later with George III of England, Frederick
William IV of Prussia and Ludwig II of Bavaria and his brother Otto
(whose mother was a Hohenzollern). In the case of Frederick William
I certainly and George III possibly, this was due to porphyria, a
hereditary affliction passed down to the House of Hanover from
the Tudors via James I and his daughter Elizabeth of the Palatinate.[1]
Although described by Hippocrates in the fifth century BC, it was not
explained biochemically until 1871 and not given its present name
until 1889.[2]

In many transmitters it lies dormant or is so mild as to escape detec-
tion, but in Frederick William I the disease unleashed its full fury. He
suffered four major attacks, nearly dying in 1707, 1718 and 1734,
before suffering a terminal bout in 1740 when he did die, at the age
of fifty-one.[3] In between times, he was prone to less disabling but still
frightful outbreaks. Some idea of the symptoms can be gained from
the expressions used by contemporaries to describe them: 'fainting
fits', 'restlessness', 'delusions', 'insanity', 'foolish fantasies' and, especially, 'explosions of rage'. At its peak, porphyria scourged him with
insomnia alternating with nightmares, paranoia, swollen genitalia
(which made urination very painful), constipation alternating with
diarrhoea, great blisters full of water, foaming at the mouth, and
intense abdominal pain. The related affliction of gout was also a frequent visitor.[4] In October 1734 Frederick reported from Potsdam to
his sister Wilhelmine that their father was in a terrible condition: his
legs were swollen right up to the top of his thighs, his feet between
calf and toes were bright scarlet and filled with pus, his arms and face
were terribly emaciated, his face was yellow and covered in blue spots
and he could barely eat or drink so great was the pain.[5]

In 1726, Frederick William wrote resignedly: 'I can do nothing
against God's will and must bear everything patiently.'[6] This submission to divine mercy was often articulated. In 1734 his son reported
him as saying, 'with a moving, tragic expression', that he was only
forty-six years old, had everything on earth that a man could ask for,
and yet was suffering the most frightful pain the world had ever
known. 'Nevertheless,' he went on, 'I wish to suffer everything
patiently. My Saviour suffered so much more for my sake and I have
probably deserved God's punishment for my sins. His will be done

and may He determine my fate according to His Holy Will. I shall always bless and praise His name.'[7] Unfortunately, this heroic resolution could not be put into practice, for patience was one virtue Frederick William conspicuously lacked. Wilful from his first breath, he had given an early indication of his temperament when, as a four-year-old, he had responded to an attempt by his governess to take away a golden shoe-buckle he was using as a toy, by swallowing it. After the initial hysteria, when his mother screamed loud enough 'to pulverise rocks', a good dose of laxative solved the problem and the buckle was sent off to be exhibited in the palace's 'chamber of curiosities'.[8] On another occasion, the little boy dealt with a threat of punishment by clambering on to the window-ledge of his upstairs nursery and supporting his negotiations with his governess with a threat to jump.[9] Handy with his fists, he had to be sent home from a visit to his grandparents at Hanover for beating up his cousin George.[10] He grew up to be round-bodied and red-faced, as short in temper as he was in stature (five feet five inches), and notorious for his violent mood swings.[11]

How much of Frederick William's coarse behaviour was due to his personality and how much was a reaction to physical pain obviously cannot be determined. It seems likely, however, that he would have been a difficult parent even if he had enjoyed the best of health. His fabled parsimony, for example, was spotted early on by his mother, who commented 'what a miser at such a tender age!' when she found the child keeping a careful account of 'my ducats'.[12] His authoritarianism was also deeply embedded and often expressed, as was his attachment to Calvinist Christianity, although he found the doctrine of predestination so awful that he rejected it with characteristic intemperance.[13]

No less contingent was Frederick William's militarism. As soon as he came to the throne he issued a new table of ranks to elevate soldiers at the expense of civilians. A field marshal now went straight to the front of the pecking-order, leapfrogging all the great offices of state and court. Further down, even mere captains rose by fifty-five places.[14] After 1725 the king himself was never seen wearing anything but uniform, rather pedantically the uniform of a colonel, because it was to that rank that his father had promoted him and Frederick William took the view that after his death there was no one authorized to promote him further.[15] He told anyone who would listen that he had never enjoyed anything so much as the murderous battle of Malplaquet; that there was no higher calling than leading an army; that he could have been a great commander himself if only he had seen more military service; and so on.[16] In his view, the people were there for the state, the state was there for the army and the army was there for the head of the House of Brandenburg.[17]

Also impossible to explain away by reference to illness was Frederick William's attitude to recreation and culture. What he liked was hunting. The next best thing to killing enemy soldiers was killing the various forms of game with which the forests around Berlin and Potsdam teemed. His meticulous records reveal that between 1717 and 1738 he shot 25,066 pheasants at Wusterhausen alone. Notoriously averse to ceremonial, Frederick William made an exception for hunting, staging an elaborate burial of a favourite falcon who had got the worst of a 'heroic struggle' with a heron.[18] The Feast of St Hubertus, the patron saint of hunters, on 3 November, was one of only two festivals he observed (the other was the anniversary of the battle of Malplaquet on 11 September).[19] Revealingly, the only building he ever commissioned for himself was a little hunting lodge to the south-east of Potsdam. Closely resembling a simple Dutch town house, 'Star', as it was known because it was placed at the centre of a radiating network of hunt drives, comprised just a dining room, kitchen, bedroom and a room for an adjutant.[20]

He had three other hunting lodges at his disposal, at Köpenick to the south-east of Berlin and now part of the metropolis, in the Grunewald forest to the west, and at Wusterhausen, twenty kilometres south of the capital. It was the last of these that was his favourite residence.[21] According to his eldest daughter, Wilhelmine, he seriously considered abdicating and living the life of a simple country squire at Wusterhausen on 10,000 talers a year. While he divided his time between prayer and farming, he announced, the rest of the family would attend to running the household, with Wilhelmine taking charge of the linen cupboard, sewing and mending.[22]

At Wusterhausen Frederick William's favourite *après*-hunting recreation was his 'tobacco parliament', an exclusively male assembly at which smoking, beer drinking and robust conversation were the order of the day. Unsurprisingly, most of those invited were army officers. According to the Austrian ambassador, Count von Seckendorf, the sessions began at five in the evening and could last until midnight.[23] A celebrated painting by Georg Lisiewski of 1737 shows a sparsely furnished whitewashed room with Frederick William at the head of a plain oak table, his guests sitting on unupholstered benches without backs. The only people present not drinking and smoking are his three youngest sons, August Wilhelm (aged fifteen), Henry (eleven) and August Ferdinand (seven).*[24] At the far end of the table sit two civilians without pipes or tankards. These are the 'comic councillors', academics invited along to be the butts of the assembled company's coarse humour. Sitting between them is a large hare with ears pricked, a contemptuous symbol of the timidity and meretricious bragging Frederick William associated with their profession.[25] On his instructions, salaries paid to academicians were entered under the rubric 'expenses for the various royal buffoons'.[26]

As this suggests, Frederick William had no time for intellectual pursuits. As one of his biographers has put it, 'his way of life was highly idiosyncratic and almost wholly devoid of culture'.[27] Even Count Seckendorf had to smuggle in books to Wusterhausen, lest he be suspected of wasting on reading time that might have been better employed in hunting, drinking or praying.[28] At the age of ten Frederick William still did not know the alphabet and could not add up to ten.[29] The *Political Testament* he composed for his heir in 1722 was not so much illiterate as dyslexic, a chaotic stream of consciousness in which even the innumerable misspellings were not consistent. Upper and lower cases were used arbitrarily, capital letters appeared in the middle of words. He dated it 17 February 1722 at 'Bostdam' (Potsdam), which on the previous page he has spelt 'Postdam'.[30] Characteristically, he began with a prayer: he had always placed his trust in God, certain of salvation, and repented of his sins. His successor must take no mistresses ('or rather whores as they should properly be termed'); he must lead a godly life and set an example to country and army; he must not indulge in excessive eating or drinking; he

---

* Greatly to his relief, Crown Prince Frederick escaped the tobacco parliament when he married and was given his own establishment at Rheinsberg. See below, pp. 49–50.

must tolerate no public entertainments, for they were all satanic; the House of Hohenzollern had always shunned such things – and that was why God had smiled on it; he must fear God and never start an unjust war, but must also stand up for the rights of the Hohenzollern dynasty.[31]

Mostly he practised what he preached, although by all accounts he never managed abstinence. The closest he came to adultery, according to his daughter Wilhelmine, was to lust after one of his wife's ladies-in-waiting, the beautiful but virtuous Frau von Pannewitz. With his usual lack of subtlety, he let his desires be known in an offensively direct manner and was rejected with equal vehemence. However, when he encountered the lady on a narrow staircase in the ducal palace at Brunswick, to which the court had moved for his son's wedding, he resumed his wooing by grabbing her breasts. The lady responded by punching him so hard that his nose and mouth bled copiously. This experience put him back on the straight and narrow, but ever after he referred to Frau von Pannewitz as 'that evil witch'.[32]

For all his boorishness, Frederick William was no fool. Sharp-witted, energetic and determined, he was a man who made things happen – usually the way he wanted. He even had a sensitive side, best expressed in the painting to which he resorted to fill his sleepless nights and to ease his physical aches and pains, labelling the finished work *Fredericus Wilhelmus in tormentis pinxit* (painted by Frederick William in his torment).[33] An expressive self-portrait reveals both talent and suffering.[34] He was also surprisingly indulgent to his wife, Sophia Dorothea, allowing her to maintain her own court at Monbijou Palace on the banks of the river Spree in Berlin, whose construction – begun during the reign of his predecessor, Frederick I – he completed.[35]

Any relationship with the mercurial Frederick William was bound to be difficult. In the case of his queen, it was made more difficult by her knowledge that he had in fact wanted to marry Caroline of Ansbach, who – just to add insult to injury – had preferred his detested cousin George of Hanover and England.[36] Cultured, pleasure-loving and fiercely proud of her Guelph pedigree, Sophia Dorothea needed all her plentiful good sense and good nature to adapt to life with Frederick William. For thirty-four years she put up with his tantrums, nursed him through his numerous illnesses and bore him fourteen children. When she died in 1757, Count von Lehndorff, who had known her very well, wrote that this 'daughter, wife, mother and sister of kings' was 'so admired, so venerated, so loved by so many' because she was good, charitable, gracious and dignified. She was also, he added, immensely corpulent and all the strength of the numerous pall-bearers, of whom he was one, was needed to transport her coffin to her final resting-place.[37]

FATHER AND SON

For a child growing up, a choice between this ill-assorted couple was not difficult to make. On the one side, there was love, attention, culture and the good things of life; on the other, duty, piety, austerity and brutality. For the first six years of his life, Crown Prince Frederick did not have to choose. He was left to the tender care of an elderly Huguenot lady, Madame de Rocoulle (who had been Frederick William's own first governess), and her daughter. As the other women in his life – his mother and his elder sister – only ever spoke French, Frederick's early – and happy – years were spent in an entirely Francophone and feminine world. Only occasional visits to his father at Wusterhausen revealed the very different German and masculine alternative that awaited him.[38] This then broke in on his cosy world when he reached the age of seven, with the appointment of two male governors, both senior army officers – General Count von Finkenstein and Colonel von Kalkstein. Princess Wilhelmine, who got to know them well, described the former as decent but dim, the latter as a deceitful bigot.[39] Fortunately for Frederick, they were complemented by Jacques Duhan de Jandun, a Huguenot who had impressed Frederick William less by his intellectual attainments than by the bravery he had shown at the siege of Stralsund.[40]

This tutorial team was instructed to train their charge to become a thrifty manager, a pious Christian and an enthusiastic soldier. Most emphasis was laid on the third: 'in particular they must both [Finkenstein and Kalkstein] take exceedingly good care to imbue my son with a love of soldiering and to impress upon him that there is nothing in the world that bestows on a prince more fame and honour than the sword and that, equally, nothing makes him more despised than if he does not love the sword and seek his glory in it alone'.[41] They faced an uphill task. For Christmas in 1717, shortly before his sixth birthday in other words, Frederick had been given by his father a whole company of lead soldiers, complete with weapons, drums, flags and standards, and even miniature cannons that could be fired. Barely favouring them with a glance, the little boy had turned away to a magnificently bound volume of French melodies and was soon entrancing his female audience with his lute.[42] Although it was not yet apparent, the second objective would also prove problematic. It was not for want of trying, as the following daily routine at Wusterhausen dictated by Frederick William in 1721 shows:

> 5.30 a.m. reveille: the Crown Prince must rise and say his prayers out loud, then he must quickly wash, dress and do his hair.
>
> 5.45 a.m. all servants and Duhan are to come in and the assembled company will recite their prayers on their knees; then Duhan shall read a chapter from the Bible and one or more good hymns are to be sung; after the servants have left, Duhan shall read the biblical text of the day, explain and discuss it, and also repeat passages from the catechism.
>
> 7–9 a.m. history lesson with Duhan.
>
> 9–10.45 a.m. religious instruction with Noltenius.
>
> 11 a.m. after washing with soap, to the King.
>
> 2–3 p.m. political geography with Duhan.
>
> 3–4 p.m. moral instruction.
>
> 4–5 p.m. writing letters in German with Duhan with a view to stylistic improvement.
>
> 5 p.m. after washing his hands he will return to the King to ride out with him.
>
> 6 p.m. free time to do what he wants if it is not against God's law.

On Sundays, Frederick was allowed to lie in until seven but was also expected to attend a (lengthy) church service with his father.[43]

It is not possible to establish precisely when Frederick William began to realize that his best-laid plans for his son and heir were going awry. Little Frederick turned out to be crafty as well as clever, adept at feigning interest in all the things his father loved but he secretly hated, notably hunting, drilling, shooting and commanding the company of 130 cadets created for him when he was just six years old.[44] Certainly by 1724 the father had begun to be suspicious, saying: 'I would very much like to know what is going on in that little head. I am well aware that Fritz doesn't share my tastes and I also know there are people who have filled him up with contrary notions and who rubbish everything I do.'[45] The Pietist Francke was disconcerted at the dinner table by the sight of Frederick and his sister Wilhelmine looking at each other with their big blue eyes but saying nothing in their father's presence. It was only when the king had gone off hunting that Frederick came alive, mocking the academics and clergy present, including Francke himself.[46] It was in 1724 that foreign diplomats began to report incidents of paternal disapproval of what was judged to be 'effeminacy' – the wearing of gloves when hunting on a cold day, for example, or the use of a silver three-pronged fork rather than the steel two-pronged implement favoured by soldiers.[47] Fear of the sound of gunfire was another discouraging sign.[48] In 1726 Frederick was transferred to Potsdam to be a captain in the King's Own Regiment, a move which meant much greater emphasis on military matters in his education with a correspondingly austere life-style and an end to what little 'comfort or pleasure' he had enjoyed hitherto. Falling off his horse on the parade ground in front of his father dramatized Finkenstein and Kalkstein's failure to turn him into a model soldier.[49]

Religion was also a divisive issue. Frederick himself probably could not have said when he began to have doubts about the Christian faith that was thrust down his throat on a daily basis. For a mind with little natural inclination to 'metaphysical fiction', as Frederick later defined Christianity, such force-feeding was probably counterproductive. There was certainly plenty of it. From the age of seven he was obliged to copy out the more important passages from the New Testament and any minor misdemeanours were punished by rote-learning of the catechism and hymns.[50] Mealtimes were especially bleak, accompanied by readings from devotional texts, sermons and psalm-singing. Only pious topics of conversation were permitted.[51] At some point in his early teens, Frederick's rejection of his father's grim religion was complete. In 1720 Frederick's tutors could still report satisfaction with his religious education, but by 1726, as confirmation approached, extra instruction was deemed to be necessary.[52] The ceremony, which eventually took place in April 1727, does not appear to have helped. By this time, with the aid of his tutor Duhan, Frederick had compiled a clandestine library which included works by John Locke, Pierre Bayle and Voltaire.[53] Tucked away in Ambrosius Haude's bookshop on the 'Liberty', a row of houses immediately opposite the Berlin Palace, it eventually ran to 3,775 volumes in fifteen bookcases.[54] Together with other little luxuries, this bibliophilia ran Frederick into debt, as he received no money of his own until he was seventeen. During the winter of 1727–8 he had to confess that he had borrowed 7,000 talers from a Berlin banker. Given his own obsessive parsimony, Frederick William cannot have been pleased by this news but he paid up. He might well not have done so, had he known that this was not the limit of his son's liabilities.[55]

Although it is conceivable that somewhere at some time a father has enjoyed a consistently harmonious relationship with his adolescent son, it is not a phenomenon often recorded. In the case of Frederick William and Frederick, the natural tensions of the latter's teenage years went way beyond what was normal to reach physical violence and climaxed with a near-filicide. It was a sustained campaign to break Frederick's will and turn him into a subservient instrument. The technique was brutal: Frederick William never praised his son, never showed him any affection and treated him worse than he did his court buffoons.[56] An army-hating, free-thinking spendthrift was the son of Frederick William's nightmares. So long as his defects were concealed behind a façade of obedience, however, some sort of *modus vivendi* could be achieved. This became more difficult as Frederick grew both more restless and more assertive. A watershed was reached with the royal visit to the Saxon capital Dresden in January 1728. Frederick William had not intended to take his son with him and it was only at the urging of his host that Frederick was allowed to join the party.[57]

The contrast between Augustus the Strong's hedonistic, not to say decadent, court and the grim austerity at home could not have been greater. Frederick enjoyed at least three experiences for the first time. He attended his first opera, Johann Adolf Hasse's *Cleofide*, one of the finest *opere serie* (grand operas) ever written. Also for the first time he heard flute playing of virtuoso standard, by Johann Joachim Quantz.[58] Last but not least, he probably had his first heterosexual experience, which may also have inspired him to start writing poetry. According to his sister Wilhelmine, Frederick was present when the Saxon king entertained his Prussian guests after a good dinner by escorting them into a lavishly decorated chamber, where he suddenly pulled back a curtain to reveal reclining on a couch in an alcove a young woman who was not only very beautiful but also stark naked. A horrified Frederick William thrust his son from the room, but not before Frederick had seen enough to make him want to see more. He was, after all, of an age – he had celebrated his sixteenth birthday while in Dresden. The carefully planned display represented an attempt by Augustus to divert Frederick's attentions away from his illegitimate daughter (and reputed mistress) Countess Anna Karolina Orzelska. He offered his guest the girl on the couch, an opera singer called La Formera, on condition he abandoned the countess. Wilhelmine concluded: 'my brother promised everything to gain possession of this beauty, who became his first lover'.[59] On his return to bleak Berlin from the flesh-pots of Dresden, Frederick fell into a deep depression, lost weight and suffered from fainting fits.[60] The reappearance of Countess Orzelska when Augustus paid a return visit to the Prussian court proved a bitter disappointment, for she was now pregnant. A frustrated Frederick turned to unspecified other forms of dissipation.[61]

Almost everything that is known about this episode stems from the memoirs of Frederick's older sister Wilhelmine. These are not to be despised as a source, for she was very close to Frederick and the sympathetic recipient of his confidences. On the other hand, she was writing long after the event and her memoirs are full of mistakes.[62] All that can be said with certainty is that Frederick William I felt very uncomfortable in Dresden. On his return, he wrote to Seckendorf that he had been appalled by the ungodly behaviour of the court there, adding piously 'but God is my witness that I took no pleasure from it and that I am as pure as when I left home and shall remain so with God's help until the end of my days'.[63] The historian's task is made more difficult by the reluctance of any of the participants to spell out exactly what they meant by 'dissipation' or who exactly was 'a kind person'. The latter was a phrase used by Frederick in a letter to Voltaire of 16 August 1737 in which he stated that it was this anonymous muse who had first inspired in him two powerful emotions: love and

the desire to write poetry, adding 'this little miracle of nature possessed every possible charm, together with good taste and delicacy.
[S]he sought to transfer these qualities to me. I succeeded well in love
but poorly in poetry. Since that time I have very often been in love and
have always been a poet.'[64] Frederick gives no date for his epiphany
beyond that it had happened 'in the first flush of youth'. In a footnote,
the editor, J. D. E. Preuss, identified the kind person as 'Madame de
Wreech' and dated the experience to 1731 on the grounds that Frederick wrote to Wilhelmine in 1734 that three years had passed since,
'as a pupil of Horace', he had stood at the foot of Mount Parnassus.[65]
That rather orotund expression does not mean, however, that he had
not started writing verses at an earlier date. Indeed, in a previous
work, Preuss had written that in his letter to Voltaire of 1737 Frederick had been referring to Countess Orzelska.[66]

The four weeks he spent in Dresden revealed to Frederick just how
narrow, parochial and philistine was the 'culture' to be found at home.
Among the Saxon courtiers he had met was Crown Prince Augustus,
a sophisticated man of the world who had been on the Grand Tour to
France and Italy, had been received at Versailles by the Sun King himself and had married into the Habsburg dynasty.[67] As he returned to
the dreary round of regimental duties at Potsdam under the ever-
watchful eye of his brutal father, how Frederick must have wished to
escape his iron cage. A minor but indicative sign that the worm was
beginning to turn was his habit of signing his letters '*Frédéric le philosophe*', which began while he was in Dresden.[68] A move towards
greater assertiveness can also be inferred from his father's increasingly
intemperate behaviour. There is general agreement among Frederick's
biographers that the Dresden visit was followed by a sharp deterioration in relations.[69] This may well have been caused in part by Frederick
William's belated discovery that Frederick's post-Dresden illness was
not physiological but stemmed from frustrated sexual desire. Sympathy at once gave way to outrage and the offer of a hundred ducats
to the first informer to report any misconduct.[70]

Driven to distraction, in the autumn of 1728 Frederick wrote a
desperate letter to his father to complain of the 'cruel hatred' to which
he was subjected at every turn. In his uncompromising reply Frederick
William denounced his son as an effeminate who could not ride or

shoot, was dirty in appearance, wore his hair too long, was wilful, and generally looked and behaved like a fool.[71] Everything Frederick said or did, whether it was riding, eating or even just walking, set his father's teeth on edge. And there were, of course, plenty of informants only too willing to tell the king what he wanted to hear – that Frederick had referred to his grenadier's uniform as his 'shroud', for example.[72] Frederick William's exasperation may well have been intensified by constant comparisons with Frederick's younger brother August Wilhelm, who was showing every sign of being a real chip off the old block, even to the point of looking like his father.[73] As for Frederick, Frederick William simply could not bear the sight of him. On 17 October 1728 the Saxon envoy von Suhm reported that Frederick had told him his situation had become intolerable. He implored Suhm to ask King Augustus to intervene with Frederick William to give him more freedom and to allow him to travel.[74] There was no prospect of that. On the contrary, Frederick William narrowed the bars of the cage still further. Early the following year he assigned two more young adjutants to Frederick with the express purpose of keeping an eye on his behaviour. Their instructions singled out Frederick's lack of 'truly manly inclinations', that is to say soldiering, hunting and hard drinking. It was their mission to bring it home to Frederick that 'all effeminate, lascivious and feminine occupations were highly unseemly in a man'.[75]

By now this clash of cultures and life-styles had been given an extra political dimension by a sharp disagreement between king and queen over their son's marriage. As the daughter of George I and sister of George II, Sophia Dorothea was naturally keen to promote closer relations between Hanover and Prussia. An ideal means, in her view, would be the double marriage of two pairs of first cousins: Frederick, Prince of Wales (born in 1707) and Wilhelmine (born 1709), and Princess Amelia (born 1711) and Crown Prince Frederick (born 1712). Frederick William did not turn this proposal down when it was first mooted in 1725, appreciating the obvious advantage in forming a stronger Protestant bloc stretching across northern Germany. Wilhelmine recorded that she exchanged letters with her English fiancé and even received an engagement ring.[76] According to the British envoy at Berlin, Brigadier Dubourgay, her brother was also

enthusiastic about his own prospective partner, sending 'loving messages to England'. When it was put to him that Amelia's younger sister
Caroline might be a better choice, 'his Royal Highness broke out into
such raptures of love and passion for the Princess Amelia, and showed
so much impatience for the conclusion of that Match, as gave the
King of Prussia a great deal of surprise, and the Queen as much satisfaction'.[77] That was written at the end of 1728, by which time
Frederick William had begun to turn against the queen's plan. So
alienated was he now from his son that he was instinctively opposed
to anything that might give him pleasure, a consideration strengthened by the thought that a separate establishment for the happy
couple would prove expensive.[78] The accession of his detested cousin
George to the English throne in 1727 was a further objection. Frederick William's prejudices were inflamed by a conspiracy at the Prussian
court conducted by the Austrian ambassador Seckendorf in cooperation with the venal Prussian minister Grumbkow.[79] To assist their
machinations, Vienna dangled the prospect of imperial support for
Frederick William's claims to the duchies of Jülich and Berg when the
childless Elector of the Palatinate died.[80] The *coup de grâce* to the
English marriage was delivered by a brief but vicious dispute with
Hanover in the summer of 1729 over the arrest of Prussian recruiting
officers, and a border dispute, to which Frederick William responded
by mobilizing an army 44,000-strong.

Marriage would have brought Frederick, if not complete liberation,
then at least some measure of release. The more unlikely it became,
the more he chafed at the bit. Frederick William responded to his
distress at the collapse of the matrimonial project by asking contemp-
tuously how on earth he could be in love with a woman he had never
met, exclaiming 'what a farce!'[81] Frederick was receiving daily reminders of his father's 'cruel hatred'. Dubourgay reported in July 1729 that
Frederick William now refused to sit with his son at dinner, consign-
ing him to a seat at the bottom of the table, where he often got nothing
to eat and so had to rely on food-parcels sent round to his room later
by his mother.[82] On 10 December 1729 Dubourgay reported that
when Frederick had responded to his father's sneer about the 'vile
clique' which supported the English by saying 'I respect the English
because I know the people there love me', Frederick William seized

him by the collar and gave him a thrashing with his cane.[83] Physical violence was now common. In the same month, Frederick was thrown to the ground and forced to kiss his father's feet.[84]

FREDERICK'S ABORTIVE FLIGHT

In the summer of 1730, soon after the painful episode recounted in the introduction,* king and crown prince travelled together to Augsburg, where Frederick's sister Frederica was to marry the Margrave of Ansbach, and then on to Württemberg and the Hohenzollern territories on the Lower Rhine. It was now that Dubourgay's prediction of the previous December – 'there is a general apprehension of something tragical taking place before long' – came to pass.[85] Frederick's future was as bleak as could be. Frederick William I was only forty-two in 1730, his father had lived to be fifty-five and his grandfather to be sixty-eight, so there was little hope in the medium term that his natural death would bring liberation. Probably the last straw was Frederick William's boast that, whereas some people were comforting Frederick with the prediction that his father would mellow as he grew older, in reality he was determined to treat his son ever more harshly, adding grimly: 'and you know I am a man of my word'. On another occasion, Frederick William added insult to injury by sneering that if he had been treated in the same manner by his own father, he would have shot himself. The physical abuse also intensified. On a visit to Radewitz in Saxony in May 1730, Frederick William punched Frederick in the face, tore his hair and then made him pass across the parade ground so that everyone could witness the visible effects of his humiliation.[86] Frederick never seems to have considered the most obvious solution – regicide – but he did plan to run away, first to France and from there to England, where he hoped the marriage plan could be realized.

The attempted escape on 5 August 1730 near Mannheim on the Rhine was a fiasco, frustrated even before it started. So ham-fisted was the enterprise that it has been suggested by one of Frederick's most

* See above, pp. xxi–xxii.

perceptive recent biographers that its main purpose was to draw attention to himself.[87] Indeed, it was so futile that it took a few days before Frederick William fully realized what had been planned. He then made up for lost time with a vengeance. Frederick was placed under close arrest and rushed back across Germany to Berlin, the route carefully chosen to avoid Hanoverian territory, for British complicity was suspected. By all accounts, Frederick was unrepentant to the point of nonchalance. Seckendorf reported him saying that he did not regret what he had done and did not care if it cost him his life. He added, however, that he would be sorry if those who had known about the plan in advance suffered as a result of his actions.[88] That proved to be Frederick's Achilles heel. Even Frederick William would have found it difficult to have his son and heir executed, although he certainly talked about it. Prussia was not Russia. But he could certainly make him suffer vicariously. Of the two main co-conspirators, Lieutenant von Keith had managed to escape to the Dutch Republic and thence to England, but Lieutenant Hans Hermann von Katte was arrested at Berlin.[89]

Also in the know had been Frederick's sister Wilhelmine, in whom he had confided long before. It was she who was the first to experience her father's wrath. When Frederick William arrived back in Berlin, she recorded,

> We all rushed to kiss his hand, but as soon as he caught sight of me, he was overcome by rage and fury. His face went black, his eyes blazed, and he foamed at the mouth: 'You loathsome villain!' he screamed, 'Do you dare to come near me? Get her out of here! She can go and join her rogue of a brother.' With these words, he grabbed my hand and punched me several times in the face, one blow striking me on the temple so hard that I fell over and would have hit my head on the edge of the panelling if Fräulein von Sonsfeld had not broken my fall by grabbing me by the hair. I lay senseless on the floor. Completely beside himself, the king wanted to let fly at me again and stamp on me, but the Queen, and my brothers and sisters held him back.

She added that when she regained consciousness she berated her protectors for saving her from the death that would have been a thousand times preferable to the life she was currently forced to lead.[90] This kind of atrocity could not be kept secret. Both the French and British ambassadors reported that the king's ranting and his victim's screams resounded through the palace.[91]

Frederick himself was taken first to Mittenwalde near Berlin, where he was interrogated on 16 September by a team led by Frederick William's closest adviser, Field Marshal Friedrich Wilhelm von Grumbkow. They put to Frederick 185 questions, all of them drafted by the king personally and many of them implying that execution was the most likely outcome of the process.[92] He was then sent off to prison in Küstrin on the river Oder, where he was kept in solitary confinement in a cell lit only by a narrow slit high in the wall. There he was left to contemplate his fate.[93] He wrote to Wilhelmine that he now knew that the worst thing life had to offer was to be hated by one's father.[94] Meanwhile, Frederick William was busy taking revenge on the minor players. Following a court martial, the fugitive Lieutenant von Keith was hanged in effigy. The daughter of a Potsdam clergyman, whose only offence was to have played music with Frederick, was ordered to be whipped outside her father's house, in the public square and 'in all four corners of the town', and was then despatched to Spandau prison 'for life'. Nor were inanimate objects spared. The large clandestine library Frederick had assembled with the help of his tutor Duhan was packed up and sent off to be sold. Duhan was banished to Memel on the Polish frontier, the Prussian equivalent of Siberia.[95]

It was Lieutenant von Katte, however, who bore the brunt of royal vengeance. After a court martial had condemned him to life imprisonment, Frederick William intervened to impose the death penalty. Not even his aristocratic connections could save him. Turning down a plea for clemency from Katte's grandfather Field Marshal von Wartensleben, Frederick William told him that it was better that one individual should die than that 'the whole world or the Empire should be destroyed', that Katte deserved to be torn apart with red-hot pincers but, being merciful, he had commuted this to decapitation.[96] This vindictive frenzy was probably due to his belief that the relationship between Katte and his son had been sexual.[97] When he met Frederick for the first time since the flight, he repeatedly asked: 'Did you seduce Katte? Or did Katte seduce you?', although the record does not make it clear whether he was referring to sex or to the flight.[98] It might appear suggestive that on 17 October 1730 a man named Andreas

Lepsch was burned at the stake at Potsdam 'for sodomy', but it seems that he had sex with a cow and not another male.[99]

After interrogation, Katte was taken to Küstrin, where on 6 November he was beheaded. When the army chaplain entered Frederick's cell to inform him that the execution was about to occur, Frederick thought that it was he himself who was to be the victim.[100] As Katte was led out, he 'caught sight of his beloved Jonathan for the last time', as the garrison chaplain Besserer recorded, for Frederick was forced to watch from a window immediately above the place of execution.[101] As the axe fell, a hysterical Frederick dropped unconscious into the arms of his warders. In close attendance was an army chaplain, under orders from Frederick William to take advantage of this anticipated mental breakdown to lead his son back to the consoling embrace of Christianity.[102]

It is impossible to say whether or not Frederick William really intended to have him killed too. The Austrian ambassador Seckendorf reported the queen saying that only imperial intervention could save Frederick. Frederick William himself later announced in public that it was Charles VI's plea for clemency that had changed his mind.[103] He was certainly in a terrible state during the autumn of 1730, drinking even more heavily than usual, roaming the palace shouting that he was haunted, and ordering his coach in the middle of the night to take him out to Wusterhausen. The British envoy Guy Dickens reported: 'The King of Prussia cannot sleep, the officers sit up with him every night, and in his slumbers he raves and talks of spirits and apparitions.'[104] On 9 November Frederick was told that he would be pardoned on condition that he took an oath of unconditional obedience to the king 'as servant, subject and son'. Moreover, this oath was not to be mumbled but to be proclaimed loud and clear without any mental reservations.[105]

THE SUBJUGATION OF FREDERICK

For the best part of a year, Frederick was kept under close observation at Küstrin. Although his conditions of incarceration were eased, he was subjected to a punishing regime of training in the practical business of government, interrupted only by lengthy sessions of religious observance, including four hours of sermons and services on Sundays. Knowing just how close had been his brush with death, Frederick submitted and dissembled. There was no more of the insouciant defiance he had shown immediately after his arrest. All the while Frederick William was taking a close interest in his rehabilitation. In May 1731, for example, the chief minder, Colonel von Wolden, was told that Frederick must clear his head of all the French and English rubbish he had picked up and replace it with exclusively Prussian matter, must be loyal to his father, have a German heart, constantly pray to God for his grace and never let God out of sight, in the hope that God would be merciful to him now and for ever.[106] On 15 August 1731, Frederick William arrived at Küstrin in person with a numerous retinue to conclude the rehabilitation process. On entering the royal presence, Frederick threw himself at his father's feet. His numerous sins of omission and commission were then rehearsed in suitably abrasive fashion. An eye-witness account by Grumbkow revealed Frederick William in all his appalling glory. Among other things, he told his son that if the flight to England had succeeded, his mother and sisters would have been confined in a place 'where never again would they have seen the sun or the moon', while he himself would have led an army to invade Hanover, burning and pillaging as they went. Along with this familiar brutality, Frederick William also revealed a rather pathetic sense of inferiority when he half-proudly, half-ruefully stated that he had no 'French manners' and could not come up with *bons mots* but would live and die as just a simple German prince. He added that Frederick had always made a point of hating what his father loved. Inevitably, his tirade ended with an awful warning about the consequences of impiety. Frederick was impeccably submissive, greeting his father's final pronouncement of forgiveness by falling to the floor weeping and kissing his feet.[107] As a token of his unconditional obedience, he reported two weeks later that he had been out hunting, had fired at a stag and a fawn, had missed both, alas, but would try to do better next time.[108]

There was one more stage in this ritual humiliation before Frederick William could consider his victory over his son complete: he had to get him married. There was no question now of a match with

George II's daughter Amelia, not least because it was clear that the British had failed to disclose their advance warning of Frederick's flight attempt. In September 1730 Frederick William had rubbed in the queen's disappointment at the final collapse of her double-marriage plans by trying to make her drink a toast to the 'downfall of England', which had made her burst into tears.[109] He also upset her by forcing Wilhelmine to marry, in November 1731, her Hohenzollern relation the Margrave of Bayreuth, a choice of mate which represented a terrible come-down from her earlier prospect of becoming Queen of England. To make matters even worse, the king's choice of bride for Frederick fell on Elizabeth Christine of Bevern, a junior branch of the House of Brunswick, in other words related to Queen Sophia Dorothea but, in her eyes at least, of appreciably lower standing than the electoral and royal House of Hanover.[110] The disappointed mother retaliated by depicting Elizabeth Christine to her son, who had never met his fiancée, in the darkest possible hues. She was just a 'silly goose', and a bad-tempered bigot with a deformed hip into the bargain.[111] To Wilhelmine she added that her prospective sister-in-law was 'as thick as two short planks and completely uneducated. Heaven knows how my son is going to put up with such a pipsqueak.'[112] Frederick William did not help by describing her as 'neither ugly nor beautiful' when announcing his choice to Frederick, who is also unlikely to have been impressed by the further recommendation that she was 'God-fearing'.[113] Frederick's siblings were, if anything, even more venomous. One of his sisters announced at the dinner table in his hearing that she had visited her prospective sister-in-law one morning when she was performing her ablutions only to find that she smelled so rank that it had taken her breath away. 'She must have a dozen or so anal fistulas, that's the only possible explanation,' his sister added.[114]

This was not a good start. In January 1732, Frederick wrote to Grumbkow that the very thought of his wife-to-be overwhelmed him with revulsion.[115] The tears in Frederick's eyes that were noted at the betrothal ceremony on 10 March were not thought to be tears of joy or anticipation. After the rings had been exchanged, he moved smartly away from his fiancée and demonstratively started a conversation with another young lady of the court. Even Seckendorf, who had worked hard to secure the match, took the view that it had all been too rushed, adding that Frederick William should at least have waited until the red spots on Elizabeth Christine's face caused by a mild attack of smallpox had disappeared.[116] The actual wedding did not take place until 10 June in the following year. The difficult question of Frederick's sexual relations with his wife will be considered in the next chapter.[117] Whatever Frederick's feelings on his wedding night may have been, his bride had performed one very important service for him. The ceremony marked the last stage in his paternal rehabilitation. He was now allowed his own income, his own establishment, his own home and, most important of all, his freedom. The making of Frederick could begin.

3

The Making of Frederick

REHABILITATION

Liberation from Frederick William's prison was a process rather than an event. Following the reconciliation ritual in August 1731,* Frederick was allowed to leave Küstrin for daily excursions, and after a while to travel further afield, albeit only within Brandenburg. In November he attended Wilhelmine's wedding at Berlin and was formally readmitted to the army.[1] At Küstrin he was put to work learning about the nuts and bolts of provincial administration, with special emphasis on the need for economy and careful accounting. This was all to be done on the job, directed Frederick William, 'because nothing can be learned from books, only practical experience will do, and it was thanks to reading too many useless books that the Crown Prince got into all those harmful and dangerous situations in the first place'. So Frederick's reading material was still confined to a hymn book, the Bible and Johann Arndt's anthology of pious meditations entitled *True Christianity*.[2]

Betrothal to Elizabeth Christine was rewarded with greater freedom. A month later, in April 1732, Frederick was made colonel of a regiment of infantry and moved to Ruppin, a small town north-west of Berlin where the headquarters of the first battalion was located (the second battalion was quartered at Nauen thirty-five kilometres to the south). Here he showed that he was taking seriously the oath of obedience to his father by applying himself diligently to military matters. So diligently indeed, that by 1734 the notoriously demanding

* See above, p. 43.

Frederick William singled out his regiment for special praise following the annual review of 1734 (and actually embraced him after the
same event the following year). Shortly after this last accolade, Frederick was promoted to major general.[3] Also in 1734 total liberation
seemed imminent when Frederick William was afflicted by a particularly severe attack of porphyria. Frederick got ready to govern, and
was deeply disappointed when his father made an unexpected
recovery.[4]

Well aware that his freedom was conditional, Frederick did all that
was asked of him. But he also began to regain his self-respect after the
humiliations of the past and to assert his own identity against the
overpowering personality of his father. He achieved this by adopting
the triple strategy identified in the introduction: creating a congenial
environment, assembling convivial company and outperforming his
father. First and foremost came culture in all its forms. Freed from a
diet of Christian piety, Frederick turned back to reading the sort of
books Frederick William had confiscated and sold in 1730. As he had
no Latin, thanks to his father's directive that he should not be taught
anything so 'useless',[5] little English, and used German only with his
social inferiors, this meant that everything had to be in the French
language. It was in French translation that Frederick read the Greek
and Roman classics, along with English and even German philosophy.
It can also be assumed that French wine, banished on the express
orders of Frederick William in 1730, returned to his dining table.[6]

A long-standing favourite author was Pierre Bayle (1647–1706),
whose works had been in the clandestine library. Although periodic
attempts are made to reclaim Bayle for Christianity, he was regarded
by the sceptics of the Enlightenment as one of their most important
founding fathers, if not *the* most important.[7] His *Philosophical and
Historical Dictionary* of 1697 went through edition after edition during the next century. 'The first dictionary that taught men to think'
was Voltaire's accolade. Frederick paid his own tribute by financing
and editing two anthologies of articles from the compendious complete work. In his view it had delivered the *coup de grâce* to religion
by 'tearing the blindfold of error from mankind's eyes'.[8] Laudatory
remarks about Bayle and his influence abound in Frederick's works
and correspondence. Among other compliments, he hailed him as 'the

true precursor of Voltaire', 'the premier dialectician in Europe', 'of all men who have ever lived, he was the one who knew how to gain most from dialectics and reasoning'.[9] In his struggle against religious intolerance, Frederick wrote, Voltaire stood on the shoulders of another giant – Bayle.[10] On campaign during the Seven Years War, Frederick complained to the Marquis d'Argens that he had inadvertently left his books by Bayle behind at Breslau. He asked for the *Various Thoughts on the Occasion of a Comet* to be sent on post-haste, for he desperately needed 'this intellectual food which heals our prejudices and provides essential nutrition to sustain our reason and good sense'.[11] This was the book he hailed later as the best guide of all for logical thinking.[12] Further evidence that Bayle was an important influence on Frederick's thinking can be found in the copy of the *Philosophical and Historical Dictionary* in his library, which is liberally covered in underlinings and marginalia.[13] During his last winter, 1785–6, he was still having passages read to him from one of the four editions of Bayle's *Dictionary* he owned.[14]

It was also at Ruppin that Frederick was able to devote to music the attention he believed it deserved. Music for him was much more than an agreeable recreation and something to entertain the private man in moments of leisure. Throughout his life, he saw it as an integral part of who he was and what he did. He identified himself with Apollo, the charismatic protector of scholarship and art in general and music in particular. It was an identification which ran through his work as a leitmotiv.[15] In 1738 he wrote an eloquent letter to the Count of Schaumburg-Lippe, stressing the centrality of music to a true nobleman's existence and his active life. He contrasted this with those contemptible Spanish nobles who believed idleness to be the true mark of gentility. Music, Frederick maintained, was unique in its ability to communicate emotions and speak to the soul.[16] No sooner had he arrived at Ruppin than he set about forming a band of instrumentalists and singers. There from the start was Johann Gottlieb Graun, a composer and violinist who had been director of music of the Prince of Waldeck. In 1735 he was joined by his brother Carl Heinrich, who taught Frederick musical theory and was to become the most important composer at his court.[17] It was very much to Frederick's credit that he should have been able to detect the Graun brothers' talent and secure their long-term employment. Both men remained in Frederick's service until their deaths in 1771 and 1759 respectively. So did two other distinguished violinist-composers, the brothers Franz and Johann Benda, who were recruited in 1733 and 1734 and died in 1786 and 1752 respectively.[18] In his autobiography Franz Benda claimed to have accompanied Frederick in 10,000 performances of flute concertos.[19] Other distinguished Ruppin musicians were the harpsichordist Christoph Schaffrath and the bass viol player Johann Gottlieb Janitsch.[20] An occasional visitor was the flautist Johann Joachim Quantz,* whom Frederick would have liked to employ had he not been retained by the King of Poland-Saxony.

Frederick's musical establishment at Ruppin eventually numbered seventeen (one more than that of Prince Leopold of Anhalt-Cöthen when Johann Sebastian Bach entered his employment).[21] In 1736 they all moved with Frederick to his new residence at Rheinsberg, some twenty kilometres to the north. Bought in 1734 by Frederick William at Frederick's request, it represented the completion of the reconciliation process. Picturesquely situated on the Grienerick Lake, fed by the river Rhin, and surrounded by forests of beech and oak, the original castle was badly in need of repair. As there were strict limits to the king's generosity, razing the existing building and starting again was not an option. Although the early modifications were supervised by the royal director of buildings, Johann Gottfried Kemmeter, from an early stage Frederick was secretly consulting his friend and chosen architect, Georg Wenzeslaus Baron von Knobelsdorff, a gifted amateur with a military background. His first commission had been to create a formal garden for Frederick at Ruppin featuring a Temple of Apollo.[22] Frederick had then sent him on an extended tour of Italy in 1736–7 to study buildings ancient and modern, especially theatres.

On his return, Knobelsdorff set about turning Rheinsberg into a residence fit for a crown prince. The result was a country house of modest size but pleasing proportions, whose exterior has survived more or less unchanged until the present day.[23] The two projecting wings of the single court are linked by an open colonnade and end in two round towers, this last unusual feature being dictated by the need

* See above, p. xxii.

to incorporate the tower already in place. Although Knobelsdorff drew plans and served as project manager, it was Frederick who supplied the ideas, especially those relating to the internal spaces. That the building was not intended for representational purposes was shown by its orientation away from the public sphere of the town (to which the palace presented its backside) to the private realm of gardens and lake. From his little library in the southern round tower Frederick could look out at lake and gardens on three sides without seeing another building. Immediately adjacent was his main library, followed by a study and a suite of eight further rooms occupying most of the south wing. On the ceiling of the tower room a painting entitled *Tranquillity in the Study* by the court painter Antoine Pesne depicted Minerva surrounded by personifications of the sciences, arts and literature, one of whom points to an open book in which are written the names of Frederick's two favourite authors: Horace and Voltaire.[24] Contemporary descriptions reveal how luxurious were the furniture and interior decoration with silver, gilt and pastel shades to the fore.[25] Outside, both the medieval moat and the river Rhin were straightened to complement the rectilinear garden created by Knobelsdorff in the French style.[26]

FREDERICK'S RELATIONS WITH HIS WIFE

Immediately adjacent to Frederick's quarters was the apartment of his wife, who joined him at Rheinsberg on 20 August 1736. Her bedroom was dominated by a massive ornate bed, a gift from her father-in-law.[27] Frederick William was anxious that it be put to good and immediate use, so keen indeed that he had promised to allow Frederick to travel abroad as soon as he sired a child.[28] A year earlier he had sent Elizabeth Christine a birthday present with a note: 'Madame, as today is your birthday, I congratulate you with my whole heart and wish you a long life and in a few months' time a plump and strapping baby son.'[29] The frustration of his hopes raises the important but murky question of Frederick's sexuality.

Until very recently this was a topic historians either did not mention or passed over swiftly and with disdain. Representative was Otto Hintze, whose single paragraph in his magisterial history of the Hohenzollerns first published in 1915 stated that the 'gossip' was contradictory and needed no refutation; that the malicious stories about 'perverted inclinations' should not be repeated; that, as a young man, Frederick had drained the cup of (heterosexual) love to the very last drop but had then abstained on health grounds; and that his indifference to women was typical of eighteenth-century intellectuals (an observation that would have come as a surprise to – say – Voltaire, Rousseau or Diderot).[30] The most eminent of the next generation's biographers, Gerhard Ritter, was even more perfunctory, recording only that there was 'little of substance to report' and that 'Frederick's sexual life was in no way abnormal', although conceding that 'psychologically as well as physically his sexual needs were unusually limited'.[31] No more expansive was Theodor Schieder, who solemnly recorded that 'in no official record' could anything be found explaining why Frederick decided at an early age that he would not have children (as if that settled anything). Although there were malicious rumours about his sexuality spread by Voltaire, Schieder added, the most convincing explanation was provided by the doctor who attended him during his last illness, the Swiss-born Johann Georg von Zimmermann, who wrote that Frederick had convinced himself that he was impotent after contracting venereal disease from a prostitute shortly before his marriage.[32] The author of the current standard biography, Johannes Kunisch, also maintains that young Frederick was completely heterosexual but that his 'homoerotic preference' became apparent after his accession to the throne and then persisted until the end of his life.[33] He also repeats the Zimmermann story.[34] However, two shorter studies published as part of the celebrations of Frederick's tercentenary birthday are quite unequivocal: 'decisive in explaining Frederick's personality was his sexuality. Frederick was homosexual' is Wolfgang Burgdorf's verdict, while Reinhard Alings's answer to the question he poses – 'Was Frederick gay?' – is: 'There can be no reasonable doubt.'[35] Their view has been confirmed most recently by Peter-Michael Hahn's excellent biography.[36] It will be argued in what follows that these last opinions accord best with what is known, although certainty can never be achieved.

The fullest contemporary account of Frederick's sexuality, and also the one with the most enduring influence, was provided by Zimmermann. According to this version, Frederick was enthusiastically heterosexual during his youth. Denied the company of respectable women by his father's brutality, of necessity he turned to prostitutes. Unfortunately, just at a time when Frederick William was due to take him off to Brunswick to meet his bride-to-be, he contracted an acute dose of gonorrhoea. On the advice of his cousin, the Margrave of Brandenburg-Schwedt, Frederick was treated by 'the doctor of Malchow', believed that he had been cured and proceeded on his journey. All his reservations about the bride forced on him by his father were dispelled by 'the incomparable' Elizabeth Christine's 'charm and beauty', so their marriage initially proved entirely satisfactory. The happy couple shared the same bed every night and all night. Alas, after six months of wedded bliss the gonorrhoea erupted again, so violently indeed that Frederick's life was in danger. The only remedy was deemed to be a surgical operation, which led to a minor deformation of his genitalia. Zimmermann stressed that this did not amount to castration, an operation which was known to make the victim 'timid, cunning and deceitful'. Although just 'a little bit mutilated', he had not been castrated, was still able to produce sperm and therefore remained what he had always been: 'a man of supreme intellectual power, the most fearless and the greatest hero of his age'. He 'must have' retained his heterosexual drive, but had convinced himself that his little defect had reduced him to being a eunuch. So it was 'completely against his inclination and completely against his will' that he felt obliged to distance himself from the wife he loved so passionately and to pretend that he had been alienated from her by a forced marriage. But Frederick went further: he *pretended* to have a liking for what Zimmermann coyly referred to as 'Socratic love' so that he would continue to appear virile and capable of sexual intercourse, albeit with men. Rather than reveal the minor deformity which made sex impossible, he put up with the belief that he engaged in 'the depraved weakness common to many Greeks and Romans'.[37]

Quite apart from its inherent implausibility, this story lacks any kind of corroboration. Most fundamentally, Zimmermann never revealed his sources, if indeed there were any. It must stand or fall by the genital deformation caused by the alleged operation in 1733. As Frederick's physician during his last illness, Zimmermann would almost certainly have had the opportunity to make the necessary inspection. However, the surgeon Gottlieb Engel, who helped to prepare Frederick's body for burial, indignantly asserted that the royal genitalia were as 'complete and perfect as those of any healthy man'.[38] This opinion was confirmed by a joint statement issued in 1790 by the three medical officers who helped to wash the body.[39] Although it does not necessarily invalidate his testimony, it needs to be recorded that Zimmermann was a long-standing and passionate admirer of Frederick, despite being Swiss by birth and Hanoverian by choice. After his first encounter with his hero in 1771 he left the room in floods of tears, exclaiming 'Oh, my love for the King of Prussia is beyond words!'[40] However, there is so much error in his account – for example, he has the newlyweds moving to Rheinsberg immediately after their marriage, rather than three years later – that his reliability must be doubted.[41] Moreover, his own apologia for Frederick often points in an unintended direction. He records, for example, that 'almost everyone' who knew Frederick – friends and enemies, princes and servants, even his closest confidants and companions – believed that he 'engaged in the same sort of relationship as that between Socrates and Alcibiades'. Even Zimmermann himself had once believed this too, not least because one of Frederick's male favourites had told him that Frederick was still active [homo]sexually in 1756.[42]

On the other hand, there is certainly some evidence of heterosexual attraction if not activity. The inconclusive Dresden episode has already been discussed.* Better documented is a flirtation with a married woman, Eléonore-Louise von Wreech, dating from the time Frederick spent at Küstrin. The seven letters which have survived from 1731–2 are ardent but light in tone, ironic, almost flippant, and highly stylized.[43] Four are in verse-form or contain verses, for example:

> Accept, Madame, a heart that is too tender
> Which impatiently awaits only your permission
> To lay before you its sweet submission,

---

* See above, pp. 34–6.

And which until now has hesitated to do so.
I count the moments, I count the minutes,
Until I can receive from you the decision,
That will determine all my actions.[44]

Evidence regarding this relationship is conflicting. On 30 August 1732 the minister von Grumbkow wrote to the Austrian ambassador von Seckendorf (often spelt 'Seckendorff') that Frederick William had told him that Frederick had got Frau von Wreech pregnant and that the cuckolded husband would refuse to recognize the child as his own. Frederick William was pleased by this sign of his son's virility and hoped that Frederick's fiancée would be equally impressed.[45] This should have come as no surprise to Seckendorf, for six months earlier he had reported to Prince Eugene in Vienna that Frederick was passionately in love with the lady and was engaging in such intense debauchery with her that he had no time to think about anything else.[46] Again the ultimate source of this story was Grumbkow, who was on the Austrian payroll, had his spies on Frederick's staff and sent back to his paymasters via Seckendorf any information that might be of value. Although it is difficult to see why he should have invented the story, he does not reveal how he came by it. He may well have had an informant on Frederick's staff, who however could hardly have been present during any such trysts. Certainly there is nothing in the surviving correspondence to indicate a physical relationship and Frau von Wreech was not pregnant. Seckendorf himself was not convinced. A month later he told Prince Eugene that, although Frederick was in an erotic mood, 'it was believed' that his physical capability did not match his ambition and consequently his amorous pursuits were more a case of showing off than genuine desire.[47]

By this time, of course, Frederick was engaged to be married. As Seckendorf lamented, Frederick's attitude wobbled between sulky resignation and vehement rejection of his bride-to-be. He wrote to his sister in March 1732 that Elizabeth Christine was not without her good points, for she had quite a pretty face, blonde hair, a good complexion, shapely breasts, and a slender figure, but on the debit side she had deeply set eyes, an ugly mouth, bad teeth, an unpleasant laugh and walked like a duck. Moreover, she was very badly educated, nervous in conversation and so almost always stayed silent. She was well-intentioned, good-natured, polite and modest, in short 'not quite as bad as I had expected and had been led to believe'. Nevertheless, he concluded, she did not please him at all, for the good reason that she was his father's choice.[48] He himself would have preferred one of the other candidates, a Princess of Saxony-Eisenach or a Princess of Mecklenburg. No sooner had he signalled his consent than he told Grumbkow: 'I have been unhappy all my life and I believe that it is my destiny to stay that way ... but I still have a last resort, and a pistol shot would simultaneously put an end to my misery and to my life.' He implored Grumbkow to get the wedding stopped. The minister replied with a stern reminder of the fate of Philip II's son Don Carlos.[49] The long engagement of eighteen months did nothing to reconcile him to his fate. In September 1732 he told Wilhelmine that, far from loving his bride-to-be, he had developed an intense aversion towards her. The marriage would never amount to anything, he added, there could be no sense of affinity, no friendship.[50]

Seckendorf remained confident that all would be well in the end because, for all his repugnance, Frederick could also grasp that marriage offered the only escape route from his current subjection.[51] He was right. Also in September 1732 Frederick delivered the definitive statement of his position in a letter to Grumbkow:

> They want to beat me into an amorous frame of mind; but as unfortunately I don't have the nature of a donkey, I doubt very much whether they will succeed ... Marriage means one comes of age and as soon as I have reached that state, I shall be the master in my own house and my wife will have nothing to say in the matter, for women should have no role in government or in anything else either! I believe that a man who allows himself to be governed by women is the greatest poltroon in the world and unworthy to bear the honourable name of man. And that is why, if I marry in the style of a gentleman, that is to say I let Madame do as she sees fit, then for my part I shall do what I like myself and long live liberty! ... I shall keep my word, I shall get married, but afterwards it will be a case of that is that, and goodbye, Madame, and fare thee well.[52]

Also indicative of Frederick's feelings as the wedding approached was a mocking letter he sent to Grumbkow at the beginning of 1733: 'my princess has sent me a snuff-box which arrived broken, and I'm not sure whether this symbolises the fragility of her hymen, her virtue or her whole person'.[53] Shortly before the ceremony he told Wilhelmine that he was only going through with it out of 'extreme necessity' and that he inwardly rejected it.[54] In view of her own unhappy forced marriage, Wilhelmine probably concurred with Frederick's likening marriage to the bubonic plague and his further observation that the very word 'marriage' caused him intense pain.[55]

There is very little evidence of what happened after the wedding. Frederick's immediate impulse on his wedding night was to write to Wilhelmine to exclaim 'Thank God that's over!', adding that his first thoughts were for his sister and that he belonged completely to her.[56] The most interesting comments on the early stages of the marriage come from a diary kept by Christoph Ludwig von Seckendorf, nephew of the Austrian ambassador, who was in Berlin in 1734–7. Although not part of Frederick's circle, he saw both him and Frederick William frequently and was generally part of Prussian high society. In October 1734 Seckendorf recorded that Frederick 'is fond of the Crown Princess' and had shown Count von der Schulenburg letters from her, adding the rather double-edged comment: 'even so, she has common sense'. Presumably it was also from Schulenburg that Seckendorf learned that 'he fucks and refucks her', for he went on to add that Schulenburg just laughed when people said that Frederick would renounce his wife when he came to the throne.[57] Seckendorf was also friendly with Count Friedrich von Wartensleben, a member of the Rheinsberg circle and singled out by Frederick in 1741 as one of the six people he had most loved in his life.[58] He recorded in June 1735: 'Friedrich Wartensleben has confided in me that Junior [Frederick] fucks his wife in the afternoon and says that she has a lovely body and a beautiful arse.' In the following month Wartensleben confirmed that Frederick was sleeping with her.[59]

Wartensleben cannot have known, of course, what was going on in the bedroom but he certainly knew what Frederick was saying about it. For his part, Seckendorf had no reason to falsify or to exaggerate what he wrote in a private diary not intended for publication. At the very least, Zimmermann's story of a Frederick shamed by a surgeon's cut is refuted. Seckendorf's reliability is strengthened by an entry in his diary made the following year which can be partly corroborated. In the summer of 1736 he recorded that after Frederick had complained of poverty, he had been told by another of his friends, Count Manteuffel, that if he wished to improve his situation, he should sire an heir. Frederick had agreed that was good advice but added: 'I cannot sleep with my wife out of desire, and when I do sleep with her, I do it out of duty rather than inclination.' Manteuffel replied that passion was not always necessary, plenty of children had been conceived without their parents liking each other at all, the crown princess was very pretty and seemed expressly made for 'that'. Frederick agreed that she was very pretty but protested that he had never been in love with her. He went on to pay tribute to her many good qualities, including an eager readiness to do whatever her husband wished, and concluded: 'In any case, she can't complain that I don't sleep with her: I have no idea why a child does not result.'[60]

Seckendorf recorded this exchange as if it had been a conversation which Manteuffel had then told him about. In reality, there had been an exchange of letters. On 26 August 1736 Manteuffel had written to Frederick to urge him to produce an heir, adding that this was what all his friends wanted. He also expressed the hope that the settled life at Rheinsberg – to which Frederick and Elizabeth Christine had just moved – would be more conducive to conception than the previous short and hurried encounters necessitated by Frederick's garrison duties at Ruppin and his wife's residence at Berlin.[61] In his reply, dated Rheinsberg 23 September, Frederick made no mention of his feelings for his wife, merely writing: 'I am very obliged to you for your concern about my propagation, and I have the same destiny as the stags who are presently in rut; in nine months from now there may happen what you ask for.'[62] Even if it did not, there was nothing to worry about: 'kingdoms always find successors and there has never been a case of a throne remaining empty'.[63] Had there been a conversation such as that recorded by Seckendorf as well as this exchange of letters? All that can be stated with certainty is that Frederick wished Manteuffel – and thus his father – to know that he was doing his best to produce an heir.

In other words, during the four years they lived together at Rheinsberg, Frederick was at pains to present his marriage to his parents as entirely normal. In his letters to his sister Wilhelmine, on the other hand, he never mentioned his wife, it was as if his marriage had not happened. In 1738 he sent Prince Leopold of Anhalt-Dessau on a secret mission to the Vice-Chancellor of the Holy Roman Empire, Friedrich Karl von Schönborn, to secure imperial assistance in getting the marriage dissolved.[64] Moreover, hitherto unpublished letters from Manteuffel to other correspondents, and from Frederick to a Lieutenant von der Groeben, indicate that he continued to maintain intimate relations with young officers of his regiment.[65] Two letters written to his mother during a journey with his father to East Prussia in the summer of 1739, also hint at play-acting. In a letter to Elizabeth Christine of 27 July which was to be passed on to his mother, Frederick went out of his way to emphasize his affection, as in: 'I very much look forward to being back in Rheinsberg and even more to the pleasure of kissing you ... May God protect you, my lady! Please do not forget me, and permit me to embrace you with all my heart, be sure that I am totally devoted to you.' But a letter written two weeks later which he expressly stated was *not* to be shown to his mother was appreciably less fulsome, ending simply with 'your most obedient servant'.[66] As soon as Frederick William died, the tone became much sharper. The very first letter he wrote to his wife as king, on 31 May 1740, issued curt instructions as to when and where she was to go and what she was to do, signing off with 'I have no time to tell you anything more. Goodbye.'[67] Any hopes Elizabeth Christine may have had of becoming Queen in Prussia in anything more than name were dashed by another letter the very next day:

> Madame, when you arrive [in Berlin] you will go first to the Queen [Mother] to pay your respects, and you will try to make a better job of it than in the past; after that you may remain here, your presence being necessary, until I write to tell you what to do. You will see few or no people. Tomorrow I shall decide on the mourning to be observed by the women and shall send details to you. Farewell, I trust that I shall have the pleasure to find you in good health.[68]

As this implied, henceforth there was to be only one woman in Frederick's life: his mother. Back in 1731 when he attended his sister

Wilhelmine's wedding, he told her that his heart would belong to her and their mother alone.[69] As Carlyle observed, Frederick was 'always his mother's boy'. When she tried to address him as 'Your Majesty', he replied 'please call me son, for that is the title of all others most agreeable to me!' and returned the compliment by insisting that she be styled 'Her Majesty the Queen Mother' not 'Queen Dowager'.[70] The diplomat who reported a week after his accession that 'the new king's devotion to his mother is very apparent' was to be proved wrong, however, when he also predicted that she would prove to be highly influential and would push Prussia in the direction of Hanover.[71] Frederick took direction from no one, not even his mother. He did, however, make it clear that she was to be regarded as the first lady of Prussia, and her court at Monbijou Palace was to be the first port of call for visiting dignitaries. It was there that Frederick went to dine when he was in Berlin.[72] The 'great affection' he always showed her mightily impressed all those who witnessed it.[73]

Left on the sidelines was Queen Elizabeth Christine, publicly humiliated by her brutal subordination to her mother-in-law. 'You can have no idea of what I have to suffer,' she wrote to her brother Duke Karl of Brunswick on 28 June 1740. 'God alone knows and only God can help me.'[74] Frederick packed her off to Schönhausen, a modest residence in what is now the Pankow district in north Berlin. It compared very unfavourably with the queen mother's palace of Monbijou. At Schönhausen she formed her own little court and eked out what was clearly a lonely and frustrated existence. In March 1744 she wrote to her cousin Ferdinand of Brunswick:

> I remain stuck in this old chateau like a prisoner, while the others have fun. I entertain myself with reading, work and music, and it is always a high day for me when I get a letter from you – that puts me in a happy frame of mind for the whole day, and the time I spend writing to you is a time of relaxation.[75]

Frederick's neglect can only be described as studied, contemptuous and spiteful. This was revealed most clearly by an episode in the summer of 1748. To celebrate the completion of a new wing at the Charlottenburg Palace, Frederick planned a festival for all the family – bar one. For although the queen mother expressly stated that she would have no objection if her daughter-in-law attended, the queen was not invited. Frederick explained why in a letter to his brother August Wilhelm: 'If my hypersensitive grouch of a wife joins the expedition to Charlottenburg, I'm afraid she will spoil the whole occasion.' His further comment that there was no adequate accommodation was particularly disingenuous, for protocol had required that a whole suite of rooms in the new wing be assigned to the queen. In a passage reeking of misogyny, Frederick concluded:

> Anyway, what would we do with the swarm of chambermaids and court ladies etc. if my delicate better-half were to be resident at Charlottenburg? How could we feed this incorrigibly sour sub-species of the female sex and accommodate all the riff-raff who mill around court establishments? What we want to do is to entertain our mother with an excursion and rural amusements. Let's stick to that resolution and not mix nettles and weeds in among the jasmine and the roses.[76]

Frederick never visited his wife at Schönhausen and never permitted her to visit him. The only time she saw Sanssouci was when she passed through Potsdam in the autumn of 1757 when being evacuated to Magdeburg to escape the invading Austrians. As her chamberlain Count Lehndorff confided acidly to his diary, it was odd that it needed the Empress Maria Theresa to send an army to Berlin to give the Queen of Prussia the opportunity of seeing her husband's favourite residence.[77]

The royal couple met on only rare occasions, usually in the royal palace at Berlin, where the queen spent the winter months, when there was a gala during the carnival season. Although Frederick made sure she lived in comfort, paid her debts and occasionally showed an awareness of her existence by sending a present on her birthday or enquiring after her health, his conduct can only be described as cruel. Not only did he fail to attend her fiftieth birthday party on 8 November 1765, but on the following day he presided over a lavish festivity in honour of the Crown Princess Elizabeth Christine at Potsdam, to which her namesake the queen was not even invited.[78] The unhappy couple's golden wedding in 1783 went unmarked and a print-maker who offered an imaginary scene of what the celebrations might have looked like had his prints confiscated by the police.[79] It must have been the public nature of her humiliation that caused Elizabeth Christine most pain. When Frederick returned to Berlin in 1763 after seven years of absence in the eponymous war, his only greeting to his wife (whom, incidentally, he never referred to as 'my wife' but always as 'the Queen'[80]) before his whole court was: 'Madame has got fat.' At the banquet which followed, he shunned her company, preferring to sit between his sister-in-law Wilhelmine and his sister Amalia.[81] His behaviour was thrown into even sharper relief by the quiet dignity with which Elizabeth Christine endured her lot. For her, he was always 'the greatest hero of the age' and she told anyone who would listen that she had been denied children only by Divine Providence.[82]

FREDERSDORF

The timing of the move from coexistence to rejection following the death of Frederick William I must cast doubt on the sincerity with which Frederick had posed as the ideal husband during the previous four years. It was also immediately after he achieved independence that Frederick bought a landed estate at Zernickow near Rheinsberg for his valet Michael Gabriel Fredersdorf. The lucky beneficiary of his largesse had been born in 1708 at Garz on the river Oder, the son of a town musician. In 1730, when serving at Frankfurt an der Oder as a musician in a regiment of musketeers, he was introduced to Frederick by his commanding officer, Count Schwerin, to lighten his captivity at Küstrin with some mutual music-making.[83] On his liberation, Frederick secured Fredersdorf's release from military service and employed him, first as a lackey and then as a valet. At Rheinsberg Fredersdorf was recognized as Frederick's 'favourite', who played only for his master.[84] Baron Bielfeld, who stayed at Rheinsberg in the autumn of 1739, wrote: 'the first valet of the Crown Prince, Fredersdorf, is a tall, handsome man who is clever and shrewd, courteous, considerate, skilful and adaptable, with an eye for the main chance but also generous. I believe that he will have a leading role to play some day.'[85]

He was right, although Fredersdorf remains a shadowy character. In 1740 Frederick appointed him Privy Treasurer and that was the office he occupied until his death in 1758.[86] Although in this capacity he did attend to Frederick's personal money matters, he was really more like a personal assistant – 'le grand factotum du roi Frédéric' was Voltaire's description.[87] He saw to the purchases of snuff boxes, objets d'art and musical instruments; assembled Frederick's personal provisions for campaigns; directed the fitting out of palaces and gardens; organized festivities, including the all-important task of issuing invitations; and so on.[88] A French visitor to Frederick's court observed that there was a chancellor who never spoke, a huntsman who would not dare to kill a quail, a butler who did not know whether there was wine in the cellar, a stable-master who did not know how to saddle a horse, a chamberlain who had never handed over a shirt, and a grand master of the wardrobe who did not know the name of the court tailor – because all these functions were performed by Fredersdorf.[89] Count Lehndorff recorded in his diary how he found 'the famous Fredersdorf' at Potsdam acting as a kind of 'prime minister', surrounded by the high and the mighty paying court to him in an antechamber filled with supplicants.[90] As this suggested, if you wanted something done at the court of King Frederick, Fredersdorf was the man to see. It was to him that the queen turned in 1748 when she tried in vain to secure an invitation to the impending festivities at Charlottenburg, asking him to transmit to Frederick her 'most humble' request to be present. She would be bringing a retinue of only five people, she pathetically added (her mother-in-law and sister-in-law, who did get invitations, took a total of forty-five).[91]

What did Elizabeth Christine make of her husband's relationship with his 'grand factotum'? Not unnaturally, the tongues at court wagged. Count Lehndorff asked rhetorically how a totally common man with no education 'from the back-end of Pomerania' had been able to rise to be second man in the kingdom, the only one after the king who could give orders and who often abused his power in a despotic fashion? The answer, he confided to his diary, was simple: Fredersdorf's 'very pretty face'.[92] Although there is no unequivocal evidence of a sexual relationship (how could there be?), there can be no doubt that Frederick felt very strong affection. Fredersdorf was another of the six men Frederick identified in 1741 as 'those I have loved the most during my life'.[93] Only once did Fredersdorf appear to have lost his position, when ejected from Frederick's tent while on campaign in favour of a handsome hussar. The mysterious suicide of his rival soon afterwards saw Fredersdorf back in Frederick's favour.[94] As we have seen, he had given concrete expression to his affection by purchasing a substantial estate for Fredersdorf as soon as he came to the throne. This was all the more remarkable a gesture in that it was a *Rittergut*, that is to say an estate reserved for the landed nobility. Moreover, it was always Frederick's firmly stated opinion that noble land should not be allowed to pass into the hands of commoners.* Fredersdorf turned out to be an energetic and enterprising landlord, buying more land to round off his original holding and establishing a silk-worm breeding plantation there. Later he branched out into commerce, buying a merchant ship that plied the Baltic ports and a plantation in Dutch Guyana. The 'Fredersdorfer beer' from the breweries he established at Spandau and Köpenick acquired a good reputation in Berlin.[95] He also took a keen interest in alchemy, building a laboratory and even persuading a sceptical Frederick to enter into an agreement with a woman called Notnagel, who claimed to be able to turn base metal into gold.[96]

Frederick's numerous letters to Fredersdorf are intimate in tone and substance – what one might expect from a doting husband. Significantly, he used the intimate second-person *Du* form, not the impersonal third-person usually employed when addressing a servant. Much of the correspondence is taken up with Frederick reporting on his own health, which was often bad, and expressing tender concern for Fredersdorf's own ailments, which were even worse. Both men suffered regularly from anal problems. 'I am suffering from haemorrhoids,' reported Frederick in March 1747, for example, adding that, as it happened after an enema, the affliction may have been caused by a defective tube.[97] In April 1754 he informed Fredersdorf that he had celebrated the latter's recovery from illness with two bottles of Hungarian wine. He added that on this occasion 'Carel' had squealed when being tickled, this being a reference to Carl Friedrich von Pirch, one of the royal pages who carried messages to and from Fredersdorf. Fifteen years old at the time, Carel was dubbed 'White Mene' by Frederick because he was blond, as opposed to 'Black Mene', Frederick's favourite dog. However, Frederick

---

* See below, pp. 402–3.

added, Carel had also been 'very naughty' and so was to have his pocket-money docked.[98] There is much more of this playful banter in the correspondence with unmistakable homoerotic overtones.

Frederick passed over Fredersdorf's marriage in 1753 to a rich heiress, with whom he then lived in some style in a grand house in Berlin near the Brandenburg Gate.[99] In 1757 he persuaded Frederick to allow him to retire. According to Lehndorff, this was due to his continuing ill health, his accumulated wealth, his wish for a quiet life, but also his jealousy of 'the famous Glasow', adding rather spitefully that he admired Fredersdorf for knowing when to quit 'just like a beautiful woman being able to spot when her beauty is fading'.[100] Christian Friedrich Glasow was famous for all the wrong reasons. He had caught Frederick's eye in 1755 when serving as a private soldier in an infantry regiment at Brieg in Silesia and was made his batman.[101] He was only one of two people to accompany Frederick on his private journey to the Dutch Republic the same year.[102] For reasons which are still not entirely clear, their relationship ended abruptly in 1757. According to Johann Wilhelm von Archenholz, who joined the Prussian army as a cadet in that year and later wrote a celebrated history of the Seven Years War, Glasow was 'a great favourite of the king's, so much so, that he was often required to sleep in the king's bedchamber'. Bribed to poison his master, he was apprehended by accident at the last moment, arrested and sent to Spandau, where he soon died.[103] An alternative version offered by Anton Friedrich Büsching held that Glasow's crime was to use the royal seal to issue unauthorized orders.[104] A petition from Glasow's father, a *Zeugleutnant* in the artillery with forty-six years' service, dated 22 June 1757, revealed that the offender was twenty years old, his youth being the only mitigating circumstance mentioned. Frederick wrote across the bottom of the petition: 'his son's crime is very great but there is some mitigation'.[105]

ALGAROTTI

Following Fredersdorf and his short-lived successor has taken us a long way from Frederick's sexual liberation on the death of his father. Another actor in this process was the Italian man of letters Francesco

Algarotti, whom Frederick first met in 1739 at Rheinsberg, when visiting in the company of the English peer Lord Baltimore. Born in the same year as Frederick, Algarotti was the son of a rich Venetian merchant and had studied at Bologna and Florence before embarking on a European tour. In 1736 he made a name for himself with the publication of *Newtonianism for Ladies*, a successful exercise in popularization which brought him to the attention of Voltaire, whom he visited at Cirey.[106] Equipped with Voltaire's letters of introduction, Algarotti then moved to London, where he very quickly made an intriguing double conquest of two aristocrats: Lady Mary Wortley Montagu (daughter of the Duke of Kingston) and Lord Hervey (son of the Earl of Bristol). Not only were these two engaged in an intermittent adulterous relationship, they were also both bisexual. As Hervey's biographer put it: 'they accepted each other for the flawed but interesting human beings that they respectively were, Lady Mary as a woman who at times wanted to be a man and Lord Hervey as the opposite'. William Pulteney described Hervey as 'Mr *Fainlove* ... such a nice Composition of the two Sexes, that it is difficult to distinguish which is more praedominant.'[107]

Even by the standards of mid-eighteenth-century London, this was an exotic *ménage à trois*. Love letters circulated in multiple permutations. 'I love you with all my Heart, & beg you never to forget the affection I have for you, nor let the affection you have expressed for me grow weaker,' wrote Hervey to Algarotti. 'Adieu, My Lord, continue to love me, and sometimes think of me,' replied the latter. Those words were written from St Petersburg, to which Algarotti and his (platonic) friend Lord Baltimore had travelled in 1739 to attend the wedding of the tsarina's niece.[108] Both Lord Hervey and Lady Mary, however, were outbid when Algarotti met Frederick. According to Marc Fumaroli, this was love at first sight, a *coup de foudre* for both parties. Algarotti wrote to Voltaire: 'I have seen, *oh me beato*, this adorable prince ... I cannot put in words the number of pleasures I have experienced!'[109] For his part, Frederick was, if anything, even more effusive. No sooner had Algarotti departed after a sojourn of just eight days than Frederick fired off letter after letter to his 'swan of Padua'. In the third one, dated 1 September 1739, he exclaimed: 'Happy are the men who can enjoy the company of clever people!

Happier still are the princes who can possess them!' Never would he forget the week they had spent together, he added at the end of October, and then broke into verse:

> Never would I have sought
> the frivolous advantage of vain honour,
> for I measure all my efforts and courage
> against my strength.
> It is said that in his seraglio the Turk
> ....
> .... [*sic*]
> Has a hundred beauties at his disposal;
> Which he can take his turn with, if he so wishes,
> That Atlas carries the world by himself,
> That Hercules tamed the giants,
> That the Gods vanquished the Titans:
> A less illustrious victory
> Will always suffice for my glory
> By honouring my talents.

Frederick signed off by declaring that he was delighted that Algarotti had happy memories of Rheinsberg 'where the memory of his presence would be eternal and where he was immortal'.[110]

Frederick also wrote to Voltaire, rhapsodizing about Algarotti's 'fire, vivacity and sweetness'. They had talked about everything under the sun, he reported, adding happily that Algarotti had promised to return as soon as possible.[111] Voltaire replied to Frederick in verse, as if he were addressing Algarotti and including the following suggestive lines:

> Cease, Algarotti, to look at other people,
> The call-girls of Venice and the rent-boys of Rome,
> In the theatres of France and at the tables of Germans,
> The ministers, kings, heroes and saints;
> Don't wear yourself out, no longer look for a man:
> He has been found. Heaven, which fashioned his virtues,
> Heaven, has placed my hero at Rheinsberg ...
> Bring your wanderings to an end at the foot of Rheinsberg,

The universe no longer counts for anything;
You have nothing left to see.[112]

Frederick William I died seven months later, on 31 May 1740. On 2 June Frederick wrote to Algarotti: 'My dear Algarotti, my lot has changed. I await you with impatience; please don't make me pine. Frederick.' He added a postscript in verse:

> Come, Algarotti, from the banks of the Thames
> Share with us our happy destiny.
> Hasten to reach this pleasant place,
> Where you will find liberty is our watchword.
> This is to let you know that four days ago Frederick II
>   succeeded Frederick William.
> All his people with us feel no joy,
> He alone, as a loving son, is prey to grief,
> Caring little for the attractions of such a flattering destiny,
> He deserves to be loved and to reign over your heart.[113]

Frederick then added a line of Latin – *Ne gaudia igitur nostra moreris. Algarotti venturo, Phosphore, redde diem*, which is an adaptation of Martial's epigram VIII/21 and can be translated as 'Don't delay our rejoicing. Algarotti return, Morning Star bring back the day.' The Morning Star is, of course, Venus.

The response was everything Frederick could have wished for. Algarotti wrote to his brother Bonomo a few days later that he had just received 'the most beautiful letter ever written'.[114] Speeded on his way by fifty guineas supplied on Frederick's instructions by 'the Jew Mendez' and a letter of credit on Amsterdam, he reached Berlin on 28 June. On 7 July the two men set off for Königsberg for Frederick's coronation as 'King in Prussia'. In 1701 his grandfather Frederick I had needed 30,000 horses and 1,800 carriages to transport the Electoral family, court and retainers, and the whole expedition cost 6,000,000 talers, or about twice the total annual revenue of the state.[115] Frederick took just three coaches and spent next to nothing.[116] Sitting in the royal coach alongside the king was Algarotti 'like a royal mistress'.[117] Needless to say, the queen was not a member of the party. On their return later that month, Algarotti wrote to his brother that the king 'gave me countless caresses, and honoured me in a thousand different ways'.[118] Among the latter were appointment as Chevalier of the newly created Order 'Pour le Mérite', the title of Kammerherr ('Chamberlain') and elevation to the nobility as count, an honour that was also granted to his brother. These were accompanied by expensive presents of porcelain, watches and snuff-boxes decorated with diamonds.[119] As Lord Baltimore commented in a letter to him on 7 June 1740: 'since you are now in the land of Canaan, nothing can be wanting to make you the happiest of men'.[120] For his part, Algarotti entertained Frederick with bawdy sonnets and songs by the Venetian patrician Giorgio Baffo, a special favourite being 'In praise of the bum'.[121] Back in London, Lady Mary and Lord Hervey realized they had been outbid. The latter wrote ruefully to Algarotti on 28 June 1740: 'There are so few people in the world whom God Almighty has made to be liked or who have made themselves to be loved, that you will not wonder when I tell you I hourly regret one of the few I find so deserving of both. Adieu.'[122]

From Charlottenburg on 29 July 1740 Frederick wrote to Voltaire announcing his return from his coronation and enclosing a poem entitled 'The Orgasm'.[123] It had been prompted by Algarotti's observation that northern Europeans were less capable of strong emotions than Italians. Frederick sought to prove poetically that this was not the case, although conceding that some experiences were as difficult to depict in words as the splendour of the sun at high noon. Long thought to be lost (or suppressed), a copy was recently unearthed in the Berlin archives.[124] Addressed to 'M. Algarotti the Swan of Padua', it begins:

> During this night, satisfying his fierce desires,
> Algarotti swam in a sea of pleasure.

The language is certainly ecstatic enough to restore the reputation of the North:

> Divine lust! Sovereign of the world!
> Mother of our pleasures, ever fertile source,
> Sing with your own voice through my verse
> The passion, the actions, the ecstasy of the senses!

Our happy lovers, in their extreme delirium,
In the fury of their love they know only each other:
Kissing,* climaxing, feeling, sighing and expiring,
Resuming, embracing, rushing back for more pleasure.

There is nothing in the poem to suggest that Frederick himself was Algarotti's partner. On the contrary, the passage just quoted is preceded by lines identifying the lover as the nymph 'Chloris', with a body more perfect than that created by the Greek sculptor Praxiteles for Aphrodite for her temple on Knidos. It should also be recorded that, in one letter at least, Frederick appeared to state explicitly that their relationship was not physical. On 29 November 1740 he wrote that he felt as much pleasure at seeing Algarotti again after a long absence as did Medoro when reunited with his beloved Angelica, 'the difference being that it is my intellect alone that participates in this pleasure, and that it seeks only to woo yours to warm itself with the fire of your sparkling genius'.[125] One possible explanation for this reticence, which points the other way, had been signalled in a letter of 24 September in which Frederick referred to Algarotti as an 'illustrious invalid of the Empire of love', wished him a speedy recovery from the 'wounds of Cythera' and expressed the hope that he would at least be able to benefit from his intellect when they met at Berlin.[126] There is also evidence of overt homosexual activity among Frederick's circle. On 15 December 1740 Voltaire wrote in verse to Frederick following his visit to Prussia in the autumn:

Great king, I predicted to you
That Berlin would become the new Athens
For both the pleasures of the flesh and the intellect;
The prophecy has turned out to be quite right.
When, at the home of fat Valori,†
I saw the loving Algarotti
Crush in a passionate embrace

---

* The word used by Frederick here, and in the next line, is '*baiser*', which can mean 'kiss', 'embrace' or, more vulgarly, 'fuck'. Although on occasions Frederick used coarse language, in the context of the poem, the more decorous words seem appropriate, albeit with a carnal overtone.
† Louis Guy Henri Marquis de Valori, the French ambassador, also spelt Valory.

The handsome Lujac,* his young friend,
I thought I was seeing Socrates fastened
To the rump of Alcibiades.[127]

By this time, Frederick was busy conquering Silesia and had other things on his mind. Algarotti was sent on a diplomatic mission to Turin, in the (forlorn) hope of inducing Piedmont to attack Austria. Yet although the relationship could only be intermittent, it remained passionate. In April 1742 Frederick wrote from his camp in Bohemia, saying he was obliged to follow war (Bellona) but feared the anger of hedonism (Epicurus) and sex (Cythera). He called on Algarotti, as the supreme representative of the last two, to intervene on his behalf to deflect the thunderbolts from one 'who was born for them'. Algarotti replied with a particularly effusive tribute to Frederick's shower of favours. They would ensure his own immortality, he added, for when talking about the feats of Achilles, posterity would always also remember his Patroclus.[128] There could hardly be a clearer indication of the relationship between the two men. It was about to go into cold storage, however, for in the autumn of 1742 Frederick became exasperated by Algarotti's reluctance to commit himself to a permanent position in Prussia.[129] It was probably sensible of Algarotti to move to the less demanding and more luxurious surroundings of the Saxon court at Dresden, where he spent the next five years. Frederick's attachment remained strong: in 1746 the British diplomat Thomas Villiers (later Earl of Clarendon) wrote to Algarotti from Berlin: 'The King bid me let you know that he should be extremely glad to see you, comparing your separation, for I can't call it a quarrel, to that of lovers whose affectionate passion continues. Amoris Redintegratio is the completion of happiness.'[130] Returning to Berlin in 1747, Algarotti once again became an influential figure on Berlin's cultural scene but the old intimacy with the king was not restored. Afflicted by chronic illness, he returned to Italy in 1753, dying at Pisa in 1764. Frederick made a substantial contribution to the erection of an elaborate memorial in the cemetery there.[131]

I shall return to the topic of Frederick's sexuality when discussing

---

* Charles Antoine de Guérin Marquis de Lujac (also spelt Lugeac), Valori's secretary.

his court. As this chapter has sought to show, this was not something peripheral, to be passed over in furtive silence or explained away. It was central to his assertion of his own personality after twenty-eight years of oppression and repression. When the crushing weight of his father's tyranny was lifted, at last he could be himself. Putting aside his wife, giving Fredersdorf an estate and making Algarotti a count were all part of a declaration of independence. On 31 May 1740 the grim reaper had brought what Frederick called his 'Egyptian servitude' to an end. He was now king and could do as he pleased. The next stage in his making was not to deny his father but to surpass him in the royal *métiers* that mattered most – war and conquest.

4

The Making of Frederick (part two)

CROSSING THE RUBICON

'I have crossed the Rubicon with flags flying and drums beating,' wrote Frederick to his minister Count Podewils on 16 December 1740. It was on that day that he led his army across the frontier separating Brandenburg from the Habsburg province of Silesia on what was to prove perhaps the most famous smash-and-grab raid in European history (until that point). His spirits were high: 'my soldiers are full of good will, the officers are fired with ambition and the generals are hungry for glory, everything is in our favour and I have reason to anticipate the best possible outcome of this enterprise'.[1]

This coup should not have come as a surprise. Barely six months had passed since he had succeeded to the throne but they had been six months in which he had caused more stir than his father had managed in twenty-seven years. The better informed or more perceptive observers of Frederick as crown prince had long predicted that he would be much more proactive. On 2 October 1736 the younger Seckendorf confided to his diary that 'Junior [Frederick] will not think in such a pacific way when he comes to the throne, but will begin with a sensational stroke [*coup d'éclat*], even at the risk of being on the receiving-end of one himself'.[2] Another well-placed observer, Count Manteuffel, agreed, adding that Frederick was so much more arrogant, lively, bold, devious and unpredictable than his father that the new reign was certain to be much more volatile. That prediction came after receipt of a letter from Frederick, who was at a training camp at Wehlau, which began: 'Alas! Must I always have to write to you from a camp of peace, and shall I never be able to address my letter from a battlefield or the trenches? Shall I spend my whole life like one of those swords which never leave the armaments shop and rust on the nail from which they hang?'[3] In the same year, the British chargé d'affaires at Berlin, Guy Dickens, reported to London that comparisons were being made between the Prussian and Macedonian armies and posed the following rhetorical question: if Alexander the Great could conquer so much with so few, what might Frederick achieve with so many more?[4] They were all correct. Frederick told his envoy sent off to Versailles in June 1740 to stress his 'dynamic and headstrong mind-set' and to warn the French that it was in the nature of young people to be enterprising and that their ambition to be heroic had often proved disruptive. Even more provocatively, Frederick added that the military expansion he had ordered might well ignite a general conflagration in Europe.[5] Although he had disbanded his father's 'Guard of Giants', at the same time he had increased the size of the army by seven infantry regiments.[6] For this expansion he had benefited from the recent end to Austria's disastrous war against the Turks, which had left a number of German princes looking for a new paymaster for their contingents.[7]

Just a week after Frederick sent his warning to the French, he advertised his intentions by intervening in a dispute between the Archbishop-Elector of Mainz and the Landgrave of Hessen-Kassel over the castle and village of Rumpenheim near Offenbach on the river Main. He protested vigorously at the Elector's pre-emptive military occupation – 'a rape', he called it – and threatened his own retaliation if the Mainz troops were not withdrawn forthwith.[8] Needless to say, he had his way. Crushing the hapless archbishop allowed Frederick to indulge two of his strongest prejudices – against the clergy and against the Holy Roman Empire.

It also gave him a taste for more of the same. He now turned his attention to another imperial prelate, the Prince-Bishop of Liège, who was contesting Prussia's right to the barony of Herstal on the river Meuse. In this case, however, David was supported by two Goliaths, France and Austria, so Frederick's advisers counselled caution. His response, scribbled in the margin of their memorandum, was dismissive: 'when the ministers talk about negotiations they show themselves to be clever people but when they talk about war it is as if an Iroquois were talking about astronomy'. He added that he was not afraid of the emperor, who might have been powerful once upon a time but was now nothing more than a *'vieux fantôme d'un idole'* ('an ancient wraith of an idol').[9] Indeed, he denied that the dispute had anything to do with the empire at all, asserting it was to be dealt with *'prince à prince'*.[10] Once again, Frederick's use of language showed him keenly aware of his superior status as a sovereign ruler lording it over the small fry. The bishop had been impertinent, insulting and offensive, he claimed.[11] Chastisement duly followed, as twelve companies of grenadiers and a squadron of dragoons were despatched to teach the offender to behave properly in future. Well might the diplomatic corps in Berlin comment that the new King of Prussia's abrasive diplomatic style was reminiscent of Louis XIV at his most imperious.[12] The intimidated prince-bishop duly capitulated.[13]

THE DEATH OF CHARLES VI

These two Catholic prelates had been easy meat, barely worth the faint effort involved. Almost immediately, however, a much more formidable target arose which did invite 'the great blow' predicted by Seckendorf. On 20 October 1740 the Emperor Charles VI died suddenly and unexpectedly of food-poisoning at the age of fifty-five. It was the kind of chance event that makes a mockery of structural explanations of historical change. For this was not just the death of an emperor, it was also the death of a dynasty. In this masculinist world, only a male could be elected Holy Roman Emperor. For nearly 300 years, since 1452, a Habsburg had been elected. Now the line was broken. Succession to the *hereditary* Habsburg lands, collectively known as the 'Habsburg Monarchy', however, was not gender-exclusive. In 1713 Charles had issued a document known as 'the Pragmatic Sanction', proclaiming the indivisibility of the family territories and directing that, if there were no male heir, they could pass to his eldest daughter. This turned out to be Maria Theresa, born in 1717 and married to Francis Stephen, Duke of Lorraine in 1736.

This 'truly revolutionary document'[14] was bound to prove problematic, not least because it (deliberately) involved passing over the two daughters of Charles's predecessor, his elder brother Joseph (Holy Roman Emperor from 1705 to 1711). Maria Josepha had married the Crown Prince of Saxony in 1719 and Maria Amalia the Elector of Bavaria in 1722, although not before accepting the Pragmatic Sanction and thus abandoning their own claims to the Habsburg inheritance. Whether these commitments were worth more than the paper on which they were inscribed, remained to be seen. The same applied to the international recognition of the Pragmatic Sanction negotiated with such effort and at the cost of so many concessions during the remainder of Charles's reign.

Among the rulers signing a guarantee was Frederick William I, in 1728, in return for a promise of imperial support for Prussian claims to the Rhenish duchies of Jülich and Berg when the current ruler died.[15] This was a promise that could not be kept, not least because a similar undertaking had been given to Saxony and also to the Sulzbach branch of the Wittelsbach dynasty. By 1732 it had become clear that Charles would renege, in 1738 it became certain.[16] Even a man less volatile than Frederick William I might have been enraged. He had always been ambivalent in his attitude to the Habsburg Emperor, and this latest act of bad faith drove him into the arms of France. On his accession to the throne, his son at once set about reasserting his claims, putting out feelers to Austria, France and Great Britain, but got nowhere. There was vague talk of Prussia getting 'something' from the Jülich–Berg inheritance, but, as Frederick put it, writing of himself in the third person: 'this was little satisfactory to the wishes of a youthful and ambitious king, who would have all, or nothing'.[17]

He was still smarting from this rebuff when news arrived of the emperor's demise. At once his attention swivelled from west to south, from the Rhine to the Oder, where a much more desirable prey was now exposed. The situation could hardly have been more favourable. The twenty-nine years of Charles VI's reign had left the Habsburg Monarchy in a truly parlous condition, at its most vulnerable since the dark days of 1618. In two crucial respects it was on its knees: financial and military. A combination of persistent over-expenditure and inadequate accounting had multiplied the total debt by around five times since the beginning of the century. So bare was the cupboard that, shortly before Charles's death, a Jewish agent was even sent up to Berlin to seek a loan.[18] With debt-servicing now consuming half the annual revenue, the army had to be reduced even in wartime, with the result that in 1740 barely one half of its paper-strength of 160,000 was actually under arms.[19] In the withering verdict of one of Charles's confidants, his reign had been one of 'torpor, indecision and mutual recrimination'.[20]

These two fundamental failures had brought disaster to the Habsburg Monarchy, first in the War of the Polish Succession (1733–8) and then in a war with the Turks (1737–9). The former ended with the loss of Naples and Sicily and the latter with the loss of large amounts of Balkan territory, including Belgrade. By all accounts, both leadership and morale were abysmal: three generals serving in the Turkish campaign ended up in prison.[21] Commenting on the lethargy of Austrian administration at the centre, a British diplomat reported in 1735: 'The least business produces a *referat* (memorandum), a *referat* produces a conference, and were the town on fire, there must be a conference to deliberate if the fire must be put out and how.'[22] As if this were not enough, the monarchy's new ruler inherited from her father a team of ministers variously described by her greatest biographer, Alfred von Arneth, as 'senile ... of limited ability ... rapaciously venal ... self-indulgent and idle ... failing mentally and physically ... old and timid'.[23] Maria Theresa's own comment on her inheritance was that she had been left 'without money, without credit, without an army, without any experience or any knowledge of my own, and finally without any kind of advice'.[24]

All this was well known, not least by Frederick. On 5 November 1740, or in other words ten days after he learned of the accession of Maria Theresa, he wrote to his envoy in Vienna, Caspar Wilhelm von Borcke: 'the Emperor is dead, the [Holy Roman] Empire and the House of Austria are leaderless, the Monarchy's finances are exhausted, the army is ruined and the provinces are drained by war, plague, famine and the terrible burden of taxation they have had to bear up to the present'. This merciless exposé had been prompted by Borcke's report that the Austrians believed they would be able to maintain their territorial integrity. Is it possible, Frederick went on to ask rhetorically, that they have overlooked the rapacious intentions of Bavaria, Saxony, France, Spain and Sardinia? Are they unaware that, of their possible allies, Great Britain is engaged in a war with Spain, Russia is restrained by threats from Sweden and the Turks, and the princes of the Holy Roman Empire are always immobilized if there is no prospect of financial assistance? In conclusion, he complained that he had become increasingly exasperated by the Austrians' failure to follow up on the friendly noises they made in the year when he came to the throne and that he would now have to think more aggressively about how to take advantage of the present situation.[25]

This ominous remark came just a few weeks after the publication at The Hague of his first major literary exercise: *Against Machiavelli or An Examination of Machiavelli's Il Principe together with historical and political notes*, better known to posterity by its original abbreviated French title *Anti-Machiavel*.[26] On completing the first draft in the previous autumn, he had told Algarotti that his intention was to show that unbounded ambition, treason, faithlessness and murder were contrary to the true interests of a monarch and that the only sound policy, from both a moral and a prudential point of view, was to be good and just.[27] In the final chapter Frederick turned his attention specifically to war. His premise was its horror: 'war is so full of misfortune, its outcome is so uncertain, and its consequences so ruinous for a country that sovereigns should think twice before undertaking it. I do not speak of the injustice and violence that they commit against their neighbours, but merely of the misfortunes that fall directly on their subjects.'[28] The only just wars, he stated, were those that were defensive, although a preventive attack might also be permissible. Also allowed were wars to assert 'disputed rights or claims' and to fulfil contractual obligations to allies.[29] Because princes must regard their subjects not as their slaves but as their equals, even as their masters, 'princes who wage unjust wars are more cruel and cold-blooded than any tyrant ever was. They sacrifice to their impetuous passions the well-being of an infinity of men whom they are duty bound to protect.'[30]

Less than three months after the publication of those fine-sounding words, Frederick invaded Silesia. Clearly the war he was starting could not be described as defensive or preventive or in support of allies. As for the 'disputed rights or pretensions', not even Frederick ever seriously maintained that he had any legal claim to Silesia. When his foreign office produced an elaborate historical justification for the invasion, he commented: 'Bravo! That is the work of a good charlatan.'[31] This hypocrisy was partly a simple case of 'do as I say, not as I do'. Voltaire certainly thought so, writing to his friend Sir Everard Falkener: 'You will know the victory of my good friend the King of Prussia, who wrote so well against Machiavel, and acted immediately like the heroes of Machiavel . . . You must know my prussian king, when he was but a man, lov'd passionately yr english gouvernement, but the king has altered the man, and now he relishes despotik power, as much as a Mustapha, a Selim, or a Soliman.'[32] Voltaire also observed: 'If Machiavelli had had a prince as a pupil, the first thing he would have recommended would have been that he write against him.'[33] That is too cynical. More persuasive was the argument advanced by Friedrich Meinecke that in Frederick humanitarian and power-political impulses coexisted in fruitful tension.[34] More persuasive still was Theodor Schieder's qualification of this insight, namely that Frederick's anti-machiavellism penetrated only the intellectual side of his nature, whereas his machiavellism was a natural force.[35]

This more considered view is supported by Frederick's own reflections long before he thought of writing *Antimachiavel*. Confined at Küstrin in 1731, following his abortive flight, the nineteen-year-old Frederick put down on paper his thoughts on 'The present political situation of Prussia'.[36] Fundamental, he argued, was the state's geopolitical situation: with so many pieces of territory strung out across northern Europe, it was especially vulnerable. Therefore good relations had to be maintained with all the numerous neighbours and conflict had to be avoided. Inaction, on the other hand, was not an option for 'if one does not advance, one retreats'. So the ruler always had to be on the look-out for opportunities to acquire territory to fill in the gaps between his fragmented possessions. Top of the shopping-list came Polish (West) Prussia, whose acquisition would link Brandenburg to East Prussia and give control of Polish trade down the river Vistula. Also highly desirable was Swedish Pomerania, valuable in its own right but also facilitating a future acquisition of Mecklenburg. 'And so,' Frederick concluded, 'I am constantly advancing from country to country, from conquest to conquest, like Alexander the Great always seeking new worlds to conquer.'[37] That may have had an ironic tone, but wholly serious was his further assertion that only through acquisitions such as these could the King of Prussia raise himself from the dust in which he currently cowered and take his place at the top table of European powers.

When he wrote this, Frederick was not thinking of Silesia but the more perceptive Austrians could sense danger. After reading a copy of Frederick's musings, the veteran general and statesman Prince Eugene observed that, although his plans had not been properly thought through, they did display 'vigour and good sense' and that in time he could become a dangerous neighbour unless he could be wooed away from current thinking.[38] Three years later he had the opportunity to confirm this impression when Frederick arrived at his camp at Philippsburg in south-west Germany to experience warfare at first hand. Prince Eugene was dismayed to find the crown prince 'wholly French-minded' and wrote to the emperor that 'much is at stake in gaining this young prince, who one day will be able to make more friends in the world than his father has and be able to do as much harm as good'.[39] After Frederick had returned to Prussia, the aged prince wrote to him, extolling the great qualities he had shown during his spell at the front and rejoicing in the wonderful things that could be expected from him in the future.[40] The object of his flattery did not repay the compliment, commenting sourly that Prince Eugene's 'body was still there but his soul had gone'.[41]

Prince Eugene was wrong. Frederick was not 'wholly French-minded'. He had only the lowest opinion of Louis XV and his ministers. When the foreign secretary Chauvelin was dismissed in 1737, Frederick wrote that he was too honest to survive 'in a ministry consisting only of wretches like the Cardinal [Fleury] who deserve to be the instruments of a king as torpid, stupid and contemptible as Louis XV'.[42] But if he despised the French, he hated the Austrians, castigating their 'excessive pride' despite their ruinous situation.[43] He was also chafing at the bit to replace the 'pernicious lethargy' that had settled on the conduct of Prussia's affairs: 'unfortunately for us, the century in which we live is better at conducting negotiations than waging war. From a military point of view we are well placed, but our diplomacy lacks vigour'.[44] It was force that was needed to cut the Gordian knot, especially over the long-festering sore that was the Jülich and Berg dispute.

The Austrians might reasonably have expected some measure of gratitude from Frederick. After all, in 1730 Charles VI had intervened to urge clemency when it looked as though Frederick William might have made Frederick suffer the same fate as his friend Katte. It was the Austrian ambassador Seckendorf who kept Frederick afloat financially during the 1730s, paying off his debts and making repeated gifts.[45] Yet all that largesse paled before Frederick's knowledge that it was Seckendorf who had been the prime mover behind his forced marriage to Elizabeth Christine of Brunswick, who was not only the Austrian candidate but also the niece of Charles VI's wife (also called Elizabeth Christine and also *née* Brunswick). It was with gloating satisfaction that the French ambassador La Chétardie reported from Berlin on 4 November 1732 that any gratitude had been stifled by the marriage business.[46]

Moreover, Seckendorf had been a close friend of Frederick William ever since they had campaigned in Flanders together during the War of the Spanish Succession and so was indelibly associated with his tyranny. He had been sent to Berlin with the express purpose of keeping Prussia in the imperial camp. This proved to be no easy task. Frederick William veered unpredictably between fawning veneration of the imperial office and characteristically violent abuse of the emperor as fellow-ruler. One communication from Charles VI was answered so abrasively that Prince Eugene exclaimed: 'if I was the Emperor and the King of Prussia had written such a letter, I would certainly declare war on him if he denied me satisfaction'.[47] By the closing years of his reign, Frederick William had turned decisively away from Austria as a result of the duplicity shown in the Jülich and Berg affair. In 1733 he could still tell Seckendorf that his devotion to Charles VI was such that the latter would have to 'kick him away with his feet'. Four years later he told his son and heir never to trust the Austrians – they would flatter him so long as he was useful and then drop him immediately he was not.[48] In this respect, Frederick proved to be a chip off the old block that flew in just the direction his father would have wanted.

THE EUROPEAN
STATES-SYSTEM IN 1740

Deciding to humble the Austrians for past insults and injuries was one thing, putting it into practice quite another. Frederick was well aware that Prussia was still 'a kind of hermaphrodite, which was rather more an electorate than a kingdom'.[49] If it were to establish its masculine credentials unequivocally, it would need to show that it could play an independent role in the European states-system. Even Frederick William the Great Elector, the most vigorous and successful of Frederick's predecessors, had found himself at the mercy of the great powers. At the Peace of Saint-Germain in 1679 he had been forced to hand back to the Swedes all the conquests he had made at their expense during the previous five years of victorious campaigning, simply because their ally Louis XIV of France had ordered him to do so.*

He had been unfortunate enough to encounter Louis XIV at the height of his power and prestige, a time when a French diplomat could boast that 'not a dog barks in Europe unless our king says he may'.[50] Sixty years later, dogs were howling without any reference to Versailles. This seismic change was due to a decline of France that was both absolute and relative and needs to be explained if Frederick's position in 1740 is to be understood. Louis XIV's long reign, the longest in European history (1643–1715), had brought substantial territorial acquisitions but at the cost of serious structural damage. So pressing had been the need to finance the wars that dominated every decade, that short-term gain had been bought at the cost of long-term pain. When the old king died, the treasury was empty, even the most pressing obligations could not be met, regular taxes had been eroded by exemptions and evasions, much of the royal domain had been sold or given away, and there was an accumulated debt in excess of a billion livres.[51] The master of requests Richer d'Aubé lamented 'a wretched situation [characterized by] immense debts ... a population crippled by taxes ... numbers diminished ... and trade less flourishing'.[52]

---

* See above, p. 13.

From that low point there was a sustained recovery. No other country in Europe boasted such depth and breadth of natural resources, no other country was so populous. But all the others were expanding too and, what was more, they were doing it faster. Most seriously, they were doing it in the all-important field of population. Starting from the relatively high base of *c.* 20 million, the population of France grew by around 30 per cent in the course of the eighteenth century – but most of her rivals managed double that rate or more. As the century wore on, what had once been French demographic supremacy gradually evaporated.[53] Nor were they making the most of what they had. The failure to develop effective financial institutions such as a national bank; the continuing privatization of state revenue collection; and the all-pervasive venality ensured the intensification of private affluence and public squalor. The court at Versailles, which had been so effective an instrument of political and social control during its brief heyday under its creator, Louis XIV, now became a dysfunctional barrier to reform.[54]

Like so many other empires whose star was (and is) waning, France failed to adapt. For the past two centuries and more, its foreign policy had been based on hostility to the House of Habsburg, first the Spanish and then the Austrian branch. To counter encirclement by the Habsburg possessions in Spain, the Holy Roman Empire and the Low Countries, the French had sought to form an 'Eastern Barrier' (*barrière de l'est*) by alliances with states on the periphery which could divert the threat: Sweden in the north, Poland in the east and the Ottoman Empire in the south-east and south. This leap-frog diplomacy had often worked well, most spectacularly in 1630 when Gustavus Adolphus of Sweden invaded northern Germany to put an end to what had looked like irresistible Habsburg expansion. By the early eighteenth century, however, both the effectiveness and the reliability of all three allies were beginning to fade. Not only did the Turkish siege of Vienna fail in 1683, the relieving army was commanded by the Polish king John Sobieski. The Great Northern War of 1700–1721 ended with the decisive defeat of Sweden and the partition of its Baltic empire.

The great beneficiaries in the short term were the Austrian Habsburgs. In the course of the 1690s their army pushed the Turks out of

Hungary. In the War of the Spanish Succession (1701–14), they may have failed to win the whole inheritance of their extinct Spanish cousins but they did take control of rich and strategically vital territory in Italy and the southern Netherlands (most of present-day Belgium). Another short but successful war against the Turks in 1716–19 pushed their frontier deeper into the Balkans, capturing Belgrade in the process. As the miserable 1730s were to show, the Austrians then fell asleep on the laurels of Prince Eugene, allowing both the French and the Turks to recover and opening up an opportunity for an even more dangerous enemy in the north. It was Russia which derived both the most spectacular and the most permanent advantage from the decay of the French alliance system. By destroying Charles XII's Swedish army at Poltava in 1709, Peter the Great ensured that the eastern Baltic became a Russian lake and Poland a Russian satellite. When the Great Northern War eventually came to an end with the Treaty of Nystad in August 1721, Russia gained the provinces of Livonia, Estonia, Ingria and a large part of Karelia. This was not so much the 'window on the west' that Peter had long sought as a whole panorama, and confirmed that Sweden had been replaced by Russia as the dominant power in north-eastern and eastern Europe.

Had they known that Russia had come to stay, the French might have responded differently. But it was still very much *terra incognita*. It was not so long ago that Louis XIV had addressed a letter to Tsar Michael unaware that he had been dead for twelve years.[55] The eastern star had blazed on occasions in the past, only then to sink back into Muscovite obscurity. When Peter the Great visited Paris in 1717, he offered the regent, the Duke of Orleans, to take the place of France's traditional allies. He told the Comte de Tessé, the government minister deputed to look after him during his stay:

> France has lost its allies in Germany; Sweden, almost destroyed, cannot be of any help to it; the power of the Emperor has grown infinitely; and I, the Tsar, come to offer myself to France to replace Sweden for her . . . I wish to guarantee your treaties; I offer you my alliance, with that of Poland . . . I see that in the future the formidable power of Austria must alarm you; put me in the place of Sweden.[56]

Neither the regent nor any other subsequent French minister was listening. They preferred to reinforce the old system; indeed hostility to Russia became almost as much an axiom of French foreign policy as was Austrophobia. An important symbolic statement of intention came in 1725 when the fifteen-year-old Louis XV was married to Marie Leszczyńska, daughter of the Polish king-in-exile Stanislas Leszczyński, expelled from his kingdom by Peter the Great after Poltava. The Polish connection was continued into the next generation when their son the dauphin was married in 1747 to Maria Josepha, daughter of Augustus III, King of Poland and Elector of Saxony. In Sweden French diplomats worked ceaselessly to dislodge from power the pro-British 'Caps' in favour of the pro-French and anti-Russian 'Hats', a change they finally helped to achieve in 1738. At Constantinople their colleagues watched over the integrity of the Ottoman Empire, encouraging the Turks to resist Russian encroachments north of the Black Sea, supervising the modernization of their army and intervening to negotiate the peace of 1739.[57]

As these events showed, French influence in northern and eastern Europe was still strong. It was having to compete for resources, however, with a colonial dimension that could only grow in importance. When Louis XIV had told Frederick William the Great Elector to hand back his conquests to Sweden, he also controlled Charles II of England. The Glorious Revolution of 1688 brought that master–slave relationship to an abrupt end and also initiated the 'Second Hundred Years War' between France and England that was only to end 127 years later at Waterloo. By the Treaty of Utrecht, which brought the Anglo-French side of the War of the Spanish Succession to an end in 1713, the British had gained enough colonial territory to whet their appetite for more. They now controlled the entire Atlantic seaboard of North America, with the exception of Spanish Florida, and also claimed a vast swathe of territory to the south of Hudson Bay. In between were the French, whose first expedition to the St Lawrence river had been made as early as 1534 and who now controlled the river valley to the Great Lakes and beyond. More recently, the French had also laid claim to territory far to the south, at the mouth of the Mississippi, naming their new possession 'Louisiana' after their king and founding New Orleans in 1718. Their obvious strategy was to link up these new acquisitions with their older colonies in the north via the Mississippi and Ohio river valleys. It was in the latter that they collided with settlers from the British seaboard colonies moving west across the Appalachians in search of new land. By the 1730s it was clear that armed struggle was inevitable.[58] It was already underway – since 1739 – between Britain and Spain, also over colonial disputes.

In short, when Frederick came to the throne, he was confronted by a very fluid international situation in which no one state was dominant. At least his geopolitical position meant that he had neither the means nor the opportunity to get involved in disputes outside Europe. Also in his favour was the eclipse of Prussia's two chief rivals for the domination of northern Germany – Sweden and Saxony-Poland. The former still held on to western Pomerania, including the large island of Rügen, but with most of its Baltic empire lost, it no longer had the demographic, financial or military resources to permit an independent policy. Saxony was quite different. Since Frederick Augustus had been elected King of Poland in 1697 as Augustus II, a sustained effort had been made to present his composite state as a major power. Dresden had been transformed, with the intention of turning it into the Venice of the North, a political, economic and cultural entrepôt between East and West. The marriage of the Saxon crown prince to a Habsburg archduchess in 1719 and his election as King of Poland as Augustus III in 1733 in succession to his father opened up the possibility of elevating a personal and elective union into something permanent. As we have seen, indicative of the Wettin dynasty's prestige and ambition was Augustus III's brilliantly successful marriage policy.*

As the numerous Polonophile historians of Poland have been eager to point out, there was nothing inevitable about the sequence of events that would see the country partitioned off the map of Europe before the century was out. It possessed many impressive assets, not the least of them being size. The 'Polish-Lithuanian Commonwealth', or even more properly the 'Kingdom of Poland and the Grand Duchy of Lithuania', was the largest country in Europe after Russia,

---

* See above, p. 19.

stretching from the Baltic almost to the Black Sea and including all or part of present-day Poland, Lithuania, Latvia, Belarus and Ukraine. Less than eighty kilometres away to the west lay the Electorate of Saxony, much smaller in size but much richer in resources, both human and material. With flourishing manufacturing, commercial, agricultural and mining sectors and one of the highest literacy rates in Europe, Saxony was the most advanced and prosperous principality in the Holy Roman Empire. When combined with Polish quantity, Saxony's quality gave its Elector-kings every hope of dominating the region, including Prussia.

History also made that seem possible, if not likely. When Albert of Hohenzollern, who was half-Polish through his mother, secularized the lands of the Teutonic Knights in 1525, it was to Krakow that he went to pay homage to the King of Poland, receiving the duchy of Prussia back as a Polish fief.[59] It was a ceremony performed by each succeeding duke, including the Electors of Brandenburg after they inherited the duchy in 1618. It was not until the Peace of Oliva in 1660 that they achieved sovereignty and thus independence from Poland.[60] In the Holy Roman Empire, the Elector of Saxony had always been regarded as more important than the Elector of Brandenburg. His dynasty was older (late ninth century versus mid-eleventh century), his territory was more extensive, at least until 1648, and much richer and his position as head of the union of Protestant princes, the *corpus envangelicorum*, was more prestigious. If his royal title was only elective, it had been obtained just before that of his Prussian neighbour (1697 versus 1701).

As we have seen,* Augustus the Strong also had a much more glamorous court than Frederick William I permitted. But that was the rub. While the former was spending vast sums on palaces, mistresses, illegitimate children, operas and all the rest of court culture, not to mention the colossal bribes required to secure the two Polish elections, the latter was building up his army and salting away cash.[61] As Frederick wrote of his father, in this way 'he travelled silently on towards grandeur'.[62] Augustus is reputed to have told Frederick William: 'when Your Majesty collects a ducat, you just add it to your

* See above, pp. 18–20.

treasure, while I prefer to spend it, so that it comes back to me three-fold'.[63] This tax-and-spend approach to economic growth could also have been supported by the parable of the talents, but created problems for his successor when confronted by the crisis following the death of Charles VI. At the beginning of the eighteenth century, the Saxon army could match the Prussian in terms of size, but by 1740 it had shrunk relatively to less than a third.[64] Any sense of gratitude for Austrian assistance in the Polish election of 1733 was destroyed by Charles VI's refusal to back Saxon claims for the Jülich and Berg inheritance.[65] As a glance at the map will show, of all the possible predators circling Maria Theresa's inheritance in 1740, Saxony had the most to gain, for it was the Habsburg province of Silesia which separated the Electorate from the Kingdom of Poland. Its acquisition would have formed an unbroken bloc of territory stretching from the river Weser in the west to the Dnieper in the east. More specifically, Silesia was an important source of raw materials for Saxony's manufacturing industries and the prime market for Saxon salt.[66]

In short, Saxony was certain to be both a potential ally and a rival for Frederick. The same could be said of the other major German prince involved, Charles Albert Elector of Bavaria. Once again, knowledge that it was Prussia that emerged triumphant should not obscure the contemporary possibility of quite a different outcome. The Wittelsbach dynasty ruled not only Bavaria but also the Electorate of the Palatinate, the Electorate of Cologne and the duchy of Zweibrücken, together with a number of other prince-bishoprics whose collective resources were considerable: Münster, Hildesheim, Paderborn and Osnabrück. This ecclesiastical complex had been assembled by Charles Albert's younger brother Clement Augustus. The Wittelsbachs left an architectural legacy that put even the Saxon Wettins in the shade: Nymphenburg, Schleissheim, Mannheim, Brühl and Poppelsdorf, just to mention the more grandiose. Within these gilded frames, a court culture was developed with no expense spared but many debts incurred. The celebrations attending Charles Albert's marriage to the Habsburg Archduchess Maria Amalia in 1722 went on for three weeks and cost 4,000,000 gulden, the equivalent of a year's annual revenue.[67] By the late 1730s Bavarian finances were in so parlous a state that the army was placed at the disposal of Charles VI for the Turkish war just to get it on to the imperial payroll. Decimated into the bargain by the failed campaigns, by 1740 it was just 10,000-strong.[68]

Yet neither insolvency nor military impotence could restrain Wittelsbach ambition, fuelled by a frustrated sense of underachievement. For all the massive expenditure on parading its splendour during the previous two or three generations, the dynasty was still anchored in the second rank of European rulers. Whereas the Guelphs of Hanover, Wettins of Saxony and Hohenzollerns of Prussia had secured royal titles, the Elector of Bavaria was still just that. But with Charles VI's death in 1740 a wonderful opportunity arose to leapfrog their rivals and secure election to what was still regarded as the most prestigious title in Europe – Holy Roman Emperor. This was not as fanciful as it sounded. After all, there had been two Wittelsbach emperors in the past, Ludwig of Bavaria (1314–47) and Ruprecht of the Palatinate (1400–1410). There was also a legal claim to be made: the Bavarians asserted that a treaty of 1546 had stipulated that if the Habsburg dynasty failed in the male line, the inheritance would pass to the Wittelsbachs. Unfortunately, when the actual document was produced from the Vienna archives, it was found to confine succession not to 'male' but 'legitimate' heirs (although of course the Bavarians claimed it to be a forgery).[69] More crucially, Charles Albert won the support of France. There was a long tradition of Franco-Bavarian cooperation, based on the secure foundation of mutual hostility to Austria. In the War of the Spanish Succession the alliance had led to disaster at Blenheim in 1704, after which Charles Albert's father, the Elector Max Emmanuel, spent ten years in exile. As it turned out, a similar fate awaited this latest joint initiative.

This proved to be a slow process. On hearing of the death of Charles VI, Louis XV's initial reaction had been entirely passive: 'I do not wish to get involved in any of this,' he said. 'I shall keep my hands in my pockets, unless there is an attempt to elect a Protestant as Emperor.'[70] When he heard that Frederick had invaded Silesia, he exclaimed: 'He's a lunatic, the man is mad.'[71] This inertia was very much to the liking of his aged chief minister, Cardinal Fleury, but not to the young bloods at Versailles who were lusting for a continental war in which they could make their mark. Their leader was the Comte de Belle-Isle, the self-appointed executor of Providence in completing the work of Richelieu and destroying the House of Habsburg once and for all.[72] Characteristically, the king chose to give each party something. The Austrians were told that the Pragmatic Sanction would be respected, so that the Habsburg Monarchy could pass to Maria Theresa, but it was also decided to support the candidacy of the Elector of Bavaria as emperor, rather than Maria Theresa's husband Francis Stephen. Promoted to be Marshal of France, Belle-Isle was sent off to Frankfurt am Main to oversee the imperial election.[73]

Fleury proved to be the more sensible of the two competing poles between which the indecisive Louis XV slithered, for his field of vision was wide enough to accommodate the global implications of a forward policy on the continent. With Spain at war with Britain from the summer of 1739, and informal clashes between British and French colonists in North America on the increase, open warfare on the high seas and overseas could only be a matter of time. In August 1739 the Duke of Newcastle wrote: 'We take for granted that France will join Spain, and that we shall be attacked at home.'[74] In September 1740 a French squadron sailed to the West Indies to warn the Royal Navy off attacking Spanish colonies in the region.[75] In the event, Fleury's prudence was disregarded. Long before he died in January 1743, the hawks had pushed him to one side at Versailles.

At the other end of Europe, a different kind of diversion was underway, caused by another death in this year of royal fatalities. This time it was Tsarina Anna of Russia, who expired on 17 October, or in other words three days before Charles VI, although it took longer for the news to reach western Europe. As Russia had not yet succeeded in establishing an ordered procedure when an imperial vacancy occurred, an extended period of instability at home and impotence abroad was likely. It was made certain by the late tsarina's choice of successor – the two-month-old baby son of her niece Anna Leopoldovna. A scramble for power predictably ensued. The late tsarina's choice of regent, her lover Biron, Duke of Courland, fell foul of senior officials and the all-important Guards regiment in St Petersburg and on 21 November he was removed by a coup engineered by two senior military men: Field Marshal Burkhard Christoph von Münnich and Admiral Johann Heinrich Ostermann. It was they who wielded real power, with Anna Leopoldovna and her husband, Prince Anton Ulrich of Brunswick, as nominal regents.[76] This was all good news for Frederick, as Anton Ulrich was his brother-in-law and Münnich was nursing a sense of betrayal at the hands of the Austrians who had negotiated away the fruits of the victories he had won against the Turks.[77] Leaving nothing to chance, Frederick sent off flattering letters to Münnich signed 'your very loyal friend' and authorized his envoy at the St Petersburg court, Mardefeld, to offer Münnich a substantial bribe in return for assistance.[78] As it turned out, it was not long before the volatile Russian faction-fighting took another and much less favourable turn, but for the time being there was no threat from that quarter. It was the death of the tsarina, Frederick wrote in *The History of My Own Times*, which finally determined his decision to invade Silesia, for, during the minority of the infant Ivan, Russian policymakers would be too pre-occupied with maintaining stability at home to think about supporting the Pragmatic Sanction abroad.[79]

THE FIRST SILESIAN WAR 1740–42

In short, as the autumn of 1740 made way for winter, Frederick was in an exceptionally favourable position. If he had no ally to lend him support, at least he had freedom of action. The three western powers were diverted by conflict actual or imminent, the only great power in the east was immobilized by domestic upheaval. His target, the Habsburg Monarchy, had never been weaker. But how long would this happy constellation endure? If the moon moved into a different quarter, the opportunity to take the tide in the affairs of men at the flood might pass and all ventures would be lost. Frederick famously despised Shakespeare, from whom this paraphrase is taken, but he knew all about Julius Caesar, as he showed in the reference to 'crossing the Rubicon' quoted in the first sentence of this chapter.* That he had a

---

* See above, p. 72. The passage is from Act IV, scene 3 of *Julius Caesar*: 'There is a tide in the affairs of men, Which, taken at the flood, leads on to fortune; / Omitted, all the voyage of their life / Is bound in shallows and in miseries. / On such a full sea are we now afloat, / And we must take the current when it serves, / Or lose our ventures.' For Frederick's views on Shakespeare, see below, p. 343.

strong sense of opportunity knocking he revealed in a letter to his minister Podewils on 1 November: 'I am giving you a problem to solve. When one is in a favourable situation, should one make use of it, or not? I am ready with my troops and everything else; if I don't take advantage of it, I shall have in my hands an asset I don't understand how to use; if I do take advantage of it, it will be said that I know how to make the superiority I enjoy over my neighbours work for me.'[80]

At a conference with Frederick and Field Marshal Schwerin, held at Rheinsberg three days earlier, Podewils had urged caution. He proposed negotiation. In return for Silesia, Maria Theresa should be offered military support in retaining her other possessions, Frederick's vote for her husband as emperor, renunciation of Prussian claims to Jülich and Berg, and a cash payment of 2 million talers.[81] Frederick would have none of it. In justifying his insistence on immediate direct action, he also revealed a motive that has not always been given due weight: 'if we wait for Saxony and Bavaria to begin hostilities [against Austria] we shall not be able to prevent Saxon aggrandisement, and that is utterly contrary to our interests . . . But if we act now, we shall keep the Saxons down, and by preventing them from acquiring a supply of horses, we shall make it impossible for them to undertake anything.'[82] In all the twists and turns that followed during the next few years, Frederick always had one eye – and often two – on competition from other German princes, especially Saxony. In early November he learned that Bavaria had lodged claims in Vienna to the Habsburg inheritance, and shortly afterwards the Saxon envoy told Podewils that his master would be obliged to follow the Bavarian example.[83] It was wariness tempered by contempt, for he was convinced that Saxony was so inadequately prepared for war that it could be eliminated at the first sign of resistance.[84]

The decades of preparatory work by Frederick William I and his staff, most notably Prince Leopold of Anhalt-Dessau, better known as 'the Old Dessauer', now paid off. Other European armies took months to mobilize – the Russians could take a year or more – but Frederick was able to put an army into the field in just a few weeks. On 26 October he had learned of the emperor's death; on 7 November he ordered the regiments to be made ready; on 2 December he returned to Berlin from Rheinsberg; on 8 December the hussars and the Kleist and Sydow regiments marched off; he himself left his capital on 13 December; and three days later he led his army across the Silesian frontier near Krossen on the river Oder.[85] As the Austrians had only 3,000 infantry and 600 cavalry in the entire province, what then followed was less a conquest than an occupation.[86] The Prussian army was divided into two columns, one under Frederick's command taking an easterly route along the Oder valley, the other further to the west under Count Schwerin. By the beginning of January 1741 Frederick had reached the Silesian capital, Breslau; by 17 January he could claim in a letter to Algarotti that the entire province was his. Only the fortresses of Glogau, Glatz, Neisse and Brieg remained in Austrian hands. The whole affair, he boasted, had cost the lives of just twenty soldiers and two officers.[87]

Frederick was in a jaunty mood. On the last day of the year he wrote to Podewils: 'you are the cleverest charlatan in the world and I am the luckiest child of fortune, our names will never be forgotten by posterity'.[88] A week later, he announced that he was off to demonstrate to the other courts of Europe that, far from being chimerical, his project would be brought to a triumphant conclusion in the most glorious manner the world had ever seen.[89] His hubris was understandable. He was now twenty-eight years old. Apart from the desultory campaign on the Rhine in 1734, he had never had the opportunity to prove himself in the most royal of royal pursuits: war. Now he found himself at the head of a large, superbly equipped and well-disciplined army, sweeping through enemy territory towards the 'rendezvous with glory' he had told his army was their destiny.[90] He was doing something his half-detested, half-admired, wholly feared father had never done. And he was in sole command. On 2 December he had told the Old Dessauer that for this initial campaign his services would not be required: 'the world should not think that the King is marching off to war accompanied by his tutor'.[91] As this implies, for all his rational analysis of the advantages to be gained from conquering Silesia, Frederick's essential motive was personal. On arriving in Silesia he wrote to Voltaire to describe the privations of campaigning, adding that he would gladly pass them on to someone else 'if that phantom called glory did not appear to me so often. In truth, it is a great lunacy, but a lunacy that is very difficult to shed once one is infatuated with it.'[92] Two months later he confessed to his friend Charles-Étienne Jordan: 'I love war for the glory.'[93] Even when he wrote his history of the war for public consumption, he acknowledged more than once that the pursuit of glory had been a prime aim.[94] Sometimes he associated his state or even his dynasty with this exercise, but at root it was for him alone.[95] It was a trait too obtrusive not to be noticed – by the French ambassador Tyrconnell, for example, who told his court that Frederick was driven by his 'love of grandeur, glory and especially anything that can enhance his reputation among foreign nations'.[96]

When standing him down, Frederick had paid Old Dessauer the compliment of adding that his services would be very much needed in 1741, when the real war would begin. His hope that the Austrians might agree to cede Silesia without a fight foundered on his underestimate of both their resources and Maria Theresa's resolution. The reaction in Vienna to Frederick's invasion was a mixture of horror, grief, anger – and determination to resist. When campaigning started in 1741, the Prussians scored an early and important success when the fortress of Glogau was taken by storm on 9 March, but by that time, Austrian light troops were already beginning to harass Prussian outposts. At the end of the month, the main army of about 16,000, commanded by General Count Wilhelm von Neipperg, crossed into Silesia from Moravia, relieved the besieged fortress at Neisse on 5 April and advanced north towards Breslau. Caught napping, Frederick had to hurry off in a pursuit that was constantly hampered by the ubiquitous Austrian hussars.[97] Neither combatant had more than a vague idea as to where the other was, the next few days providing a good illustration of Clausewitz's observation that the unreliability of all intelligence meant that 'action takes place in a kind of twilight, which, like fog or moonlight, often tends to make things seem grotesque and larger than they really are'.[98]

When the mists cleared both metaphorically and literally near the village of Mollwitz near Brieg on the morning of 10 April, it was Frederick who had achieved tactical surprise, helped by intelligence reports from Austrian prisoners of war and sympathetic Protestant peasants. He then threw it away and showed his inexperience by

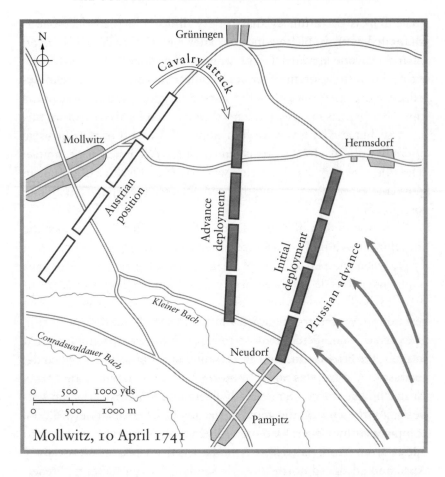

Mollwitz, 10 April 1741

taking more than an hour and a half to carry out his deployment, doing it all by the book. It was not until 1.30 in the afternoon that the Prussian artillery bombardment began. What then followed was a contest to establish whether the superior Austrian cavalry or the superior Prussian infantry would win the day. At first the former gained the upper hand, scattering their counterparts on the Prussian right. All accounts agree that Frederick himself showed great personal courage in trying to rescue the situation, so much so in fact that his second-in-command, Schwerin, feared for his life and pleaded with him to leave the battlefield for a place of safety. Whether his consent amounted to a flight, as the Austrians – and their historians – claimed

afterwards, is doubtful. What is not in dispute is that the veteran
Schwerin was now able to concentrate on winning the battle by sending his infantry forward in the centre. This decisive advance was
described by an Austrian officer in an account written four days after
the battle:

> The enemy army now advanced from all sides. As they enjoyed a
> numerical superiority of up to 3,000 men and there was a strong
> reserve corps situated behind the two lines, they overlapped us on both
> flanks. I can safely say that never in my life did I see anything finer.
> They marched forward with the greatest steadiness, with their lines as
> straight as a die, as if they were on the parade ground. Their polished
> weapons glinting in the sunlight made a stunning impression, and their
> volleys were like a constant roll of thunder. Our army became com-
> pletely demoralised; our infantry could no longer be kept together in
> their ranks and our cavalry no longer had any wish to form up against
> the enemy.[99]

As Clausewitz observed, in this advance the Prussian infantry achieved
'a level of perfection in the use of firepower that still has not been
surpassed'.[100] With his army falling apart, Neipperg ordered the
retreat. By five o'clock Schwerin could send a messenger off to find
the king and announce the victory. Unimpeded by the weak and desultory Prussian pursuit, the Austrians fell back to Neisse.[101]

It was not until the following morning that Frederick could be
located and told of his good fortune. He had spent an adventurous
night riding around the Silesian countryside in search of a safe haven,
a fifty-kilometre odyssey that included a narrow escape from capture
by Austrian hussars. His mood should not have been exultant. By his
inexperience he had thrown away the priceless advantage of surprise
and with it the chance of a swift, total and cheap victory, inflicting
instead on his army a murderous battle which killed some 1,500 on
the battlefield and wounded probably double that number, many of
whom succumbed later to the ever-present danger of gangrene. Austrian casualties were of the same order.[102] The account of the battle
Frederick sent back to his ministers in Berlin two days later was rather
different: 'after a violent four-hour battle, the army of Field Marshal
von Neipperg, despite being 6,000-men stronger and having three

times as many cavalry as mine, has been utterly put to flight and forced to retreat back to Neisse'.[103] There was no mention of Schwerin or of his own premature departure from the battlefield. Nor did he mention the latter in letters to intimates such as Jordan, Algarotti or Wilhelmine.[104] It was Frederick's victory that was now to be trumpeted to the other courts of Europe.

He was less triumphalist in a letter he wrote to his brother August Wilhelm a week later: 'we have beaten the enemy, but everyone is weeping, one over a lost brother, another over a lost friend. In short, we are the most depressed victors imaginable. May God preserve us from a second battle as bloody as Mollwitz! My heart bleeds when I think about it.'[105] But even then he could not bring himself to give credit where it was due. In 1754, while on military manoeuvres, he did admit to the Comte de Gisors that he had been an absolute novice at Mollwitz and would have been lost without Schwerin, who had saved him from his errors.[106] In the account of the battle he wrote for posterity, first drafted in 1742, revised in 1745 and again in 1775 but not published until after his death, Frederick was more self-critical. He confessed that he should have concentrated his forces earlier in the campaign, that at Mollwitz he had lost two hours in deploying his army, that by failing to attack at once he had missed the opportunity to score a second Blenheim, and that he had been saved only by the valour and discipline of the Prussian infantry. On the other hand, he conceded only that Schwerin was 'an able man and an experienced general' and again failed to mention that it was he who had been in command during the crucial phase of the battle.[107]

'Mollwitz educated the King and his army: this prince reflected deeply on all the mistakes he had made, and subsequently tried to correct them,' wrote Frederick in the same passage, referring to himself in the third person (as Julius Caesar had done in his histories). One lesson he had learned was that the Austrians were a force to be reckoned with. In Clausewitz's view, Frederick had missed a trick by not following up his victory with a further attack.[108] That respite allowed the Austrians to withdraw south to lick their wounds. They were clearly resting not dying and would soon be reinforced as the Habsburg Monarchy's rusty war machine was cranked into first gear. In the short term, victory at Mollwitz allowed the nearby fortress of Brieg on the river Oder to be invested, besieged and captured, on 4 May, while the main Prussian army recuperated in fortified camps at Mollwitz itself and at Grottkau on the road to Neisse.[109] Some indication of the state of Austrian preparedness can be gained from the fact that at Brieg the only piece of artillery was made of leather and had been 'abandoned here by the Swedes ninety-nine years ago. It was said to have been left loaded all this time. The garrison artillery captain did not want to fire, but an army gunner touched the gun off without his knowledge, whereupon it burst, wounding twelve people.'[110]

It need hardly be added that news of Mollwitz caused a sensation in Europe. Louis XV had not been alone in thinking that Frederick's audacity in invading Silesia amounted to lunacy. If the Prussians invariably underestimated the Austrians, the Europeans invariably underestimated the Prussians. Just as in later wars between the two, observers both well- and ill-informed expected the superior weight of the Habsburg Monarchy to be decisive. So the impact of the battle was out of all proportion to the numbers involved. As Frederick himself wrote: '[10 April] was one of the most momentous days of the century, because two little armies decided the fate of Silesia, and the soldiers of the King acquired a reputation which neither time nor envy could take away from them'.[111]

In the shorter term, Mollwitz precipitated a chain of events that was to unleash the War of the Austrian Succession on the world. If the Austrians had won and expelled Frederick from Silesia, they might well have deterred other potential predators. In the event, the advertisement of their fragility brought a flock of vultures flapping down. Carlyle employed a mineral metaphor, identifying Mollwitz as the loose pebble that precipitated the avalanche, 'hitting other stones big and little, which again hit others with their leaping and rolling – till the whole mountain-side was in motion under law of gravity'.[112] The biggest boulder was France. Thanks to its military and diplomatic victories in the 1730s – and the inaction or failures of its rivals – France was now the dominant power in the European states-system again, although this proved to be the last blaze of the ember.[113] With the advantage of hindsight, we can see that 1740–41 represented a pinnacle of French power that was never to be reached again under the old regime.

What followed was a prolonged period of diplomatic activity as intense as any previous episode in European history. For those who enjoy the shadow-boxing, double-dealing and horse-trading involved, events can be followed on a daily basis in the plethora of documentation available. Happily for this biographer of Frederick, the essentials can be quickly told. Holding firm in the maelstrom of events that swirled around them were the war aims of the three main combatants. Austria wanted to get Silesia back and defend the integrity of the rest of the Habsburg Monarchy. Prussia wanted to gain international recognition of its Silesian conquest. The objectives of France were rather more complicated. Top of the list was preventing the election of Maria Theresa's husband, Francis Stephen, as Holy Roman Emperor, for that would have threatened France's eventual acquisition of his duchy of Lorraine.* The increasingly dominant hawks, led by Belle-Isle, however, wanted to go further and reduce the old enemy to permanent second-rank status. This was to be accomplished by a partition of the Habsburg Monarchy between the three principal claimants. Although there were several variations on this main theme, what was finally agreed in a treaty signed at Frankfurt am Main on 19 September 1741 was that Bohemia and part of Upper Austria should go to Bavaria, together with the imperial title; Moravia, part of Upper Austria and Lower Austria should go to Saxony, together with a royal title; and the rest of Silesia to Prussia.[114] Maria Theresa would have been left as Queen of Hungary, a kingdom whose corpulence could not compensate for its lack of muscle. In other words, Central Europe would have been divided into four states of roughly equal size, thus allowing France to hold the ring. It was Napoleon's plan for Central Europe sixty years early.

Unfortunately for the visionaries of Versailles, they had no Bonaparte to command their armies. Nor were they confronted by the pliable puppets the Emperor Napoleon bullied so ruthlessly. The Elector Charles Albert of Bavaria and King Augustus III of Saxony-Poland were the feeblest of their respective houses,[115] but Frederick

---

* By the Treaty of Vienna in 1738, which brought the War of the Polish Succession to an end, Lorraine had been ceded by Francis Stephen to Louis XV's father-in-law, ex-King Stanislas of Poland. On his death it was to pass to France.

and Maria Theresa were made of sterner stuff than their hapless successors. Frederick was eager to receive the assistance of the French, but only on his terms. Bavaria and Saxony he regarded as rivals more than allies. As he wrote in *The History of My Own Times*, the French partition plan was clean contrary to his interests: 'if the King had allowed himself to become the servile instrument of French policy, he would have created a yoke for himself and would have done everything for France and nothing for himself'. Success for their joint venture would have made Louis XV the hegemon of Europe and turned Prussia from ally into vassal.[116] It was clearly in Frederick's interests to save Maria Theresa from total defeat at the hands of the coalition put together by Belle-Isle. A voluntary cession of Silesia would have suited Frederick best. So when Belle-Isle came to his camp at Mollwitz at the end of April 1741 seeking an alliance, Frederick sent him away empty-handed, greatly to his annoyance. It was only when an emphatic rejection of negotiations arrived from Vienna a month later that Frederick succumbed to the French approach. A treaty was signed at Breslau on 4 June.[117] Even then, Frederick was careful to spell out with an explicitness bordering on rudeness that the alliance was dependent on the French keeping their side of the bargain. From his camp at Grottkau on 6 June he wrote to Belle-Isle that he awaited 'with all the passion and all the impatience imaginable' the despatch of two army corps, one to help him and the other to invade Bohemia, not forgetting the alliance with Sweden to keep the Russians away from Frederick's exposed eastern flank.[118]

Apart from taking control of Breslau on 4 August, he stayed passive throughout the summer of 1741, using the time to sort out the faults exposed at Mollwitz. Rising at 4 a.m. he began his day with a searching inspection, imposing on his fellow-officers a regime so rigorous that many sought to resign. One suitably impressed eye-witness was Belle-Isle, who described Frederick drilling a guards battalion in person: 'the weather was frightful and the snow was falling in large flakes, which did not prevent the battalion from exercising as if it had been a fine day. I had some inkling before I came of the army's discipline, obedience and exactitude, but I must say that they were driven to such a degree that I was ill-prepared for the reality.'[119] Special attention was paid to the arm which had performed worst in the battle: the cavalry. In May the French envoy, the Marquis de Valori, had found their horses malnourished and their riders ill-trained. By the end of July he was greatly impressed by the sixty-two well-trained, well-equipped and well-mounted squadrons Frederick paraded at the camp at Strehlen.[120] Not for the last time, the benefits of 'unity of command', that is to say the combination of supreme civilian and military authority in one individual, were apparent. Reinforcements for branches kept arriving, so that by the end of the year the total number of Prussian combatants in Silesia had risen to 117,600.[121]

A new phase of the war began when the French armies crossed the Rhine in August 1741. Technically, they were just an auxiliary force sent to support the claims of the Elector of Bavaria. In reality, everyone knew that what was intended to be the final showdown in the centuries-old struggle between the houses of Valois-Bourbon and Habsburg had begun. As with most coalitions, divisions became apparent at once. Frederick wanted the Franco-Bavarian force to march straight down the Danube valley to Vienna. That would have forced the Austrians to withdraw their remaining troops from Silesia, leaving Frederick in complete control of the province. Belle-Isle, however, wanted to concentrate on the conquest of Bohemia, which would have allowed Charles Albert to be crowned there as king. That in turn would have given him the additional Bohemian vote and made his election as Holy Roman Emperor certain.[122]

At first the Franco-Bavarian army took the Danube route, advancing to Linz by the middle of September. With Vienna now threatened, Maria Theresa had to swallow her pride and do a deal with Frederick. He was in a receptive mood because his attempt to seize Neisse with an audacious outflanking manoeuvre had just failed.[123] On 9 October he met Neipperg at Klein-Schnellendorf, a castle belonging to the Austrian Prince Starhemberg near the Neisse river, after elaborate precautions to ensure that no one – especially not the French envoy Valori – knew where he was going or what he was doing. The convention signed that day in effect was a truce. Frederick would cease military operations, the Austrians would abandon the fortress of Neisse after a sham siege and withdraw to Moravia. At the peace settlement to be negotiated, Maria Theresa would cede Lower (northern) Silesia up to and including Neisse.[124] The latter was duly surrendered on 2 November, although not before the mock siege had caused a number of casualties and inflicted considerable material damage.

The troops released for the Austrians were badly needed. On 21 October the Franco-Bavarian army had reached St Pölten, just sixty kilometres from Vienna. But then it turned more than ninety degrees to the left and marched north into Bohemia in pursuit of the royal crown and electoral vote. Reinforced on 20 November by the arrival of 20,000 Saxon troops, it took Prague six days later in a surprise attack led by the Marshal de Saxe, illegitimate son of Augustus the Strong.[125] Charles Albert was proclaimed King of Bohemia on 7 December and twelve days later received the homage of 400 Bohemian nobles.[126] To lose the monarchy's second city after a campaign lasting less than a month was a terrible blow for Maria Theresa, who burst into tears when the news arrived. Not even three days of ritual supplications to the Almighty had helped.[127] News of the collaboration of many of the most notable Bohemian magnates, including the Archbishop of Prague, only rubbed salt in her wounds. As it turned out, however, this was to be the lowest point of her misfortunes. By this time she had been crowned Queen of Hungary and that country's leading nobles had promised to raise 40,000 fresh troops. In the event, only around half that number were actually mobilized, but they proved to be enough to turn the tide.[128]

After Klein-Schnellendorf, Frederick did not stay neutral for long. He had no intention of allowing the French and their Bavarian and Saxon satraps to take control of the situation. That he had signed a piece of paper pledging this or that was of no concern to him. In *Antimachiavel* he had written that it was not only wrong but politically stupid to be a cheat (*fourbe*) and deceive (*duper*) everyone, because, once destroyed, trust could never be regained.[129] In the autumn of 1741, however, he wrote to Podewils: 'if there is advantage to be gained from being honest, then that is what we shall be; but if we have to deceive (*duper*), then let us be cheats (*fourbes*)'. Unfortunately, this letter was part of a package intercepted by the Austrians and sent on to Vienna by Neipperg, where it was gratefully received by the Austrian propagandists.[130] In December Frederick was on the move again, taking first Troppau and before the end of the year Olmütz in

Moravia. He could justify his unilateral breach of the convention on the grounds that the Austrians had broken the final article requiring '*un secret inviolable*'. He should not have been surprised: Vienna was a notoriously leaky place. Within a couple of weeks of the signing every court in Europe knew about it.[131]

His allies needed him back in the war urgently, for their plans were going seriously awry. Frederick had been right to predict that the move north to Bohemia would prove a serious mistake, for it exposed their eastern flank in Austria. At just the same time that Frederick was invading Moravia, the Austrians were moving west. With an army of about 16,000 formed by regiments recently arrived from Italy, Field Marshal Count Ludwig Andreas Khevenhüller advanced rapidly through Austria, trapping the French General Ségur and an army of 10,000 in Linz, the capital of Upper (western) Austria. After a brief siege, it fell on 24 January. By that time a Bavarian army had been defeated at Schärding, south of Passau. Marching rapidly further west, the Austrians took Munich on 12 February.[132] Ironically, it was on that very day that the city's absent ruler, the Elector Charles Albert, was crowned as Holy Roman Emperor at Frankfurt am Main. In terms of precedence, he was now first among European sovereigns, in reality he had no state, no army and no resources and was utterly dependent on his French paymasters.

As the fortunes of war waxed and waned, Frederick held steady to one main aim – the retention of Silesia – and one subsidiary aim – to make sure that neither Bavaria nor Saxony made gains at his expense. The first moved a step closer on 17 January 1742 when the town of Glatz fell, although an Austrian garrison stubbornly remained in the citadel until April, by which time their numbers had shrunk from 2,000 to 200.[133] To force the Austrians to recognize their loss, in February Frederick launched a full-scale invasion of Moravia in conjunction with a Saxon army. This was the first time that Frederick had attempted an operation with an ally and he did not enjoy the experience. He claimed that the Saxons supplied only 14,000 as opposed to the 22,000 promised, were poorly supplied and uncooperative.[134] When they reached Iglau (present-day Jihlava) to the north-west of Brünn (Brno), the Saxons regarded their mission as accomplished and refused to go any further. Although Prussian hussars were within a few kilometres of

Vienna on 1 March,[135] by this time the campaign was beginning to fall apart. Knowing that Moravia was destined for Saxony at any eventual peace settlement, Frederick had been particularly ruthless in bleeding it white with levies and requisitions, a self-defeating tactic that could only yield diminishing returns. It also provoked fierce opposition from the local population, encouraged by the supply of weapons and a promise by Maria Theresa that resistance would be rewarded with a reduction of dues. On 8 March the Prussians began to retreat from the Austrian frontier back to Brünn, harassed all the way by Hungarian irregulars and peasant partisans. Less than a month later, the approach of an Austrian army sent them north again, the Saxons home and the Prussians to Bohemia.[136] This was not to be the last time that Frederick failed in Moravia.

Denied a military solution, Frederick turned back to diplomacy. But with so much now reconquered, the mood in Vienna was not accommodating. Frederick complained in *The History of My Own Times*: 'in all ages, the spirit of the court of Austria has been seen to follow the brute impressions of nature. Inflated in good fortune, crouching in adversity, never could it arrive at that sage moderation which renders man invulnerable to the good or evil that chance distributes.'[137] To this basic Austrian failing Maria Theresa added a virulence that was both personal and gender-determined: 'an ambitious and vindictive enemy, who was the more dangerous because she was a woman, headlong in her opinions, and implacable ... devoured by ambition'.[138] Indeed, so determined was she, to employ an adjective less loaded than those favoured by the misogynist Frederick, that in May she took the war to him. Reducing their army in Bohemia, the Austrians sent a large reinforcement to Prince Charles of Lorraine in Moravia with orders to advance against Frederick in his camp at Chrudim. Denied reliable intelligence, it was not until 10 May that he realized he was the target of a major operation. It was only just in time that he managed to concentrate his forces and confront the approaching Austrians at the village of Chotusitz a week later. When the battle began at around eight in the morning, the Prussian cavalry on the right under General Buddenbrock at first drove the Austrians back before being forced to retreat themselves in some disorder, with neither side able to gain the upper hand. Meanwhile, the main action had moved to the other side of the battlefield, where the Austrians advanced to take Chotusitz village and penetrated the Prussian camp, before being distracted by the lure of plunder. They were then driven back by determined counterattacks. The decisive moment came at around 11.30 when Frederick sent the main mass of his infantry battalions forward in the centre. Wheeling left, they took the Austrian right in the flank. With his line of retreat now threatened, Prince Charles gave the order to retreat.[139] It was high noon.

Unlike Mollwitz, Chotusitz was undoubtedly a victory for Frederick personally and he made the most of it. Instead of the breast-beating that had followed the former, he now indulged himself in chest-thumping. On the day of the battle, he wrote to his 'tutor', the Old Dessauer, that he and his army had scored 'a complete victory' over the Austrians, killing 3,000 on the battlefield and then engaging in a

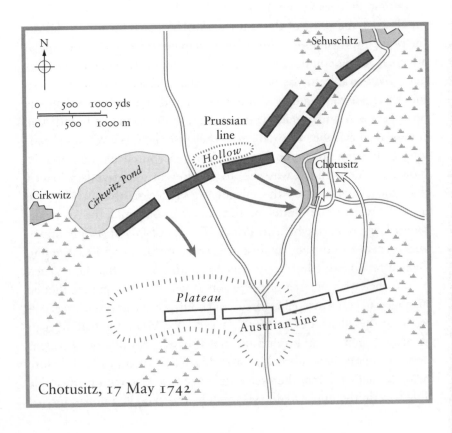

Chotusitz, 17 May 1742

hot pursuit. His own side had lost just 2,000 in dead and wounded. Several pieces of artillery had been captured. The entire infantry and 'various cavalry regiments' had distinguished themselves.[140] In a letter to his close friend Charles-Étienne Jordan, written three days later, he was more expansive: the victory was all the more pleasing because 'not very bloody' for his side. The rout of the Austrians had been terrible, their dismay, grief and demoralization without precedent. Total Prussian casualties amounted to only 1,000–1,200, whereas the enemy had lost six or seven times that number.[141] Although Frederick claimed that his account of the battle 'stuck strictly to the truth', he must have known that it did anything but. In reality, he had lost 4,800. Of the 6,330 Austrian casualties, most were prisoners, indeed the Prussians had suffered 1,000 more casualties in the actual battle.[142]

The Austrians had withdrawn in good order, ready to fight again another day. Back in Vienna, however, the realization was dawning that Frederick could not be eliminated militarily. If the French and their allies were to be ejected from Bohemia, another deal would have to be struck with him.[143] Eager to broker it was the new British Secretary of State Lord Carteret, whose self-appointed mission was to rescue Maria Theresa and with it the balance of power on the continent.[144] This meant bringing to a close her war with Frederick so that all Austrian resources could be concentrated on France. That in turn involved the sacrifice of Silesia. To ease it down the craw in which it currently stuck, the British supplied the necessary lubricant – money. By treaties concluded in 1741, they promised annual subsidies of £300,000 for three years. By the spring of 1742 this was desperately needed, as the Austrian treasury was empty. The British envoy James Porter reported on the very day that Chotusitz was fought that the first payment had arrived 'so opportunely, that it sav'd their whole army from disbanding; so that not only as Count Starhemberg, Count Kinsky, Baron Hildebrand but all the ministry honestly Confess'd, that single £300,000 sav'd the House of Austria from total ruin'.[145] The mediation was led by the Earl of Hyndford, who had already performed a similar role at Klein-Schnellendorf the previous autumn. Peace preliminaries were signed at Breslau on 11 June.

So pleased was Frederick that he brought himself to attend a *Te Deum* in the cathedral conducted by the Cardinal-Archbishop Count

Sinzendorff. Never one to miss an opportunity for a gesture that would play well with the public, Frederick declined to sit on the throne installed in front of the high altar, saying, 'I am a man like any other and shall sit in an ordinary pew.'[146] A definitive treaty at Berlin followed on 28 July after a few loose ends had been tidied up. Among the latter was which title should be given to Frederick in Lower Silesia, the Austrians being willing only to concede 'sovereign Duke'. Frederick's response was characteristically pithy: 'I don't give a fuck about titles,' he told Podewils, 'so long as I get the territory.'[147]

Frederick had done it. Both Lower and Upper Silesia, plus the fortress and County of Glatz, technically part of Bohemia, were his. He had not had everything his own way. Hard bargaining by the Austrians had been rewarded by their retention of the southern part of the duchy of Jägerndorf, the duchy of Teschen, the districts of Troppau and Krnov south of the Opava river and the southern part of the duchy of Nysa, which were all amalgamated to form the new Habsburg province of Austrian Silesia, but the lion's share was now Prussian.[148] The security of Frederick's hold remained to be seen. Although she had accepted her loss, Maria Theresa was not reconciled to it. For the time being, all her energies would have to be concentrated on the French in Bohemia, but the day might well come when she could turn her attention north to Silesia again. Frederick knew that, of course, and set about increasing his army, restocking his treasury and making the Silesian fortresses impregnable.[149]

THE SECOND SILESIAN WAR

·These precautions soon turned out to be necessary. By the end of 1742 the Austrians had expelled the French from Bohemia and reoccupied Bavaria, which they set about incorporating into the Habsburg Monarchy. In 1743, moreover, the British added military intervention to the financial support they were already providing. On 27 June the 'Pragmatic Army', commanded in person by George II, won a decisive victory over the French at Dettingen near Frankfurt am Main. Although that success was not followed up, Frederick became increasingly alarmed. He also knew that Saxony was in the process of changing sides. For this defection he was himself largely to blame. Not only had he treated them brutally during their joint expedition to Moravia in the spring of 1742, he had also made sure that they had been left empty-handed when he negotiated his separate peace in June. The knowledge that he had derided both their military and diplomatic skills, telling anyone who would listen that they were cowards, cretins and knaves, helped to push Augustus III and his all-powerful chief minister Count Brühl into reconciliation with Maria Theresa. On 20 December 1743 they signed an alliance, which although technically defensive was squarely aimed at Frederick.[150] This was a serious loss. Saxony's strategic position was enormously important, for Russia could intervene in the west only through Poland; the Electorate itself formed the bridge between Hanover and Bohemia; and the French, Prussians and Bavarians could combine only if Saxony was with them.[151] In navigating the notoriously treacherous waters of the Holy Roman Empire, Frederick's hand on the tiller had been more firm than deft.

During the two years of peace that followed the Peace of Breslau, Frederick devoted a great deal of time and effort to constructing a bloc of German princes to oppose the Austro-British coalition. He failed, partly because Dettingen made it too dangerous; partly because no one believed his trumpeting about the need to defend the German nation and German liberties; partly because Maria Theresa could draw on what was still a deep reservoir of loyalty to the Habsburgs, especially among the Catholics; and partly because of his own mistakes. In particular, his well-publicized encouragement to the Emperor Charles VII to secularize a number of ecclesiastical states to increase his territorial base caused great alarm among all the smaller imperial fry.[152] In February 1744 he learned that a secret treaty had been signed at Worms the previous autumn by Austria, Great Britain and Sardinia, which he believed, not without reason, to be aimed at him.[153] Not for the last time, he decided to get his retaliation in first. On 5 June he signed an offensive alliance with France. His chief war aim was to weaken Austria and strengthen the Bavarian Emperor by conquering Bohemia and transferring it to the latter. As he put it in his manifesto, he was acting to secure 'the liberty of the Holy Roman Empire, the dignity of the Emperor and the peace of Europe'.[154] But of course there was going to be something in it for him too, namely a good slice of Bohemian territory adjoining Glatz, including Königgrätz and Pardubitz.[155] He had nothing in common with Bavaria beyond the tried and tested principle that 'my enemy's enemy is my friend'.

The prospects looked good. During the previous two years, while his Austrian enemies had been losing men and spending money, Frederick had been accumulating both. When he and his two oldest brothers left Potsdam on 15 August to start the campaign, he had at his disposal a field army of 80,000, backed up by 468 provision wagons to feed them and 6 million talers in cash to pay them.[156] The plan was to take Prague and then to continue south into the heart of the Habsburg Monarchy. With the bulk of the Austrian army away on the Rhine fighting the French and Bavarians, a clear run to Vienna beckoned. The first part was easy. Weakly garrisoned, fortified and led, Prague fell on 16 September. The Prussian advance guard then moved rapidly south, taking Tabor on 23 September and Budweis a week later. At this point, things began to go badly wrong. As Frederick himself was to write in *The History of My Own Times*, 'No general committed more faults than did the king, during this campaign.'[157] The first and most serious was to assume that the French would cooperate in keeping the Austrians occupied in the west. In the event, they did nothing, thus allowing Prince Charles of Lorraine to march his army back from the Rhine to Bohemia with a speed usually thought to be uncharacteristic of the Austrians. There they joined with Count Batthyány's force of 18,000. To make matters worse, this formidable army of around 50,000 was then joined on 21 October by 20,000 Saxons thirsting for revenge against their erstwhile ally.[158]

With winter approaching and supplies running low, Frederick needed a battle. The Austrians did not oblige. Although Prince Charles was urged by a belligerent Maria Theresa to defeat the outnumbered Prussians in open battle, his second-in-command, the wily veteran Count Traun, persuaded him to let time, distance and hunger do his work for him. An outmanoeuvred Frederick's best chance came on 25 October at Marschowitz, some forty kilometres south of Prague, but there his enemies had taken up a position that he deemed to be impregnable.[159] Cutting his losses, he sounded the retreat. With the army decimated by disease and desertion, an ever-diminishing number of Prussians straggled back through Bohemia, reaching Silesia in early December. The Austrians were amazed by the scale of desertion: between 26 November and 6 December, wrote a Hungarian officer, at least 9,000 had come over.[160] By the end of the year perhaps as many as 30,000 had deserted, including many officers. Of the 17,000 Prussians who abandoned Prague on 26 November, only 2,000 ever got back to Silesia as an organized force.[161] Without a major engagement, the campaign had cost the Prussian army over 15 per cent of its total strength.[162] Count Ludwig Wilhelm von Münchow lamented: 'we no longer have an army, what we have is nothing more than a bunch of men held together by habit and the authority of their officers, and even these officers are discontented, many of them in a desperate condition indeed. All we need is the slightest setback, or a decision to continue the war during the winter, for there to be a mutiny.'[163] For a mutiny in the Prussian army even to be mooted as a possibility was a sign of how disastrous the campaign had become. Leaving Old Dessauer to deal with the Austrians who had penetrated Silesia, with their light troops ranging almost up to Breslau, Frederick returned to Berlin with his tail between his legs.

In his memoirs, the French ambassador Valori wrote a scathing account of Frederick's generalship in 1744, although the indictment was softened by the comment that at least he knew how to learn from his mistakes.[164] Although Valori might not have agreed, the first lesson Frederick learned was: never again undertake an operation that depended on the French. The second was: never again underestimate the military prowess of the Austrians or the mischief potential of the Saxons. A third should have been: never again try to conquer Bohemia. Frederick himself wrote in *The History of My Own Times*: 'it must be allowed that it is more difficult to make war in Bohemia than in any other country'. He went on to explain that this was due partly to geography – 'this kingdom is surrounded by a chain of mountains, which render invasion and retreat alike dangerous'; partly to the devotion to the Habsburgs of the nobles, priests and officials; and partly to the 'aversion invincible' to the Protestant Prussians of the Catholic inhabitants 'who are as stupid as they are superstitious'. It had been a fatal combination when Vienna had called on the Bohemian peasants 'to leave their hamlets at the approach of the Prussians,

hide their corn under ground, and fly into the neighbouring forests . . .
Thus the army found wildernesses only, on its passage, and deserted
villages.'[165]

Valori also observed that everyone now thought Frederick was finished. His main enemy was positively looking forward to the next
campaign ('That is the Austrian way of thinking about things,' Valori
added laconically).[166] The bad news kept on coming. On 8 January
1745 a Quadruple Alliance between Great Britain, Austria, the Dutch
Republic and Saxony was signed, which among other things provided
the necessary finance to increase the Saxon contingent to 30,000.[167]
On 20 January the Emperor Charles VII died and his son and heir, the
eighteen-year-old Maximilian III Joseph, ordered negotiations with
Maria Theresa, which led to the Peace of Füssen on 22 April. Frederick's nominal French ally was concentrating on the familiar
battlegrounds of the Low Countries and, although it maintained an
army between the Main and the Lahn, in effect had withdrawn from
the war in Germany. Attempts by an increasingly desperate Frederick
to secure British or Russian mediation failed.[168] He would have been
more anxious still if he had known that his enemies were now con-
sidering the partition of Prussia.[169] It would no longer be enough to
deprive him of Silesia, he had to be reduced to 'a nullity', so destruc-
tive had his impact on the European states-system been. The British
diplomat Thomas Villiers explained that 'this means nothing but his
destruction, and they [would] sacrifice the liberties of mankind to
compass it'.[170] For the first time, he was seriously short of ready
money and was having to melt down anything silver that could be
found in the royal palaces and impose a forced loan. He also
tried – and failed – to raise a loan in Amsterdam and tried – and
failed – to sell the port of Emden in East Frisia to the British.[171]

So far Frederick's military career had been a sad story of inexperience, overconfidence and ineptitude. His avoidable mistakes had cost
the lives of thousands of his subjects, thrown away the inheritance
bequeathed by his father and brought his state to the brink of disaster.
What he had been able to show on the positive side was a capacity for
taking decisions and an iron resolution in seeing them through. This
was well summed up by Carlyle in his characteristically orotund but
perceptive way: 'intellect sun-clear, wholly practical (need not be

specially deep), and entirely loyal to the fact before it; this – if you add rapidity and energy, prompt weight of stroke, such as was seldom met with – will render a man very dangerous to his adversary in the game of war'.[172] During the early spring of 1745, it was these personal assets which came to his rescue. On 15 March he left Berlin for Silesia, reaching Breslau on the 17th and Neisse a week later. There he set about reorganizing his battered forces, organizing new recruitment drives, luring back deserters with an amnesty and ordering up reinforcements of men and matériel. Above all, by his constant presence in the main Silesian camps at Kamenz and Frankenstein he rebuilt the army and restored its morale.[173] All the advantages of unity of command were apparent. To them he brought his own special charisma, laced with a powerful dose of do-or-die nihilism. On 27 April he wrote a long and revealing letter to Podewils from his headquarters at Pomsdorf:

> I have made it a question of personal honour to contribute more to the aggrandisement of my house than any of my predecessors; so far I have played a distinguished role among the crowned heads of Europe. This has all become a personal obligation for me and I am determined to uphold it, even at the cost of my happiness and my life … I have crossed the Rubicon and now I want either to maintain my position of power or to see everything perish and be buried with me right down to the very name of Prussia … If the enemy moves against us, then it is certain that either we shall defeat him utterly or we shall all be wiped out, for the salvation of the fatherland and the glory of my house.[174]

In the course of the next six weeks he turned these bold words into action, although it has to be said that he was helped greatly by the Austrians. Brimming with confidence and driven on by orders from Vienna, they planned to do to Frederick in Silesia what they had done to him in Bohemia the previous year. They planned to make a feint into Upper Silesia to prompt Frederick to divide his forces, while their main army crossed the passes through the Giant Mountains further north and headed for Breslau. On 29 May they reached Landeshut, where they were joined by a substantial force of Saxons.[175] This played straight into Frederick's hands. After the Bohemian débâcle of 1744, what he wanted was to lure his enemy down on to the Silesian plains and bring them to battle. To that purpose he had deliberately left the mountain passes unguarded and had let it be known through a double-agent in the Austrian camp that it was his intention to retreat to Breslau for one last desperate stand. As Carlyle put it, he had 'left the mousetrap open; – and latterly has been baiting it with a pleasant spicing of toasted cheese'.[176] Enjoying, for once, excellent intelligence from his roaming hussars, he declined to be diverted by the southern feint and concentrated his forces at Schweidnitz. It was the Austrians who were fumbling in the dark, believing they were facing only 40,000 demoralized Prussians who would retreat north at the first sign of action. In reality, there were 58,000, led by a commander eager for action.[177]

On the evening of 3 June 1745 Frederick told his friend Chasot: 'now at last I have got what I wanted. I have just seen the enemy army leave the hills and spread out in the plain. Tomorrow will be an important day for me.'[178] Leaving the tents erected and the campfires burning, he sent his army off on a perilous night-march to take the Saxons and Austrians by surprise. Much that could go wrong did go wrong, but shortly after 4 a.m. the first Prussian cavalry units were attacking the Saxons on the allied left. A series of fierce and murderous engagements followed, ending around 7 a.m. with the defeat and flight of the surviving Saxons. Meanwhile, the main battle in the centre was only just getting underway. For the first time, the Prussian cavalry showed they were now superior, as they overwhelmed the Austrians on the right between Thomaswaldau and Halbendorf, a vital role being played by the hussars led by the tiny but terrifying Hans Joachim von Zieten. It was also horse power that delivered the *coup de grâce*, when at around 8.15 a.m. the twin squadrons of the elite Bayreuth dragoons launched a charge in the centre which put the Austrian infantry to flight. In just twenty minutes they captured five cannon, sixty-seven colours and 2,500 prisoners.[179] By 9 a.m. the battle was over. So there was plenty of time for Frederick to sit down and spread the glad tidings to the rest of Europe. Top of the list of correspondents was Louis XV, who only recently had sent him news of the French victory at Fontenoy near Tournai in the Austrian Netherlands on 11 May. A special pleasure must also have been writing a letter to his erstwhile tutor in military matters, the Old Dessauer. At the cost of 1,200 casualties, Frederick proudly told him, the Austrians had lost 3,000 dead and 5,000 prisoners, including four generals. Two days later he added that the victory had been 'one of the most complete of all times, the like of which has not been seen since Blenheim'. He was also able to update him on the decimation of the Austrian generals – four dead, four captured and six mortally wounded.

In his letter to Podewils, also written on the battlefield, Frederick added: 'you know the use to which you can and should put this news'.[180]

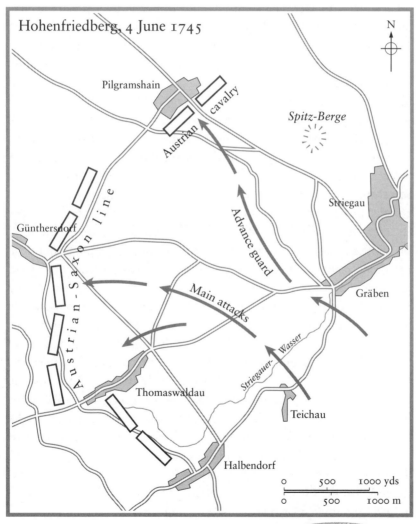

Hohenfriedberg, 4 June 1745

N

Pilgramshain

cavalry

Spitz-Berge

Austrian

Striegau

Günthersdorf

Austrian-Saxon line

Advance guard

Main attacks

Gräben

Striegauer-Wasser

Thomaswaldau

Teichau

Halbendorf

| 0 | 500 | 1000 yds |
| 0 | 500 | 1000 m |

Leabharlanna Chonndae

Unfortunately, Prussia's main enemy was not as impressed by this defeat as she ought to have been. Maria Theresa was certainly dismayed but, if anything, was even more determined to pursue the war à outrance. She ordered reinforcements to be diverted from Italy to Bohemia forthwith, wrote personally to her allies to reassure them that the situation was not as bad as it looked, and implored them not to desert the common cause.[181] An anxious George II, however, hurried to do a deal with Frederick. On 26 August the Convention of Hanover was concluded on the basis of a mutual guarantee of each other's territory. George promised to try to persuade Austria and Saxony to settle too, while Frederick agreed not to vote against Maria Theresa's husband Francis Stephen at the impending imperial election.[182] Neither party bothered to tell his main ally about this separate peace, an omission which was to cause great annoyance at Vienna and Versailles respectively.

The next three months Frederick spent in northern Bohemia, both living at the expense of his enemies and ensuring there would be nothing left for them when he decided to leave. His sojourn was brought to an abrupt end when he was caught napping again, at the end of September. Showing uncharacteristic enterprise, the Austrian commander Prince Charles of Lorraine surprised Frederick at his camp at Staudenz and moreover with superior numbers (39,000 to 22,000). The battle at Soor which resulted on 30 September could easily have been a disaster. The Prussians were saved partly by Frederick's speed of decision and aggression once he woke up to the danger, but mainly by the iron discipline and courage of his soldiers, no less remarkable for being habitual.[183] He described the battle variously as 'terrible but very glorious', 'very hot', 'the fiercest of the four I have fought', and 'bloodier than Hohenfriedberg'.[184] Even in the immediate aftermath of the battle, a time when he was most likely to be triumphalist, he paid tribute to his opponents: 'their plan was conceived very shrewdly. It was also carried out very well, and it was only the daring of the Prussians and their being so used to winning that allowed them to overcome their incredible difficulties'.[185] Among the 856 Prussian dead was his wife's brother, Duke Albrecht of Brunswick, yet he failed to send Elizabeth Christine even a letter of condolence, an omission so unfeeling that even she was roused to anger.[186]

Despite this success, Frederick was still in danger. With supplies exhausted, he was obliged to take his army back to Silesia in early October and get ready for yet another round, for he knew that even now the Austrians were not ready to negotiate, especially not since Maria Theresa's husband had been elected Holy Roman Emperor on 13 September. Although written long after the event, the relevant passage in *The History of My Own Times* clearly shows his

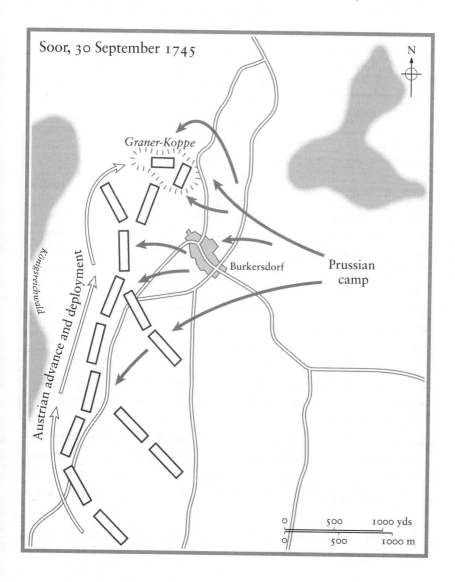

Soor, 30 September 1745

N

Graner-Koppe

Königsreichwald

Austrian advance and deployment

Burkersdorf

Prussian camp

500   1000 yds

500   1000 m

exasperation: 'the fortitude of the empress degenerated sometimes into obstinacy. She was as a woman intoxicated at having recovered the Imperial dignity for her descendants. Occupied solely by the smiling prospects of futurity, she thought her grandeur would be degraded, should she negotiate with a prince, whom she accused of rebellion, as with an equal.'[187] Thanks to the indiscretion of the Saxon minister Count Brühl, Frederick knew that the next attack would be coming from Saxony, directed at Berlin. In Valori's opinion, what followed represented Frederick's greatest achievement hitherto.[188] As soon as he learned that Austrian troops had crossed the Saxon frontier from Bohemia, he sent Zieten with a force of hussars and heavy cavalry to prevent their junction with the Saxon allies awaiting their arrival. A victory over the Saxons at Katholisch-Hennersdorf on 23 November sent Prince Charles and his army back where they had come from. That left the northern Saxon army, reinforced by Austrians detached from the army on the Rhine, to be dealt with. At Kesselsdorf on 15 December, an army commanded by Old Dessauer achieved a hard-fought but decisive victory. Three days later, he and Frederick rode into Dresden together.[189] It was to be the last battle of the war, and Old Dessauer's last battle ever (he died in 1747). At long last Maria Theresa accepted that a military solution could not be found. On Christmas Day 1745 the Peace of Dresden brought the Second Silesian War to an end. Silesia and Glatz remained Prussian. All the Austrians had achieved was Frederick's recognition of the election of Francis I as emperor. Their Saxon ally recovered all his territory but had to pay Frederick an indemnity of 1,000,000 talers.[190] Peace did not come a moment too soon for Frederick, for according to his account in *The History of My Own Times*, these last sixteen months of campaigning had cost him 8,000,000 talers and he had just 15,000 left in his treasury.[191]

Although the War of the Austrian Succession was to continue for another three years until brought to an end by the Peace of Aachen in October 1748, Frederick's part in it was over.* He could return to his capital in triumph, which he promptly did, arriving on 28 December.

---

* Significantly, the Prussian share of what had become a world war has always been known in Germany as the First and Second Silesian Wars.

He was given a hero's reception – banners, crowds, delegations, processions, illuminations, the full panoply of baroque triumphalism. For the first time in public he was hailed as 'Frederick the Great', a sobriquet which became permanent. Indeed, the most popular slogan to be found displayed on the streets of Berlin in various media was '*Vivat Fridericus Magnus!*' (Long live Frederick the Great!).[192] A choir of schoolchildren sang: '*Vivat, vivat, Friedericus Rex, Victor, Augustus, Magnus, Felix, pater Patriae!*'. The burghers of the Dorotheenstadt district erected a triumphal arch dedicated to 'Frederick the Invincible, the Greatest of the Great'.[193] To ensure that the word was spread to the rest of Europe, an official account and two commemorative volumes were published.[194] In his distinguished and influential biography of 1983, Theodor Schieder concluded that it was 'highly unlikely, if not to be discounted entirely', that Frederick had a hand in his proclamation as 'the Great'.[195] More recently, Jürgen Luh has argued persuasively that Frederick knew very well what he was doing and that his acquisition of the coveted sobriquet was the result of long and careful manipulation. In this process, Voltaire played a crucial role, proclaiming to Europe that his royal friend and correspondent should be hailed as '*le Grand*', an appellation he first used in a letter to Frederick in July 1742 following the Treaty of Berlin.[196] Moreover, there is abundant evidence to suggest that the Berlin celebrations of 28 December were carefully choreographed by the authorities, although Frederick's personal involvement is less clear.[197] As we shall see in a later chapter, he was certainly very well aware of the importance of public recognition and took great care to foster it. For the time being, he can be left to savour his triumph, proclaimed by his people as 'the Great', a title he shared only with his great-grandfather Frederick William the Great Elector.

5

The Masterful Servant of the State

Frederick William I had confined his aggression to his own subjects, the chief victim being his eldest son. In this respect, if no other, 1740 marked a watershed. Before the year was out, Frederick had shown that his own lust for power would be turned outwards. From being a quiescent dinghy, bobbing along behind the great powers, Prussia became the most daring destroyer in the European states-system. Would there be an equally radical change in domestic politics? At the level of theory, it certainly looked that way. As their political testaments revealed, father and son had very little in common as to how they viewed the foundations of the state. The following observations on the nature of political obligation give a fair indication of the rudimentary nature of what passed for Frederick William's political thought: 'So long as God gives me breath, I shall assert my rule like a despot'; 'My subjects must dance to my tune or the Devil take me: I'll treat them as rebels and have them hanged and roasted like the Tsar does' and – most eloquent of all – 'After all, we are lord and king and can do what we like.'[1] Yet he also acknowledged three important restrictions. Firstly, he had a strong attachment to the House of Hohenzollern. When he succeeded in 1713, one of his first actions was to promulgate a dynastic law which placed every last possession of the family, right down to the jewels, in an entail. In other words, rather in the manner of an English landowner, he sought to guard against the accident of a profligate successor by making everything the Hohenzollerns owned inalienable.[2] The current head of the family would enjoy only a life interest. Nothing could have advertised better Frederick William's patrimonial attitude. When he spoke of 'the state',

118

he meant his own domains and when he referred to 'matters of state' he meant foreign policy.[3] Secondly, for all his disagreements with Charles VI, he entertained a respect bordering on veneration for the imperial office per se and the Holy Roman Empire, commanding his successor never to enter into an alliance directed against either. The awful fate of Bavaria and Cologne following their traitorous dealings with the French in the War of the Spanish Succession provided sufficient warning, he added.[4] Thirdly and crucially, he was restrained by a belief that he was under constant surveillance from an omnipotent, omnipresent and punitive God:

> never start an unjust war and do not be an aggressor, because God has ruled against unjust wars and you will have to report to him, and his justice is severe, just think of what became of those who started unjust wars such as Louis XIV, King Augustus II of Poland, the Elector of Bavaria etc., these last two were chased out of their territories and Augustus II was punished by the hand of God.[5]

Of these restraints, the second and third certainly meant nothing to his successor, although it is less clear that Frederick had no sense of dynastic pride. In an important letter written to his brother and heir-apparent, August Wilhelm, in February 1744, he stressed that his only interest was the promotion of 'the future welfare of the state and the glory of the House of Brandenburg'.[6] Despite that coupling, he was always insistent that the greater whole must take priority. Three independent eye-witness accounts agree that when he met his ministers for the first time as king, on 2 June 1740, he told them that, whereas his father had drawn a distinction between his own interests and those of his country, 'I look upon the interests of the state as my own: I can have no interests which are not equally those of my people. If the two are incompatible, the preference is always to be given to the welfare and advantage of the country.'[7] This insistence on the subordination of self to country became the most celebrated leitmotiv of Frederick's political discourse. Many literary sources have been identified, including the *Meditations* of the Stoic Roman Emperor Marcus Aurelius (whose bust he placed in his bedroom at Sanssouci and another in his library at Charlottenburg);[8] François Fénelon's *Telemachus* (1699), whose first acquaintance he made when he was only nine years old;[9] and Voltaire's *Henriade*, whose praises he sang to the author from the moment their correspondence began.[10]

An early theoretical fruit was harvested in *Antimachiavel*, with Frederick's statement that a prince should subordinate all personal emotions to love of the fatherland and the promotion of the state.[11] Variations on this theme were played again and again for the rest of the reign. As the media chosen for his views included documents not intended for publication (private correspondence and the political testaments), their sincerity can be accepted. They also marked a sharp break with the past. Where his father's thinking had been prescriptive (looking to past practice), particularist (anchored in the here and now) and pious, Frederick's was rational, universal and secular. To legitimate his authority, he postulated a social contract, by which the luckless inhabitants of a state of nature delegated to a sovereign sufficient authority to maintain external security and internal order. By the middle of the eighteenth century, such a concept was hardly original, but its advocacy by a ruler of a backward and hitherto minor principality of the Holy Roman Empire certainly was. Frederick's clearest exposition was given in the course of a discussion of religious toleration in his *Essay on the forms of government and the duties of sovereigns* of 1777, where he identified the origin of the state in an agreement between all members of society to appoint one of their number as their sovereign. Obviously, he argued, they did not renounce their natural freedom because they wished to embrace servitude. All they were seeking was the maintenance of law and order, wise legislation and defence against foreign enemies. That was to be the limit of the sovereign's authority. All the other liberties they had enjoyed in their pre-political state of nature were unaffected. Chief among them was freedom of conscience, the right to worship any god in any way they saw fit, or indeed no god at all. Coercion was pointless anyway: anyone could be forced to parrot a doctrine but, if it were done without 'inner consent', the act would have no value. He added, however, 'once this agreement had been made, it could not be altered'.[12]

This is, of course, an authoritarian interpretation of the social contract. The grant of sovereignty is irrevocable and unconditional, the subjects have no right of resistance. On the other hand, the ruler is obliged to serve the interests of the whole. Frederick made that explicit in a passage following that just quoted:

Here we have, in general, the duties which a prince should carry out. So that he never neglects them, he should often recall to mind that he is a man just like the least of his subjects; if he is the first judge, the first general, the first minister of society, it is not so that he can indulge himself, but so that he can fulfil the duties involved. He is only the first servant of the state, obliged to act with honesty, wisdom and with a complete lack of self-interest, as if at every moment he might be called upon to render an account of his stewardship to his fellow-citizens.[13]

In a letter to Voltaire written the year before he came to the throne, he used a striking simile to identify the role of the ruler: he likened him to the heart in the human body, receiving blood from all the members and then pumping it out again to the furthest extremities of the body politic; he received loyalty and obedience, he sent out security, prosperity and everything else which could further the welfare of the community. Apologists for Frederick's regime pointed to this identification of ruler with state to rescue him from accusations of despotism. The essence of despotic power, they pointed out, was its arbitrary, capricious character, its sole dependence on the whim of its wielder. That was what led contemporaries to castigate the Russian and Ottoman empires as 'oriental despotisms'. In Prussia, on the other hand, the absolute power of the king was limited by the obligations imposed by the social contract, especially by the rule of law. Nothing could be more misleading, they maintained, than to confuse authoritarian government with despotism. In a speech delivered to the Prussian Academy shortly after the outbreak of the French Revolution, the foreign minister Count Hertzberg recorded indignantly that especially the British and the French depicted Prussia as 'purely despotic, arbitrary, militarist and oriental' with its own version of the Bastille in the form of Spandau prison. The reality was quite different: 'from its inception the Prussian government has been formed on the principles of a *free and moderate monarchy* [his emphasis], composed of a sovereign; intermediary bodies in the form of provincial Estates; a Council of State and all the necessary subordinate bodies for public administration'. In other words, the Prussia of Frederick the Great ticked all the boxes of Montesquieu's *Spirit of the Laws*. Not unreasonably, Hertzberg awarded his state a self-congratulatory pat on the back by pointing out that, at a time when all the states of Europe were being shaken to their foundations, Prussia enjoyed 'profound peace at home and abroad'.[14]

Many European sovereigns had put pen to paper, or had had pens put to paper on their behalf, to proclaim the purity of their principles. Whether they practised what they preached is a different matter. The Frederick presented to the world in *Antimachiavel* was soon shown to have little in common with the Frederick who invaded Silesia. Nor did his domestic rule always fit the theoretical template. That the tone would be imperious, not to say domineering, was clear from the start. Although Frederick had been on the throne barely six months before he went off to war, he had had plenty of time to advertise what sort of ruler he was going to be. Any hope on the part of his subjects that the iron grip of his tyrannical father would be relaxed was soon dashed. The reign opened with a flurry of eye-catching initiatives – the recall of the exiled philosopher Christian Wolff, the abolition of torture, the relaxation of censorship and the opening of royal granaries to bring down the price of bread* – but the style of government remained the same. There was no dilution of the previous autocracy, if anything the reverse. On 2 October 1740 the Danish General Prätorius reported that Frederick was doing everything himself, exceeding even his predecessor in his jealous hoarding of decision-making.[15]

So close did Frederick keep his cards to his chest that foreign diplomats could find nothing beyond gossip and idle speculation to send back to their courts. The Austrian ambassador lamented in 1749 that not even the notional foreign minister, Podewils, had any idea as to what his master's intentions were. Frederick himself was reported to have said that, if he discovered that his own skin knew what he was going to do, he would have it peeled off and thrown away.[16] A royal interview was not only pointless, it also exposed the unwelcome guest to Frederick's notoriously acid tongue. According to the French envoy, the Duc de Guînes, very few of his intimidated colleagues were brave enough even to ask for an audience at Potsdam.[17] It was not only

---

* For more on all of these initiatives, see below, pp. 319–21, 368–9, 387–9.

foreign affairs that were kept so secret. Soon after the beginning of the reign, another French diplomat, the Marquis de Beauvau, predicted that 'the generals of his army will never be anything more than his adjutants; the ministers nothing more than his clerks; his chancellors of the exchequer nothing more than his tax collectors; and the German princes nothing more than his slaves'.[18] Moreover, it was Frederick who made the selection. Towards the end of his reign, he reminded a senior minister that he was the man in charge of appointments: 'it is my custom to select for my service people I can make use of, and I appoint them as I see fit, and no one can have any sort of claim to a post, but it all depends on me and me alone'.[19]

As in the previous reign, there was no discussion, no consultation. No minister dared twice to wait on his royal master without an express summons.[20] 'Frederick was definitely the autocrat and his ministers only the instruments of his will,' wrote a senior minister, Graf von der Schulenburg.[21] The minister, or rather clerk, always had to submit his report in writing. Frederick read it, scribbled a decision in the margin and handed it back to a secretary for execution. More than any of his more polished reflections on policy, these marginalia reveal his speed of decision, penetrating intellect, equally sharp wit and occasional spite. They can also be quite entertaining. For example: the members of a town council asked what punishment would be appropriate for a man who had slandered God, the king and themselves. Frederick's comment was that, while the offender's blasphemous remark about the Almighty merely demonstrated that he did not know Him and so should be excused, and his *lèse-majesté* could also be forgiven, his attack on the city-fathers deserved exemplary punishment, which in this case meant half-an-hour's confinement in Spandau.[22] As we shall see more than once, Frederick loved nothing more than to indulge his scepticism and anti-clericalism.

The compulsive wish to keep secret everything important and to monopolize decision-making probably had its roots in his childhood and adolescent experiences. Forced to keep his true self and opinions concealed from his fearsome father, he created for himself an iron mask which he took off only among his *cercle intime*, and even there political issues remained taboo. It was an attitude he proclaimed from the start. In the letter to his brother cited earlier he declared firmly: 'What our state needs is a ruler who sees with his own eyes and governs by himself.'[23] In both the political testaments he wrote for his successor, he elevated this advice to the status of an axiom: 'a well-run government must have a firmly established system constructed like a philosophical system in which finance, policy and military all combine to promote the same end, the strengthening of the state and the expansion of its power. Such a system can only derive from one brain' (1752).[24] He returned to the theme at greater length in 1768. He had never convened councils, he stated, because nothing could be more damaging than exposing matters of state for general discussion. Only a single ruler could achieve an overall view and maintain the necessary confidentiality. In seventeenth-century France, both Richelieu and Mazarin had failed in the long run; only Louis XIV had been able to show that essential singleness of purpose. As for his own contemporary, Louis XV, his sloth and incompetence had allowed French policy to slip and slide through ever-changing ministers before reaching its nadir when 'a wretched whore' (Madame de Pompadour) got her hands on it. The situation was even worse in those enfeebled countries where monarchy had turned republican and 'the love of fame had become the spirit of faction'.[25] The other great parliamentary monarchy, Great Britain, may have looked more virile, but closer inspection revealed a stew of depravity. In his satirical poem *Palladium* he sent the hero to visit Parliament, depicting it as a talking-shop where fine words were not matched with action and where freedom of speech concealed the fact that all members had been corrupted. So the Hanoverian tail was allowed to wag the British dog, he added ('The Electorate rules the Kingdom').[26] On another occasion he dismissed the British constitution as 'turbulent and wild'.[27] The acid test of sole rule he also applied to his own predecessors, with Frederick William the Great Elector and Frederick William I getting top marks but Frederick I failing miserably.[28] Towards the end of his reign he did occasionally summon to Potsdam from Berlin his two ministers in charge of foreign affairs, Hertzberg and Finckenstein, to discuss business, but even then he jealously rationed the information he passed on to them.[29]

Even in an industrial enterprise of modest size, it is necessary for the CEO to delegate. Frederick was trying to run a state which stretched for a thousand kilometres across Europe and included more than 2 million subjects even at the beginning of his reign. That he was able to exercise even some measure of control was due to his exceptional capacity for hard work. Needing only five to six hours sleep, he was up between three and four in the morning (an hour later in winter), going straight to his desk to deal first with the deciphered despatches of his envoys. After dictating replies to the secretary responsible, he turned to domestic business, scribbling marginalia and dictating directives. While this was being done, another secretary was preparing a digest of the less important material and petitions from private individuals. The secretaries then retired to prepare the necessary letters or decrees which were brought back later in the day for perusal and signature.[30] This was *Kabinettsregierung*, the very opposite of the 'cabinet government' that was evolving in Great Britain at about the same time, despite the verbal similarity. 'Government from the closet' would be a better translation. In the authoritative view of one of Frederick's most recent biographers, the only person to whose advice Frederick was prepared to listen was Voltaire – and then only on cultural matters.[31] This was a system he had inherited from his father and he took it even further, often corresponding directly with diplomats and senior provincial officials. Frederick's aim was to achieve a 'monopoly of information'.[32]

It is something of a truism that influence in government is determined more by proximity to power than formal office. In the case of Prussia, it was Frederick's private secretaries who enjoyed daily access to their master. It can never be known just how much influence they exerted. That they were the passive instruments of the royal will must certainly be doubted. Chief among them was August Friedrich Eichel, one of three secretaries inherited from the previous reign. Never far from Frederick's side, even when on campaign, he was surrounded by a mystique all the more towering for being nebulous. 'No mortal knew him' was the verdict of the French envoy, the Jacobite Duke of Tyrconnell.[33] No one knew exactly what he did, but everyone thought his influence was colossal. The official ministers in Berlin certainly believed so, as they sought to ingratiate themselves, hoping that Eichel would pave the way for the acceptance of the proposals they were submitting for royal approval.[34] The courtier Count Lehndorff dubbed him 'the Mazarin of our country', a tribute to his dominance but not really an appropriate sobriquet for, unlike the cardinal who dominated French politics during the minority of Louis XIV, Eichel was very rarely seen and discreet to the point of invisibility. The Abbé Carlo Denina described him as 'a kind of prime minister'.[35] He achieved this status by making himself indispensable, not least by his industry. Rising even earlier than Frederick, he worked from 4 a.m. until 2 p.m. and, following a lengthy lunch break, again from 8 p.m. until midnight.[36] As on a normal day a dozen or more royal orders with the force of law were being issued, Eichel and the other secretaries had plenty of opportunity to draft them in the manner they saw fit and 'interpret' the royal will. This was undoubtedly a risky exercise given the autocratic will and short temper of their master, but Frederick could not read every document brought back to him for signature.[37] Especially when he was away at the war, their freedom of action swelled to fill the vacuum. Theirs cannot have been an agreeable existence, as the secretaries were on call at all hours of night and day and transacted most of their business standing up. When one tried to evade appointment on the grounds that he was married (Eichel and the others were bachelors), Frederick replied: 'Your wife doesn't need to know everything.'[38] Although the salaries were meagre, there must have been other opportunities for making money: despite his reputation for incorruptibility, Eichel left a large fortune to the family of his friend, the Chancellor Jariges, when he died in 1768.[39]

In this relentless insistence on retaining personal control, Frederick showed that he was a political anachronism. At a time when the world was becoming so much more complex thanks to demographic and economic expansion, and when Prussia in particular was expanding so rapidly, the need for delegation of decision-making grew correspondingly. Frederick's doubling the number of private secretaries after his return from the Seven Years War, and allocating each of them specific responsibilities, could not solve the problem.[40] Advancing age meant that his grasp of business necessarily slackened while the volume inexorably increased. When the system he bequeathed was shipwrecked by the disasters of 1806, the chief complaint levelled at the old order by reformers such as Stein was the influence of the cabinet secretaries (who enjoyed 'power without responsibility') and the distance between sovereign and ministers.[41] It was a vice which Frederick passed down the chain of command. When he found officials he could trust, he overloaded them with responsibilities. Friedrich Wilhelm von der Schulenburg-Kehnert, for example, or Friedrich Anton von Heinitz, were left to their own devices most of the time. The former accumulated so much business that he could master it only with the help of twenty-five secretaries housed in his private residence. Unable to read, let alone master, all the reports that poured into his office on a daily basis, he in turn was obliged to give subordinates a great deal of leeway.[42] On occasions Frederick could show awareness of the need to delegate. When David Lenz was sent to the newly acquired territory of East Frisia in 1744, he was told that the king was giving him only general advice about conduct and policy because he himself had no knowledge of local conditions. Lenz was to decide what was appropriate when he had settled in.[43] This seems to have been the exception that proved the rule. As Frederick grew older, his taste for micro-management kept pace. A cabinet order of August 1783 told his officials they must not 'do anything off your own bat, but ask me first, about absolutely everything, even if it is only about trivial things'.[44]

Frederick tried to get some movement into this ponderous system by constant tours of inspection. In this, as in so many other respects, he was following – but intensifying – his father's practice. En route to Königsberg in the summer of 1740, whenever he stopped in an administrative district he expected to find the *Landrat* (local official) waiting for him, equipped with a report on local conditions and needs. The common people were also authorized to contribute their opinions and information.[45] That set the pattern for the reign. Over the next four and half decades, he criss-crossed his possessions repeatedly, cajoling, bullying, often criticizing, sometimes praising and always asking questions. Some idea of what this involved was given by the record made by a local official called Fromme of Fehrbellin when Frederick came to call in the summer of 1779. Among other things, Frederick enquired about why nothing appeared to be growing on a particular plot of land; the number of cattle and the incidence of bovine epidemics (Frederick advised the use of rock salt for the latter); drainage, land reclamation and water transport; land ownership; why an officer had retired from royal service (he kept coming back to this topic);

wheat yields and manuring; why hemp and woad were not cultivated; the prosperity, protection and insolence of peasants; immigrants; a mule stud; and timber management. If the account can be trusted, Fromme spoke frankly when he thought the king was wrong and stuck to his guns when contradicted. He got nowhere, however, when he lamented that he had received no remission of taxes when his own herd was decimated by foot-and-mouth disease, Frederick saying: 'My son, today something is wrong with my left ear; I can't hear well.'[46] The overriding concern with military matters, together with the ubiquity of the Kleist clan, came out clearly in the following exchange:

KING: What is the name of the village ahead?
FROMME: Protzen.
KING: Who is the owner?
FROMME: Herr von Kleist.
KING: Which Kleist?
FROMME: A son of General von Kleist.
KING: Which General von Kleist?[47]

The news that the king was on his way must have struck fear into every official heart, but at the same time cheered the subjects in his charge, especially those selected to provide hospitality, for Frederick paid 50 talers for a meal and 100 talers for bed and breakfast.[48] They also had the opportunity to air their grievances, even when horses were being changed at a posting-station. This royal reputation for accessibility may well have done something to restrain the more brutal landlords. In 1779, for example, the peasants of Marzahn, a village east of Berlin, threatened to send a deputation to find Frederick on his Bohemian tour of inspection and present a remonstrance.[49] What happened after the – usually very small – royal party passed on was a different matter, of course. As for all royal visits, past and present, the improvements hurriedly made by nervous officials often proved to be cosmetic and temporary. One of Frederick's favourite officials, Carl Georg Heinrich, Count von Hoym, the minister in charge of Silesia, went to great lengths to discover in advance Frederick's likely route through the province. Subordinate personnel were briefed on likely questions; stray dogs and beggars were rounded up and removed;

houses on the route were painted; peasants were loaned smart clothes for the day; and so on. Especially where shortcomings had been noted on a previous visit, action was taken to indicate that the matter was in hand – scaffolding was erected around a decrepit building, for example (only to be taken down again when Frederick moved on).[50] Knowing that his master liked nothing more than to be told that the population of his state was increasing, Hoym added 20,000 fictional immigrants with a stroke of his pen.[51]

Frederick must have suspected that the wool was being pulled over his eyes. Despite his energy and application, he could not be everywhere. To the Rhenish provinces or East Frisia he went only seldom. In most communities of his sprawling possessions, life could roll quietly along, untroubled by orders issued from the centre. Every now and again, his frustration at the sclerotic nature of his administration led to outbursts against his officials, whom he variously dubbed in his marginalia as thieves, apes, rascals, lackeys, scallywags, jokers, idiots, cheats and rogues.[52] The officials of the War and Domains Chambers (the main administrative bodies in the provinces) he viewed as 'idiots', characterized by 'indolence' and 'carelessness', good only at hatching 'institutionalised conspiracies' against him. Gratefully receiving the anonymous denunciations which seemed to confirm his low opinion, he was quick to take punitive action. Of the forty-one provincial presidents who served during his reign, he cashiered eleven.[53] Essential qualifications for a tolerable life in the Prussian civil service were, therefore, a broad back and a thick skin. Officials had to be ready for periodic blasts of denunciation, as for example when Frederick told the West Prussian administration, following the discovery of a trivial peccadillo: 'with good conscience one can always hang ninety-nine out of a hundred war commissaries; it is already saying a good deal if a single honest man is among them'.[54]

It is a truism, albeit one confirmed by experience, that bullies were once the victims of bullying. In the case of Frederick, his father's verbal excesses directed at people weaker than himself were certainly reprised. A good example was provided early in the reign when Frederick jumped to the conclusion that his foreign minister, Count Podewils, had let slip to the Prussian envoy at Stockholm secret information about negotiations being conducted between the two countries. Enraged, he fired off a letter from his camp in Saxony telling Podewils that if he could not retrieve the situation, he would be 'a man lost for ever'. This was followed up the next day by an even more intemperate tirade, in which Frederick voiced his suspicion that Podewils had sold himself to the English, adding that there were enough prisons in Prussia to accommodate ministers who disobeyed him and that even his head was at risk.[55] In a dignified reply, Podewils stated that his poverty and reputation provided sufficient defence against the charge of corruption; that Frederick's threats could make no impression on one who valued his honour more than his life; and that he had informed von der Linde of the Swedish negotiations on the direct orders of Frederick himself. And just to rub it in, Podewils added that this was not the first time he had had occasion to complain about orders being given orally and then forgotten. Great must have been the embarrassment when this devastating riposte arrived. Eichel was told to reply that it had all been the result of 'a little over-hastiness' and that the whole thing was now regretted and forgotten.[56]

Podewils was notionally Frederick's most senior minister (although Frederick was always his own foreign minister).[57] Suitably cowed by Frederick's abrasive style of man-management, Prussian officials lower down the chain of command usually kept their heads below the parapet. What might happen if they were brave enough to question a royal decision was dramatized in 1766 when a senior financial official, Erhard Ursinus, was instructed to conduct an inquiry into the economic crisis that had been afflicting Prussia since the end of the Seven Years War three years earlier. In his report, Ursinus identified three main culprits: the inevitable after-effects of war; growing competition from other countries; and the king's misguided economic policy. Although diplomatically drafted, the criticism of the last-named was radical. Singled out for being especially damaging to the Prussian economy was the monopoly granted to the Levant Company; the trade war with Saxony; the restrictions on transit trade; the rise in taxation occasioned by the new excise regulations; and, more generally, the protectionist measures which had made Prussian manufactures expensive, poor in quality and impossible to sell abroad.[58] This exposé amounted to nothing less than an indictment of Frederick's whole economic policy and he reacted with corresponding vehemence. He wrote to the General Directory: 'I am astounded by the impertinent report they have sent me. I can excuse the ministers on the grounds of ignorance, but the malice and corruption of the author [of the report] must be punished in exemplary fashion, otherwise I shall never succeed in subjecting the villains'.[59] The exemplary punishment he had in mind turned out to be instant dismissal and imprisonment in Spandau for a year.[60] It appears to have encouraged the others to keep their criticisms of royal policy to themselves in future.

It was unfortunate that the greatest single positive influence on Frederick's youth was Voltaire, from whom he took much wit but also much spite. From Ruppin in 1732 Count Schulenburg reported that Frederick's preoccupation with finding something ridiculous in everyone he met and his penchant for wounding mockery would cause him trouble later in life.[61] Once he was king, he had endless opportunities to demonstrate his power over individuals in a mean and petty way. The diary of the flamboyant bisexual courtier Count Lehndorff is particularly revealing. He venerated Frederick, whom he regarded as the greatest sovereign of the century, so charismatic that he would stand out in a crowd of thousands in a foreign city.[62] Yet he also recorded some episodes of Frederickian malice that make painful reading. On 29 January 1756, being the birthday of the Princess of Prussia (the wife of his heir-apparent), Frederick held a gala dinner at court, which ended in 'a truly terrible way'. An unmarried lady, Fräulein von Brand, sitting on the top table, contrived to make Frederick so angry that he threatened to have her thrown out. He then added insult to injury by announcing to the assembled company that it was only the pretty ladies who managed to hook a husband, the ugly ones just hung around the court 'and you can smell these horrible cows ten miles away'. When this dreadful meal was over, Lehndorff added, there was a mass rush for the exit, the Princess of Hessen-Darmstadt announcing she would even accept a sedan-chair (rather than a carriage) if only she could get away.[63] Lehndorff himself was on the receiving end of Frederick's ill-nature in that same year. He had fallen in love with an English aristocrat, Sir Charles Hotham, who was not only very handsome but also highly intelligent ('even by English standards', he added mysteriously). Invited to return to England with him, Lehndorff first had to obtain royal permission. After a week of palpitating anxiety, he received from Eichel the terrible news that his request had been denied, with no reason given, leaving poor Lehndorff in the depths of despair: 'I cry, and I cry, and I cry.'[64] But he was also very angry, raging to his diary that there was nothing he would not do for his king, but he never received anything in return. It must have occurred to him that his senior position in the queen's household was not calculated to endear him to Frederick.

There is just too much evidence from both public and private life to avoid the conclusion that Frederick's relations with other people were authoritarian to the point of being dictatorial. This can be seen with special clarity in the cultural sphere to which he devoted so much time and money. In his opera house Frederick chose not to sit in the royal box but preferred a seat immediately in front of the orchestra pit, so that he could keep a sharp eye on both the stage and the musical director's score.[65] Visiting the opera for a performance of Graun's *Alessandro e Poro* in 1744, Johann Friedrich Borchmann described how Frederick took up position in the front stalls immediately behind the brothers Graun – Carl Heinrich, who conducted operations from the keyboard, and the leader of the orchestra, the violinist Johann Gottlieb, both of whom wore red coats to distinguish them from the rest of the orchestra.[66] A graphic eye-witness account of what this could involve for the performers was provided by the English musicologist Charles Burney, who visited Berlin in 1772:

> The king always stands behind the *maestro di capella*, in sight of the score, which he frequently looks at, and indeed performs the part of director-general here, as much as of generalissimo in the field ... In the opera house, as in the field, his majesty is such a rigid disciplinarian, that if a mistake is made in a single movement or evolution, he immediately marks, and rebukes the offender; and if any of his Italian troops dare to deviate from strict discipline, by adding, altering, or diminishing a single passage in the parts they have to perform, an order is sent, *de par le Roi*, for them to adhere strictly to the notes written by the composer, at their peril. This, when compositions are good, and a singer is licentious, may be an excellent method; but certainly shuts out all taste and refinement. So that music is truly stationary in this country,

his majesty allowing no more liberty in that, than he does in civil matters of government: not contented with being sole monarch of the lives,
fortunes, and business of his subjects, he even prescribes rules to their
most innocent pleasures.[67]

The same taste for micro-management already noted in administrative
matters was indulged in even greater detail in cultural matters. 'Dictatorial' or 'despotic' are adjectives often applied by both contemporaries
and historians. It was a musical regime that was 'an astonishing instance
of artistic despotism, of an almost obsessive control by a monarch
over the least detail of music-making for the gratification of his own
firmly delineated and unvarying musical taste'.[68] It was not unusual for
he who paid the piper to call the tune, but Frederick went further. According to his last *Kapellmeister*, Johann Friedrich Reichardt, Frederick
interfered in every aspect of music-making, whether it was tempo, key
(no minor keys!) or orchestration. 'There was nothing he did not
decide,' concluded Reichardt, 'and the punishment for transgressors
was severe.'[69] As Frederick wrote to his *directeur des spectacles*, Graf
von Zierotin-Lilgenau: 'The singers and the musicians are subject
entirely to my choice, together with many other objects connected with
the theatre, which I order and pay for myself' and, on another occasion,
'You would act much more sensibly if you did what I told you and
didn't argue, because that's something I will not tolerate.'[70] This imperious attitude was overlaid with an even less agreeable element of spite.
So when he sacked his ballet master, Potier, he also published a letter in
the Berlin press denouncing him as a fool and a scoundrel.[71] The word
spread: in 1777 the famous Italian singer Ferrandini declined an engagement in Berlin on the grounds that it was well known that Frederick
treated his singers as if they were soldiers.[72]

One singer who felt the full force of this attitude was Gertrude
Elizabeth Mara (*née* Schmeling), one of the greatest sopranos of her
day. As she recorded in her autobiography, in 1774 she received from
London the kind of offer Prussian singers could only dream of: 1,200
guineas for twelve evenings, plus 200 guineas travel expenses and a
benefit concert. At first Frederick gave his permission, although insisting that her husband stay behind in Berlin as a guarantee that she
would return, but then reneged at the last moment. When the couple

tried to escape to fulfil the engagement, they were arrested at the gates of Berlin and her husband was imprisoned for ten weeks. It was not his first confinement, for Frederick had jailed him earlier for writing to complain about his wife being made to sing an aria she did not like. The royal retort was that Madame Mara was paid to sing not to write. The aria – by the court composer Reichardt – was duly sung.[73] In 1780 she fell ill, but Frederick refused to allow her to go to a Bohemian spa for a cure. 'But now I began to feel the weight of slavery,' she wrote in her autobiography. 'Not only was I having to bury my fame and fortune with him [Frederick] but also now my health,' so this time she and her husband planned their flight carefully. Describing her emotions on waking up for the first time in the safety of Bohemia, she wrote: 'a magnificent morning awaited my awakening, there was a lawn in front of the house, so I had my tea served there and felt completely happy – O Liberté!'[74]

'La Mara' was also the subject of a celebrated anecdote making the rounds in Prussia which exemplified Frederick's contempt for German culture. When first told about a local girl with a wonderful voice, he is said to have snorted: 'A German singer? I should as soon expect to receive pleasure from the neighing of my horse.'[75] Another version of the same story had him saying: 'I'd rather have the arias of my operas neighed by a horse than to have a German prima donna' and refusing even to hear her, on the grounds that she would have an 'accent tudesque'.[76] In fact 'howled by a dog' would have been a more appropriate metaphor, because La Mara recorded that when eventually she did get an audition she found Frederick sitting on a sofa with General Tauentzien and three Italian greyhounds who at once started howling – as they always did when they caught sight of a woman.[77] It ought to be added, however, that she was writing her autobiography more than forty years later and omitted to mention the problems caused for her employer by her disreputable husband and her own troubled relationship with her father.[78]

In a world reminiscent of Alice in Wonderland, where the Queen of Hearts was constantly crying 'Off with their heads!', disgrace was an ever present danger. Of Frederick's numerous readers-cum-librarians, only two – the first (Jordan) and the last (Dantal) – were not cashiered.[79] When the long-serving building director Heinrich Ludwig

Manger submitted an estimate deemed to be excessive, he found himself denounced as a thief and a swindler and despatched to prison. He was soon released, but only because Frederick died the following month.[80] Not every victim of royal caprice was so fortunate, a peasant by the name of Havenbroek, for example, who so badly beat a neighbour who failed to comply with a court ruling that his victim died. He was sentenced to three years in prison for manslaughter. Frederick's enraged marginal directive ran: 'You ought to be ashamed to call yourselves judges, men of learning and officers of the court and hand down a verdict and sentence such as this. In accordance with the dictates of reason and natural law, I want Havenbroek beheaded.'[81] More offensive was the summary hanging of a Catholic army chaplain in Silesia alleged to have given the wrong advice to two Prussian soldiers who had revealed during confession their intention to desert. The body swung from the roadside gallows for the next four years before being cut down by the Austrians in 1760.[82]

These episodes in the life of an autocrat could not have made Frederick loved by those on the receiving end, but they certainly made him feared and respected. Popular among foreigners was the negative opinion of the British envoy Hugh Elliot: 'the Prussian monarchy reminds me of a vast prison in the centre of which appears the great keeper occupied in the care of his captives'.[83] As the well-heeled son of a Scottish baronet commissioned into a Guards regiment at the age of ten and given his first diplomatic posting at the age of twenty-two, Elliot could afford to be disdainful.[84] The Prussian-born art historian Johann Joachim Winckelmann excoriated the land of his birth as the quintessence of despotism and emigrated, first to Saxony and then to Rome.* But this is not the complete picture. It is not so much justice as the need to understand how Frederick's Prussia worked as well as it did that requires the other side to be addressed too. Throughout Frederick's reign, there was a stream of immigrants. As we shall see, at one end of the social scale these included princes seeking commissions in the most prestigious army in Europe and, at the other end, impoverished economic migrants attracted by offers of free land. In

* See also below, p. 142.

between, there was a surprising number who believed that Prussia was a state worth serving.

The most famous was the Imperial Knight Karl vom Stein, the future Prussian reformer. He was one of many. Indeed, Stein's most recent biographer has written of an 'abrupt turn of an entire generation of young people in the direction of Berlin'.[85] Stein's decision in 1780 to seek employment as a Prussian bureaucrat paid a handsome compliment to the ethos Frederick had created. In the past, most Imperial Knights, even the Protestants among them, had looked to Vienna, for the good reason that the Habsburg Emperor was the order's chief protector in the Reich. These 'Prussians by choice' would make a powerful contribution to their adopted country's recovery from the disastrous defeats of 1806, including as they did Hardenberg, Fichte, Hegel, Scharnhorst, Gneisenau and Blücher.[86]

Representative of the professional middle class was Christian Wilhelm Dohm, born at Lemgo as a subject of the Count of Lippe. After graduating, he turned down the offer of a post in Hanover because he hoped for an offer from Prussia. Only the most enticing terms, he added, would deflect him from 'a state which I consider to be the best for oppressed humanity and which offers the greatest scope for constructive activity free from intrigues and other obstacles'. Eventually he did accept a teaching post elsewhere, at Kassel, but only in the expectation that it would accelerate his move to Berlin. He wrote to his friend, the Prussian writer Gleim: 'it is my firm intention, or rather my desire, to serve your great Frederick. This I see as my main objective in life.'[87] He achieved his goal three years later, in 1779, and he remained a loyal 'Prussian-by-choice' until his death in 1820. Direct experience of his adopted country did not curb his enthusiasm; on the contrary, Dohm became one of its most effective propagandists. To another intellectual friend, Friedrich Heinrich Jacobi, he wrote in 1781:

> My principles are truly republican; but of all monarchies I consider ours to be the best, because a great man stands at its head and because in no other country is there less oppression or injustice, and if oppression is to be found, at least it is orderly and regular, and depends as little as possible on personal circumstances. Is it not a great good that every subject has the right to petition the King if he wants to?[88]

If he had been born a Briton, a Swiss or even a citizen of a Free Imperial City, he added, he would not have moved to Prussia, but of all monarchies this was the best. Dohm even managed to get published his ground-breaking treatise on the emancipation of the Jews, even though Frederick disapproved of the contents.[89]

Dohm was well educated, intelligent and articulate. He could have found a good position in any one of a dozen German states. His choice of Frederick's Prussia has to be respected. He was attracted by the ethos of duty, service, self-sacrifice, fairness and efficiency propagated by the king. As he conceded in his memoirs, he had also been impressed by his idol's military success.[90] As we shall see, Dohm and his colleagues were also convinced that they lived in a state which, for all its limitations, promoted enlightened progress and the rule of law.* This seductive combination of culture and power stood out in stark contrast to the self-indulgence and weakness of so many princes of the Holy Roman Empire.

* See below, p. 398.

6

Culture

OPERA

Frederick's accession to the throne made him a very rich young man. The fortune bequeathed by his father was not just colossal, it was in ready money.* Unlike contemporaries such as Maria Theresa of Austria or Frederick, Prince of Wales, he could now indulge himself in any way he chose. In view of his invasion of Silesia later that year, most attention has been paid to the military activity this great hoard made possible, but he also found time to continue on a much grander scale the process of self-fashioning he had begun following his marriage. As we have seen, his first indulgence was to send money to London to bring back his lover, Algarotti, and then to shower him with presents.† This sexual liberation was accompanied by the creation of an aesthetic environment, both cultural and material, in which he could feel comfortable.

A crucial part of that construction was played by music. At Ruppin and then at Rheinsberg, Frederick had to cut his coat according to the limited cloth allowed him by his parsimonious father. Now he could luxuriate. The poverty of the musical establishment he inherited was painfully advertised when soloists had to be borrowed from the Saxon court to perform the oratorio written for Frederick William I's funeral.[1] Its composer, Carl Heinrich Graun, was promptly despatched to Italy to recruit the best singers money could buy.[2] He returned in March 1741 with five male and three female singers.[3] Also sent off

---

* See above, p. 24.
† See above, p. 68.

was Frederick's architect-friend Georg Wenzeslaus von Knobelsdorff, in his case to look at theatres at Dresden and Paris as preparation for building a great new opera house at Berlin.[4] This was a plan of long standing, already discussed intensively at Rheinsberg. Frederick had prepared carefully by sending Knobelsdorff to Dresden in 1732, where four years earlier he himself had been greatly impressed by Augustus the Strong's theatre, and then to Italy in 1736–7 to study the great theatres of Naples, Rome, Florence and Venice.[5] A longer-range influence was English Palladianism, mediated through Colen Campbell's *Vitruvius Britannicus*, a lavishly illustrated compendium of designs published in three volumes between 1715 and 1725 and in Frederick's possession. Also in his library was *Fabbriche Antiche disegnate da Andrea Palladio,* assembled and edited by Campbell's patron, the architect-peer Lord Burlington. It was an influence encouraged by the ubiquitous Algarotti, whose own enthusiasm for Palladio had drawn him to the Burlington circle during his sojourn in London. He obtained for Frederick Palladio's *Quattro libri dell'architettura,* reprinted in Venice with magnificent new engravings rather than woodcuts.[6]

The opera house which Knobelsdorff and Frederick then created has been hailed as 'the first important monument of Neo-Palladianism in Germany'.[7] Architect and patron needed to be yoked together, for the former wrote on the plans that Frederick had provided the design and he, Knobelsdorff, had merely turned it into architectural drawings.[8] In actual fact, the building was highly derivative, for the north façade is a direct copy of Colen Campbell's design for Stourhead in Wiltshire and the west façade was taken from Campbell's design for Wanstead House in Essex.[9] Its construction, however, proved to be problematic. Partly responsible was the reluctance of Frederick's kinsman, the Margrave of Brandenburg-Schwedt, to sell the property which formed part of the site. Further delay was caused by the import from Poland of the very large timbers for the deep foundations necessitated by the marshy soil.[10] Frederick's absence campaigning in Silesia from December 1740 did not help. It was his brother, the fifteen-year-old Prince Henry, who laid the foundation stone on 5 September 1741. Chivvied by a stream of orders from Frederick, work was then driven on apace, so much so that the first performance could be staged on 5 December

1742.[11] By that time, what proved to be the first of three Silesian wars had been brought to a successful conclusion, with Silesia ceded by the defeated Austrians.* With a triumphalist gesture worthy of Louis XIV, Frederick's choice of opera to inaugurate his new theatre was Graun's *Cesare e Cleopatra*, although it may be doubted whether he intended to follow the example of his Roman model to the extent of making love to his own vanquished empress, Maria Theresa.

Much more work was needed to fit out the new opera house, which was still covered in scaffolding on the first night, although the sets by Giacomo Fabris were magnificent and there was an orchestra of forty players.[12] By the time it was complete, a year later, it was hailed by Voltaire in a letter to Maupertuis as 'the finest in Europe'.[13] It was also one of the biggest, capable of seating an audience of 2,000, admitted through five great entrances through which five people could pass simultaneously.[14] On the same grand scale were the interior passage-ways, allowing sedan chairs to be carried straight in and up to even the topmost tier. Also praised by visitors were the spacious boxes ('more like boudoirs'), the good sight-lines, the effective ventilation and the excellent acoustics. Cutting-edge technology allowed the speedy transformation of the raked auditorium into a level surface for balls. Great tanks of water in the roof doubled as reservoirs for special effects on stage, cooling the refreshment rooms with fountains and extinguishing fires.[15]

As intended, the fame of Frederick's new opera house was spread across Europe by the increasing number of foreigners persuaded that Berlin '*vaut le voyage*', to employ the parlance of a Michelin guide. The English merchant and philanthropist Jonas Hanway, who called in to Berlin on his way back from Persia, reported in 1750: 'The extreme delight which the king takes in music, and the great personal knowledge he has of that science, have carried this entertainment [opera] to a great perfection. The dresses, the scenes, and the machinery in the opera of *Phaeton*, were indeed most elegant and magnificent.'[16] Those denied first-hand experience could see for themselves through the medium of the numerous pictorial depictions produced. What these emphasized, so much more clearly than present-

* See above, p. 116.

day illustrations, was the fact that this was a *free-standing* building, so free-standing indeed that it was said to have space around it for 1,000 coaches.[17] It was in fact the first free-standing opera house in Europe.[18] Every previous royal theatre had been located either within the fabric of the royal palace – Versailles, Munich, Mannheim, for example – or immediately adjoining it, allowing the royals to access their box via a private passage – Vienna, Turin, Naples, for example. Moreover, these interiors were dominated by a massive royal box, directly facing the stage and usually rising through two or more floors. There was a royal box in the Berlin theatre too, but Frederick made no use of it.[19]

SACRALIZATION

There is more to this than meets the eye. The primary purpose of the Real Teatro di San Carlo (Royal Theatre of Saint Charles), for example, built for Charles IV of Naples in 1737, was representational, proclaiming the majesty of the patron. Frederick's opera house too was intended to impress his contemporaries, especially the sovereigns among them, and was also a place for his personal recreation. But it also represented his homage to the arts in general and music in particular. The inscription he placed above the portico was not Théâtre Royale de Saint Frédéric but Fridericus Rex Apollini et Musis. This was an aesthetic temple 'dedicated to Apollo and the Muses by King Frederick', their self-appointed high-priest. The gable on the street side depicted Apollo with Thalia (the muse of comedy) and Melpomene (the muse of tragedy), while the south side presented Orpheus, the musical son of Apollo and Calliope.[20] As we shall see later, Apollo was to put in another appearance when Frederick built the New Palace at Potsdam after the Seven Years War.*

The construction of this autonomous temple of the arts was an early harbinger of what was to become a powerful movement, especially in German-speaking Europe: the sacralization of culture. By that is meant the emancipation of high culture from any representational

* See below, p. 167.

and recreational function and its elevation to become a sacralized activity to be worshipped in its own right. At its heart, paradoxically, was its apparent opposite: secularization. As traditional forms of organized religion went into retreat, a growing number of intellectuals began to look elsewhere for metaphysical and spiritual sustenance. Art was promoted from being an instrument for the glory of God to being God itself. The most influential single exponent of this new art-religion was Johann Joachim Winckelmann (1717–68), a Prussian by birth, who spent most of his adult life in Rome. He hated Frederick and everything he stood for – 'I shudder from head to foot when I think of Prussian despotism and of that oppressor of nations, who will make his country ... an object of eternal curse and horror among men'[21] – but in fact the two men had much in common, not least in their sexual orientation and enthusiasm for classical sculpture. By marrying Pietist introspection to sensualist paganism, Winckelmann created an aesthetic religion. His account of the Apollo Belvedere, for example, is more than an appreciation of a statue, it is a religious exercise, because for him the statue does not represent a god, it *is* a god.[22]

Frederick experienced the same mixture of sensual delight and high-minded aestheticism. From his camp in Bohemia in April 1742 he wrote to Algarotti, who was on a diplomatic mission to Piedmont, to ask him to try to engage the singer Pinti, authorizing the very generous offer of 4,000 talers per annum. He then broke into verse to extol his devotion to the arts:

> O company of sweet pleasures, children beloved of the gods
> Hurry to satisfy my voluptuous senses:
> Open up to me, you gates of life.
> Assuage the flames aroused by my passions.
> And you, the perfumes of Araby,
> And you the nectars of Hungary,
> Lavish on me your delicious tastes.
> And you, ravishing melody,
> Whose miraculous effects
> Spread their magic through the organs to the heart,
> Whether the flattering sweetness of melancholy,

Or the powerful rush of joyous emotions.
When the soul is all alone in tranquillity,
Taking leave of futile care,
It knows how to savour this ecstasy, and these happy moments
Enjoyed by the heavenly throng,
Come O company of the arts, company always welcome,
And make your immortal abode with me for ever.[23]

The Berlin opera house was the metropolitan cathedral of Frederick's art-religion. It was there that the great liturgical set-pieces were performed, in the shape of the grand operas staged during the carnival season. These were lavish, multi-media productions, presenting a combination of drama, music and ballet which appealed as much to the eye through the gorgeous costumes and elaborate sets as to the ear. They were also multi-national: most of the singers were Italian, the dancers French and the musicians German. Although so often described as a Francophile, Frederick in fact had a generally low opinion of contemporary French culture. During the golden age of the mid-seventeenth century, he believed, French writers, led by Corneille and Racine, had produced dramatic works of unsurpassable quality, but since then their star had waned. Dismissing their music as 'puerile', he told Graun to stop composing overtures in the French style. Modern Italian music was mellifluous when sung properly but essentially 'stupid'.[24] What Frederick demanded was music in the Italian style but written by Germans. Ascribed to him was the dictum: 'The French only know how to write drama and the Italians only know how to sing; the Germans alone understand how to write music.'[25] In practice, this meant that the operatic repertoire throughout his reign was dominated by Graun, his first *Kapellmeister*; by Johann Friedrich Agricola, who succeeded Graun on his death in 1759; and by Johann Adolf Hasse, whom Frederick never employed but had admired greatly ever since he had heard his opera *Cleofide* in Dresden in 1728.[26] As the distinguished English music critic and historian Charles Burney pointed out: 'the music of this country is more truly German than that of any other part of the empire; for though there are constantly Italian operas here, in carnival time, his Prussian majesty will suffer none to be performed but those of Graun, Agricola or Hasse'.[27]

THE DELIGHTS OF MUSIC

The contrast with the other courts of Europe was striking. Many of his fellow-sovereigns were just as knowledgeable, enthusiastic and dictatorial but none of them had such untrammelled access to ready money. When Frederick made up his mind that he wanted a particular singer, he had the wherewithal to have his way. As we have seen,* Frederick always had a substantial pot of money at his disposal, administered by his factotum Fredersdorf, completely independent of the regular state finances. It was cash from this source that brought, among many others, Carl Philipp Emmanuel Bach to Berlin in 1740.[28] Ironically, the flow of top-flight singers from Italy – Giovanni Carestini, Antonio Uberi ('Porporino'), Felice Salimbeni, Paolo Bedeschi ('Paulino'), Benedetta Molteni, Giovanna Astrua – was made possible by the penny-pinching of his predecessor. How Frederick William I would have raged, had he known that his savings were being squandered on Italian castrati and French ballet dancers. As ever in the musical world, there was a chasm between the salaries of the stars on the stage and the orchestral players in the pit. Porporino was paid over 2,000 talers a year, Salimbeni and Carestini more than double that, and Giovanna Astrua even more, perhaps as much as 6,000.[29]

Even the most cursory of glances at Frederick's correspondence reveals how much time and trouble he devoted to the world of grand opera. It was more than a question of display, of keeping up with his monarchical competitors. It was a psychological necessity to create for himself a visual, dramatic and sonic world in the theatre. Frederick was scornful of the excessive display of the operas staged at Dresden, which he dismissed as all show and no substance, effects without causes. In January 1755 he wrote to his sister Wilhelmine about a performance there of Porpora's *Ezio*, which had brought on stage two companies of grenadiers and two squadrons of light cavalry in Roman dress, twenty camels, four mules and a carriage drawn by four white horses. These Saxon extravaganzas, he observed, were aimed only at the eyes and failed to touch the heart. For him, one

* See above, p. 62.

moving scene was worth more than all that triumphalist braggadocio: 'woe to those who have never known the rapture of tears!'[30] Yet, his was a passion informed by self-knowledge and tempered by an awareness of alternatives. This can be seen, with special clarity, in his revealing but neglected poem entitled simply 'On pleasures', addressed in 1749 to his *directeur des spectacles,* Ernst Maximilian Sweerts, Baron von Reist.* Two hundred lines long, it begins with a dismissal of the intense but short-lived and dangerous carnal delights offered by prostitutes, before putting in the mouth of Sweerts the command:

> Go to the palace of enchantment and magic,
> Where spectacle, dance and the art of music
> Combine a hundred different pleasures to create just one.[31]

Frederick replies to Sweerts that he is only too happy to obey, for he loves all the pleasures condemned by *'un faux mystique'* (Christianity) and would always follow the Epicurean gospel. He adds that he only wishes that his soul had a hundred doors, like the ancient city of Thebes, through which every possible pleasure could enter. But then, at some considerable length, Frederick extolls the superior attractions of natural phenomena – dawn, mists, mountains, flowers, birds – and concludes that they outpointed the artificial beauties offered by Sweerts ('nature has the right to triumph over art'). Frederick also took the opportunity to advocate pluralism:

> We are left cold by the pleasures of others,
> And if our instincts compel us to prefer our own,
> Let us tolerate those of everyone else:
> Like everything about human beings, they are all different.
> Rather let us bless wise Providence,
> Which has given such an abundance and such a variety of tastes
> that there are enough to go round for everyone.

The poem ended with an attack on the notion of the theatre as a school of morals. We go there to enjoy ourselves, wrote Frederick, not

---

* I have been able to find out very little about him, apart from the fact that his name has been spelt in a dozen different ways. Neither he nor this poem appears to have been discussed previously.

to hear a sermon. In any case, no one had ever been converted to virtue there. Self-improvement could only be achieved by personal struggle and introspection. So Frederick ended with the cheerful observation that what Sweerts had to offer was just 'vains plaisirs' to be enjoyed when the daily toil was over.

Not for the first or last time, it is difficult to know whether Frederick's habitual irony is shading into insincerity. The poem appeared in Œuvres du philosophe de Sanssouci in 1750, in a small printed edition aimed exclusively at close friends, although a pirated edition appeared in France ten years later.[32] Close friend number one was of course Voltaire, whose mocking tone Frederick sought to imitate and whom he was always trying to impress. A more serious-minded and probably more sincere expression of his devotion to the arts was to be found in the verse epistle to Algarotti quoted above. Both works had in common a sensual not to say erotic vocabulary. In the case of that nominally directed to Sweerts there was 'lovely God of the island of love ... getting drunk with a hundred blazing pleasures ... lustful atmosphere ... voluptuous senses ...' – and that is just the first page.

MUSIC AND ENLIGHTENMENT

Certainly Frederick did not follow his own observation to Sweerts that the theatre should eschew preaching. All the libretti of the grand operas performed during his reign promoted virtues, especially those associated with the idealized rulers of classical antiquity: courage in adversity, moderation, selflessness and, above all, clemency. As they were usually adaptations of texts first composed by the Austrian court poet, Pietro Metastasio, this was not surprising. Frederick did however give an entirely personal flavour to at least one of his libretti. This was Montezuma, which he wrote in French and had translated into Italian by his court poet Giampietro Tagliazucchi and set to music by the prolific Carl Heinrich Graun, whose twenty-fourth Berlin opera this was.[33] Heavily influenced by Voltaire's Alzire, ou les Américains (1736), it was given its première at the Berlin opera house in 1755 with lavish sets designed by Carl Friedrich Fechhelm.[34] One of Graun's best operas, it proved to be a considerable success. It was performed eight times in 1755 and was revived on several occasions after the Seven Years War.[35] It can also claim to have been a 'reform opera'. On Frederick's orders, da capo arias were replaced by two-section cavatinas, and ensembles were used to push the action along in a manner that anticipates Mozart.[36] Observing the unities required by classical aesthetics, it recounts the last day in the life of the eponymous Mexican king and his killing by the Spanish *conquistador* Hernán Cortés. The plot is not subtle, it is a statement not a nuance. The Catholic Spaniards are uniformly intolerant, arrogant, cruel, lecherous and treacherous; the pagan Mexicans are uniformly gentle, courteous, hospitable, enlightened and tolerant. A representative sample is provided by the following exchange, which comes after Cortés has succeeded in tricking his way into the royal palace:

CORTÉS: Everyone and everything must bow the knee to the Almighty God I worship.

MONTEZUMA: Is this how you show your gratitude?

CORTÉS: Our laws command us to exterminate barbarians who still make human sacrifices. We take the field not to make conquests but in the name of our God, and we seek to convert you to this sublime faith which is so pleasing to the Almighty.

MONTEZUMA: What! Am I to believe in a God who condones deceit. What am I to make of a faith which commands you to condemn everyone who does not share your opinion? What am I to make of a God who approves of all your atrocities?

CORTÉS: You are not worthy of the religion you outrage.

MONTEZUMA: But our religion is greatly superior. For it commands us to love every living being and forbids us to hold in contempt those who do not share our faith. It requires us to prove our virtue by deeds and imposes severest penalties for the sort of crimes you commit. Oh, what a difference! Oh barbarous enemy![37]

An impeccably enlightened Deist, Montezuma sings as he is being dragged off to execution: 'Without fear I return a pure soul to nature's bosom; and without fear I return my body to the elements which gave it birth', words which were repeated almost exactly in Frederick's own last will and testament.[38] Eupaforice, a Mexican princess betrothed to Montezuma, frustrates Cortés' lust by committing suicide, but not before she has organized the incineration of the city. An infuriated Cortés declares that the only way to handle the natives is to exterminate them, ordering his soldiers to put the city to the sword, killing every living being within it, adding as the final words of the opera: 'And so Mexico will be conquered for the King of Spain and the True Faith.'[39] In the theatre, this final scene of looting, murder, rape and general mayhem was enhanced by a ballet and special stage effects.[40]

As if it were necessary, Frederick explained the polemic point of his libretto in a letter to Algarotti of October 1753:

> If your operas [in Italy] are bad, you will find one here that perhaps will not surpass them. It is *Montezuma*. I chose the subject and I am working it out at present. You realise, I'm sure, that my sympathies are with Montezuma; Cortés will be the tyrant and consequently one can let fly, in music as well, some jibes against the barbarity of the Christian religion. But I forget that you are now in a land of the Inquisition, and I make my excuses, hoping to see you soon again in a heretic land where even the opera can serve to reform morals and destroy superstitions.[41]

He might also have added that Montezuma should have maintained a strong army to defend his country against foreign predators. At least it could be said that Frederick was entirely sincere in his aversion to Catholicism and support for toleration. The same could not be said for the message of another of his operas, *Silla*, also translated into Italian by Tagliazucchi and composed by Graun, for in this the hero renounces his dictatorship when the emergency is over, returns Rome to constitutional rule and retires into private life – not the sort of scenario one might expect Frederick to enact in real life.[42]

Opera seria represented only one part of Frederick's musical life, albeit the most formal. He also devoted a great deal of time and trouble to the other side of the coin, *opera buffa* or comic opera. Frederick's reign coincided with the golden age of the genre. Beginning in Naples during the first decade of the eighteenth century, it spread quickly northwards, carrying all before it. Among other things it unleashed a furious controversy in France – the '*Querelle des*

Bouffons' – between supporters of French and Italian music. Frederick was very much on the side of the latter, establishing a troupe of performers without equal north of the Alps. Among other things, this involved building for them a magnificent new theatre in the north-eastern wing of the Town Palace at Potsdam. Conceived by Frederick and executed by Knobelsdorff, this departed from the traditional horseshoe design and hierarchical structure in favour of an amphitheatre which gave everyone present a good view of the stage and no obtrusive royal box.[43] In keeping with this egalitarian seating-plan, the plots of the operas, mostly taken from Goldoni, often presented the tricking of aristocrats by crafty servants. In *Bertoldo*, for example, the eponymous peasant tells King Alboino: 'we are all born naked and naked shall die; take off your gilded robes and you will see that our estate is the same'.[44] Potsdam remained the headquarters of the *bouffonistes*, although they also performed in the opera house at Berlin during the carnival season. As Sabine Henze-Döhring has demonstrated, *opera buffa* was not a private exercise for Frederick but an integral part of his aesthetic programme. When the son and heir of Catherine the Great of Russia paid a visit to Berlin in 1776 and the representational boat was well and truly pushed out, it was comic not grand opera that was the centrepiece of the musical festivities.[45]

MUSIC IN PRIVATE

At the other end of the scale from opera was Frederick's solo and solitary flute-playing in his bedroom-cum-study. From the moment he first heard the virtuoso Johann Joachim Quantz play at Dresden in 1728* until he lost his teeth in old age, a flute was never far from his side. The Austrian ambassador reported that immediately on rising at – or before – the crack of dawn, Frederick paced up and down playing his flute while waiting for his coffee to appear. Once the morning military and political business had been completed, he returned to his inner sanctum and his instrument until it was time for the main meal of the day.[46] He told d'Alembert that he never knew what he was

---

* See above, p. 34.

playing, but that his improvisations helped him to think.[47] Every evening, starting between six and seven o'clock, there was a private concert lasting around two hours and usually attended only by the seven to ten musicians involved, although occasionally guests were admitted. At these, Frederick performed three to five concertos and a number of sonatas, composed either by himself or by Quantz. He then listened to another performed by Quantz, occasionally a solo piece for cello, and usually an aria, which brought the concert to a conclusion.[48] As this suggests, Quantz played a central role in Frederick's life, so much so that it was said that Prussia was really ruled by Mrs Quantz's lapdog, for Frederick did what Quantz told him, Quantz did what his wife told him, and she was in thrall to her pet.[49] A better indication of his importance was the 299 flute concertos he composed for Frederick, denied his third century only by his death in 1773. The bereaved Frederick now abandoned the orchestral concerts, henceforth confining himself to solo performances with keyboard accompaniment.[50]

By all accounts, Frederick was an accomplished flautist. This can be inferred from the works written by or for him and is confirmed by the select few who actually heard him play. Among them was Charles Burney, whose expert opinion must be treated with respect. He wrote of the concert he attended at Potsdam:

> The concert began by a German flute concerto, in which his majesty executed the solo parts with great precision; his *embouchure* was clear and even, his finger brilliant, and his taste pure and simple. I was much pleased, and even surprised with the neatness of his execution in the *allegros*, as well as by his expression and feeling in the *adagios*. In short, his performance surpassed, in many particulars anything I had ever heard among *Dilettanti*, or even professors. His majesty played three long and difficult concertos successively, and all with equal perfection.[51]

Also authoritative was the verdict of Johann Friedrich Reichardt, not least because in general he disliked both Frederick and his regime. He criticized Frederick's playing of the fast passages, because he tended to lag behind the orchestra, despite the musicians' best efforts to adjust their tempo, but acknowledged that in an adagio 'he really was a great virtuoso ... It was unmistakable that he felt what he played;

melting transitions, exceedingly nuanced accents and little melodic embellishments expressed very clearly a sophisticated and tender feeling . . . His entire adagio was a gentle effusion and had pure, graceful, often moving, singing tone – the surest proof that his performance came from his soul.'[52] The distinguished music teacher Karl Friedrich Zelter, who numbered Mendelssohn among his pupils, recorded that Frederick's keyboard player Karl Friedrich Christian Fasch, 'who served the King for thirty years and outlived him by fourteen, told me repeatedly that he had only ever heard an adagio performed in a truly moving and elevated manner by three virtuosi. The first was his friend Emanuel Bach on the keyboard, the second was Franz Benda on the violin and the third was the King on the flute'.[53]

Like his tutor Quantz, Frederick was a composer as well as a performer. Despite his father's opposition to anything so 'effeminate', he had been given a solid grounding in thorough bass and four-part composition from the age of seven.[54] His most ambitious orchestral works – four flute concertos and a symphony in D major – he composed while still crown prince. By 1738 he had reached the painful conclusion that he would never acquire the necessary technique to make a mark in this genre and gave up, a decision probably hastened by the presence in his household of a genuinely top-flight composer, Carl Heinrich Graun, not to mention the occasional visits of Quantz, his superior both as a performer and a composer.[55] From then on he confined himself to operatic arias, courtly dances and especially flute sonatas.[56] By the time he abandoned composition altogether, on the outbreak of the Seven Years War in 1756, he had composed 121 of the last-named. Not one was published in his lifetime, they were all written just for him and Quantz to play.[57] These agreeable if lightweight and unoriginal pieces are available in many different recordings and filmed performances.[58]

Frederick and the musicians of his court were making music in the 'galant' style that had come to dominate Europe. By this was meant 'music with lightly accompanied, periodic melodies, and the appropriate manner of performing the same', as the leading modern historian of the style, Daniel Heartz, has put it.[59] In the place of the complex counterpoint and fugues of its opposite, 'the learned style', galant music 'means seeking to please' (Voltaire).[60] This it certainly does, as the numerous recordings of Frederick's compositions testify. His musical team was also the centre of galant theory, as C. P. E. Bach, Quantz, Agricola, Friedrich Wilhelm Marpurg, Johann Philipp Kirnberger and Johann Georg Sulzer articulated the style's objectives. In the words of C. P. E. Bach, music should express human nature, for it is the language of the emotions (*Affekten*). It holds up a mirror to the emotional world of humankind with the task of 'transforming the heart into a tender sensibility' (*sanfte Empfindsamkeit*). The 'gentle tears' it called forth were not self-indulgent emotionalism but promoted virtue.[61] In other words, galant music sought the same sort of effect achieved by Samuel Richardson's hugely successful contemporary novels. Frederick was very much part of this world of sensibility, as his letters to his sister Wilhelmine demonstrate, telling her, for example, that a piece of music he had written was inspired by the pain of separation from her, which accounted for its melancholic character.[62]

So Frederick had music in the opera house, concert room and even bedroom. He also took it to war with him, not just his trusty flutes (which Fredersdorf took care of) but selected musicians too, who no doubt cursed their fate as they looked forward to the privations inseparable from campaigning. Among them was Fasch, who accompanied Frederick on the portable keyboard which was always part of the royal baggage-train. Of Parisian manufacture, it could be dismantled into three sections for transport.[63] Following his triumphal entry into Dresden after the defeat of the Saxon army at the battle of Kesseldorf on 15 December 1745, one right of conquest he was quick to exercise was the command to the Saxon musical establishment to stage Hasse's opera *Arminio* the next evening. This was duly performed, with the composer directing and his wife, the star soprano Faustina, singing. Both husband and wife were then obliged to perform chamber concerts for Frederick each evening during his nine-day sojourn.[64] Back in the city during the winter of 1760–61, he found that five years of devastating war, during which the Prussians had lived at Saxon expense, had destroyed the musical establishment, and so was obliged to send for his own orchestra from Berlin.[65] The musical establishment was also deployed as a weapon of foreign policy. When Frederick met the Holy Roman Emperor Joseph II at Neisse in Silesia in August

1769, he had a temporary theatre erected for the performance of comic opera, both to entertain himself and to impress his visitor.[66] An operatic troupe also accompanied him for the return fixture at Neustadt in Moravia the following year.[67]

MUSIC IN PUBLIC

At home or away, Frederick's world was suffused with music, for recreation, representation, expression, therapy and even diplomacy. But this was a confined world. It was limited geographically to Berlin, Potsdam and wherever Frederick happened to be, and was restricted socially by being accessible only by invitation. So large was the new opera house in Berlin that not even the entire court could fill it, and decently dressed citizens could gain admission to the pit by tipping the doorman. They could also buy tickets for the uppermost tier of boxes, those lower down being reserved for the nobility. The *Berlin Journal* greeted the 1743 carnival season with the news that 'foreigners as well as native-born [Prussians], no matter what their estate, will be permitted to attend for free the operas, plays and masked balls'.[68] As elsewhere in Prussia, here too the military element was obtrusive. On the opening night in December 1743, all the generals and staff officers attended at Frederick's express order, standing in ranks in the pit behind two rows of armchairs reserved for the king and his top brass.[69] Thereafter, each regiment billeted in the city had the right to claim a certain number of tickets, which necessarily limited the number available to civilians.[70] They were limited further by the preference given to foreign visitors to the city.[71] According to the soprano Elizabeth Mara, when the weather was cold, soldiers were drafted into the theatre to warm up the auditorium with their body heat.[72]

Concerts were held elsewhere in Berlin, by the queen, queen mother and other members of the royal family, borrowing musicians from the king's orchestra, but these were socially exclusive. So were performances by the small separate bands maintained by Frederick's brothers, Prince Henry and Prince August Ferdinand.[73] None of the Prussian noble families commanded the resources which allowed Austrian equivalents such as Prince Esterházy or Prince Lobkowitz to finance orchestras fit for a Haydn or a Beethoven. Nor was there a public sphere large enough to allow a free-lance musician to make a living, as Mozart did in Vienna in the 1780s. Nevertheless, the example set at the top did encourage the development of a quasi-independent musical culture.[74] It has to be called *quasi*-independent because so many of those involved, especially in a directing capacity, were royal employees. It was in their often extensive leisure time that they were able to organize musical associations and events. As early as 1755, Friedrich Wilhelm Marpurg, who scratched a living in Berlin as a musical journalist, reported that since Frederick's accession the city had developed into an important musical centre, the scene of frequent concerts and musical societies. The Music Performing Society, for example, formed by the royal organist Johann Philipp Sack, gave concerts every Saturday, 'attended by ladies and gentlemen of rank'.[75] These were modest affairs, with just a few dozen present at most, but by the 1780s a series of concerts comparable to the *Concerts Spirituels* of Paris or Salomon's subscription concerts in London were being organized.[76] It has to be conceded, however, that Berlin never developed into a symphonic centre on a par with either city, or even Mannheim or Vienna.[77]

There was a similar development in the theatrical world, although this was necessarily more formal thanks to the need to obtain an official 'privilege' to operate. Two entrepreneurs, Heinrich Gottfried Koch from 1733 to 1735 and then Carl Theophil Döbbelin, ran a commercial company in a theatre in Behrens Street with a broad appeal to the plain people of Berlin. By 1776 it numbered fifty-eight actors, singers and musicians, presenting a mixture of French, Italian and German comic operas.[78] Frederick's dissolution of his French theatre company when the War of the Bavarian Succession broke out in 1778 made more performers available. By 1781 it was the largest company in Germany. From being initially 'by and large a scruffy, sorry lot' (Thomas Bauman),[79] the Döbbelin company developed into the best in northern Germany, including a star soprano in Marie Sophie Niklas, a gifted composer in Johann André and a prolific librettist in Christoph Friedrich Bretzner.[80] Together they gave the public what they wanted, which was strong meat, as the journalist Christian Friedrich von Bonin put it: 'high tragedy and comedy that approaches farce are now most effective here. Our public no longer desires weak fare; one wants either to be shaken or to laugh from the belly – everything that is simply *sentimental* won't do.'[81]

In short, Frederick's influence on the musical life of his capital diminished as his reign progressed and the public sphere expanded. This was especially apparent in the one genre which Frederick not so much neglected as despised – church music. When Charles Burney visited Berlin in 1772 he was told that sacred music was neglected in Berlin because Frederick refused to listen to it and that he 'carries his prejudice against this kind of music so far, that when he hears of any composer having written an anthem, or oratorio, he fancies his taste is contaminated with it, and says, of his other productions, "Oh! This smells of the church."'[82] That was not quite accurate, for Frederick's most favoured composer was also responsible for the most popular Passion of the eighteenth century in German-speaking Europe, far outstripping any of the great Passions of Johann Sebastian Bach. This was *The Death of Jesus (Der Tod Jesu)*, by Carl Heinrich Graun, first performed in Berlin Cathedral on the Wednesday of Holy Week in 1755, shortly after the première in Hamburg of Telemann's setting of the same text by the poet Karl Wilhelm Ramler. So well received was the oratorio that its performance at Easter became an annual event in Berlin throughout the rest of the century and almost to the end of the nineteenth. It has proved the most durable of all Graun's compositions, often performed, available in several audio recordings and with numerous extracts uploaded to YouTube.

This was a relative, not an absolute decline in the importance of the royal music. There is no truth in the popular view that Frederick lost interest in old age and scaled down his establishment. Reichardt's memoirs have a lot to answer for here. It does seem that Frederick had a low opinion of Reichardt's ability and treated him accordingly, but his memoirs contained much falsehood. For example, his statement that Frederick detested *opera buffa* and rarely attended it is 'pure fiction'.[83] The musical establishment listed by Friedrich Nicolai in 1779 was certainly substantial: an orchestra of around forty players, an *opera seria* company of eight soloists and a chorus of twenty-four, an *opera buffa* company of five soloists, a French theatre company of ten, and a *corps de ballet* consisting of a ballet master, three principals and a dozen dancers, not to mention the numerous back-stage staff, including carpenters, hairdressers, wardrobe mistresses and the like.[84] Towards the end of his life, however, Frederick went ever more rarely to the opera in Berlin, attending for the last time in 1781.[85]

MUSICAL CONSERVATISM

Frederick carried on until the end, regardless of changing fashions. Nothing if not opinionated, he was quick to criticize his fellow-musicians. He always had been. 'Handel's great days are over, his inspiration is exhausted and his taste is behind the fashion,' he had opined in 1737, that is to say before Handel had composed *Serse, Messiah, Semele,* etc.[86] As he grew older, his range of enthusiasms, never generous at the best of times, narrowed further. Increasingly he lamented that European culture had gone to the dogs. In 1771 he told Voltaire that the kind of opera currently in fashion would never have won approval in the palmy days of Louis XIV. But now it passed for high quality 'in this age of triviality, when genius is as rare as common sense and when general mediocrity reveals the bad taste that will thrust Europe back into the barbarism from which it was rescued by an army of great men'. He added piously that for the time being, there was nothing to fear, because they had Voltaire, 'the Atlas whose efforts alone keep the ruinous building standing'.[87] Six years later he wrote a revealing letter to his musically gifted confidante, Maria Antonia, the Dowager Electress of Saxony:

> Here the public is being entertained by Hasse's opera *Cleofide,* which is being revived in the opera house. Good things endure, and, even though we have heard them in the past, we like to hear them again. In any case, music today has degenerated into a hullabaloo, assaulting our ears rather than caressing them, and the noble art of singing is lost to the present generation. To rediscover it, we have to go back to Vinci, Hasse and Graun.[88]

In keeping with his forthright approach to everything else in life, Frederick knew what he liked and did not like. French music he could not abide; Haydn's symphonies were 'a shindy that flays the ears'; Gluck he abused 'with violent expressions and insults'; Reichardt was refused permission to write an opera for the Berlin carnival season 'because he doesn't know how to do it or does everything wrong'; Mozart he never mentioned.[89] In May 1780 the Marchese Lucchesini recorded in his diary that Frederick had delivered a diatribe against all 'modern music'.[90] Even his favoured composers were not immune from his harrying. Ordered repeatedly to rewrite arias, Carl Heinrich Graun eventually rebelled, saying that his setting of *'Misero pargoletto'* in the opera *Demofoonte* was excellent and that he could not improve it. Frederick promptly ordered that it be replaced in performance by Johann Adolf Hasse's version of the same aria.[91] According to Fasch, the public made known its preference for Graun's original, although he does not explain how this implicit criticism of the royal interference was expressed.[92]

Frederick's limitations as connoisseur and patron were revealed most obviously in a negative manner, by his inability to appreciate that he was the employer of 'one of the most influential composers, authors, teachers, and performers in the musical world of the later eighteenth century'.[93] This was Carl Philipp Emanuel Bach, the most gifted of Johann Sebastian's numerous sons.[94] First employed on a temporary basis by Frederick as crown prince, he was a permanent member of the musical establishment from 1740 until 1768. During that period he composed more than 300 works, mainly keyboard and chamber music, but also nine symphonies, thirty-eight keyboard concertos, a *Magnificat*, an *Easter Cantata* and numerous songs.[95] As this productivity suggests, he had plenty of time for his own work, not least when Frederick was away on manoeuvres or fighting a war. Even when his employer was back at Potsdam, Bach could take it in turns with the second harpsichordist to provide the keyboard accompaniment for Frederick's concerts.[96]

Less agreeable was the gnawing sense of being underestimated. As he ground his way through the accompaniment to yet another of Quantz's flute sonatas, how he must have yearned for the opportunity to display his own greater talent. Matters came to a head in 1755 when he submitted a remonstrance comprising 'too many complaints to mention' according to Fredersdorf, who presented it to Frederick. The crucial grievance was financial. His pitiful salary of 300 talers per annum was not only inadequate for a decent standard of living, it was also insulting, for he knew that his former pupils Christoph Nichelmann and Johann Friedrich Agricola were being paid twice as much. Frederick's marginal comment was terse: 'Bach is lying; Agricola gets only 500 talers.' Adding that Bach was also 'getting cocky', Frederick did agree grudgingly to an increase, adding that it would have to wait for the next spending round.[97] That kept him in Prussia for another decade, but in 1768 he finally left for Hamburg to replace his godfather Georg Philipp Telemann as director of the city's church music. At least able to appreciate Bach's skill as a keyboard player, Frederick gave him permission to leave only 'after repeated [and] respectful expostulation'.[98]

For his contemporaries, Carl Philipp Emanuel was 'the great Bach'; for posterity, it has been his father Johann Sebastian.[99] In 1747 the latter went to see his son at Potsdam. Of all the visits to Frederick's court, this was the one that left the most enduring memorial, in the shape of *The Musical Offering* (BWV 1079). On 7 May Bach *père* presented himself at the Town Palace in Potsdam, requesting permission to attend Frederick's evening concert. The story later put around by Johann Nikolaus Forkel, Bach's first biographer, that it was Frederick who sent for Bach, on learning that he was in town, seems to be apocryphal.[100] In any event, he was duly admitted and shown Frederick's fine collection of fortepianos built by Gottfried Silbermann. (Their very existence shows that, in this respect at least, Frederick was at the cutting edge of musical technology, for the instrument had been invented, by Bartolomeo Cristofori of Padua, only around 1700.) According to the press release which appeared in a Berlin newspaper, Frederick then sat down at one of them, played a theme and invited Bach to improvise a fugue on it:

> This was done so happily by the aforementioned *Kapellmeister* that not only His Majesty was pleased to show his satisfaction thereat, but also all those present were seized with astonishment. Mr. Bach found the theme propounded to him so exceedingly beautiful that he intends to set it down on paper as a regular fugue and have it engraved on copper.[101]

On the following evening, Bach was again in attendance, and this time was asked to improvise a fugue in six parts. In 1774 the Austrian envoy Gottfried van Swieten recorded that Frederick had enthused about Bach's powers 'and to prove it to me he sang aloud a chromatic fugue subject that he had given this old Bach, who on the spot had made of it a fugue in four parts, then in five parts, and finally in eight parts'.[102] This story had probably grown with the telling, but there is no doubt that within a few weeks of his return to Leipzig, Bach had turned Frederick's theme into a highly complex work. His dedication, dated 7 July 1747, stated that 'the noblest part' of his musical offering was from the hand of the king himself.[103]

ROOMS FOR MUSIC

One of the numerous Silbermann fortepianos owned by Frederick and played by Bach was to be found in the magnificent new music room of the Town Palace in Potsdam. Executed by the sculptor and stuccist Johann August Nahl 'according to guidelines laid down by the King', the room was located in the south-eastern corner, immediately adjacent to Frederick's study and bedroom.[104] Its decorative scheme was a typical example of 'Frederician rococo' – narrow and shallow wall pilasters framing a mixture of delicate, elaborate, asymmetrical motifs, some abstract and some derived from plants, animals (especially birds) and music, all in silver-gilt, with similar motifs spread across the ceiling. Two paintings by Lancret, *The Swing* and *Dancing by a Fountain*, are incorporated in the decorative scheme, together with a small copy of a painting by Rubens, which might seem out of place but in fact is singularly appropriate for a room created for Frederick, for it shows Venus vainly restraining Mars.[105] The decorative scheme is complemented by matching furniture resting on a parquet floor of symmetrical contrasting lozenges. The overall effect is light, elegant, sophisticated and refined. To a less sympathetic eye, especially one peering back from the present, it can also seem excessively ornate. The same could be said of a second and similar music room, created in the south-western corner of the palace. Room after room of swirling rococo decoration of the kind to be found in the Town Palace can certainly be enervating. But it was what Frederick liked and his taste never changed. It can be found at his first major architectural project, at Rheinsberg, and at his last, the Potsdam New Palace.*

It was at Rheinsberg that Frederick had first demonstrated his enthusiasm for music architecturally, by assigning the largest space in the building to the room devoted to its pursuit, the Hall of Mirrors. Musical motifs abound there, including scenes from Ovid's *Metamorphoses* revealing the transforming power of music.[106] Nothing if not consistent in his tastes, Frederick was to repeat these Ovidian musical references in many of his other building projects.[107] In addition to this large concert hall, he also had at Rheinsberg a smaller dedicated music room in his private suite of apartments. And so it continued. A music room was included in the suite of rooms created for him between 1745 and 1747 on the first floor of the royal palace in Berlin, overlooking the river Spree.[108] It was in use for only a few days a year, for Frederick was there only during part of the carnival season, from late December until his birthday on 24 January, and spent even less time in his capital after 1763.[109]

CHARLOTTENBURG AND POTSDAM

Clearly, Frederick felt most at home at Potsdam. In peacetime, when he was not away on one of his numerous tours of inspection or directing military manoeuvres, he spent the winter there in the Town Palace and the summer at Sanssouci. This was not the obvious choice when he came to the throne. At first it seemed more likely that he would favour Charlottenburg, out in the country but close to the capital, easily accessible by water and with plenty of room for expansion. It was there that he went the day after the death of his father.[110] It was also there that he commissioned his first major building project the following month. This must have been planned well in advance by Frederick and Knobelsdorff, for construction began straight away. Absence on campaigning after December did not prevent Frederick from taking a close interest in the progress of the work. 'Tell

* See above, pp. 49–50 and below, pp. 167–8.

Knobelsdorff to entertain me by writing about my buildings, gardens, furniture and opera house,' he wrote to his friend Charles-Étienne Jordan from Silesia in April 1742.[111] Knobelsdorff duly obliged, but Frederick found his letter inadequate: 'it's all too dry, there aren't any details. I want a description of each and every astragal at Charlottenburg covering four quarto pages, that would give me a lot of pleasure.'[112] The demands kept coming. At the end of May, Frederick told Jordan to make Knobelsdorff tell him how things were coming on at Charlottenburg, in the gardens and at the opera house, adding 'I am like a child in these things; these are my toys I amuse myself with.'[113]

All this hectoring had the desired effect. On 25 August 1742, Frederick returned from the war, following conclusion of the Treaty of Breslau, and went straight out to Charlottenburg to inspect the new wing Knobelsdorff had been building there. Sufficient progress had been made to allow the formal opening of his private apartments, together with the grand dining room known as the 'White Hall' four days later.[114] Behind the restrained classicism of the façade, completed by the end of 1743, the interiors were in Frederick's favoured rococo style. Particularly striking was the enormous reception room later known as the 'Golden Gallery', forty-two metres long and stretching right across the building. It need hardly be added that there was also a music room, an elegant combination of white-and-grey panelled walls and a gilded ceiling, designed and executed by Johann August Nahl and Johann Michael Hoppenhaupt.[115] More surprisingly, a large suite of rooms was reserved on the ground floor for the queen, although she never used them and, as we have seen, was refused an invitation to attend the celebrations marking the completion of the new wing in 1748.*

Despite this major expenditure, Charlottenburg never did become anything more than an occasional destination for Frederick. Another possibility mooted in 1740 was the expansion of his existing residence at Rheinsberg, probably rejected for being nearly 100 kilometres from Berlin. It was Potsdam that gradually emerged as the favourite.

* See above, p. 60.

Although a suite of rooms in the Town Palace there was renovated for him in the first year of his reign, this project was no more than basic accommodation, for use when he was in the town attending to military matters. It was not until late 1743 that orders were given for work to begin on a more permanent – and splendid – set of apartments.[116] By the following year, the scale of the building operations indicated that his choice had finally settled on Potsdam as his main residence. Over the next decade, the Town Palace was reconstructed both inside and out. Its celebration of the conquest of Silesia was advertised by the expanded coat of arms on the façade and the lavish use of Silesian marble.[117] Although the basic ground-plan of the old building was retained, the only part of the exterior to survive was the Fortuna Gate, erected in 1701 by Frederick's grandfather to mark the elevation of the Electorate of Brandenburg to royal status as the Kingdom of Prussia.[118] Elsewhere, Frederick's architect Knobelsdorff raised the wings by a storey, created an entirely new exterior, and on the garden side added a grand façade with exterior staircase and the free-standing colonnades Frederick liked so much.[119] Inside, for the first time in the history of a Hohenzollern residence, no provision was made for quarters for the queen, although apartments were created for Frederick's brothers; the director of the Berlin Academy, Maupertuis; and even the Prince-Bishop of Breslau (given the suggestive sobriquet 'The Bishop of Sodom' by Count Lehndorff).[120] Room was also found for a small but richly decorated theatre. Unsurprisingly, the space previously occupied by the chapel was secularized and turned into guest rooms.[121]

SANSSOUCI

The definitive break came in the summer of 1744. In June, Frederick gave Rheinsberg to his younger brother, Prince Henry, and on 10 August he issued the order that led to the construction of Sanssouci. It is this latter palace that has always been most closely associated with him, and rightly so. All his other numerous buildings were derivative: elegant and sophisticated certainly, but outshone by better examples of late baroque/rococo elsewhere in the Holy Roman

Empire. Neither the Town Palace nor the New Palace at Potsdam could hold a candle to, say, the Würzburg Residence, completed in 1744. Antoine Pesne, who painted most of the ceilings in Frederick's palaces, was accomplished, but not in the same class as, say, Giovanni Battista Tiepolo, who painted the great ceiling frescoes at Würzburg in 1751–3. The opera house in Berlin was very big and also had the distinction of being free-standing, but in terms of aesthetic appeal it fell a long way behind the theatres at Bayreuth (1744–8) or Munich (1751–3). In terms of sheer size, nothing Frederick built could compete with the gargantuan palace at Mannheim, with its 450-metre-long façade, constructed by the Palatine Electors between 1720 and 1760. For a combination of size and sumptuous interior display, the prize must go to the Habsburg summer palace of Schönbrunn, rebuilt by the Empress Maria Theresa in the 1740s and 50s.

Yet Frederick's little palace of Sanssouci can lay claim to pride of place for charm and originality. Moreover, it was very much his personal creation. The venue he chose was a greenfield site, a hill outside Potsdam overlooking the town and the river Havel, where his father had kept a kitchen garden and a small summer house which he derisively called 'Marly' after the palace built by Louis XIV in the park of Versailles. Frederick's order of 10 August was for the excavation of six terraces on the hillside, to accommodate the large quantity of fruit trees and vines ordered from France the previous year.[122] Although it was not until January 1745 that building materials were ordered, it is very likely that his own version of Marly was always intended. As usual with Frederick's pet projects, the work was driven on apace. The foundation stone was laid on 14 April 1745 and by the autumn the roof was going on. Frederick's rooms in the east wing were ready for occupation in April 1747 and the last major room, the Marble Hall, was completed the following year. Assigning responsibility for the design is not as easy as it looks. Although two drawings in Frederick's hand have survived, it is not clear whether they were produced before or after the building was completed. The best guess is that he supplied all the ideas, right down to decorative details, and Knobelsdorff and his assistants produced the necessary drawings.[123] There was sharp disagreement between patron and architect. Knobelsdorff urged the installation of a cellar, to guard against damp, and also wanted to bring the building forward to the corner of the terrace and to place it on an elevated base, to improve views of it from below. He was overruled.[124] The only view of Sanssouci Frederick cared about was his own, from inside.[125] That it was not to perform a representational function was made clear by the position, the approach road being too steep for carriages.[126]

By royal standards, this is a small building, a very small building. In effect it is the suite of private rooms occupied by Frederick at Rheinsberg or the Potsdam Town Palace turned into a separate dwelling, with a second suite added for a handful of guests. That Rheinsberg was in his mind was shown by his instruction to Knobelsdorff written on his own sketch – 'the colonnade to be Corinthian but the rest to be as at Rheinsberg [where the colonnade was Ionic]'. Even the rounded ends of the building are reminiscent of the towers at Rheinsberg, one of which Frederick had used as a library. For this room too, he has written on the plan 'as at Rheinsberg'.* Stylistically, there is a striking contrast between the relatively austere north façade, which has a French appearance, and the more exuberant garden front, where the concave central pavilion and eighteen pairs of caryatids bearing the cornice give a sculptural, Italianate feel to the whole.[127]

As usual, the interiors are far more extravagantly decorated. Whether because of the smaller scale of the building or the greater care taken, the result is the most successful of all Frederick's projects, ranking as one of the great architectural achievements of the century. Even the most austere of puritan tastes must surely succumb to the charms of these enchanting rooms. They vary from the representational splendour of the entrance hall and Marble Hall to the intimacy of Frederick's library, as at Rheinsberg the last room in the sequence and also the most intimate, to which access was granted very seldom and only to the likes of Voltaire and d'Alembert.[128] In every room the superlative quality of the craftsmanship is evident, on the mosaic and parquet floors as much as on the richly decorated ceilings. Frederick's fabled liking for marble, especially the rare varieties once reserved for the use of Roman emperors, was very prominent.[129]

The same attention to detail is also evident in the garden and park

* See above, p. 50.

that grew up around the little palace. As he had never been allowed to go on a grand tour as a young man, Frederick had to rely on engravings of the great European gardens for inspiration.[130] At the bottom of the flight of steps running down through six terraces of vines was a formal parterre garden in the French style, the plants in flowerbeds arranged in swirling arabesques and the whole ensemble framed by multiple rows of cherry trees. At its centre, the point at which the path from the palace joined an avenue running from east to west at right angles, was an ornamental pond embellished with a group of statues depicting the sea goddess Thetis and her retinue. Everywhere could be found evidence of Frederick's love of statues: around the Obelisk Portal which marked the eastern entrance to the park, around the colonnade which marked the western end and in the roundels which punctuated the avenue joining the two.[131] Over the years Frederick added numerous small buildings to his park, the most spectacular being the exquisite – and wildly extravagant – Chinese Pavilion built by Johann Gottfried Büring between 1755 and 1764, one of the finest architectural examples in Europe of the contemporary fashion for chinoiserie.[132] More authentically Chinese was the Dragon House built on the edge of the park in 1769–70, the design inspired by Sir William Chambers's *Designs of Chinese Buildings*.[133] Frederick also showed his awareness of changing tastes when he extended the park to the east after the Seven Years War to make room for the New Palace. This involved the extension westwards of the axial avenue, which measured two and a half kilometres by the time it reached the eastern extremity.

The coordination of an army of artists and workers by Frederick, Knobelsdorff and the project manager, Johann Boumann, to create such a masterpiece as Sanssouci and its park in so short a space of time commands respect. Moreover, the original buildings can still be appreciated almost in their entirety. Of Frederick's personal rooms in the palace, only the study-bedroom was altered significantly after his death; the palace as a whole escaped the bombs of the Second World War; and much of the furniture and most of the paintings have been returned to their rightful places.[134] The gardens and park, alas, have come off much less well, although more due to changes in fashion in the nineteenth century than to enemy action.

PALACES

Frederick would probably have been happier, and his state would certainly have been richer, if he had stuck to small-scale architectural projects like Rheinsberg or Sanssouci. His ventures into large-scale representational palaces must be regarded as failures. The first was entirely abortive. At the very beginning of his reign he planned a massive complex of buildings on Unter den Linden, christened *foro di federigo* (Frederick's Forum) by Algarotti, to the west of the existing royal palace.[135] Although the latter was one of the largest in Europe and less than fifty years old, Frederick had no desire to live there, possibly because he had suffered so much there at the hands of his father.[136] While still crown prince, he had planned an *additional* palace just a couple of hundred metres to the west. This '*Pallais* [*sic*] *du Roy*', as he called it, was to be gigantic, 300 metres wide and 150 metres deep, fronting a square 500 metres wide, and would have involved the demolition of all buildings down Unter den Linden as far as the Friedrichstrasse. It was probably inspired by the recently completed Würzburg Residenz, although it was to be twice as big as even that Behemoth.[137] The refusal of Frederick's brother-in-law, the Margrave of Brandenburg-Schwedt, to sell his palace then forced an adaptation. The palace was pushed further north, the opera house was reoriented 90°, and the tennis court was dropped in favour of a large building for the Academy of Sciences. This was baroque town-planning on the grandest of scales. The veritable forest of 112 columns twenty metres high in front of the palace were clearly inspired by Bernini's colonnade for St Peter's Square in Rome.[138] In the end, nothing came of it, as Frederick's interest switched to Potsdam. In 1744 his gift of Rheinsberg to his brother Prince Henry signalled that he would not be returning to his previous home; in 1747 the commission of a palace opposite the new opera house for the same favoured (if ungrateful) sibling confirmed that he would not be making Berlin his main residence.

Frederick did build a great new palace, but at Potsdam. This was the New Palace, planned in the early 1750s, delayed by the Seven Years War and promptly begun when peace returned in 1763, as a three-dimensional symbol of victory and an advertisement that

Prussia was so well governed that it still had the resources for grandiose display. And the palace *was* grandiose – the façade is 220 metres long, 55 metres high and adorned with 220 pilasters, 312 windows and 468 sculptures. Inside there are some 200 decorated rooms and 638 in total.[139] It is also tediously uniform, as one window follows one giant pilaster again and again. James Lees-Milne's withering comment on the even larger palace of Caserta near Naples is appropriate: 'The serried windows and the detailed ornament are lost in the enormous bulk like a small necklace upon the bosom of an immoderately fat woman.'[140] The interior is unusual in its spatial arrangements because so was the palace's purpose. It was never intended to be a royal residence, rather a guest-house to accommodate Frederick's family members and other dignitaries when they visited during the summer.[141] So there was no grand staircase, just four relatively utilitarian flights to provide private access to private apartments. A suite of rooms was created for the king, tucked away in the south wing on the ground floor. There were, however, four major representational rooms: on the ground floor a grotto, also known as the 'Shell Room', and 'Marble Gallery', and on the first floor a ballroom, known as 'The Upper Gallery', and 'Marble Hall'. The latter is a very large room, extending across the breadth of the building and rising through two storeys. There were also, of course, two music rooms, one on each floor.[142] The most successful room in the building was the theatre, which recaptured the intimate elegance of Sanssouci. Seating only a hundred or so, its private nature was highlighted by the lack of a royal box, Frederick choosing to sit in the third row of the stalls.[143] Every room was decorated and furnished extravagantly, as an anonymous Hungarian noble reported in 1784: 'the interior of the palace exceeds all expectations in its magnificence and taste. At no other court have I witnessed such valuable tables, vases, statues and floors.' The walls 'are of purple and white marble', the floors 'are of black, white, yellow and violet jaspis and amethyst', the tables 'are inlaid with kalcedon, achate and lapis lazuli', and so on.[144]

Neither the exterior nor the interior of the New Palace has the charm or originality of Sanssouci at the other end of the park. Indeed they are downright derivative, not to say old-fashioned. The façade was clearly copied from Vanbrugh and Hawksmoor's Castle Howard in Yorkshire, built between 1699 and 1712 for the Earl of Carlisle, but is less interesting.[145] Also a generation or so behind the times was the Shell Room, anticipated by a dozen similar rooms across Germany. Overall, the triumphalist character was more in keeping with Louis XIV's Versailles than with the residence of an enlightened ruler. Prominently on display were valuable artefacts recently removed from Saxony as spoils of war, including twenty-four 'snowball vases' of Meissen porcelain, and mirrors looted from the palace of the Saxon chief minister, Frederick's hate-figure Count Brühl.[146] In the Marble Hall, the statues of eight Electors of Brandenburg look imperiously at four great emperors: Julius Caesar, Constantine, Charlemagne and (rather anti-climactically) Rudolf II. The New Palace was the last major baroque palace to be built in the Holy Roman Empire, and it looks like it.[147] Construction work on the south wing, which contained Frederick's own apartments, was rushed along so that he was able to move in and direct operations on the rest of the site.[148] The architect usually credited is Carl von Gontard, but, as usual, the real directing hand was Frederick's. His imperious but ignorant interventions often led to problems. When his design of the two staircases in the main vestibule turned out to be impracticable, much remedial and expensive demolition and rebuilding proved necessary. A more permanent problem resulted from his refusal to listen to the experts who told him that the high water table necessitated a deep basement. The inevitable flooding was not to be corrected until the late twentieth century.[149]

Much more innovative, architecturally speaking, was the Communs, a gigantic complex of two grand service buildings, linked by a colonnade and designed by the French architect Jean-Laurent Legeay. Containing kitchens and accommodation for servants and courtiers not grand enough to qualify for the main palace, it also served to screen off the unappealing marshy landscape that lay beyond.[150]

In architecture, as in music, Frederick's tastes were set early and did not develop. Sanssouci is a later version of Rheinsberg, and the New Palace is a later version of the Potsdam Town Palace. Looking at the ceilings or wall decorations produced for him, it is impossible to say whether they stem from the 1740s or 1770s.[151] One might go further and add that the New Palace showed that Frederick's taste was not so much conservative as retro. From the large collection of architectural compendia and engravings he assembled, as a substitute for the Grand Tour refused him by his father, he selected designs from earlier periods for implementation by his architects.[152] So the Old Market outside the Town Palace in Potsdam took on a Roman appearance as the church of St Nicholas (Nikolaikirche) was given a façade taken from Santa Maria Maggiore and its vicarage and school were based on Ferdinando Fuga's Palazzo della Sagra Consulta sul Quirinale in Rome. An ideological point was also being made: the religious culture embodied by these Roman-baroque buildings was contrasted with the rational secularism of the Palladian Town Palace opposite.[153] The Town Hall was modelled on Palladio's unexecuted design for the Palazzo Angarano in Vicenza. Other Palladian buildings to find an echo in the square were the Palazzi Valmarano and Giulio Capra, both in Vicenza, and the Villa Barbaro in the Veneto. To provide a focal point of unity, Knobelsdorff cleverly installed in the centre of the piazza an obelisk, whose four bronze medallions of Frederick and his three immediate predecessors clad in Roman armour also served as a proclamation of Hohenzollern power and Frederick's dynastic pride.[154] Elsewhere in Potsdam could be found imitations of two great Roman palaces: Bramante's Palazzo Caprini and Raphael's Palazzo Vidoni.[155] As Algarotti observed, it seemed as if Frederick was seeking to make Potsdam as much a school of architecture as it was already of military art.[156] In the course of his reign more than twenty façades were copied directly from classical Italian, Chinese or English originals.[157]

Of Frederick's buildings, the most retrogressive was also his last major project: the Royal Library in Berlin. It was only after he had been on the throne for three decades that Frederick took steps to provide a dedicated building for the large royal collection comprising some 150,000 volumes, previously housed in a wing of the main palace. As it consisted mainly of works in Latin, which he could not read, or in German, which he did not want to read, it is not surprising that it had to wait so long for his attention. He seems to have been persuaded to act by a member of his inner circle, Charles Théophile Guichard, whom Frederick had renamed 'Quintus Icilius' in 1759 as a joke, after losing a wager to him about the correct name of one of Caesar's generals.[158] Although the architects directed to put up a building on a site near the opera house were notionally Michael Philipp Boumann and Georg Christian Unger, their task was simply to translate into working drawings a design first produced in 1726 by the celebrated Austrian baroque architect Johann Bernhard Fischer von Erlach. As only a part of Erlach's designs had actually been carried out in Vienna, either because they would have involved the demolition of the Court Theatre and/or because of shortage of funds, Frederick was probably making the point that he could do in practice what his Habsburg rivals could only do on paper. What works well as an integrated part of the Hofburg in Vienna is less successful as a stand-alone building in Berlin. In particular, the concave shape of the new library prompted irreverent Berliners to dub it the 'chest-of-drawers'.

This derivative character of Frederick's building operations recurs frequently. The French Church at Potsdam, for example, was lifted straight from Robert Morris's illustration in *The Architectural Remembrancer* of 1751. In the park of Sanssouci, the Temple of Antiquities was copied from William Kent's Temple of Ancient Virtue at Stowe, built in 1734; the Chinese Pavilion was modelled on the Maison du trèfle, built in 1738 by the French architect Emmanuel Héré de Corny for the Duke of Lorraine, Stanislas Leszczyński; and the Dragon House was taken from two books of architectural drawings presented to Frederick by Sir William Chambers – *Designs of Chinese Buildings* (1757) and *Plans, Elevations, Sections and Perspective Views of the Gardens and Buildings at Kew* (1763).[159] English influence could also be seen in two other buildings at Potsdam: the Hiller-Brandtsche House, based on an (unexecuted) design by Inigo Jones for a new palace of Whitehall, and the neo-Gothic Nauener Gate.[160]

PAINTINGS AND SCULPTURES

To fill these palaces great and small, Frederick became 'one of the most important art collectors of the mid-eighteenth century in Europe'.[161] Indeed, he was the first Hohenzollern ruler to form a collection of paintings.[162] Although never allowed to travel abroad, his appetite may have been whetted by the important collections he had seen at Salzdahlum, home of his Brunswick relations; Pommersfelden, the

Franconian palace of the Schönborns; and, of course, Dresden.[163] Although his slender resources as crown prince meant that he had to start in a small way, he was already buying pictures while at Rheinsberg.[164] As we have seen, it was there that he set about creating an Arcadian world in which he could recover from his father's brutality.* There could be no greater contrast than that between the hard, hypermasculinity of Frederick William's militarist regime and the soft, gentle, languid, hedonistic world of the *fête galante* paintings favoured by Frederick. Once he came to the throne, he could indulge this taste to the full, although he was always insistent that his agents should not pay over the odds, a concern which did not of course prevent him being often overcharged and/or palmed off with fakes.[165] Among his early purchases was a great masterpiece, Antoine Watteau's *The Shop-Sign of Gersaint* (*L'Enseigne de Gersaint*), acquired in 1744. Eventually he came to own twenty-four by (or, rather, attributed to) Watteau, the acknowledged master of the genre, thirty-two by Nicolas Lancret and thirty-one by Jean-Baptiste Pater.[166] The last major acquisition in the genre was another painting of supreme quality, Watteau's *Embarkation for the Island of Cythera*, bought at a sale at The Hague in 1763.

Frederick hung the painting in his private rooms in the Potsdam Town Palace, where perhaps it served as a nostalgic visual reminder of his younger, less careworn days and formed an agreeable counterpoint to the soldiers drilling on the parade-ground below his window.[167] By that time his taste had moved on and he was concentrating on earlier and grander styles. His approach to aesthetic quality in the visual arts was robust: he knew what he liked. As he told his sister Wilhelmine, he considered beautiful what gave him pleasure, and anything that did not, had no value, however old it might be.[168] However, for all his imperiousness, it seems that he was more amenable to influence when it came to painting than in music or literature, where his knowledge, talent and self-confidence were greater. The *fête galante* genre was certainly calculated to appeal to his feminine side, but it was also encouraged by Antoine Pesne, a friend of Lancret, and Pesne's pupil, Knobelsdorff.[169] Frederick fell out with both Pesne and

* See above, p. 50.

Knobelsdorff in the late 1740s. In 1748 he hired from Paris two painters of a younger generation, Charles-Amédée-Philippe van Loo and
Blaise Nicolas Le Sueur, although neither of them proved to be as
good as the old guard.[170] By this time Frederick had come under the
influence of Algarotti, Voltaire and the Marquis d'Argens, all of
whom disliked the rococo frivolity of Watteau and his imitators and
encouraged Frederick to switch his purchasing patronage to the old
masters.[171] When offered a parcel of paintings by Lancret in 1754, he
replied that he had lost his taste for that sort of art and was now more
interested in the great Italian and Flemish masters of the sixteenth and
seventeenth centuries.[172]

He was quickly into his stride, telling Wilhelmine in November
1755 that his old master collection had reached three figures, including two Correggios, two Guido Renis, two Veroneses, a Tintoretto, a
Solimena and no fewer than twelve Rubens and eleven Van Dycks.
Fifty more were needed, he added, to be obtained from Italy and the
Low Countries: 'so you see, my dear sister, that philosophy does not
banish folly from the heads of men'. He did not expect this craze to
last long in his case, however, because when the walls were full, he
would stop buying.[173] His purchases included some very fine works,
notably Correggio's *Leda and the Swan* (1531), Rubens's *Saint Cecilia*
(1640) and Rembrandt's *Moses Breaking the Tablets of the Law*
(1659).[174] To house them, Frederick built a dedicated gallery just
below Sanssouci on a site previously occupied by greenhouses. The
earliest free-standing gallery to have survived in Europe, it was
designed by Knobelsdorff's pupil Johann Gottfried Büring, although,
as usual, he was working within strict stylistic parameters set by Frederick.[175] Begun in the spring of 1755, work was driven on with
Frederick's customary impatience, to such effect that by the autumn
of the same year the shell was complete, except for the central dome.
A major influence in both the decision to build it and the manner in
which it was built was Algarotti, who was the author of a manifesto
advocating an autonomous temple of art.[176]

The entire project might well have been finished within two years,
had the Seven Years War not intervened. As it was, it was opened in
1764, an architectural and pictorial celebration of its builder's survival against all the odds. No expense was spared, with rare and very

expensive marble brought from North Africa and Siena for the walls and floors.[177] It had a dual function, to provide Frederick with a space for recreation and exercise when inclement weather ruled out the garden, and also to show the world that anything other European rulers could do, he could do just as well, if not better. Every single picture in the new gallery had been acquired by him personally. He spurned the opportunity to put together a good collection from the paintings he had inherited and which hung in the Berlin Palace. Nor were there any portraits of his Hohenzollern ancestors.[178] This had to be exclusively his own achievement.[179]

It was especially important to keep up with Dresden, where Augustus III of Saxony-Poland had rebuilt his gallery in 1745–7 to show off his fabulous collection to best advantage. It had quickly acquired the reputation of being one of the best publicly accessible museums in Europe, helping to make the city an essential port of call for the Grand Tourists.[180]

Anxious not to be left behind in this cultural competition, Frederick took great care to publicize his own collection, even though it was greatly inferior to that of his Saxon rival. Mathias Oesterreich was poached from Dresden to serve as curator, and his first task was to prepare and publish a *Description of the Royal Picture Gallery and Private Collection [Kabinett] at Sanssouci*, which went through numerous updated editions.[181] Oesterreich also served as the guide to the collection, admitting anyone decently dressed, in return, of course, for a tip.[182] An ambitious plan to publish two large volumes containing engraved reproductions of the collection was begun by a team of seven artists but later abandoned, probably on grounds of cost.[183] This autonomous temple, adjacent to but spatially separate from the palace, provided another illustration of the sacralization of art discussed earlier in this chapter. Although his tongue was in his cheek, d'Argens told Frederick in 1760 that everyone of taste was making the pilgrimage from Berlin to Potsdam to see the gallery with as much zeal as Christian pilgrims journeyed to Loreto and Santiago de Compostela.[184] Frederick did not commission paintings of his victories in the triumphalist style of Louis XIV, but he did present art as a suitable subject for veneration. More frivolously, the new gallery also gave him the opportunity to indulge his contempt for Christianity, by juxtaposing Carlo Maratta's *Madonna* with Guido Reni's *Toilet of Venus*.[185] (He played the same sort of trick in the Potsdam Town Palace, where Correggio's *The Repentant Mary Magdalene* was placed among a group of erotic *fête galante* pictures, including Watteau's *Cythera*.)[186]

There were very few contemporary paintings in the gallery, a notable exception being Pompeo Batoni's *The Marriage of Cupid and Psyche*, which Frederick commissioned in 1756 and which accompanied him on all the campaigns of the next seven years.[187] There were more to be found in the Potsdam Town Palace and the New Palace, where French artists were to the fore. Ironically, Frederick owned more early eighteenth-century French paintings than did the King of France.[188] He also commissioned four large history paintings by French artists for display in the New Palace. One of them, Carle Vanloo's monumental *The Sacrifice of Iphigenia*, has been hailed as 'the most important French painting of the mid-eighteenth century'.[189] Commissioned in 1755 and exhibited at the Paris Salon of 1757 before despatch to Prussia, the painting caused something of a sensation in the European art world.[190] The Comte de Caylus, one of the founding fathers of neo-classicism, published a pamphlet praising it warmly: 'M. Vanloo has achieved what Euripides would have done if he had had a brush rather than a pen in his hand.'[191] A visitor to the Salon that year wrote in another pamphlet that as soon as he entered the exhibition hall, he was struck at once by Vanloo's painting, thanks to its size and location. He went on to describe and analyse it in detail with a critical eye and to speak disapprovingly of the excessive enthusiasm it had aroused among the public.[192] The controversy surrounding the painting was then summarized and broadcast across Europe in his *Correspondance littéraire* by Baron Grimm, who also took the opportunity to imply that it was the King of France who ought to have been patronizing French history painting rather than the King of Prussia.[193]

Quantitatively, Frederick was an even more enthusiastic collector of sculpture. One improbable estimate maintained that his palaces housed 5,000 three-dimensional objects.[194] These were acquired in four main stages. In 1742 he bought for 80,000 livres the collection of the recently deceased Cardinal Melchior de Polignac, who had put his time in Rome as French ambassador to good use by accumulating a first-rate collection of around 300 pieces, most of them classical antiquities.[195] In 1758 Frederick inherited 130 objects from his sister Wilhelmine. A very large number of items, mainly consisting of engraved precious stones, was bought in 1764 from the heir of the notorious Baron Philipp von Stosch for 30,000 talers plus a pension of 400 talers per annum for life.[196] Stosch was a Prussian by birth but had spent most of his adult life in Italy, dealing in the flood of classical arte-facts, both real and fake, that reached the market from the numerous excavations underway. Among other things, he had been paid by the British government to spy on the Stuart Pretender, despite Walpole's view that he was 'a man of most infamous character in every respect', which seems to have been an oblique reference to Stosch's flagrant homosexuality.[197] A final burst of purchasing was launched in the late 1760s to fill Frederick's new buildings, especially the New Palace. These latest sculptures were obtained mainly from agents in Rome.[198]

As this suggests, Frederick very much liked his buildings, gardens and interiors to be adorned by statues. The rebuilt Potsdam Town Pal-ace, for example, boasted seventy-six figures, ninety-two vases, sixteen trophies and three large cartouches.[199] He took a great deal of care to arrange them in a coherent manner. At Sanssouci the paintings of his personal 'small gallery' were complemented by statues of Apollo, Dio-nysus, Athena and Marsyas, the last-named being the flute-playing satyr who unwisely challenged Apollo to a contest. On the wall opposite were placed twelve portrait busts, including three Romans especially admired by Frederick: the emperors Marcus Aurelius and Hadrian, and the latter's catamite Antinous in the style of the statue discovered at the Villa Mondragone earlier in the century.[200]

FREDERICK'S HOMOEROTIC SOCIETY

As we have seen, as soon as Frederick was liberated from paternal tyranny by Frederick William's death in 1740, he put away his wife and showered presents and favours on his two favourite men,

Fredersdorf and Algarotti.* He also set about creating a physical, social and cultural environment in which he could feel comfortable and recover from the horrors of the previous twenty-eight years. This was a soft, luxurious world, in which his new-found wealth allowed him to indulge the tastes his father had found effeminate. It was homosocial, homoerotic and probably homosexual too. Of course care must be taken not to apply anachronistic perspectives. What seems 'camp' to twenty-first-century eyes, could appear impeccably virile to mid-eighteenth-century patrons. No European ruler was more enthusiastically heterosexual than the priapic Louis XV, but he was also the lavish patron of rococo art just as refined as anything commissioned by Frederick. Even so, the ambience at Potsdam was very different from the court of Versailles, or any other European court for that matter.

A visitor to Sanssouci approached the palace from the northern side, across a courtyard – the *cour d'honneur* – encircled by a colonnade, one of Frederick's favourite architectural forms, which had also featured earlier at Rheinsberg, the new palace planned for Berlin and the Potsdam Town Palace. It is clearly reminiscent of the Grand Trianon at Versailles. The main doors led into an entrance hall in which two statues confronted each other, to the west Mars and to the east Mercury. The former was a modern French copy of the statue in the Ludovisi collection in Rome, itself a second-century AD copy of the Greek original of the fourth century BC. Mars is depicted as a naked, athletic young man, his sword of war sheathed, as a cupid plays about his feet, indicating that military activity should make way for love-making. On the eastern side was Mercury, a classical statue inherited from Frederick's sister Wilhelmine. He was chosen perhaps because he was the god of commerce (among other things) and so implied that the Prussian economy was in good shape,[201] or more likely because he was a beautiful naked youth awaiting the attention of Mars opposite. On Frederick's death, his heir had the statue removed and it has never returned.[202] The erotic, bacchanalian mood of the room is enhanced by gilded bas-reliefs of the overdoor spaces, whose scenes of drunken debauchery show satyrs making music to honour Bacchus and nymphs

* See above, pp. 61–71.

dancing around the god Pan.[203] From the vestibule, the visitor entered the largest room in the palace, the Marble Hall. Prominently displayed here was a bust by Jacques-Philippe Bouchardon of Charles XII of Sweden, autocrat, military hero and homosexual, about whom both Voltaire and Frederick himself wrote enthusiastically.[204]

Charles 'personified the conjunction of military and royalty, victory and calamity, together with a world without women and homosexual orientation'.[205] Languid eroticism was the theme of the ante-chamber, which also served as an informal dining room, and also of the music room, decorated by Antoine Pesne with scenes from Ovid's *Metamorphoses* – Pygmalion and Galatea; Vertumnus and Pomona; Pan and Syrinx; Bacchus and Ariadne – and a large painting of Diana bathing. One perhaps rather speculative interpretation is:

> The concert room at Sanssouci is the threshold between the official and the more 'private' rooms of Frederick's apartments. Frederick intended to make a clear, although not too precise, statement about the nature of love at this specific point in the sequence of rooms, where his own, private realm began. As displayed in the paintings, love is either terrifying, irreal or utterly unsuccessful. Women cannot or should not be approached. The most hopeful scene, featuring a *deus ex machina* rescuing the desolate lover Ariadne, is immediately adjacent to the door leading into the king's study and bedroom. The king himself, turned away from the love of women, deserted by his love, waits for the god to rescue him.[206]

From his library, which is also immediately adjacent to Fredersdorf's room, Frederick looked out at a statue of Antinous which he had placed inside an elaborate wrought-iron pavilion. This was undoubtedly the finest piece of sculpture in Frederick's collection, indeed one of the finest in any European gallery. Dating from *c.* 300 BC, it was discovered on the island of Rhodes in 1503. Although the identity of the boy must be uncertain, in Frederick's day it was always referred to as Antinous and was thus given a homosexual connotation: 'Frederick thus purchased an icon of pederastic, male desire in males which had already long been defined as such.'[207] It was only after his death that the statue was renamed 'The Praying Boy' and hastily removed to a museum.[208] Hadrian was so grief-stricken when Antinous died that he made him a god and instituted a cult in his memory. The statue passed through several hands before reaching the Austrian Field Marshal Prince Eugene, who was famously homosexual. On campaign in the Rhineland in 1734 he welcomed Crown Prince Frederick to his camp. Frederick was well aware of Eugene's proclivities, writing later in *History of My Own Times* that the prince had been refused a military commission by Louis XIV because the courtiers had given him the derisive nickname 'Lady Claude'.[209] Christoph Ludwig von Seckendorf wrote in his secret diary for 1734 that Frederick was imitating Eugene's laconic manner. He also recorded the following conversation: 'The Prince of Anhalt-Dessau: "Does Your Highness still get an erection?" Prince Eugene, taking a pinch of snuff: "No, I do not get an erection."'[210] Also present on the Rhine in 1734 was Prince Joseph Wenzel von Liechtenstein, who struck up a friendship with Frederick, corresponded with him when he returned to Prussia and even lent him money.[211] It was Liechtenstein who bought the statue of Antinous from Prince Eugene's heir and then sold it to Frederick, who knew of the statue already from an engraving by Giuseppe Camerata, for the large sum of 5,000 talers.[212] Delighted with his acquisition, Frederick took great care over its transport from Vienna, instructing his embassy there to give every assistance to the member of his staff he sent down to collect it.[213]

To place this statue so that it was in direct line of view from his study was to make an unmistakable statement. This was no secret but plainly visible to anyone taking advantage of the easy accessibility offered to visitors to Sanssouci. As it was located immediately adjacent to the vault intended by Frederick for his remains, it could be interpreted as his tribute to Lieutenant Hans Hermann von Katte, who had sacrificed himself for his lover just as Antinous had for Hadrian.[214] Also accessible was the Temple of Friendship erected at the western end of the park as a memorial to Frederick's sister Wilhelmine, who died in 1758. Four medallions on the columns depict four pairs of male lovers from classical antiquity: Orestes and Pylades, Nisus and Euryalus, Heracles and Philoctetes, and Theseus and Pirithous.[215]

The same homoerotic theme could also be found in the two most important paintings commissioned for the New Palace nearby. The first was Pompeo Batoni's *The Family of Darius*, which depicts another celebrated pair of male lovers, Alexander the Great and Hephaestion, bringing comfort to the wife and children of the vanquished King of Persia, a perennially popular subject among history painters. In Batoni's version, the intimacy of the relationship between the two men is emphasized by Hephaestion placing his hand on Alexander's wrist.[216] Commissioned in 1763, it was not delivered until 1775, but such was the importance Frederick attached to it that the allocated space was kept vacant.[217] This was in the Blue Antechamber, which led to Frederick's apartments.

Even more prominent was the fresco *Ganymede is introduced to Olympus* by Charles Vanloo in the Marble Hall. That Frederick should choose such a well-known homoerotic subject for the largest fresco in the largest room in his largest palace could hardly be more revealing about how he chose to represent himself.* It was also of long standing, for the same subject had been painted by Antoine Pesne for Frederick's tower room adjoining the music room at Rheinsberg.[218]

Frederick's homosexuality is a subject that was once taboo, remains fraught, but is too important to be ignored. Reluctance to accept it has been justified by the allegedly anachronistic character of the concept, for the word 'homosexual' and its cognates were late-nineteenth-century inventions. This does not convince. Many phenomena have existed before a particular word has been used to describe them – 'nationalism' and 'liberalism' spring to mind as examples. It can certainly be allowed that in early modern Europe, the boundaries between the unequivocally heterosexual and the unequivocally homosexual were more fluid. But they existed. When Frederick William I called his son 'effeminate' and a 'sodomite', he knew quite well what he meant. It has also been stressed that the period also saw a 'cult of friendship' between males which could be intensely emotional without being sexual, although this is usually seen as a form of 'bourgeois' reaction to the formalities of aristocratic culture.[219] It is just not possible to say when a Platonic relationship became Socratic. When the Prussian officer Ewald von Kleist wrote to Johann Wilhelm Ludwig

---

* Franziska Windt's attempt, in 'Künstlerische Inszenierung von Grösse', to present Ganymede as a 'beautiful soul' does not convince. She ignores the homoerotic reference.

Gleim that his professions of desire were not exaggerated 'for I truly love you more than all the girls in the world', was there not some sexual ingredient?[220] In Frederick's case, he certainly enjoyed intense friendships. These were almost all with men, although there were some notable exceptions – his sister Wilhelmine, the Countess Camas and the dowager Electress of Saxony Maria Antonia. Unless a document can be found in which Frederick relates what he did, when and with whom, a residual doubt must remain. The cumulative weight of evidence, however, is difficult to resist.

PART II

War and Peace

7

Peace and War 1745–1756

25 December 1745 was a happy day for Frederick. He was celebrating, not the birth of Christ, in whom he did not believe, but peace with Austria and Saxony, in which he certainly did believe. His cupboard was bare. It was high time to leave a war from which nothing more could be gained. He knew that he had been lucky, that Maria Theresa would have preferred to make a separate peace with Louis XV. She had favoured Frederick only because she found the French intransigent, their backbones stiffened by recent victories in the Low Countries and the Jacobite rebellion that was diverting the British.[1] The French looked forward to clinching victory in 1746. Despite this confidence, they were appalled to learn in mid-December that their Prussian ally was about to desert them once again. The French ambassador in Berlin, Valori, mounted a last-ditch attempt to frustrate the negotiations underway at Dresden by sending off his secretary, Claude Etienne Darget.

Why would a mere secretary be entrusted with such an important mission? The probable explanation is that Darget had already caught Frederick's roving eye, making such an impression, indeed, that his transfer to Prussian service had been requested.[2] As we shall see, Darget was to feature as the anti-hero of Frederick's homoerotic poem *Palladium*.* Alas, Frederick knew how to keep sex and politics separate. In the detailed report of their encounter sent back to Valori, Darget had to register total failure, in his diplomatic mission at least.[3] Franco-Prussian relations had been uneasy since Frederick's first uni-

---

* See below, pp. 447–8. Darget moved to become Frederick's librarian the following month, January 1746.

lateral desertion of his ally back in November 1741.* The separate
peace of Breslau in 1742 and the Convention of Hanover of August
1745, both concluded secretly and unilaterally, had reinforced the
French conviction that their occasional Prussian ally was not to be
trusted. For his part, Frederick then rejected with fierce contempt a
French offer of a subsidy in lieu of military assistance, commenting
that so pitifully small a sum, barely enough to finance three battalions, might be appropriate for a minor prince such as the Landgrave
of Hessen-Darmstadt, but was just an insult to the King of Prussia.⁴
The rejoinder sent back in the name of Louis XV was equally chilly,
in effect telling Frederick that he was now on his own: 'Who is better
qualified to give advice to Your Majesty than you yourself? You only
have to follow what you are told by your intelligence, your experience
and – above all – your honour.'⁵

This exchange exemplified Frederick's problematic situation at the
end of the Second Silesian War. He had won for the time being, but
the future was uncertain. His seizure of Silesia in 1740, and successful
defence of his booty in the five years that followed, had alarmed every
other major European power. What had been most disturbing? The
brutal aggression of the original invasion? The astounding feats of the
Prussian army? The speed of decision and execution? The devious
diplomacy? The repeated abandoning of allies? The reputation for
cynicism and godlessness? Into the staid, slow-moving world of great-
power diplomacy, which liked to take its time when sorting out
disputes, there had barged a disruptive intruder, a parvenu upstart
with boundless presumption. Louis XV may have thought that the
invasion of Silesia was the act of a lunatic,† but Frederick had shown
that when madness succeeds, it has to be renamed audacity.

Of all those who wanted to see Frederick back where he belonged,
in the asylum, Maria Theresa was the most implacable. He was, of
course, under no illusions. In his account of the next war, which eventually broke out just over ten years later, he described how he set
about getting ready before the ink was dry on the peace treaty, commenting 'the ant amasses in summer what it consumes in winter'. If

---

* See above, p. 105.
† See above, p. 88.

the resources of his state had allowed it, he added, he would have done even more, for Maria Theresa was implacably hostile.* One of her objectives had been attained, for with the election of her adored husband Francis Stephen as emperor in September 1745, the briefly interrupted nexus between the House of Habsburg (now more properly Habsburg-Lorraine) and the Holy Roman Empire had been restored. That mattered to her a lot, for both dynastic and personal reasons. The greater prize, the reconquest of Silesia, however, still eluded her. News of the peace treaty had been greeted in Vienna with dismay, 'among all sections of the population' according to the Venetian ambassador Erizzo.[6]

Their depression is easily understandable. The loss of Silesia was momentous, for several reasons. Most obviously, the addition of its *c.* 1.1 million inhabitants increased the population of Prussia by about 50 per cent.[7] It covered more than half a million square kilometres, that is to say an area as large as about a third of England.[8] Along with the width came quality. It was the most prosperous of all the Habsburg provinces, thanks to a productive agriculture, abundant mineral resources and a thriving textile industry.[9] Frederick wrote in his *Political Testament* of 1752 that Silesian linen was to Prussia what Peruvian gold was to Spain. Having provided around a quarter of the Habsburg Monarchy's tax revenue, Silesia was to perform the same service for its new ruler – more so, indeed, for it was to yield around 40 per cent of Prussian revenues.[10]

Nature had helped by providing the river Oder, which bisects the province as it runs north-west to Brandenburg before reaching the Baltic at Stettin. Navigable for most of its length, it gave Frederick a priceless military asset, allowing the relatively rapid transport of men and matériel and enabling him to fight on interior lines.† More generally, the strategic importance of Silesia is revealed by a glance at any contemporary map of the region. In the hands of the Habsburgs, it was a tongue of territory stretching into northern Germany, putting Austrian armies within 150 kilometres of Berlin; its loss not only reduced Habsburg influence in northern Germany, it also put Prussian

---

* See above, p. 114.
† See below, p. 264.

armies within 150 kilometres of Prague and 200 of Vienna. It was guarded by several major fortresses: Glogau, Breslau, Brieg and Cosel on the Oder, Schweidnitz in the south-west on the Weistritz, and Glatz and Neisse on the river Neisse (confusingly, there were four rivers called 'Neisse', all of them tributaries of the Oder).[11] Moreover, the fact that this great asset had passed to Prussia doubled the depth of the wound inflicted on the Austrians, for if all the various resources of Silesia were added together and expressed by the algebraic symbol 'x', the power relationship between the two states changed as a result of its transfer not by 'x' but by two times 'x', for what had been taken away from the one was added to the other. In footballing parlance, the conquest of Silesia was a 'six-pointer' for Frederick. As Maria Theresa complained in a memorandum to Field Marshal Daun in the middle of the Seven Years War, the loss of Silesia had both increased Frederick's army by 40,000 and diminished her own by a similar number.[12]

Prussian rule proved to be a mixed blessing for the Silesians. The economy had been closely integrated with the two other parts of the 'Crown of St Wenceslas': Bohemia and Moravia. Although the peace treaty had promised a commercial treaty to allow the network to continue, it was never honoured. On the contrary, Frederick's aggressive protectionism forced the Silesian merchants to reorientate their commerce north to the Oder and the Elbe, which proved a long and painful process. Full integration into the Prussian economy was not achieved until the 1780s.[13] Culturally, the main beneficiaries were the Protestants who made up around half the population.[14] Indeed Ranke hailed Frederick's victory over the Austrians at Leuthen in December 1757 as the delayed Protestant response to the battle of the White Mountain, a reference to the Catholic victory of 1620 which had ushered in a century and more of vigorous persecution of heretics.[15] Frederick not only put a stop to that, he also prevented any reprisals. Keeping his promise to freeze the confessional status quo, however, could mean disappointing the Protestants, who complained that they often still had to travel away from their communities to find a church, while in their own village a handful of Catholics continued to monopolize a building much too big for their needs.[16]

Loyalty to the Habsburgs lingered in some regions, especially in

Upper (southern) Silesia, where dense forests and poor-quality agricultural land had encouraged the development of serf-run latifundia, where Catholicism was the norm and where the majority of the Polish-speaking population (28 per cent of the total) lived.[17] A special problem was posed by the 300-odd noble estate-owners who lived outside the province and were mainly in Habsburg service.[18] Frederick certainly did his best to win over his new acquisition. Silesia may have been conquered but it was never treated as such and was never exploited as temporarily occupied territories such as Mecklenburg or Saxony.[19] Indeed, it was treated with special favour, being placed directly under Frederick's supervision, rather than being assigned to the General Directory.[20] A symbolic earnest of his intention was the acquisition of a noble town house in the centre of the Silesian capital, Breslau, and its conversion into a royal palace.[21] He visited twice a year, touring tirelessly to seek information, although, as we have seen, he was too often told what he wanted to hear.* Of course he moved quickly to make the most of his new asset, introducing Prussian administration and the canton system for recruitment. Two hundred young Silesian nobles were despatched to the cadet school in Berlin for officer training.[22]

In short, Silesia was a real prize, one worth every exertion to retain – and to regain. For the time being, the Austrians had their hands full, fighting the French in Italy and the Low Countries. Negotiations for a general peace began at Breda in the autumn of 1746 but fizzled out the following year. Neither of the two groups of allies – Austria, Sardinia, Great Britain and the Dutch Republic on one side, France and Spain on the other – could achieve decisive superiority. The French won in India and the Austrian Netherlands but lost in Canada, Italy and on the high seas. Eventually, financial exhaustion imposed peace. By the Treaty of Aachen of 18 October 1748, a complex series of deals was done, but with only minor adjustments to the map. Nearly ten years of ruinously expensive fighting across the globe had yielded very little change. The French and British exchanged conquests in Canada and India and the French handed back their conquests in the Low Countries to Austria and the Dutch Republic

* See above, p. 129.

respectively. Their only gains were by proxy, with the Austrian duchies of Parma, Piacenza and Guastalla passing to Louis XV's Spanish
son-in-law Don Philip. The only unequivocal victor of the War of the
Austrian Succession was the King of Prussia, who had left it three
years earlier. His possession of Silesia, however, was expressly guaranteed by the Treaty of Aachen.[23]

Frederick knew that nothing had been resolved, neither the conflict
between France and Great Britain for the domination of the world
overseas, nor his own existential struggle with the Habsburgs for the
domination of Central Europe. The peace, he wrote, 'was the work of
men in a hurry and was concluded in haste, as the powers resolved
their present embarrassment at the cost of sacrificing their long-term
interests: they extinguished part of the fire that was consuming Europe, but only by piling up combustible material that would catch light
at the first opportunity'.[24] Had he known what the Austrian policymakers were thinking, he might have used an even more inflammatory
metaphor. A memorandum from the senior minister, Johann Christof
von Bartenstein, stated that in the past the Habsburg Monarchy had
been confronted by two deadly enemies – France in the west and the
Ottoman Turks in the east. But now they had been joined by an even
more dangerous and malevolent predator. This required a reassess-
ment of the monarchy's alliance system. The Maritime Powers (Great
Britain and the Dutch Republic) had always been able and willing to
help against France, but were of little use against the eastern enemies.
The only power, Bartenstein concluded, with both the interest and the
ability to help was Russia.[25]

He was right, as Frederick knew only too well. He had a low opinion of the Russian people ('stupid, drunken, superstitious, and
wretched') but a healthy respect for the Russian Empire, unassailable
itself because of physical distance but a terrible menace to others,
thanks to the swarms of marauding irregulars it could unleash in time
of war.[26] He told his man in St Petersburg, Baron Mardefeld, in June
1743 that 'there is nothing in the world I would not do to maintain in
perpetuity harmonious relations with the Russian Empire'.[27] He also
knew that Russian foreign policy was directed by the implacably
Prussophobe vice-chancellor, Count Alexey Petrovich Bestuzhev,
denounced by Frederick as 'a man without genius, little able in

administration, haughty from ignorance, deceitful from character, and double in his dealings even to those by whom he had been bribed'.[28] In August 1743, Mardefeld was told to do his best to secure Bestuzhev's dismissal.[29] That initiative failed, like all the others Frederick attempted in the years that followed. No more successful was the switch to bribery in June 1744 when Mardefeld was authorized to offer '100,000, 120,000 or even 150,000 crowns [*écus*]'.[30] In August an untempted Bestuzhev was promoted to grand chancellor and remained in office until 1758, a constant thorn in Frederick's flesh.

Policy towards Russia was difficult for all the other European powers because the situation in St Petersburg was fluid, not to say chaotic. The old saw that the Russian system of government was 'despotism tempered by assassination' was never more valid than when it came to the fundamental issue of succession. Peter the Great's decision in 1722 to leave the choice of successor to the current incumbent opened the way for a destabilizing scramble whenever a vacancy occurred. He himself was succeeded by his widow as Catherine I (1725–7), his grandson Peter II (1727–30) and his niece Anna (1730–40). As we have seen, it was the death of the last-named, on 17 October 1740, that prompted Frederick to invade Silesia.* Her own choice of the two-month-old son of her niece Anna Leopoldovna (granddaughter of Tsar Ivan V and great-niece of Peter the Great) to rule as Ivan VI brought a prolonged period of instability. In November 1741 the infant tsar and his parents were removed from power in a *coup d'état* which put Peter the Great's daughter Elizabeth on the throne, where she remained until 1761.[31] Unmarried herself, she quickly appointed as successor her twelve-year-old nephew Karl Peter Ulrich, son of her late sister Anna and Karl Friedrich, Duke of Holstein. He was brought to St Petersburg, converted to Orthodoxy and was renamed 'Peter Fedorovich'. In return for the Russian succession, he was obliged to renounce his claims to the Swedish throne, which passed to his uncle Adolf Friedrich.

The fortunes of Frederick were deeply involved in these comings and goings of the Romanov and Holstein families. He appeared to have brought off a great coup in August 1744 when Grand Duke

* See above, p. 90.

Peter was betrothed to Princess Sophie of Anhalt-Zerbst, renamed Catherine when she converted to Orthodoxy. As Frederick complacently put it: 'no one better suited the intentions of Russia, and the interests of Prussia'.[32] Her father was a general in the Prussian army, her mother was a Holstein, sister of Adolf Friedrich, now heir-apparent to the crown of Sweden. Just to add to this matrimonial conquest of northern Europe, in the same month Frederick's sister Luise Ulrike was married to Adolf Friedrich and became Queen of Sweden when her husband succeeded in 1751. After a turbulent engagement, Grand Duke Peter and Catherine were eventually married in August 1745.

Alas, this triangular family nexus between Prussia, Sweden and Russia did not translate into political harmony between the three powers. Just as Ulrike was getting married to Crown Prince Adolf Friedrich in August 1744, Frederick was launching the invasion of Bohemia which began the Second Silesian War.* Sensing that *raison d'état* might count for more than family ties at St Petersburg, Frederick tried to enlist his new allies at the Russian court. In letters congratulating the Princess of Anhalt-Zerbst and her daughter Catherine on their 'triumph', which he hailed as 'one of the happiest days of my life', he expressed the pious hope that the Tsarina Elizabeth would wake up to her true interests, take the necessary action to secure her regime and her family, and not allow the enemies of Prussia at her court to misrepresent his resumption of hostilities against Austria.[33]

His hopes came to nothing. It was Frederick's resumption of hostilities in support of the French coalition that confirmed Bestuzhev's 'furious hatred' of him.[34] In this Bestuzhev was aided and abetted by his own family connections. Cunningly, he married his son Andrey to the Countess Avdotya Razumovsky, officially the niece of Count Aleksey Razumovsky but in reality his daughter. Her mother was none other than the Tsarina Elizabeth, who was secretly and morganatically married to Razumovsky (an intellectual weakling but a 'Hercules of Cythera', as Mardefeld delicately put it).[35] Partly, it was due to the intense personal dislike Elizabeth felt for Frederick.[36] As the two never met, this antipathy may have been caused by the reports

* See above, pp. 107–8.

carefully fed to her by Bestuzhev that Frederick had been making merry about her well-known taste for strong drink and strong men. Certainly Bestuzhev had been instructing Russian diplomatic representatives to include in their despatches anything that would put Frederick in a bad light.[37] She also took violent exception to Frederick equating her in public with the other great oriental despot, the Turkish Sultan.[38] So Frederick's attempts to curry favour with gifts – a portrait of himself by Antoine Pesne and a magnificent gala coach – were not favoured with even an acknowledgement.[39]

Although such apparent trivia were undoubtedly important in such a Byzantine environment as the Russian court, behind the rift lay more fundamental considerations. On the one hand, the rise of Prussia and Russia to great-power status had been mutually supportive. It was Peter the Great who had dealt with the two great rivals of the House of Hohenzollern, by defeating Charles XII of Sweden and Augustus the Strong of Saxony-Poland in the Great Northern War. The victory made Russia the dominant power in the eastern Baltic but also created a vacuum in north-eastern Germany, into which Prussia gratefully moved. It has even been argued that Prussia was the real victor of the war, despite its modest and intermittent military contribution.[40] It bears repeating that the 'hereditary enemy' of Prussia was not so much Austria as Saxony-Poland.*

In short, Poland was not the filling in the sandwich but the mortar between two bricks. It could only be adhesive, however, so long as Prussia was seen to be the junior partner. In 1716 Peter the Great had intervened in the tumultuous affairs of Poland, to bang heads together and to force both the king and representatives of the *Sejm* (Parliament) to agree to a settlement which Russia then guaranteed (thus obtaining the right to intervene at any point in the future, should the agreement be broken). On 30 January 1717 the 'Silent *Sejm*', cowed by the Russian soldiers surrounding their building, gave their assent. From that date, Russian supremacy continued in one form or another until the late twentieth century.[41] More often than not, it was supported by Prussia. Frederick William I set the example by concluding an agreement with Peter the Great in 1720 to maintain 'Polish

---

* See above, pp. 85–6.

liberties'. First among the latter was the *liberum veto*, the requirement that all legislation of the *Sejm* be voted unanimously, which predictably led to paralysis.[42] Together, Russia and Prussia were able to frustrate French attempts to create an 'Eastern Barrier' comprising Sweden, Poland and Turkey and to get Louis XV's father-in-law, Stanislas Leszczyński, elected as King of Poland when Augustus II ('the Strong') died in 1733.[43] That 'election' also showed which was the senior partner in the Russo-Prussian relationship. Only a few months previously, a Russian envoy, Count Löwenwolde, had been sent to Berlin to sign an agreement committing both parties not to vote for either Stanislas Leszczyński or Augustus's son but to promote instead the candidacy of a Portuguese prince.[44] In the event, the Russians reneged and engineered the election of the new Saxon Elector as Augustus III, although not before securing a promise that he would not try to reform the Polish constitution.[45] Such a choice was fundamentally opposed to Prussian interests (not to mention Poland's), and an indignant Frederick William I offered the Austrians a force of 50,000 to overturn it. Interestingly, they declined: unwilling to accept Prussia as a full ally, they took only 10,000.[46]

In other words, Prussian and Russian interests overlapped but were not identical. Only when the Saxon–Polish connection was broken would an alliance seem more natural. In the meantime, the Russians watched with concern and then anger as Frederick, first treated his Saxon ally shabbily during the First Silesian War and then attacked him in the Second.* They were deeply disturbed by Frederick's alliance with France, which seemed to make Prussia part of the *barrière de l'est*.[47] Another bone of contention was Sweden. Hoping to exploit the domestic turmoil in Russia, the Swedes declared war in August 1741 and invaded Finland. They had miscalculated. The war turned out disastrously, leading to the Peace of Åbo in January 1743 which ceded to Russia southern Finland east of the river Kymmene, including the fortresses of Vilmanstrand and Frederikshamn.[48] This latest attempt to overturn the achievements of Peter the Great made the Russians hypersensitive about the volatile Swedish political situation. As Frederick was allied (off and on) with France, and as his sister was

---

* See above, pp. 106–7, 116.

Queen-apparent of Sweden after August 1744, he was viewed with deep suspicion in St Petersburg. The conclusion of a formal alliance between Sweden and Prussia in 1747 confirmed it.

By now fully in control of the tsarina, Bestuzhev set about plotting a *coup d'état* in Sweden to switch the succession from Adolf Friedrich to the present king's nephew, the Crown Prince of Hessen-Kassel. In the course of 1748 this developed into a grandiose plan for a major war: a coalition of Denmark, Russia, Saxony and Hessen-Kassel would invade Sweden, supported by a British fleet, while Austria would take the opportunity to reconquer Silesia, with Russian assistance.[49] In the course of 1749 the project fell apart. Neither the British nor the Austrians would agree to such a belligerent policy. Their reluctance was stiffened by vigorous – and well publicized – military preparations undertaken by Frederick, and by the diplomatic intervention of France in his support. Even if the French had not forgotten and forgiven his treachery, they had no wish to see Sweden fall under Russian control.

By the spring of 1750 the crisis was over. The sigh of relief breathed by Frederick would have been less confident if his intelligence reports from Vienna had been better. Unknown to him, in March 1749 the Empress Maria Theresa had asked all her senior ministers to submit reports on what their foreign policy should be, now that the War of the Austrian Succession was over. The youngest member of her cabinet, Count Wenzel Anton von Kaunitz, proved to be both the most prolix and the most radical. He brought to the task formidable diplomatic experience. From service in Italy (1741–4), the Austrian Netherlands (1744–8) and as the Austrian representative at the peace negotiations in 1748, he drew two main conclusions: firstly, that in future Austria must concentrate on the German-speaking core of her dominions, and, secondly, that Great Britain must cease to be the foundation of the alliance system. As early as March 1743, he wrote:

Austria should be looking more to the security of her German lands and the removal of a perpetual enemy, dangerous neighbour and rival to the imperial crown [Prussia], than to expansion in Italy and the acquisition of such lands which carry many difficulties with them, and are far removed, and whose conquest and maintenance are essentially dependent on England.[50]

The Peace of Dresden of 1745 he regarded as a 'necessary evil', adding that when the time was ripe, Prussia should be 'extinguished'.[51]

His report to Maria Theresa of 24 March 1749 was twice as long as those of the other five ministers consulted put together.[52] Its fundamental premise was the absolute necessity of regaining Silesia, so organic a part of the Habsburg body politic that its amputation had inflicted a wound that would not heal. As the existing alliance system had failed, he concluded, a fundamental rethink was needed. Number one enemy was now Prussia, their 'most terrible, dangerous and implacable enemy' now and in the future.[53] Far from resting on his laurels, Frederick would go on trying to weaken Austria further to ensure the retention of his booty. There was no point relying on the Maritime Powers in future. The Dutch Republic was a broken reed, while perfidious Albion had left Austria in the lurch time and again. Moreover, this 'Old System' was fundamentally flawed because it was directed not against Prussia but against France and Spain. George II and his Hanoverian ministers might hate the Prussian upstart, but British public opinion was very much in his favour.

Kaunitz went on to argue that only a continental ally could help now, and that could only mean France. Overturning Habsburg–Bourbon hostility, the central plank of the European states-system for more than two centuries, he acknowledged, would be very difficult, especially as the French only ever consulted their own selfish interest. On the other hand, they were not the threat they had once been. Louis XV was ignorant and lazy, while his foreign minister, the Marquis de Puysieux, was inexperienced, passive and less Austrophobe than his predecessors. And they were both still smarting from Frederick's triple desertion during the last war. To overcome French objections, Kaunitz recommended a multiple exchange of territory: Louis XV's son-in-law, Don Philip, would receive Savoy from the King of Sardinia, who would be compensated by Austria with the duchy of Milan. Don Philip would then return to Austria his duchies of Parma, Piacenza and Guastalla, ceded in 1748. If that did not appeal, the Habsburg duchy of Luxembourg was a possible bait for France. Other allies – Russia, Saxony, the Palatinate and Hanover – could then be added to the coalition by promises of Prussian territory.[54]

With the Habsburg Monarchy desperately short of money and

embarking on a programme of domestic reform to repair the manifold defects revealed by the war against Prussia, this was not a
propitious time for such a revolution, as the more conservative ministers pointed out. Maria Theresa, however, was impressed, not least
because she harboured such an intense dislike for Frederick. In 1750
Kaunitz was sent off to Versailles as Austrian ambassador.[55] There he
found a once dominant power whose feet of clay were beginning to
crumble. The Peace of Aachen, which handed back all the conquests
in India and the Low Countries, had been greeted by French public
opinion with consternation and anger: '*bête comme la paix*' (as stupid
as the peace) became a popular simile.[56] As it was believed that the
chief minister *de facto* was the royal mistress, Madame de Pompadour, sleaze was added to incompetence.[57] Just how much influence
on policy (as opposed to patronage) she actually exercised has been
much debated.[58] In any event, she was a useful whipping girl for all
who opposed the apparent incoherence and indecision of royal policy.[59] Frederick had a low opinion of Louis XV* and even less time
for his *maîtresse-en-titre*, his contempt fuelled by a potent combination of misogyny and snobbery (Madame de Pompadour *née* Poisson
came from the world of finance). When Voltaire conveyed greetings
from her in 1750, Frederick responded with a disdainful 'I do not
know her.' This was foolish. Maria Theresa, for all her prudishness,
brought herself to address La Pompadour in correspondence as '*Ma
Cousine*' or even '*Madame, ma très chère soeur*'.[60] As we shall see, her
politeness was to pay a handsome political dividend in 1756.[61]

In general, Frederick's dealings with France showed his limitations as a statesman. Until much too late in the day he remained
convinced that there was a natural community of interest between
Prussia and France that could never be broken. In one of his first letters to the French foreign minister, Cardinal Fleury, in 1740, he stated
unequivocally: 'the interests of France and my own are identical;
everything combines to unite us'.[62] That did not stop him abandoning
France unilaterally three times between 1741 and 1745. As we have
seen, he had good reasons for doing so,† but he does not seem to have

---

* See above, p. 79.
† See above, pp. 100, 105–6, 116.

appreciated just how much offence his conduct caused at Versailles, not even when told that Fleury had wept tears of rage on hearing of the Treaty of Breslau in June 1742.[63] He believed that both countries were bound together by that most adhesive of ties: 'my enemy's enemy is my friend'. As he put it in his *Political Testament* of 1752, they had both taken large chunks of territory from the House of Habsburg-Lorraine: he had married the elder daughter (Silesia) while France had taken the younger (Lorraine).[64]

That Austria had replaced Saxony as Prussia's paramount enemy was undoubtedly true. It was less obvious that Austria still played the same contrapuntal role for France. As Frederick himself recognized in his *Political Testament*, a better candidate had been emerging in the west ever since the Glorious Revolution of 1688 had transformed England from France's junior partner into her bitter rival. Charles II had been Louis XIV's satrap, William III was his hammer. In India, Africa, the Caribbean and, above all, North America, French and British interests clashed ever more frequently and violently. Between 1744 and 1748 they had fought a localized but intense conflict around the Gulf of St Lawrence. The most spectacular event was the British capture of Louisburg in 1745, although it had to be handed back when the war ended. With so much at stake, the peace could only be a truce: North America was not big enough for both aspiring world powers. As the British settlers continued to pour west from the seaboard colonies in search of new land, their progress was challenged by their equally rapacious French rivals moving south from the St Lawrence river valley. Had the latter succeeded in their mission of linking up with their fellow-countrymen moving north from Louisiana, the British would have been blocked from further expansion across the Mississippi and on to the prairies beyond. In the spring of 1749 a French expedition was sent down the Ohio river with orders to remove British traders.[65] In 1752 a new governor, the Marquis de Duquesne, was despatched to French Canada, with instructions to take possession of the Ohio valley and thus the geographical link with Louisiana. In 1754 he built a fort at the confluence of the Allegheny and Monongahela rivers, which together form the Ohio river, and named it after himself.

With war inevitable, both parties now looked to neutralize the continent to allow a free hand overseas. The more nervous of the two was

Great Britain, for George II's adored Electorate of Hanover was a tempting target for the French. Sitting on the north German plain without natural frontiers, it might be easily occupied and used as a bargaining chip in any peace negotiation.[66] To secure their position in general, and Hanover in particular, from 1749 the British had been seeking to strengthen their Austrian ally in the Holy Roman Empire. This mainly took the form of promoting the election of Maria Theresa's eldest son, Joseph, as King of Romans. This would have guaranteed his succession to the imperial title when his father died and thus have avoided any repetition of the events of 1740–45. Unfortunately, the negotiations with the Electors did not go well and the whole project collapsed ignominiously in 1752.[67] Perhaps surprisingly, the initiative had not been helped much by the Austrians, who considered the whole project misguided and resented the most junior of the Electors – the Elector of Hanover – arrogating a leading role in imperial affairs.[68] Needless to say, in this respect, if no other, Frederick heartily agreed with them and helped to shipwreck the Duke of Newcastle's grand scheme.[69]

With the advantage of hindsight, we can see that both the British and the Austrians were fumbling their way to a recognition that their interests were now essentially different – not necessarily opposed, but definitely different. The British had no interest in Silesia; the Austrians had no interest in the world outside Europe. The Austrians could not send an army to America; the British could not send a fleet up the river Oder. Kaunitz, of course, had reached that conclusion long ago. At Versailles he had been cultivating Madame de Pompadour, visiting her frequently at her Château Bellevue, showering her with flattery, and telling her what he knew would be passed straight back to Louis XV[70] (or 'France', as she is reported to have called him during the ecstasy of their most intimate moments). Returning to Vienna early in 1753, Kaunitz found that all his more senior colleagues still adhered to the alliance with Great Britain. Shortly afterwards promoted to chancellor of state and thus placed in charge of foreign affairs, he also had the satisfaction of seeing two of the old guard, his predecessor Ulfeld and the veteran councillor Bartenstein, shuffled off to retirement.[71] As usual, the Viennese mills ground slowly. It was not until the middle of August 1755 that negotiations between Austria and Britain for an alliance finally collapsed.[72] It was then that the decision was taken to implement an aggressive plan aimed at the reconquest of Silesia. In a memorandum dated 28 August, Kaunitz asserted that Prussia would have to be destroyed if the Habsburg Monarchy were to survive. The latter had already lost influence and prestige both in Europe and the Holy Roman Empire. It was a case of kill or be killed, for Frederick was planning the total destruction of the dynasty.[73]

The military action would be taken by Austria and Russia. France was to be kept neutral by the promise of a part of the Austrian Netherlands for Don Philip; support for the French Prince de Conti when the Polish throne fell vacant; the use of the Channel ports of Ostende and Nieuport during the war against Great Britain; and slices of Prussia for French allies (Sweden, Saxony, the Palatinate) with the aim of reducing that turbulent power to the third-rate status it had occupied before Frederick William the Great Elector (r. 1640–88).[74] The Austrian ambassador at Versailles, Count Starhemberg, was instructed to make the necessary approach.[75]

The response was confused, not least because there were two rival organizations involved in the conduct of French policy: the official foreign office, headed since 1754 by Antoine-Louis Rouillé, Comte de Jouy, and an informal group around Madame de Pompadour, the most important member being her protégé the Abbé Bernis. The king was the nominal head of both groups. It was symptomatic of his irresolution and secretiveness that he should be responsible for two organizations often at odds with each other. And so it was in the autumn of 1755. Rouillé was unimpressed by the Austrian approach, preferred to revive the Prussian alliance and decided to send a high-ranking ambassador, the Duc de Nivernais (often spelt Nivernois), off to Potsdam.[76] According to Bernis, however, both the king and his mistress were much more favourably inclined. Louis stated that he had always wanted an Austrian alliance, because it would secure peace; because it would unite the two major Catholic powers in support of the True Faith; because of his respect for Maria Theresa; and because of his equally heartfelt distrust and dislike of the King of Prussia. In particular he had been irked by the way the 'Margrave of Brandenburg', as he called him, addressed the King of France as if he were his equal.[77] Bernis added that an Austrian alliance would secure

France from any hostile action from the Low Countries or the Holy Roman Empire, enhance her influence in Italy and remove Great Britain's main ally.[78]

He was very likely encouraged by Madame de Pompadour, who had been flattered by Kaunitz but insulted by Frederick. According to Starhemberg, she nursed 'an indescribable hatred for the King of Prussia'.[79] It was at her Château Bellevue that the first negotiating meeting took place on 3 September 1755 between Starhemberg and Bernis.[80] No one seemed to be in much of a hurry. Despite the belligerence of the British, most recently demonstrated by their seizure of two French ships off the Canadian coast, Rouillé still hoped that the crisis in the colonies could be resolved without an all-out war.[81] Opposition to an Austrian alliance from a pro-Prussian group at Versailles, led by the Duc de Belle-Isle and the Marquis d'Argenson, may also have slowed the lethargic pace still further.[82] Soon the French were overtaken by events elsewhere in Europe. The Duc de Nivernais did not actually leave for Prussia until 22 December 1755. By the time he got there on 12 January, the pass had been sold.

It was one of the many ironies of the ensuing chapter of accidents that the pebble that brought down the landslide was dislodged by the timorous, slow-thinking Duke of Newcastle, the British foreign secretary. Although a keen supporter of the Old System, he had to conclude by the autumn of 1755 that Austria would not help in the war with the French, not even if the latter invaded the Low Countries. As ever, his main concern in continental Europe was the security of Hanover. Fearing that France would induce Frederick to attack, Newcastle turned to Russia for help: 'everybody knows, that the king of Prussia acts only from interest or fear; by interest we cannot gain him, by fear we may have no means of doing it but by Russia'.[83] For several years Bestuzhev had been advocating such an alliance with the object of 'clipping still further the wings of the King of Prussia' but the Tsarina Elizabeth had been less enthusiastic. On 19 September 1755, however, she did agree to a convention, signed at St Petersburg, which provided an annual subsidy from Britain of £100,000 to keep an army of 50,000 and a naval force of fifty galleys permanently stationed on Russia's western frontier, plus the promise of £400,000 extra if they were actually deployed in anger.[84]

Although the tsarina delayed ratification, it was enough to put the fear of the Supreme Being into Frederick. On 20 December he took his minister Podewils to task for suggesting that the St Petersburg agreement was essentially defensive. On the contrary, he stated, he had reliable intelligence that at a council held in October in the presence of the tsarina, it had been decided to get ready at once for military action, should either Prussia attack an ally of Russia or – 'nota bene', added Frederick for emphasis – should an ally of Russia attack Prussia. Since then, preparations for war in cooperation with Austria had been driven on apace.[85] With France inactive, isolation threatened, so Frederick turned willy-nilly to Britain. Fortunately, relations with Uncle George (II) had thawed slightly from their normal state of deep freeze. Back in 1751 Frederick had gone out of his way to upset him by sending the Jacobite Earl Marischal George Keith to Versailles as Prussian ambassador. When his foreign minister, Podewils, asked how George might react, Frederick replied coarsely 'I don't give a fuck!'[86] In late 1754, however, the two kings had cooperated to contain the damage to the Protestant party in the Holy Roman Empire threatened by the conversion of the Crown Prince of Hessen-Kassel to Catholicism.[87] The ice was dissolved further when Frederick travelled across Germany to his territories in the west in May 1755, passing close to George, who was in residence at Herrenhausen. Although the two kings did not meet, amicable messages were exchanged. Frederick also used a visit by the Duchess of Brunswick to the Hanoverian court, on a matrimonial mission of her own, to convey informally the assurance that he would never attack his uncle's territories.[88]

With Tsarina Elizabeth still delaying ratification of the St Petersburg agreement, by the end of 1755 the British were in a receptive mood for the Prussian approach. Huddling together for warmth, the two isolated powers came together in the Convention of Westminster, signed in London on 16 January 1756. Its intention was to neutralize Germany for the duration of the colonial war, underway de facto for many months although not yet formally declared. This was emphatically not an alliance. It was a specific agreement by Britain and Prussia not to attack each other and to keep foreign armies away, or in other words to stop the French attacking Hanover and the Russians attacking Prussia. There were two secret articles, the first excluding the

1. A self-portrait by Frederick's father, King Frederick William I, who practised painting as a form of therapy. This dates from 1737 and is marked 'painted by F.W. in his torment'.

2. The hunting lodge Wusterhausen, where King Frederick William I was happiest and his son Frederick most miserable.

3. Frederick (*left*) in 1737, aged twenty-five, and his brothers: Ferdinand (born 1730), August Wilhelm (1720) and Henry (1726).

4. This engraving of 1740 shows the château at Rheinsberg, where Frederick lived from 1736 until his accession in 1740.

5. Schönhausen, the modest château on the outskirts of Berlin assigned by Frederick to his queen after his accession.

6. Francesco Algarotti, the bisexual Venetian connoisseur and man of letters with whom Frederick fell in love in 1739 and whom he made a count when he came to the throne the following year.

7. Carl Friedrich Fechheim's set for Act III of Frederick's opera *Montezuma*.

8. The 'Golden Gallery' in the Charlottenburg Palace, completed in 1746.

9. The garden (south) front of the Potsdam Town Palace.

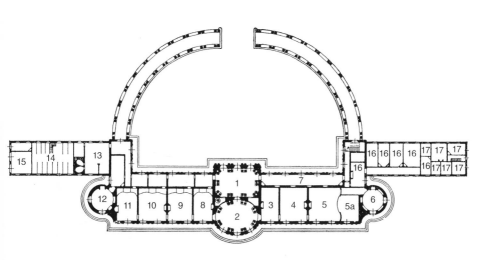

10. Sanssouci ground plan: 1. entrance hall, 2. Marble Hall/formal dining hall, 3. ante-room/small dining room, 4. music room, 5. study and bedroom with alcove for bed (5a), 6. library, 7. picture gallery, 8–12. Guest rooms, 13. kitchen, 14. stables, 15. outbuilding, 16. rooms for secretaries and servants (first room occupied by Fredersdorf), 17. rooms for gardeners and custodian.

11. Sanssouci, terraces and parterre garden, *c*. 1765.

12. Sanssouci, the music room.

13. The free-standing picture gallery next to Sanssouci, not to be confused with the small gallery inside the palace.

14. *The New Palace at Potsdam from the Klausberg*, by Karl Christian Wilhelm Baron (1775). The avenue in the foreground is planted with mulberry trees.

15. Sanssouci, entrance hall, Mercury.

16. Sanssouci, entrance hall, Mars. These two statues faced each other across the entrance hall of Sanssouci, perhaps conveying the message that the time for war was over and that the reign of love should begin.

Austrian Netherlands (which was why 'Germany' was mentioned in the main text, not the Holy Roman Empire), the second obliged Britain to pay £20,000 compensation for Prussian ships which had been seized during the War of the Austrian Succession.[89]

The convention was defensive, not to say pacific, but it turned out to be a major step towards world war. In all European capitals there was consternation; at St Petersburg and Versailles there was fury. For the Russians, the whole point of the subsidy treaty negotiated with the British the previous September had been its anti-Prussian direction. Yet now they found that the British were actually guaranteeing Frederick's security! For the French, it was the last straw, the final proof – if it were needed – that their Prussian 'ally' was a treacherous villain. They also concluded, quite wrongly, that if the British had not been reassured about the security of Hanover, they would have come to terms over America.[90] In truth, the French had only themselves to blame. Five months were allowed to elapse between the appointment of the Duc de Nivernais as ambassador and his actual arrival in Berlin. Knyphausen reported from Versailles on 8 December 1755 that he was still in Paris and showing no signs of departure.[91] He actually arrived in Prussia just a few days before the Convention of Westminster was signed. Had he turned up the previous autumn and offered Frederick the neutralization of Germany, all that followed might well have been avoided.

Great was the satisfaction in Vienna. For months they had been telling the French that Frederick was going to do a deal with the British and had not been believed. Sensibly, they resisted the temptation to rub it in. In private, of course, they hugged themselves – 'the decisive event in the delivery of Austria' crowed Kaunitz. In fact Louis XV proved so indignant at Frederick's betrayal that from being pursued for an alliance, he became the pursuer. On 19 February 1756 Bernis presented Starhemberg with a declaration that France would seek an agreement with Austria to promote the peace of Europe, the salvation of the Catholic religion and the mutual benefit of the two courts.[92] Yet the road to an alliance treaty proved to be bumpy. There were several ministers at Versailles who had misgivings. As Frederick pointed out, there was nothing in the Convention of Westminster to stop the French occupying the Austrian Netherlands, for the province had been deliberately excluded to allow for just such an eventuality.[93] Louis XV was not listening. Once he had made up his mind to abandon Prussia, he showed uncharacteristic resolution in insisting on a full alliance with Austria. Not one of his ministers dared to oppose him.[94] On 1 May 1756 the Treaty of Versailles was signed by Rouillé, Bernis and Starhemberg.

This was the great 'diplomatic revolution', known more temperately in France as *'le renversement des alliances'*. At its core was a mutual guarantee of territory and a commitment to contribute an army 24,000-strong should either country be attacked by a third party. The existing conflict between France and Great Britain was excluded. In other words, it was entirely defensive. However, the French made it clear that they were prepared to proceed to a more aggressive undertaking directed against Prussia. These further negotiations would take time, probably several months, so on 22 May 1756 Kaunitz told his ambassador in St Petersburg to ask the Russians to postpone their planned assault on Prussia until the following spring.[95]

Frederick's initial response was perplexity: 'I do not understand what France and the Court of Vienna expect to gain from all this,' he wrote to Knyphausen on 11 May, telling him to affect an air of complete indifference in the presence of French ministers.[96] On that day he also gave a first audience to the new British ambassador, Andrew Mitchell, and was optimistic, at least in the short term. He assured Mitchell that 'nothing will happen this year, I can answer for it with my head, but I do not pretend to say what may happen the next'. But he also expressed his main anxiety: 'are you sure of the Russians?', to which Mitchell replied: 'The king, my master, thought so.' Frederick could not leave it at that and later in the interview asked again 'whether we were absolutely sure of the Russians?' and was again reassured by Mitchell, more emphatically this time. Frederick certainly wanted to believe that and probably did, for he also talked about the Russian army of 30,000 provided for by the Anglo-Russian agreement of the previous autumn being moved by sea to Pomerania.[97] A week later he was less sure, telling his man in London, Abraham Ludwig Michell, that he had received reliable intelligence that the tsarina was 'more disaffected than ever' about the Convention of Westminster.[98]

In the course of June and July the scales gradually dropped from

Frederick's eyes.[99] Events can be followed on a daily basis through the documents reprinted in volumes twelve and thirteen of the *Politische Correspondenz*. Frederick was receiving good intelligence from two spies, a secretary in the Austrian embassy in Berlin and an official in the Saxon cabinet office in Dresden. In addition, the correspondence from the Dutch envoy in St Petersburg was being intercepted and deciphered in Berlin en route for The Hague.[100] The key information reaching Frederick can be summarized as follows:

17 June: the Russians are assembling 170,000 regular troops and 70,000 irregulars on their western frontier.

'late June': the Austrians are concentrating troops in Bohemia and Moravia.

27 June: the Russians have halted military preparations.

16 July: Austrian troops in Hungary have been ordered to move to Bohemia and Moravia.

21 July: the Russians have stopped mobilizing, but only because the attack has been postponed until 1757.

It is not entirely clear which of these two last pieces of information decided Frederick to launch a pre-emptive strike in 1756.[101] It is certain that by 23 July he had concluded that, as war was certain, '*melius est praevenire quam praeveniri*' (better to forestall than to be forestalled).[102] Action was delayed until late August only to make sure that the Russians and French could not campaign that year. On 13 August he ordered General Prince Ferdinand of Brunswick at Magdeburg to cancel all leave and get ready to march by the 19th. On 26 August he ordered him to cross the Saxon frontier three days later.[103] Mitchell reported to London on 28 August: 'this morning between four and five o'clock, I took leave of the King of Prussia [at Potsdam]. He went immediately to the parade, mounted on horseback, and, after a very short exercise of his troops, put himself at their head and marched directly for Belitz, whence, to-morrow, he will enter the Saxon territory.'[104] This time his 'rendezvous with glory'* would take him to the very

* See above, p. 92.

brink of total disaster and the consideration of suicide and end in muted triumph only after six and a half long years of constant danger and anxiety.

The immediate effect of the invasion of Saxony was the activation of the alliance between France and Austria. Far from wishing to confine their contribution to the 24,000 specified in the Versailles treaty of 1 May 1756, the French proved positively eager to send a major army against Frederick. Partly this was due to a concern not to be seen as the junior partner in the continental war and partly to a wish to reserve a seat at the top negotiating table when the time came to dictate terms to an enemy whose quick defeat was thought to be certain. Sheer folly may have had something to do with it too: a clash between those who demanded resources for a maritime war and those who wanted them for a land war was resolved by the simple expedient of giving both parties what they demanded. It is some measure of the irresponsibility of the French ministers that the controller general of finance, Moras, was told not to point out to the king that the funds were simply not available for all this largesse. Although negotiations took a while, in a second Treaty of Versailles, of 1 May 1757, a force 105,000-strong was promised, plus 4,000 Bavarian and 6,000 Württemberg troops financed by French subsidies. In return, Maria Theresa agreed to cede her possessions in the Netherlands, in part directly to France but with the lion's share going to Louis XV's son-in-law Don Philip. Silesia would return to the Habsburg Monarchy, of course, Magdeburg would go to Saxony and Prussian Pomerania to Sweden if it joined the war. Also mentioned was the possibility of Prussian territory being ceded to the Dutch Republic, the Palatinate and Bavaria. As if all that were not enough, France also undertook to pay to Austria an annual subsidy of 12 million gulden.[105]

In other words, the pebble dislodged by the Duke of Newcastle in the autumn of 1755* had brought crashing down on Frederick the most formidable coalition ever seen in Europe – the three great continental land powers – France, Austria and Russia – aided and abetted by Sweden and most of the princes of the Holy Roman Empire. All Prussia could muster in return was a limited agreement with Great

---

* See above, p. 199.

Britain, which was preoccupied with the colonial struggle. Frederick had only himself to blame. Back in 1742, following the Peace of Breslau, he had told his foreign minister, Podewils, that 'so far as the future security of our new possessions is concerned, I shall rely on a good and large army, a well-stocked treasury and impregnable fortresses, together with some alliances for show to impress the others'. He added that the worst that could ever happen would be an alliance between France and Austria, but even if that were to come about, Prussia would be supported by the Maritime Powers and Russia.[106] In 1756 the worst had indeed happened, except that one of the Maritime Powers – the Dutch Republic – had declared its neutrality, and Russia had become a particularly implacable enemy. Until much too late in the day, Frederick had believed that France and Austria were such natural enemies that they could never combine. But, as Friedrich Meinecke pointed out, even oil and water can mix briefly when shaken hard enough.[107]

It was Frederick who had done the shaking. While it is easy for an armchair statesman to move pieces around as if part of a board-game, it cannot be denied that Frederick made several serious mistakes. So ignorant was he of what was at stake overseas that he consistently failed to understand British and, to a lesser extent, French policy. Typical was his comment to the British ambassador, Andrew Mitchell: 'with regard to the war in America, he said he could not help wondering at the absurdity of both nations to exhaust their strength and wealth for an object that did not appear to him to be worth the while, that he was persuaded by next year both nations would be sick of it'.[108] Unable to appreciate how long were the tentacles of the American connection, he complacently observed in September 1755: 'it's a long way from the Ohio to the Spree'.[109] By completely misreading the likely impact of the Convention of Westminster on Louis XV, he played straight into the hands of Kaunitz. If he could not be held responsible for the ensuing folly of French policymakers, he should certainly have taken the possibility into account. His third error was the mistaken conviction that the British could control Russia with bribes and subsidies.[110] He failed to appreciate the hostility aroused in St Petersburg by his meteoric rise in the first two Silesian Wars and the personal hatred shared by the Tsarina Elizabeth and her first minister Bestuzhev. A fourth error – the overestimate of his military superiority – must await examination in the next chapter.*

In conclusion, three questions suggest themselves. Firstly: could Frederick have kept out of a continental war? He denied it, emphatically and repeatedly. In 1753 his brother and heir-apparent, August Wilhelm, congratulated him on the security he had achieved because 'your enemies fear you as much as your friends respect you'. Frederick replied that this assessment was too optimistic, for war was coming. It might not come soon, but come it would. He added that, because the Prussians were so much better disciplined and so much quicker than their enemies, they would survive – but only if they had as many allies as enemies.[111] Although he was right that war was inevitable, his treatment of the French in general, and the Convention of Westminster in particular, ensured that he would start this third Silesian war in a much less favourable situation than in 1740 or 1744.

Secondly: was the pre-emptive strike a foolish gamble that failed to pay off ('lunatic' in the judgement of one English historian)?[112] Here the answer is less straightforward than it might seem. Certainly it activated the Franco-Austrian alliance and also failed to knock the Austrians out of the war before the Russians could join in. On the other hand, the French were looking for an offensive alliance even before the invasion of Saxony and the lure of the Austrian Netherlands might well have brought them in anyway. In an important letter to William Pitt written in July 1761 when the outcome of the war was still very uncertain, Frederick stated emphatically that he had attacked only because he had conclusive proof that a great conspiracy had been formed against him. Not even the most stupid ruler, he added, would sit back and wait until his enemies had completed their plans to destroy him. Not everything had gone his way in the war, he conceded, but at least he was in possession of a good part of Saxony and he would not be giving that up until the French, Russians and Austrians had returned everything they had taken from him.[113]

Finally, was the war that Frederick began essentially defensive, or did he have a plan to annex further territory? This was a question which greatly exercised nineteenth-century German historians but

* See below, pp. 208–11.

cannot be resolved.[114] That he had raised the desirability of obtaining Saxony in his *Political Testament* of 1752 is not conclusive. The most persuasive answer is that Frederick did not go to war to annex Saxony, West Prussia or Mecklenburg, but to break up the gathering coalition before it could break him. However, if he had achieved total victory, he would undoubtedly have helped himself to as much as he could.[115]

A longer view is needed to identify the source of Frederick's problems. We have to go back to November 1740 and the decision to invade Silesia. This was his original sin, for which no amount of suffering could atone.[116] As we have seen, he did it primarily for the sake of his glory, to make a name for himself, to show he was a man, and moreover a man superior to his father. From that moment he would know no peace. He would always be looking over his shoulder for the retribution he knew was coming. He had barged his way on to the European top table, but would never be able to relax there, as the current occupants were always looking for ways to push him off it again. It was a burden of anxiety he condemned himself to carry for the rest of his life. As Talleyrand observed about Napoleon's murder of the Duc d'Enghien: 'It was worse than a crime, it was a mistake.'

8

The Seven Years War: the First Three Campaigns

1756

In the course of explaining the all-important role of 'friction' in the conduct of war, Carl von Clausewitz wrote: 'Everything in war is very simple, but the simplest thing is difficult.'[1] The war in which he himself was blooded in 1793, as a thirteen-year-old ensign in the Prussian army, was supposed to last only a few months. In the event, it was not until 1815 that the Prussians and their allies could hold a final victory parade in Paris. *Mutatis mutandis*, his idol Frederick made the same discovery in 1756. This was the last of his four errors identified at the end of the last chapter:* an overestimate of his military capability. On 27 August 1756, he told the British envoy that his plan was to pass rapidly through Saxony, where he expected little or no opposition, to cross the mountains into Bohemia and occupy Prague, so that 'as the winter approaches, he can have good quarters in Bohemia, which will disorder the finances at Vienna and perhaps render that court more reasonable'.[2]

Two days later this plan was put into operation. Unfortunately, the Saxons were following a different script. Refusing either to stand and fight, or to capitulate, they retreated to the south to a fortified camp on the river Elbe at Pirna. Had they taken the trouble to stockpile provisions there, they might have kept Frederick waiting for many months, such was the impregnable nature of 'one of the most tactically strong positions in Central Europe'.[3] In his satirical poem *Palladium* of 1750, Frederick had derided the Saxons as a fighting

---

* See above, pp. 205–6.

208

force: when they meet the Prussians in battle, they turn around and display their bottoms, whereupon their merciful opponents tell this 'timid band, soppy and sugary' to run off home and go back to manufacturing porcelain.[4] So it was an unpleasant surprise that they proved able to delay him long enough to tear up the timetable outlined to Mitchell. Memories of the catastrophe of 1744 convinced Frederick that he could not push on regardless, leaving a Saxon army in his rear.* He reached Dresden on 9 September, but there he had to wait. Meanwhile his main enemy had been quicker off the mark than expected. So unaware had Maria Theresa been of Frederick's impending invasion that she was at a country retreat at Holitsch on the Moravian–Hungarian border when news first arrived. Rushing back to Vienna, she set about organizing the necessary mobilization with a sense of urgency not always associated with Habsburg governance.[5] By 20 September, Field Marshal Maximilian Ulysses von Browne and the main army had reached Budin (Budyně nad Ohří) in northern Bohemia, halfway between Prague and Teplitz.[6]

Browne's mission was to rescue the beleaguered Saxons at Pirna. The plan was for the latter to break out across the Elbe to the right (eastern) bank and then march south to Schandau for a rendezvous with the Austrian relieving force. But when the latter moved north on 30 September from Budin, they ran straight into Frederick at Lobositz on the Elbe. Not for the first or last time, his intelligence was defective. Believing he was facing only an Austrian rearguard moving away from him, it was some time before he realized the danger he was facing from a numerically superior foe (c. 28,500 Prussians versus c. 34,000 Austrians).[7] A very sharp battle ensued, with each side suffering around 10 per cent casualties. After inconclusive artillery exchanges and cavalry engagements, once again it was the steadiness of the Prussian infantry which tipped the balance. After the Austrians had been forced back into the little town of Lobositz, which was also set ablaze by Prussian artillery fire, Browne ordered the retreat back to Budin.

As it was the Prussian army which camped on the field of battle, among the dead and dying, it was technically a Prussian victory. Frederick was quick to talk it up, telling his sister Wilhelmine that he had

* See above, p. 108.

put the Austrians to flight, and boasting to Field Marshal Schwerin (in command of a second Prussian army in Silesia) that it was 'the unvarnished truth' that he had defeated an army more than twice as numerous (24,000 to 60,000, he claimed).[8] He told another of his senior officers, Prince Moritz of Anhalt-Dessau, that such had been the feats of arms of his soldiers that he now believed they were capable of anything.[9] But the battle had also shown that the gap between

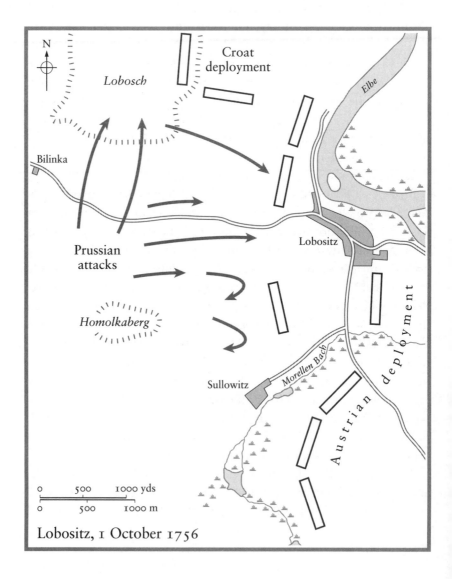

N

Lobosch

Croat
deployment

Elbe

Bilinka

Prussian
attacks

Lobositz

Homolkaberg

Austrian deployment

Morellen Bach

Sullowitz

| 0 | 500 | 1000 yds |
| 0 | 500 | 1000 m |

Lobositz, 1 October 1756

the two armies had narrowed. A Prussian officer named Retzow commented ruefully:

On this occasion Frederick did not come up against the same kind of Austrians he had beaten in four battles in a row. He was not dealing with people like Neipperg or the blustering Prince Charles of Lorraine. He faced Field-Marshal Browne, who had grown grey in the service, and whose talent and experience had raised him to be one of the heroes of his time. He faced an artillery which Prince Liechtenstein had brought to perfection at his own expense. He faced an army which during ten years of peace had attained a greater mastery of the arts of war, and had striven to adopt the methods of its former victors and shape itself according to their discipline.[10]

That Lobositz was not the decisive victory Frederick needed so badly was then shown by Browne's renewed attempt to relieve the beleaguered Saxons. Four days after the battle he took personal command of a detachment 8,000-strong, leading it across the Elbe and up the right bank to Schandau, which he reached on 11 October, the day agreed with the Saxons. Alas, the Saxons had proved unable – or perhaps unwilling – to break out from Pirna. On the 14th their demoralized commanders surrendered.[11] If not the finest hour of the Saxon army, the six-week delay it had enforced on Frederick meant that it was Field Marshal von Browne who spent the winter in Prague. Frederick had to make do with Dresden.

1757

Frederick knew that in 1757 he would be facing invasions by the Russians from the east, the Swedes from the north, the French from the west and the army of the Holy Roman Empire from the south-west. If this mighty coalition's belligerence were to be dampened, the initial failure to knock the Austrians out of the war would have to be made good very quickly. With this in mind, in mid-April 1757 Frederick sent his main field army of some 120,000 down into Bohemia. Anticipating Napoleonic warfare, it marched in four separate units across a hundred-mile front before concentrating just to the north of Prague at

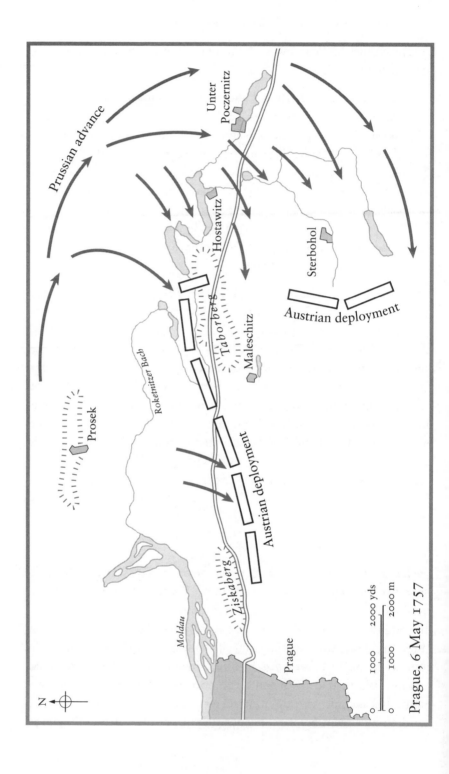

Prague, 6 May 1757

the beginning of May.[12] Displaying once again his taste for classical parallels, Frederick told his brother Prince Henry that a victory on the White Mountain would prove as decisive for the fate of present-day empires as Caesar's defeat of Pompey at Pharsalus in 48 BC had been for Rome.[13]

Fortune soon claimed the hostage. Frederick got his victory, on 6 May, but it left a great deal to be desired. The Battle of Prague was such a muddled affair that it has challenged even the most lucid of military historians.[14] Coherent direction on both sides was impeded by the death or wounding of several senior officers. Frederick himself was repeatedly incapacitated by the effects of food poisoning, Field Marshal Schwerin was blown apart while leading his regiment in a counterattack and another senior commander, General Winterfeldt, was seriously wounded. On the Austrian side, Field Marshal Browne had his leg shattered and Prince Charles of Lorraine suffered some sort of a seizure that rendered him unconscious. Ironically, it was the very success of what proved to be Browne's last charge that opened the way for other Prussian units to take the Austrians in the flank.[15] The initiatives taken at battalion level by colonels and majors showed that the Prussian army was anything but the automaton of legend.[16] Casualties on both sides were horrendous, so much so that the battle became a byword for slaughter, commemorated in ballads and plays. Two days later the Prussians counted 3,099 dead, 8,208 wounded (many of whom died later) and 1,657 missing.[17] Even that dreadful toll was incomplete and continued to grow as the dust of battle settled. Their enemy had lost almost as many, although a significant proportion were prisoners of war.[18]

Although dejected, the Austrians once again showed impressive resilience.[19] They still commanded superior human resources. The garrison inside Prague was now some 46,000 strong, swollen by the survivors of the battle, while to the south-east, another army was being assembled by Marshal Daun. By 12 June it numbered around 55,000 and was on the move. Meanwhile, Frederick was finding that he lacked both the necessary manpower and the firepower to capture Prague, which also proved to be much better provisioned than he had expected. On 13 June he moved off to counter Daun's advance. The two armies clashed at Kolin near the river Elbe five days later. If

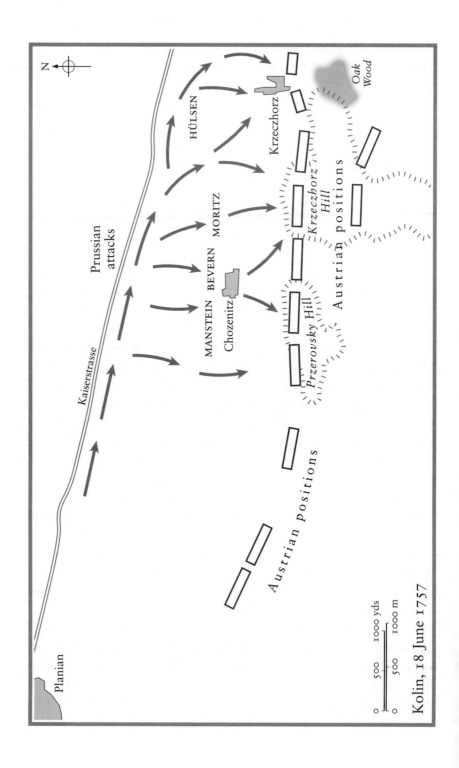

N

Planian

Kaiserstrasse

Prussian
attacks

HÜLSEN

MANSTEIN BEVERN MORITZ

Chozenitz

Krzeczhorz

Oak
Wood

Krzeczhorz
Hill

Przerovsky Hill

Austrian positions

Austrian positions

0   500   1000 yds
0   500   1000 m

Kolin, 18 June 1757

anything, this battle was even more bewildering in its twists and turns than its predecessor. But the result was clear enough. The defeat of the Prussian army was complete, bloody and momentous. Of the infantry, 8,755 were killed or went missing and 3,568 were wounded; of the cavalry, 1,450 men and 1,667 horses were killed: a horrifying total representing about 40 per cent of the pre-battle strength of 34,000. Austrian casualties were appreciably fewer at 8,114 (1,002 dead, 5,472 wounded and 1,640 missing) or 15 per cent of their pre-battle strength of 54,000. The Austrians buried 6,500 Prussians and took 5,380 prisoners.[20]

No wonder that the glad tidings were received in Vienna with ecstatic celebrations at every level of society. A *Te Deum* was offered up to the God of Battles, while gifts and titles were showered down on his warriors. The empress created the eponymous Order of Maria Theresa to celebrate the victory and conferred its first Grand Cross on Daun.[21] The court poet, Metastasio, wrote an allegorical work in which Kyllene (Saxony) dreams how Atalanta (Maria Theresa) kills the Calydonian Boar (Frederick) and together with Euadne (Russia) and Tegea (France) sets off for a joyful hunt.[22] In Rome, Pope Benedict XIV expressed his 'indescribable jubilation'.[23] In Berlin, on the other hand, Count Lehndorff found everyone in tears, for seventeen years of unbroken success had spoilt them all.[24] In truth, Frederick had lost a lot more than a battle. In just a few hours, his superhuman reputation had collapsed. The Austrian cavalryman Jacob de Cognazo wrote that everyone could now see that the Prussians could be made to flee and Frederick could be beaten. Until that moment, the very appearance of the Prussian infantry had been enough to spread panic through the Austrian ranks.[25]

What had gone wrong? In his own accounts, Frederick blamed his subordinate commanders, especially Manstein, the Duke of Bevern and Prince Moritz of Anhalt-Dessau, for not carrying out his orders,[26] This was the view faithfully repeated by the Prussophile historians of the nineteenth century,[27] but a careful reworking of all the numerous accounts, official and private, revealed that the responsibility was his alone. When trying to outflank the Austrian position, Frederick had suddenly and fatally ordered the division commanded by Prince Moritz of Anhalt-Dessau to form a line and attack the enemy position frontally. Overruled by his king, the prince commented: 'now the battle is lost!' In fact, the battle was not finally lost for some hours to come, but that change of heart probably made eventual victory impossible. At every stage subsequently, the Prussians found their enemy making the most of superior numbers and a superior defensive position.[28] Frederick was more candid in a letter he wrote to Marshal Keith the day after the battle, in which he conceded that he had tried to do too much with too few, that the Austrians had defended their well-chosen positions tenaciously and that their artillery, as recently reformed by Prince Liechtenstein, had proved too effective. He ended on a characteristically misogynistic note: 'Fortune has turned her back on me. She has it in for me; she is a woman, and I am not that way inclined.'[29] He also commented that his brother Henry had 'performed miracles', adding that he trembled for him because he was 'too brave'. That was a compliment not returned by Prince Henry, who crowed in a letter to their sister Amalia: 'At last Phaeton has crashed!'[30]

Frederick had landed with such a bump that for a while he did not know what to do with himself. Dejected and disorientated, he told Prince Henry to make arrangements for lifting the siege of Prague and the retreat of what remained of his army to the north. He tried to put a brave face on it, telling Keith in the letter just quoted that success bred overconfidence and they would do better next time. 'Don't you know that every man must have his setbacks, and it seems that I shall have mine' was another rueful comment, made to an officer immediately after the battle.[31] But this was a setback of potentially catastrophic dimensions, for it completely disrupted his strategy. Reinvigorated by their victory, the Austrians now prepared to finish him off. Encouraged by this revelation that Frederick was not invincible, all his other enemies rushed to be in at the death and to claim their share of the spoils.[32] Looking back on events when he wrote his *Political Testament* of 1768, Frederick stated that if he had won the battle of Kolin, the Austrian army in Prague would have had to capitulate, a French army would not have crossed the Rhine, the Russians would have stayed at home and Austria would have had to make peace on Prussian terms.[33]

In the event, the opposites of all those things happened, and with them the very nature of the war was transformed. Put most simply, a war of movement became a war of attrition. As Theodor Schieder observed, Kolin was to Frederick what the Marne was to the Kaiser in 1914 or Moscow to Hitler in 1941.[34] In its aftermath, one bit of bad news rapidly followed another. On 23 July the Austrians advanced to Zittau in Saxony and destroyed a large Prussian depot. Three days later a French army commanded by Marshal d'Estrées defeated a Hanoverian and Hessian army commanded by George II's son, the Duke of Cumberland, at Hastenbeck near Hamelin on the river Weser. After much diplomatic wrangling, this led to the conclusion of the Convention of Kloster Zeven on 10 September. Had it been implemented, it would have disbanded the allied army, withdrawn the British from the continental war and opened up Frederick's western flank. By that time a large Russian army under Marshal Apraksin had moved into East Prussia and brushed aside a much smaller Prussian army at Gross-Jägerndorf on 30 August. More bad news followed. On 7 September, at Moys, to the east of Görlitz, a Prussian corps of 10,000 was crushed by a larger Austrian force under General Nádasti, the most serious loss being General Hans Karl von Winterfeldt, whose death left Frederick distraught.[35] A week later the Swedes crossed the Prussian frontier and headed south. To emphasize Prussia's fragility, on 16 October an Austrian flying corps of 3,400 under General Hadick moved into a virtually undefended Berlin. They left the next day but not before extracting a stiff ransom.[36]

Frederick's only chance was to prevent the French and the Austrians uniting their armies, so he hurried west to meet the former, commanded by the Prince de Soubise. On 4 November he found them at Mücheln, some twenty-five kilometres west of Leipzig. They were 30,200-strong, an imposing total swelled further by 10,900 imperial troops under the command of Prince Joseph Friedrich of Saxony-Hildburghausen. Although outnumbered almost two-to-one, Frederick was anxious for a battle and took up position facing west between the villages of Bedra and Rossbach about four kilometres from the French camp. The relative strengths of the two armies were as follows:

	Infantry	Cavalry	Total	Artillery
Prussians	16,600	5,400	22,000	79
French	33,770	7,340	41,110	114[37]

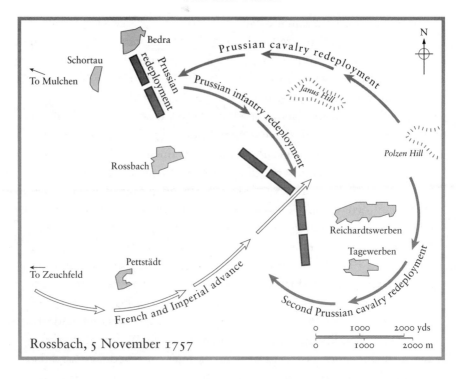

Rossbach, 5 November 1757

At this point, both sides miscalculated. Prince Joseph Friedrich concluded that Frederick was trying to avoid an engagement and
persuaded his reluctant superior, Soubise, to launch an attack on the
following day. Early on 5 November, the French duly marched south,
with the intention of wheeling to the east and taking the Prussians in
their flank. For his part, Frederick believed that the French would try
to escape, a conclusion which was strengthened by the news that they
had struck camp and were moving off to the south. It was only after
they had turned east and had marched several kilometres in this new
direction that his scepticism could be overcome by increasingly anxious staff officers. Now the Prussians did move quickly, lucky that the
painfully slow French advance was giving them the opportunity to
make amends. It was now three in the afternoon. Taking advantage of
the cover provided by a long ridge, the Prussian cavalry commanded
by General von Seydlitz was able to move first east and then south
to confront their opposite numbers head-on. Their first charge was
stoutly resisted by a force of Austrian cuirassiers, allowing the French

cavalry to be rushed up in support, but a renewed charge by Seydlitz's reserves proved irresistible.

Still in marching order, the French and imperial infantry had already been unnerved by a bombardment from the Prussian artillery positioned above them to the north-east on the Janus Hill by the commander of the left wing, Frederick's brother Prince Henry.[38] The sight of their cavalry being worsted completed their demoralization. So when the dreaded Prussian infantry advanced into view in battle order, there was little resistance. The imperial troops simply dropped their weapons and ran. Some of their French comrades stayed long enough to discharge their weapons but they too were soon swept away in headlong flight. It was at this point that Seydlitz's cavalry charged again from the south, to complete the rout. Only the mercifully quick onset of nightfall put an end to the slaughter. So quick, easy and complete was the Prussian victory that most of the infantry never even had to fire. 'That was a tame battle!' exclaimed Frederick in a letter to his sister Wilhelmine, written immediately after it was over.[39] To d'Argens he wrote that they had taken prisoner eight French generals, 260 officers and 6,000 soldiers at the cost of one colonel, two other officers and sixty-seven soldiers killed and 223 wounded.[40]

It was a famous victory.[41] Everything had gone wrong at Kolin; everything went right at Rossbach. A major difference, of course, lay in the relative calibre of Frederick's opponents. At Kolin he had faced battle-hardened Austrians, supported by Saxons seeking revenge for the humiliations inflicted on them by the Prussians during the Second Silesian War. At a crucial stage in the battle, the Saxon cavalry had charged screaming: 'This is for Striegau!', referring to their defeat at Hohenfriedberg in 1745.[42] At Rossbach, the French were exhausted after a long march across Germany and disorganized by the persistent looting for which they had become notorious. The Comte de Saint-Germain, who had the thankless task of commanding the rearguard, wrote to a friend in Paris:

No doubt you, like me, were able to predict the Rossbach disaster five months ago. Never has there been such a defective army, and the first cannon-shot determined our rout and humiliation. I am leading a gang of robbers, of murderers fit only for the gallows, who run away at the sound of the first gunshot and who are always ready to mutiny. The King has the worst infantry under the sun, and the worst-disciplined – there is just nothing to be done with troops such as these.[43]

As for the imperial troops, they were a ragtag collection from many different principalities of the Holy Roman Empire. The commander reported to Maria Theresa's husband, the Emperor Francis, that everything about them was defective: training, administration, armaments, equipment, pay, logistics, discipline and leadership – everything![44]

Moreover, many if not most of them believed they were fighting for the wrong side. So detested were the French, especially after their misbehaviour on the march east, that cooperation between the two allies was always difficult.[45] This hostility was especially marked among Protestants: at both Stuttgart and Nuremberg there was violent resistance when attempts were made to send contingents off to fight Prussia.[46] Georg Jakob Gegel recalled that Frederick's manifesto depicting the war as a confessional struggle had made an impact in south-west Germany: 'in Stuttgart it made such a powerful impression on the common people that everywhere it was read with the same sort of veneration as was the Bible'. He added that the young Württembergers detailed to march off in support of the French were told in no uncertain fashion that they could not fight with a clear conscience against Frederick, the protector of the Protestant faith.[47] Reluctance to fight Prussia was not peculiar to Protestants, however. The secretary of the imperial Field Marshal Georg Wilhelm of Hessen-Darmstadt reported from Fürth (near Nuremberg) on 11 July 1757 that almost all the imperial soldiers, no matter what their confession or where they came from, were pro-Prussian and told anyone who would listen that they would not fight against Frederick.[48] The tide of Francophobe derision that washed through the German public sphere after Rossbach showed that this was a current that ran broad and deep.[49]

When Frederick wrote to his sister Wilhelmine about his victory, he added that he could now go to his grave in peace because the reputation and honour of his people had been saved.[50] That was wishful thinking. True, he never again had to face a direct threat from the French. Dealing with them could be left to his brother-in-law

Ferdinand, Duke of Brunswick, who had commanded the right wing at Rossbach and was now sent to replace the hapless Duke of Cumberland as commander of the British-financed army on the western front. The Russians too had retreated, withdrawing at the end of October into winter quarters in Livonia and Courland. In the north, a modest Prussian force of ten militia battalions, a squadron of hussars and a cavalry unit recruited from foresters and gamekeepers had proved sufficient to keep the unenthusiastic Swedes in check. 'They were brave once, but now their time is past' was the Russian General Saltykov's dismissive comment on his Swedish allies.[51] By the end of 1757 they had been pushed back into Swedish Pomerania.[52] But the Austrians were still very much a danger, a point they rubbed home just a week after Rossbach when they captured the important Silesian fortress at Schweidnitz, together with 180 artillery pieces and more than 6,000 prisoners of war – men Frederick could ill afford to lose. That in turn opened their way to Breslau, which surrendered in turn on 24 November, after a sharp engagement that cost the Prussians 9,000 more casualties in dead, wounded and prisoners.[53] The ultimate Austrian goal of the reconquest of Silesia seemed to have been reached at last.

Winter had now arrived. The days were short, the weather freezing. By rights, all combatants should have gone into winter quarters. But Frederick knew that would have been tantamount to conceding defeat. In his *History of the Seven Years War*, he wrote: 'under these circumstances, time was of all things the most precious: not a moment must be lost, the Austrians must incessantly be attacked, however great the hazard, and expelled from Silesia, or the province given up eternally'.[54] He now led the victors of Rossbach from Leipzig to Silesia, a distance of some 300 kilometres as the crow flies, in twelve days. Reaching Parchwitz on the western bank of the Oder at the end of November, he was joined during the next few days by the demoralized remnants of the army that been repeatedly battered by the Austrians during the autumn campaign in Silesia. By 4 December he had assembled an army of around 35,000 and moved south towards Breslau. On the same day, the Austrian army, commanded by the emperor's brother, Prince Charles of Lorraine, advanced north from the city.[55]

They met at Leuthen on the following day. The battle that ensued was

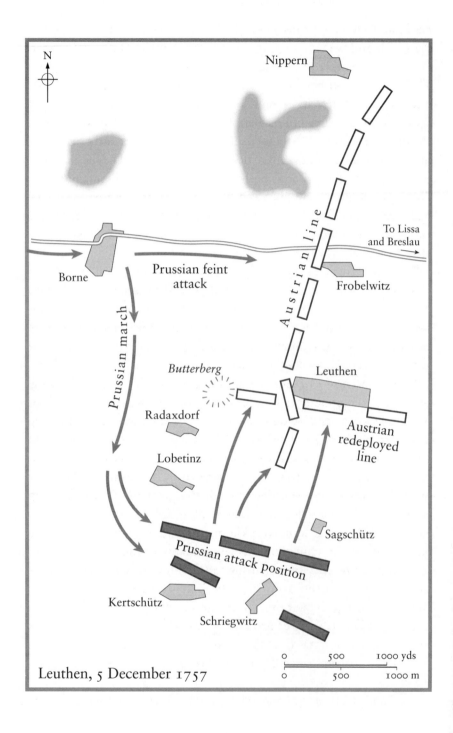

N

Nippern

Austrian line

To Lissa
and Breslau

Borne

Prussian feint
attack

Frobelwitz

Prussian march

Butterberg

Leuthen

Radaxdorf

Austrian
redeployed
line

Lobetinz

Sagschütz

Prussian attack position

Kertschütz

Schriegwitz

0	500	1000 yds
0	500	1000 m

Leuthen, 5 December 1757

undoubtedly Frederick's finest hour.[56] This was a verdict anticipated by no less an authority than Napoleon: 'This Battle is a masterpiece of movements, of manoeuvres and of resolution; enough to immortalise Friedrich, and rank him among the greatest Generals. Manifests, in the highest degree, both his moral qualities and his military.'[57] Everything went right for him. The enemy cooperated by extending their line across two kilometres. The terrain allowed him to move his battalions and squadrons around unnoticed. As the battlefield had been the site of Prussian manoeuvres in the past, Frederick and his subordinate generals knew its every inch and so the chance of orders being misunderstood (a notorious source of problems on other occasions) was reduced if not eliminated. On at least three crucial moments during the battle, subordinates took initiatives which turned the tide the Prussians' way. All three arms – infantry, cavalry, artillery – cooperated effectively.[58]

It was just as well that Frederick enjoyed all these advantages, for he had seriously underestimated the size of the Austrian army. His belief that numbers were about equal once again exposed his defective intelligence. In reality, the 35,000 Prussians were facing around 65,000 Austrians.[59] The disparity was overcome by tactical surprise. As the map demonstrates, instead of attacking the Austrian right, as they expected, he turned a sizeable part of his army to his own right, marched them unnoticed a mile to the south and then turned them again to take the Austrians in the flank. That battle-winning attack was given decisive momentum by the use of the 'oblique order of battle', with a staggered line of infantry battalions extending to the left at fifty-pace intervals. It was given powerful assistance by the mobile field artillery positioned first on the Glanz-Berg, then on the Judenberg and finally on the Butter-Berg. The *coup de grâce* was delivered by General von Driesen's cavalry. As at Rossbach, the victory was complete, all the better savoured for being won against a well-motivated army flushed with recent success. Prussian casualties totalled 6,382, the majority being wounded. The Austrians lost 22,000 (the majority of them – 12,000 – prisoners), including seventeen generals dead or wounded, 116 pieces of artillery and fifty-one standards.[60]

Although Rossbach had serious long-term consequences for the French, it had done little for Frederick. Leuthen was different, although he himself described it as only a palliative.[61] Had he lost, it would have been all over. In the event, Prince Charles took his army out of Silesia back to Bohemia, Breslau surrendered on 21 December and Liegnitz a week later. In Vienna there was consternation at this sudden change in the fortunes of war. The Venetian ambassador, Ruzzini, reported: 'every face is marked by anguish and panic, and the general dismay is much more intense than it was back in May following the defeat at Prague'.[62] For the Prussians, this stunning victory despite the numerical odds gave birth to an enduring legend. In one of his most sonorous passages, Thomas Carlyle related the march of the Prussians down the road to Lissa following the battle:

> Thick darkness; silence; tramp, tramp: a Prussian grenadier broke out, with solemn tenor voice again, into Church-Music; a known Church-Hymn, of the homely Te Deum kind; in which five-and-twenty thousand other voices, and all the regimental bands, soon join:
>
> > Now thank we all our God,
> > With heart and hands and voices,
> > Who wondrous things has done,
> > In whom this world rejoices.
>
> And thus they advance; melodious, far-sounding, through the hollow Night, once more in a highly remarkable manner. A pious people, of right Teutsch stuff, tender though stout; and except perhaps for Oliver Cromwell's handful of Ironsides, probably the most perfect soldiers ever seen hitherto.[63]

Originally intended as a simple domestic thanksgiving at the end of a meal, 'Now thank we all our God' was henceforth elevated into a triumphalist anthem and became known as 'The Leuthen Chorale'.[64] Whenever Prussian or (later) German armies triumphed, it was roared out on the battlefield by the victorious survivors.[65]

1758

At the end of 1757, however, Frederick was not in a triumphalist mood (not that he would ever have relished singing a Christian hymn). On 19 December he told d'Argens that Leuthen had been 'a sticking-plaster on my wounds; but it has not healed everything'.[66] On the home front too, the mood was sombre. Leuthen and the recapture of Breslau, recorded Count Lehndorff, meant that everything in Silesia was back on a secure footing but that did not prevent the more far-sighted Berliners from yearning for a quick peace before the weight of the enemy coalition could crush them.[67] Of that coalition's three main components, the French were to prove the least threatening. The enterprising Ferdinand of Brunswick took the fight to them early, unleashing a campaign in mid-February 1758 which in the space of just six weeks sent them reeling back 300 kilometres across western Germany to the Rhine and beyond. In the process they lost about a third of their army or about 26,000 to desertion, disease or capture. Another French advance was abruptly terminated by Ferdinand's army at Krefeld on 23 June, after which they were again driven back across the Rhine and the Lahn.[68] From Pomerania the Swedes moved south again and even reached Fehrbellin, but once again turned tail when confronted by even a modest Prussian force – just 5,000 on this occasion.[69] It was from the east that a much more dangerous enemy loomed. In 1757 the Russians had overwhelmed a small Prussian army at Gross-Jägerndorf in East Prussia at the end of August, but very soon afterwards had retreated east into winter quarters. As Frederick recorded derisively in his *History of the Seven Years War*, they had won a battle, 'yet had retreated as if they had been vanquished'.[70]

Although the Russians had not gone far away, to their winter quarters in Courland and Livonia, Frederick could assume that it would take them many months before they reached the Prussian heartland. So his strategy for the new year was essentially the same as the previous years: strike hard and fast at Austria. This time, however, the main thrust was moved to the east. Instead of invading Bohemia from Saxony, this time he invaded Moravia from Silesia. The first target was Olmütz (Olomouc), where he hoped to bring the Austrians to battle, inflict a decisive defeat in the style of Leuthen and then advance south to Vienna. At first all went well. After a bit of unfinished business from the previous years was cleared up when Schweidnitz was taken on 18 April after a lengthy siege, the Austrian frontier was crossed on 29 April and Olmütz reached on 3 May.[71] It was the last fortress on the road to the Austrian capital. But then all the forms of friction that made warfare such an inexact science began to intervene. The most problematic was literal: the friction between wheel and rutted track that impeded delivery of everything the army needed. The necessary siege artillery did not arrive until 20 May and the bombardment could not begin until the last day of the month.[72]

Friction was also applied by the Austrians, once again fatally underestimated by Frederick. Swiftly recovering from the dejection caused by the Leuthen disaster, Maria Theresa and her ministers had taken vigorous action to repair the damage. Recruits were raised, especially from Hungary and Bohemia; a general staff was created with Count Franz Moritz Lacy as chief of staff; and Prince Charles of Lorraine was replaced as commander-in-chief by the cautious but wily Count Leopold Joseph von Daun.[73] A sign of the times was the argument used by the Emperor Francis when telling his brother he would have to resign: the force of public opinion was against him. It is some indication of the different military cultures prevailing in Prussia and Austria that Prince Charles had to lose five major battles (Chotusitz, Hohenfriedberg, Soor, Prague and Leuthen) before he could be sacked, whereas Frederick broke his brother August Wilhelm after just one botched retreat.

Back in Olmütz, Frederick was making the unhappy discovery that the Austrians could be just as resolute as his own troops when it came to defending hearth and home. More so, in fact. Unlike the spineless Prussians who had surrendered Breslau the previous November, the local Austrian commander, General Marschall, had delivered an object lesson in how to resist a siege: reinforcing his garrison, stocking up on vital supplies, reducing the civilian population, demolishing the suburbs, and so on. He was helped by Daun, who took advantage of a gap in the Prussian besieging force to send fresh supplies and 1,200 reinforcements into the garrison. The most potent Austrian ally, however, proved to be logistics. Everything the Prussian siege effort needed had to be transported across the hills and through the forests that separated Olmütz from their base at Troppau (Opava). This was territory ideally suited to the excellent light troops which formed the single most effective arm of the Austrian army and they duly took advantage. The decisive blow was struck on 30 June when a massive

Prussian convoy strung out along many kilometres was ambushed at Domstadl by units led by Daun's most enterprising commanders – Janus, Laudon and Ziskowitz. In the chaos that followed, most of the conscripted Moravian peasants fled into the forests, taking their horses and oxen and – where possible – their carts with them. The Prussians gave a good account of themselves, but could not prevent the convoy dispersing in disorder. Of the more than 4,000 wagons that set out from Troppau, only some 250 eventually arrived at Olmütz.[74]

On the day before the disaster at Domstadl, Frederick had written to General Keith that he expected the convoy to arrive and then to get his long-desired battle with Daun.[75] Two days later he had to tell him that '*ce terrible contretemps*' meant that the siege would have to be lifted and the retreat back to Silesia begun.[76] Unlike the retreat from Bohemia in 1744,* this proved to be an orderly withdrawal and moreover one which allowed occasional counter-thrusts at the pursuing Austrians. Nathaniel Wraxall found the appropriate metaphor: 'he retired; but it was the retreat of the lion, who turns upon his pursuers. Frustrated, not vanquished; formidable even in defeat; carrying with him all his artillery and baggage, he left to Daun little more than a negative triumph.'[77] Nevertheless, there could be no doubt that the campaign had failed. It also proved to be Frederick's final attempt to invade the Habsburg Monarchy.[78] Present at Olmütz on the day the siege was abandoned was Prince Charles Joseph de Ligne, a junior officer in his father's Austrian regiment who had already seen action at Kolin and Leuthen.[79] He expressed surprise that a siege should ever have been attempted, given that the besieged could always be reinforced and resupplied. He was also sharply critical of the manner in which Frederick had conducted the siege.[80]

It was now time for Frederick to turn his attention to the north-east. There the situation had been developing at its usual slow pace, albeit after an unusually quick start. The new Russian commander, Count Villim Villimovich Fermor, who had replaced Apraksin the previous October, was under orders to start early. In the middle of January 1758 a corps under Count Nicolai Petrovich Rumyantsev crossed the

* See above, pp. 108–9.

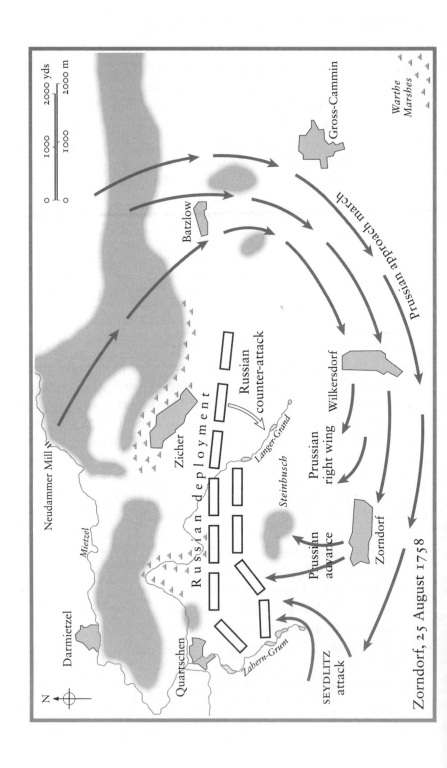

Zorndorf, 25 August 1758

Prussian frontier, took Tilsit and advanced towards Königsberg. The weak Prussian forces in the province fell back on the Vistula without offering resistance. As a result, Fermor was able to move his troops some 200 kilometres in little more than a week.[81] Underestimating the likely strength of the Russian effort in 1758, Frederick had transferred his senior commander in East Prussia, Lehwaldt, together with most of his corps, to Pomerania to deal with the Swedes.[82] It was just as well for him that after their first headlong rush, the Russians reverted to their old pace. By 1 July they had only got as far as Posen and it was not until the middle of August that they got across Poland and reached the river Oder at Küstrin.

It was there, just to the north of the town, at the village of Zorndorf, that Frederick confronted them on 25 August. His army had covered 250 kilometres in twelve days, ten of marching and two of resting, or an average of twenty kilometres per day, a truly impressive feat. The battle which followed had several distinguishing features: it was very protracted, lasting all day for a total of ten hours; it was exceptionally murderous, with the Russians suffering 42 per cent casualties and the Prussians 35 per cent (31,000 of the 80,000 soldiers engaged on both sides were casualties); it was more than usually confused, with the two armies swivelling 180 degrees, so that the day ended with each occupying the other's original position; and it was also more than usually decentralized, with both commanders losing control of events.[83] The modest Prussian numerical inferiority (37,000 to 44,500) was modified by superior artillery, the usual steadfast infantry performance and the timely cavalry charges directed at crucial moments by General von Seydlitz. Modified but not overcome, for the outcome of the battle was really a bloody draw. A *Te Deum* was sung in both Berlin and St Petersburg.[84] The Russian infantry in particular proved to be every bit as resolute as their opponents. The Saxon artillery captain Johann Gottlieb Tielke, who had been seconded to the Russian army, recorded admiringly that

> The extraordinary steadiness and intrepidity of the Russians on this occasion is not to be described; it surpassed everything that one has heard of the bravest troops. Although the Prussian balls mowed down whole ranks, yet not a man discovered any symptoms of unsteadiness,

or inclination to give way, and the openings in the first line were instantly filled up from the second or the reserve.[85]

Two further features of the battle deserve comment. The first was the exceptional tenacity, not to say ferocity, displayed by the rank-and-file on both sides. Contemporary observers all agreed that the Prussians were fired up by the devastation inflicted on the region by the Russians.[86] As one combatant recorded:

> We were all smouldering with anger over the destruction of Küstrin and the sufferings of the poor country people. The enemy had wasted and destroyed everything, and even broken into churches and robbed them. The poor farmers were scattered over the woods and fields like sheep with their wives and children. The children were crying for bread, so we gave them most of our rations, for which they brought us water in return. Many of the people had been horribly injured or even killed by the Cossacks' whips.[87]

The second is that the thousands of Russians and Prussians died needlessly. There is general agreement among military historians that Frederick could have achieved his objective – sending the Russians home – by capturing the wagon park they had carelessly left exposed at Gross-Kammin (see map).[88] He had not one but three golden opportunities to do this, the last of them actually during the battle, but he preferred to seek a military victory.[89] Writing about the episode in his *History of the Seven Years War* he conceded: 'The enemy had left their heavy baggage under a small escort between this village [Batzlow] and Cammin. Had the king been in less haste, he might easily have taken it, and have obliged the Russians by some marches to quit the country; but decision was necessary and every thing was to be hoped.'[90]

The Russians had had enough. Quite apart from the blood-letting at Zorndorf, they had so devastated the surrounding countryside that food and fodder had been exhausted. So Fermor took his army back east to Landsberg. His reluctance to resume the offensive was stiffened by a dispute with the Austrian representative in his camp, St André. While the latter doubted the Russian commander's competence and goodwill, Fermor was understandably enraged that the

Austrians had not sent even an auxiliary corps to his assistance.[91] Instead, they were preparing for a decisive thrust against the weak Prussian army Frederick had left behind in Saxony under the command of his brother Prince Henry. But, as usual, they were moving much too slowly. All they managed to achieve during Frederick's absence in the north was the capture of the minor fortress of Sonnenstein and its Prussian garrison of 1,400, and even that modest feat was achieved by imperial, not Austrian, forces. Just as Marshal Daun was preparing to move against Prince Henry, news reached him that Frederick had returned to Saxony and on 11 September had concentrated his forces once more around Dresden. That was enough to persuade Daun to stay on the defensive in a fortified camp at Stolpen to the east of Dresden. His timidity (he called it caution) earned him a sharp rebuke from an impatient Maria Theresa in Vienna.[92]

But it was Daun who had the last laugh. Throughout September, an increasingly frustrated Frederick tried to get round him to threaten his eastern supply lines. Daun did eventually move from Stolpen, but only to take up another defensive position at Kittlitz near Bautzen, which he reached on 7 October. Frederick now made the catastrophic mistake of underestimating the Austrian capacity for sudden action. He formed his own camp around the village of Hochkirch but in such an extended fashion as to invite an attack. Here, on 14 October, he was well and truly caught napping. Once again his intelligence had proved lamentably inadequate. Ably advised by his enterprising chief of staff, Count Lacy, as dawn broke Daun launched an attack which took full advantage of his massive numerical superiority (c. 80,000 to 36,000). Anxious Prussian staff officers had difficulty in getting Frederick out of bed and even then he dismissed the sounds of combat as the usual early-morning skirmishing with which the Croatians liked to start the day. It was his generals who tried to organize resistance. It said a good deal for the fabled discipline of the Prussian rank-and-file that they did not collapse altogether. Even so, the slaughter was terrible. One of the streets in Hochkirch was known from then on as 'Blood Alley', after the river of blood that poured down the gutters from bodies so densely packed together that the dead could not fall down.[93] By 10 a.m. it was all over. The Prussian survivors had withdrawn to the north-west, leaving behind more than 9,000 comrades.

The retreat was organized by Zieten and Seydlitz, who had ignored Frederick's instructions and had prudently kept their horses saddled all night.[94]

The casualties included Frederick's brother-in-law Duke Friedrich Franz of Brunswick (decapitated by a cannon-ball), General Geist, Prince Moritz of Anhalt-Dessau (who never recovered from his wounds sufficiently to return to service) and – the cruellest of all – his close friend Field Marshal James Keith. This haemorrhage of senior commanders was not uncommon but was certainly serious. Frederick had lost four dead at Lobositz, four at Prague, one each at Kolin and Moys, three at Breslau, two at Leuthen, three at Zorndorf and now three more at Hochkirch.[95] Requiring his generals to set personal examples of courage undoubtedly inspired their subordinates but also ensured that this was an asset that necessarily had to yield diminishing returns. The same rate of attrition applied further down the officer corps, which had lost almost half its strength in the first three campaigns.[96]

Frederick was badly shaken by Hochkirch, not so much by the military consequences, for Daun failed to follow up his brilliant success, as by the knowledge that he had been solely to blame for the defeat. The usually admiring British envoy Andrew Mitchell explained it by reference to 'the very great contempt he had of the enemy, and the unwillingness I have long observed in him to give any degree of credit to intelligence that is not agreeable to his own imaginations'.[97] Frederick took refuge in literature. At three o'clock in the afternoon on the same day as the battle, he summoned his librarian-cum-personal-assistant Henri de Catt. Not surprisingly, a trembling de Catt entered the room with deep apprehension. Frederick approached declaiming a speech by the eponymous hero of Racine's *Mithridate*, one of the many he knew off by heart. The words were uncannily appropriate:

> So, after one
> Whole year, although thou seest me here again, Arbates –
> No more the fortune-favoured Mithridates,
> Who in the balances of destiny
> Was weighed with Rome for the world's mastery,
> Which long was doubtful. I have met defeat!
> Alert was Pompey, his success complete,

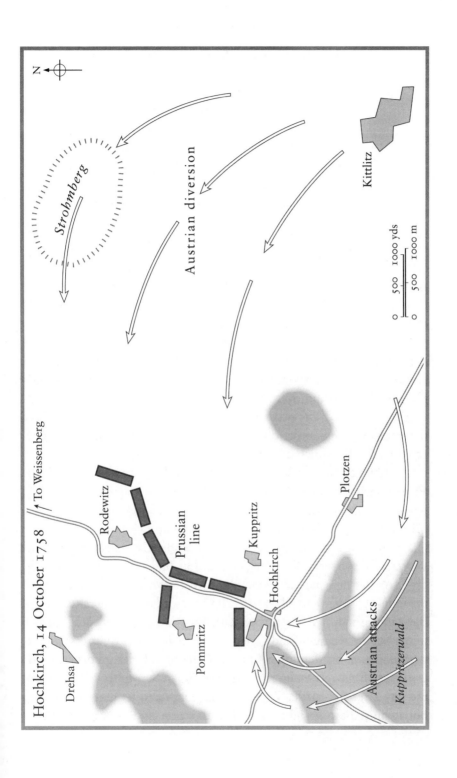

Hochkirch, 14 October 1758

To Weissenberg

Strohmberg

Austrian diversion

Kittlitz

Rodewitz

Prussian line

Drehsa

Pommritz

Kuppritz

Hochkirch

Plotzen

Austrian attacks

Kuppritzerwald

N

0   500   1000 yds
0   500   1000 m

In darkness which for courage left scant room.
Our soldiers were half-clad amid night's gloom,
Their ranks ill formed, ill maintained everywhere,
By their confusion making worse their fear,
Turning their weapons 'gainst each other, cries
Re-echoing from the rocks and from the skies –
With all such horrors of a midnight fray,
What good was valour? Panic held full sway.
Some died, flight saved the rest, and I no doubt
Owed my life solely in the general rout,
To the report of my own death, which I
Had spread.[98]

At the words 'I have met defeat!' he broke off, visibly agitated. He then lamented the death of Keith especially, praising his exploits and character, as tears streamed down his face.[99]

His grief intensified when he learned two days later that his beloved sister Wilhelmine had died on the day of the battle. Behind drawn curtains, Frederick sought consolation in books such as Bossuet's *Funeral Orations* and '*un volume de Young*' (probably Edward Young's *Night Thoughts*).[100] It was also on this occasion that he showed Catt the small oval tin he wore on a chain around his neck, containing eighteen opium pills, which he carefully counted, saying they would suffice to send him to that dark place from which there was no return.[101] In Vienna, news of Hochkirch arrived on Maria Theresa's name-day, when the whole court and high nobility were assembled at Schönbrunn Palace to celebrate the event, so her cup overflowed.[102]

Yet although the campaign of 1758 ended in defeat, death and depression, the overall strategic situation had changed remarkably little. As the Prussian army chaplain Küster wrote in his account of the fighting, never had a lost battle had such a favourable outcome for the vanquished.[103] After toying with Austrian requests for a further initiative, the Russians had gone back to their winter quarters beyond the Vistula. Soon shaking off his post-Hochkirch despondency, Frederick set about retrieving the situation. As he wrote to Prince Henry the day after the battle, 'In truth, I have suffered a great misfortune, but it must be put right with determination and courage.'[104] On 5

November, the anniversary of Rossbach, the Austrians abandoned the siege of Neisse at Frederick's approach. At the end of the month, a further march west to Saxony prompted Daun to take his army back into winter quarters in Bohemia. Frederick thus remained in possession of both Saxony and Silesia. That Hochkirch should have brought so little reward naturally led to sharp criticism of Daun, but not from the two people who mattered most: Kaunitz and Maria Theresa. Indeed, the latter gave material backing to her warm praise by creating an endowment of 250,000 gulden for Daun and his heirs.[105] She remained optimistic about the eventual outcome of the war, not least because both Russia and France had recently repeated their determination to see it through *à outrance*.

9

The Seven Years War: Disaster and Survival

1759

Vigorous recruiting during the winter of 1758–9 meant that Frederick faced the new campaigning season with an army roughly the same size as he had had a year earlier: about 163,000.[1] Whether the soldiers were of the same quality was a different matter. Even the veterans among them could stand only so much exertion and slaughter. The main problem, however, was the growing numerical disparity, as the Russians in particular began to make their superiority in manpower resources felt. There was also the fear that at long last the various allies might start to coordinate their war efforts. As Frederick wrote to d'Argens from Zuckmantel on the Bohemian frontier: 'my great difficulty is this: in previous years, our enemies have failed to act together, so that they could be fought one after the other. This year they intend to act simultaneously.'[2]

An early success was scored in the far west. Despite growing financial problems, the French had resolved to make a major effort to conquer Hanover and bring the war with Great Britain to a quick end. At first, all went well. On 13 April a secondary French army, commanded by the Duc de Broglie, defeated Prince Ferdinand of Brunswick at Bergen near Frankfurt am Main. This allowed the main force under the Marquis de Contades to recross the Rhine and advance into Hessen. Early in June they took Kassel and advanced towards the river Weser, occupying the crucial fortress of Minden a month later.[3] It was there, on 1 August, that Ferdinand's army of some 42,000 British, Hanoverians and Hessians inflicted a decisive defeat on Contades's 54,000 French. The latter suffered around 7,000 casualties, the allies only about 2,800.[4] In a secondary action on the same day, Ferdinand's nephew, the Crown Prince of Brunswick, defeated another French force under the Duc de Brissac and so threatened French communications with their supply bases. The demoralized French began a retreat which took them back west to the river Lahn north of Frankfurt am Main. The Duc de Choiseul, who had replaced the defeatist Abbé de Bernis as French foreign minister in October 1758, wrote apologetically to Kaunitz: 'I blush when I speak of our army. I simply cannot get it into my head, much less into my heart, that a pack of Hanoverians etc. could defeat the army of the King.'[5] By the time the two armies went into winter quarters, rather belatedly, in January 1760, they were virtually back to where they had started a year earlier, minus of course the thousands of men they had lost to death, disease and desertion.

For the belligerents in the centre and the east, the west was a sideshow, although a French victory at Minden might well have brought complete disaster for Frederick. His main problem remained the convergence of enemies from four different directions. To his south-west, a combined army of imperialists and Austrians was to advance into Saxony; to the south and south-east, there was Daun and the main Austrian army, with orders to retake Silesia; in the north the plan was for the Swedes, reinforced by a Russian corps, to advance on Berlin; in the east there was the lowering presence of the Russian hordes. When they all met in the middle, Frederick would be crushed. His only chance was to strike quickly and repeatedly at his individual enemies. As he told Prince Ferdinand at the end of March, his strategic situation was '*extrêmement embarrassante*', his only hope being to score so decisive a success against one of his tormentors as to allow him a free hand to deal with the next.[6]

The enterprising Prince Henry got this off to a good start by, first destroying Austrian supply depots in northern Bohemia, and then swivelling west to raid deep into Franconia, seizing recruits and supplies and disrupting the plans of the imperial army to advance on Saxony.[7] A second Prussian detachment, under General Heinrich August de la Motte-Fouqué, inflicted the same sort of damage on Austrian depots in Upper Silesia around Troppau and Jägerndorf. The Austrians were in no hurry anyway, waiting in northern Bohemia until the time was ripe. They certainly had no intention of descending to the Lower Silesian plains and giving Frederick the chance to score another Hohenfriedberg or Leuthen. It was their Russian allies who got things moving. On 25 June they began their march to the river Oder from Posen, where an army of 60,000 under a new commander, Prince Nikolai Ivanovich Saltykov, had concentrated during the early summer. From Silesia Frederick sent General Carl Heinrich von Wedel and a modest army of 28,000 to arrest the Russian advance. They were not enough, although Wedel's bone-headed aggression did not help. At the battle of Kay (sometimes called Paltzig) near Züllichau

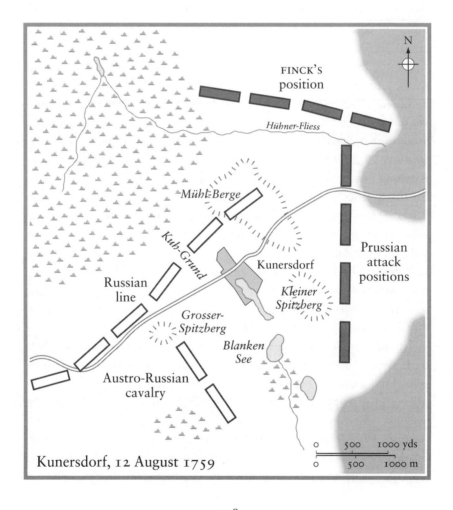

N

FINCK'S
position

Hühner-Fliess

Mühl-Berge

Kub-Grund

Russian
line

Kunersdorf

Kleiner
Spitzberg

Prussian
attack
positions

Grosser-
Spitzberg

Blanken
See

Austro-Russian
cavalry

0   500   1000 yds
0   500   1000 m

Kunersdorf, 12 August 1759

east of the Oder they were crushed, losing 8,000 in casualties.[8] On 1 August Saltykov occupied Frankfurt an der Oder.

With the road to Berlin (only eighty kilometres away) now open, Frederick had to take a hand himself. He was fortunate that the ever-cautious Daun had detached only 24,000 under Laudon to join Saltykov. Together they had about 64,000. Just as before Zorndorf the previous year, Frederick marched his army up the west bank of the Oder, crossing near Küstrin and then marching south. The two armies met at Kunersdorf, to the north-east of Frankfurt an der Oder, on 12 August. What followed was Frederick's greatest military disaster and 'the greatest Russian feat of arms of the eighteenth century'.[9] Immediately after the battle, Frederick wrote to his minister Finckenstein:

> My coat is riddled with musket balls, and I have had two horses killed beneath me. It is my misfortune to be still alive. Our losses are very great, and I have only 3,000 men left out of an army of 48,000. At the moment that I am writing everybody is in flight, and I can exercise no control over my men. At Berlin you ought to be thinking of your safety. I shall not survive this cruel turn of fortune. The consequences will be worse than the defeat itself. I have no resources left, and, to speak quite frankly, I believe everything is lost. I shall not outlive the downfall of my fatherland. Farewell for ever![10]

What had gone wrong? In his own account of the battle, Frederick wrote that it was all a matter of chance – 'who can but remark the slender thread by which victory is suspended!' If only the Austrian General Laudon had arrived a couple of minutes later at the Russian battery, the tide of battle would not have turned his way.[11] He told the Marquis d'Argens 'we have been unlucky, but it was not my fault',[12] but, in reality, Frederick was the author of his downfall. His intelligence was faulty, his own reconnaissance inadequate. He failed to read the opposing disposition correctly and so was obliged to alter the line of his attack at the last moment. The time taken by this manoeuvre allowed Saltykov to take appropriate counter-action. His refusal to call a halt before it was too late was fatal. A combination of artillery fire followed by infantry assault had seized the Russian positions on the heights of the Mühl-Berge (see map). To attack the main Russian positions, the Prussians would now have to descend into the valley known as the 'Kuh-Grund' and up the other side, all the while exposed to enemy artillery fire. Frederick refused to listen to his senior officers who urged him to stop, arguing that the enemy would soon be obliged to withdraw and that his own soldiers were exhausted.[13] As at Zorndorf, Frederick was determined to have his outright victory. But this was different: his situation was less favourable, the enemy better led and his own troops less numerous and less effective. The fabled steadiness of the Prussian infantry eventually collapsed. Four days after the battle, Frederick wrote to Finckenstein: 'the victory was ours when all of a sudden my wretched infantry wavered. The ridiculous fear of being sent to Siberia [if taken prisoner] turned their heads and there was no way of stopping them.'[14] He himself was more liable to a charge of reckless courage than cowardice. Two horses had been shot under him during the battle and a third as he was about to mount it.[15]

Once the rot set in, the Prussian army just fell apart. Immediately after the battle, Frederick was left with just 3,000 men in some sort of organized military formation. The rest were scattered to the four winds – or were lying dead or dying on the battlefield. More than 6,000 had been killed outright and total casualties amounted to 19,000 or 40 per cent.[16] Among the mortally wounded was Ewald von Kleist, one of the most anthologized German poets of the century.* Also lost were 172 guns and twenty-eight flags and standards, symbolizing the scale of the disaster.[17] There was nothing now to stop the Russians linking with the rest of the Austrian army and advancing on Berlin. Yet nothing happened. In a much quoted letter to his brother Prince Henry, Frederick wrote on 1 September from Waldow, roughly halfway between Berlin and Bautzen:

> I can announce to you the miracle of the House of Brandenburg: just when the enemy had crossed the Oder and could have finished the war by risking a [second] battle, he marched from Müllrose to Lieberose. I marched first to Trebatsch, and from there yesterday to Waldow, where my position cuts him off from Lübben which I have had occupied. So I am cutting him off from that part of Lusatia which was being obliged to keep him supplied.[18]

---

* On Kleist, see below, p. 274.

As this suggests, a lot had happened during the past fortnight. After plumbing the depths of despair after the battle to the extent of contemplating suicide, Frederick had quickly pulled himself together and set about rounding up the survivors. It says a great deal for the discipline of the Prussian soldiers that the survivors were a fighting force again within a couple of days.[19] A week after the battle Frederick could put together an army of about 28,000 at Madlitz, a few kilometres west of Frankfurt an der Oder, covering the road to Berlin. If the allies wanted to reach his capital, they would have to fight him for it. They did not. The Russians had lost about a third of their army – 4,700 at Kay and another 19,000 at Kunersdorf.[20] Not unreasonably, they took the view that it was high time their Austrian allies assumed more of the risk. The surrender of Dresden on 4 September, which meant that effectively all of Saxony was now in Austrian hands, should have triggered a long-term plan for an Austro-Russian invasion of Silesia. By this time, however, relations between Saltykov and Daun had deteriorated to the point where no joint action was possible. The two allies were also kept apart by some inspired manoeuvring by Prince Henry in northern Silesia. On 7 September Saltykov announced that lack of supplies compelled him to retreat eastwards to the Oder, which he reached on the 25th. On 15 October the Russians began their long withdrawal to winter quarters on the Vistula.[21] Hugely expensive in terms of men, money and matériel, their campaign had come within a hair's breadth of total victory but ultimately had yielded nothing.

Meanwhile, the focus of the campaign had switched to Saxony. With the Russians gone, Frederick was able to concentrate on regaining control of the Electorate and pushing the Austrians back into Bohemia. At first everything went well. By the end of September, all the Saxon territory lost in the previous month was back in Prussian hands, with the notable exception of the capital, Dresden. The Prussians were helped by Austrian inactivity. Despite intense pressure from his increasingly exasperated superiors in Vienna, Daun refused to risk battle, preferring a stately sequence of manoeuvres to dislodge Prince Henry from his fortified position at Torgau on the Elbe. This failed, and it began to look as though the campaign would end as it had begun, with Frederick back in control of Saxony and Daun back in Bohemia. Then Frederick came to his enemy's assistance with a daring but disastrous initiative. General Friedrich August von Finck and a corps of 15,000 were sent to Maxen south of Dresden to apply pressure to Austrian supply lines and thus accelerate their departure. Despite repeated warnings from his senior generals, Frederick insisted. The result was that Finck's force was cut off, surrounded, attacked and forced to capitulate. Frederick's bone-headed obstinacy had inflicted a loss of 2,000 casualties, 13,000 prisoners of war, including nine generals, and seventy-one artillery pieces, or in other words the greatest numerical loss he ever did suffer, apart from Kunersdorf.[22] Not even the most enthusiastic of Frederick's admirers can find anything to offer by way of extenuation. It says very little for Frederick's capacity for self-knowledge that he should have heaped all the blame on the hapless Finck, who was merely obeying orders he knew to be misguided. When he returned from Austrian captivity, he was court-martialled, imprisoned for a year and then dismissed from the service.[23] Even Frederick's ultra-loyal private secretary, Eichel, took the view that Finck was not to blame. Just to put the tin lid on this year of disaster, two weeks after Maxen another if smaller Prussian corps of 3,500 was cut off near Meissen and forced to surrender. As the Austrians were now refusing to exchange prisoners, aware that they held a natural numerical advantage and that one Prussian veteran was worth a good deal more than his Austrian equivalent, the net loss of these two capitulations was greater still. Frederick himself wrote:

> The regiments lost at the battle of Maxen and the action fought by Direcke had indeed been replaced, during the winter; but these were neither veterans nor troops fit for service: they were there for show. What might be effected with a cluster of men, the one half Saxon peasants, the other deserters, who were headed by officers engaged from necessity, and because no better were to be obtained?[24]

1760

After four campaigns of ceaseless activity and intense stress, during which he had had to witness tens of thousands of dead and dying, all victims of his ambition, Frederick was beginning to feel the strain.

Rarely healthy at the best of times,* he was now increasingly prone to disabling bouts of illness, with gout and haemorrhoids to the fore. So fierce had been the attack of gout and attendant fever the previous autumn that his journey to Silesia at a crucial time had to be delayed. He had told Prince Henry: 'I shall fly to you on the wings of patriotism and duty, but when I arrive you will find only a skeleton,' although he added that his feeble body would still be activated by his indomitable spirit.[25] By January 1760 the spirit had wilted too. He wrote to d'Argens to thank him for the trouble he was taking to publish his 'twaddle', but asked how he could be expected to write good verse when his mind was 'too disturbed, too agitated, too depressed'. There was no prospect of securing peace, he cried, and one more defeat would deliver the *coup de grâce*. Weighed down by care, surrounded by implacable enemies, life had become an insupportable burden . . . and so he went on in the same vein lamenting his fate.[26]

It was not quite yet a case of 'darkest before dawn', because Frederick had one even more tenebrous moment to survive. His overall strategy remained the same – to keep control of Saxony and Silesia – and so did his prime objective – the recapture of Dresden. How many troops he had at his disposal is a matter of dispute. The best guess is that he never had more than 110,000 on active duty, so his numerical inferiority was of the order of at least two to one.[27] That disparity increased on 23 June when General de la Motte-Fouqué was overwhelmed at Landeshut by a greatly superior Austrian force under Laudon, losing 2,000 on the field of battle and another 8,000 in prisoners of war. Fewer than 1,500 managed to escape. Once again, a Prussian general had obeyed his royal master well but not wisely. Frederick had had second thoughts about his original order to hold Landeshut come what may, but his change of heart came too late to save Fouqué's corps.[28]

Back in Saxony, Frederick had been very active but without achieving anything. All his attempts to bring either Lacy or Daun to battle failed. So did his siege of Dresden, which began on 19 July only to be abandoned four days later. Three days after that, the Austrians showed him how a siege should be conducted when Laudon's army took the

* See below, pp. 453–4.

great Silesian fortress of Glatz by storm. Admittedly, Dresden had been garrisoned by 14,000 veterans commanded by the determined Major General Macguire (sic), whereas the luckless Glatz commandant, Lieutenant-Colonel Bartolomei d'O (also sic), had only 3,000 ill-motivated Saxons and Austrian deserters at his disposal. That did not save him from court martial and execution when he eventually returned from Austrian captivity.[29] The difference between the two defences showed that the greater demographic resources of the Austrians were beginning to make themselves felt.

Frederick's situation was now perilous in the extreme. He was losing control of both Saxony and Silesia and was running out of men, thanks to his own numerous mistakes. To make matters worse, a Russian corps under General Chernyshev had crossed the Oder and was advancing through Silesia to join up with Daun. Nothing, it seemed, lay between the allies and total victory but a few weakly defended Silesian fortresses. As soon as he had taken Glatz, Laudon moved off to Breslau, the greatest prize of all, confident that he could repeat his triumph. Now at last chinks of light began to shine through the gloom for Frederick: his commander at Breslau, General Bogislav Friedrich von Tauentzien, proved to be made of sterner stuff than his colleague d'O at Glatz; in a lightning march which took his army corps of around 35,000 over a hundred kilometres in three days, Prince Henry marched to Breslau's relief; and the Russians failed to link up with Laudon.[30] Meanwhile, Frederick had embarked on an epic march from Saxony to Silesia, which took up the first week of August, not so much pursued as accompanied by the main Austrian army commanded by Daun and a subsidiary corps under Lacy. So close were the three armies that they appeared to be one force. Urged on by Maria Theresa and Kaunitz, who demanded a battle to finish Frederick off, it was Daun's intention to force an engagement on the Katzbach, a tributary of the Oder, north of Breslau.[31]

That was what Daun got, on 15 August, but not in the manner he had expected. As his combined forces of 90,000 enjoyed a three-to-one superiority, he was confident he could encircle and eliminate Frederick's army, which was camped a couple of kilometres north-east of Liegnitz. On this occasion, Frederick was not caught napping. On the contrary, during the night of 14–15 August he moved his army to the

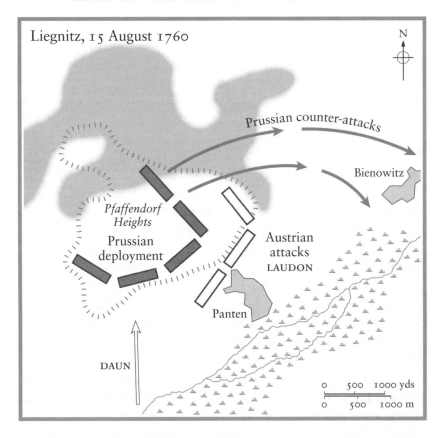

Liegnitz, 15 August 1760

north, leaving his campfires burning to confuse the enemy. So when it began to get light shortly after 3 a.m., it was General Laudon who was taken by surprise. Expecting to be supported by Lacy and Daun, who were supposed to be advancing from the west and south respectively, and unaware that he was facing the main Prussian army, Laudon attacked. Decimated by artillery, then taken in the flank, the Austrians were forced back to the Katzbach. By six a.m. the battle was all over.[32] It had been short but sharp. It cost Laudon around 10,000, including 4,000 prisoners of war, among them two generals and eighty officers, and eighty-three pieces of artillery. The Prussians lost 775 dead and 2,500 wounded, most of them to two late cavalry charges which covered the Austrian withdrawal.[33]

As the battles of the Seven Years War went, Liegnitz was not a particularly grand affair. Most of the Austrians never fired a shot in anger. Yet its importance was colossal. This was a battle Frederick had to win, or rather it was a battle he could not afford to lose. If Daun and Lacy's hammer had smashed down on Laudon's anvil, as had been intended, the Prussians in between would have been pulverized, to an even greater extent than at Kunersdorf. Any remnants would have been mopped up by a Russian force under Chernyshev which Saltykov had promised to send across the Oder on the 15th. In the event, the Russians now prudently went east rather than west, while Daun and the Austrians moved off to besiege the fortress of Schweidnitz to the west of Breslau. With the advantage of hindsight, we can see that Liegnitz was a pivotal moment in the Seven Years War. It brought to an end a sequence of military defeats stretching back to Hochkirch nearly two years previously (although some of Frederick's subordinate generals, notably Prince Henry, had won minor engagements in the interim). Napoleon was not the first to realize the importance for an army's morale of the belief that luck (also known variously as Providence, Fortune and God) was on its commander's side. As Jomini observed, Liegnitz restored '*toute sa force morale*'.[34] It also restored his reputation among the powers. The British secretary of state, Lord Holdernesse, wrote: 'the superior genius of that great prince never appeared in a higher light than during this last expedition into Silesia. The whole manoeuvre is looked upon here as the masterpiece of military skill.'[35] This was the best chance the Austro-Russians had had since Kunersdorf of bringing the war to an abrupt end and they knew it. Thereafter their offensive never regained momentum.[36]

In the short term, this brief but violent flurry of activity was followed by several weeks of stalemate, as Daun and Frederick manoeuvred around each other in the hills of western Silesia. At the end of September, Frederick complained to Prince Henry that he was getting nowhere. Daun was in one camp, Frederick in another, and both were invulnerable.[37] The impasse was broken further north by an unusually vigorous if brief initiative on the part of the Russians, spurred on by the French military attaché in their camp. In the first week of October, a force led by Chernyshev occupied Berlin, where they were joined by 18,000 Austrians and Saxons detached from

Daun's army. Although this was an expensive and disagreeable experience for the inhabitants, and a good deal of vandalism was perpetrated at the palaces of Charlottenburg and Schönhausen, the three-day occupation had no military consequences. The main casualties were the fifteen Russian soldiers killed during an incompetent attempt to blow up the powder mill.[38] As Showalter has commented, 'it was a raid as opposed to an operational manoeuvre'.[39]

Liegnitz did nothing to repair Frederick's personal morale. He lamented to Prince Henry that his resources were too narrow and shallow to resist the overwhelming numerical superiority of his various enemies, adding 'and if we perish, you can date our eclipse to that pernicious affair at Maxen'.[40] He now had to realize that the ever-cautious Daun had got the better of him in Silesia and that he must march back to Saxony if the campaign was not to end in total failure. It was in a grim mood that he set out, telling Prince Henry on 7 October that 'given my present situation, my only motto can be: conquer or die'.[41] Daun was also under pressure from Vienna, from where an increasingly impatient Maria Theresa sent an express order to maintain control of Saxony against Frederick and to seek the necessary battle no matter what the circumstances.[42] In the event, Frederick took the battle to him, on 3 November at Torgau to the north-east of Leipzig, where the Austrians had taken up a strong defensive position. If they could not be dislodged, Saxony and its resources would be lost. To attack head-on invited a disaster on the lines of Kunersdorf, so Frederick embarked on an imaginative outflanking movement designed to take the bulk of his army – 24,000 infantry, 6,500 cavalry and fifty twelve-pound guns – to attack the Austrians in the rear. Their attention would be diverted to their front by a smaller force of 11,000 infantry and 7,000 cavalry commanded by General von Zieten. The drawback turned out to be the long march needed to get the main army into position. Too much could and did go wrong, so that it all took too long and allowed Daun to take effective counter-action.

The battle that ensued was even more ferocious than previous encounters between the two sides. Frederick himself was stunned when hit by a spent bullet and had to be carried from the field for a time. What turned out to be the bloodiest victory of his career was won by a combination of individual initiatives by junior officers at crucial

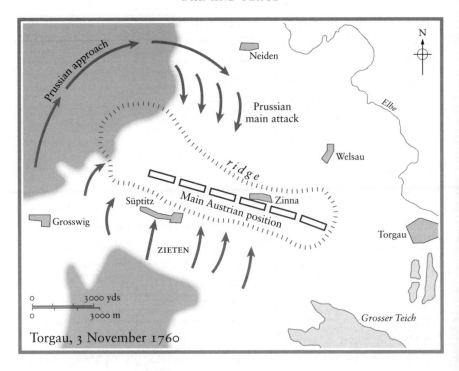

Torgau, 3 November 1760

moments and the timely advance of Zieten's corps. Until almost literally one minute to midnight, the result was in the balance. Indeed, Daun had already sent off a courier announcing a victory when the tide turned, a mistake which caused intense despondency in Vienna when the initial rejoicing turned to ashes.[43] The losses on both sides were horrific. In a letter to Prince Henry written the following day, Frederick claimed that in this 'rough and stubborn' battle he had inflicted 20,000–25,000 casualties.[44] He did not even mention his own. When his adjutant, Georg Heinrich von Berenhorst, produced the final score some days after the battle, Frederick told him: 'it will cost you your head, if this figure ever gets out!' It cannot be known just how high it really was, the estimates ranging from 16,670 to 24,700, but even the lowest exceeded the Austrian total (which Frederick greatly exaggerated).[45]

Although he talked up his victory, Frederick was not in a victorious mood. The losses had been so heavy that in future such offensive tactics simply could not be afforded.[46] As he wrote to d'Argens on 5

November, he had secured a period of peace for the winter but that was all. Five days later he added that the Austrians had been sent back to Dresden but from there they could not be dislodged for the time being. He went on:

> In truth, this is a wretched prospect and a poor reward for all the exhaustion and colossal effort which this campaign has cost us. My only support in the midst of all these aggravations is my philosophy; this is the staff on which I lean and my only source of consolation at this time of trouble when everything is falling apart. As you will see, my dear marquis, I am not inflating my success. I am just telling it like it is; perhaps the rest of the world will be dazzled by the glamour a victory bestows, but 'From afar we are envied, on the spot we tremble.'[47]

This was just the sort of gloomy mood in which he had begun the year.* He was perhaps being too hard on himself; 1760 had been a decidedly better year than 1759. The Austrians and Russians had failed to combine effectively, he had won two major engagements and the only net loss was the fortress of Glatz. A more judicious assessment would be given by Clausewitz. While disagreeing with those who saw the campaign as a work of art and a masterpiece, he did find admirable

> the King's wisdom: pursuing a major objective with limited resources, he did not try to undertake anything beyond his strength, but always *just enough* to get him what he wanted ... His whole conduct ... shows an element of restrained strength, which was always in balance, never lacking in vigour, rising to remarkable heights in moments of crisis, but immediately afterward reverting to a state of calm oscillation, always ready to adjust to the smallest shift in the political situation. Neither vanity, nor ambition, nor vindictiveness could move him from this course, and it was this course alone that brought him success.[48]

Much less satisfactory was the situation on the western front. French losses overseas in 1759 forced them to seek victory in Germany as a bargaining counter for the eventual peace negotiations. A large army of around 150,000 was unleashed in June 1760. Prince Ferdinand was

* See above, p. 243.

forced back from Hessen and much of Westphalia, despite winning a number of engagements. Victory at Warburg on 31 July could not stop the French taking Göttingen a week later, although that proved to be the limit of their advance into Hanoverian territory.[49] More ominous in the long term for Frederick was the diminishing enthusiasm on the part of his British allies for the continental war. They had achieved virtually all their war aims in North America, the Caribbean and India and were now looking for an early end to what had become a ruinously expensive war. Moreover, the death of George II on 25 October brought to the throne a king who the previous year had referred to Hanover as 'that horrid Electorate which has always liv'd upon the very vitals of this poor Country'.[50] It could be only a matter of time before the invaluable British subsidies to Frederick were halted. In December the Prussian representative in London, Knyphausen, warned Frederick of the growing opposition in Parliament to the continental war and corresponding enthusiasm for a separate peace with France.[51]

1761

1761 turned out to be a year without a major battle on the main eastern front. There is a weary sense of déjà vu about the allied strategy. Marshal Daun, still recovering from the wound sustained at Torgau, anxious to resign and more static than ever, was in command in Saxony. His more enterprising subordinate, Laudon, was to join forces with a Russian army, now commanded by the tsarina's favourite, Count Alexander Borisovich Buturlin, and seek to win a second Kunersdorf. Frederick left Prince Henry and 28,000 in Saxony to keep an eye on Daun, while he headed off to Silesia with the main army of about 55,000. His attempt to keep his two enemies apart failed, not least because he ducked an opportunity to attack the Russians at Liegnitz on 15 August.[52] As things turned out, this was probably wise. Buturlin linked up with Laudon four days later but then proved very reluctant to go on the attack. On the day before their junction, Frederick told Prince Henry that 'the Russians still have no desire to attack, but I think Laudon will force them to'.[53]

The Austrian commander certainly tried but Frederick mounted a persuasive counter-argument by taking his army into a fortified camp at Bunzelwitz to the north-west of Schweidnitz. Nature was given a helping hand by intensive spade-work. Working in twelve-hour shifts around the clock, the Prussian soldiers created a formidable network of trenches and palisades. The Saxon Captain Tielke reported admiringly:

> In this location the Prussian army stood on a series of low and mostly gentle eminences, which were utilised in a masterly fashion. The approaches were by no means physically insurmountable, but what rendered them difficult to reach were the little streams, the swampy meadows, and the enfilading and grazing fire from the batteries on every side.[54]

Breaking into this fortress would have proved extremely costly, given the 460 pieces of artillery that guarded it. The Russians blinked first. First Buturlin told Laudon he would cooperate in a joint attack, then he had second thoughts. On 9 September he finally gave up and took his army back east to the river Oder and beyond.

At this point, this uneventful campaign should have come to an end with the two sides going into winter quarters. Frederick certainly thought it was all over. From Pilzen on 27 September he wrote to Prince Henry that it was next to impossible that the Austrians in Saxony would attempt another raid on Berlin, now that the Russians had gone, and as for those in Silesia 'I believe you do not need to have any worries about us because essentially the campaign is over, given that neither we nor the Austrians intend to undertake anything.'[55] He was wrong. There were three more incidents to come, one welcome, the other two decidedly not. The first was a brilliant piece of work by General Dubislav Friedrich von Platen and a corps of about 8,000, sent by Frederick to harry the retreating Russians and already underway. On 15 September they had attacked the main Russian supply base at Gostyn in Poland, destroying 5,000 wagons and taking 1,845 prisoners and seven artillery pieces. From there they moved on towards the Prussian fortress of Colberg (often spelt Kolberg) on the Pomeranian coast, disrupting the Russian supply lines as they went.[56] But no sooner had Frederick sent off congratulations on this coup than the truly terrible news arrived that on 1 October Laudon had taken the great fortress of Schweidnitz with a sudden night attack. Frederick was completely nonplussed by this 'so extraordinary and almost incredible turn of events'.[57] It was indeed a devastating blow, for Schweidnitz covered the passes from Bohemia via Friedland and so was 'the key to Lower Silesia', especially since Glatz, which covered the routes from Königgrätz to Neisse, was already in Austrian hands.[58] Given all he had suffered at Laudon's hands in the past, most notably at Glatz and Hochkirch,* Frederick's complacency was as surprising as it was damaging. The third piece of bad news which arrived just before the end of the year was that Colberg had fallen to the Russians on 16 December, which gave them for the first time a port through which they could bring up supplies. For the first time, the Russians could winter in Pomerania and the Austrians in Silesia. Meanwhile in Saxony, Prince Henry had been forced out of his camp at Meissen by Daun.[59]

The only chink of light was visible in the west, where the French had gone into winter quarters in the middle of November, having achieved nothing durable in the course of a long campaign. This was all the more disappointing for them because a major effort had been made that year. Two large armies were sent east, one totalling c. 95,000 from the Lower Rhine commanded by the Prince de Soubise and the other with some 65,000 from further south commanded by the Duc de Broglie. They thus outnumbered Prince Ferdinand's forces by at least two to one.[60] What then followed was a bewildering succession of marches and counter-marches, manoeuvres and counter-manoeuvres, the only real point of contact being the battle of Vellinghausen near Hamm on the river Lippe on 15–16 July, which was a clear victory for Prince Ferdinand. Although this did not end the campaign, it helped to ensure that there would be no conquest of Hanover in 1761.[61]

* See above, p. 232.

1762

On 6 January 1762 a depressed Frederick wrote from Breslau to his chief minister, Finckenstein, that if the Turks could not be induced to open a second front against the Austrians in the Balkans, he was finished. So negotiations would have to be initiated in the hope of saving something from the wreckage for his successor, which was a hint that Frederick was contemplating suicide – again.[62] Just two weeks later, on the 19th, he received news from his man in Warsaw that at long last the Tsarina Elizabeth had died, on the 5th. His immediate reaction was cautious. He wrote to Finckenstein that they could not be sure how her successor, Peter III, would act and whether he would succumb to the blandishments of Russia's existing allies. The indolent British ambassador in St Petersburg, Sir Robert Keith, should be stirred up to counter French and Austrian influence. He ended by adding gloomily that he did not suppose this change of ruler would do him any more good than had the accession of Charles III in Spain three years previously.[63]

He could not have been more wrong. As the French complained, the new tsar had not so much an attachment as an 'inexpressible passion' for Frederick, whom he hailed in a personal letter 'one of the greatest heroes the world has ever seen'.[64] He often wore the uniform of a Prussian major-general, displayed in his apartment all the portraits of his hero he could find and repeatedly kissed Frederick's image on a ring sent from Potsdam as a present.[65] This was partly hero-worship and partly motivated by Peter's need for Prussian assistance in regaining the duchy of Schleswig from Denmark for the House of Holstein from which he descended.[66] It was not long before very good news was bringing cheer to Frederick. At a dinner at the Russian court on 5 February, Peter had expressed himself so intemperately about the shortcomings of his Austrian ally that the Austrian ambassador, Count Mercy, felt unable to repeat his actual words in his despatch to Vienna.[67] Orders were sent to the Russian generals to cease all hostile action against Prussia. The Turks and Tartars were encouraged to attack Austria. A treaty of alliance with Prussia was signed on 5 May. Peace between Prussia and Sweden was brokered by Russian diplomats and signed on 22 May.[68] Frederick had to rub his eyes. Within just a few weeks, the north and east had been neutralized and Russia turned from enemy into ally. No wonder that he exulted when he came to write up his history of the episode:

> The summary of events we have related will present to our view Prussia on the brink of ruin, at the end of the last campaign; past recovery in the judgment of all politicians, yet one woman dies, and the nation revives; nay is sustained by that power which had been the most eager to seek her destruction . . . What dependence may be placed on human affairs, if the veriest trifles can influence, can change, the fate of empires? Such are the sports of fortune, who, laughing at the vain prudence of mortals, of some excites the hopes, and of others pulls down the high-raised expectations.[69]

Whether or not Frederick was saved by the death of the tsarina is so contentious an issue that it deserves separate treatment.* Here it need only be remarked that Frederick was overdoing it. Had he known just how desperate was the situation of his enemies, he might have modified his view. When he heard that 20,000 men had been discharged from the Austrian army, he assumed it was because Maria Theresa was so confident of total victory.[70] In fact it was because there was no money to pay for them.[71] So many new taxes had been imposed and so many old ones increased, so many loans had been raised, that the Austrian well was bone-dry. Around 40 per cent of annual revenue was now needed just to service the accumulated debt. By the time the war ended the following year, the debt had reached a total equivalent to seven to eight years' regular income.[72] The situation was no better in France, where a state bankruptcy began to look like a real possibility.[73] When the Austrian financial expert Count Ludwig Zinzendorf was asked by the French ambassador about the fiscal structure of the Habsburg Monarchy, his response was: 'Can one blind man show another the way?'[74]

Once it became clear just how much had changed in St Petersburg, Frederick turned positively jaunty. On 6 March 1762 he wrote to d'Argens that peace with Russia was certain, that this had caused

---

* See below, pp. 279–80.

great alarm in Vienna and that 'the storm clouds are breaking up and we can look forward to a beautiful calm day, shining with rays bursting from the sun'.[75] But there was still work to be done. Pomerania was being evacuated by the Russians. That left Silesia and Saxony to be regained. The chief target had to be Schweidnitz, for if the Austrians remained in control of Lower Silesia, they would have a strong hand to play at the peace negotiations. Leaving Prince Henry and 30,000 to keep an eye on Saxony, Frederick took an army variously estimated at between 66,000 and 72,000 to Silesia, where he found Daun and about 82,000 in defensive positions around Schweidnitz. There he was joined by 15,000 to 20,000 Russians under Chernyshev. Together, they pushed Daun back to Burkersdorf, south-west of Schweidnitz.

During the first two weeks of July, Frederick tried to induce Daun to move away by sending General Franz Karl Ludwig von Wied zu Neuwied (the younger son of a German prince) and a corps of 20,000 to cause mayhem in north-eastern Bohemia. Daun appeared not to move, so most of this force was recalled. In fact, substantial numbers had been sent off to guard communications, with the result that when battle was joined at Burkersdorf, Frederick for once enjoyed numerical superiority. This would have been even greater if the Russians had been actively involved. On 18 July, however, Chernyshev had to tell Frederick that a palace revolution in St Petersburg had deposed and killed Peter III and that he and his army had been recalled. With the aid of what amounted to a large bribe, Frederick persuaded him to stay put for three days, albeit in a non-combatant role. In fact, Chernyshev's corps played a crucial role when the battle began on 21 July. Frederick placed it, together with eleven battalions of his own, opposite the Austrian army to fool Daun into thinking that it was there that the main attack would be launched (see map). Meanwhile, the main Prussian brigades were sent off to take up positions to the north-east and east, which were weakly guarded. It was their assault which threatened to turn Daun's flank and forced him to order a general retreat. As battles of the war went, this was a relatively bloodless affair, with each side suffering around 1,600 casualties but the effects were of the greatest political and strategic importance.[76] Burkersdorf would also turn out to be Frederick's last battle. Daun was pushed

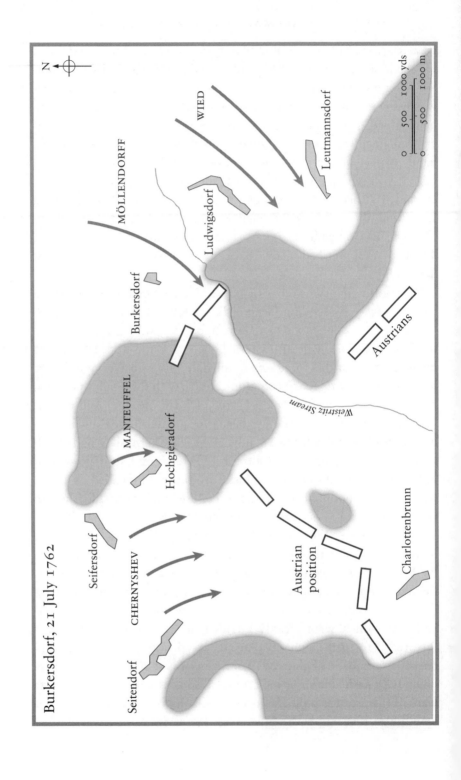

Burkersdorf, 21 July 1762

back into the Bohemian mountains and was cut off from Schweidnitz. The siege lasted sixty-three days, as the Austrian garrison commanded by General Peter Guasco, an experienced engineer, defended the fortress with enterprise and resolution. Only after a lucky Prussian bomb blew up a magazine and opened the way for an assault did he surrender, on 9 October.[77] This was a crucial moment, for in effect it returned Silesia to Prussian control. Commenting on Daun's inactivity as the siege progressed, Jomini wrote: 'modern history offers no comparable example of cowardice'.[78] In the west, the campaign ended with the capitulation of the French garrison at Kassel on 1 November.

By this time, Kaunitz's great coalition was falling apart. It was clear that Great Britain and France would soon negotiate a peace (a preliminary treaty was signed on 3 November 1762) and also that the new ruler of Russia, Peter's widow, Catherine, would not resume hostilities against Frederick, for the good reason that Russia was financially exhausted.[79] Austria was soon going to be on her own. The last straw was the decisive victory achieved by Prince Henry on 29 October at Freiberg, south-west of Dresden, which in effect restored Prussian control of Saxony.[80] An exultant Frederick wrote to tell him that the news had made him feel forty years younger: 'yesterday I was sixty, today I am eighteen again'.[81] He told the Duchess of Saxony-Gotha that Fortune, having persecuted him for seven campaigns, now seemed to have decided to treat him more leniently, and that peace was within his grasp.[82] He was right. At Vienna, even the hardest of hard-liners could now see that he could not be defeated. Of all the combatants, it was Saxony which had suffered most and so it was appropriate that a Saxon, Karl Thomas von Fritsch, should have been chosen to inform Frederick that Austria was ready to negotiate. That happened on 25 November at Meissen.[83]

1763 – THE PEACE OF HUBERTUSBURG

Formal negotiations began on 30 December 1762 at the Saxon palace of Hubertusburg near Leipzig. Fritsch acted for Saxony, Heinrich Gabriel von Collenbach for Austria and Ewald Count von Hertzberg for Prussia. The Austrian negotiating position was not strong. Even before news of Freiberg had arrived, Daun had told Maria Theresa that 'if there is no hope of peace, then I cannot see how Your Majesty can continue the war, as the current situation is such that it is to be feared that the army cannot be kept in one piece throughout the winter'. Supplies were so scarce that the soldiers had to be scattered across a wide area, thus inviting an irresistible Prussian assault. The officer corps in particular was 'totally demoralised'.[84] In 1760 Kaunitz had written that the worst possible peace would be one that left all Silesia in Prussian hands. That was what he now got. Not even the fortress and county of Glatz, in Austrian hands since July 1760, could be retained.[85] However, it was not Austrian obduracy which postponed the signature of the treaty until 15 February 1763, it was Frederick who spun things out with a view to extracting the last ounce of Saxon resources in men, money and supplies. And women too, for large numbers of Saxon women were carried off to Prussia to aid the repopulation of war zones.[86]

Of the twenty-one articles of the Peace of Hubertusburg, the most important was number twelve, which confirmed the treaties of Breslau, Berlin and Dresden of 1742 and 1745 which had brought the first two Silesian Wars to an end. In other words, peace had been concluded on the basis of the *status quo ante bellum*. It seemed that six and a half years of ruinously expensive and murderous fighting had been for nothing. That was not how the more far-sighted contemporaries viewed it. The most acute was the Danish chief minister, Count Johann Hartwig Ernst von Bernstorff, who had managed to keep his country out of the war. In December 1759, when the outcome was still unknown, he offered a penetrating analysis in a letter to the French foreign minister, the Duc de Choiseul. Discussing the prospects of peace between France and the Anglo-Prussian alliance, he commented: 'but what conditions will they want, what will they be able to offer? That is the stumbling-block. The King of England wants to win, the King of Prussia does not want to lose, because, if he doesn't lose, he will have won everything.' There was so much territory available in North America that a settlement there could be achieved, but

> this is not the case with the King of Prussia, whose grandeur or abasement is the sole point of the German war. As you know so well, that is

what makes this war so cruel, so dynamic and so difficult to resolve. It did not erupt for a petty or passing interest, for this or that province or city, but for the very existence of the new monarchy which the King of Prussia has raised with a skill and speed that has astonished one part of Europe and fooled the other.

Moreover, Bernstorff went on, it was a different kind of state 'completely militarist and still possessing all the vigour, all the agility and all the greed of a young and slender body'. What was at stake was nothing less than German dualism, whether the Holy Roman Empire in future was to have, along with its official emperor, a second ruler in the north, who had turned his states into a garrison and his people into an army and who could hold the balance between the other great powers of Europe.[87]

Had he ever had the chance to read this analysis, Frederick might well have kept nodding his head in approval. He knew what had been at stake, knew how close his gamble had come to total failure and was in anything but an aggressive mood. He told Prince Henry that he would now set about paying his state's debts 'and after that I shall be able to die if I feel like it'.[88] Although he believed that Maria Theresa and Kaunitz had had enough of war and genuinely wished to restore good relations, he added that he would never forget the fable of the cat and the mice.[89] Despite having been away for the best part of seven years, he was not looking forward to his return home. He told the Marquis d'Argens that his subjects should rejoice at the peace, but 'for me, a poor old man, I shall be going back to a town where only the walls will be familiar, where I shall meet no one I know, and where colossal labour is waiting and from where in a short while I shall leave my old bones in a resting-place untroubled by war, disasters or human villainy'.[90]

10

The Seven Years War: Why Frederick Won

Frederick may not have been triumphalist after the Treaty of Hubertusburg, but everyone else in Europe knew that he had every right to be. As the French Foreign Office conceded when sending a new envoy to Prussia in 1772, for Frederick the Peace of Hubertusburg had been '*glorieuse*'. The Seven Years War had been many things for many countries;[1] for Prussia it had been 'The Third Silesian War', an existential struggle about great-power status. Ranke summed this up well:

> If one could establish as a definition of a great power that it must be able to maintain itself against all others, even when they are united, then Frederick had raised Prussia to that position. For the first time since the days of the Saxon emperors and Henry the Lion [1129–95] a self-sufficient power was found in northern Germany, needing no alliance, dependent only upon itself.[2]

Moreover, this third Silesian war was also the final Silesian war. As Austria had failed to win back the province, despite the support of France, Russia, Sweden and the Holy Roman Empire, there was no prospect of ever achieving that in the future. Kaunitz's aim 'to reduce the house of Brandenburg to its original rank of a second-rate power' had to be abandoned.[3] Even before the war ended, in March 1762, Maria Theresa had told her ambassador in France, Prince Starhemberg, that reconquest was 'a chimerical idea and impossible to achieve'.[4] By that time, the best she could hope for was the county and fortress of Glatz, and even that proved unattainable.

The account of the seven campaigns of 1756–62 has indicated some of the reasons for their outcome; it is now time to pull the threads together. The first concerns Saxony. Frederick's pre-emptive strike of

August 1756 looks very much like a gamble that failed. Held up longer than expected by local resistance, he did not have enough time to deliver a mortal blow against the main enemy before the end of the campaigning season. Moreover, it activated what until then had been merely a defensive alliance between France and Austria, obliging the former to come to the latter's aid. But was it so 'lunatic', as has often been asserted?[5] It is clear that the French would have joined in an aggressive war against Prussia anyway.* It was even more obvious that the Russians were determined to attack and had only been deterred from acting in 1756 by Austria's insistence on the need for delay.†

There were three more positive reasons for Frederick's decision. The first was strategic. For the Austrians, the obvious invasion route into Brandenburg was down the river Elbe through Saxony. As Berlin was unfortified and no more than two or three days' march from the Saxon frontier, Prussian occupation of the Electorate provided a badly needed buffer.[6] It was all the more necessary for Frederick to get in first, for Saxon hostility was intense. Augustus III, King of Poland and Elector of Saxony, was tied to the House of Habsburg by marriage (he had married a daughter of the Emperor Joseph I); by religion (a convert to Catholicism, he showed all the zeal of the neophyte); and by resentment at having been betrayed and exploited during the first two Silesian wars. Greed had prompted him to join Prussia and Bavaria in the attempted partition of Maria Theresa's inheritance in 1740, but by 1744 he was back in the Austrian camp, a sadder if not wiser man.[7] He was both led and kept there by his chief minister, Count Heinrich von Brühl, who nursed a personal hatred of Frederick that was heartily reciprocated.[8] The Saxons hoped that their share of the spoils when Frederick was crushed, as seemed inevitable in 1756, would be a land-bridge across Silesia to link Saxony to Poland.[9] For his part, Frederick had only the greatest contempt for his neighbour, dismissing Augustus as 'the successor of kings from whom he has inherited only pride' and likened his state 'to a ship without a compass, a prey to wind and waves.'[10]

---

* See above, pp. 204–5.
† See above, p. 202.

Secondly, and as a necessary corollary, an immediate occupation of Saxony was an enormous logistical advantage, allowing the river Elbe to be monopolized along virtually its entire navigable length. Crucial here was the great Prussian fortress of Magdeburg on the Elbe just north of the Saxon frontier, which Frederick's predecessors had made the biggest and strongest in the kingdom.[11] Not only did it dominate the Elbe crossing, it was also the gateway to the lowlands of Lower Saxony, and allowed the domination of Hanover and Mecklenburg as well as Saxony.[12] In the course of the Seven Years War it proved to be 'of incalculable value' in the view of Jürgen Luh, while Christopher Duffy has written that without it, Prussia would almost certainly have gone under.[13] From Magdeburg up the Elbe were sent the shiploads of food, forage and ammunition that kept the Prussian armies in the war zone. If the river upstream had been in Austrian hands, this great asset would have been a liability of equivalent severity.

Finally, and most importantly, the seizure of Saxony opened up the richest province in Central Europe to the Prussian foragers. In the course of the next six and a half years, it was bled white to sustain Frederick's war effort. Every state, of course, did the same to the territories it occupied in the course of a war. What singled out Frederick's treatment of Saxony was its intensity, duration and success. This was a result of careful planning. Even before the invasion had been launched, a detailed instruction had been issued to Friedrich Wilhelm von Borcke, the official from the General Directory appointed to supervise the operation. He was authorized to take control of every source of public revenue in the conquered territories, while reassuring Saxon taxpayers that it was not the Prussians' intention to ruin them. Indeed, it was promised that less would be paid than under the previous regime, for a flat tax yielding 5,000,000 talers would replace the great diversity that was estimated to have extracted appreciably more than that in the past. Receipts would be issued for requisitioned food or forage and would be taken into account when assessing taxation.[14] Borcke and his small team of Prussians conscripted the local Saxon officials into their administration and went to work with a will, although never efficiently enough for their exacting royal master. It has been estimated that at least a third of Frederick's total costs during the war was covered by the involuntary sacrifices of the Saxons, in other words the single largest source of income. Moreover, it was significantly greater than anything France or Russia managed to squeeze out of the Prussian territories in the west (Cleves, Mark, etc.) or east (East Prussia) respectively. By putting experienced bureaucrats in charge of the operation Frederick maximized the returns.[15] Needless to say, his stated commitment not to inflict ruin on his new subjects could not be honoured in wartime. He himself famously observed that Saxony was like a flour sack, for no matter how often one hit it, a puff always came out.[16] When Prince Henry proved too considerate to the local population, the task of requisitioning was reassigned to three civilian specialists, prompting the prince to complain that three villains had been authorized to loot and pillage.[17]

The control of the Elbe through possession of Saxony was mirrored by the control of the river Oder through possession of Silesia. Just as the pre-emptive strike of August 1756 had brought occupation of the Saxon fortresses, so had the pre-emptive strike of December 1740 put the Silesian fortresses into Frederick's hands. Indeed, it has been argued cogently by Peter-Michael Hahn that the fundamental reason for Frederick's military success during his reign was that early conquest.[18] So when the Third Silesian War began in earnest, he was already in a strong position.

The Austrians on the other hand were handicapped by serious structural problems. Neither Bohemia nor Moravia was as fertile as Silesia or Saxony, nor were they as well equipped with navigable rivers. The routes up into the Bohemian mountains from their main base at Königgrätz were relatively straightforward, but coming down the other side through the narrow ravines that served as passes was much more problematic and in winter often impossible.[19] And once any Austrian army reached the Silesian plains, it was confronted by Prussian fortresses, the most formidable being Neisse, Glatz and Schweidnitz. That was why the loss of Glatz in 1757 and again in 1760 and Schweidnitz in 1761 were regarded by Frederick as such serious blows – and their recaptures such causes for celebration.* It also explains why he was so insistent that he must have Glatz back when peace was negotiated. It was the fortresses not the battles which kept

* See above, pp. 255–7.

Silesia in Prussian hands.[20] Other fortresses of importance were Colberg on the Baltic, Küstrin on the Oder east of Berlin, Stettin at the mouth of the Oder and Magdeburg on the Elbe.[21]* Together, this network of 'mighty nails', as Frederick described them, bound the provinces together and allowed him to exploit his central position and to fight on 'interior lines'.[22] This latter concept, much favoured by military historians, is really a matter of common sense: a defender in a central position enjoys a natural advantage over several converging enemies because their lines of supply and communication lengthen while his own shortens. Frederick demonstrated this on several occasions during the war, most spectacularly in 1757 with Rossbach followed by Leuthen. It is all the more remarkable therefore that he was so cavalier in his treatment of fortresses. This was well put by Carlyle: 'Nothing so surprises me in Friedrich as his habitual inattention to the state of his Garrisons, he has the best of Commandants and also the worst: Tauentzien in Breslau, Heyde in Colberg, unsurpassable in the world; in Glatz a d'O; in Schweidnitz a Zastrow, both of whom cost him dear.'[23]

Another obvious but important asset enjoyed by Frederick was unity of command.[24] As he was both absolutist head of state and commander-in-chief of the army, he concentrated all authority in his own person. His actual presence meant not only that his own orders were implemented forthwith but also those issued by subordinates acting in his name.[25] Consequently, he could move very much more quickly than his opponents at both the strategic and the tactical level. He was very well aware of this, extolling the feats of similarly advantaged predecessors – Charles XII of Sweden, for example, 'that Alexander of the North, who would have resembled the Macedonian conqueror in all respects if he had had the same luck'.[26] There was no need for Frederick to consult ministers or ask parliament for funds! For him the gap between decision, order and implementation was prolonged only by the shortcomings of his agents (although they were plentiful). How different was the situation at Versailles, St Petersburg or Vienna. Even such a strong and intelligent ruler as Maria Theresa found herself in toils, having to consult her husband Francis I (who

* See above, p. 186.

was after all the Holy Roman Emperor), her son Joseph, her chancellor Kaunitz, and all the other grandees who sat on her Council.[27]

At the other two allied courts, the vicious combination of weak rulers and strong factions made decision-making incoherent. So timid, irresolute and secretive was Louis XV that he had developed a personal and clandestine foreign service, the *'secret du roi'*, which was often at odds with the official institution.[28] So a French envoy might find himself in the difficult situation of receiving two instructions, both signed by his royal master but incompatible in content. The senior French generals in Germany – the Duc de Broglie, the Marquis de Contades, the Prince de Soubise – seem to have spent as much time manoeuvring against each other as against Prince Ferdinand.[29] Although more energetic, the Tsarina Elizabeth was frequently immobilized by illness and just as susceptible to court intrigue. As a result there was a different commander-in-chief for each of the five campaigns the Russians fought.[30] That the last of them, Count Alexander Borisovich Buturlin, was appointed because he had once been the tsarina's lover graphically encapsulates the Russian military underperformance. Not only could he not read a map, he had no battlefield experience.[31]

The importance of unity of command seems self-evident. Georg Friedrich von Tempelhoff, who served in the Prussian army throughout the war, first as an artilleryman and later as an officer, and wrote a six-volume history of the conflict, stated firmly that 'it is the army led by its sovereign which enjoys the decisive advantage. Even the greatest general cannot and may not risk what a king who stands at the head of his troops can venture.'[32] That was ruefully recognized by Field Marshal Daun, who had better reason than most to complain about the handicap of *dis*unity of command.[33] His main objective was the defence of the Habsburg Monarchy and that meant first and foremost keeping the army intact; as he wrote: 'an army can soon be ruined but not so quickly put together again, and without armed force, the Monarchy has no means of support'.[34] Napoleon, a keen student of the Seven Years War, agreed. From an early stage in his career, after observing the disunity of the allied coalition against revolutionary France, he saw that 'a house divided against itself cannot stand'. Looking back on his military career, he proclaimed: 'unity of

command is the most important thing in war'.[35] However, the fact
that Napoleon was languishing in exile on St Helena when he uttered
those words should give pause for further thought. Unity of command
had allowed him to conduct the Austerlitz campaign, but it had also
allowed him to enforce a misguided strategy in Spain in 1808, Russia
in 1812, Saxony in 1813 and Belgium in 1815. Similarly, for Frederick unity of command made Hohenfriedberg, Rossbach, Leuthen and
Torgau possible, but also Kolin, Hochkirch, Kunersdorf and Maxen.
Unity of command proved to be a double-edged sword. When it
worked, it could turn opportunity into triumph. But it could also elevate a reverse into a disaster. This was doubly dangerous for Frederick
because, as we have seen, he was an inveterate risk-taker, a gambler
who liked to call 'Va banque!' During the dark days of the summer of
1760, he wrote to the Marquis d'Argens: 'our affairs are taking a
terrible turn; whether I like it or not, I must now embark on a great
adventure and play double or quits'.[36]

To continue Frederick's metaphor, it could be said that the cards
with which he played the first two Silesian wars were inherited, as he
freely admitted.* By the time the third war ended, he had been on the
throne for almost a quarter of a century and it must be conceded that
he was dealing from a pack he had drawn himself. Not that he was a
great innovator. Rather he took the 'walking battery' bequeathed by
his father and Old Dessauer, polished and refined it further and greatly
increased its size. As with the civilian administration, he imitated but
also intensified his father's personal attention to business. Drill, drill
and more drill; training, training and more training; exercises, exercises and more exercises – that was the lot of the Prussian soldier of
all ranks. Special attention was paid to loading drill – a daily
ritual – with the result that a Prussian musketeer could fire at a rate
of rather more than twice a minute, which meant that a battalion
could fire twelve times a minute, by some margin the fastest rate in
Europe.[37] The Austrian General Neipperg lamented that the Prussian
infantry had fired five times before his own men had got off two
shots.[38] Frederick's experiences in the Seven Years War did not change
his mind on this point, all evidence of the importance of cold steel

* See above, p. 14.

notwithstanding. In his *Political Testament* of 1768 he emphasized that battles are won by superior firepower, that therefore the infantry that loads fastest will prevail and so daily practice was essential.[39]

To enforce this iron regime, Frederick's hypercritical eye was never far away. No one was safe, no one knew when or where he was going to pop up. And when he did, he was very much hands-on, riding with the cavalry, for example, when it charged on manoeuvres, to make sure his orders were being followed.[40] Even the cadets at the Berlin Military Academy might expect to find him appearing at examination time to ensure rigour and ask his own questions.[41] In peacetime, the military year began in February with exercises held simultaneously in Brandenburg, Magdeburg and Pomerania, followed by major reviews held at Berlin and Potsdam in May, Magdeburg in June, Stargard in Pomerania in July, and Silesia in August or September.[42] During an actual campaign, Frederick's personal attention was legendary. Johann Wilhelm von Archenholz, who served in the Prussian army during the war, recorded:

> The king himself set an example of ceaseless vigilance. One was never safe from him, as little in the most desolate places as in the most dangerous, as little on a starlit night as during the most terrible thunderstorm, and he had succeeded in making both senior and junior officers fear him more than enemy bullets, so that the mere possibility of a visit was enough to redouble vigilance. Often he made his inspections without revealing his presence.[43]

In three areas Frederick improved his inheritance. We have already seen that right at the start he transformed the regular cavalry of cuirassiers and dragoons. Subsequently, he greatly increased the numbers and importance of light mounted troops in the shape of hussars, who had numbered only around 1,000 in 1740. The deadly effectiveness of the Croats operating with the Austrian armies demanded imitation. In quantitative terms, the response was certainly impressive – by the end of the reign about 9 per cent of the total military strength comprised hussars – but qualitatively much less so. The autonomy, independence and relaxed discipline of the light troops did not accord well with the Prussian ethos. So the new units were quickly reined in and turned into something barely distinguishable from the regular cavalry.[44] After

1756 Frederick did however allow the formation of so-called 'free-battalions', quasi-private gangs of quasi-criminals, who could cause havoc behind enemy lines but also became notorious for their looting and other offences.[45] In 1778 a British observer, Nathaniel Wraxall, reported from Vienna:

> It is in the irregular forces which Maria Theresa can bring into the field, that she possesses a great superiority over her adversary. The Croats and Hungarians, fierce, undisciplined, and subjected to scarcely any military laws, are attached to the House of Austria by prejudices and predilections of religion, manners, and education, peculiar to themselves. Frederic has no troops of a similar description to oppose to them, equally faithful and loyal. The Croat rarely or never deserts.[46]

More impressive were the improvements he made to his artillery. In this department, Frederick William I had lagged a long way behind the rest of Europe and Frederick had to sprint to catch up. Improved casting techniques, lighter barrels and carriages, more mobility and standardization of calibres and parts had brought a massive increase in the number of pieces deployed on the battlefield. In the Thirty Years War, each side had boasted no more than a couple of dozen; at Malplaquet in 1709 the Austro-British allies fielded over a hundred against the sixty of the French.[47] In his *Political Testament* of 1768, Frederick complained that he had inherited just one field artillery battalion, which he immediately doubled.[48] This early initiative was not followed through, however. The expansion announced in 1744 was not implemented after the peace, with the result that in 1756 the Prussian army had no more artillery than ten years before.[49] Moreover, the quality was poor. The arms manufacturers of Berlin and Breslau had not yet developed the modern technique of boring out a solid core (rather than casting over a core). So now Frederick found himself on a steep learning curve, as in battle after battle it was the cannon not the musket that inflicted the heaviest casualties.[50] But learn he did. By the last year of the Seven Years War he had 662 pieces of artillery available, not counting the heavy siege guns. Moreover, he had also proved himself an innovator by introducing a horse artillery unit consisting of six six-pounders, each pulled by four horses and serviced by three NCOs and forty-two artillerymen. It was lost at Kunersdorf, promptly replaced, lost again at Maxen and replaced again. From June 1759 Prince Henry had his own similar unit, which he did not lose. The effectiveness of this ultra-mobile artillery was advertised when it was imitated, first by the Austrians – hitherto leaders in artillery development – and then by other European armies.[51] Frederick was now a firm believer in the battle-winning potential of artillery, as he told his generals in his treatise on 'Fortifications and tactics' of 1771, for example.[52] So important did he consider it, indeed, that he moved the training centre for gunners to Berlin, so that he could keep an eye on it.[53]

In the final analysis, success or failure in the war depended on the infantry. As the accounts of the seven campaigns have shown, the Prussians were by no means invincible. Of the sixteen major battles, they lost eight.[54] Nevertheless, despite being usually outnumbered, often heavily, they were still standing at the end of the 1762 campaign when their enemies had given up. The fearful casualties suffered during the bloodbaths of 1757 and 1759 meant that many, if not most, of the highly trained veterans who had marched off in August 1756 had been killed or invalided out by the time the fifth campaign began. As each year passed, it became more difficult to fill the gaps during the winter, so that each campaigning season began with fewer men than the year before. With so much of the Holy Roman Empire shut off from the recruiting sergeants by enemy armies, it was the cantonal system at home which had to bear the brunt. Increasingly, the conscripts it sent to the armies were younger and less well trained. This did not mean they were ineffective. As the engagement at Domstadl in June 1758 showed, raw recruits could give a good account of themselves, even in defeat.[55] Expedients such as the impressment of prisoners of war, on the other hand, proved to be self-defeating, as they were notoriously unreliable and deserted or surrendered at the first opportunity. By the end of the war, 'almost all' soldiers still at the colours were native-born Prussians.[56] Well might Frederick record with gratitude after the war that 'these cantons constitute the pure essence of the state'.[57] It had been his ability to keep on raising armies that had seen him through.[58]

'In the land of the blind, the one-eyed man is king,' wrote Erasmus. Nowhere is that more true than in the fuzzy-edged field of military

history, where every generalization is qualified and every plus coun-
tered by a minus. The Prussian infantryman looted, deserted, cheated,
ran away and even on occasions disobeyed, but of his *relative* superiority there is too much contemporary evidence to be ignored. Ulrich
Bräker, a Swiss who had been tricked into joining the Prussian army
and was anything but well intentioned towards it, recorded that when
he and his comrades first saw action at Lobositz in October 1756,
'our native-born Prussians and Brandenburgers set about the Austrians like furies. I myself was so violent and excited that I felt neither
fear nor horror but blazed away with all my ammunition until my
musket was red-hot and I had to hold it by the strap; although I don't
think I hit a living soul and all my shots went wild.'[59] Major General
Henry Lloyd, who had served in the Austrian army and had first-hand
experience of the Seven Years War, described the Prussian army as 'a
vast and regular machine . . . They have a facility in manoeuvring
beyond any other troops . . . and their victories must be ascribed to
this chiefly for all the genius of the leader can do nothing without it,
and almost everything with it.'[60]

The familiar image of the Prussian rank-and-file is of mindless
automata programmed by brutal discipline to advance into the jaws
of death without flinching. Frederick himself bore responsibility for
this by issuing his famous (and often repeated) instruction that the
soldiers should be taught to fear their officers more than the enemy.[61]
By devoting the whole of the first chapter of his *General Principles of
War* of 1748 to the problem of desertion and identifying fourteen
ways in which it could be reduced, he announced the essentially
coercive nature of his army.[62] Even an observer as well disposed
to Frederick as the French General Guibert believed that the non-
Prussians in the army, who he thought counted for 50 per cent of the
rank-and-file, would desert at once if not deterred by the near-
certainty of capture and the horrific punishment that followed.[63]
Frederick's army on the march was 'a mobile prison'.[64]

More recently, however, this grim picture has been much modified.
Life in the ranks has been shown to be not just terror, privation and
violence. There is also evidence of loyalty or even devotion to Frederick and Prussia more generally. Much of this is anecdotal, and so has
to be taken with a good pinch of salt, but not all of it. When the

Austrians tried to recruit from the 11,000 prisoners of war they were holding in camps in Styria, they got only a feeble response, and none at all from the native-born Prussians, despite the conditions in which they were being held.[65] It has long been known that the Prussian soldiers were better fed than their enemies, thanks to their ability to fight on interior lines and the relative efficiency of their logistics. Ensign von Barsewisch, who served throughout the war and saw action at Rossbach, Leuthen and Torgau, claimed:

> We were never short of bread, and it frequently happened that we had a surplus of meat. It is true that coffee, sugar and beer were often not to be had even at high prices, while in Moravia we sometimes ran out of wine. But in Bohemia we had local wine in plenty, especially in the camp at Melnik in 1757. You know how things are in wartime: if you want to be really comfortable, you ought to stay at home.[66]

Johann Wilhelm von Archenholz, who also served during the war, agreed: 'the Prussian army was never without pay, never without bread or forage, very rarely without vegetables and even more rarely without meat'.[67] The half-pound of meat issued each week to every soldier is reported to have attracted many starving deserters from the allied armies to the Prussian camps.[68]

How many went the other way? There were certainly episodes when thousands took flight, the retreat from Moravia in 1744 being the most notorious.* On the other hand, even a catastrophic defeat did not lead to the permanent dissolution of the army. Within two days of Kunersdorf, for example, most survivors had returned to the colours and reformed as disciplined units ready to fight another day.[69] Recent research has shown that the harshness of Prussian discipline has been exaggerated and that the soldiers were motivated by honour, *esprit de corps*, professionalism, Protestantism and patriotism as well as fear.[70]

The relative quality of the rank-and-file was repeated in the echelons above. Although impossible to prove, it is at least very likely that an important advantage enjoyed by Frederick was the number and quality of his non-commissioned officers. There were fourteen per

* See above, pp. 108–9.

company, more than double the rate of the Austrian army, mostly the literate sons of free peasants. They were encouraged by the prospect of winning commissioned rank and even noble status if they distinguished themselves in wartime.[71] A legend in his own lifetime was the fifty-year-old grenadier David Krauel, who was first over the ramparts of the Ziskaberg fortifications at Prague on 12 August 1744 and was rewarded with an immediate commission and ennoblement as 'Krauel von Ziskaberg'.[72] These commoners were joined by nobles, all of whom had to start as ensigns, performing the duties and sharing the quarters of the other NCOs and receiving the pay of a sergeant.[73] An anonymous English report composed after the Seven Years War stated that 'the vigour of the Army is in the Subalterns and Non-Commissioned Officers, who are undoubtedly the best in the world.'[74]

The same report went on to observe that 'it seems to decline as the ranks ascend, and as other qualifications than those of mere execution become requisite'. This verdict seems much less justified. On many occasions in Frederick's battles, as he himself ruefully admitted, initiatives launched by subordinates proved decisive.[75] Most of the officers were native Prussians, most were nobles from the same sort of background, they had all had the same education and training, apart from those who had risen from the ranks, and consequently enjoyed a much greater cohesion than their colleagues in other armies.[76] Convinced that 'the valour of the troops consists solely in the valour of the officers',[77] Frederick used both stick and carrot to keep his officers on their toes. At the annual reviews, any deemed to be incompetent, unfit or too old were weeded out, sent off to garrison regiments and replaced by the best ensigns.[78] Moreover, no matter what their rank or status, they were obliged to be on duty with their regiments for most of the year, even in peacetime. It was this requirement which most impressed French observers, accustomed to a world in which many officers spent most of their time at Versailles or on their estates.[79] No matter how august his background or elevated his rank, the Prussian officer had to share the privations of his men. In July 1753, Count Lehndorff visited Frederick's brother August Wilhelm, who was with his cavalry regiment at Kyritz, west of Neuruppin. He recorded in his diary:

The town is terrible, it really is a miserable dump, and so is the house in which the Prince lives. It is comic to find him in a room whose furniture consists of a wooden table and three chairs. There are no curtains! His kitchen-boy in Berlin is better housed. But the Prince is devoted to training his regiment and is very satisfied. He is very kind to his officers and as a result is extraordinarily loved by them. And this is what distinguishes our army from all the others: our princes are soldiers themselves and have to put up with just the same hardships as the common soldiers do.[80]

The example was set right at the top. As we have seen, at home at Sanssouci or in the Potsdam Town Palace, Frederick was positively self-indulgent. But once he took the campaigning trail, or even went on peacetime exercises, quite a different regime was followed. Anticipating Napoleon, he went out of his way to impress on all ranks that he was one of them, that they were all in it together, sharing the dangers, the discomforts and the triumphs. This meant riding with the men, talking to them in dialect, visiting them as they sat around the campfire, laughing at their jokes, however crude, sleeping under canvas at the centre of the camp, remembering their names, and so on.[81] Although it can be assumed that he drew the line at joining them on church parade, he allowed his pious subordinates to organize prayer meetings and the troops to sing Lutheran hymns.[82] According to the Prussian soldier Johann Friedrich Dreyer, he and his comrades sang 'A Mighty Fortress is Our God' as they went into battle and 'Now Thank We All Our God' if they survived.[83] Before the battle of Leuthen, Frederick even joined in himself, to sing:

> Do not be faint-hearted, O little band,
> Although your enemies are of the will
> To upset you completely,
> And seek your downfall, of which
> You are most distressed and perplexed:
> It will not last long.[84]

Christian Tage, a chaplain serving in the Russian army, recorded after the battle of Zorndorf 'the dreadful and terrifying moment' when the

Prussian line wheeled into oblique order to the sound of drums. As they advanced, first the fife band became audible and then a thousand voices roaring out the Lutheran hymn 'Ich bin ja, Herr, in Deiner Macht' (Lord, I am in your power).[85] Prussian soldiers were famous for their singing. The poet-officer Ewald von Kleist wrote to his friend Johann Wilhelm Ludwig Gleim in 1758 that on the march they liked to sing hymns first, before moving on to songs in praise of Frederick.[86] Obviously it is impossible to quantify the impact of this close relationship between the warlord and his men, which has been likened to that between a highland chief and his clan, but it was probably considerable. Visiting Prussia at the very end of the reign, the Marquis de Toulongeon, a French officer, concluded that 'the fundamental basis on which the great edifice of military power in Prussia resides is the example set by the King and his generals'.[87] The Austrian cavalryman Jacob de Cognazo was very impressed:

> The king treated his common soldiers with a degree of comradeship which in our army would not have been shown by a noble captain let alone a high and mighty general, and so they knew that there was no grievance, no hunger, no cold, no watch-keeping, no daily burden, in short no danger or discomfort of the war however great that was not shared by their 'Great Fritz', as they dubbed him with their child-like veneration and love.[88]

Certainly there were plenty of anecdotes making the rounds to advertise it. For example, Count Lehndorff recorded in his diary in November 1759 that, when Frederick fell ill en route from Silesia to Saxony, he was placed in a litter to be carried by thirty men, to avoid the jolting of a carriage. When the time came for the first team to be replaced, they refused to make way and insisted on carrying their king the whole way. 'Such is the veneration paid to him by his army,' proclaimed Lehndorff.[89]

In short, for all his snobbery and contempt for humanity,* Frederick showed a sharp awareness of the need to cultivate an intimate bond with his army. Although fear reinforced by punishment was an important ingredient, he also knew how to reward. As with Daniel

---

* See below, pp. 336–7.

Krauel von Ziskaberg, conspicuous gallantry on the field of battle could be recognized at once. Promotions, public or written expressions of appreciation, the medal of the Order *'Pour le Mérite'* (better known later as the 'Blue Max') and straight cash payments were all used. After victory at Liegnitz, for example, every regiment received 137 talers for captured cannons and fifty talers for captured standards and flags.[90] This was one of the many aspects of Frederick's leadership to catch the approving eye of the Comte de Guibert. After Hohenfriedberg, he noted, Frederick wrote out in his own hand a diploma of thanks for the 'Bayreuth' regiment of dragoons in which every officer was mentioned by name.[91] The 'Pour le Mérite' was not only a battlefield decoration. It was also awarded to Lieutenant von Freytag, for example, the inventor of the funnel-shaped powder hole that made charging muskets easier.[92]

The other side of the coin, of course, was equally instant punishment for cowardice or incompetence. The most prominent casualty was Frederick's brother August Wilhelm, ruthlessly disgraced in 1757 with the words: 'you will never be anything more than a pitiful general. Command a harem of maids of honour, if you wish; but I shall never again entrust you with the command of ten men.'[93] Further down the hierarchy, the most notorious collective disgrace was that inflicted on the Anhalt-Bernburg regiment after it broke and ran from an Austrian attack outside Dresden in July 1760. Redemption was achieved the following month at Liegnitz when to shouts of 'Honour or death!' the same soldiers launched a devastating counterattack with bayonets, 'one of the few occasions in military history in which infantry have ever taken the offensive against cavalry'.[94] After the battle, Frederick rode over to the survivors of the regiment:

> The officers uttered not a word, in the silent expectation that the king would render them justice. But four old soldiers rushed to his stirrups, clasped his knee and begged him to restore them to favour in recognition of how well they had done their duty this day. Frederick was moved. He answered: 'Yes, lads, everything will be given back to you. All is forgotten!'[95]

Things were very different in the Austrian army, where there was not one court martial in the course of the war.[96]

One more ingredient in Frederick's recipe for success in the Seven Years War needs to be mentioned. It both encapsulates and transcends the points already made. That is charisma, no less important for being difficult to pin down. It was famously defined by Max Weber as:

> a certain quality of an individual personality by virtue of which he is set apart from ordinary men and treated as endowed with supernatural, superhuman, or at least specifically exceptional power or qualities. These are such as are not accessible to the ordinary person, but are regarded as of divine origin or as exemplary, and on the basis of them the individual concerned is treated as a leader.[97]

Weber was thinking of religious leaders such as Christ or Joan of Arc, and in politics – rather surprisingly – had Mr Gladstone in mind as an exemplar, but Frederick certainly fits well. This was a major theme of Theodor Schieder, who pointed out that Maria Theresa was just as popular as her rival and was greatly his superior when it came to humanity and integrity, but lacked 'the charisma of a personality driven by his inner demon'.[98] He also drew attention to the example provided by Frederick's famous speech delivered to his generals and staff officers at Parchwitz on 3 December 1757 just before the battle of Leuthen. It was short, to the point, eloquent and revealing. He started by emphasizing the desperate plight in which they found themselves: Schweidnitz and Breslau had fallen; their supplies had been captured; the Duke of Bevern had been defeated and taken prisoner; most of Silesia was under Austrian occupation. He would be desperate, he declared, without the knowledge that he could count on the steadfastness, courage and patriotism of the men who stood before him and those they commanded. The hour had struck, it was now: do or die!:

> Against all the rules of war I shall attack Prince Charles wherever I find him, even though his army is three times as numerous. Now it is a question of how many enemies there are or the strength of the position they have taken up; all this can be overcome by the enthusiasm of my troops and the precise execution of my orders. I have to risk this operation, or everything is lost; we must defeat the enemy or all of us must perish before his batteries. This is what I think, and this is what I shall

do. Make my decision known to all your officers and prepare the rank
and file for the events that must follow, and tell them that I am counting on their unconditional obedience. Remember that you are Prussians
and you will prove worthy of that distinction; but if there is any one
among you afraid of sharing the dangers with me, then let him take his
leave and he will suffer not the slightest reproach from me.[99]

He ended by brandishing the stick: a cavalry regiment failing to charge
when given the order would be unhorsed and sent off to man a garrison, any infantry unit that even wavered would lose sabres, flags
and regimental insignia (the disgrace inflicted on the Anhalt-Bernburg
regiment after Dresden).

Charismatic authority or legitimacy is both immensely potent and
notoriously fragile, for the good reason that it relies on the individual's performance. If the miracles stop happening, the prophecies fail to
materialize or the victories stop coming, it can collapse very quickly.
Napoleon and Hitler provide good examples, although even they
managed to retain some measure of support until the end (and even
beyond). But Frederick was peculiar in that his defeats did not erode
his charisma, rather the reverse. If he had died at Zorndorf or if Kunersdorf had been followed by total collapse and the dismemberment
of his state, it might have been different. It was just because he kept
on going in the face of apparently overwhelming odds that occasional
failure could be absorbed by the ever-burgeoning myth. The chaplain
Küster, for example, was an eye-witness of the disaster of Hochkirch,
about which he wrote a graphic account. Yet it only enhanced his
veneration of his king, for – he asked rhetorically – when was a lost
battle ever rewarded with such wonderful results? The Austrians did
not follow up; Neisse and Kosel were relieved; the Swedes left Pomerania; the Russians went home; and by the end of the year the Austrians
had evacuated both Silesia and Saxony.[100]

This leads naturally to a consideration of what was perhaps the
main reason for Frederick's survival: the failure of the allies to coordinate their war efforts. All five continental allies had different war
aims. Four sought territorial gains, either to be kept or traded: Silesia
for Austria, Belgium and Hanover for France, East Prussia for Russia
and Prussian Pomerania for Sweden, while the Holy Roman Empire

sought to uphold the imperial constitution contravened by Frederick's invasion of Saxony. Ironically, it was only the last named and weakest of the five which achieved its objective, despite a fitful military performance. All might well have succeeded if Frederick had been crushed quickly and completely. The longer the war went on, the more the rifts began to show. As the later Prussian reformer Scharnhorst sagely observed, every coalition carried within it the germ of a secret betrayal.[101] One serious worm had been in the bud from the start. *Two* diplomatic revolutions had occurred at the start of the war – not just the alliance between France and Austria, but also that between France and Russia, concluded when the latter acceded to the first Treaty of Versailles on 11 January 1757. Yet, as we have seen,* traditional French policy had been devoted to constructing an 'Eastern Barrier' against any form of Russian expansion.[102] Sweden was an especial bone of contention, as the French supported the faction known as the 'Hats' and the Russians the 'Caps'.

The Austrians too had reservations about Russian expansion. At the end of 1760 Kaunitz told Maria Theresa that Russia should not be allowed to expand westwards lest it turn out to pose more of a threat to the Habsburg Monarchy than did Prussia.[103] Moreover, the Russian military performance was sporadic. Partly this was a question of distance. So far away was the front that reinforcements melted away en route. Of a contingent of 20,799 that set off in 1759, 5,539 (26 per cent) fell ill or died and 849 deserted.[104] Although improvements were made in the course of the war, the immense Russian potential was never realized.[105] Part of the problem was political. There was always a strong party at St Petersburg whose members did not share the tsarina's personal antipathy to Frederick. They argued very reasonably that in any alliance with him, Russia would always be the dominant partner and able to play him off against Austria.[106]

The same sort of flaw weakened the Franco-Austrian alliance. So radical was the change of direction imposed by the first Treaty of Versailles that opposition to its reversal of two and a half centuries of hostility to the House of Habsburg was inevitable. As the policy was closely associated with the royal mistress Madame de Pompadour, it naturally

---

* See above, p. 82.

attracted the full venom of Versailles faction-fighting. The minister she had put in place to negotiate the diplomatic revolution, the Abbé Bernis, lamented in April 1758: 'our nation is more than ever worked up against the war. The King of Prussia is loved to the point of madness, because those who run their business successfully are always popular. The court of Vienna is hated because it is seen as the bloodsucker of our state.'[107] Just as the Russian national interest had been distorted by Tsarina Elizabeth's fierce hatred of Frederick, so was French national interest distorted by Louis XV's deep affection for Maria Theresa.[108] Almost everyone, with the important exception of the king, his mistress and their chosen ministers, could see that a strong Prussia was needed in the Holy Roman Empire to balance Austria. The Comte de Vergennes, foreign minister of Louis XVI, asked rhetorically where France would have found herself if 'les efforts monstrueux' of the Seven Years War had succeeded and Prussia had been eliminated.[109]

Four days after his letter to Prince Henry of 1 September 1759 announcing 'the miracle of the House of Brandenburg',* Frederick wrote to Prince Ferdinand in the same vein. The campaign could only end well, he stated, if there were either a miracle or his enemies committed some 'divine idiocy' (divine ânerie).[110] The latter took the form of a refusal by the Russians and the Austrians to combine to deliver the final blow. It was not the first or last time. Napoleon observed: 'everything tends to prove that he [Frederick] could not have resisted France, Austria and Russia for one campaign, if these powers had acted in earnest; and that he could not have sustained two campaigns against Austria and Russia, if the Cabinet of St Petersburg had allowed its army to winter on the theatre of operations'.[111] This was not contingent, explicable in terms of the personalities of Elizabeth, Maria Theresa or Louis XV. It was an inherent part of coalition warfare. The same sort of structural flaw saved Louis XIV at the end of the War of the Spanish Succession and would have saved Napoleon in 1814 if he had not been so stupid. As Clausewitz observed in On War: 'one country may support another's cause, but will never take it so seriously as it takes its own. A moderately-sized force will be sent to

* See above, p. 240.

its help; but if things go wrong the operation is pretty well written off, and one tries to withdraw at the smallest possible cost.'[112]

That in itself should guard against the facile assumption that Frederick was saved from perdition only by a fluke – the death of the Tsarina Elizabeth on 5 January 1762.* First put into print by Frederick himself, this is a myth which continues to be repeated.[113] As we have seen, by that time *all* the continental combatants were exhausted, out of money and out of willpower. It was the Prussian state that could still generate the necessary funds and manpower to win the last battles. Moreover, it was a death long anticipated. Even before the war began, it was reported from St Petersburg that the tsarina's health was very bad, that she was often short of breath, was spitting blood, had swollen legs, water on the chest, and so on.[114] The likelihood that she would die sooner rather than later was in everyone's minds as the war unfolded, not least in the minds of the Russian commanders who knew that her heir was passionately pro-Frederick.[115]

Frederick had won – just – because of the strength of his inheritance, the involuntary sacrifices of his subjects, the '*ânerie*' of his enemies and the inherent problems of coalition warfare. The final question is, of course, how much of a contribution did he make himself? Undoubtedly, the army that saw him through to the bitter end was in good measure his creation. A more flaccid hand would have allowed Frederick William I's inheritance to go to seed – in the same way that his own successors did. Frederick ratcheted the military machine up still higher, made important improvements and greatly increased the size. The effect of the personal example he set in galvanizing both the civilian and the military administrations was 'incalculable'.[116] It was on the battlefield that the picture begins to blur. The horrific mistakes he made at Kolin, Hochkirch, Kunersdorf and Maxen (just to mention the more obvious) surely negates any claim to the genius rating claimed by his more enthusiastic admirers. Time and again he was saved from defeat only by the enterprise of his subordinates and the sacrifices of the rank-and-file. The much vaunted 'oblique attack' only really worked once, at Leuthen. Every other attempt failed because conditions on the parade ground could not be

* See above, pp. 253–4.

replicated on the battlefield.[117] In the course of the war, Prince Henry proved himself to be the more talented commander by far, both in tactical manoeuvring and on the field of battle. Frederick himself recognized that, toasting his brother at a banquet after the war as 'the only general never to have made a mistake'.[118] It was an admiration that was definitely not reciprocated. Henry hated his royal brother with a pathological intensity that probably traced back to Frederick's poaching of his beloved catamite, the page von der Marwitz.[119]

Prince Henry was indeed the better general, but he would have lost the war. If Frederick had been killed at Kunersdorf or had committed suicide afterwards (which he seems to have contemplated), Henry would have made a peace that returned Silesia to Austria and Prussia to second-rank status.[120] And that, ultimately, was Frederick's greatest contribution to his success: his indomitable will and ruthless determination to keep going, no matter how desperate the situation looked. In short, he was an indifferent general but a brilliant warlord.

I I

A Long Peace, a Short War
and Double Diplomacy

THE FIRST PARTITION OF POLAND

The miracle of Brandenburg was also the debacle of Poland.[1]

When the Second Silesian War ended in 1745, Frederick had written to his foreign minister, Podewils: 'now that we have escaped from the storm, let us stay in port and never leave it'.[2] In the event, he had been driven out to sea again in 1756 when the mighty fleets of Austria, France and Russia appeared on the horizon, not to mention the smaller squadrons of Sweden and the German princes. When the surviving vessels limped back to their respective havens seven years later, Frederick was in anything but a confident mood. He knew all too well just how close he had come to being blown out of the water. The miracle that saved him was not the fortuitous death of the tsarina, although that certainly helped, but the failure of the Russian and Austrian armies to combine their operations. They had managed that only once, at Kunersdorf on 12 August 1759, which was the closest Frederick ever came to drowning.* So when peace returned, he was even more determined never to weigh anchor again.

The key to calm seas and a prosperous voyage, as he saw it, lay in finding shelter from the wind that blew from the east. In 1739, in *Antimachiavel*, he had derided Russia as a country just emerging from barbarism, scarcely more formidable than the Dutch Republic in naval and military power and greatly inferior in wealth and resources.[3] Thirty years later a sadder and wiser Frederick told his brother Prince

---

* See above, pp. 239–40.

Henry that Russia was 'a terrible power'. It was all the fault of the Austrians, of course, he went on, for it was they who had first called into the European states-system a power from the east to redress the balance of the west.[4] Unlike Charles XII (or Napoleon or Hitler), Frederick could grasp that the sheer size of the Russian Empire made it invulnerable in defence, while its inexhaustible manpower allowed it to wreak havoc in offence. As the events of 1756 had shown, the Austrians would never have dared to attack Prussia without Russian assistance.[5] So Frederick's top priority always had to be keeping Austria and Russia apart.

His task was made both easier and more complex by events in Poland very soon after the Seven Years War ended. On 5 October 1763, the amiable if indolent Polish King Augustus III died. At once Frederick fired off a letter to St Petersburg, telling the Tsarina Catherine that he would do anything in his power to help her in the election campaign for a new monarch that now began.[6] In subsequent letters he fell over himself with assurances of assistance, including an order to his man at Warsaw to follow the Russian line. 'Our alliance has not yet been concluded,' he told her, 'but I consider myself to be your ally and am behaving accordingly.'[7] Ever alert to the threat posed by a personal union between Saxony and Poland,* he was particularly anxious that the nexus should now be broken.

On this point he need not have worried. Catherine had decided more than a year earlier that her former lover Prince Stanisław Poniatowski would be the next King of Poland.[8] He was selected not because of his strength in the bedchamber but for his weakness of character. Of all the possible candidates, Catherine observed, he was the one with the worst chance of winning by himself, so would owe her the most. Just to make sure, he was obliged to promise to regard Russia's interests as his own, to maintain constant 'devotion' to his benefactress and never to refuse her 'just intentions'.[9] But to make sure of her satrap's election, she needed the help of another power. As both France and Austria were too tied to Saxony by dynastic and confessional solidarity and Britain was not interested, that left only Frederick. 'Don't laugh at me because I leapt from my chair when I

* See above, p. 87.

heard of the death of the King of Poland,' she told her foreign minister Count Nikita Panin, 'the King of Prussia jumped up from his table.'[10]

It was some months, however, before an actual embrace could be negotiated. Frederick was not interested in an *ad hoc* agreement, he wanted a proper permanent alliance, and that was what he got, eventually. In November 1763 it was beginning to look as if Catherine thought she might secure Poniatowski's election without buying Prussian help, so Frederick applied some rather crude diplomatic pressure by giving a lavish reception to a Turkish envoy.[11] Although he had no intention of concluding an alliance with the Ottoman Empire, Frederick made a great show of giving it careful consideration, in the full knowledge that such a connection would be extremely unwelcome in St Petersburg. Catherine now hurried things along. On 26 January 1764, the Prussian ambassador was presented with a draft defensive alliance that Frederick could broadly accept.[12] After the small print was sorted out, the definitive treaty was signed on 11 April, committing the two sovereigns to backing Poniatowski in the impending election and also guaranteeing each other's European possessions against any third-party attack. In other words, the previous Russian commitment to Austria to support the reconquest of Silesia had been reversed.[13] Well might Frederick celebrate. So long as this Russian alliance lasted, his haven was safe.

At first, all went well. The election of Stanisław Poniatowski as King of Poland on 6 September was 'the least troublesome in the Republic's history', as he himself claimed.[14] But the Russians and their Prussian allies then paraded their power too nakedly. When the Polish *Sejm* modernized the country's customs system, Frederick blocked its shipping on the Vistula at Marienwerder with a battery of ten heavy cannon until this was revoked.[15] For the most part, however, Frederick was content to let Catherine take charge. This she did with a will, treating Poland not so much as a client as a puppet. The new king's attempt to reform the anarchic political structure was quickly snuffed out. Knowing that the Catholic nobility would never submit to Russian control, she sought to use her self-appointed role as protector of the Orthodox and Protestants to create an alternative client-base. In December 1767 a *Sejm* intimidated by Russian soldiers passed into law 'the most comprehensive statutory enactment of religious toleration in Europe'.[16] The result was civil war, as the mainly – and intensely – Catholic Polish nobles took up arms. A Confederation formed at Bar in Podolia in the south-east early in 1768 began a rising that took the Russians four years to bring under control. Even more seriously, the flagrance of Russian intervention in Poland provoked the Turks into declaring war in October.[17]

This was the last thing Frederick wanted, just as his country was struggling to recover from the Seven Years War. He told his man in Vienna, Count von Rohde, that the news was 'infinitely unpleasant' because there was a real danger that the war would drag in the other European powers, including Prussia.[18] He was already involved in-directly, because the Turkish declaration of war had activated his defensive alliance with Catherine. Although no Prussian troops had to be sent, a substantial annual subsidy of 400,000 roubles (or 480,000 talers), amounting to some 3 per cent of the gross revenue of his state, had to be paid for the duration of the war.[19] This was money he would much rather have spent on projects such as the New Palace, now nearing completion at Potsdam. Both nightmarish and probable was a scenario which had the Russian armies achieving military superior-ity, Catherine demanding large territorial gains – and the Austrians entering the war to stop her. That would have forced Frederick into a conflict in which he had nothing to gain but everything to lose.

The war went just as Frederick had feared. By the end of 1769 the Russians had taken control of the Sea of Azov in the south-east and had occupied Bucharest in the south-west. The following year proved to be an *annus mirabilis*. In July Count Peter Alexandrovich Rumy-antsev scored two crushing victories over much larger Turkish armies, on the 7th at the junction of the Larga and Pruth rivers and two weeks later on the Kagul river. This dazzling operation opened up the whole of the vast area between the Dniestr and the Danube. By the end of the campaign, the Russians had conquered all the main Turkish fortresses there, most notably Bender, and had reached the Danube delta. Perhaps even more spectacular was the naval victory won at Chesme off the Anatolian coast near the island of Chios, achieved on 5 July by a Russian fleet which had sailed all the way from the Baltic via the English Channel and the Straits of Gibraltar. This astonishing feat at once established itself as the Russian equivalent of Lepanto and caused both rejoicing at home and respect everywhere else in Europe.[20]

As the Russian steamroller powered through Moldavia and Wallachia towards the Danube, Frederick needed to satisfy Catherine's territorial appetite without making the Austrians feel threatened. One way to do so, which had the additional attraction of giving Prussia something too, was to divert her rapacity from the Turks to the Poles. After all, he reasoned, it was the latter who had provoked the Turkish attack on Russia in the first place.[21] So much outrage did the partition arouse subsequently that it is easy to forget just how long it had been on the agenda of the other powers of central-eastern Europe. First mooted during the chaotic reign of John Casimir (r. 1648–68), it was then discussed by Russia, Prussia, Sweden and Austria.[22] Although taken off the drawing-board for a generation or two by a Polish revival under John Sobieski (r. 1674–96), whose feats included lifting the Turkish siege of Vienna in 1683, partition moved back towards the top of the list during the Great Northern War of 1700–1721. It was during that long and devastating conflict, much of which took place in Poland, that the country's descent into dependence on foreign powers became irreversible.[23] The Saxon King of Poland Augustus II repeatedly *offered* partitions to his neighbours in return for their guarantee of his hereditary possession of what remained.[24] Even before he died, Russia, Prussia and Austria had signed the Treaty of Löwenwold in 1732 to stitch up the succession (although in the event Russia reneged on the agreement not to elect another Saxon).[25]

Frederick himself set his sights on Polish territory at a very early stage. In February 1731, shortly after his nineteenth birthday, he wrote a remarkable letter to Dubislav Gneomar von Natzmer, in which he discussed Prussia's geopolitical situation. So vulnerable were the Hohenzollern territories, strung out in bits and pieces across the North European Plain, that good relations must be maintained with the neighbours that were also potential predators. On the other hand, 'when one does not advance, one retreats', so every opportunity should be seized to fill in the gaps. The most yawning was that part of Poland separating Pomerania from East Prussia. Its annexation would create an unbroken bloc of territory from the Elbe to the Niemen and deliver into Prussian hands control of Polish trade down the Vistula.[26] He returned to the theme in the *Political Testaments* of 1752 and 1768, predicting in the latter: 'it is clear to me that in the long run the over-mighty neighbours will come to an agreement on the partition of the booty [Poland]. Perhaps a radically reduced kingdom hemmed in by these three powers, that is to say Russia, Prussia and Austria, will continue to exist.'[27]

Power-political considerations were reinforced by simple prejudice: religious, historical, social, political and national. Frederick had a very low opinion of the Poles, which he often expressed, the most definitive statement coming in *The History of My Own Times*:

> Poland is in a perpetual state of anarchy; the great families are all divided by interest; their individual advantage is preferred to the public welfare; and they are unanimous only in the severity with which they oppress their subjects, whom they rather treat as beasts of burden than as men. The Poles are vain, haughty when fortune smiles upon them, and mean in adversity; capable of any act to amass money, which, having obtained, they scatter without care; frivolous, wanting in judgment, ever ready to change parties without a motive, and by their inconsistent conduct to plunge themselves into the most disagreeable situations . . . The human mind in this kingdom is become feminine, the women are the supporters of all factions, and dispose of everything while their husbands are getting drunk.[28]

The only Poles good for anything, he opined, were the horses.[29] His correspondence with the philosophes was peppered with anti-Polish remarks. In January 1772, for example, he told Voltaire that Montesquieu would struggle to find republican principles in the 'Republic of Poland', for the prevailing anarchy had allowed only egotism, pride, corruption and faintheartedness to flourish. There were no philosophes to be found there, he went on, only rascals brutalized by the most stupid superstition and capable of every crime a coward could commit.[30] He was following his friend Voltaire's celebrated quip: 'One Pole – a charmer; two Poles – a brawl; three Poles – ah, that is the Polish Question.'[31] Polish opposition to Catherine's attempts to force them to be tolerant inspired one of Frederick's longest and most tedious poems – 'Ode to the Confederates', which consumes sixty pages of his collected works. In one scene, Folly returns to visit Poland and is delighted to find that the inhabitants had not changed a bit: 'Brutish, stupid and uneducated, / Notable, Jew, serf, and drunken magnate, / All are vegetables and without shame.'[32] Frederick sent it off to Count Solms at St Petersburg to be circulated among the Russian court, but got cold feet when his ambassador urged him to desist.[33] Solms may have been right, although the Russians were no less Polonophobe than the Prussians. They did however have more options when dealing with their neighbour. In fact, they had a dilemma: should they continue to exercise sole but loose control over Poland? Or should they annex directly part of it, even if that meant allowing Prussia, and perhaps Austria too, to take a share?

The Polish endgame began separately but almost simultaneously at Vienna and Potsdam. The civil war unleashed in Poland by the Confederation of Bar in the summer of 1768 brought armed conflict close to the north-eastern frontier of the Habsburg Monarchy. It was made all the more dangerous by a simultaneous outbreak of plague which the armed bands helped to spread. In response, the Austrians organized a protective military cordon stretching along the whole frontier with Poland. That left stranded on their side a number of enclaves which had been mortgaged by the Kingdom of Hungary to Poland in 1412 but never redeemed. The most important, joined to Poland by a narrow strip of territory, was the county of Zips. Following confederate agitation there, King Stanisław actually asked the Austrians to intervene. In the event, when they ordered the incorporation of the territory, they justified their action by reference to their claimed sovereign rights.[34] At about the same time, Frederick wrote to Count Solms in St Petersburg that the Danish diplomat Count Lynar had recently visited Berlin to attend the wedding of his daughter and had floated 'an extraordinary idea' for sorting out the problems of eastern Europe: Austria would receive Polish territory contiguous with its existing frontier, together with Zips; Prussia would get Polish Prussia, Ermland (also known as 'Warmia') and the port of Danzig as a 'protectorate'; and Russia would take whatever part of Poland it saw fit. This plan was startling but seductive, Frederick added, perhaps more brilliant than solid. He left it up to Solms whether to pass it on to the Russian government or not.[35] This wonderfully disingenuous communication had Frederick's own fingerprints all over it, it need hardly be added.[36]

Frederick's reasoning is easy to follow. Catherine's thirst for territory could not be slaked entirely at the expense of the Turks, for that would bring Austria – and Prussia – into the war. So it would have to be redirected to hapless and helpless Poland, whose territory could also be used to buy off Austria. His own reward, or what he preferred to call 'compensation for the costs incurred by the Russian subsidy', would be the long-coveted prize of West Prussia. The weak link in this chain was obviously Austria, which had most to lose and least to gain from a weakened Poland and a strengthened Prussia. With every Russian success, Frederick's anxiety grew. He was not alone. In August 1769 an equally concerned Emperor Joseph went to see Frederick at Neisse in Silesia to discuss their common interests in the face of Russian expansion. Both men were impeccably polite, falling over each other with protestations of goodwill and hopes for eternal peace. Frederick confessed to his visitor that he had been driven by ambition when young but claimed to have put all that behind him: 'You believe I am imbued with bad faith,' he told Joseph, 'and I know that I did deserve such a charge once, but that was when the situation required it, and now everything has changed.'[37] Privately, he formed the opinion that the young emperor (he was twenty-eight, the same age at which Frederick came to the throne and invaded Silesia) was 'consumed with ambition' and would launch some great project as soon as he was freed from his mother Maria Theresa's apron-strings.[38] Joseph's repeated assurance that the Austrians had given up Silesia once and for all was greeted with scepticism.

It must be allowed that Frederick showed impressive skill in navigating his frigate between the two neighbouring battleships without being crushed or swamped. First, he used his apparent rapprochement with Austria to hurry on negotiations with Russia for a proleptic renewal of the alliance due to expire in 1772. That he obtained on 12 October 1769 with a treaty that not only prolonged his sense of security until 1780 but also gave him a promise of Russian support for his claims to the south German principalities of Ansbach and Bayreuth, currently ruled by heirless junior branches of the Hohenzollern family.[39] Secondly, he kept up the Austrian charm offensive with a further meeting with Joseph, at Neustadt in Moravia in September 1770. This time the Austrian foreign minister, Prince Kaunitz, came too and did most of the talking, as was his wont. Once again, no clear agreement resulted beyond a general commitment to seek to mediate between Russia and the Turks.[40]

That last-named initiative got nowhere. Further military success expanded Catherine's appetite to embrace the independence of the Crimea, extensive territory around the Sea of Azov and the two Danubian principalities of Moldavia and Wallachia. Although the latter would only be 'leased' to Russia by the Turks for twenty-five years, the obvious result would be annexation.[41] Just as everything seemed to be going wrong, Frederick enjoyed what looked like a massive stroke of luck. On 24 December 1770 Louis XV dismissed his foreign minister, the Duc de Choiseul, whose forward policy in support of Spain against Great Britain had looked like taking France into a war for which it was completely unprepared.[42] For the next six months or so, French foreign policy was under the direct control of the king, which is another way of saying that it ceased to operate. This was a crucial development at a critical stage, for it immobilized the power that had always been the great support of both the Poles and the Turks against Russia. It was Choiseul – 'the great fire-raiser of Europe', as Frederick called him – who had incited the Turks to attack Russia in 1768.[43] In Vienna, only Maria Theresa was sorry to see him go. She could appreciate that nothing could deflect Austria from the perilous route now being taken by 'the wild ambition of Joseph, the blind folly of Kaunitz and the Machiavellian cunning with which the King of Prussia knew how to exploit the passions and weaknesses of men'.[44] Actually, the collapse of French diplomacy was less fortuitous than it seemed. Long-term developments in the European states-system had redirected French interests away from the continent to the extra-European struggle with the British. Both symptom and cause of that shift was 'the emergence of the eastern powers', with Prussia to the fore.*

With the restraining hand of France removed, the pace of events began to accelerate in 1771. The main Prussian agent was the king's

---

* This is the central theme of Scott's eponymous book.

younger brother, Prince Henry, who had been sent off by Frederick to Stockholm in the summer of 1770 to warn their sister, Queen Ulrike, that Prussia was now committed to occupying Swedish Pomerania if Sweden attacked Russia or changed its constitution. While there, Henry had secured an invitation to St Petersburg to see at first hand how the land lay.[45] He had his own agenda, which was a good deal more acquisitive than Frederick's at this time: 'I want to see you lord of the Baltic coast . . . If this is only a dream, it is at least a very happy one, and you may well believe that the interest I take in your glory makes me wish it were true.' Frederick replied that the 'wind of fortune' was not yet blowing strongly enough to overcome the likely objections of the other powers.[46] So far as he was concerned, Henry's main task in St Petersburg was to promote the scheme for an Austro-Prussian mediation in the Turkish war.

It cannot be determined just how much Prince Henry encouraged the Russians to say what he wanted them to say. What is certain is that on 8 January 1771 he reported to Frederick a conversation with the tsarina he had enjoyed very much. It began with Catherine remarking that the Austrians had occupied Polish territory and put up their insignia to mark the new frontier. She went on: 'Why shouldn't everyone take something too?' Henry replied that Frederick had established a military cordon like the Austrians but had not taken any territory. 'But,' said Catherine, smiling, 'why don't you occupy it?' A moment or two later, Count Chernyshev approached Henry and addressed the same subject: 'Why don't you seize the bishopric of Ermland? After all, it is necessary that everyone should get something.' All this may have been said in jest, Henry commented, but he did not doubt that Frederick would be able to turn it to his advantage.[47]

Prince Henry arrived back at Potsdam on 18 February 1771 and was soon able to persuade Frederick that the 'wind of fortune' was now blowing so strongly in favour of partition that anchor could be weighed. 'You hold the balance between Austria and Russia,' he told him, 'and in the long run Russia will have to come to terms with having to give you something in return for what you have done for her; when the Austrians see that happening, they will look for their own share too, and in this way the three powers will reach a reciprocal agreement based on their true advantages.'[48] On 27 February

Frederick told his man at St Petersburg, Count Solms, that Russia might just as well seek territorial gains from Poland, given that it was there that the war started. As for Prussia, it would be necessary to take 'some little piece' to maintain the balance against Austria and to cover the costs of the subsidies paid to Russia since the war began.[49] The 'little piece' turned out to comprise 36,000 square kilometres.[50]

Gallons of ink had to be used before that result was achieved more than a year later.[51] In the age of the quadruped, negotiations could only proceed at the pace of the couriers struggling along roads that were glutinous quagmires when it rained and bottomless dust-bowls when the sun shone. Frederick was helped to achieve his essential goal by being the man in the middle between two warring parties, or *Der lachende Dritte* ('the rejoicing third'), to use an expressive German idiom.* He was helped by the Turks, who slowed the Russian advance in 1771 and by the Austrians, who made a show of negotiating an alliance with the Turks, which they concluded on 25 June but never ratified. Especially helpful was the well meant but clumsy intervention by the Empress Maria Theresa in September 1771 when she assured the Prussian ambassador at Vienna, Count von Rohde, that she would never allow Austria to go to war. Her furious son and co-regent Joseph wrote to his brother Leopold, the Grand Duke of Tuscany, that 'she overturned our whole system – we who wanted to put pressure on Russia, perhaps ally with the Turks, threaten them with war etc. She strongly assured him that she would never want or permit war, that the possession of the Crimea seemed to her only a small point, that she didn't mind at all if Russia retained it.'[52] In the end, all three powers had to give up something: Frederick had to abandon his claim to Danzig; Russia had to agree to evacuate the Danubian principalities; Austria had to accept that the Russians would take some Turkish territory when peace was negotiated.

Agreement in principle on the partition was reached between Frederick and Catherine in July 1771 and a convention was signed on 17 February 1772. Just before signature of the latter document, news arrived that the Austrians now agreed to the principle of partition. Working out exactly what they meant by the 'complete equality' they

---

* *Tertius gaudens* in its Latin form.

demanded took further time and it was not until 5 August that the tripartite partition treaties were signed at St Petersburg.[53] Although the last to come to the table, the Austrians took most away, as the following statistics demonstrate:

	Population	Area (square kilometres)
Prussia	580,000	36,000
Austria	2,650,000	83,000
Russia	1,300,000	92,000[54]

Yet it was the Austrians who were least pleased by the outcome. Maria Theresa lamented the 'cruel necessity' that had forced her to approve

Poland, 1772

actions she knew to be 'immoral' and 'unfortunate'; even Kaunitz, the most enthusiastic member of the Austrian triumvirate, saw the partition as '*louche*'; Joseph was afraid the rest of the world would conclude he was 'a man of loose and unsettled principles'.[55] Frederick remarked with frank cynicism: 'Catherine and I are simply brigands; but I wonder how the Queen-Empress managed to square her confessor! ... She wept as she took, and the more she wept, the more she took.'[56] Once they had overcome their various scruples, the Austrians then squeezed the last drop out of their share. The river Podgórze, up to which they had been allocated territory, turned out not to exist, so they chose the river Zbrucz instead, which lay thirty kilometres further into Poland.[57] For his part, Frederick decided that 'the river Netze' meant 'the flood-plain of the river Netze' and so extended his frontier several kilometres to cover it.[58]

Even before he took formal possession, Frederick had inspected his prize, which of course he had also seen numerous times when en route to East Prussia. He wrote to Prince Henry in June 1772 that he was trying to avoid jealousy on the part of the other powers by talking down the value of West Prussia, saying that all he had found there was 'sand, pine trees, moorland and Jews'. In reality, he added, 'it is a very good and advantageous acquisition, both for its strategic position and its financial resources'.[59] In another letter, he refined and expanded this assessment:

> I have now seen a large part of what comes to us through the partition; the biggest advantage of our portion is commercial. We become the masters of everything Poland produces and imports; and the greatest advantage of all is that, as we become masters of its grain trade, so we shall never again be exposed to the threat of famine. The population of this acquisition amounts to 620,000 souls, and that can soon be raised to 700,000, especially because all the [religious] dissidents in Poland will seek refuge here.[60]

Expanding the power, prosperity and population of Prussia could hardly be used to justify his rapacity against a harmless neighbour. Instead, Frederick adopted a dual defence. The partition was necessary to avoid a war, he told Voltaire, and war was a scourge which brought misery and every kind of crime.[61] In another letter, he added a more positive spin, assigning to himself a civilizing mission. He had gone to Poland 'to abolish serfdom, to reform barbaric laws, to introduce more rational legislation, to cut a canal to join the rivers Vistula, Netze, Warthe, Oder and Elbe, to rebuild towns derelict since the plague of 1709, to drain 100 miles of swamp, and to establish some law and order in a country where even the concept was unknown'.[62] As it turned out, West Prussia proved very resistant to assimilation, as the local elites stubbornly – and effectively – defended their traditional institutions and culture against Prussian centralization.[63] By the time Frederick died, there was little if any sign that his 'civilizing mission' had achieved anything. Neither the peasants nor the numerous Jews had experienced any improvement in their wretched lot.[64]

Perhaps surprisingly, European reaction was muted, determined more by national interest than ethical principle. So the French were outraged, and for just that reason the British were indifferent.[65] David Hume lamented that 'the two most civilised nations, the English and the French, should be on the decline; and the barbarians, the Goths and Vandals of Germany and Russia, should be rising in power and influence' but took consolation in the thought that it was the French who had been humiliated, crowing about 'the affronts offered to France, where this partition treaty was not even notified. How that formidable monarchy is fallen, debased.'[66] William Pitt the Elder, now the Earl of Chatham, added: 'I am quite a Russ. I trust the Ottoman will pull down the House of Bourbon in his fall.'[67] In Germany, condemnation was loudest in Catholic regions, although even there Austrian involvement drew the sting of criticism. Protestants were clear that the partitioned Poles should count themselves lucky to have escaped a priest-ridden hell. The radical Swabian journalist Christian Friedrich Daniel Schubart wrote in his *German Chronicle*:

> Bend the knee Poland, and remain silent! Irrational superstition has not yet been eradicated from this country. Reason can achieve nothing while this hostile deity builds its temples . . . With few exceptions, the Poles still believe in witches, spirits and poltergeists, know only the exterior and not the inner meaning of religion and nurse a deadly hatred for anyone who does not share their faith. Their behaviour towards

the Jews is disgusting. Many hundreds of the latter have been executed in the most gruesome manner on the mere suspicion that they need Christian blood to celebrate their Easter; a Christian child only needs to go missing or drown accidentally, and a Jew is seized by his beard, executed or even burnt to death.[68]

Inside Prussia, Count Lehndorff probably spoke for many when he rejoiced in the conquest of a province without a shot being fired, and hailed it as a personal triumph for Frederick.[69]

Most subsequent verdicts on the partition have been critical, although German nationalists continued to celebrate throughout the following century and well into the next. In Treitschke's opinion, 1772 signalled that 'the five hundred-year struggle between Germans and Poles for possession of the Baltic coast had been decided in Germany's favour'.[70] Representative of the opposing camp was the metaphor employed by the Polonophile English historian Norman Davies, writing in 1981: 'Poland was the victim of political vivisection – by mutilation, amputation, and in the end total dismemberment; and the only excuse given was that the patient had not been feeling well.'[71] Yet Davies also cited Bismarck's observation that the partitions of Poland were no different from the partitions inflicted *by* the Poles on their neighbours in the later Middle Ages. What prompted accusations that this episode was 'the horror of our age' (Jacques Mallet du Pan) or 'a shameful crime' (Macaulay) was that it was followed by a period when national integrity became the master-concept of political discourse.[72] The multi-ethnic, multi-lingual and multi-confessional nature of the composite state that should properly be called 'the Polish-Lithuanian Commonwealth' was conveniently forgotten by these liberal critics. As Paul Schroeder has pointed out, partitions were commonplace in eighteenth-century Europe. What made this one special was that Poland was treated like a colonial territory, to be carved up as an aid to conflict resolution – just like Africa in the later nineteenth century. Yet, Schroeder added, essentially it was in accordance with the system that had evolved in the course of the previous century: 'the "crime" of the first Polish partition rose directly from the rules and needs of standard eighteenth-century politics'.[73]

THE HOLY ROMAN EMPIRE

As the dust settled on the Polish imbroglio, contemporaries speculated as to the identity of the next victim. 'Poland was but a breakfast,
and there are not many Polands to be found. Where will they dine?'
asked Edmund Burke.[74] In the event, the next course was served up by
the Turks, whose reprieve courtesy of the Poles proved to be short-
lived. The Peace of Kuchuk-Kainarji that brought their disastrous war
with the Russians to an end in July 1774 gave the victors important
gains around the northern coastline of the Black Sea: to the east, control of the entrance to the Sea of Azov; to the west, control of the
Bug-Dniester estuaries; and in between 'independence' from the Turks
for the Khanate of the Crimea. Freedom of navigation and the right
to send merchant ships into the Mediterranean meant that the Black
Sea was no longer a Turkish lake and Russia could now become a
force in the eastern Mediterranean. As the river-systems draining
central and southern Poland and western Russia flow south, the
commercial potential of the new acquisitions was colossal. No one
supposed that this marked the limit of Catherine's ambitions. As Lord
Rosebery wrote:

> If there is one point on which history repeats itself, it is this: that at
> certain fixed intervals the Russian Empire feels a need of expansion;
> that that necessity is usually gratified at the expense of the Turk; that
> the other Powers, or some of them, take alarm, and attempt measures
> for curtailing the operation, with much the same result that the process
> of pruning produces on a healthy young tree.[75]

As we have seen, during the most recent Russo-Turkish war, the prun-
ing shears had been operated by the Austrians. It was thanks to them
that the Danubian principalities had to be evacuated by the Russians.
But now Emperor Joseph and his chancellor, Prince Kaunitz, were
beginning to consider an alternative strategy, namely *joining*, not
stopping, the Russian despoliation of the Ottoman Empire. In 1774
they launched a campaign of intimidation in Constantinople to
extract the cession of Bukovina, a substantial wedge of territory to the

south-east of their share of the recent partition. Although thinly populated ('a real desert' in Joseph's opinion), it had considerable strategic
value in forming a link between existing Austrian possessions in Galicia and Transylvania. The claim was based on a promise made in the
draft alliance treaty of 1771, a pretext all the more outrageous because
it was the Austrians who had refused to ratify it.* As they knew full
well, the Turks were in no position to offer resistance and signed the
necessary treaty in April 1775.[76]

After this flurry of activity during the first half of the 1770s, it was
all quiet on the eastern front. Attention switched to the world overseas, where the rebellion of the American colonists became the War of
American Independence in February 1778 when France entered the
fighting, to be joined by Spain in 1779 and the Dutch Republic in
1780. Frederick however remained uneasy, aware that the Polish partition and the Russo-Turkish war had created a new and deadly peril:
the possibility of a rapprochement between the other two eastern
powers at his expense. Satiated as Catherine was (for the time being)
with her share of Poland in the west, her acquisitive gaze had shifted
south, aided and abetted by her new lover, Grigory Aleksandrovich
Potemkin, whom she made viceroy of southern Russia in 1774–5.[77]
Frederick wrote to Prince Henry in March 1774 that this changing of
the guard in the imperial bedroom 'greatly displeases me', adding in
October the characteristically misogynistic comment 'a woman is
always a woman and, in feminine government, the cunt has more
influence than a firm policy guided by sound reason'.[78]

Potemkin (whom Frederick derisively referred to as 'Patukin' or
'Tapuquin') and Catherine came round to the view that in regard to
advancing their frontier in the Danubian region and the Balkans,
there was little to be hoped for from Prussia, but a great deal from
Austria, if only current hostility could be reversed. Catherine knew
that would be impossible so long as 'Saint Theresa' (as she dubbed
Maria Theresa) was alive, but the latter had been prematurely aged by
sixteen pregnancies and was now an old woman (born 1717) by the
standards of the time. In a receptive mood for Russian advances was
her son Joseph, Holy Roman Emperor in his own right since 1765 but

---

* See above, p. 292.

only co-regent in Austria, and looking forward eagerly to being undisputed master of both his houses. His enthusiasm for joint action against the Turks was of long standing: in 1772, for example, he would have preferred to partition the Ottoman Empire rather than Poland.[79]

The attraction of a Russian alliance was then reinforced by events in the Holy Roman Empire in the late 1770s. Not for the first time, it was the ailing House of Wittelsbach that became the centre of conflict. As the Elector Maximilian III Joseph of Bavaria had no male heir and was now in his fifties, a succession crisis was inevitable sooner or later. It came quite suddenly, on 30 December 1777, when a particularly virulent strain of smallpox carried him off after a very short illness. It might be thought that the most obvious heir was the Elector of the Palatinate, Karl Theodor, the head of the senior branch of the Wittelsbachs. In the wonderful world of imperial law, however, nothing was ever that simple. As the two Wittelsbach lines had been separate since 1323, there was much room for argument as to whether they still constituted a single dynasty.[80] Moreover, the Bavarian lands did not form a coherent bloc but had been accumulated over a long period of time under many different conditions. In short, the Wittelsbach inheritance was a lawyer's dream and a statesman's nightmare.

In Vienna, forward planning had begun in 1764 with a lengthy memorandum from Kaunitz.[81] Frederick too was on the alert. In the summer of 1777 he told his ambassador at the French court, Baron Goltz, that Joseph was 'filled with boundless ambition' and would move to annex Bavaria as soon as the present ruler died.[82] This would be just the next round in an existential struggle, he wrote to his brother Prince Henry: 'I have certain knowledge that Prince Kaunitz has said "Never can the imperial court tolerate Prussian power; to dominate it, we have to eliminate it."' Frederick added 'these sacramental words should be preserved in the heart of every Prussian, to stop us falling asleep with a false sense of security'.[83]

Neither Frederick nor Joseph was inhibited by any respect for the Holy Roman Empire, its constitution and its laws. After a well-meant but fruitless attempt to reform the imperial courts in the early 1770s, Joseph made no secret of his contempt. The imperial office, he opined, was 'a ghost of an honorific power', its business was 'loathsome', the

imperial constitution was 'vicious', the princes were spineless ignor-
amuses, putty in the hands of their pedantic and venal ministers.[84]
Frederick was no less dismissive. If Joseph called the imperial office 'a
ghost of an honorific power', Frederick called the emperor 'an old
ghost of an idol who once had power but now counts for nothing'.[85]
Continuing the supernatural metaphor, he added that the Imperial
Parliament (*Reichstag*) 'is but a kind of phantom . . . The envoy which
a sovereign sends thither resembles a yard-dog who bays at the
moon.'[86] Early in his reign he had used his dominant influence on the
Wittelsbach Emperor Charles VII to sever the remaining judicial and
ceremonial ties binding Brandenburg in feudal subjection. Of great
symbolic importance was liberation from the obligation of the Prussian representative to kneel in homage to a newly elected emperor.[87]
The right of Prussian subjects to appeal to imperial law courts went
the same way.[88] Charles VII was also obliged to recognize the validity
across the empire of all patents of nobility issued by Frederick.[89]
Indulging both his anti-imperial and anti-Christian prejudices, Frederick also put a stop to the saying of prayers for the emperor in
Prussian churches – 'an old and silly custom' he called it.[90] His most
celebrated symbolic rejection of the Holy Roman Empire was performed by proxy by his representative at Regensburg, Erich Christoph
von Plotho, on 14 October 1757, when the imperial notary Georg
Mathias Joseph Aprill arrived at the Brandenburg residence to deliver
the *Reichstag*'s condemnation of Frederick's invasion of Saxony.[91]
Plotho seized the document, shoved it down Aprill's shirt-front 'with
all possible violence' and summoned his servants to throw the messenger down the stairs and out into the street. This they did not
actually accomplish, although the pro-Prussians chose to believe they
had. By his own account, Aprill went home in tears.[92] Needless to say,
this episode soon made the rounds and grew with the telling. To pun
the name of the unfortunate notary, it was later claimed that it had
happened on April Fool's Day.[93] Lurid accounts in the press were supported with visual illustrations. According to Goethe, when Plotho
travelled to Frankfurt am Main in 1764 he was lionized by the local
people as the personification of Frederick's victory over Catholic
Austria.[94]

For an enlightened rationalist such as Frederick, the Holy Roman

Empire was 'bizarre and superannuated', 'a republic of princes', 'a chaos of little states'.[95] That did not mean he missed any opportunity to exploit its complexities to frustrate Austrian policy. This he did very effectively when impeding Joseph's plans to reform the Imperial Cameral Tribunal. The formation of a Catholic bloc of great powers by the Franco-Spanish 'Family Compact' and the Franco-Austrian alliance of 1756 facilitated what has been called the 'reconfessionalization' of imperial politics. The requirement of the Peace of Westphalia of 1648 that any contentious issue with a confessional element had to be settled by negotiation, delivered into the hands of Frederick and the Protestant princes a powerfully obstructive constitutional weapon.[96] Such was the intensity of religious fear and hatred in Germany that not even Frederick's invasion of Saxony in 1756 could destroy entirely his credibility as a Protestant hero.[97]

It took quite some time before Frederick became an effective imperial politician. During the brief reign of the Wittelsbach Emperor Charles VII (1742–5), he managed to alienate almost everyone with his clumsy proposals for the secularization of several prince-bishoprics.[98] Gradually, however, he learned how to use the considerable assets at his command. Not only was he one of the nine members of the Electoral College of the Imperial Parliament, he also had several votes in the Princes' College (as Duke of Magdeburg, Prince of Halberstadt, Duke of Pomerania, Prince of Minden, Prince of East Frisia, etc.). He also exercised considerable if not dominant influence on three of the Imperial Circles into which the Holy Roman Empire was divided, namely those which covered North Germany – the Westphalian, Lower Saxon and Upper Saxon.[99] Matrimonial alliances provided another means of expanding Hohenzollern influence, as Frederick was every bit as ruthless as his father in directing family members to advantageous matches.* Surprising though it may seem to an anti-militarist age, the Prussian officer corps was also a magnet for non-Prussian princes, especially after the victories of the first two Silesian wars. In 1756 Count Lehndorff recorded in his diary that the Crown Prince of Hessen-Darmstadt was beside himself with joy at being made a lieutenant-general, counting the prestige of serving the

---

* See below, pp. 443–4.

King of Prussia far higher than being the heir to a fine principality of his own. His kinsman the Crown Prince of Hessen-Kassel, however, was devastated at being passed over for the command of the von Hacke regiment. These men were fools, commented Lehndorff, clamouring for posts in Prussia when they could have been doing so much better at home, which was where they belonged.[100] Lesser nobles were also attracted: of the 689 officers above the rank of major in 1786, 203 were non-Prussians, most of them Germans from the principalities of Frederick's dynastic partners.[101]

THE WAR OF THE BAVARIAN SUCCESSION

Before the Seven Years War, Frederick's imperial strategy was largely negative. But when Joseph's brief enthusiasm for his imperial office faded away in the early 1770s,[102] he could see the opportunities for more positive action. As the Habsburg gamekeeper turned poacher, the Hohenzollern poacher could – perhaps even had to – turn gamekeeper. The first climax in this reversal of roles came with the death of the Elector of Bavaria. Frederick's immediate response was cautious. As he wrote to the Dowager Queen of Denmark, he would follow the advice of the Emperor Augustus: *festina lente* ('Make haste slowly').[103] That did not mean he would be passive. According to the French envoy, the Chevalier Gaussen, when news arrived that an Austrian army had entered Bavaria in support of Joseph's claims, he exclaimed: 'These people must think I am dead, I shall prove the contrary.'[104] With the Turks about to declare war on Russia (or so he believed) and France and Spain about to join in the American war, the melting pot was bubbling over. Crucial in the Bavarian business, he realized, was going to be the attitude of the other Wittelsbach heirs, led by the Elector of the Palatinate, Karl Theodor. So Count Goertz was sent off to Mannheim to find out whether the latter had already done a deal with the Austrians.[105]

He had. Afraid that he might lose the whole inheritance, Karl Theodor had signed a convention recognizing Austrian claims to most of Lower Bavaria, the duchy of Mindelheim in Swabia and the

Bohemian fiefs in the Upper Palatinate (northern Bavaria). Further negotiations were envisaged to round off the Austrian acquisitions.[106] There was much back-slapping in Vienna, where Maria Theresa hailed Kaunitz as 'the greatest statesman in Europe' and Joseph congratulated himself on having pulled off a famous diplomatic coup.[107] They also looked forward to acquiring later *all* of Bavaria in exchange for Habsburg territory in south-western Germany and the Netherlands. Given all they knew about Frederick, one wonders how they could have miscalculated so badly. Did they really imagine he would have allowed such a shift in the German balance of power to go unchallenged? He may have referred to himself in a letter to Prince Henry as an 'old carcase' but simultaneously was issuing orders to get the army ready. The foreign office was told to prepare a protest against the 'injustice and violence' of Austrian conduct with a view to initiating 'a kind of negotiation' to keep things ticking over until the spring. On the pretext of bringing forward the usual military reviews, the Silesian regiments were told to be in position by 1 April. As he told one of his generals on 26 January, it looked very much as though war was inevitable.[108]

So it proved. The Austrians might have ensnared Karl Theodor, but as he too had no heir of his own, the consent of the next Wittelsbach in line, Karl August, Duke of Zweibrücken, was also needed. Luckily for Frederick, he was a hopeless spendthrift, financially dependent on French subsidies to stay afloat, and the last thing his paymasters wanted was Austrian expansion in Germany. In February 1778, the French foreign minister, Vergennes, made it known that the Austrians were on their own. On 24 March they were informed that the proposed Bavarian partition was not covered by the treaty of 1756 and that no French diplomatic or military assistance would be forthcoming. This was very bad news for Joseph and Kaunitz, always more forward in their policy than Maria Theresa. It ruled out the complete exchange and made problematic even the retention of what Karl Theodor had conceded already.[109] Even though he could not induce his Russian ally to provide military support, Frederick fancied his chances in a straight contest with Austria. As he observed to Finckenstein in April, in the previous war he had held off so many powers all at once, that just the one should not prove a problem.[110] So he felt able to move decisively. Mobilization was ordered on 18 March, and on 6 April he left Potsdam for Silesia. Three months of diplomatic manoeuvring followed but, after receiving an evasive reply to his latest ultimatum, on 3 July Frederick declared war and two days later crossed the frontier.[111]

What followed for Prussia was inglorious in the short term, satisfactory in the medium term and alarming in the long term. Frederick was sixty-six years old when he went off to war for the last time and was in particularly frail health. He was so weak, recorded General von Schmettau, that he could barely sit on his horse, even at walking pace.[112] That did not stop him from going straight on to the offensive (thus anticipating Prussian armies in 1792, 1806, 1813, 1866, 1870, 1914, 1939 and 1941). He had every reason to be confident. Unlike in 1756, the Austrians had no allies to create diversions to the west, north and east, while Frederick was reinforced by 22,000 Saxons supporting their own ruler's claim to part of the Bavarian inheritance. So the ensuing stalemate was a terrible disappointment. Prince Henry's army on the western front achieved an early success, crossing into Bohemia via passes wrongly thought to be impassable, taking Marshal Laudon by surprise and forcing him back to Münchengrätz.[113] Perhaps because he disapproved of the war in the first place, Henry then went on the defensive. Meanwhile, Frederick's eastern army was making no progress at all in Moravia. The Austrians under Marshal Lacy took up a strong defensive position on the Upper Elbe to the north of Königgrätz and sat it out.[114] It may be recalled that Frederick had written about his disastrous campaign of 1744: 'it must be allowed that it is more difficult to make war in Bohemia than in any other country'.* Thirty-four years later it was just as difficult and for all the same reasons, or rather even more difficult because the military gap between the two combatants had narrowed appreciably in the meantime.

As autumn approached, supplies were getting lower, the desertion rate was getting higher and the weather was getting worse. Snowfall at the beginning of September heralded an early and hard winter. In the middle of the month Prince Henry began to retreat back to

* See above, p. 109.

Saxony, blaming an acute shortage of provisions, and Frederick followed to Silesia at the beginning of October.[115] There had been no battle, only low-level skirmishing in which the Prussians usually came off worst. Three months of inaction had brought Frederick's army only demoralization, disease and desertion, which combined to reduce his army by 40,000.[116] This was the inglorious part. But Frederick had done enough to achieve his political objective, which had always been the main object of the exercise. He had been helped by sharp divisions within the opposing camp. So anxious was Maria Theresa to avoid war that, even after Frederick had invaded, she sent him a personal plea from a mother whose 'maternal heart' was distressed to see two of her sons and a son-in-law going off to war.[117] She also sent Baron Thugut as a special envoy to the Prussian camp to try to find a compromise solution.[118] Understandably, Joseph was outraged at his mother going behind his back: 'we are telling him [Frederick] that all the forces of the Monarchy are nothing and that, when he wants something, we're obliged to consent . . . I declare I find the action as injurious as possible.'[119]

Divided and incoherent, the Austrian triumvirate was no match for Frederick's solo voice. The attempt to make a renunciation of the Bavarian claim conditional on him giving up his (much better-founded) reversionary interest in Ansbach and Bayreuth was particularly clumsy, serving only to advertise the weakness of the Austrian position.[120] It is pointless to speculate what might have happened if the war had resumed in 1779. By November 1778, Maria Theresa had had enough. As she told Count Mercy, her ambassador at Versailles, the experience of the Seven Years War and the much stronger financial resources of Prussia disqualified any thought of a war of attrition.[121] Austria had already spent 100,000,000 gulden just to get to this point and the treasury was bare.[122] By this time, a way out was being offered by the other two great continental powers. With France now fully engaged in war with Great Britain, it was the tsarina who took control of events. When the war began, Frederick had been angered by her refusal to send military assistance on the grounds that Prussia had not been attacked on its own territory, a view that was technically correct but hardly in keeping with the spirit of the alliance.[123] She made amends in October by sending Prince Repnin on a diplomatic mission to seek to mediate, with the further instruction to liaise with Frederick on military assistance if the Austrians proved obdurate. The simultaneous despatch of 30,000 soldiers to western Poland added the necessary muscle.[124]

The negotiations conducted by the Franco-Russian mediators dragged on through the winter and into the spring, as the two sides sniped at each other both verbally and literally. 'Never did there exist so strange a mixture of Warfare and Negotiation,' commented the British ambassador in Vienna.[125] Not until 13 May 1779 did a treaty signed at Teschen in Saxony bring the war formally to an end. In territorial terms, Elector Karl Theodor of the Palatinate got most, namely everything he had ceded in his treaty with Austria of 3 January 1778, apart from a modest strip of territory to the east of the river Inn with a population of about 120,000. This was named the 'Inn Quarter' by Emperor Joseph and was all he had to show for his efforts. As in the case of the Polish Partition, the real victor was Frederick. Not only had he averted a game-changing shift in the German balance of power, he also now had a great-power guarantee of his own succession to Ansbach and Bayreuth. In 1772 West Prussia had been worth a lot more than Galicia, and now in 1779 Ansbach and Bayreuth were worth a lot more than the Innviertel.[126] Also flushed with success was Catherine, rewarded for her mediation with the status of guarantor of the treaty. As the Treaty of Teschen renewed the Peace of Westphalia of 1648, this not only raised Russia to equal status with France but also opened the way for further intervention in imperial affairs.[127]

So far, so good, but the long-term prospects for Frederick's Prussia were alarming. The army's performance had been dismal, as many of the participants recorded. 'The Prussian army bears no resemblance to what it was before. There is no life in the generals and as for the officers, they are all demoralised and nowhere can the least order be found' was one verdict.[128] Prince Henry complained that several of his subordinate generals were unfit for service and simply a burden: von Britzke was eighty years old and physically unable to go to war; Lossau had been carrying a bullet in his head since the battle of Torgau in 1760 and had no memory; old age made Kleist immobile; three of the major-generals were well over seventy; the general supposed to be commanding the rearguard could only travel by carriage;

and so on.[129] The quality of the rank-and-file was also thought to be deteriorating, not least because an increasing number of native Prussian subjects were exempted from military service.[130] For all his emphasis on the need for service and duty, Frederick could never bring himself to clear out the dead wood – and neither could his successors until the catastrophe of 1806 forced their hand. Queen Luise famously remarked after that event that Prussia 'had fallen asleep on the laurels of Frederick the Great', but in reality it was Frederick who had dozed off after 1763.[131] In 1767 he wrote to Prince Henry that the Seven Years War had 'ruined the troops and destroyed discipline' but that he was making good progress in restoring the situation and that in three years everything would be back to normal.[132] The campaign of 1778 disproved that forecast. During the second half of his reign the size of the army increased but there was no equivalent qualitative increase.[133]

On 4 May 1779, Frederick's negotiator at Teschen, Baron Johann Wilhelm von Riedesel, reported that the French and Russian mediators had predicted that the treaty about to be signed would guarantee a 'stable, secure and long-lasting' peace in Germany. They also summed up the outcome of the episode as follows: Frederick had demonstrated how quickly and resolutely he responded to Austrian usurpations; France and Russia had shown how effective their diplomatic intervention could be; the Austrians would need at least fifteen years to repair their tattered finances; and Joseph's undoubted territorial ambitions in the Balkans would be restrained by the knowledge that Russia would intervene to put a stop to any expansion.[134] In his reply, Frederick agreed that Germany would remain undisturbed so long as France, Russia and Prussia acted together, but could not resist adding that he was naturally a sceptic and quoted the wise advice from the Norman father to his son: 'Have trust!' 'But whom should I trust, father?' 'No one!'[135]

JOSEPH II

Frederick's scepticism turned out to be entirely justified. The mediators' final prediction was soon proved to be completely wrong. Far from opposing any Austrian designs, Catherine was now looking for an alliance to promote a joint partition of the Ottoman Empire. She knew that would not be possible during Maria Theresa's lifetime but could afford to wait for her death. It came on 29 November 1780. Less than a month later, Joseph told his ambassador in St Petersburg: 'Russia with us, and we with Russia, can achieve anything we like, but without each other we find it very difficult to achieve anything important and worthwhile.'[136] With both partners so eager, consummation was not long delayed: by an exchange of letters in May 1781 the alliance was sealed.[137] The most important provision obliged the two powers to come to each other's aid with equal forces – but only if the attack came from the Turks. Any other aggressor required only modest assistance: 10,000 infantry, 2,000 cavalry plus appropriate artillery, or a cash subsidy of 400,000 roubles if the theatre of operations was too remote for direct intervention. The Italian and Asiatic possessions of Austria and Russia respectively were excluded altogether.[138] It is very likely that this alliance would have happened anyway, but Frederick had certainly helped to alienate Catherine and push her towards Joseph by his sharp practice over the Polish frontiers following the partition, his consistent underestimate of both her ability and her determination, and his incorrigible habit of making offensive remarks about female sovereigns' sex-lives.*[139]

It was not long before Catherine moved to take advantage of her obviously lopsided alliance with Austria. With Britain, France, Spain and the Dutch Republic all fully committed to the war over America, she enjoyed complete freedom of action. In April 1783 the annexation of the Crimea was announced. This was the biggest staging-post so far on what was looking increasingly like a road-map ending in Constantinople. She had advertised her intention in 1779 when her younger grandson was christened 'Constantine' and a commemorative medal was struck depicting Hagia Sophia on one side and the Black Sea surmounted by a star on the other.[140] The Crimea was an acquisition of colossal importance, among other things confirming and accelerating the redirection of Russian commerce from north to south. Yet the Austrians went away empty-handed, for Joseph rejected Kaunitz's advice to annex the Danubian principalities.[141]

---

* See above, p. 191.

Poor Frederick was left out in the cold. Of course he had seen this latest diplomatic revolution coming. An early signal that the Russian weathercock was swinging southwards was a visit Joseph paid to Catherine in the summer of 1780, which turned out to be 'a public as well as a private triumph for both rulers'.[142] Frederick did his best to keep his alliance intact by joining Catherine's anti-British 'Armed Neutrality' in May 1781, or in other words at exactly the same time that she was dropping him in favour of Joseph.[143] Two months later he told Finckenstein that the Austro-Russian negotiations had been broken off without result and went on believing that for the next year.[144] It was not until July 1783 that the Russian ambassador, Prince Dolgoruki, informed the Prussian minister Hertzberg that Russia and Austria had 'renewed their ancient treaties'.[145] By that time, Frederick was well aware that he had been jilted. Joseph's diplomatic support for the seizure of the Crimea dispelled any lingering illusions.[146] All he could hope for now was to wait for the tsarina's death and, in the meantime, cultivate her mercurial, not to say unbalanced, son, the Grand Duke Paul, who was known to be a Prussophile who venerated Frederick.[147] Given Catherine's self-indulgent life-style, this was not a forlorn hope, although in the event her robust constitution kept her going until 1796.

From May 1781 Frederick was on his own. The harbour walls of the safe haven he seemed to have reached with his Russian alliance of 1764 had been breached and his modest craft expelled to face peril on the high seas once more. The most obvious cure for this inglorious isolation was to ally with the other friendless power, Great Britain. He refused to take it, for three reasons. Firstly, he had long nursed an aversion to the English, often referring to them as corrupt, decadent, materialistic, spendthrift, gluttonous and – above all – arrogant.[148] Since the time of Cromwell, he told Prince Henry, they had succumbed to 'rampant debauchery and licentiousness'.[149] Secondly, he never forgot the way in which they had betrayed him in 1762 by making a separate peace, his particular *bête noire* being the 'infamous' Lord Bute. Long after the latter had exercised any influence on George III, Frederick went on believing he was 'the minister behind the curtain' pulling all the strings.[150] Finally, the American war convinced him that Britain was a spent force in the European states-system, exhausted, bankrupt and faction-ridden.[151] So he rejected the periodic approaches made by the British for an alliance, comparing the two countries to two drowning men: if they clasped each other, they would only go down all the faster.[152] This misconception was widely shared in Europe after the American war: by Joseph II, for example, who believed that Britain was now a second- or third-rate power.[153]

Paradoxically, the Austro-Russian alliance turned out to be, not the existential threat it seemed, but the springboard for a last diplomatic victory. It had two planks. The first was the reaction of the French. For two and a half centuries they had regarded the Ottoman Turks as their natural allies in eastern Europe and were horrified by the Russian seizure of the Crimea. Having just concluded a ruinously expensive war against the British on behalf of the American rebels, they were in no position to intervene militarily, but they did launch a diplomatic offensive. In this, they demanded – and had every right to expect – the assistance of their Austrian ally, and so were suitably angry when they discovered that not only was Joseph doing everything he could to *support* Catherine but had been secretly allied to her for the past two years. No wonder that the hapless Austrian ambassador at Versailles, Count Mercy, was subjected to several 'warm exchanges' with the French foreign minister, Vergennes.[154] So the most secure of diplomatic adhesives – 'my enemy's enemy is my friend' – then brought France and Prussia together in informal cooperation.[155]

The other plank was the encouragement the Russian alliance gave to Joseph's restless ambition. He was full of bright ideas, some of them sensible, all of them impracticable, especially when promoted simultaneously. Such was his reputation for indiscriminate expansion that, when he asked about the size of the population of Verona when changing horses in that city in 1784, the rumour immediately spread that he had designs on the Republic of Venice.[156] Real or imagined, his plans generated such fear and anger in the Holy Roman Empire that Frederick could step forward as a knight in shining armour. Joseph was a man in a hurry, the exemplar of Lessing's definition of the modern man: 'He often achieves very accurate insights into the future, but he cannot wait for the future to come.'[157] For thirty-nine frustrating years he had been restrained by his formidable mother; now all his pent-up energy was unleashed. In a mere two or three years he managed to alienate just about everyone, apart from the small number who thought like he did. Inside the Habsburg Monarchy, the clergy, nobility and all the numerous commoners with a vested interest or conservative opinion to defend were soon protesting noisily. In the Holy Roman Empire, even the princes traditionally loyal to the emperor were driven out of his camp by his clumsy initiatives. As a young man he had preached the gospel of state power: 'everything exists for the state; this word contains everything, so all who live in it should come together to promote its interests'.[158] This objective inspired a programme of centralization, standardization, secularization, Germanization – and all the other '-izations' associated with modernization. Given the wonderful diversity of the two polities he headed, the Habsburg Monarchy and the Holy Roman Empire, he was attempting the impossible.

When Austrian *raison d'état* collided with imperial law, all those whose very existence depended on the maintenance of the latter had to look elsewhere for protection. First in Joseph's firing-line were those neighbouring prince-bishops whose diocesan responsibilities extended over the Habsburg territories. Joseph moved quickly to exclude such 'foreign' jurisdiction and make the territorial and episcopal frontiers of his state coincide. His expropriation of the Austrian estates of the Bishop of Passau in 1783 was a particularly brutal infringement of imperial law.[159] More alarming for all princes was his vigorous expansion of Austrian power (as opposed to imperial influence) in the empire. Even before Maria Theresa's death, the election of Joseph's brother Maximilian Franz as 'coadjutor' to the Archbishop-Elector of Cologne and Prince-Bishop of Münster had been secured. This meant that on the death of the present incumbent (the two bishoprics were held in plurality by the same man), a Habsburg archduke would succeed automatically to two large, prosperous and strategically important principalities in north-west Germany. Many other ecclesiastical states were thought to be on the list of the pluralist archduke.[160]

That was bad enough. Much worse was the news that broke in 1784 that Joseph was reviving his plan to exchange his possessions in the Netherlands for the Electorate of Bavaria. Only a glance at the map is needed to appreciate the colossal benefit this would have brought. From being a wedge of territory separating the Habsburg possessions in Bohemia and the Tyrol, Bavaria would have become a link between the two. The domination of southern Germany would inevitably have followed.* In all respects, Bavaria would have been the perfect substitute for Silesia. If Joseph had kept things simple, he might have pulled it off. The current Elector of Bavaria, Karl Theodor, was keen to move: he did not like Munich, to which he had had to transfer in 1778 (the feeling was mutual); he had been born in Brussels and his mother was an Arenberg, one of the great families of the region; he fancied himself as 'King of Belgium'; and did not want to move back to Mannheim and his estranged wife.[161]

Frederick had been on constant and anxious alert ever since the end of the War of the Bavarian Succession. In September 1779 he had told his ambassador in St Petersburg that Karl Theodor was pathologically timid and completely under the thumb of the Austrians, who had bought up all his advisers, including his father confessor. It was only a matter of time, he predicted, before Joseph tried again to annex the Electorate. Only the guarantee given by France and Russia in the Treaty of Teschen restrained him.[162] Three years later he complained to his nephew, the Duke of Brunswick, about the crushing weight thrust on to his septuagenarian shoulders by the plethora of intrigues unleashed by Joseph from every direction.[163] Moreover, the situation was deteriorating. France had been weakened by the ruinously expensive war over America and Russia had become an Austrian ally. As Joseph had supported Catherine to the hilt over the Crimean annexation without asking for anything for himself, he now felt entitled to reciprocity. In May 1784 he told her about the Bavarian exchange project and asked for help. She agreed promptly, promising 'all possible help'.[164]

Luckily for Frederick, the incorrigible Joseph had been tripping over his own feet again. No sooner had he made the offer than he began having second thoughts about whether he would give up all of his possessions in the Netherlands. Much confused fine-tuning followed, only serving to exasperate Karl Theodor. More damagingly, he also decided this would be a good time to put pressure on the Dutch

* See the map on p. xiv.

Republic to open the river Scheldt to international shipping, to which it had been closed *de facto* since the Dutch captured the river's mouth in 1585 and *de jure* since the Peace of Westphalia in 1648. This had meant that the once great port of Antwerp had contracted into a backwater. There was of course some connection with the Bavarian exchange, because the liberation of Antwerp would make the Austrian Netherlands that much more attractive to Karl Theodor. Unfortunately for Joseph, his *démarche* coincided with a determined attempt by France to secure an alliance with the Dutch. They believed that, if only the Dutch naval bases at the Cape of Good Hope and in Ceylon could be added to the French islands in the Indian Ocean, they would be in a position to do to the British in India what they had just done to them in America. It is not too much to say that the future of the world overseas was thought to be at stake in this project. So when forced to choose between their existing ally, Austria, and their prospective ally, the Dutch Republic, the French did not hesitate in opting for the latter.[165]

Joseph certainly tried hard. An Austrian ship was sent up the Scheldt to force the issue (the Dutch called his bluff and forced it to turn round); he offered to drop his demands on the Dutch in return for French support for the Bavarian exchange (they declined); and he got his sister Marie Antoinette to put pressure on Louis XVI (who, it turned out, could never be influenced by her on policy issues).[166] It was all to no avail. He could find no way round the opposition of the French, who displayed impressive resolution and skill. In the twilight of the *ancien régime*, they ignited a last sunburst of decisive action. At a meeting of the Council of State held at Versailles on 2 January 1785, every single minister voted against the exchange, with the exception of the foreign minister, Vergennes, and even he was only covering his back against the queen's anger.[167] The key player turned out to be Karl Theodor's heir, the Duke of Zweibrücken, whose Francophilia had recently been encouraged by a grant of 6 million livres and the promise of more to come. So when the Russian envoy Count Nicolai Petrovich Rumyantsev went to seek approval of the exchange, he was summarily dismissed. To add insult to injury, the duke then sent an 'insolent and ridiculous' letter to Joseph confirming his refusal.[168] He also sent a letter off to Potsdam, informing Frederick of what had happened and asking for his support.[169] That of course was readily given. With France technically still an ally of Austria, Russia actively promoting the exchange, and Great Britain apparently a broken reed, Frederick had to look to a league of German princes to frustrate Joseph. This was a plan with a long history. Frederick may have considered it as early as 1780, although there is a continuous history of interest only from the spring of 1783 when he first discussed it with Hertzberg.[170] Unknown to him, a similar confederation was also being planned by a number of smaller princes seeking a third way between the two German super powers.[171] They loathed Joseph, but feared Frederick: 'a skiff crushed between two battleships' was the metaphor employed by Goethe to describe the uncomfortable situation of his employer, the Duke of Saxony-Weimar, one of the princes involved.[172] These small craft stood no chance of independent action once Frederick took command, but most of them preferred him to Austria and fell into line.[173] Frederick made it easy for them by stressing that all he wanted was to protect the traditional constitution of the empire against violent innovation.[174] The final constitution of the league, drafted by Hertzberg and dated 15 March 1785, guaranteed protection against any 'encroachments, secularisations or exchanges' to all members of the empire, and not just to those who actually joined.[175]

Recruitment to the league began at once. In one sense this was a pointless exercise, for Joseph had abandoned the exchange as hopeless as soon as he learned of French opposition and Zweibrücken resistance.[176] More importantly, Joseph's ham-fisted campaign – 'as contemptible in its manner as in its achievements'[177] – had delivered into Frederick's hands a golden opportunity to stand forth as the saviour of the empire. A shoal of princes swarmed into his protective shadow: Saxony-Weimar, Saxony-Gotha, Zweibrücken, Brunswick, Baden, Hessen-Kassel, three Anhalt princes, Ansbach, Pfalz-Birkenfeld, Mecklenburg Schwerin, Mecklenburg Strelitz and Hessen-Darmstadt. To these small fry must be added three major catches: the Archbishop-Elector of Mainz, low in power but high in prestige as the Arch-Chancellor of the Empire and Primate of the Church in Germany; the Elector of Saxony; and the Elector of Hanover.[178] Particularly gratifying was the enthusiastic participation of George III, who showered 'the greatest praise possible on Your Majesty's patriotic zeal', as the Prussian ambassador to London, Count Lusi, reported to a gratified if surprised Frederick.[179] Blithely ignoring the clash that resulted with his British ministers, who at just this time were moving heaven and earth to obtain an *Austrian* alliance, George went on to play a major constructive role in the development of the league.[180]

When the League of Princes was formally initiated on 23 July 1785, Frederick had just a year to live. Although Prussia was still without a great-power ally, it was no longer isolated and the Hanoverian connection gave some sort of bridge to Britain. Just a year after Frederick's death this would lead to a great Anglo-Prussian triumph in the Dutch Republic. Just as gratifying was the defeat and humiliation inflicted on the old enemy, Austria. How Frederick would have rejoiced, had he lived to see Joseph embroiled in a hugely expensive and pointless war in the Balkans after 1787, which brought the Habsburg Monarchy to the very verge of total collapse. In his own lifetime he could savour the public relations triumph the league brought him. With the pump primed by Hertzberg's team of publicists, there was a flood of pamphlets, poems, plays and pictures to praise his patriotism. Frederick was acclaimed as a second Herman, defending German liberties.[181]* The whole episode inspired a surge of patriotic discourse in the 1780s, anticipating the more famous debates occasioned by the French Revolution.[182] The real significance of the League of Princes was the part it played in the development of German national consciousness.[183]

Frederick had undoubtedly scored a great diplomatic victory. Moreover, he could present it as his very own, even though the most punishing blows landed on Joseph had been self-inflicted. He was also lucky that the French could not publicize their own crucial contribution without upsetting Joseph even more than they had already. Indeed, both the guarantor powers of the Treaty of Teschen had been sidelined, much to the fury of Catherine, for whom the league was a 'crushing blow' to her German policy.[184] Frederick's policy towards the Holy Roman Empire, and the League of Princes in particular, has perhaps been the only aspect of his reign to earn unqualified praise from historians, the accolades ranging from 'a brilliant achievement'

---

* See below, p. 364.

(von Aretin) to 'a very successful Reich politician' (Peter Baumgart) to 'one of the most successful Reich politicians ever' (Volker Press) to 'a brilliant *Reichspolitiker*' (Joachim Whaley).[185] Soon everything would be back in the melting-pot again, as France slid into bankruptcy, the Eastern Question was reopened with war between Russia, Austria and the Turks, and the Wars of the French Revolution erupted, but that was all left to his successor. Frederick had timed his exit from this world to perfection.

PART III

On the Home Front

12

Public and Nation

CENSORSHIP AND THE
LIMITS OF FREEDOM

As we have seen, Frederick began his reign with two bold gestures – the public commitment to the Enlightenment and the private advertisement of his homosexuality.* A third was his recognition of the existence of a public that needed to be managed. The public sphere was not a new phenomenon, of course. Especially in the urbanized regions of Italy, England and the Low Countries, a self-conscious public had existed for centuries. However, it was during the seventeenth and eighteenth centuries that it became an established – and increasingly important – cultural and political force. In rural Central and Eastern Europe it was a newcomer. By 'public sphere' is meant a virtual space, in which private individuals came together to form a whole greater than the sum of the parts. By exchanging information, ideas and criticism, they cohered to form a cultural actor – the public – which has dominated European culture ever since. Many, if not most, of the cultural institutions of the modern world derive from this period – the periodical, the newspaper, the novel, the journalist, the critic, the public library, the concert, the art exhibition, the public museum, the national theatre, just to list a sample. Of course almost all of these can be found in earlier periods, but it was in the eighteenth century that they came to maturity and fused to trigger what can reasonably be called a cultural revolution. Perhaps most important of

---

* See above, pp. 61–71 and below, pp. 368–72.

all, it was then that 'public opinion' came to be recognized as the ultimate arbiter in matters of taste and politics.[1]

Frederick William I had shown a characteristically brutal attitude to the public. On his own ascension to the throne he had banned all newspapers because the 'bloody scribblers' led their readers astray by encouraging them to form their own opinions. One or two periodicals were later permitted, for the sake of the fees that were paid to the recruitment fund, but the slightest sign of dissent brought immediate closure.[2] So it must have afforded his son special pleasure in 1740 to give Ambrosius Haude permission to publish newspapers in both the German and French languages, for it was Haude who had helped the teenaged Frederick to form his clandestine collection of books and had housed it in his bookshop.* Not only was Haude allowed to break the existing monopoly of Johann Andreas Rüdiger (who did not dare to complain), he was also freed from censorship. This audacious innovation caused some head-shaking among senior Prussian officials. The foreign minister, Podewils, reminded Frederick that foreign courts, and the Russian court in particular, were very sensitive about anything critical appearing in the public prints. Frederick's reply was in the form of a marginal comment as memorable as that on toleration: 'if newspapers are to be interesting, they must not be interfered with'.[3]

Frederick may well have believed that when he scribbled it down, but it was not long before he was having second thoughts. It was not that Haude abused his privilege. Although claiming to be objective, the editorial line adopted by his *Berlin News of Political and Cultural Matters (Berlinische Nachrichten von Staats- und gelehrten Sachen)* was uncritical veneration. The first issue opened with the verse:

> A wise Frederick wishes to protect
> This paper with his wonted graciousness,
> And may what his order has created
> Be of benefit to the common good!

Each issue was headed with the image of a Prussian eagle bearing the palm of victory and a parcel of books as it flies over the globe,

* See above, pp. 34, 41.

accompanied by the slogan 'Truth and Liberty'.[4] The fact was that in all aspects of Frederick's dealings with his subjects, control was his dominant consideration. By the end of 1740, Haude was subject to the same censorship as every other journalist, his reports on the war having been deemed too revealing.[5] His appeals to Frederick for relaxation and complaints that even book reviews were now being censored fell on deaf ears.[6] In July 1743 Frederick finally conceded that Podewils had been right all along when he confirmed the reimposition of pre-censorship on the grounds that 'slanders' offensive to foreign courts had been published.[7] In 1749 a censorship commission was established and the sale of all 'scandalous and offensive books' published outside Prussia was prohibited.[8] Subsequently, he intervened every now and again to tell the censors they were getting slack; in August 1750, for example, when he told Podewils that a lot of objectionable material was getting into print.[9] In the following February, the distinguished writer Gotthold Ephraim Lessing wrote to his father from Berlin that there was no point in sending copies of the local newspapers because oppressive censorship made them so dull as to be unreadable.[10]

Frederick's imperious attitude to journalists extended beyond the Prussian frontiers. It is an indication of how much importance he attached to the public sphere that he should have taken so much trouble to silence dissenting voices. One notorious victim was Johann Ignaz Roderique, who from 1734 had published a highly successful bi-weekly newspaper, the *Gazette de Cologne*, in the eponymous Free Imperial City. The knowledge that it was distributed all over Europe added to Frederick's anger when it proved to be vigorously pro-Austrian after war broke out in 1740. When appeals to the Cologne City Council to suppress it proved fruitless, Frederick resorted to direct action. He authorized his agent in the city, von Rohde, to spend a hundred ducats hiring a local thug to give Roderique 'a good thrashing'. The thrifty von Rohde found someone willing to do it for half that amount. A suitably chastened – and bruised – Roderique promptly fell into line, publishing Prussian reports on the war as well as the enemy's. It was not long, however, before his bias was deemed to be swinging back to the Austrian side, so von Rohde pointed out to him that he still had fifty ducats in the bank with which to repeat the dose. An apology swiftly followed.[11] This crude intimidation continued. In 1749, von Rohde's successor, von Diest, was told to pay another visit on Roderique and inquire whether he really fancied a periodic thrashing.[12]

This muscular approach to dissent was not so uncommon in eighteenth-century Europe. Frederick must have known that the young Voltaire's verbal skewering of the Chevalier de Rohan in 1725 had been punished by a public flogging conducted by his target's lackeys.[13] Only in England, to which Voltaire then moved, was it possible for journalists to offer radical political criticism with (relative) immunity. Yet the regime imposed by Frederick after his early flirtation with freedom of the press may not have been as bleak in practice as the draconic language of the laws indicated, although it must be conceded that the most celebrated comment on freedom of expression in Prussia, made by Lessing in 1769, was entirely negative. To understand fully his verdict, only part of which is usually quoted, it is necessary to know the context: the poet Friedrich Gottlieb Klopstock had drawn up a plan for an academy at Vienna, to promote the arts and sciences, and had submitted it to the Austrian court. If it had been implemented, Lessing would have been entrusted with the supervision of the Viennese theatres. In a letter to Lessing, Friedrich Nicolai – Berlin bookseller, prolific author and warm admirer of Frederick – had poured cold water on the plan, pointing out that a work by Moses Mendelssohn, like Nicolai a prominent member of the Berlin Enlightenment, had just been confiscated by the Austrian censors. Lessing replied:

> Vienna may be what it is, but there is more to be hoped for there than in your Frenchified Berlin. If Mendelssohn's book has been confiscated in Vienna, then it was only because it was published in Berlin and it could not be conceived that anyone in Berlin would write in favour of the immortality of the soul. And don't talk to me about your Berlin freedom to think and write. It's just the freedom to market as many insults about religion as one likes. An honest man should be ashamed to avail himself of it. Just let someone in Berlin try to write about other matters as freely as [Joseph von] Sonnenfels has done in Vienna. Let him try to tell the truth about the rabble of courtiers as Sonnenfels has

done. Let him try to make a stand for the rights of the subject and against exploitation and despotism, as is being done in Denmark and in France – then you will soon see which country is the most slavish in Europe.[14]

Against that punishing verdict must be set other more friendly assessments. The Scottish physician John Moore, accompanying the Duke of Hamilton on his grand tour, wrote of Berlin in 1775:

> Nothing surprised me more, when I first came to Berlin, than the freedom with which many people speak of the measures of government, and the conduct of the King. I have heard political topics, and others which I should have thought still more ticklish, discussed here with as little ceremony as at a London coffee-house. The same freedom appears in the booksellers' shops, where literary productions of all kinds are sold openly. The pamphlet lately published on the division of Poland, wherein the King is very roughly treated, is to be had without difficulty, as well as other performances, which attack some of the most conspicuous characters with all the bitterness of satire. A government, supported by an army of 180,000 men, may safely disregard the criticisms of a few speculative politicians, and the pen of the satirist.[15]

This is an opinion that deserves to be taken seriously, for Moore was a learned, impartial and acute observer. He and his charge spent some time in Berlin and Potsdam, even being accorded the unusual favour of a personal interview with Frederick. The book he wrote recording his experience in Prussia and elsewhere – *A View of Society and Manners in France, Switzerland and Germany* – was a bestseller, going through twenty-one editions in Moore's lifetime.[16] It should also be noted that the last sentence uncannily anticipates Immanuel Kant's observation in his essay 'What is Enlightenment?' of 1784, in support of his argument that 'a lesser degree of civil freedom gives intellectual freedom enough room to expand to its fullest extent', for 'only a ruler who is himself enlightened and has no fear of phantoms, yet who likewise has at hand a well-disciplined and numerous army to guarantee public security, may say what no republic would dare to say: *Argue as much as you like and about whatever you like, but obey!*'[17]

The Abbé Denina, who was in Prussia for the last four years of the reign, reported that Frederick treated criticism of himself with amused contempt, even to the extent of having critical pamphlets reprinted at his expense and ordering abusive posters moved lower on the gates of Sanssouci so that everyone could read them.[18] Also characteristic was his admonition to a Lutheran pastor who had persisted in vigorous attacks on Frederick's impiety, despite warnings from his superiors to moderate his tone: 'you want me to persecute you but I have not the slightest desire to grant you the honour of becoming a martyr: your pose is not appropriate for this day and age, so live in peace and seek happiness by contributing to the welfare of your flock'.[19] Another beneficiary of this relaxed attitude was a schoolteacher who in his cups made offensive remarks about his king. Asked what would be an appropriate punishment, Frederick replied that, as alcohol had clouded his reason, the offender should be merely despised – but should be given a warning about the dangers of drink.[20] This indifference to criticism extended to gossip about his sexual orientation. In 1753 he told his representative in London to treat a scurrilous pamphlet in circulation with the contempt it deserved. As he wrote to George Keith on the same occasion: 'I have always despised the verdict of the public and in judging my conduct I have only ever answered to my conscience.'[21] This disdain was well publicized, by d'Alembert, for example, who observed that Frederick had placed himself above satire by his talent and his fame.[22]

Against Lessing's curt dismissal must also be set less lapidary but more numerous opinions such as that of the Berlin pastor Daniel Jenisch:

> What chiefly elevates the eighteenth century above previous epochs is the degree and diffusion of intellectual endeavour: and it was the Prussian monarch who strove to arouse and invigorate it, with incalculable power; indeed, it can be said without exaggeration that he did more, and in more ways, than any other of the most notable men of the enlightenment.[23]

Evidence of a different but compelling kind can be found in the essays written by young Prussian students taking the *Abitur* (university entrance examination) in the early 1790s. All revealed a belief that they lived in a free country and that the French Revolution had been caused by the French monarchy's despotism.[24]

LA METTRIE

This was not, of course, freedom as it would be understood by a twenty-first century liberal, or even a nineteenth-century liberal for that matter, but in eighteenth-century continental Europe it marked a significant advance on current practice in most states, especially those where the Catholic Church dictated cultural policy. The freedom to be heterodox in matters of religion (or 'to market as many insults about religion as one likes' as Lessing put it) could also be crucial for some. The most prominent beneficiary of Frederick's relaxed attitude was Julien Jean Offray de La Mettrie (1709–51), whose materialist work *L'Homme machine* (*Man a machine*) was deemed so offensive that he was chased not only from his native France but also even from the Dutch Republic ('the great ark of the refugees' as Pierre Bayle had called it). In both countries his book was ceremonially burned by the public executioner, whose axe would have been applied to La Mettrie's neck, if he had been caught.[25] Frederick gave him asylum, a position in the Berlin Academy, a pension and a place at his dining table as a member of his *cercle intime*.[26] The eulogy of La Mettrie he wrote and had read to a meeting of the Academy caused a sensation. Not just devout Christians were scandalized by praise being heaped on a materialist in the royal palace (where the Academy met) before an audience that included a number of young princes.[27] While in Prussia, La Mettrie collaborated with the Marquis d'Argens on one of the most notorious – and popular – pornographic books of the eighteenth century, *Thérèse philosophe*. Indeed, the materialist views of the lecherous Jesuit Father Dirrag are those of La Mettrie.[28]

As this suggests, La Mettrie was a hedonist as well as a materialist. Both aspects appealed to his patron. Frederick's view of nature was also mechanistic, determinist and fatalistic.[29] He probably also enjoyed La Mettrie's treatise *De la volupté*, having written himself to Voltaire:

Oh, God of sensual delight
You, my one and only divinity,
Come, crown my fidelity.[30]

He may have approved as well of the defence of homosexuality in La Mettrie's *Discourse on happiness* of 1748.[31] When La Mettrie died suddenly in 1751, after reportedly over-indulging in pheasant pie, Frederick's eulogy contained the memorable line: 'The title of philosopher and the reputation of being unfortunate were enough to procure for La Mettrie a refuge in Prussia with a pension from the king.' The opportunity was also seized to use La Mettrie's persecutions as a stick with which to beat the Christians, for example:

> This work [*Man a machine*], which was bound to displease men whose profession makes them declared enemies of the progress of human reason, roused all the priests of Leyden against its author. Calvinists, Catholics and Lutherans forgot for the time being that transubstantiation, free will, masses for the dead, and the infallibility of the pope divided them: they all united to persecute a philosopher.

Frederick concluded that 'Nature had made him [La Mettrie] an orator and a philosopher; but a yet more precious gift he received from her was a pure soul and an obliging heart.'[32] This was too much even for the docile academicians, who received the eulogy in stony silence.[33] Frederick was rather less generous when he wrote to his sister Wilhelmine: 'he was jolly, a good chap, a good doctor and a very bad writer'.[34]

JEAN-JACQUES ROUSSEAU

Frederick gave La Mettrie and other radicals a refuge, but not unlimited freedom to write. La Mettrie's *Discourse on happiness* was burned publicly in Berlin and publication of his *Œuvres philosophiques* prohibited.[35] The same policy was adopted towards someone even more subversive than La Mettrie, namely Jean-Jacques Rousseau, arguably the most subversive thinker of the century. Having published *Julie, ou la nouvelle Héloïse* in 1761, *The Social Contract* in 1762 and *Émile* in the same year, Rousseau was the most famous and the most

persecuted intellectual in Europe. In both Paris and Geneva, his home-
town, his books had been burned and warrants for his arrest issued.[36]
At his wits' end, Rousseau was now even prepared to consider an
offer of sanctuary in the Swiss principality of Neuchâtel, a Prussian
possession by inheritance since 1707. In *The Confessions* Rousseau
paid Frederick a characteristically barbed compliment:

> This offer was particularly opportune because on the King of Prussia's
> territory I should naturally be safe from persecutions; at least religion
> could hardly be used as an excuse for them. But a secret objection, which
> I did not care to state, was quite enough to make me hesitate. That inborn
> love of justice that always consumed my heart, together with my covert
> sympathy for France, had inspired me with an aversion for the King of
> Prussia. He seemed to me, both in his principles and his conduct, to show
> violent disrespect for both natural law and human obligation.[37]

Above his desk he had displayed a portrait of the Prussian king but
adorned with an inscription reading 'Glory and self-regard, those are
his God, his law; he thinks like a philosopher but behaves like a
king.'[38] On arrival in Neuchâtel in July 1762, Rousseau wrote to the
governor of the province, Frederick's close friend George Keith, the
Jacobite Earl Marischal of Scotland, asking for asylum, adding pathetically: 'Determine my fate: I submit to your orders, although if you
order me to leave, I shall not know where to go.'[39] As sceptical and
anti-clerical as his king, Keith forwarded the request to Frederick,
who was campaigning in Silesia. Frederick knew plenty about the
refugee, having read and disliked some of his works.[40] D'Argens had
warned him in 1760 that Rousseau was a dangerous lunatic, whose
views on social equality were not just weird but subversive.[41]

Although preoccupied with tidying up after his victory at Burkersdorf* and organizing the siege of Schweidnitz, Frederick found time
to tell Keith to grant asylum 'to this unfortunate man', although he
added that everything should be done to stop him writing, lest he
upset the plain people of the province.[42] A month later he wrote again:
'we ought to give relief to this poor, unfortunate creature, whose only
sin is to have strange opinions which he thinks are good'. He also

* See above, pp. 255–6.

enclosed a hundred crowns (*écus*) to provide for Rousseau's needs, adding sagely that the intended recipient would be more likely to accept help if it were presented in kind rather than cash. If only the war had not depleted his resources, he added ironically, he would build for Rousseau a hermitage with a garden where he could imitate the life-style of his noble savages. As for himself, he wrote, his views were as different from those of Rousseau as finite is from infinite and he had no intention of giving up the good things of life. He concluded by identifying Rousseau as a man born out of his time: he should have been a hermit of the desert, living on a column, performing miracles, being proclaimed a saint – and adding his name to the long roll of martyrs.[43] This was the sort of letter, mixing generosity with irony, that Frederick did best.

It all ended in tears, of course, as it always did with Rousseau. Keith was unwise enough to offer him an annuity, provoking the stinging reply: 'I have enough to live on for the next two or three years, and I have never pushed foresight that far ahead. But even if I were starving to death, in the present situation of that good prince, and my worthlessness to him, I would rather eat grass and dig up roots than accept a morsel of bread from him.' To Frederick himself he wrote: 'you wish to give me bread. Is there not one of your subjects who lacks it?'[44] In the autumn of 1765, after his house had been stoned by local people enraged by his alleged impiety, Rousseau was on the move again, this time to England, assisted by the philosopher David Hume. There he fell out with everyone as usual, including his host. In a bizarre footnote, Horace Walpole was responsible for a mischievous letter purporting to have been written by Frederick to Rousseau:

> I wish you well and will treat you well if you wish me to. But if you persist in rejecting my help, believe me, I shall tell no one. If you go racking your brains to find new misfortunes, choose the one you would like. I am a King and can provide you with as much suffering as you desire and – something you will not obtain from your enemies – I shall cease persecuting you when you cease to seek glory in being persecuted.[45]

The real Frederick never did appreciate Rousseau. During the peace negotiations of the winter of 1762–3, he read *Émile*, but found it

worthless, as he told the Duchess of Saxony-Coburg.[46] When Dieudonné Thiébault came to Prussia in 1765 to take up his appointment
as professor at the new Military Academy, Frederick asked him which
French prose writers he admired most. When Rousseau's name was
mentioned, Frederick interrupted him with the cry: 'Oh! That man is
a lunatic!'[47] But he continued to have sympathy for his plight, telling
Voltaire sternly in 1766: 'My view is that he is an unfortunate man for
whom we ought to feel sorry ... We ought to respect the unfortunate;
it is only the depraved who condemn them.'[48] As Voltaire habitually
and vehemently condemned Rousseau, he must have felt the force of
this particular thrust.

VOLTAIRE

Voltaire himself was of course the most celebrated of all subversive writers to have found refuge in Prussia. Not the least important reason for
Frederick's frequent and urgent invitations was the wish to have his own
French prose and poetry corrected and polished.[49] One does not need to
be a native speaker to spot how defective were his spelling, grammar
and syntax. The relationship between the two men was contentious but
fruitful, perhaps the most absorbing of any between intellectual and
sovereign. From Frederick's first communication of 8 August 1736 to
Voltaire's last of 1 April 1778 (he died two months later), they exchanged
enough letters to fill three fat volumes of Frederick's *Œuvres*, Frederick
himself writing 654, many of them long.[50] At one level this was a mutual
admiration society. Voltaire variously likened Frederick to Julius Caesar, Augustus, Marcus Aurelius, Trajan, Antoninus Pius, Titus, Julian,
Virgil, Pliny, Horace, Maecenas, Cicero, Catullus, Homer, La Rochefou-
cauld, La Bruyère, Boileau, Solomon, Prometheus, Apollo, Patroclus,
Socrates, Alcibiades, Alexander, Henry IV and Francis I.[51] 'He thinks like
Marcus Aurelius and writes like Cicero' was a typical accolade.[52]

Frederick's reciprocal admiration was of long standing. The clandestine library he assembled as a teenager* included the first volume
of Voltaire's collected works, two editions of the *Henriade* and the

* See above, p. 34.

Histoire de Charles XII.[53] On the ceiling of his study at Rheinsberg he had Antoine Pesne paint an open book displaying the names of the two writers he venerated most: Horace and Voltaire.[54] The two men met for the first time on 11 September 1740 at the Château de Meuse near the Prussian territory of Cleves. Afterwards, Frederick wrote to his close friend Jordan: '[Voltaire] has the eloquence of Cicero, the mildness of Pliny, the wisdom of Agrippa; he combines, in short, what is to be collected of virtues and talents from the three greatest men of Antiquity.'[55] But the sincerest form of flattery Frederick had to offer was imitation. From adolescence to death Voltaire and his works were the objects of his most intense fascination and admiration.[56]

Also imitated was Voltaire's verse, not least in its profusion. Both men possessed an extraordinary fluency in turning out page after page of short rhyming lines on every kind of subject. Even their prose correspondence breaks repeatedly into verse. For Frederick this was more than showing off his command of the French language, it was also a form of therapy. If he could versify an experience, he could also come to terms with it. So he was especially prolific during the critical periods of the Seven Years War.[57] When it came to quality, however, there was a chasm between them. Frederick's seemingly interminable epistles, eulogies, odes and satires are at the same time plodding and irritating, clumsy and facetious. It is easy to imagine Voltaire becoming exasperated when obliged to correct, polish and supplement them. Theodore Besterman's withering comment on Frederick's *Art de la guerre* of 1749 was 'confused in structure, feeble in execution, commonplace in poetic style'. After it had been sent to Voltaire for revision, the author studied his amendments 'in the spirit of an uninspired schoolboy', adopting all of them word for word. Yet this work was the most successful of all Frederick's long poems, Besterman added, for the good reason that of the 1,600 lines, 300 were entirely the work of Voltaire.[58] More unkind still was Lytton Strachey:

> He filled volumes, and the contents of those volumes afford probably the most complete illustration in literature of the very trite proverb – *Poeta nascitur, non fit.* The spectacle of that heavy German Muse, with her feet crammed into pointed slippers, executing, with incredible conscientiousness, now the stately measure of a Versailles minuet, and now

the spritely steps of a Parisian jig, would be either ludicrous or pathetic – one hardly knows which – were it not so certainly neither the one nor the other, but simply dreary with an unutterable dreariness, from which the eyes of men avert themselves in shuddering dismay.[59]

To a certain extent, this was a complementary relationship: between Frederick's political power and intellect on the one hand, and Voltaire's literary talent and intellect on the other. It worked well when all that was required was an exchange of compliments. As Voltaire wrote: 'he called me a divine being and I called him a Solomon. These sobriquets cost us nothing.'[60] But mutual admiration also involved mutual exploitation. For Voltaire, the well-publicized veneration of such a renowned sovereign gave him a status no other philosophe could boast. 'Ordinarily, we men of letters flatter kings,' wrote Voltaire, 'this one praised me from head to toe.'[61] At a time when he was out of favour at Versailles, out of fashion at Paris and in constant danger of prosecution for impiety, a foreign asylum was very welcome.[62] For Frederick, to be called 'the Great' by the most famous intellectual of the day was to be raised to lonely eminence as a philosopher on the throne. Like every amateur author, he craved recognition from the professionals. So when Voltaire reported to his friends in Paris that his employer was a combination of Apollo and Marcus Aurelius and had turned Berlin into a new Athens, he could preen himself on having gained admission to the elite of the Republic of Letters.[63]

Two such clever, wilful, arrogant men could not coexist easily. By the time Voltaire arrived for his extended stay in 1750, both knew enough about each other to be on guard. Knowing that Voltaire had been showing his Parisian friends a garbled version of one of his letters, Frederick had lamented to Algarotti in September 1749 that Voltaire was as mischievous as a monkey, adding that he admired his intellect while distrusting his character.[64] As Strachey observed, 'If any man ever acted with his eyes wide open, it was Frederick when he invited Voltaire to Berlin.'[65] Voltaire's own illusions had been shattered by Frederick's invasion of Silesia in 1740 just as his *Antimachiavel* was being prepared for publication. He also knew that Frederick had lured his young protégé Baculard d'Arnaud to Berlin with the flattering comment that he was the rising sun of French literature just as Voltaire's sun was setting.[66] The prospect of becoming Frederick's resident tutor in literary matters cannot have been inviting. Yet he still went, offering the following explanation a year later to the Duc de Richelieu:

> I arrived in Potsdam, the big blue eyes of the King, his lovely smile, his seductive voice, the aura of his five victories, his avowed pleasure in seclusion, in work, in writing verse and prose, and finally also the marks of his friendship which made my head spin, also a delightful gift for conversation, broadmindedness, a complete lack of majesty in his discourse, a thousand attentions that would bewitch even if made by a private citizen – all this turned my head: I surrendered to him out of passion, out of infatuation and without qualification.[67]

As his letters from Berlin and Potsdam make clear, at first Voltaire enjoyed himself thoroughly, basking in the adulation of king, court and public, enjoying his comfortable quarters, revelling in his status as royal chamberlain and banking his 4,000 talers of removal expenses and princely annual salary of 5,000.[68] Once he formally entered royal service in August 1750, however, his status changed from honoured guest to servant.[69] On 12 September he told his niece (and lover) Madame Denis that he was not the king's chamberlain but his grammarian.[70] As the days shortened and the bleak Prussian winter threatened, he began to have second thoughts. In another letter written two months later, he listed all the reasons he had for being happy but added after each one '... but ... but ...', ending 'the weather is beginning to get really cold'.[71] He then did something extraordinarily stupid. Although very rich already – his annual income from writing and investments had reached 75,000 livres by 1749[72] – what can only be called avarice led him into a fraudulent and illegal transaction with a Berlin Jew called Abraham Hirschel involving Saxon war debts.[73] As the two protagonists sued each other, a public scandal resulted, which caused Frederick embarrassment and irritation in equal measure. He told Wilhelmine that it was a case of a rogue trying to cheat a swindler.[74] In February 1751 he wrote Voltaire a stern letter, accusing him of causing 'a frightful disturbance' and warning him as to his future conduct.[75]

The atmosphere was poisoned further by two bits of malicious gossip eagerly passed on to each man by wagging tongues. Voltaire was told by La Mettrie that Frederick had said about him: 'I shall have need of him for another year at most, no longer. One squeezes the orange and then one throws away the peel.'[76] On the other hand, Frederick was told that Voltaire had been telling anyone who would listen that Frederick's verses were rubbish and, when receiving a further instalment of royal writings for correction, had sighed: 'Will he never get tired of sending me his dirty linen to wash?'[77] Voltaire believed that this last sally had been both invented and spread by Pierre Louis Maupertuis, director of the Royal Academy of Berlin. Originally, the two men had been friends, indeed it was Voltaire who had recommended Maupertuis to Frederick in the first place. Berlin-Potsdam, however, proved to be not big enough for the two of them. Maupertuis had been the leading French intellectual in Prussia until the arrival of the more glamorous Voltaire and deeply resented his demotion. As Maupertuis had elevated the Berlin Academy to high standing in the European intellectual world, he had every reason to feel aggrieved.[78] For his part, 'Voltaire could not stand importance unless it was his own.'[79] The furious quarrel that resulted confirmed once again the validity of the familiar adage that academic disputes are so vicious because there is so little at stake.

After a great deal of sniping by both sides, what proved to be the terminal tiff erupted over an academic dispute between Maupertuis and Samuel König about 'the principle of least action'. Voltaire naturally took the latter's side. In the summer of 1752 he published in a Dutch periodical an attack which also derided some of Maupertuis's more speculative projects. These included boring a hole to the centre of the earth, and dissecting the brains of the giants believed to live in Patagonia.[80] Unfortunately for Voltaire, Frederick aligned himself on the side of Maupertuis, not surprisingly as the reputation of the director of his Academy was at stake. So he entered the public sphere with *A letter from a Fellow of the Academy of Berlin* (Frederick) *to a Fellow of the Academy of Paris* (Voltaire). Recklessly, Voltaire responded with a supportive letter to König that he must have known would be made public. He also rushed out one of his most venomous pamphlets, *Diatribe of Doctor Akakia*. 'Akakia' means without malice, making the title particularly ironic. Needless to say, all this caused a tremendous public stir, not just in Berlin but across Germany and even Europe.[81] Count Lehndorff recorded in his diary that the Berliners had been kept royally entertained, adding sagely 'all these great minds are bad characters'.[82] Frederick had had enough. If nothing else, the episode now demonstrated the limits of his toleration of dissent. In a gesture that would not have been out of place in the most unenlightened of contemporary states, he had Voltaire's pamphlet burned on several public squares in Berlin by the public hangman and then sent the ashes to Maupertuis.[83] In letters to his sister Wilhelmine, Frederick denounced Voltaire with real passion, branding him as 'contemptible', 'false', 'vile', 'disgusting', 'an indecent villain'.[84] Voltaire was less intemperate, sending back his insignia of office accompanied by a verse:

> I received them with tenderness;
> I return them to you with sorrow;
> This is how a lover, in his extreme passion,
> Returns the portrait of his mistress.[85]

Predictably perhaps, the love-affair between philosophe and philosopher-king had ended in bitter tears. More were shed during the extended and equally unpleasant coda. Voltaire finally shook off the dust of Prussia on 26 March 1753 but, having reached the safety of Saxony, promptly re-ignited the feud by reprinting the *Akakia* pamphlet. But he had underestimated Frederick's reach. At Frankfurt am Main, Voltaire was apprehended, placed under house arrest and his luggage was seized and searched. Frederick's main concern was to retrieve a copy of the (very) limited edition of his *Œuvres*, which included *Palladium*. Voltaire now spent five very disagreeable weeks (29 May–7 July) at Frankfurt before he was allowed to proceed.[86] Voltaire had undoubtedly behaved very provocatively, but Frederick had responded in a manner that can only be described as despotic and also illegal (Frankfurt was a Free Imperial City not subject to Prussian jurisdiction).

A prolonged period of cooling off was required before the two men could resume relations. Although they never saw each other again, they did restart their correspondence in the spring of 1754.[87] At least Frederick showed he was able to distinguish between the man and the writer, continuing to despise the former while admiring the latter: 'the world has produced no finer genius than Voltaire, but I utterly despise him because he is not honest'.[88] Throughout the rest of his life Voltaire remained his favourite author and dramatist. In 1770, when subscribing generously to an appeal to erect a monument in honour of Voltaire, he wrote to Baron Grimm: 'no writer has ever possessed so perfect a taste as this great man; Ancient Greece would have made him a god and raised a temple in his honour'. To d'Alembert on the same occasion he added that Voltaire's works were his best memorial, for they would outlast St Peter's Basilica, the Louvre and all the other structures 'dedicated to eternity by the vanity of mankind'.[89] When the famous French actor Henri-Louis Cain, known as 'Le Kain', performed at Potsdam in the summer of 1775, Frederick reported to Voltaire that he himself knew his plays so well that he could have acted as prompter without a text and that he wept during the performances of *Œdipe* and *Zaïre*.[90] The last reading he ever heard before he died was from Voltaire's *Louis XIV*.[91]

THE PRUSSIAN PUBLIC SPHERE

Limited but well-publicized generosity to stars of the European intelligentsia was not matched by patronage of the home-grown literary scene. The public sphere greatly expanded in depth and breadth during Frederick's long reign but more in spite of, than because of, his encouragement. His official attitude was certainly supportive. In his own first major publication, *Antimachiavel*, he wrote: 'it is well-known just how curious the public is; it is a creature that sees everything and hears everything and passes on everything it hears and sees. When public curiosity is applied to the conduct of private citizens, it is done only for entertainment during idle moments, but when it passes judgment on the character of rulers, it is pursuing its own interest.' So it was just as well that the public was a 'sound judge' of reputations.[92] In the preface to the revised edition of his *Memoirs to serve as a history of the house of Brandenburg*, published in 1751, he stated that he had made corrections 'out of consideration for the public, which every author ought to respect' and in the opening paragraph announced that he would not be repeating fairy stories about the origins of the dynasty because they were unworthy of 'the judicious and enlightened public of this century'.[93] His friend Jordan he commended for showing the 'respect and deference owed to the public'.[94]

The public may have had 'a penetrating eye from which nothing escapes', as he told the young Duke Karl Eugen of Württemberg in the instruction manual (*Miroir des princes*) he composed for him, but his perspective was very much top–down. It was the task of the men of letters to instruct the public and of the philosophers to disseminate truth.[95] Nothing could have been more elitist than his model of cultural transmission, which saw right thinking spreading imperceptibly 'from those who cultivate the arts and the sciences to the public and thence to the common people; it passes from the court to the town, and from the town to the provinces'.[96] By the time enlightened thinking reached its final destination, however, he thought that no one would be listening. In a revealing letter to d'Alembert of January 1770 he estimated that in a state with a population of 10 million, the peasants, labourers, artisans and soldiers would be beyond reach of the educator. Of the 50,000 remaining, half could also be excluded because they were women. Of the remaining nobles and educated bourgeois, the shiftless, the imbecilic, the faint-hearted and the debauched would have to be weeded out, leaving no more than 1,000 well-read people. Even among that residue there would be a great variety of talent. So, Frederick concluded wearily: 'in every age the number of philosophes will always be tiny, and the universe will be dominated by some form of superstition.'[97]

This crushing verdict on the general public came in a private letter and it was only when he knew he would not be overheard that Frederick gave full vent to his jaundiced view of humanity, as the following brief but representative selection reveals:

- How often has one seen clever charlatans confirm the errors of the stupid public!
- Three quarters of the world are ignorant and stupid.
- The public is blind and born to be misled.
- The idiot public is enslaved for life to its vacuous prejudices.
- Alas! Just look closely at the public, it is stupid, ignorant, foolish, contemptible and bestial.

- The idiot public is born to vegetate.
- Appearances are deceptive but that is the only way the public judges.
- I have always despised the verdicts of the public.
- There must be a king to direct the stupid mass, a beast with a long tongue but short sight.[98]

What made Frederick really angry as well as disillusioned, however, was the knowledge that these ignorant and stupid people thought they were entitled to criticize their betters. In a verse epistle entitled 'On Reputation' sent to General Asmus Ehrenreich von Bredow, an East Prussian Junker, he fulminated:

> Everyone, even women, think they are entitled to decide
> Off their own back on the great issues of the day;
> Before their tribunal, ministers, generals,
> Kings who are aggressors, and kings who are their enemies,
> Receive their verdict in less than a minute,
> Reputations are made and destroyed;
> Virtue, talent, crown and sceptre,
> Nothing is spared in this bizarre century of ours.
> ....
> Bredow, such are the people and the idiot public,
> Nothing can escape their barbed tongues.
> ....
> So, what do you think? Is it sensible for a man
> To devote all his effort, trouble and industry,
> To forgo his pleasures, his time and his leisure,
> Just to bring down on himself the attention and the censure
> Of these ignorant, thoughtless and unfaithful people,
> Imbued with prejudice, enslaved to error,
> The wholly fallacious adjudicator of contemporary reputation?[99]

Time and again, Frederick revealed his sensitivity to criticism. After the Peace of Breslau in June 1742, for example, he told Jordan that he knew he would be attacked by the 'foolish and the ignorant' but he did not care a fig for the 'absurd prattle of the public'. Evidently he *did* care. A week later he asked Jordan to report everything the Berlin public was saying about the peace and not to leave anything out.[100]

337

One defence mechanism was along the lines of the 'I-never-read-my-reviews' claim still popular today, as in his letter to Voltaire at a particularly bleak time in 1759: 'I go my own way; I do nothing contrary to my inner voice and conscience; and I pay no attention to how my actions are depicted by the brainless.'[101] Another was the assertion that he could not defend his policies in public without compromising state security, so was content to leave the verdict to posterity.[102] In the event, the latter has proved to be a rather unreliable umpire.

The same could be said of his contemporaries. As the brevity of his honeymoon with freedom of expression had demonstrated, Frederick would have dearly liked to control the Prussian public sphere, especially in his capital. He was defeated by both its width and quality. In 1648 the population of Berlin had been only c. 10,000.[103] Thanks to the highest birth-rate in Germany in the second half of the seventeenth century, this had more than quintupled by 1709 to about 55,000, including the garrison.[104] Frederick William I's dismantling of the court and austerity drive had led to an exodus of some 17,000 artisans and dependants, although the rapid increase in the garrison was some compensation.[105] By the time Frederick succeeded in 1740, both natural growth and immigration had brought the total to 90,000, including 21,000 soldiers and dependants.[106] It kept growing, reaching 132,365 by 1770 and 145,000–148,000 by the end of the reign.[107] Literacy rates are hard to come by, although a few straws in the wind suggest they were high: 94.1 per cent of owner-occupiers could sign their names in 1782 and 'probably' 60–70 per cent of children between the ages of six and fourteen were attending school throughout the Potsdam-Berlin region.[108] The *Berlinische Monatsschrift* claimed in 1783 that in general the city's schools were excellent.[109] The high percentage of Berliners with a Huguenot background (20 per cent in 1720) may also account in part for the high ranking in the European literacy league table.[110]

Among the many revolutions identifiable in the eighteenth century, a 'reading revolution' deserves a place. For the first time across a significant part of the continent, albeit on a falling west–east and north–south gradient, the ability to read became a mass phenomenon. Moreover, this was also a perceived revolution, as contemporaries noticed, usually with approval, that more and more people were reading. In the course of a review of the Leipzig book fair in 1780, the influential periodical *German Museum* wrote: 'Sixty years ago the only people who bought books were academics, but today there is hardly a woman with some claim to education who does not read. Readers are to be found in every class, both in the towns and in the country, even the common soldiers in the large cities take out books from the lending libraries.'[111] The painter and print-maker Daniel Chodowiecki, born in Danzig but for most of his adult life a resident of Berlin, gave pictorial expression to this development in two contrasting but eloquent studies of a single peasant and a middle-class group reading. Literate people created a literary market which entrepreneurs were quick to supply. By the time Lessing arrived in Berlin in 1748, there were thirteen bookshops, four of them also book publishers and five of them specializing in French literature.[112] The most prominent publisher, Friedrich Nicolai, was responsible as well for two of the most successful literary German periodicals – the *Letters concerning the latest literature* (1759–65) and *The General German Library* (1765–1806).[113] The former immediately established itself as the most influential organ of the German Enlightenment, engaging high-profile contributors such as Lessing, Herder and Moses Mendelssohn.[114] It was a status maintained by its successor, which in the course of its long career reviewed around 80,000 books, making its editor a small fortune into the bargain, as it rarely dropped below the break-even circulation of 1,000 and often achieved two or three times that.[115] Nicolai was also on the receiving end of one of Goethe and Schiller's *Xenien*:

> If you deserve little credit for the education of the Germans,
> Fritz Nicolai, you have earned a great deal of money in the process.[116]

If the total circulation seems modest, it should be remembered that, to achieve a total *readership* figure, a multiplier of at least ten, probably twenty and perhaps even thirty to forty, can be used.[117] Nicolai and his fellow editors were able to take advantage of the greatly improved postal services provided by the Imperial Post-Master (the Prince of Thurn and Taxis) and the rival Prussian and Saxon services (with 760 and 140 post offices respectively). This allowed the letter-post, including periodicals, to be moved at speeds of between 130 and 150 kilometres per day.[118] By the end of the century, no German community was further than half-a-day's walk from a postal station.[119]

Reading could be individual, collective or even institutional, for the eighteenth century was also the century of reading clubs. Although increased print runs brought the unit cost of books down, technological constraints – especially in the production of paper – imposed limits to price reductions. One solution was for readers to pool their funds to form a reading group, passing the purchased volumes around. Most of these associations were informal, but in cities like Berlin more permanent clubs were founded, with a committee of management and their own premises. The first reading club in Berlin was founded in 1764; by the end of the reign they could be found in several other towns.[120] Also usually informal were the cultural societies which met regularly to discuss books and even, more daringly, the issues of the day. In Berlin they were known after the days of the week on which they met – the Monday Club, founded in 1749 by a Lutheran pastor, and the Society of Friends of Enlightenment or Wednesday Society, founded in 1783 and comprising the leading lights of the Berlin Enlightenment, including Nicolai, Mendelssohn, Christian Wilhelm von Dohm, Carl Gottlieb Suarez, Ernst Ferdinand Klein, Johann Joachim Spalding, Johann Friedrich Zöllner, Johann Erich Biester and Friedrich Gedike. The last two were co-editors of the city's other major periodical, the *Berlin Monthly*, which also enjoyed a pan-German circulation and has been hailed as 'the most important journal of the Enlightenment'.[121] This was much more than a collection of book reviews and dealt with all manner of topics, from the Montgolfier balloon to the latest opera, and included political issues such as Prussia's new judicial system.[122]

Given his notorious disdain for literature written in the German language, it may be doubted whether any of these periodicals were to be found on Frederick's desk. Nor did he play a direct role in any of the other media that made up the public sphere. That did not, however, prevent him exerting influence at one remove. As we have seen, his musical establishment had a considerable impact on his capital's musical life.* In one important part of the public sphere he did how-

---

* See above, pp. 153–6.

ever set a direct example. This was Freemasonry, which in its modern form was the creation of the eighteenth century, dating from the foundation of the Grand Lodge of England in London in 1717. Admitted to the order at Minden in 1738 while still crown prince, by Count Albert Wolfgang of Schaumburg-Lippe, Frederick founded his own lodge at Rheinsberg on his return home.[123] His enthusiasm for Freemasonry would not have been diminished by his father's intense and well-publicized hostility to it.[124] Frederick was very much a pioneer, for the first Masonic Lodge in Germany had been founded as recently as December 1737, in Hamburg.[125] On his accession to the throne he was instrumental in founding a lodge at Berlin – 'At the Three Globes' – and personally inducted two of his brothers and other members of the Prussian aristocracy.[126] This royal public endorsement gave Masonry 'an enormous expansion boost' throughout the Holy Roman Empire, not least in Prussia, where there were twenty-eight lodges in 1764.[127] By the end of the reign the Berlin lodges alone numbered more than 400 members.[128]

Although his active participation later waned, Frederick's continuing support for the movement was well advertised. In 1774, for example, he informed a Berlin lodge: 'His Majesty will always count it a special pleasure that he enjoys the opportunity to give his strong support to the promotion of the objectives of all true Masonry, namely the intellectual elevation of men as members of society and making them more virtuous and more charitable.'[129] The masons returned the compliment by including the name of Frederick in a dozen of their lodges ('Frederick at the Golden Sceptre', for example) and by stressing the duty of their members to serve him and his state. In the year of his death, a masonic address stated: 'whosoever fails to serve his king and his state loyally and honestly ... is unworthy to be a mason'.[130] When he died, a masonic funeral oration hailed him as 'a man of whom not just Masonry but all humanity will eternally be proud, not just the greatest ruler but, what is more, the greatest man that history has ever known'.[131]

FREDERICK ON GERMAN
LANGUAGE AND LITERATURE

This expanded and rapidly growing public sphere was both an opportunity and a threat for all regimes. More scrutiny could bring negative criticism, or positive engagement, or both. One reason for the collapse of the absolute monarchy in France but the survival of the equally troubled Habsburg Monarchy in 1789–90 was the relative ability of the two sovereigns involved to project an effective image to the public.[132] Frederick proved to be far more adept than either Louis XVI or Joseph II, although he certainly did not go out of his way to woo the leading lights of the Berlin republic of letters. On the contrary, his attitude to the great German-language literary renaissance that coincided with his reign was both hostile and ill-informed. While still crown prince, he had written to Voltaire that Germany could never expect to develop a vernacular culture of any value. He conceded that the Germans had some virtues, for they did not lack intellect, they had ample good sense (being rather like the English in this regard), were industrious and even profound. On the other hand, they were also ponderous, long-winded and boring. The main – indeed the insuperable – problem was linguistic: because Germany was divided into an infinity of territories, he stated, it would never be possible to reach agreement on which of the regional dialects would become the standard form.[133] This aversion to the German language became a recurrent theme of both his public works and private correspondence, as in 'if we still retain some vestige of our ancient republican liberty, it consists of the worthless opportunity to murder at our leisure a language that is coarse and still virtually barbaric'.[134] He confirmed his own prejudice by using a form of German which, for all its characteristic vigour, was crude, misspelt and ungrammatical.[135] The literature created in this primitive medium naturally attracted his corresponding contempt. As he wrote to Voltaire in 1775 (the year after the publication of Goethe's bestselling novel *The Sorrows of Young Werther*), German literature was nothing more than a 'farrago of inflated phrases', German history was pedantic, and even German philosophy had died out since the days of Leibniz and Wolff. In short, he claimed, Germany's current cultural level was about two and a half centuries behind that of France.[136]

It was one thing to convey this abuse in private letters to Voltaire, it was quite another to broadcast it publicly in the form of a pamphlet, which is just what he did with *Concerning German Literature; the faults of which it can be accused; the causes of the same and the means of rectifying them*, published in 1780. As if to rub in his alienation from German culture, he wrote it in French, leaving one of his officials (Christian Wilhelm von Dohm) to translate it into German.[137] He expressly denied that German literature was making progress: 'I do not believe that any writer can write well in a language which has not yet been refined.' From that point the insults came thick and fast:

> The German language is still semi-barbaric and divided into as many dialects as Germany has provinces . . . The German language is confusing, difficult to use, does not sound pleasant and is not rich in metaphors . . . The endings sound so harsh in German and would be much improved by the addition of an 'a', so that '*sagen*' would become '*sagena*', and so on . . . [138]

At least he had the good grace to concede that this last fatuous suggestion would prove unacceptable. As if seeking to cause maximum offence, Frederick then singled out the boy-wonder of German letters – Goethe – for a special insult:

> To see just how bad contemporary taste in Germany is, just visit any theatre. There you will see the abominable plays of Shakespeare being performed in German translations and the audiences deriving great pleasure from these ridiculous farces which merit only to be performed in front of savages in Canada . . . Shakespeare can be forgiven because he lived at a time when English culture had developed but little. However, there is no excuse for our contemporaries making the same mistakes – as has been done, for example, in Goethe's *Götz von Berlichingen*, an abominable imitation of those bad English plays. Yet the public warmly applauds this rubbish and demands that it be repeated. I know one shouldn't argue about matters of taste, but I have to say that someone who can derive as much pleasure from a puppet-show as from the tragedies of Racine is just looking for a way of killing time.[139]

Predictably, the pamphlet was greeted with (mostly) outrage.[140] Within a year, nine refutations had been published.[141] Yet there was no real surprise, for throughout his reign Frederick had flaunted his low opinion of German culture. When he revived the Academy in 1743, he gave it a French title (Académie Royale des Sciences et Belles-Lettres), French statutes, a French president (Maupertuis), a mainly French membership and decreed that French should be the language of both oral and written communications.[142] This did not change: between the end of the Seven Years War and his death Frederick appointed only eighteen full members of his Academy, of whom only five were Germans.[143] No wonder that a German intelligentsia rapidly growing in numbers and self-confidence should take offence: as they saw it, he had the cream of a native culture both rich and fresh at his disposal, but preferred the sour and thin dregs of France. The fiasco of the appointment of Antoine Joseph Pernety as his librarian, mistaking him for Jacques Pernety, exemplified the problem.[144] In similar fashion the sculptor François Gaspard Balthasar Adam was brought to Berlin in mistake for his more famous elder brother Nicolas Sébastien.[145] French was of course the language of choice of most aristocratic Europeans, at least on the continent, but in German-speaking Europe, Frederick's studied preference was beginning to seem increasingly anachronistic.

As *Concerning German Literature* revealed, Frederick was a living fossil, a relic of the generation before last. Baron von Grimm found a good simile: Frederick wrote of German literature like a blind man trying to describe colours.[146] His cultural tastes had been formed before he came to the throne and had simply not developed. As Werner Langer pointed out, in the most penetrating of the studies of Frederick's cultural formation, it was crucial that Frederick's intimate friends during his all-important sojourn at Rheinsberg (1736–40) – Jordan, Keyserlingk, de la Motte Fouqué – were twelve to fifteen years older than he was. In other words, they belonged to a generation born around 1700 and were contemporaries of Voltaire. Indeed, it was Frederick's conscious decision to have mature men around him, from whom he could learn, and it was his avowed aim that he should grasp things quickly – but then never let them go.[147] As we have seen, Voltaire himself exercised profound influence on his development, making, among many other things, an important contribution to Frederick's first major work, *Antimachiavel*.[148] The result was deep cultural conservatism.*

In every branch of the arts Frederick had been overtaken by his subjects. The Berliners in particular were quick to embrace innovation, from *opera buffa* in music to *Sturm und Drang* in literature. In 1777 the celebrated actor Johann Franz Brockmann ('The German Garrick') visited Berlin en route for an appointment at the National Theatre in Vienna. Of course he was excluded from any of the royal stages, from which only Italian was sung or French declaimed, so he appeared at the public theatre in Behren Street run by the actor-manager Carl Theophil Döbbelin. Brockmann's appearance as Hamlet was a sensation. Each of his twelve performances was sold out. Anyone wanting a seat had to be at the theatre hours in advance.[149] He was lionized by high society and his visit was recorded visually in a number of engravings by the enterprising Daniel Chodowiecki. It was a revealing episode and some at least of the theatregoing public must have appreciated its significance: the most famous actor of his day was confined to a brief season at a public theatre in Berlin while on his way to the state-funded *National* Theatre in Vienna. 'Those bad English plays' were derided by Frederick but hailed by the Berliners, who were also entertained by *Romeo and Juliet*, *Richard III*, *Othello*, *Macbeth* and *Henry IV*.[150]

It was a conservatism shot through with pessimism. In a letter to Voltaire of 1771 he abused the newfangled comic operas as 'platitudes set to music, shouted and sung out of tune just to make the audience laugh'. 'Frederick's pessimistic narrative of modern culture traced a steady decline from the golden age of Louis XIV towards a decadence of taste that would inexorably end in reverting back to outright barbarism. What the present-day believed to be of quality was just trivial rubbish and genius was as rare as good sense.'[151] Increasingly out of joint with the times, Frederick despised such new forms as the *comédie larmoyante* and the *drame bourgeois*, while he did not regard the novel as a literary genre at all, dismissing it as a mere 'diversion'.[152] A man who derided the great German epic – the *Nibelungenlied* – as

---

* See his remark about modern music quoted earlier, pp. 156–7.

'not worth a shot of gunpowder' and dismissed the Middle Ages as 'twelve centuries of stupidity' was not likely to appreciate Herder or Goethe.[153] No more adventurous in the visual arts, his taste changed only by going backwards – from near-contemporaries such as Watteau, Pater and Lancret to Dutch, Flemish and Italian old masters.[154]*

For someone who often showed an acute awareness of which way the public wind was blowing, Frederick was remarkably obtuse when it came to matters theatrical. In particular, he missed a relatively cheap and easy means of mobilizing support in the German-speaking world by failing to notice the growing popularity of 'national theatres'. A clear signal was given when one French troupe after another was closed down – at Hanover in 1757, Munich in 1758, Stuttgart in 1767, Dresden in 1769, Mannheim in 1770, Vienna and Bayreuth in 1772, and so on.[155] A trail-blazing initiative was taken by Joseph II in 1776 when he turned his court theatre into a *Nationaltheater* with a repertoire devoted to works in the German language (one of them was to be Mozart's *The Abduction from the Seraglio* or rather *Die Entführung aus dem Serail*). This played well with the German intelligentsia. Tobias von Gebler wrote to Friedrich Nicolai: 'Every patriot must rejoice that our German Joseph has designated the national stage as his *Court theatre*. He will certainly employ no Frenchman until German plays are performed at Versailles.'[156] A periodical devoted to the theatre rejoiced: 'The Germans now have a national theatre, and it is their Emperor who has founded it. What a delightful, what a magnificent thought for everyone capable of feeling that he is a German! Everyone thanks the Emperor with a feeling of the deepest reverence for the great example he has given to the German princes.'[157] It was not often that Vienna could celebrate stealing a march on Berlin at the cultural cutting-edge. Frederick had built a new theatre on the Gendarmenmarkt in 1774 but assigned it to a French company, which was disbanded on the outbreak of war in 1778. The theatre was barred to German actors and remained dark until the end of the reign.[158]

* See above, pp. 172–3.

FREDERICK AS PROPAGANDIST

If Frederick thought it vital to stop the wrong sort of information reaching the public, he was equally concerned to propagate the right version. He was his own first minister – and he was also his own first journalist. The favour granted to Ambrosius Haude* was not just gratitude for services rendered. He needed the newspapers to get his message across. In his very first venture in foreign affairs, the dispute with the Prince-Bishop of Liège, he gave instructions that the Prussian case be presented in the public prints.[159] He knew all about the crescent of publishing houses that extended from the Low Countries around the Rhineland to Switzerland, from which mainly French-language periodicals and pamphlets were diffused across Europe, and was determined to get his own words in.[160] Right from the start, Frederick's busy pen was turning out articles and pamphlets. Soon after the conquest of Silesia he set up *Silesian News* (*Schlesische Zeitung*), which among other things published his own (unsigned) accounts of victories over the Austrians and even sold as supplements engravings of his portrait. Remarkably, it was to enjoy an unbroken existence until the end of the Second World War.[161] In particular, he was eager to counter the mainly anti-Prussian Dutch press, the most sophisticated and widely distributed in Europe. When the Second Silesian War began in 1744, he charged the Marquis d'Argens with creating *L'Observateur Holandois*, which – for added authenticity – claimed to be published in Leiden. Promptly banned in the Dutch Republic, it folded the following year.[162] Undaunted, Frederick continued to use the press throughout his reign, especially in wartime. With the number of newspapers in the Holy Roman Empire increasing from sixty to over 200 during his reign, this was a hotly contested medium, whose temperature rose as the public sphere expanded. The intensification of political and confessional controversies during the Seven Years War proved especially good for business.[163]

Nowhere in Europe was there a more lively or larger public sphere than in England, whose capital was the largest metropolis in Europe

* See above, p. 320.

by mid-century and was expanding rapidly towards seven figures. To this key ally after 1756 Frederick was careful to send exultant reports of victories and down-playing explanations of defeats for onward transmission to the British public.[164] In a country where anti-Catholicism was an essential part of the political culture, he could be paraded as a second Gustavus Adolphus, a Protestant champion defending Europe's liberties against the fell designs of the tyrannical Catholic triumvirate of France, Austria and Spain. The British needed a hero to bring them confidence in the perilous times of war abroad and rebellion on the Celtic fringe, and Frederick was much better suited for that role than their own ageing and uncharismatic sovereign, George II. So Frederick became the beneficiary of a wave of public adulation expressed in countless poems, songs, sermons, ceramic artefacts, medallions and engravings. Especially ubiquitous and durable was the renaming of hundreds of inns as 'The King of Prussia' (some even survived the Germanophobe waves of 1914 and 1939 and remain to this day). His birthday was celebrated across the length and breadth of the land, even including Scotland.[165]

It was no different in Germany. A torrent of artefacts, from tablecloths to snuff-boxes, from knives to bracelets, all adorned with Frederick's image, were produced for the market. Iserlohn in the Prussian duchy of Cleves emerged as the main centre for the mass production of items as various as brass and copper boxes depicting battle plans, decorated spoons, enamelled tobacco tins and tobacco scissors shaped like Frederick, to be exported all over the empire and indeed 'to all parts of the world'. Especially popular, not least because of their low cost, were the 'vivat ribbons' inscribed with patriotic motifs, images and verses and worn pinned to a waistcoat or the brim of a hat.[166] Illustrations of battle scenes were often accompanied by an adulatory poem and a narrative, so that the engravings were more like illustrated pamphlets.[167] If Frederick was aware of this dimension, he did not comment. Given his disdain for the public, noted earlier in this chapter, it is unlikely to have met with his approval. Although he commissioned portraits of himself, especially during the early years of his reign, he would not sit for a painter, although he probably made an exception for the Brunswick court painter Johann Georg Ziesenis when on a visit to his sister Amalia in 1769 and also for Anna Dorothea Therbusch in 1775.[168] They seem to show two different men.

Contemporaries generally agreed that the best likeness was the portrait painted by Anton Graff in 1781, based on the artist's careful study of his subject at many Potsdam parades. It was engraved many times and sold in 'countless' copies.[169] In this respect too, Frederick knew what he liked and, especially, disliked. So Daniel Chodowiecki's luxuriant baroque depiction of him as bringer of peace in 1763 was suppressed on his direct orders: the plates were purchased and broken up and any copies that could be found were burned.[170] Royal disapproval, however, could not diminish the appeal of Chodowiecki, whose popularity 'can hardly be over-estimated' in the authoritative opinion of Eckhart Hellmuth.[171]

Frederick's attitude to the public was inconsistent. When he returned to his capital on 30 March 1763 after seven years away, he deliberately kept the crowds waiting for several hours and then made his way to the royal palace by a different route. Not surprisingly, this caused considerable resentment in those who had devoted a great deal of time and money to preparing a welcome fit for a hero. Even 'the people's poet', Anna Louise Karsch, whose devotion and popularity rivalled even Gleim's, was offended by his 'indifference', commenting: 'he disappointed the expectation of a hundred thousand people . . . At that moment he seemed to me to be something less than great.'[172] On other occasions Frederick showed that he could work a crowd as effectively as any modern politician. He may never have kissed babies, pretended to enjoy fast food or worn a baseball cap, but he did make a point of showing himself in public. At a time when it was unheard of for a man to raise his hat to a social inferior, Frederick's habit of doffing his to anyone he rode past made a deep impression. Friedrich August Ludwig von der Marwitz, later a prominent conservative, was only eight years old in 1785 when he first saw the aged Frederick doing it as he rode through Berlin, but he never forgot. Between the Halle Gate and Koch Street, he estimated, Frederick must have raised his hat at least 200 times.[173] Observing the same ritual ten years earlier, Anna Louisa Karsch commented: 'it was in this situation that he seemed to me to be completely the Great

Frederick'.[174] This helps to explain the immense popularity of Heinrich Franke's portrait of Frederick raising his hat, which the enterprising artist repainted many times and of course had engraved.

Frederick's other trademark gesture was a willingness to accept petitions, either directly when on one of his many travels or as letters when he was back at Potsdam. According to Wraxall, anyone could write, in the confident knowledge that a reply would be sent. He cited the case of a complaint from a tailor of Königsberg who could not persuade the governor, Count Dohna, to pay his bill. Frederick replied telling him to try again, for by that time the count would have received the necessary reprimand.[175]

In both Britain and Germany, much of Frederick's appeal was due to his identification with Protestantism. If the natural tendency to see the eighteenth century as an increasingly secular age has any validity, it is only when applied to the upper echelons of society, and perhaps not even there. Cynics or agnostics such as Kaunitz, Catherine the Great or Frederick may have been guided solely by *raison d'état*, but society at large was still living in a confessional age.[176] The popular sobriquet to describe the eighteenth century – 'the age of reason' – has less justification than 'the age of religion' or 'the Christian century'.[177] Moreover, at least during the first half of the century, it was the Catholic Church that appeared to be in the ascendancy and gaining ground, exemplified by the construction of the great baroque monasteries and churches of Austria, Bavaria and Swabia. In the Holy Roman Empire, the political balance seemed to have shifted decisively away from the Protestants. Of their major bulwarks, the Electorate of the Palatinate had been ruled by Catholics since 1685, the Electorate of Saxony since 1697 and the duchy of Württemberg since 1733. Between the middle of the seventeenth and the middle of the eighteenth centuries, at least thirty-one German princes converted to Catholicism.[178] When the revelation in 1754 that the Landgrave of Hessen-Kassel had converted (allegedly to allow him to be reunited with a mistress in Paradise) was followed by the Austro-French alliance two years later, Protestants across Europe feared the worst. So Frederick not surprisingly played the confessional card for all it was worth, assuring anyone who would listen that he was the champion of Protestantism against Popery.[179] However fictitious, it certainly had an impact. The

Hanoverian master baker Eberhard Jürgen Abelmann revealed in his diary a strong confessional element, believing that German liberty and the Protestant faith had been in danger.[180] In Switzerland Frederick was even presented in the improbable guise of a latter-day William Tell, defending liberty against the would-be tyrants of the Catholic coalition.[181]

This resonance was well earned. Not only was he the 'first servant of the state', as he frequently claimed, he was also the first participant in the public sphere he helped to create. His approach to culture was not that of the passive patron of representational art, but that of the active creator. As political theorist, historian, poet, dramatist, composer and flautist, he would deserve his niche in any cultural history of the eighteenth century, even if he had not been also King of Prussia. Whatever one might think about his regime or its impact on the subsequent course of German history, no one can read his works or listen to his music without realizing that he possessed extraordinary gifts. Although he did not call it such, the importance he attached to 'Bildung' – individual self-cultivation – placed him squarely in the mainstream of German culture. A man who took Lucretius' De Rerum natura into battle and whiled away the intervals in the negotiations leading to the Peace of Hubertusburg by reading Rousseau's Émile was a man who gave a high priority to the intellect.[182] Along with music-making, reading was his favourite occupation: 'I have read a lot today and am as happy as a king,' he told his reader de Catt.[183] In 1771 he observed that at his age the only festivities that suited him were good books.[184] Substantial libraries were to be found in all six of his major palaces (Berlin, Charlottenburg, Breslau, Potsdam Town Palace, Sanssouci, New Palace) plus a portable collection that went with him on his travels and on campaigns.[185]

There is no reason to doubt the sincerity of his numerous declarations of faith such as: 'Since my childhood I have loved the arts, literature and the sciences, and if I can contribute to their propagation, I dedicate myself with all the zeal at my disposal, because there can be no true happiness in this world without them.'[186] For the sceptical non-believer Frederick, as for many other members of the German intelligentsia, art in its widest sense took the place of the revealed religion to which they could not subscribe. It filled a transcendental vacuum. Many of those who articulated this new aesthetic religion – Winckelmann, Lessing, Goethe, Schiller – had serious reservations about Frederick and his regime, but one thing they all had in common was a belief in the sacralization of art. Frederick's credo just quoted anticipated many such, by the Romantic poet Novalis (the *nom de plume* of Georg Philipp Friedrich von Hardenberg), for example: 'Whoever feels unhappy in this world, whoever fails to find what he seeks – then let him enter the world of books, art and nature, this eternal domain which is both ancient and modern simultaneously, and let him live there in this secret church of a better world. There he will surely find a lover and a friend, a fatherland and a God.'[187] Moreover, the intellectualism Frederick flaunted made him a role model. As the Piedmontese Abbé Carlo Giovanni Maria Denina, summoned to Berlin by Frederick to become a member of the Academy, wrote: 'The enthusiasm generated by a king who was an author, by a king who was an academician in the fullest sense of the word ... by a king who kept the company of men of letters every day and everywhere, certainly gave a great momentum to every kind of intellectual endeavour.'[188] This point is worth belabouring, because it narrows the gap often assumed between the Francophile monarch and the German intelligentsia.

But Frederick was not only activist in his approach to culture, he was also critical. From his first major publication – *Antimachiavel* – he entered the public arena repeatedly to engage in debate. As Goethe noted, by simply publishing a pamphlet about German literature Frederick gave intellectual debate a momentum which no other living person could have matched. His declared aversion to their culture was paradoxically 'highly beneficial' for German writers, because it spurred them on by provoking a reaction. Goethe continued: 'Moreover, in the same way, Frederick's aversion to the German language as the medium for literature was a good thing for German writers. They did everything they could to make the King take notice of them.'[189] That Frederick's remarks about German literature were ill-informed, one-sided and even at times absurd, did not matter. What was important was the entry of the King of Prussia to the public domain to take on all-comers. Moreover, his treatise was directed at the public, as he sought to arouse curiosity in advance of publication by releasing trails to the Berlin press.[190] It was not his first appearance in the public sphere, of course. He had already taken up his pen to attack Holbach's *Essai sur les préjugés* and *Le Système de la nature*, Rousseau's *Discours sur les sciences et les arts* and *Émile*, and the philosophes in general.[191] Moreover, he encouraged others to enter the public sphere in a critical spirit by having the Academy organize annual prize-essay competitions after 1744, setting such subjects as 'What has been the influence of governments on culture in nations where it has flourished?' (won by Herder) and 'What has made French the universal language of Europe and does it deserve this supremacy?'[192] The most successful was 'Whether it can be expedient to deceive the people?' of 1777, which attracted forty-two entries and was much discussed in the German periodicals.[193] Frederick continued to engage critically with the latest works sent from Paris throughout his reign.[194]

Paradoxically, this combination of goad and encouragement does seem to have promoted German literature. Not every intellectual on the receiving end of his barbs thought they were unmerited. No less a person than Goethe himself sometimes employed similar language. In 1785, Goethe found himself responding negatively to Mozart's *Die Entführung aus dem Serail*, only coming to terms with the work when he put out of his mind the fact that the libretto was written in German. At about the same time he abandoned the German libretto he was working on himself, his thoughts even turning to writing a substitute in Italian rather than 'this barbaric tongue'.[195] The Prussian writer Leonard Meister maintained that there was a broad measure of agreement among the German intelligentsia that Frederick's criticisms were justified, claiming they had won 'the applause of the majority of the nation'.[196] He could even find a beneficial side to Frederick's alleged Francophilia: 'even his preference for the French seems to have had a beneficial effect on the Germans. Not only did they learn from them, but there also developed a noble spirit of competition, with German intellectuals seeking to be worthy associates of their gifted French counterparts.'[197] The ever-loyal 'Prussian by choice' Thomas Abbt believed that if German literature had attained its current excellence when Frederick had been a young man, he too would have written in the German language.[198]

Looking back at the controversy at the end of the century, the

Silesian-born philosopher Christian Garve was more measured in his comments. On the one hand, he believed that Frederick had exaggerated the mutual incomprehensibility of the various regions of Germany, for every language had its national written 'high' form, which everyone could understand, and German was no exception. On the other hand, Garve was prepared to concede that the gap in Germany was greater than in other countries, with the result that there was a sense of artificiality when there was a change from written comment to reported speech, from high German to dialect. Nor was he starry-eyed about the current level of literature: 'As an honest German, who loves truth more than the reputation of his fatherland, I cannot avoid agreeing with the King when he says that, so far as literature is concerned, we lag behind foreigners.' As yet, Germany had not produced playwrights capable of gaining the same level of universal acceptance as Racine or Molière in France or Shakespeare in England. He concluded with the following judicious assessment: 'The faults he found were real faults. But he also accused us of sins we were no longer committing, and he had not read enough of our literature to be able to find the many beautiful things that were really there.'[199]

If some German intellectuals were ready to admit that Frederick had been right – or at least half-right – they were also convinced that his establishment of Prussia as a great power had given German culture a major impetus. The classic statement was provided by Goethe in his autobiography: 'The first true and really vital material of the higher order came into German literature through Frederick the Great and the deeds of the Seven Years War.'[200] Frederick's heroic feats, he argued further, gave Prussia, and with it all Protestant Germany, a priceless cultural advantage which Austria and the Catholics were never able to match.[201]

Whether Goethe was right simply cannot be proved one way or the other. One could point to Quattrocento and Cinquecento Venice, to Elizabethan England, to the 'Golden Age' of Spain, to Louis XIV's France, to the baroque culture of late seventeenth-century Austria, or to twentieth-century America, to support the hypothesis that power and culture march in step. On the other hand, one might point to fifteenth-century Burgundy, eighteenth-century Venice, *fin-de-siècle* Vienna or early twentieth-century Paris to support Hegel's aphorism that 'only in the twilight of history does the owl of Minerva begin her flight'. What is important is the fact that so many of Frederick's contemporaries echoed Goethe's assessment of the relationship. As the translator of his pamphlet *Concerning German literature*, Christian Wilhelm von Dohm, put it: 'Frederick's mighty deeds elevated the nation and inspired a patriotism of which previously there had been no inkling; and this had a beneficial effect on literature too.'[202] Achim von Arnim was more concerned to stress the paradoxical nature of this process:

> Frederick the Great belonged to that large number of German princes who were only prepared to support foreign drama with favour and funds. Yet because it was just during his reign that his victories over the French reawakened in Germans a sense of their own value, it was under his nose that a powerful reaction began the development of mighty German dramatic talents which led to the expulsion of foreign influence, without Frederick himself or any of those entrusted with the implementation of his policies having the slightest inkling of it.[203]

Frederick himself made the same point more pithily when he said to Mirabeau: 'What greater service could I have performed for German literature than that I didn't bother with it?'[204]

Frederick was more aware of the importance of the public sphere than any other European monarch hitherto.[205] So aware indeed, that towards the end of his reign he gave permission for extracts from a draft of the projected General Law Code to be discussed in public. In a printed proclamation dated 24 March 1784, the Grand Chancellor Johann Heinrich Casimir von Carmer announced that, as this was a matter of great importance and affected the whole population, it was only proper that the public voice should be heard. Experts at home and abroad were invited to submit opinions. In an article published in the *Berlinische Monatsschrift*, 'A Patriot' used the occasion to boast that one of the great advantages enjoyed by Prussians was that important political topics could be discussed in public 'quite freely', even if the line adopted was contrary to the regime's principles. Already demonstrated by numerous publications, he went on, this freedom of opinion was now confirmed by Carmer's consultation exercise, for which the king had given his express approval. The author added:

'contemporaries and posterity must esteem this open, free and noble conduct, by which the people are made aware of their interest and the Rights of Man and the Citizen are honoured'.[206] Thus the language of the French Revolution was anticipated five years in advance. Writing in 1787, Leonard Meister advanced this initiative as evidence that Prussia was a *Rechtsstaat*, a state governed by the rule of law:

> And this king unique among kings did still more. Not only did he pro-
> mote order and security by introducing a wise legal code, when drawing
> it up, he sought the advice of all those who had advice to give, both Prus-
> sian citizens and foreigners, and he himself submitted himself to the laws.
> He proclaimed loudly and publicly that in matters of justice a peasant
> counted for as much as a prince ... With views such as these and with a
> regime such as this, could the national spirit fail to be elevated? And this
> national spirit could take wing all the more boldly because nothing
> dazzled and nothing intimidated it, neither wanton display around the
> throne nor papal anathema from the altar. In this manner – and we can-
> not make the point often enough – Frederick gave the arts and the
> sciences the best possible wet-nurses: security, liberty and toleration![207]

This was all very well so long as Frederick was on the throne, but what might a less enlightened successor do? In 1785 the *Berlinische Monatsschrift* went a step further towards a constitutional state, arguing that any future changes should be made only with the consent of the whole nation.[208] It can safely be assumed that the autocratic Frederick would never have even contemplated ceding one jot of his absolute authority. Much troubled water would have to pass under the Spree bridges before Prussians were ready to seize (in 1848) what their kings would not grant.

FREDERICK THE GERMAN

Had they known Frederick better, they would have been less optimistic about the prospects for further liberalization. Such was the spell
cast by his charisma that the illusion not only survived his reign
but went on growing, as reputation morphed into myth. Not until
the frightful shocks of the twentieth century did disenchantment

begin. What was true of the public applied equally, if not more so, to another powerful abstraction that acquired ever more momentum during the eighteenth century: the nation. It is a common but egregious error to assume that, because he had a low opinion of German culture and admired Voltaire, Frederick was a Frenchman by choice. On the contrary, he was clearly aware of his German nationality. If he was torn between two national identities, it was not between a French and a German, but between a German and a Prussian.[209] Frederick told the French ambassador, the Marquis de Valori, in 1742: 'born a German prince, I have all the feelings of a good patriot and a good citizen towards my fatherland'.[210] In his correspondence with Voltaire, where one might expect him to be at his most cosmopolitan, he refers repeatedly to his nationality, as in: 'I am only a good German and I do not blush to express myself with the candour which is an inseparable part of our national character' or:

> I wager that you will think, when reading this: 'that's just like a German, he shows all the phlegm of his bloodless nation'. It's true we are vegetable-like when compared with the French; nor have we produced a *Henriade* [Voltaire's epic poem]. Since the Emperor Charlemagne took it into his head to turn us into Christians by slitting our throats, we have always been the same; and our cloudy skies and cold winters have done their bit too.[211]

As that last remark indicated, Frederick had not been a keen student of Montesquieu for nothing. In his own treatise on the subject he argued that the culture of every country had its own special flavour, as a result of 'the indelible character of each nation'. Books published in Padua, London or Paris, for example, could easily be distinguished, even if written in the same language and on the same subject. Education could modify but never change fundamentally a national character.[212]

If Frederick was a merciless and (some might think) perceptive critic of German failings – pedantry, lack of humour, clumsiness and *'le mal qu'on appelle logon diarrhœa'*[213] – he was no less severe on the French. He repeatedly subjected his alleged models to withering attacks, especially on account of their incorrigible taste for persecuting dissidents. 'The Englishman can think out loud,' he claimed, 'but a Frenchman hardly dares to betray an inkling of his ideas.'[214] It was for that reason that France could produce a Descartes or a Male-branche but never a really intrepid thinker such as a Leibniz, a Locke or a Newton. As this suggests, Frederick had a very good knowledge of English writers, including Francis Bacon, Alexander Pope and Jonathan Swift.[215] Moreover, France's day was done. There had been a few years during the ministry of Richelieu and during the reign of Louis XIV when its star had shone, but these were brief moments of wisdom in a long history of folly.[216] It was not just flattery which prompted him to tell Voltaire often that he was the last French writer of distinction.[217] Modern French literature, he told him, was a waste of time, fit only to be burned.[218] Rousseau he thought was 'mad', Diderot he seems not to have read at all, certainly there were none of his works in Frederick's personal library.[219] Special venom was reserved for the French avant-garde, for Holbach, against whom he wrote two counter-blasts, and for the 'encyclopaedists', against whom he launched one of his satires, in which he dismissed them as superficial and arrogant.[220]

During the golden age of the mid-seventeenth century, he believed, French writers had produced dramatic works of unsurpassable quality, but he did not allow them supremacy in any other branch of the arts. As we have seen, he had a low opinion of French music; for architectural style (or rather styles, for he was nothing if not eclectic), he looked not to France but to Italy and Great Britain.[221] The most important cultural influence on him was not French but classical, indeed he assimilated French writers only in so far as the classics permitted.[222] Moreover, as he grew older he turned his back on the decadent culture of contemporary France, the shift becoming especially marked after the Seven Years War.[223] Far from advocating France as a model, he castigated its uncritical imitators in terms just as strong as anything employed by the *Sturm und Drang*:

> The taste for French drama was imported into Germany together with French fashions: enthused by the magnificence which Louis XIV impressed on all his actions, by the sophistication of his court and by the great names who were the ornaments of his reign, all Europe sought to imitate the France it admired. All Germany went there: a young man counted for a fool if he had not spent some time at the court of

Versailles. French taste ruled our kitchens, our furniture, our clothes and all those knick-knacks which are so at the mercy of the tyranny of fashion. Carried to excess, this passion degenerated into a frenzy; women, who are often prey to exaggeration, pushed it to the point of extravagance.[224]

On the other hand, Frederick had a clear sense that German culture was beginning at long last to develop in the right direction. As he rightly appreciated and recorded in *Concerning German Literature*, the devastations caused by the Thirty Years War, by religious conflict and by the wars of Louis XIV had inflicted wounds on Germany which had taken a long time to heal. Recovery had not begun in earnest until after the War of the Spanish Succession and initially all effort had had to be concentrated on material reconstruction. But the process had been rapid, Germany was now flourishing again, everyone was getting richer and eventually this would lead to cultural renewal too, he believed. Indeed, there were a few promising straws in the wind, for German intellectuals were no longer ashamed to write in the vernacular, the first German dictionary had been published and, more generally, there was a growing sense of excitement, reflected in the public discussion of Germany's national reputation. If sufficient patrons could be found, then Germany too would have its fair share of geniuses and would create its own classical literature. So he ended his pamphlet on the following wistful but optimistic note: 'These halcyon days of our literature have not yet arrived; but they are approaching and their arrival seems certain. I serve as their herald, although my advanced age robs me of the hope of seeing them myself. I am like Moses, I see the promised land from afar, but shall not enter it myself.'[225]

Any residual belief that Frederick was a Francophile cannot survive a reading of his verse epistle entitled 'Ode to Prince Ferdinand of Brunswick on the retreat of the French in 1758', as revealing as it has been neglected.[226] This parades a series of epithets to characterize the French and their king that might have come from the most Francophobe of popular pamphlets: 'insolence ... bombast ... pride [repeated four times] ... arrogance ... rapacity ... haughtiness ...

frivolity ... vacuity ... feebleness ... decadence ... violence ... criminality'. Frederick recounts how an enormous French army had crossed the Rhine, expecting to blow away the Germans without effort. Yet all they had proved good at was pillage: 'gorged with loot, they measured their courage by the size of their booty'.[227] When they ran into the heroic Ferdinand and his mighty warriors, they turned turtle and swam back across the Rhine. For an analogy Frederick significantly turned to Germanic myth and the defeat of the Roman legions by Herman the German ('Arminius' in the Latin form) in the Teutoburg Forest in AD 9:

> This great horde
> Which flooded in from France,
> Led by a second Varus,
> As it made its triumphant progress,
> It encountered, much to its surprise,
> A second Herman.[228]

Herman was a role model for Frederick. When excoriating the decadence of present-day youth in his *Letter on education,* he asked rhetorically what Herman – 'that proud defender of Germany' – would make of them.[229] Wittingly or not, Frederick was again operating very much in the mainstream of contemporary German literature, for a major revival of interest in the Herman episode both coincided with and was encouraged by his reign. Dramas and epic poems included Johann Elias Schlegel's *Herman* (1740), Justus Möser's *Arminius* (1749), Christoph Otto Freiherr von Schönaich's *Herman, or Germany Liberated* (1751), and Friedrich Gottlob Klopstock's *Herman's Battle* (1768).[230] Among the many pictorial depictions, Johann Heinrich Tischbein's *Hermann with his trophies following his victory over Varus* (1772) stands out. In his ode to Ferdinand, Frederick directed special venom against Louis XV, the personification of his nation's vices, deriding him as an enervated, idle voluptuary, the plaything of his mistress, Madame de Pompadour, but presuming to give the law to Europe. This was a national struggle, Frederick wrote:

> Frenchmen, flaunt your riches,
> Your luxury, and your languor,

And all the gifts that Plutus brought you;
Against the behaviour of Sardanapalus,
My more frugal nation,
Can only oppose its virtues.[231]

The ferocity of the language used in this poem shows how deeply Frederick felt about the French. In more informal vein, he told Ferdinand in a prose letter to imprint the mark of his boot on the fleeing French bottoms.[232] He was particularly enraged by the yawning gulf between their overweening pretension and feeble achievement. A poem written at the end of the previous year and called sarcastically 'To the crushers' was prefaced by the note: 'When he marched off to Rossbach, the Prince de Soubise wrote back to France that he was off to pick a posy of flowers for the Dauphine.'[233]

The dauphine never did get her flowers, of course, because Rossbach turned out to be the most catastrophic military defeat suffered by France in the eighteenth century – a greater national humiliation than Crécy, Poitiers or Agincourt according to Voltaire.[234] That was how other contemporaries saw it too. They did not care that a significant number of the defeated army had been German-speaking imperial troops. This was seen first and foremost as a national victory over the self-proclaimed French 'gendarme of the Holy Roman Empire', who repeatedly over the past century had come across the Rhine, bringing death and destruction.[235] A flood of triumphalist pamphlets, songs, poems and prints followed. Among the many composers setting verses to music was Carl Philipp Emanuel Bach, who set Johann Wilhelm Ludwig Gleim's 'Song of challenge before the Battle of Rossbach' (Wq 199/20).[236] In December 1757 Gleim received a letter from his friend and poet, Karl Wilhelm Ramler, reporting on a service of thanksgiving held at the cathedral in Berlin:

I have just come out from hearing the victory sermon of our incomparable [court chaplain] Sack. Almost all eyes were weeping for love, for gratitude ... Our young men have not stopped firing off victory shots and there is shooting all around me as I write these lines. Our merchants have produced every sort of silk ribbon in honour of both victories and we have festooned our vests, hats and swords with them.[237]

Sack's sermons preached during the Seven Years War were particularly popular, not just printed and reprinted but also declaimed aloud to assemblies across Prussia.[238] In an age when most people of all ages went to church both frequently and regularly, the sermon as a public medium was as important as it has been neglected by most historians. In Prussia during Frederick's reign, the Protestant pastors played a central role in the formation of opinion. The language and imagery they used were of course biblical. Frederick was presented as King David, God's instrument in smiting the Philistines (Catholics) hip and thigh, and the Prussian nation as God's elect, the latter-day Children of Israel.[239] Meanwhile, in contemporary Britain, preachers were performing the same service for the House of Hanover, and Handel was giving majestic expression to the narrative in his Israelite oratorios.[240] Whatever Frederick may have thought about it, most of his subjects liked him best clad in the armour of a Protestant champion. Indeed, anecdotes circulated that he was really a good Christian, who insisted that his soldiers attend church parades and joined in singing hymns.*

Frederick's victories inspired or spawned, according to taste, a whole sub-genre of literature: battle verse. Most popular were the *Prussian war-songs of the campaigns of 1756 and 1757*, allegedly written 'by a grenadier' but in fact from the hand of Gleim, who believed that Frederick was fighting 'the most just war that has ever been waged'.[241] The fiction was repeated by Lessing in his preface to a collected edition he published in 1758 when he claimed that the author was 'a common soldier blessed with as much heroism as poetic genius'.[242] At least Gleim had direct military experience, having served as secretary to a Prussian general, the Margrave of Brandenburg-Schwedt, following his employer on campaign until the latter was killed in battle at the siege of Prague in 1744.[243] Written in simple, direct, vivid language, his verses were also intended to be sung, based as they were on the metre of the English folk-ballad 'Chevy Chase', transmitted to Gleim by Addison's *Spectator* via Klopstock.[244] The tone was aggressive, violent, even bloodthirsty, from the opening lines of the first poem 'On the opening of the campaign of 1756':

---

* See above, p. 273.

War is my song! Because all the world
Wants war, let there be war!
Let Berlin be Sparta! May Prussia's hero
Be crowned with glory and victory![245]

At the beginning of the campaign of the following year, the grenadier looks forward to drinking Hungarian wine from goblets made from the skulls of Hungarian soldiers.[246] At the centre stands the indomitable figure of Frederick, venerated as the fearless and peerless hero, as great in defeat as in victory. The traditional cry of 'For God and Fatherland' is extended to become 'For God, Fatherland and Frederick'.[247] With the aid of God, who is often invoked, he triumphs over apparently impossible odds, yet always cares as tenderly as a father for his soldiers. Despite their militarism, Gleim's poems achieved not only enduring popular success but also applause from his fellow-intellectuals, even from Lessing, although his attitude to Frederick was admittedly ambivalent, not least because of his lingering loyalty to Saxony.[248] Genuinely popular in the social sense were the poems of Anna Louisa Karsch, who moved to Magdeburg from war-torn Breslau in February 1761 and was taken under the wing of Gleim. Her simple celebrations of Frederick's victories – Torgau was a special favourite – were published as an anthology with the help of Gleim and achieved a notable success with both public and intelligentsia.[249]

Frederick's appeal was not confined to Prussia. Right across Protestant Germany and German-speaking Switzerland there came evidence of enthusiastic support.[250] The Seven Years War did not create German nationalism, but it did anchor it in a heroic episode, gave it a powerful twist towards Prussia, extended its vocabulary and sank it deeper into German society and literature.[251] A flood of literature showed that almost none of the active poets were able to disengage from the war.[252] So long had educated Germans smarted from a sense of cultural inferiority and political weakness, especially over and against the dominant French, that they were ready to respond to anyone who turned the tables. Among the more interesting was Christian Friedrich Daniel Schubart, born in a midget Swabian principality (Obersontheim) and brought up in a midget Swabian Free Imperial City (Aalen). He was one of many Protestants in southern Germany who supported Frederick and Prussia without having any direct knowledge of either. Schubart wrote in his autobiography that at school in Nuremberg during the Seven Years War 'all my enthusiasm was totally dedicated to Prussia'. The songs he wrote there to celebrate Frederick's victories were sung by the locals but earned him a thrashing from the Austrian troops occupying the city.[253] In the periodical he founded in 1774, *German Chronicle*, Schubart rejoiced at the revolutionary change in Germany's standing in the world: 'if we ever had reason to be proud of our fatherland, then that time is now. Foreigners view with envy a nation they sought to subdue by fomenting discord and insinuating their fashions' (France for example). In large measure, he asserted, this was due to Frederick 'who in his right hand holds the scales of Europe and in his left the sceptre – who can speak his name without enthusiasm? He is the cynosure of the world, the great original of present and future heroes, he is a German and still in the prime of life.'[254] In that article Schubart made Frederick share his laurels with the Emperor Joseph II ('who could be more active, wise, brave, or sensitive than our sublime Joseph?') but the latter's policies directed against the Holy Roman Empire in the 1780s changed Schubart's mind. In a poem he called simply 'Frederick the Great', he hailed Frederick's foundation of the League of Princes to frustrate Joseph's plans:

> Germany's princes rushed
> To Frederick's stone fortress, where the giant
> Lay brooding on his bed of iron.
> They stretched out their hands to him, hailed him as
> The guardian of their fundamental rights, and cried:
> 'Be our leader, Frederick Herman!'
> He gave his consent and the German League was formed.[255]

Just to enhance his mythic power Frederick appeared in the poem not only as Herman but also as Wotan.

It is important to note that Schubart was a radical by the standards of his times, paying for his outspoken criticism of abuses in the duchy of Württemberg with ten years in prison. As one standard general history of German literature in the eighteenth century put it: 'Schubart gave concrete expression to the idea of "liberty" by his struggle against feudal despotism and oppression, against clerical obscurantism and against the exploitation of the peasantry.'[256] Less often emphasized are Schubart's credentials as a nationalist. He gloried not only in the superiority of German culture, he also gloried in German power. It was the Germans, he claimed, who now gave the law to Europe, and he gloried in the quarter of a million men that Frederick had under arms.[257] Anyone lucky enough to attend his military manoeuvres he added later, could only exclaim: 'Here is more than Athens and Sparta!'[258] Happily, he went on, where Frederick had led, others had followed, and now (1774) even the smaller principalities had attained military perfection: German cavalry was on a par with the British, and German artillery was a match for that of any other country in the world. If only, Schubart sighed, every prince in the Holy Roman Empire could be induced to act together, such a gigantic German power would be invincible.[259]

In Prussia too, militarism was popular, despite the enormous financial and social cost. It was not only Junker officers who were seduced by the siren call of martial glory. A particularly acute French observer, the Comte de Guibert, wrote after a visit to Prussia a year after Frederick's death that 'the ordinary people in Prussia, even among the lowest classes, are imbued with the military spirit, speak with respect of their army, know the names of their generals, refer to their feats of arms and the times they have distinguished themselves'.[260] Recalling his childhood in Berlin, the Romantic poet Ludwig Tieck wrote in his memoirs:

> The King appeared at military parades and reviews as the great warlord, who had defied successfully a coalition of all of the rest of Europe, and at the head of his troops, who had won so many battles. When there were military exercises or manoeuvres outside one of Berlin's city-gates, perhaps the Hallesche or the Prenzlauer, then the citizens of Berlin streamed out in their hordes to watch. My father [a master carpenter] also used to take his children out to these popular festivals. Among the pressing crowds of people, the rush of artillery-trains and the marching soldiers, we were prepared to put up with the dust and the heat for hours on end, just to catch sight of our old Fritz surrounded by his dazzling retinue of celebrated generals.[261]

More by luck than design, Frederick promoted the public sphere, German nationalism and popular militarism. When the three fused during the roller-coaster ride that was to be Prussian history between 1806 and 1815, his mythical status as 'Frederick the Unique' (a sobriquet first invented by Ramler, for whom 'Frederick the Great' was inadequate[262]) was assured. As with Napoleon, to whose nemesis at Leipzig and Waterloo the Prussians contributed so much, Frederick's warts fell away like scabs with the passage of time, leaving only unblemished heroism in a nostalgic haze. Visual expression was given by the equestrian statue commissioned in 1836 to mark the fiftieth anniversary of Frederick's death. Forced on a reluctant Frederick William III by the Estates of Brandenburg, it was the work of Christian Daniel Rauch. His original design for the base called for attributes of peace on the front, the sciences and the arts on each side and war at the back. The king, however, insisted on three sides for the military, with the three peaceful elements confined to the rear.[263] Even so, room was found for the names of Pesne, Knobelsdorff, Wolff, Ramler, Gleim, Garve, Kleist (as poet rather than soldier), Maupertuis and (very oddly, given his detestation of Frederick) Winckelmann. There were three-dimensional representations of Graun, Lessing and Kant.[264] Three bas-relief images demonstrated Frederick's devotion to promoting the economy and the arts: in the first, he inspects cloth; in the second, he plays the flute; and in the third, he admires his statue of Antinous.

13

Light and Dark on the Home Front

ENLIGHTENMENT

One of Frederick's favourite metaphors was 'light' (*lumière*). It peppers his correspondence, poems and prose works. Revealingly, he used the plural form – *lumières* – twice as often as the singular, for it is also the French word for Enlightenment with a capital E (as opposed to enlightenment meaning more light in a general sense, for which *éclaircissement* or *illumination* would be used).* Also prominent in his vocabulary was the antonym *superstition* and its cognates. As this suggests, he had a very clear image of himself as a beacon of reason, shining all the more brightly for being projected into a darkly irrational world. As he put it succinctly in his preface to Voltaire's verse epic *La Henriade*: 'the more one is enlightened, the less one is superstitious'.[1] Light was a metaphor which dominated eighteenth-century discourse, as its romantic detractors pointed out. Writing in 1799, Georg Philipp Friedrich von Hardenberg, better known by his *nom de plume* 'Novalis', looked back in scorn at the enlightened rationalists: 'light became their favourite subject on account of its mathematical obedience and freedom of movement. They were more interested in the refraction of its rays than in the play of its colours, and so they named after it their great enterprise, Enlightenment.'[2] It was just because this new enlightened faith had been pieced together by 'mere knowledge', Novalis argued, that Frederick's state – or rather 'factory' (*Fabrik*) – was doomed to collapse.[3]

---

* The search engine of the online edition of Frederick's *Œuvres* returns 160 hits for *lumière* and 358 for *lumières*.

Back in 1740, before the horrors of the French Revolution had revealed to the romantics the dangers of a regime founded on reason, it was easier to believe in rational progress. Frederick began his reign with a grand gesture announcing that a new era had begun. This was the recall to Prussian employment of the most influential philosopher of the age, Christian Wolff (1679–1754). His expulsion from the University of Halle in 1723 had been a great academic scandal. Persuaded that Wolff had been teaching atheism, Frederick William I had shown his habitual impetuosity by ordering him to leave Prussia within twenty-four hours on pain of execution.[4] Benefiting from the *de facto* pluralism that was one of the many attractive features of the Holy Roman Empire, Wolff simply moved to the University of Marburg in Hessen-Kassel, whose landgrave was only too pleased to give refuge and employment to such a celebrated academic. From there his philosophy and his pupils colonized the German university world. Frederick William came to regret his hastiness, making three attempts in the 1730s to entice him back and even reading some of his work in 1739.[5]

By that time the crown prince had already immersed himself in Wolffian philosophy, introduced to it by his mentor Count Ernst Christoph von Manteuffel, the founder of a society at Berlin for its promotion with the slogan '*sapere aude*' ('dare to know' or 'dare to be wise').[6] As Wolff wrote only in Latin or German, Frederick had to have his works translated into French. In April 1736 Frederick wrote to the translator, the Saxon academic Ulrich Friedrich von Suhm: 'I am studying Wolff with very great assiduity and am fashioning myself more and more in accordance with his way of reasoning, which is very profound and very just.'[7] In a later letter he exclaimed: 'what profundity! What consistency of reasoning to unravel all the secrets of nature and to bring clarity and precision to places which up till now have been plunged in shadow and darkness!'[8] Frederick was twenty-four years old in 1736 but his enthusiasm had all the intensity of a teenager. In letters to his new friend, Voltaire, and his old love, his sister Wilhelmine, he extolled Wolff's philosophy as superior to anything that had appeared so far: Descartes had blazed the trail, Newton had perfected natural philosophy but Wolff alone was convincing.[9] On 23 May 1740, Frederick wrote to Wolff to thank him for his latest work on natural law. As he must have known that it would soon be broadcast far and wide, it deserves to be quoted in full:

> Every man who thinks and loves truth must take an interest in your book; every man of integrity and every good citizen must regard it as a treasure-house, which your generosity has given to the world and which your acumen has discovered. I am all the more moved by it because you have dedicated it to me. Philosophers should be the teachers of the world and the teachers of princes. They must think logically and we must act logically. They must teach the world by their powers of judgment, we must teach the world by our example. They must discover, and we must translate their discoveries into practice. I have been reading and studying your works for a long time now and am convinced that all who read them must esteem their author. That can be denied to you by no one, and it is in this sense, please believe me, that I remain with all the complete esteem that your services deserve, your well-beloved Frederick, Crown Prince.[10]

As a declaration of intent to rule as a '*roi philosophe*', that could not be beaten. Eight days later Frederick ascended the throne and promptly turned verbal praise into action. On 6 June, he wrote to Johann Gustav Reinbeck, the provost and pastor of St Peter's Church, Berlin, asking him to negotiate his friend Wolff's return to Prussia and authorizing 'all reasonable conditions'. Frederick added as a postscript in his own hand in German: 'I am asking him to make every effort over Wolff. Anyone who seeks and loves truth is worthy of esteem in human society; and I believe that he who persuades Wolff to return here will have made a conquest in the land of truth.'[11] This demonstrated once again that Frederick had a journalist's eye for the striking phrase and it was rewarded by constant repetition in the public sphere. Forty years later, the geographer Anton Friedrich Büsching was still repeating the phrase, adding the comment that it did Wolff more honour than any other eulogy written about him and also conferred 'immortal honour' on its author.[12] It may also have helped Frederick to land the prize. On 6 December 1740, Wolff returned to the scene of his former persecution at Halle 'almost like the triumphant Entry to Jerusalem', as Carlyle put it.[13] In 1743 he became chancellor of the university; also in 1743 he bought a large country house and noble estate near Leipzig; in 1745 he was ennobled as a *Freiherr* (baron). He died in 1754 at the age of seventy-five, having shown that a combination of talent and hard work could take the son of a Breslau artisan to fame and fortune. He was also a man of the future:

> [Wolff] is the first representative of a species which in the twentieth century is still under no threat of extinction: the professor, especially of philosophy, who establishes through his pupils an empire extending over many universities and who acquires in the eyes of the public some-thing of the role of a secular preacher, a preceptor of the nation. After Wolff, the pattern is continuous from Kant to Habermas, for of all Ger-man institutions, the universities, in the last 300 years, have changed least.[14]

Wolff was not the only prodigal to return. He was joined by Professor Fischer, expelled from Königsberg in 1725 for expressing doubts about the Trinity, the Devil and original sin.[15]

TOLERATION

'A conquest in the land of truth' was memorable. Even more so was the marginal comment of 22 June 1740 in response to an enquiry from an official about Protestant discrimination against Catholic schools: 'all religions must be tolerated and the official's only task is to make sure that no one [religion] interferes with another, for here everyone must be allowed to seek salvation in any way they choose'.[16] This was a maxim that could perhaps be accepted even by the ortho-dox Lutherans who made up the majority of his subjects. More controversial was another marginal comment dating from the same month and occasioned by an enquiry from the General Directory as to whether a Catholic could be granted citizenship rights: 'all religions are equal and good, if only the people professing them are honest, and if Turks and heathens came here and wished to populate the land, we would build mosques and places of worship for them'.[17] Almost cer-tainly unacceptable to most was the extension of toleration to sexual conduct: 'I want everyone in my state to be able to pray to God and to make love as they see fit' or, in another version reported by Voltaire: 'in my domains there is freedom of conscience and the cock'.[18] This libertarian sentiment was given a more precise orientation in a letter to d'Alembert of 1774: 'I don't know whether Paris can be compared with Sodom, or Sodom with Paris; in any event, it is certain that I wouldn't wish to burn either of these two cities, and would rather say with the Angel Ituriel: if everything is not good, everything is acceptable.'[19]

Not all of Frederick's remarks reached the public in their original form. The marginal comment beginning 'all religions must be tolerated', for example, was not published until after his death, although its gist 'flew abroad all over the world' (Carlyle).[20] What did reach the public consciousness was Frederick's contempt for all forms of revealed religion, Protestant or Catholic, Christian or Moslem. A Danish diplomat reported in 1740 that the new king's flagrant indifference towards religion was causing 'amazement and dismay' among the plain people of Berlin.[21] As in every other European city, most people were devout believers and easily roused by accusations of impiety. In 1748, after hearing a sermon preached against freethinkers, a mob went out on to the street and broke the windows of a local citizen known to be a keen supporter of the Enlightenment.[22] Although the windows of the royal palace were never in danger, no one could have been in any doubt about the views of their sovereign. He just could not resist turning toleration into derision. For example, a request from conservative Lutherans to be allowed to go on singing their old hymns, rather than the new ones wished on them by the ecclesiastical authorities, received the marginal comment: 'with me everyone can believe what he likes so long as he is honest'. No one could object to that, but he also added: 'so far as the hymn book is concerned, anyone can sing "Now All The Forests Are At Peace" or any other sort of stupid and fatuous nonsense'.[23] How much more shocked and angry his pious subjects would have been, had they been able to read in Frederick's *Political Testament* of 1768 his views on Christianity: 'an old metaphysical fiction, stuffed with wonders, contradictions and absurdities. It was spawned in the fevered imagination of the Orientals, and then spread to our Europe, where some fanatics espoused it, where some intriguers pretended to be convinced by it and where some imbeciles actually believed it.'[24] Too hot even for posterity to handle, the *Political Testaments* were kept under lock and key in the Hohenzollern archives until the twentieth century.

No Christian could take refuge in the comfortable belief that Frederick's hostility stemmed from ignorance of the faith. His grim education had left him with a formidable knowledge of the Bible (he knew it 'off by heart' according to the Abbé Denina) which he enjoyed deploying in the best Voltairean manner.[25] For example, in the margin of a letter from a young applicant for a pastor's position that was hotly competed for by more senior contenders, he simply wrote '2 Samuel 10:5', a verse which closes with the words 'and the king said, Tarry at Jericho until your beards be grown, and then return'.[26] To another clerical supplicant seeking a better-endowed parish he wrote that the first Apostles enjoyed no material reward for preaching Christ's Gospel and that he should go and do likewise.[27] He also enjoyed reminding his subjects that constitutionally he was the head of both the Lutheran and the Reformed (Calvinist) churches in his dominions. Adjudicating a petition from a man refused permission by the church authorities to marry his widowed aunt, he wrote: 'The Consistory is an ass. As Vicar of Jesus Christ and Archbishop of Magdeburg, I decree that the couple shall be joined together in holy matrimony.'[28] The parishioners of a Pomeranian village who asked for the dismissal of a pastor who did not believe in the resurrection of the body were told that on the Day of Judgment it was up to him if he wished to just lie there prostrate while everyone else got up.[29] Ordering the reappointment of a pastor dismissed because his parishioners objected to his preaching against the eternity of Hell, he commented that if they wished to be damned for all eternity, he had nothing against it.[30] And so on.

Frederick cannot have been the first nominally Christian European sovereign not to have believed in Christian doctrine, but he was surely the first to parade his scepticism so brazenly. After an extended visit to Prussia in 1756, the Duke de Nivernais wrote a lengthy account of Frederick's character and opinions.[31] Pride of place went to his lack of religion, which Frederick had 'elevated to a system'. Nivernais was not impressed by the depth of Frederick's views, dismissing them as a mishmash of Bayle's arguments and Voltaire's jibes, but he was certainly struck by the vigour and frequency with which they were expressed. One *tête-à-tête* on the subject lasted for more than three hours.[32] It could be said, Nivernais went on, that Frederick had turned himself into a kind of anti-legislator on religion by parading publicly his contempt for it. In this manner he proclaimed his complete neutrality between all the various denominations to be found in his kingdom. This meant that 'Prussia is the only country in Europe where toleration is absolute, universal and unlimited. One is permitted to profess whatever religion one likes; and one is permitted to profess none; one is even permitted to profess irreligion.' The Calvinists, Lutherans, Anabaptists, Catholics might abuse each other as much as they liked but were not permitted to do each other any harm: 'Prussia is the only country in the known world where several religions coexist without it being a problem, and it is also the country in the universe where there is least religion to be found. The principles of Protestantism, the indifference of North Europeans towards intellectual matters and the royal example have made irreligion very common at Berlin.'[33]

'I am neutral between Rome and Geneva,' stated Frederick in his *Political Testament* of 1752, misquoting slightly a line from Voltaire's *La Henriade*, where it was spoken by the eponymous hero, Henry IV of France: 'I do not take sides between Geneva and Rome.'[34] Early in his reign Frederick advertised his neutrality by allocating a prime site in the centre of Berlin for the building of a new Catholic church, to be as big as the faithful of the city needed or wanted, with one or more towers, big or small bells, without restriction.[35] Located immediately adjacent to Frederick's own preferred place of worship – the Opera House – it formed part of the planned *Forum Fridericianum*.* It is worth pausing for a moment to reflect on the radicalism of this decision. This was a century when an anti-Catholic mob could take control of London for a week and inflict *ten times* more damage on property than was achieved in Paris during the entire French Revolution.[36] Frederick's Catholic church could not have been built either in London or in the other supposedly tolerant European city, Amsterdam.[37] The

---

* See above, pp. 166–7.

Berlin church was to be named 'St Hedwig', after the patron saint of Silesia, to reassure Frederick's new Catholic subjects there that they had nothing to fear from their change of ownership.

It was a grand gesture and it was made in a grand manner. The foundation stone was laid on 13 June 1747 to the accompaniment of festivities at least as elaborate as those which had marked the victory celebration staged at the end of the Silesian War two years previously. Grandstands were erected for spectators, a brass band and the royal chapel choir supplied the music, and the service of dedication was conducted by Abbot Turno, prelate of the Cistercian Abbey at Premet, at an altar erected under a massive baldacchino. Jean-Laurent Legeay, who had recently arrived in Prussia to work for Frederick, produced an album of seven engravings recording the ceremony and illustrating what the church would look like when it was finished. Legeay included on the first engraving the statement that the design for the church was the handiwork of the king himself. As we have seen, Frederick was very much in charge when it came to buildings,* and it is at least very likely that he provided the basic idea, notably the circular shape and dome reminiscent of the Pantheon (Temple of all the Gods) in Rome. His original intention to create a place of worship for all faiths had to be scaled down to just the one, although that was controversial enough in an overwhelmingly Protestant city.[38] It was also Frederick who choreographed the ceremony and had a commemorative medal struck.[39]

He provided the site, and also gave access to royal stocks of building materials, but was not prepared to finance construction. The necessary money had to be raised by an appeal to Catholic Europe. At first all went well. Aided by Legeay's encouraging illustrations, over 100,000 talers had been collected before the Seven Years War brought work to an abrupt halt.[40] But it was not until 1 November 1773, 233 years to the day since Catholicism had been formally abolished in Brandenburg, that the finished building could be consecrated by Prince Ignatius Krasicki, Bishop of Ermland, a Prussian subject since the partition of Poland the previous year.[41] Once again, the ceremonial boat was pushed out. Although Frederick did not attend in

* See above, pp. 139, 163–4, 167.

person, he did send his heir, his nephew Frederick William, known as 'The Prince of Prussia', together with the Duke of Brunswick, the Prince of Hessen-Darmstadt, generals and senior officials. The royal orchestra and chorus were also on hand.[42] To mark the event and to assist the European public to learn the right lesson, a seventy-four-page account was published, which began: 'Toleration, freedom of religion and the impartial love for all his subjects are what make up the character of a philosophical ruler; and it is just that combination in a high degree that is personified by our most gracious sovereign King Frederick the Great.'[43] During the ceremony, the bishop placed in a concealed space in the altar a memorial dedicated 'to Frederick the Great, the Invincible, the Father of His Country, who does not hate people because they serve God differently but has founded and built this Church for them'. One can only wonder how Frederick reacted when he learned that his dedication would be sharing the space with a casket of holy relics, including St Hedwig's skull.[44] The account of the consecration ended with the resounding tribute:

> Frederick the Great has set an example to the other princes and rulers of Europe. His name, already immortalised by his victories, his legislation, his promotion of the arts and sciences, the wonders he has wrought in peace and war, will be preserved for all eternity because of the gracious and solemn wisdom which have made him tolerant. This has made him the inclusive father and protector of his people, whatever their background and beliefs.[45]

By this time, the handsome classical exterior of St Hedwig's was already well known across Europe, for the numerous engravings of the new opera house usually included an artist's impression of what the Catholic church would look like when completed. A particularly good example was the popular print dating from 1750 engraved by Georg Balthasar Probst of Augsburg, one of the finest of contemporary illustrators.[46]

The relics had been supplied by the Cistercian convent at Trebnitz, founded in 1202 by St Hedwig's husband, Duke Henry. To the official communication of gratitude, sent first to the Abbé Bastiani at Breslau, Frederick added in his own hand in French:

The church is going to be inaugurated in a few days time and all that mumbo jumbo will be celebrated. If people are not now convinced by my toleration, they are difficult to please; no Lutheran or Calvinist church would ever be built at Bamberg, Würzburg or Salzburg, or at ---- or at ---- or anywhere else for that matter. The rest of you, whatever you say, you are still driven by the hatreds of a burning fanaticism, and so you are just half-humans.[47]

Statistical support for Frederick's policy was provided by the rapid increase in the number of Catholics at Berlin during his reign. In 1740 there were only about fifty in the city, by 1786 more than 8,000.[48] At the other end of the confessional spectrum, he readmitted the Mennonites, expelled by his father in 1732, and even exempted them from the military service their faith prohibited, albeit in return for an annual payment of 5,000 talers to the cadet school at Kulm.[49] The *Berlinische Monatsschrift* proudly claimed in 1784 that adherents of 'all kinds' of religion could be found in Berlin, including Moravians, Mennonites, Gichtelianer, Separatists, Arians, Unitarians and Socinians, all of whom had been ejected from other parts of Europe.[50] A few more could have been added, including the Schwenckfelder and Hussites. Prussia under Frederick was Europe's 'great ark of the refugees', the accolade originally awarded to the Dutch Republic by Pierre Bayle.

In the early twenty-first century, when growing religious intolerance inflicts misery on so many, the benefits of Frederick's policy are more apparent than, say, fifty years ago, when the triumph of tolerant secularism appeared to be inevitable. His progressive contemporaries knew what blessings toleration brought. The distinguished physician Johann Friedrich Karl Grimm of Gotha wrote that, although Prussia boasted the greatest variety of religious groups, it was also characterized by 'serene tranquillity'. So long as the political constitution was not criticized, everyone could express their opinion freely about religion. He added: 'freedom of thought is one of the main reasons for the great enlightenment that prevails in Frederick's state. It is really magnificent that at Berlin one can speak according to one's conviction, see with one's own eyes and investigate anything that seems to warrant it.' However, Grimm was not the only Christian visitor to note a negative effect of this relaxed atmosphere. He had encountered not just indifference but also open contempt for the truths of religion. In some social gatherings, his hair had stood on end at what he had heard. Even artisans showed neither shame nor inhibition when deriding Christianity.[51] Although he was careful to add that all this impiety was the legacy of Voltaire's sojourn in the city, the context made it clear that he held Frederick responsible.

No one could reasonably doubt the intensity of Frederick's commitment to religious toleration. His motivation is less straightforward. He himself might well have found it hard to be confident about any self-diagnosis. So many years of force-feeding from his father and his father's pastors, especially at the time of his flight and ensuing dark night of the soul, may well have implanted an aversion to all matters religious. If so, it was something he shared with his siblings, who had suffered a similar regime of indoctrination. In January 1755, the pious Count Lehndorff attended a dinner party at which Frederick's three younger brothers – August Wilhelm, Henry and Ferdinand – were present and recorded in his diary: 'there was talk about religion, and some very strong things were said about it. Most present admitted that they had none.'[52] Frederick's attitude was not one of indifference. As his repeated barbs indicated, he held revealed religion to be not only worthless but pernicious, because of the suffering inflicted by the mutual intolerance of the competing sects. Persecution he condemned for both prudential and principled reasons. In his *Memoirs of the House of Brandenburg*, Frederick wrote that the revocation of the Edict of Nantes by Louis XIV in 1685, which removed the limited freedom of worship enjoyed by Protestants, had led to the emigration of 400,000 of France's most enterprising and wealthy subjects. The majority went to Great Britain and the Dutch Republic, thus strengthening what proved to be Louis's two greatest enemies, and 20,000 went to Brandenburg, which they thus helped to repopulate.[53]

In 1773 Frederick was given the opportunity to practise what he preached when Pope Clement XIV dissolved the Society of Jesus. The Jesuits had been expelled already from Portugal in 1759, France in 1764 and Spain, Naples, Parma and Malta in 1767. Frederick's response to those earlier ejections of the religious group most closely identified with the papacy had been predictably enthusiastic. In 1761

377

he told d'Argens: 'in truth, my dear marquis, the better I know the world, the more it seems vicious, imbecilic and perverse. I never expected to see the Jesuits being persecuted. It would be good if this order were abolished altogether, just like the Templars were but with less reason.'[54] But when it came to expelling them from his own dominions, he thought better of it. After failing to get a special dispensation from the papal bull of dissolution, he forbade its publication. As he explained to his disapproving French friends, Catholic education in Silesia depended entirely on the Jesuits at the University of Breslau. If they were removed, all his Catholic ordinands would be obliged to go to Bohemia for their training. Moreover, he added with tongue in cheek, the Treaty of Breslau obliged him to maintain the religious status quo in Silesia. Whereas the Catholic sovereigns had the Pope to absolve them from their breach of faith, he had no one and so was obliged to keep his word.[55] To d'Alembert he exclaimed: 'By all means accuse me of being too tolerant, I shall glory in the fault; if only this were the only defect to be laid at the door of sovereigns!'[56]

Quite apart from these prudential considerations, he also believed that persecution was fundamentally wrong. The clearest statement came in his *Essay on the forms of government and the duties of sovereigns* of 1777:

> One can compel by force some poor wretch to utter a certain form of words, yet he will deny to it his inner consent; thus the persecutor has gained nothing. But if one goes back to the origins of society, it is completely clear that the sovereign has no right to dictate the way in which the citizens will think. Would not one have to be demented to suppose that men said to one of their number: we are raising you above us because we like being slaves, and so we are giving you the power to direct our thoughts as you like? On the contrary, what they said was: we need you to maintain the laws which we wish to obey, to govern us wisely, to defend us; for the rest, we require that you respect our liberty. Once this agreement had been made, it could not be altered.[57]

It was not common in eighteenth-century Europe for such a resounding statement of principle to be translated into practice so firmly. To the Empress Maria Theresa, whose own intolerance inflicted vigorous persecution on her heterodox subjects, Frederick wrote: 'from my subjects

I demand nothing more than civil obedience and loyalty. So long as they perform their duty in this respect, I consider myself obliged to give them all equal favour, protection and justice, no matter what speculative opinions in religious matters they might entertain.'[58] So the new Protestant ministers sent to Silesia were instructed not to use churches reserved for Catholics but to preach in town halls or even barns.[59] The various confessions were prevented from abusing each other, but otherwise were allowed to run their own affairs. Unlike his father, who wished to eliminate differences between Lutheran and Calvinist worship, he had no interest in interfering with internal Church matters and so granted a petition from the Lutherans asking to be allowed once more to wear surplices, carry crucifixes at burials and the like.[60] Although he wrote in his *Political Testament* of 1752 that Catholicism was 'the most ridiculous' of all religions,[61] he was careful not to discriminate against it. Sticking to the letter of the Peace of Breslau, he refused to allow Protestants to take over, or even share, Catholic churches, even in communities where they formed a large majority.[62]

JEWS

Frederick did not discriminate against the numerous varieties of Christianity to be found in Prussia, but he did discriminate against the Jews.[63] His anti-Semitism was made quite explicit in numerous public and private statements, most directly in his *Political Testaments*:

> Of all these [religious] sects, the Jews are the most dangerous, because they do harm to the trade of Christians and are of no use to the state. It is true we need Jews for trade with Poland, but we must prevent any increase in their numbers. Not only must we restrict the number of families, we must also put a limit on the total numbers. We must also confine their commercial activity, so that they are kept away from wholesale trade and only engage in retailing. [1752]

> There are too many Jews in the towns. They are needed in towns close to Poland because only Jews are involved in commerce there but the further one gets away from the frontier, the more damaging they

379

become. They are engaged in usury, smuggling and a thousand kinds of mischief, to the detriment of citizens and Christian merchants. I have never persecuted them or indeed any other group for that matter, but we need to keep an eye on them and make sure they do not increase in numbers. [1768][64]

This particular prejudice was shared of course with all but a small minority of contemporaries, but in Frederick's case it may well have been strengthened by his admiration of the notoriously anti-Semitic Voltaire. In the *Henriade*, Voltaire had derided the superstition, barbarism, ignorance and prejudices of the Jewish people.[65] For both men, hostility to the Jews of the Old Testament was just one facet of their hostility to the Christians of the New.[66] This can be seen, for example, in Frederick's satirical piece entitled *Report of Phihihu, envoy to Europe of the Emperor of China*, which he completed in March 1760. In the style of Montesquieu's *Persian Letters*, the envoy reports on the absurdities he encounters in Europe, especially those connected with the Catholic Church. In Rome he meets a Portuguese Jew, who tells him: 'the Christians base their own book of laws on ours; and they admit that their religion comes from ours; but these ungrateful children attack and abuse their mother. To avoid being burnt to death at Lisbon, my family has had to submit to the practice of this religion.'[67] Moreover, this was written for publication, which swiftly followed, accompanied by advertisements in the Berlin newspapers.[68]

At least Frederick was less abusive verbally than his father, who had written in his own *Political Testament* that 'the Jews betrayed Christ and even the most honest Jew is a rogue'. On the other hand, Frederick was initially more severe in practice than his father. His declared willingness to build mosques and temples to attract Turkish and pagan immigrants did not extend to synagogues.* In 1671 his more enlightened great-grandfather, Frederick William the Great Elector, had asked his agent in Vienna to recruit forty to fifty Jewish families for settlement in Berlin, taking advantage of one of those periodic pogroms that have been such a depressingly regular feature of Aus-

---

* See above, p. 370.

trian history. Although in the event far fewer came, this marked the return of Jews to Berlin, from which they had been expelled almost exactly a century earlier.[69] By 1700, 117 families totalling some 600 individuals had settled.[70] In 1714 a fine new synagogue was dedicated, acclaimed as one of the most beautiful in Europe. Although Frederick William I and his court attended the ceremony, the rest of his reign was marked by periodic bouts of persecution. A package of measures enforced in 1737 envisaged the progressive diminution and final extinction of the Jewish community in the city.[71]

Frederick did not interfere with the Jews' freedom of worship, but he did tighten restrictions on their numbers. A comprehensive new regulation imposed in 1750 confirmed and reinforced the various categories to which the Jews had been assigned.[72] At the apex stood a handful of specially favoured families with a 'general privilege', giving the right to reside anywhere in the kingdom. Next came the 150 families classified as 'regulars' and thus qualified to pass their right of residence on to one family member, but to a second or third only if fortunes worth 1,000 and 2,000 talers respectively could be proved.[73] 'Extraordinary' Jews, mostly professional people, enjoyed only a personal and non-transmissible residence. And so the concessions diminished down through another four categories until reaching at the bottom of the heap the Jews' servants, who had no rights at all. In theory, any Jews in Berlin in excess of the official quota should have been deported, together with any destitute beggars, but enforcement proved difficult. Despite all the periodic reminders, the numbers increased inexorably.[74] Given the enormous Jewish population of adjacent Poland, this was inevitable, especially after the first partition of 1772. Between 1750 and the end of the reign the Jewish community grew by 54 per cent from 2,188 to 3,379, which represented 2.3 per cent of the city's total population.[75] In Brandenburg as a whole, the rate of increase was even higher at 61.75 per cent.[76]

The royal attitude also softened in the middle of the reign, although only temporarily and only because Frederick found Jews helpful in two key areas. The first was the currency debasement which helped to finance the Seven Years War. This was organized by a consortium led by Daniel Itzig, Veitel Heine Ephraim and Moses Isaac, who generated a profit of 29,000,000 talers for Frederick and an undisclosed sum for themselves.[77] Unsurprisingly, it was the latter who attracted most public opprobrium.[78] The debased coins were dubbed 'Ephraims' and were derided in the couplet:

> Von aussen schön, von innen schlimm,
> Von aussen Friedrich, von innen Ephraim.
> (On the outside fine, on the inside bad,
> On the outside Frederick, on the inside Ephraim.)[79]

The second area of mutually beneficial cooperation was manufacturing, financed partly by the profits made during the war. Aided by generous subsidies and monopolies, a group of Jewish entrepreneurs emerged at Berlin and Potsdam, mainly engaged in textile production.[80] Ephraim took over the gold and silver manufactory at Berlin and turned it into a flourishing concern; Daniel Itzig remained primarily a financier but also ran the royal leather factory at Potsdam, while Moses Isaac concentrated on silk manufacturing.[81]

Among the Jewish entrepreneurs was one of the most celebrated Jews of his time, or any other time for that matter: the philosopher Moses Mendelssohn. He arrived in Berlin from Dessau in 1743 at the age of fourteen and lived there until his death in 1786. His career demonstrated the highs and lows of Frederick's relationship with the Jews. He arrived penniless but died rich, propertied and esteemed across enlightened Europe, leaving a well-educated and integrated family. Among his six children who survived to adulthood, Dorothea married, first Simon Veit and then Friedrich Schlegel. The former union produced the distinguished artists Jonas and Philipp, founders of the Nazarene movement. Moses' son Joseph founded the Mendelssohn Bank, which flourished until expropriated by the Nazis in 1939. Another son, Abraham, was the father of the composer-musicians Felix and Fanny Mendelssohn. A prolific author on a wide range of philosophical and religious topics, Moses took full advantage of the cultural and intellectual facilities on offer in Berlin. His generous hospitality and tireless correspondence helped to make the city the centre of the Jewish Enlightenment in western Europe.[82] In few other European cities could he have achieved or contributed as much, as he recognized:

I live in a state in which one of the wisest sovereigns who ever ruled mankind has made the arts and the sciences blossom and a sensible freedom of thought so widespread that their effects have reached down to the humblest inhabitant of his dominions. Under his glorious rule I have found both opportunity and inspiration to reflect on my own destiny and that of my fellow-citizens, and to present observations to the best of my ability on the fate of mankind and providence.[83]

In sermons preached to welcome victories in the Seven Years War, Mendelssohn hailed Frederick as the instrument of divine providence.[84] On the other hand, his distinction was thrown into sharp relief by the various forms of discrimination he suffered. Like all his fellow-Jews, he had to pay higher dues than Christians just for the privilege of residing; like them, he could not marry a Christian or employ a Christian; like them, he was excluded from state employment, higher education, the guilds and the purchase of a landed estate; like them, he had to buy an expensive porcelain dinner set from the royal manufactory when he got married; like them, he was subject to a number of humiliating regulations such as only being admitted to Berlin through the Prenzlau and Halle gates.[85] To get married to Fromet Gugenheim of Hamburg required great patience while waiting for special royal permission.[86] There was also the constant awareness that Jews were second-class citizens, or rather not citizens at all, just 'tolerated' outsiders. This sense Mendelssohn expressed clearly in a letter to the Swiss philosopher Isaak Iselin in 1762:

> Under Frederick's rule freedom of thought does indeed flourish in almost republican splendour; but you know how small is the share in the freedoms of this country enjoyed by my co-religionists. Civil oppression, to which we are condemned by a prejudice that is all too general, lies like a dead burden on the elevation of the spirit, and prevents it from ever attempting the flight of the free-born.[87]

On at least two occasions, Mendelssohn was dealt personal experience of Frederick's disdain for Jews. In 1771 the Saxon minister von Fritsch was invited by Frederick to Sanssouci. As he was about to set out for home, he mentioned that he would be travelling via Berlin to visit 'the famous Moses Mendelssohn', of whom he had a very high opinion. Frederick replied that a detour would not be necessary, as he would order Mendelssohn to be summoned to Potsdam. Although requiring a special dispensation to travel on a Jewish festival, Mendelssohn duly obliged and on the following day presented himself at the Potsdam city gate, where he was interrogated by a young officer. Shown the royal command, the latter asked Mendelssohn why he was called 'famous'. Knowing that a military mind might find a Jewish 'philosopher' difficult to appreciate, Mendelssohn replied: 'I am a conjurer.' That was good enough and he was allowed in. It was this episode at the gate which then formed one of the many anecdotes Friedrich Nicolai retold so often and so profitably, especially when engraved by Chodowiecki. The real point of the story, however, is that Mendelssohn did get to see Fritsch – twice – but Frederick would not see him.[88]

More serious were the insult and injury inflicted on him in 1771 when the Berlin Academy voted to recommend to Frederick that Mendelssohn be admitted to their ranks. Their request was simply ignored and eventually was dropped. Everyone knew that the tacit royal veto was imposed because Mendelssohn was a Jew.[89] Some amends were made in 1783 when a circular bearing the royal signature was sent to the courts announcing an improved form of oath for Jews and stating that it had been drafted with the assistance of 'a Jewish scholar famous for his knowledge and upright way of thinking'. Although not named, there could be no doubt that Mendelssohn was meant.[90] More striking was Frederick's intervention in 1778 when petitioned by six Jewish students at the University of Frankfurt an der Oder asking for their ban on lecturing to be lifted. When the university authorities informed Frederick that, as in every other German university, Jews could not be admitted to the doctoral status necessary, he told them this was mere prejudice and that anyone qualified should be allowed to lecture, whether baptized or not.[91]

Informally, the situation of the Jews in Prussia did improve during the course of Frederick's reign. It is worth remembering that, at a time when Jews were not allowed even to enter the Saxon city of Leipzig except when the trade fairs were being held, at Berlin Jews and Christians could work together on editing periodicals.[92] By 1786 there were more Jews in Prussia, many of them were better off and they were better educated, although none of this was due to royal policy.[93] On the contrary, the closing years of Frederick's reign were marked by an intensification of the requirement to buy large amounts of porcelain. This was imposed on the direct orders of the king himself, convinced that his officials had been getting slack. The enormous sum of 200,000 talers was extorted, resulting in the forced sale of property and the expulsion of whole families.[94] The progress the Jews undoubtedly made was due to the vigorous self-help they organized themselves, especially in the field of education.[95] One result was a more diverse – and liberal – social ambience within the community. Until mid-century, this had been very conservative, especially in relation to social practices such as the wearing of beards. In the 1740s the appearance in the synagogue of a clean-shaven Jew wearing a wig could still evoke a storm of disapproval.[96] Peter the Great of Russia famously made the removal of beards by his nobility an important symbol of modernization. Less well known is Frederick's decree of 1748 that Jews should *not* shave off their beards entirely, lest they be taken for criminals.[97] As insults go, this ranked high, for it was underpinned by the assumption that any Jew choosing to be clean-shaven must be masquerading as a Christian for nefarious purposes.

Yet the offensive decree also revealed another, if modest, way in which the Jewish situation was improving, for it evoked a response from the finest playwright of his day, Gotthold Ephraim Lessing. In his one-act comedy *The Jews*, written a year later and almost certainly a response to Frederick's decree, two rascally employees of a baron disguise themselves as Jews by donning false beards and try to rob him on the highway as he returns home in his carriage. They are frustrated by the intervention of an anonymous traveller. Assuming his assailants to have been Jews, the baron denounces a people whose only goal is profit, who will commit any crime to achieve it and are 'the most evil and villainous' of all creatures.[98] In the final scene he is suitably chastened to discover that the assailants were his own Christian employees and that his rescuer, who in the meantime has revealed himself to be educated, enlightened and generally a paragon, was a Jew. 'Oh, how estimable the Jews would be,' he exclaims, 'if they were all like you!' This double-edged compliment is echoed more crudely by a Christian servant: 'What the Devil! So there are actually Jews who aren't Jews!'[99] One of the many ironies in the play is the denunciation of the Jews by the actual criminal, aptly named Martin Krumm ('crook'), who also calls for their extermination.[100]

The Jews was not performed until 1766. It was one of several plays to present Jews in a favourable light, although the older negative stereotype remained popular. When revived in 1806, it was the rant of Martin Krumm that was greeted with acclamation by the anti-Semitic audience.[101] By then Lessing was recognized as the most eloquent advocate of Jewish emancipation in Germany. In 1753 he encouraged his friend Aaron Salomon Gumpertz to write a pamphlet calling for Jews to be given the same rights in Prussia that they already enjoyed in Great Britain or the Dutch Republic. He also arranged for it to be published and wrote a favourable review.[102] His most enduring service of course was the play Nathan the Wise, written thirty years after The Jews, and given its première at Berlin in 1783 (at about the same time it was banned in Vienna).[103] At one of its many levels it can be taken as a rebuke to Frederick and the limits of his Enlightenment. The hero was based on Lessing's friend Moses Mendelssohn, who many years earlier had delivered a more frontal assault on the prejudices of his day. It was occasioned by a hostile review of The Jews, by the distinguished Göttingen biblical scholar Johann David Michaelis. As Mendelssohn wrote to Gumpertz in a letter which Lessing then published:

> The common Christian people have always regarded Jews as the rejects of nature, as warts on human society. But I would have expected a fairer verdict from educated people ... We go on being oppressed, we are forced to live under restrictions among free and fortunate citizens, we go on being exposed to derision and contempt; what they can't take away from us is virtue, the only comfort remaining to tortured souls, the only refuge of the abandoned.[104]

It is sad that there was no prospect of these words ever reaching Frederick. As in so many other respects, he did not change. In 1780 he told his Silesian minister, Karl Georg Heinrich von Hoym, that he knew all about his 'secret proclivity' for the Jews, adding: 'but for my part I see things differently and believe it would be for the best if the Jews could be got rid of and their business taken by Christians'.[105]

If there was no prospect of any legislative move towards emancipation during Frederick's reign, a least a few shuffling steps were taken in the public sphere. The most explicit and influential was a pamphlet published in 1781 by Christian Wilhelm von Dohm, an official in the Prussian Foreign Office, with the title *On the civil improvement of the Jews*.[106] This was an important moment, for it 'inaugurated the era of Jewish emancipation in Germany ... The book so exercised public opinion that it established the contours of the emancipation debate for the entire century to come.'[107] It took Lessing's arguments from the realm of fiction into concrete legal, economic and educational proposals. At the heart of both men's analysis of the Jewish predicament was the belief that 'everything the Jews are blamed for is caused by the political conditions under which they now live, and any other group of men, under such conditions, would be guilty of identical errors'.[108] Removal of discrimination, and integration, would benefit state and society as much as the Jews themselves. Dohm's nine-point programme was lent additional weight by the almost simultaneous publication of Joseph II's decree introducing a very similar programme to the Habsburg Monarchy, where Jews could now attend Christian schools and universities, learn and practise a trade, engage in wholesale and retail business, open factories, employ Christian servants, rent houses, stay where they pleased, visit theatres, leave their homes on Christian festivals, and remove the yellow star of David from their clothes.[109] Starting further back, Austrian Jews were now appreciably better off than their Prussian co-religionists.

CRIME AND PUNISHMENT

The recall of Christian Wolff to Prussia in 1740 had announced the inauguration of an age of reason.* Almost simultaneously, Frederick gave another earnest of his intentions by abolishing the use of torture. As with some of his other innovations, some knowledge of contemporary practice is needed to appreciate its impact. What looks like extreme, not so say unimaginable, cruelty to twenty-first-century eyes,

---

* See above, p. 369.

was commonplace across eighteenth-century Europe. The terrible end of Robert-François Damiens, the failed assassin of Louis XV, whose live body was pulled apart by four horses after being tortured by the application of 'melted lead, boiling oil, burning pitch, and melted wax and sulphur' to his mutilated limbs, epitomized the eighteenth-century approach to criminal justice.[110] Just three days after he came to the throne, Frederick told his minister Samuel von Cocceji that in future torture could be applied only in cases of *lèse majesté*, high treason or mass murder.[111] It was abolished altogether in 1755.[112] His judicial officials were vehemently opposed to losing their 'Queen of Proofs', as it was known.[113] Across continental Europe torture was still widely employed. That its use was formally terminated in several countries during the second half of the eighteenth century has been attributed to the example set by Frederick; indeed the Empress Maria Theresa alluded to him specifically when banning it in the Habsburg Monarchy in 1776.[114]

Also during the first year of his reign, one of the most gruesome of traditional punishments was prohibited. This was 'sacking', the drowning of a woman convicted of infanticide in a sack she had been obliged to sew herself.[115] Frederick's attitude to infanticide exemplified the combination of enlightenment and practicality which distinguished his regime from those of most of his contemporaries. In view of the common historiographical tendency to talk up the continuities of Prussian history, it is worth pointing out the sea-change that occurred in 1740. Frederick William I had regarded crime as a sin against a vengeful Old Testament God whose wrath had to be propitiated lest he take action against the whole community. Not only did the punishment have to be public, it also had to be extreme, to make the greatest impact on the spectators (and God). So the criminal was dragged to the place of execution and tormented with red-hot pincers before being put to death. For Frederick, crime was entirely secular, an anti-social act whose punishment must always be proportionate, for its essential purpose was to lend support to the rational faculty in controlling human passions.[116] Public executions must not be so horrific as to excite pity for the criminal or dangerous curiosity:

> It is undeniable that through frightful public capital punishments, many young and innocent spirits, who naturally want to know the reason for

such a terrible execution, especially if they are also unaware of the finer sentiments (just as the criminal is), will be scandalized rather than improved, and it is even possible that evil tendencies may be awakened in them, tendencies of which they previously had no inkling.[117]

It will come as no surprise that the religious element in the new-style 'rituals of retribution' was reduced. From now on, unmarried mothers were no longer subjected to public penance in church, a degrading ritual Frederick believed to be responsible for both abortions and infanticide. Parents and employers were not only directed to refrain from punishing the pregnant girls but were also required to help them with counselling and material support, with the intention of keeping mother and baby together.[118] The motive here was less humanitarian than practical, given Frederick's concern, or rather obsession, with increasing Prussia's population. In his *Political Testament* of 1768, he lamented the number of abortions, 'the most common crime' in towns. He expressed the pious hope that foundling homes could be established in Berlin, Königsberg and Breslau, but added wistfully that this would prove expensive.[119]

On the other hand, any woman declining her demographic duty, and reducing the Prussian population by even one, was executed to encourage the others, albeit by decapitation rather than drowning.[120] Executions for infanticide formed the most numerous category of capital punishments, as the figures for the four years 1775–8 show:

Murder	12
Concocting poison	4
Highway robbery	2
Infanticide	18
Arson	8
Soliciting desertion	2
Total	46[121]

As these figures reveal, capital punishment was used sparingly. In contemporary England, the *annual* average for executions in London alone was forty-eight in the 1770s.[122] Moreover, whereas two-thirds of capital convictions in England were for simple crimes against property such as the theft of a sheep (or a lamb), in Prussia only serious crimes were punished with death.[123]

In an ocean heaving with irrational cruelty, a sovereign who was merely severe stood out as an island of humanity: 'justice, regularity, order were the watchwords of the new policy. And humanity too. A civilized society meant for an Enlightened monarch such as the Prussian king a society in which people were not routinely subjected to barbarous and painful tortures either on the scaffold or in the inquisitorial chamber.'[124] That did not mean that Frederick's Prussia was a twenty-first-century liberal democracy *avant la lettre*. Breaking on the wheel continued to be employed, although the victim was discreetly strangled first.[125] Characteristically, Frederick also insisted on retaining control of what punishments were inflicted on whom. In 1743 Cocceji suggested that in future, to save time, criminal sentences involving deportation, imprisonment, corporal or capital punishment should no longer be referred for royal approval. The reply was unequivocal: 'No! All criminal verdicts are to be forwarded; otherwise all sorts of problems would arise, and the people in the provinces would just bumble around as they liked.'[126]

Although it seems barely credible that Frederick should have reviewed all serious criminal sentences handed down in his dominions, there is plenty of evidence that he made full use of his prerogative.[127] In 1753, for example, he intervened to reduce a six-year prison sentence for poaching.[128] On occasions he seems to have been sickened by the constant demands to decide the life or death of criminals. In 1748 he confirmed the death penalty for two members of a Silesian bandit gang, but complained that they were the ninth and tenth he had despatched already and yet there were said to be fifty-odd more waiting his verdict. Could not they be simply deported or sent off for hard labour?[129] But he often went the other way. In 1750 he quintupled a sentence of two years' imprisonment for attempted highway robbery, also taking the opportunity to remind the head of the criminal justice department, Levin Friedrich von Bismarck, of his sentencing policy: those who stole because of folly or poverty were not to be punished with full rigour, especially if there was hope of rehabilitation and no violence had been involved. Robbery with violence, however, especially if planned in advance and committed by a gang, should be penalized by death or life imprisonment.[130] Also at odds with a benign image was his occasional authorization of the use of torture and infliction of cruel and unnatural punishment.[131] In 1746 the decapitated head of the Prussian consul at Danzig, von Ferber, was displayed on a pike outside Spandau prison, as an awful warning to anyone else contemplating high treason.[132] According to the Piedmontese Abbé Denina, who was living in Berlin at the time, an arsonist was burned at the stake there towards the end of the reign. Denina added that in his old age Frederick had concluded that too much leniency had led to a crime wave and was increasingly substituting the death penalty for terms of imprisonment.[133] Death might well have been preferable, given the state of Prussian prisons. A contemporary exposé claimed they were overcrowded, pestilential, filthy, dark, unheated, unsupervised, violent academies of crime.[134]

LAW AND JUSTICE

The same mixture of light and dark characterized Frederick's approach to civil law. After military matters, it was the sphere of government to which he devoted most time. In *Antimachiavel* he proclaimed in the first chapter: 'justice is the principal task of the sovereign; he should place the welfare of the people he governs above every other interest'.[135] Those words were written while he was still crown prince; when he came to the throne, it took a little while before he began to show he meant them. Attending to the opera house and then the Austrians had to come first. The short breathing space granted by the Convention of Klein-Schnellendorf in October 1741 allowed him to start thinking about the judicial arrangements in his new province, but it was not until the general peace in 1745 that he could really put his mind to it. In Samuel von Cocceji he was lucky to have inherited from his father a reformer of distinction. Emphatically not a man of the Enlightenment, Cocceji was elderly (born in 1679), devout (he believed that all law was divine by origin) and conservative (he opposed Frederick's abolition of torture).[136] But he did hold that justice should be administered fairly, quickly and cheaply, and that the laws should be clear, concise and uniform. Most importantly, he proved to be a brilliant administrator, particularly good at banging thick heads together and making things happen.

That made him Frederick's ideal collaborator. There was plenty for the two of them to do. Despite intermittent and half-hearted attempts at reform by Frederick William I, by Cocceji's own account, justice in Prussia was a disgrace: expensive, very slow, corrupt and arbitrary. Anticipating 'Jarndyce *versus* Jarndyce' in Dickens's *Bleak House*, a case in Pomerania between the royal taxation authorities and the town of Kantereck had been ambling along for two centuries without resolution.[137] Many millions of words were written in the course of the reforms which followed, many of them to be found in the volumes of *Acta Borussica*, but the salient points can be summarized quite quickly. An early success was the nationalization of the system by banning the referral of cases to the law faculties of non-Prussian universities for adjudication, and the exclusion of imperial jurisdiction in 1746.[138] Both symbolically and substantively, this was a major step on the road that led to full sovereignty and separation from the Holy Roman Empire.

The main problem was finance. Dependent on fees for their livelihood, few judges resisted the temptation to spin cases out or even to take bribes. Crucial therefore to the success of his project was Cocceji's skill in persuading the provincial Estates to provide the necessary funds.[139] He himself was very much an interventionist reformer, moving from one province to another, weeding out the corrupt and incompetent and dragooning the survivors into addressing the backlog. His first target was Pomerania, where in eight months in 1746–7 he supervised the settlement of 2,400 old cases.[140] From there he moved on to Cleves and East Frisia in 1749, Silesia in 1750 and East Prussia in 1751.[141] Everywhere, a transparent hierarchy was established, the upper courts were reorganized, ecclesiastical jurisdiction was abolished and one appeal court (*Regierung*) recognized as the sole court of appeal for the province. Over them all was placed a Supreme Court (*Obertribunal*) with jurisdiction for the whole state.[142] All judges seeking appointment or reappointment were subjected to an examination organized by a central board.[143] Needless to say, a reform so comprehensive ran into stiff opposition. Frederick deserves credit for giving Cocceji unstinting support. In 1748 he crisply told the leader of the old guard, Georg Dietloff von Arnim, to submit, adding that he would receive no more remonstrances from someone so clearly motivated by 'personal jealousy'.[144] Of Cocceji he wrote that his wisdom, integrity, enlightenment and industry would have made him stand out in the Greek and Roman republics at their peak. When Cocceji died in 1755 Frederick placed a marble bust of him in the courtyard of the justice ministry to inspire emulation.[145]

Cocceji's death and the outbreak of war in 1756 brought the reform movement to a halt. Ironically, it was revived by what was called 'a judicial catastrophe' by one of those involved.[146] This was the famous Miller Arnold affair, which paradoxically did more both to confirm *and* deny Frederick's status as a just ruler than any other episode during his reign. It took almost a decade to come to the boil. In 1770 a noble landowner and justice of the peace (*Landrat*) called von Gersdorf (his first name is never mentioned) had a fish-pond dug on his estate at Kay near Züllichau on the river Oder, diverting a mill-stream to fill it. In 1773 Christian Arnold claimed that this had reduced the water-flow so much that his mill downstream was no longer viable and so brought a case against his own lord, Count von Schmettau, for a reduction in dues until the offending pond was filled in. He was told by the courts to sue Gersdorf instead. In 1778 Schmettau lost patience with Arnold for not paying his dues, repossessed the mill and put it up for auction. It was bought by Gersdorf, who sold it on to a third party. Arnold now appealed direct to Frederick, who appointed a two-man commission to investigate. One of its members, Colonel von Heucking, wrote a report in favour of Arnold; the other, an official from the court at Küstrin, took the view that the case should go through due process in the courts first.[147]

Probably because the report came from a military man and not from the judicial officials he despised, Frederick chose to believe Heucking. The affair now became a struggle between the king, determined that Arnold should be given all he asked for, and the judges in Berlin and Küstrin, determined that the law should be upheld. Even after making every allowance for bias in the accounts of the judges, it seems clear that Arnold was in the wrong (or rather 'the Arnolds', for it was Mrs Rosine Arnold who was the driving force in the case).[148] As a contemporary map shows, the water diverted to the fish-pond flowed back into the main stream above the Arnold mill. Consequently, the water-loss through seepage and evaporation would have been minimal. The experts who inspected the site found that the water-flow was entirely adequate to run the mill-wheel, a finding that was confirmed by the new owner. Heucking, who had got to know the Arnolds when they first tried to petition Frederick in 1778, also greatly exaggerated the ill-treatment they had suffered, alleging that Schmettau had imprisoned the miller for seven weeks and had given Mrs Arnold a thrashing.[149] Frederick was wholly convinced however. The Arnolds seem to have known about his deep-rooted suspicion and dislike of lawyers and cleverly played on it.[150] According to Christian Wilhelm von Dohm, Frederick already knew Arnold, who had acted as a scout during the Seven Years War.[151]

After much toing and froing, Frederick took the law into his own hands. On 11 December 1779 he summoned Chancellor von Fürst and the three councillors who had confirmed the lower court's verdict to Potsdam. His temper was not improved by one of his periodic bouts of gout. After screaming insults at them – 'riff-raff, rogues, scoundrels' – he told them they all deserved to be strung up. Fürst's attempt to defend himself was cut off by the shout: 'Get out! Your post is vacant!'[152] The others were sacked too, along with the six Küstrin judges who had opposed Heucking's conclusions. One of the latter recorded that when they reached Berlin under close arrest they were confined in a dark, wet, unheated cell barely big enough for one.[153] And there they lingered until the following autumn. Just to add financial insult to physical injury, they were also required to pay the Arnolds compensation and costs out of their own pockets.[154]

No wonder the case caused such a sensation. At the very least, it destroyed any notion that the King of Prussia's officials were mindless automatons. Both at the centre and in the provinces they acted with courage and integrity. Their example was followed by the Minister of Justice, Karl Abraham von Zedlitz, who refused Frederick's direct order to enforce the royal will, telling him that the Heucking report was erroneous, the Arnolds were cheats and the judges should be reinstated forthwith. Frederick's reply was revealing: 'You pen-pusher, you don't understand anything; when soldiers get an order to look into something, they take the direct route and get to the bottom of things, and really know how to get to grips with it. But you can be quite certain that I place more trust in an honest officer, who acts out of honour, than in all you lawyers and your rights.' He added that if Zedlitz would not do what he wanted, he would find someone else who would. It was without any obvious irony that he then signed himself: 'otherwise I am your very affectionate king'. Zedlitz replied with dignity that he had always counted the favour of the king to be the greatest happiness of his life and had always done his utmost to deserve it, but he would not act against his convictions.[155] Even the imperious Frederick knew that he had met his match and did not press it further.[156]

Frederick may have lost that skirmish, but he won the public relations battle. He showed that he was a politician as well as a sovereign when he published his own account of the affair. After a resumé as highly coloured as it was inaccurate, he thundered: 'everyone, be he high or low, rich or poor, shall receive prompt justice, and every one of my subjects shall always find the law administered impartially, without regard for person or status'. He promised to make an example of the officials who had conspired against Miller Arnold so that their colleagues would take note, 'for they must grasp that the most humble peasant, yes, and what is more, the beggar, is just as much a human being as is His Majesty, and all must get justice, for in the eyes of the law all people are equal, whether a prince sues a peasant or a peasant sues a prince'. He concluded: 'a court of judges which acts unjustly is more dangerous and worse than a gang of bandits, for protective measures can be taken against the latter, whereas villains who don the mantle of the law to be able to act out their evil passions are invulnerable, they are the worst rogues in the world and deserve to be punished with double severity'.[157] This ringing affirmation of equality before the law was published in all the Berlin newspapers and soon went round Europe if not the world, attracting admiring attention as far south as Naples and Morocco.[158] In 1780 a Prussian mariner visiting Lisbon witnessed a dramatic re-enactment of the affair in Portuguese. When the audience discovered his nationality, they crowded round him, shouting 'Glory to the King of Prussia!' and 'Long live just kings!'[159] He also found an effigy of Frederick displayed in a local waxworks gallery.[160]

In Prussia, opinion was mixed. Representative of the enlightened intelligentsia was the withering verdict delivered by Christian Wilhelm von Dohm:

This episode made a numbing impression on both the capital and the rest of the country. With horror it was realised that we were living under a ruler who was capable of acting arbitrarily according to his whim of the moment, and that nothing seemed to restrain him, for he no longer respected the dignity of the law and would not listen to the representations and arguments of his civil servants.[161]

But for the bulk of the population, Frederick was a heroic figure who stuck up for the poor and weak against the rich and powerful. As the Lutheran pastor and writer Daniel Jenisch commented, Frederick may have been in the wrong in the Miller Arnold affair but his intervention transfigured him in the eyes of the common man.[162] So, as officials visited the homes of the dismissed judges to demonstrate their solidarity, outside the royal palace a large crowd acclaimed the 'Peasant King' and many windows were illuminated and decorated with his portrait.[163]

The affair was also captured visually in several prints. The most elaborate, by Vincenzo Vangelisti, showed Frederick holding the scales of justice, as the petitioning Arnold family kneel gratefully before him and an avenging angel drives the wicked judges from the scene. Beneath the picture is the title 'Frederick's Scales', a short history of the episode taken from the *Gazette de France*, and the full text of the royal proclamation of 11 December. An English version – 'The Justice of Frederick' – was published in London in 1782.[164]

Undoubtedly Frederick had wanted to see justice done, but equally certainly he had acted unjustly, despotically even.[165] He had also contravened his own firmly declared principles: 'I have resolved never to interfere with due process, in the courts it is the laws that must speak and the sovereign must remain silent' (*Political Testament* of 1752) and 'it is not at all fitting that a sovereign should exercise his authority to interfere with decisions in court cases; there the laws alone should rule and the duty of the sovereign is confined to protecting them' (*Political Testament* of 1768).[166] At least the episode refocused his mind on the need to resume law reform, which had fallen into abeyance with the death of Cocceji in 1755 and the outbreak of the Seven Years War the following year. The sacking of the Chancellor Fürst brought in his place Johann Heinrich Casimir von Carmer, a Cocceji protégé who had been Silesian Minister of Justice since 1768. Adding an enlightened outlook to his mentor's fabled capacity for organization, Carmer supervised during the closing years of Frederick's reign 'the most significant achievement of enlightened absolutism in Prussia'.[167]

The programme was spelt out in a royal memorandum of 14 April 1780. This had been drafted by Carmer's most important associate, Carl Gottlieb Suarez, but it was the royal support which put it into action. Frederick told the reformers: 'I leave it to you to think further about what should be done and to take the necessary steps to put it all into effect; but I do promise you my emphatic protection against all the intrigues and resistance you will encounter.'[168] The easiest part was procedural. The earlier objectives of quicker, simpler, cheaper and more transparent justice were taken up again. The investigating role of judges was enhanced at the expense of advocates, the War and Domains Chambers were assigned judicial departments staffed by trained lawyers and the appeals system was further centralized.[169]

The major task, however, was codification, which Cocceji had begun but not taken very far. By 1784 the reformers had completed a draft which ten years later had developed into the General Law Code, one of the most celebrated of all German legal-cum-constitutional documents. As has often been pointed out, the Code was essentially conservative, especially in its social aspects: 'Frederick and his legal advisers came to their task with ambivalent intentions and incompatible motives. They wanted to create clock-like order and coherence, but also to preserve special rights and social privileges.'[170] Yet their enlightened views also shone through.[171] There were enough progressive elements to allow educated Prussians to believe that they lived in a state embodying the rule of law and to persuade them to prefer it when it came under pressure from revolutionary France after 1789. They were encouraged by the active participation of the public in the reforming process. Voluntary associations such as the Wednesday

Society served as the interface for writers, journalists and officials, whose discussions prepared 'practically all' the reform projects.[172] In particular, the public consultation exercise launched by Carmer in 1784 with Frederick's approval was a revolutionary step and was held to be a sign that Prussia was moving towards a constitutional state.[173]*

Whether or not that was possible can never be resolved. In the event, it was derailed by the French Revolution and the wars which followed. At the time, there was enough rhetoric at least to surround Frederick's memory in a warm glow of political optimism. The same Dohm who had been so scathing about Frederick's role in the Miller Arnold affair also wrote that, although Frederick did not live to see the General Law Code completed, he deserved the credit for promoting an enterprise based on the principles of true philosophy and humanity.[174] Jenisch added to the tribute quoted earlier† the more general observation that 'the severity and security of the administration of justice gave the Prussian subject a certain noble defiance and a rare self-confidence that one finds among the common people only in England and Holland'.[175] More precise was the anonymous report published in the *Berlinische Monatsschrift* in 1784 which not only repeated the claim that Frederick always insisted that peasants and nobles be treated equally but added that the courts even found against the king himself. It cited a case brought by a landowner over the extraction of chalk. In the course of the dispute, Frederick had ordered the closure of the sluices on the canal she used to get her chalk to market. The Chamber Court in Berlin found in her favour and ordered the royal officials to comply forthwith.[176]

So well established did Frederick's image as 'Peasant King' become that it resurfaced in Goethe's play *Breme von Bremenfeld* in 1792. The leading character recounted how he had met Frederick at a field-hospital after the battle of Leuthen. Eight years later the two men met again, allowing Frederick to show off his fabled memory for names and faces. Breme von Bremenfeld told Frederick that he was having to work just as hard in peacetime as in war. When his drinking

---

* See above, pp. 355–6.
† See above, p. 324.

companion expressed surprise that he could speak to the king so freely, he replied: 'Certainly one could. And one person was just the same to him as the next, it was the peasant he cared most about. "I well know," he said to his ministers, when they tried to talk him round to this or that, "rich people have lots of lawyers, but the poor have only one, and that is me." '[177] If nothing else, this demonstrates Frederick's ability to project a favourable public image. He was also the beneficiary of freelance work on the part of his admirers. In 1784, for example, Gleim published an account by his nephew Johann Fromme, who was district commissioner at Fehrbellin, of one of Frederick's famous inspection tours. As we have seen,* Frederick took a keen interest in every aspect of the district, displaying strong if not expert opinions. The episode then found its way into one of the many collections of anecdotes which probably did more for Frederick's image than any other medium, especially when illustrated by Daniel Chodowiecki.[178]

It continued through the next two centuries, as he was often presented as the exemplar of 'enlightened absolutism'. Twenty or thirty years ago much attention was paid by historians to the validity of this concept.[179] With regard to Frederick, this chapter has shown that it is impossible to deny some influence of enlightened ideas on his policies, although other motives were at work. This is no more negated by actions at odds with enlightened values than is the importance of Christianity for – say – Philip II of Spain by his occasional contraventions of the Ten Commandments or the Sermon on the Mount. Frederick shared the central belief of the philosophes that reason could understand, change and improve the natural world. One final illustration must suffice. In a letter to the Dowager Electress of Saxony Maria Antonia in 1763 Frederick deplored the tenacity of 'ancient prejudices' stemming from ignorance which had prompted the Parlement of Paris to prohibit vaccination against smallpox. Of the thousands inoculated in Berlin, he added, not one had died.[180] In her reply, the Electress thanked Frederick for giving her the courage to have herself and her family inoculated, adding that her subjects would now follow her example and thus thank Frederick for saving their

* See above, pp. 127–8.

lives.[181] This provides as good an illustration as one could seek of the contrast between the political cultures of France and Prussia in the middle of the eighteenth century: in the former, Louis XV continued to touch sufferers from the 'King's Evil' (unless of course he was not in a state of grace, which was often); in the latter, Frederick took direct and successful action against the century's great killer.

14

Country and Town

NOBLES AND PEASANTS

Frederick cared. There are too many examples of his concern to get justice for the peasants for it to be dismissed as a pose. In 1777, for example, he sent a sharply worded directive to the ministers of justice that poor supplicants must be treated properly. This was occasioned by a petition from Jacob Dreher, who had journeyed all the way from Liebemühl in East Prussia to seek justice in Berlin but had been threatened with arrest by the police. Frederick reminded his officials: 'in my eyes a poor peasant is worth just as much as the highest-born count or the richest noble, and the law is there for high and low alike'. The poor, he added, must be given a fair hearing, must not be mistreated and must be granted prompt justice.[1] Among the Prussian peasants he found a receptive audience. The old image of downtrodden rural masses oppressed by omnipotent Junker landlords was exploded long ago. The authority of the king did *not* stop at the gates of the noble estate. The lord could not punish a subject for a criminal offence and a civil case tried in his manorial court could be appealed to royal justice.[2] So much did peasants make use of this right that, in the year after Frederick's death, the new king complained about their 'unbridled passion for litigation'.[3] A detailed study of the Stavenow estate east of the river Elbe, owned by a member of the von Kleist clan, showed that the peasants made full use of their legal rights in their long-running dispute with their lord, eventually settled by 'an embittered compromise'. It was the improved access to the royal courts introduced by Frederick's legal reforms which had enabled the Stavenow villagers to mount their judicial campaign. They trusted the courts to give them a fair verdict and resisted if they were not satisfied.[4]

Yet, if Frederick qualified for acclamation as the 'Peasant King', he gave even more reason for the alternative sobriquet of 'Junker King'. He lived so long, and wrote so much, that his *œuvre* can be mined for gold as well as lead. In his *Political Testament* of 1752, not written for the public, he made it quite clear which social group he put first: 'a sovereign should regard it as his duty to protect the nobility, which forms the finest jewel in his crown and the lustre of his army'.[5] His father had done his best to expand the royal domains at the expense of his nobles, buying and repossessing land. Frederick put an immediate stop to that, telling the General Directory:

> The officials shall be forbidden on pain of death to harass the nobility and to resurrect old claims against them. All a noble landowner has to do is to prove that he was actually in possession of a piece of land before 1740. And if any disputes arise between noble landowners and officials of the royal domains, then not only shall the General Directory make sure that justice is done, but it shall also make sure that it is I rather than the nobles who suffers any injustice. For what for me is a small loss can be a great gain for the nobles, whose sons it is who defend this country and whose quality is such that they deserve to be protected in every way.[6]

When Prince Leopold of Anhalt-Dessau boasted of the amount of land he had acquired from his nobles in his own principality, Frederick tartly replied that was why it was overrun by Jews and beggars.[7] Frederick might have argued that he himself was able to distinguish between the actions of individual nobles and the interests of the nobility as a class. He provided a fine example in October 1750 when he told Cocceji that the prison sentence of six years imposed on Countess Gessner for cruelly mistreating her servants was inadequate, less than a commoner might have received and must be increased. Yet two months later he told his chancellor that he had noted with displeasure that landed estates belonging to old noble families were being bought up by commoners and that action must be taken to prevent it in future.[8] It was an aspiration often expressed but rarely fulfilled, as its repetition demonstrated. Shortly before his death he was still fulminating against the haemorrhage of noble property.[9] He was very keen to promote entails, to guard noble estates against being squandered by a spendthrift heir. It was one of the few aspects of the Habsburg Monarchy he thought worth copying.[10] As the number of wealthy commoners increased rapidly during the second half of the century, so market forces burst open Frederick's protective carapace. By 1800, commoners had purchased 745 noble estates, to which must be added those bought by the recently ennobled and the noble men of straw buying on behalf of their social inferiors but material superiors. By that time, almost 20 per cent of 'noble' estates were in non-noble hands.[11] On the other hand, he could not save unlucky or untalented nobles from drifting down into commoner occupations such as postmaster or apothecary.[12]

Warding off the bourgeoisie proved beyond Frederick's power. Easier to control was access to the officer corps, the bedrock of the state as he saw it. In 1757 a senior official asked Frederick to ennoble his son, who had enlisted in the von Thadden regiment, had shown such promise that he had been commissioned as a lieutenant, but had then been transferred to a low-status garrison regiment because he was a commoner. Frederick wrote on the petition in his own hand: 'I will not tolerate non-noble vermin in the officer corps, it ought to be enough that his son can be an officer in a garrison regiment.'[13] The horrendous casualties of the Seven Years War then forced him to commission 'vermin', but he soon had them purged when peace came, on the grounds that 'most of them are small-minded and make bad officers'.[14] Although all nobles had to start at the bottom, when not on duty they were forbidden to consort with commoners.[15] In 1786, of the 711 officers of the rank of major and above, only twenty-two were not noble.[16] This apparently almost total predominance is more than a little misleading, however. Although impossible to quantify, a significant number of those bearing the prefix 'von' were not of noble origin at all but had surreptitiously added it to their surnames in the hope that usage would eventually convey legitimacy. It often did. Among others to have inveigled their way upwards were some of the most famous names in Prussian history: Humboldt, Clausewitz, Yorck and Gneisenau.[17] On the other hand, distinguished military service could lead to ennoblement as well as promotion. As we have seen, the most spectacular example was David Krauel, who became David Krauel von Ziskaberg after leading the assault on Prague in 1744, but there were plenty more. Many generals in the less fashionable hussar and artillery regiments were commoners by birth.[18]

As this suggests, Frederick's prejudice was less that of the aristocrat against the *nouveaux riches* than of the military man against the pen-pushers. In the margin of a request from a long-serving civilian official he scribbled: 'one cannot earn nobility by the pen, only by the sword'. When the self-styled Major von Holtzendorff asked for his noble status to be 'renewed', Frederick replied testily that he never had been a noble in the first place but that, because his father had been a regimental surgeon and a good officer, his request would be granted.[19] Service not birth was the key to unlocking Frederick's favour, as he told his Minister for Silesia, Ernst von Schlabrendorff:

> Let me make it plain once and for all that I will not sell titles and still less noble estates for money, to the debasement of the nobility. Noble status can only be gained by the sword, by bravery and by other outstanding behaviour and services. I will tolerate as vassals only those who are at all times capable of rendering me useful service in the army, and those who because of exceptionally good conduct and exceptional service I choose to raise into the estate of the nobility.[20]

So he had only a low opinion of nobles who believed that the length of their pedigree exempted them from service of the state. *Grafen* (counts) were a special *bête noire*, although there were relatively few in Prussia. The great majority of Prussian nobles were untitled, that is to say they simply added 'von' ('of') to their surnames, although a number enjoyed the title of *Freiherr* (baron). In Frederick's view 'the counts of no account' served only long enough to acquire a little martial glamour and then resigned.[21] When Count von der Schulenburg asked for a promotion for his son simply because he was a count, Frederick replied that he had a standing order in place that no more counts were even to be admitted to the officer corps.[22]

What Frederick wanted was a nobility dependent on military service for their livelihood. Fortunately, very few nobles in any of the Prussian territories owned estates big enough to allow an independent existence. Most estates were only 1,000–1,500 acres. In East Prussia, where unusually there were a few rich magnates, the average size of 420 noble estates was 667.5 acres.[23] As all sons inherited noble status, there were around three times as many young nobles as there were estates.[24] In the Kurmark province only 17 per cent of the nobles were directly and permanently associated with their estates.[25] So most went into the army, where they were given a good education in the cadet schools, social prestige and the prospect of a good income, eventually.* In 1752 one noble, von Bonin, told Frederick proudly that he had seven sons already serving in the army and another ready to join when he was old enough.[26] They all began right at the bottom, with three months of basic training as a common soldier, which only those with previous military experience were allowed to skip. This was followed by at least three years as an NCO with the rank of corporal or ensign. So when Charles von Lindenberg asked Frederick to admit his son to the Prussian army with the rank of lieutenant, he was told: 'it doesn't work like that here. Everyone must start at the bottom as a corporal before becoming a cadet.'[27]

As we have seen, Frederick William I combined stick and carrot to drive underemployed Junkers into the ever-expanding officer corps.† This was intensified under Frederick. During the course of his reign the number of officers increased by 77 per cent from 3,116 to 5,511.[28] Moreover, Frederick's insistence that officers of all ranks lead from the front and his bull-in-a-china-shop approach to battlefield tactics meant there were plenty of vacancies in wartime. Between 1740 and 1763 1,550 noble officers were killed, including sixty generals. The von Kleists lost twenty-three members, the Münchows fourteen, the Seydlitzes, Frankenbergs and Schenkendorffs eight each, the Winterfelds, Krosigks, Arnims, Bredows, Schulenburgs, Sydows and Puttkamers seven each, and so on.[29] When Frederick visited Pomerania after the Seven Years War he expressed surprise that no member of the von Wedel family had waited on him, only to be told: 'They were all killed in the wars, Your Majesty.'[30]

It can be speculated with confidence that the torrid times of the three Silesian wars formed a close bond between the survivors and

* See above, p. 8.
† See above, p. 8.

their warlord. They had gone through hell together, had faced apparently impossible odds but had triumphed. Although the tenor of Friedrich Meinecke's observation of 1906 may seem dated, the essence is shrewd:

> Of all elements in Prussian society, the nobility became the first to enter into a true relationship with the new concept of the state, a relationship based on conviction, not mere passive obedience, and one that forcefully expressed genuine beliefs. From a merely social and politically self-serving elite, the nobility became something akin to a national class. To use Frederick's own words, it was being infused not only with *esprit de corps* but with an *esprit de nation*. Its narrow provincial pride melted on the battlegrounds of Frederick's wars. The bond between nobility and the crown grew to be so strong that it survived all changes.[31]

The phrase '*Esprit de Corps et de Nation*' appeared in Frederick's *Political Testament* of 1752 when he wrote that he had tried to encourage his nobles to think of themselves as Prussians no matter what province they came from.[32] It was the third and final Silesian war that turned this aspiration into reality. This was two-way traffic. Frederick's emotional attachment to his noble officers mounted with every sacrifice they made. It was both instinctive and considered. He had read Montesquieu's *The Spirit of the Laws* and knew that at the heart of monarchy was honour, the virtue he found only in the nobility. When explaining why he purged the officer corps of commoners after 1763, he wrote in *Memoirs from the Peace of Hubertusburg to the Partition of Poland*:

> It is more necessary than is imagined to pay such attention to the choice of officers; because, in general, the nobility are possessed of honour. Not but that it must be allowed merit and abilities are sometimes met with in persons of low birth; though such incidents are rare; and when men of this description are found they ought to be cherished. In general, however, the nobility have no means of obtaining distinction except by the sword; if they lose their honour they do not find refuge, not even in their paternal mansions. Whereas a man of mean birth, after having been guilty of mean actions, returns to the occupation of his father without blushing, or without supposing himself dishonoured.[33]

Honour, duty, service: these were the watchwords of the ethos Frederick sought to inculcate. The life that resulted for a Prussian noble was grim: early entry to the cadet school and its ferocious discipline, a long period of penury, and a career in which extreme danger alternated with extreme tedium. He was excluded from renting the very numerous estates belonging to the royal domain.[34] His personal freedom was also severely restricted. He could not travel abroad without permission, which was rarely given, and was barred from pursuing a career in business or commerce.[35] He also needed royal permission to marry, which was almost always delayed until he reached the rank of captain (of 463 officers of the Berlin garrison in 1752, only sixty-four were married).[36] On the positive side, Frederick intervened vigorously after the Seven Years War to rescue the numerous noble landowners afflicted by a combination of long-term market forces and the short-term disruption caused by the war and the economic crisis which ensued. Cash gifts, grants of seed and cattle; a moratorium on interest payments to creditors; and a halt to bankruptcy proceedings were some of the ways he tried to get them back on their feet.[37] Longer-term assistance came in the form of mortgage institutions which gave nobles easier access to loans by making the estate owners of an entire province guarantors of the credit of an individual. Predictably, this had the unintended consequence of making the land market even more volatile by encouraging speculation.[38] Intentionally on the debit side after 1763 was the centralization of the recruitment of non-Prussian soldiers, for this reduced appreciably the cash at the disposal of company commanders.[39]

Most important of all, at least in the eyes of the Junkers, was Frederick's reluctance to reform lord–peasant relations. In principle, Frederick the philosophe was utterly opposed to serfdom, but Frederick the sovereign knew that abolition would shake the social system until its teeth rattled. He issued the following pragmatic statement in his *Essay on the forms of government and the duties of sovereigns* of 1777:

In parts of most European countries there are peasants who are the serfs of their lords, bound to the soil; of all conditions, this is the most wretched and the one which the rest of mankind finds repellent. It is certain that no man was born to be the slave of a fellow human being; such an abuse is rightly detested and it is believed that all that is required to abolish it is to will it; but it is not like that, for it stems from ancient contracts made between the owners of the land and those who settled it. Agriculture has been organised on the basis of peasant services; in seeking to abolish all of a sudden this hateful arrangement, one would completely overturn the landed economy, and it would be necessary to indemnify the nobility for the loss of income they would suffer.[40]

Frederick was reasoning from bitter experience. Immediately after the Seven Years War he decreed that serfdom was to be abolished 'absolutely' in Pomerania on all land, whether royal, noble or municipal. If there were resistance from the lords, coercion was to be used.[41] In reply the Pomeranian Estates denied emphatically that the lord–peasant relationship could be described as 'serfdom'. On the contrary it was a benign, mutually beneficial contractual relationship, by which the peasants received property and security in return for appropriate services. Abolition could only be on the basis of compensation, which would be ruinously expensive for the peasants and bring social breakdown. Probably more convincing was their further argument that they and their sons would no longer be able to serve in the army if peasant services were removed.[42] Frederick backed down. He did not live long enough to see the Habsburg Monarchy brought to the very edge of destruction by Joseph II's attempt to enforce abolition, an episode he might well have observed with grim satisfaction.

Nowhere did the absolute monarch reach the limits of his authority so obviously as in his attempts to improve the social conditions of the peasants without harming the interests of the nobility on which he saw himself dependent.[43] The need to protect the most numerous class of his subjects against both their lords and his own officials was constantly repeated.[44] Yet the very repetition revealed the intractability of the problem. As we saw earlier, the latter were notorious for telling him what he wanted to hear,* so the rough edges of rural life were smoothed and planed out of their reports. In Silesia, where conditions

---

* See above, pp. 128–9.

were particularly grim, Ernst Wilhelm von Schlabrendorff's determined attempts to implement Frederick's wish to see the peasants
granted hereditary tenure aroused fierce opposition from the landowners. Calm returned when he died in 1769 and his successor, Carl
Georg Heinrich, Count von Hoym, reported that all peasants now
enjoyed the desired secure status. It was only in 1785 that a special
commission could report that this claim was a complete fiction. Hoym
pretended to be outraged at having been deceived for so many years
by the justices of the peace.[45] When asked by a traveller: who obeyed
the peasant protection edict displayed in an inn, the publican replied:
'Only the nail that holds it up!'[46]

The average Prussian peasant's lot was unhappy in 1740, and it was
still unhappy in 1786. Only in the western provinces and East Prussia
were significant numbers of them free. Elsewhere, obligations to lord
and state were manifold. Most onerous were dues in cash and kind,
together with the obligation to work on the domain for several days
per week. The lord's permission was required for marriage, education,
choice of profession and relocation. All civil law suits were adjudi-
cated in the first instance in the manorial courts. Fixed amounts of
grain at fixed prices had to be delivered annually to the royal granaries. For four months of the year cavalry horses were grazed on the
open fields, or 'cavalry money' had to be paid in lieu. Draught animals
were liable to be requisitioned for work on fortifications and the
transport of royal officials.[47] Worst affected of all, of course, were the
quarter of a million or so peasant-soldiers who died during the three
Silesian wars.[48] Beyond Frederick's control was the growing population pressure which brought a sharp increase in the number of landless
labourers in the second half of the century.[49]

Formally, the rural world did not change much during Frederick's
reign. The upheavals brought by the French Revolution, the defeats of
1806 and longer-term socio-economic developments would be needed
before it could be transformed. It would be misleading, however, to
paint too dark a picture. On the royal domains, which covered around
a third of the total land mass, peasant tenures were made more secure.
Everywhere the outright expropriation of peasants was restrained if
not eliminated.[50] That might not sound much, but it was a good deal
more than was achieved in neighbouring principalities such as

Mecklenburg, Holstein or Swedish Pomerania, not to mention Poland, where serfdom amounted to slavery.[51] It should also be remembered that unfavourable legal conditions did not necessarily translate into inferior material conditions, or indeed the reverse – as many 'free' Irish or Scottish peasants would have confirmed.[52] Moreover, the Prussian manorial system was 'a system of *mutual* rights and responsibilities' from which the peasants drew many benefits: 'the relationship for the most part worked well, and suited both parties'.[53]

EDUCATION

Culturally, the rural landscape changed little. Here too the gap between declared policy and actual implementation was a chasm. A 'general school regulation' issued in 1763 required parents to send their children from the age of five to school every day in winter and for two days a week in summer. They were to remain until they had learned the basics of Christianity, reading and writing, or at least until they were thirteen or fourteen. Landowners entitled to the domestic service of their peasants' children were not permitted to enlist them until this basic education was complete. The poor were to have their school fees paid from parish funds. There was to be a teacher in every parish, paid by the community and supervised by the ecclesiastical authorities.[54] Given that comparable legislation in the United Kingdom, for example, did not come until 1880, this looks like a project well in advance of its time. In fact, even on its own terms it was deeply conservative, being based mainly on Frederick William I's ordinance of 1717, itself little more than a codification of existing practice.[55] In accordance with Frederick's express wish, the curriculum was traditional, dominated by Pietist Christianity.[56] As he wrote to the minister in charge, Karl Abraham von Zedlitz, in 1779,

> It is absolutely right that the school-teachers in the country should teach religion and morals to the young people, so that they stay loyal to their religion and do not go over to Catholicism, for the Protestant religion is much better than the Catholic, and so the school-teachers

must make sure the people remain devoted to their religion and educate them in it to the point that they do not go stealing and murdering.[57]

A little learning was a good thing, because it helped social control, but too much was dangerous. As he also told von Zedlitz in the directive just mentioned:

> In the countryside it is quite enough if a little reading and writing is taught, because if they get to know too much, they run off to the towns and try to become clerks and the like; therefore in the countryside the children's curriculum must be organised so that they learn what is necessary for them, not what makes them want to leave the villages but what makes them happy to stay where they are.[58]

In the event, rural life ambled along untroubled by what the central authorities might be thinking. One of the most energetic of educational reformers, Johann Ignaz Felbiger, wrote just before he left Prussia to take up a senior post in the Habsburg Monarchy: 'it is almost inconceivable that such a great monarch's most emphatic orders, whose implementation has engaged a senior minister and two departments of state for the past five years, should have had the desired effect in so few places'.[59] Frederick himself complained in the *Political Testament* of 1768 that the rural schools were still 'very defective'.[60] In some places they did not exist at all: in 337 of the 1,997 villages in the Kurmark, for example.[61] A well-informed witness was the headmaster of the Greyfriars Grammar School at Berlin, the distinguished geographer Anton Friedrich Büsching. Anticipating critically Frederick's remark just quoted, he lamented that the education of the common people had been either neglected entirely or organized in a brutish manner, because it was believed that their occupations required no enlightened understanding, whereas too much insight might make them question the yoke they bore.[62] The schoolteachers, he complained, suffered from low status, low pay and inadequate housing, so no wonder so many of them were incompetent:

> It is with pity that I think of the great number of school-age children, of whom only a few attend state schools or are taught by competent tutors. Most get their instruction from debauched clerics or ordinands, from

soldiers or veterans, from artisans and old women, but they are not so much educated as deceived and misled; or they don't go to school at all.[63]

The excellent schools he came upon at Rekahn near Brandenburg, founded and financed by the enlightened noble landowner von Rochow, were flashes of light that served only to make the general darkness seem more opaque. His statistics showed that, of the 1,760 teachers in the Kurmark, only eighty-two were paid 100 talers or more per annum, 1,031 got less than forty talers and 163 nothing at all.[64] Büsching ended his exposé with the heartfelt cry: 'If only the great Frederick would devote time and money to schools!'[65]

AGRICULTURE

One aspect of rural life to which Frederick did devote a great deal of time and money was agriculture. In a letter to Voltaire of December 1775 he hailed it as 'the first of the arts, without which there would be no merchants, no courtiers, no kings, no philosophers. The only true wealth is that created by the soil. To improve the quality of the soil, to clear waste land, to drain the marshes, is to score a victory over barbarism.'[66] His correspondence and directives make clear that he had a good knowledge of the agricultural improvements introduced to England and the Low Countries and he sent numerous Prussian farmers off to study them at first hand.[67] He commended all their techniques to his officials and landowners: convertible husbandry, rotations that reduced or even eliminated fallow, stall-feeding, artificial pastures, the growing of root crops on the fallow, the use of seed drills, market gardening, selective breeding, and so on.[68] Practical assistance was given by the distribution of seed, the import of merino rams from Spain and bulls from Holstein, and the award of prizes and subsidies to the enterprising.[69]

One special concern, almost an obsession, was the promotion of the potato as a field crop, still remembered today by the tubers placed by admirers on his grave at Sanssouci.[70] This was eminently sensible, for the potato was European agriculture's most powerful weapon in breaking the age-old overdependence on grain as the staple crop. It has been estimated that in the eighteenth century the yield of the potato per acre was 10.5 times higher than wheat and 9.6 times higher than rye, which more than compensated for its lower calorific value. To put that statistic another way, the net calorific value of the potato is 3.6 times that of grain.[71] It has been estimated that ten square metres of land would produce 500 kilocalories in meat, 2,000 in cereals, 6,300 in cabbage and 7,200 in potatoes.[72]

Knowing what to do was one thing. Getting the cultivators to do it was quite another. As Voltaire wrote: 'many useful publications are written about agriculture and everyone reads them, with the exception of the peasants'.[73] Instinctively hostile to any change, especially resistant to anything that might reduce the acreage available for cereals and deterred by the unpleasant appearance and texture of the only varieties of potato available, the peasants considered the new crop fit only for their livestock. As Frederick sighed in exasperation: 'custom, empress of the earth, reigns with imperious despotism over the narrow-minded'.[74] Unfortunately for him, Prussian agriculture was still organized on a communal basis. The village community formed a legal corporation, with the power to sue innovators.[75] So the crucial ingredient for any rise in productivity – individualism – was missing and the convoy could only move at the pace of its slowest member.[76] Fortunately for Frederick, however, his royal domains were under his direct control, although even there the tenants had to be convinced rather than coerced. Here he undoubtedly enjoyed some success. In the Kurmark, potato production increased from 5,200 (metric) tons in 1765 to 19,000 in 1779 (and 103,000 by the end of the century).[77] In 1776 the royal tenant of the Rügenwalde estate in Pomerania wrote that 'encouragement for the cultivation of potatoes is unnecessary, because on this estate in particular it has been pushed as far as it can go, not only in the field but also in the village gardens, the local people having been convinced of their advantages by the [grain] harvest failures [of 1771–2]'.[78] If the potato was not yet a common field-crop by Frederick's death, it was well on the way to becoming such.[79]

As well as seeking to increase the fertility of the existing agricultural land, Frederick also pursued a sustained and vigorous campaign to increase the acreage available through land reclamation. This was one facet of the foundation of his domestic policy, namely the expansion of population: 'new subjects [are] the true wealth of princes' (*Political Testament* of 1752) and 'the first, most general and the truest principle is that the true strength of a state lies in a high population' (*Political Testament* of 1768).[80] Especially in the thinly populated lands of Central and Eastern Europe, devastated repeatedly in the seventeenth century by war, plague and famine, 'population policy' was at the top of every regime's agenda. It was underpinned by the belief that the population of the world had been declining since classical times and would go on declining, so the attraction of immigrants was a zero-sum game. It was personified by Count Georg Friedrich von Castell, who stood in the road outside his castle at Rüdenhausen in Franconia, pleading with passers-by to settle in his depopulated territory.[81]

Land reclamation is one of the very few aspects of Frederick's domestic policy to have attracted uniformly positive accounts from historians. The draining of the marshlands along the Oder, Warthe, Netze and later Vistula rivers, initially supervised by a Dutch expert, began in 1747.[82] The Oder Wetlands comprised an enormous area fifty kilometres long and up to sixteen wide, through which the eponymous river wandered via many different channels, flooding twice a year and altering course almost as often. A paradise for birds, fish and amphibious mammals, it also swarmed with the mosquitoes that made malaria endemic. Tamed and confined within a single channel, its floodplains could be drained and turned into the most fertile arable land in Prussia, 'the market garden of Berlin', at the expense of much of the flora and fauna and most of the fishermen.[83] Although estimates of the acreage reclaimed vary considerably, even the lowest are substantial.[84] If the figure provided by Günther Franz of 400,000 hectares (*c.* 1 million acres) is correct, then Frederick was justified in claiming that he had 'conquered a province in peace-time'.[85] Moreover, the combination of highly fertile alluvial soil and the immediate proximity of water transport encouraged the growing of high-yielding commercial crops.

To populate these and other empty spaces, Frederick made every effort to attract immigrants. He was not fussy about where they came from: 'if Turks and heathens came here and wished to populate the land, we would build mosques and places of worship for them'.* In

---

* See above, p. 370.

the event, most came from adjoining principalities – Bohemia, Saxony, Mecklenburg, Anhalt, Brunswick – and the German-speaking parts of Poland, although the lure of free land brought them from as far afield as Switzerland and the Palatinate. Prussian consulates became in effect recruiting offices, publicizing Frederick's enticing manifestos, advancing money for the journey and organizing itineraries. Transit camps were set up at Hamburg and Frankfurt am Main.[86] Especially for those peasants and artisans suffering religious discrimination (a special problem in the Palatinate where the Elector had converted to Catholicism) or land shortage (a common problem in the overpopulated west of Germany), the prospect of land, settlement grants, free seed, livestock and equipment, personal freedom and exemption from military service was sufficiently alluring to compensate for the uncertainty and discomfort of the journey.[87] They brought with them not only their all-important labour, but also financial and cultural capital and substantial numbers of livestock. According to one suspiciously precise set of statistics, these amounted to 6,392 horses, 7,875 cattle, 20,548 sheep and 3,227 pigs.[88] All in all, around a quarter of a million immigrants entered Prussia during the course of Frederick's reign.[89] Not all of them made a positive contribution. According to von Dohm, some were unprepared for the rigours of rural life in the Prussian climate and turned to begging in towns.[90] Frederick claimed, at least, that he did not mind: it was only the second generation that would bring a return on his investment.[91]

TRADE AND MANUFACTURING

Agriculture was the bedrock of the Prussian economy, employing around 80 per cent of the population, but Frederick knew that, when it came to ready money, trade and manufacturing could be tapped more easily. He also appreciated that Prussia's peculiar geography put a premium on communications. We have already seen how the rivers Elbe and Oder assisted his military operations.* They were equally important for the economy, but needed a helping hand to add lateral

* See above, p. 262.

connections to their vertical flows from south-east to north-west. Before 1740, the Elbe trade had been dominated by Hamburg, the Oder trade by Saxony and Breslau.[92] Not the least important benefit of the conquest of Silesia was that the whole length of the Oder was now in Prussian hands. At once Frederick set about creating a new network of waterways that would give him control of the whole Elbe-Oder region. With remarkable speed, in 1743-5 a new canal was dug between Parey on the Elbe and Plauen on the Havel. Thirty-two kilometres long and with three locks to handle the five-metre west–east drop, it cut in half the travelling distance from Berlin to Magdeburg.[93] At the same time, the Finow Canal, which had fallen into disuse a century earlier, was reconstructed. Also thirty-two kilometres long, it needed seventeen locks for the higher fall. Together these two canals allowed ships from Breslau to travel to the North Sea and vessels from Hamburg to reach the Baltic through Prussian territory. Lying at the centre of the network was Berlin, which benefited accordingly.[94] A third major project was the Bromberg Canal, built after the acquisition of West Prussia in 1772 to link the Vistula to the Oder. By any standard, Frederick's canal-building programme was a massive feat of civil engineering, and a tangible sign of what determined government action could accomplish.[95] Of the thousand-odd kilometres of artificial waterways in Germany in 1785, most (85 per cent) were in Prussia.[96] Contemporaries were impressed too. The completion of the Bromberg Canal in 1774 was greeted with a celebratory article in Christian Friedrich Daniel Schubart's *German Chronicle*, published in Augsburg:

> The newly opened canal in West Prussia, which from Bromberg connects the Vistula with the Netze, Warthe, Oder and Spree, and therefore also with the Havel, Elbe and North Sea, is one of the most remarkable achievements of the age. In no state in Germany has the ruler's foresight brought such advantage to domestic and foreign trade by means of navigation as Brandenburg.[97]

Schubart then added that travellers who knew only Prussia's roads also completely misjudged the extent of Prussia's trade. As this implies, the roads were notoriously primitive.[98] In 1786 there was not one single properly constructed highway comparable to a *route royale* in

France or a turnpike in England.[99] It was reported that Frederick took the view that the longer travellers had to remain inside his dominions, the more money they would spend. If so, it does not seem to have occurred to him that they might choose not to come in the first place.[100] One who did persevere was Voltaire, who reported on his arrival that he had been through purgatory to get there.[101] Travelling north from Berlin in 1779, Anton Friedrich Büsching found that as soon as they passed through the Oranienburg Gate they came on to a road so sandy that only slow progress could be made. He also recorded a fine example of unintended consequences: to improve the roads around the capital, it had been decreed that all peasants travelling there had to bring with them two cobbles, to be deposited at the city gate. Reluctant to burden themselves with the additional weight during their journey, they waited until they were just outside the city before picking up the required cobbles. The result was predictable: the roads around Berlin were denuded of stones.[102]

Once the traveller had struggled through mud or sand to his destination, his problems were only just beginning. The requirements of excise collection dictated an absolute separation between town and country and rigorous inspection of anyone coming from the latter to the former. So long and porous were Prussia's frontiers that excise could only be collected at city gates. Around Berlin that meant a six-metre-high wall.[103] It also meant interrogation both at the gate and in the hotel, as the Russian Nikolai Karamzin discovered: 'A sergeant came out of the sentry box and asked: "Who are you? Where have you come from? Why have you come to Berlin? Where will you live? Will you remain here long? Where will you go from Berlin?"'[104] The same questions were repeated on a form presented by his innkeeper, but this time the answers had to be recorded in writing. Native Prussians were treated just the same. When Büsching travelled to Rekahn near Brandenburg, he and his party preferred to make a lengthy detour around Potsdam to avoid having their belongings searched at the gates when arriving and leaving.[105]

This kind of treatment gave the regime an unappealing image. The need for control stemmed essentially from Frederick's determination to build up a war-chest. This was yet another trait inherited from his father. Frederick had been left 8 million talers in hard cash, which he had spent mainly on the seizure of Silesia. Every sinew was then strained to replace this treasure and to increase it, for Frederick agreed with Cicero that 'the sinews of war are infinite money'.[106] His ideas about how to do it were conservative. As we have seen, his father had done his level best to turn him into a military man and had eventually succeeded. Frederick had even spent some time on active service with the Austrian army of Prince Eugene.* But there had been no comparable instruction on how to run an economy. The director of the Küstrin War and Domains Chamber, Hille, reported that Frederick had shown no interest in economic matters while under his direction in 1731–2. He may have succeeded better than he knew, however, for Frederick turned out to share his mercantilist views.[107]

Essentially, mercantilists assumed that the European economy was a zero-sum game. In other words, they believed there was a fixed amount of wealth in the world and one state could improve its share only at the expense of its rivals. To pursue a mercantilist policy was the continuation of warfare by other means.[108] A favourable balance of trade was all-important. If more could be exported than imported, then a larger share of the world's treasure could be won. This was Frederick's version of what had been a trope of continental economists for a century and more:

> When a country has but few products to export, and is obliged to have recourse to the industry of its neighbours, the balance of trade must necessarily be unfavourable to such a country; it must pay more money to foreigners than it receives; and if the practice be continued, it will necessarily, after a certain number of years, find itself destitute of specie. If money be daily taken out of a purse into which money is not again returned, it must soon be emptied.[109]

His predecessors he criticized for not doing enough to prevent this haemorrhage of cash. When he came to the throne, he complained, Prussia was running an annual balance of trade deficit amounting to 1.2 million talers, all of which flowed out of the country and into the coffers of its rivals.[110] The solution was the promotion of manufacturing:

---

* See above, p. 79.

The exodus of money can best be prevented by producing in Prussia all kinds of goods which were formerly imported . . . Manufacture results in large quantities of money within the country . . . The ruler of Prussia must encourage manufacture and trade, whether through direct subsidies or through tax exemptions, so that they may be in a position for large scale production and trade.[111]

So, less than a month after coming to the throne, Frederick established a new department of the General Directory under Samuel von Marschall with instructions to improve manufacturing, introduce branches currently lacking and attract skilled immigrant workers. To demonstrate the importance he attached to it, he made Marschall a member of his newly created Order '*Pour le Mérite*'.[112]

Marschall was the first Minister of Trade and Industry, and also the last. When he died in 1749 he was not replaced and Frederick became his own minister. Under both men, most of the emphasis was on domestic industry. Free trade was promoted inside Prussia by the abolition of the rights of staple enjoyed by Stettin, Frankfurt an der Oder and Breslau but that was the limit of commercial liberalization. The right of staple of Magdeburg was actually restored in 1747 as a weapon in the continuous trade war waged against Saxony and Hamburg.[113] The only significant initiative to promote foreign trade was the foundation in 1751 of a Royal Prussian Asian Company at the newly acquired port of Emden in East Frisia for trade with China. Four ships managed six highly lucrative voyages to the East before the outbreak of war at sea between France and Great Britain in 1755 put an end to it.[114] There was to be no revival when peace returned in 1763 and the Fifth Department remained concerned mainly with industry.

Frederick inherited two major branches of manufacturing and added two more. The most traditional was woollens, for the good reason that it was in woollen uniforms that the ever-expanding Prussian army went about its business. At the *Lagerhaus* (Warehouse) established by Frederick William I at Berlin, 500 weavers used 240 looms to manufacture cloth from the yarn spun by 5,000 outworkers.[115] Although its best customer was of course the Prussian army, a significant amount of cloth was exported: enough to clothe the entire

Russian infantry in 1725, for example.[116] Although not formally a monopoly, the Warehouse was the dominant institution by virtue of its size and access to the state for capital. It also enjoyed vigorous protection. In 1740 all exports of unfinished wool were banned. Preventing its escape through the porous Prussian frontiers proved difficult, as the renewed prohibition in 1766 and 1774 showed. That the death penalty had to be threatened on the last occasion testified to the policy's failure.[117] More recent but just as traditional was the linen industry, mainly centred in Silesia. So lucrative was the Silesian linen export trade that Frederick claimed it was as valuable to Prussia as Peru was to Spain.[118] It was competitive because the state-supported serf–lord relations kept labour costs low, an advantage revealed by serious labour unrest in the 1780s.[119] The Silesian lords also held up technological innovation, so as to be able to extract as much as possible from their indentured labour force, and were helped in this by Frederick's intervention to prevent the importation of spinning machines.[120] Both of these textile branches expanded during the course of Frederick's reign, especially after recovery from the economic catastrophe inflicted by the Seven Years War. Two years after Frederick's death, Hertzberg claimed that the linen industry was worth 9 million talers a year and employed 80,000 people. The equivalent figures for wool were 8 million and 58,000.[121]

Frederick added silk to wool and linen. Strictly speaking, this was a revival rather than an innovation, for the planting of mulberry trees, on whose leaves the silkworms fed, had first been promoted in the previous century by Frederick William the Great Elector. By 1740 production had fallen to 200 *Pfund* (*c.* 93 kilograms). As silk was so much more expensive than other textiles, it was especially appealing to Frederick's mercantilist ambitions. He quickly set about promoting mulberry cultivation in every churchyard in his dominions, offering the clergy free saplings, instruction manuals and financial rewards for success. Happily, the mulberry trees flourished on Brandenburg's sandy soil.[122] In his *Political Testament* of 1752 he claimed that in ten years he had increased production ten times, with the result that silk to the value of 400,000 talers was being produced.[123] In 1775 he boasted to Voltaire that the total had now reached 10,000 *Pfund* (*c.* 4,650 kilograms).[124] That was a lot of silk and required a commensurate expansion in the number of looms to turn it into cloth. Once again Frederick was to the fore, subsidizing entrepreneurs and stepping in with grants or outright nationalization if they failed.[125] It has been estimated that he spent more than 2 million talers subsidizing the silk industry in the course of his reign.[126] There were certainly some successes to record. In Berlin the number of looms increased from 238 in 1748 to 802 in 1769.[127] There is plenty of visual evidence of Frederick's enthusiastic promotion of mulberry trees. Johann Friedrich Meyer's painting of the Wilhelmsplatz at Potsdam of 1773, for example, shows the square covered in mulberry trees, with more in the process of being planted.[128]

Entirely new in Prussia was Frederick's favourite manufacturing project: porcelain. This was an enthusiasm common to many crowned heads of Europe. Porcelain had the advantage of being expensive, beautiful and even practical. Today the collecting of paintings is the preferred means of demonstrating great wealth and good taste, but in the eighteenth century it was porcelain that commanded the highest prices and the most prestige.[129] Between 1747 and 1761 no fewer than six German princes founded porcelain manufactories.[130] They were trying to repeat the success of their colleague in Saxony, where the discovery in 1708 of how to make porcelain, a secret jealously guarded hitherto by the Chinese, had led to the rapid expansion of its manufacture at Meissen near Dresden. In a characteristic demonstration of his priorities, Frederick William I had given 150 large pieces of Chinese porcelain to Augustus the Strong in exchange for 600 Saxon dragoons.[131] As part of his eventful visit to Dresden in 1728,* Frederick acquired a taste for the local product and started to form a collection. His first plans for his own manufactory date from 1737, when he was still crown prince.[132] The capture of the Saxon capital in the Second Silesian War allowed Frederick to add to his collection spectacularly. Fifty-two crates of best Meissen porcelain were despatched to Berlin.[133] The best pieces he kept for himself, the rest were given to Fredersdorf to be sold for whatever he could get.[134] Despite this windfall, the manufacturing secret could not be sent off with them. So Frederick responded with enthusiasm when the wool mer-

* See above, pp. 34–5.

chant Wilhelm Caspar Wegely claimed to be able to produce porcelain that would be just as good as, but cheaper than, Meissen. Regular production began in 1754 with craftsmen recruited mainly from the factory of the Elector of Mainz at Höchst.[135] The high quality of the surviving items shows that Wegely was as good as his word. Unfortunately, the outbreak of war in 1756 not only disrupted the market in general but ironically caused special problems for a Prussian manufacturer. Frederick's capture of Dresden in August 1756 brought him huge stocks of Meissen porcelain and also the opportunity to lease the manufacturing rights for a large sum.[136] Although not yet ruined, Wegely could read the writing on the wall and went back to making woollens. His abandoned business continued on a very much smaller scale under the direction of his chief modeller.

Frederick knew he would have to leave Saxony sooner or later, so he sought to revive his own full-scale manufacturing enterprise to avoid having to import expensive Meissen products. In 1761 he persuaded Johann Ernst Gotzkowsky, a wealthy Berlin silk merchant, who also dealt in luxury goods and paintings, to take it on. Production began at the end 1762, quickly achieved outstanding results but within less than a year threatened to stop when Gotzkowsky fell victim to the financial crisis that afflicted many parts of northern Europe and became insolvent.[137] As Frederick's debasement of the coinage and currency manipulation had been major contributions to the crisis, it was only fitting that he should take over the business himself, paying Gotzkowsky 225,000 talers.[138] On this new acquisition he now lavished attention, injecting a further capital sum of 140,000 talers.[139] The domestic market was reserved by a monopoly of production and a ban on foreign imports, not only of porcelain but also of any other ceramics, such as Wedgwood earthenware, that might provide competition.[140] The deposits of kaolin discovered near Halle and in Silesia were promptly reserved for the Berlin factory's exclusive use.[141] Only felling and delivery costs were charged for the other vital raw material, firewood.[142] Given his concern to micromanage every other aspect of his state, it will come as no surprise to learn that Frederick was very much an activist proprietor, combining the roles of chairman of the board and chief executive officer. Although he could not always be there in person, he insisted on being sent monthly accounts and often visited the factory in what is now the Leipzigerstrasse.[143] His correspondence suggests that an important part of his enthusiasm was a familiar wish to outdo the detested Saxons. One of the first artefacts to be made in his factory inspired the comment: 'my porcelain factory is much better than the one at Meissen. We are already making much more beautiful objects than Meissen has even thought about.'[144] In the Neues Palais he put on display porcelain chandeliers and mirrors in close proximity to Meissen products to demonstrate the superiority of the former.

Although Frederick always insisted that it be run as a commercial business, producing what the customers wanted, promptly and at a competitive price, in reality he was his own best customer, accounting for around a quarter of all sales during the first decade.[145] By 1786 more than twenty complete seventy-two-piece dinner services had been made for his various palaces at a cost of 5,000–7,000 talers each.[146] Similar sets were presented to foreign potentates, to the Turkish envoy Ahmed Reis Effendi in 1764, for example.[147] The most elaborate of all was created for Catherine the Great in 1770–72 with an iconographical scheme devised by Frederick himself. Sitting on a throne under a baldacchino, surrounded by allegorical figures personifying her numerous virtues, the tsarina receives the homage of the various national groups of the Russian Empire.[148]

Before its despatch to St Petersburg, it created a sensation in Berlin when put on public display.[149] Another flattering set, this time for Catherine's son, the Grand Duke Paul, was decorated with scenes of Russian triumphs against the Turks, including the great naval victory at Chesme.[150] Unlike some other entrepreneurs who liked the product so much that they bought the company, Frederick had the resources to keep it afloat even in the turbulent times following the Seven Years War. He also had the power to force potential customers to buy the products. As we have seen, Jews were obliged to buy a fixed amount of porcelain for export whenever they were granted a concession or got married.* Their compulsory purchases amounted to 25 per cent

---

* See above, pp. 383–5. Ironically, ownership of a porcelain monkey became especially prized among American Jews as a badge of old Berlin lineage – private communication from Prof. Jonathan Steinberg.

of turnover in 1779.[151] Later in the reign, the lessees of the lottery were made to do the same at a rate of 6,000 talers worth per annum, rising to 9,600 talers in 1783.[152]

Berlin porcelain with its distinctive mark of the electoral sceptre was undoubtedly a hot-house flower. But it survived, indeed has survived until the present day. This was due not just to the friendly conditions created by the owner but also to its quality. Rococo porcelain ornaments, vases and tableware are not to everyone's taste, but only the most resolute of modernists can fail to appreciate their delicate sophistication. In the authoritative view of one expert, Berlin porcelain soon came to outrank Meissen, by attracting superior modellers, painters and craftsmen.[153] The accounts certainly show a success story, with annual turnover increasing from some 12,000 talers in the first year, 1763–4, to 94,500 talers in 1771–2, and the labour force expanding from 146 in 1763 to 354 in the same period. After a brief crisis in 1778 resulting from the War of the Bavarian Succession, turnover went up to 124,000 in 1779–80.[154] Other figures give a total profit of 464,050 talers for the period 1763–86 and a workforce of 500 in 1786.[155] Between 1763 and the end of the reign, Frederick spent more than 2 million talers on porcelain.[156]

The question of course is: was this manufacturing success because of, or in spite of, Frederick's mercantilist policies? No conclusive answer is possible. He could have argued that Prussia was not England and that, where capital and entrepreneurs were lacking, the state had to step in. Without his exertions, there would have been no porcelain industry and at least a much smaller silk industry. Yet, as we have seen, a private entrepreneur such as Johann Georg Wegely was able to build up a woollen manufacturing business even bigger than the state-run *Lagerhaus* without any assistance.[157] In Krefeld in the west, the textile concern run by two Mennonite brothers, Friedrich and Heinrich von der Leyen, developed into one of the largest in Germany, employing over 3,000 people (not counting the numerous children who often worked looms part-time). They informed a government commission sent from Berlin to promote the local economy that they had learned all they needed to know from the Dutch, whom they had first imitated and then surpassed.[158] More generally, the cotton-manufacturing sector, which expanded rapidly after 1763, owed

17. Antinous, renamed 'The Praying Boy' after Frederick's death. This is the original, now in the Altes Museum, Berlin.

18. A copy of Antinous. Removed swiftly after Frederick's death, it is back in its original position at Sanssouci, looking towards the window of Frederick's study.

19. Part of the table service manufactured by the Royal Porcelain Factory and presented by Frederick to Catherine the Great of Russia in 1772.

20. Potsdam, Sanssouci Park, the Temple of Friendship, dedicated to Frederick's sister Wilhelmine and adorned with medallions depicting male lovers of antiquity.

21. *Ganymede is Inducted into Olympus,* the ceiling fresco of the Marble Hall in the New Palace at Potsdam, by Charles Vanloo.

22. 'Dispatch of Dr Aprill when he notified the Prussian ambassador Baron von Plotho of the Imperial declaration of outlawry'. Plotho's servants can been seen waiting outside the door. In the alcove to the right, Frederick's bust raises his hat in a gesture of applause.

23. (*above*) *Allegory on the Foundation of the League of Princes by Frederick the Great*, b Bernhard Rode (1786). Assisted l Germania (or perhaps Herman's wife, Thusnelda), the victorious Frederick uses the olive branches handed to him by the lady in white, symbolizing political wisdom, to bind the individual spears of the German princes to form an unbreakable fasces and thus maintain the peace. From the right, a horn of plenty is carried in by the spirit of harmon as, below, the swords are forged into ploughshares.

24. (*left*) Vivat ribbons, a cheap and popular way of celebrating Frederick's victories.

25. (*left*) Frederick portrayed by Heinrich Franke (1764). Doffing his hat to his subjects as he rode past them became one of Frederick's most famous and popular gestures.

26. (*below*) 'Frederick the Victorious at Rossbach on 5 November 1757. The battle was almost won, and Frederick was looking down on its completion from the battery on the Janus hill. An adjutant from his retinue with a telescope and posted near him reported on what happened during the engagement. The French army was attacked by Prussian cavalry in its flank and rear and it was this which decided the victory, which is being announced by two guardsmen riding up with a captured French flag'.

27. Equestrian statue of Frederick the Great, by Christian Daniel Rauch. After his death the debate over what sort of memorial should be constructed was long and fierce. Not until 1851 was it unveiled, in the middle of Unter den Linden. Frederick is riding east.

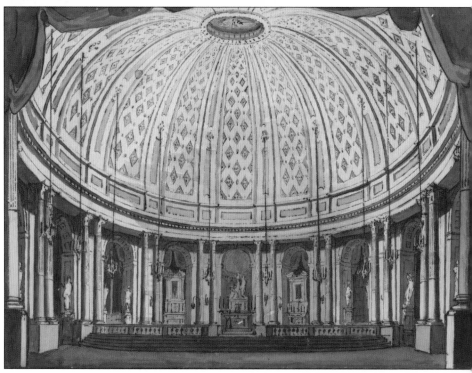

28. The interior of the Roman Catholic cathedral in Berlin, dedicated to the Silesian Saint Hedwig. An architectural expression of Frederick's insistence on the need for religious toleration, it was completed in 1773.

29. *The scales of Frederick*, by Vincenzo Vangelisti (1780), depicting Frederick's intervention in the judicial process on behalf of Miller Arnold. A despotic act it may have been, but it was a public relations coup for Frederick with most of his subjects.

30. A reconstruction of the pisang house at Sanssouci. Frederick liked his exotic fruit and spent very large sums to ensure a regular supply in and out of season.

31. The dying Frederick takes the air on the terrace of Sanssouci, as his two Italian greyhounds gambol around him.

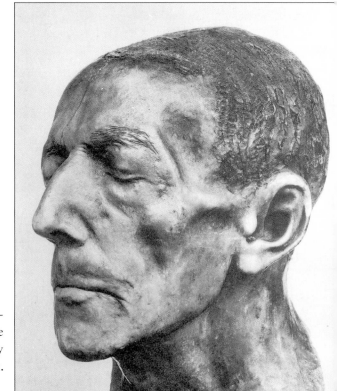

32. Frederick's death-mask, taken on the day of his death by Johann Eckstein.

nothing to the government, which preferred woollens.[159] Not a single industrial region developed in the central and eastern provinces of Prussia before 1800 and the only success story – cotton – was the one branch almost wholly neglected by the state.[160] The tension between state and *laissez-faire* capitalism was revealed in 1779 when a delegation of Berlin entrepreneurs went to the General Directory to complain about recent government interference.[161]

Within the Prussian business community there was sharp disagreement about protectionism. Most manufacturers seem to have felt comfortable sheltering behind the tariff wall which kept out predatory English or Dutch competitors. It was the merchants and those engaged in newer branches such as cotton who wanted to see liberalization.[162] There was also a geographical division, with the entrepreneurs of the far west in Cleves and the far east in Königsberg most eager to do business with the Low Countries and Poland respectively.[163] All could agree that Frederick's actions at the end of the Seven Years War had been disastrous. Inevitably, the aftermath of every major war has been difficult for both victors and vanquished. In the case of Prussia, it was made worse by Frederick's ruthless monetary manipulation to finance his war effort. The sudden revaluation of the coinage, following the debasement of the war years, brought turmoil to all and ruin to many. Gotzkowsky was only one of a host of casualties: a Berlin baker recorded that his savings of 2,293 talers had shrunk overnight to 908.[164] It was also after 1763 that Frederick launched an ambitious plan to reshape the Prussian economy from the top down. Drafted by Antonio di Calzabigi, a financier originally brought from Livorno to run the lottery, the plan called for a central bank operating in association with a network of trading monopolies and an insurance company. Together they were supposed to form a giant trust to run the economy.[165]

It turned out to be a flop. Despite heavy pressure from above, the Berlin businessmen refused to invest in the bank. When eventually founded, in 1765, it was entirely dependent on state support. Of the projected companies, only those for tobacco, timber and firewood could be realized, along with a herring company at Emden in East Frisia.[166] Indicative of the lack of confidence was the failure to place more than 822 of the 4,000 shares in the Levant Company on offer in

May 1765.[167] It was now that Frederick ordered the inquiry which led to the senior financial official Erhard Ursinus being packed off to Spandau for reporting critically on Frederick's policies.* Matters were made worse by the simultaneous trade war with Saxony and the Habsburg Monarchy. In a region in which each state was as protectionist as the next, it is impossible to determine who started it, for it had always been like that. Equally clearly, there could only be losers: the merchants who were hassled by customs officials at every frontier they crossed, the manufacturers who could not get access to international markets, the consumers who had to pay inflated prices, even the governments whose gains in rates were more than eroded by losses in volume. Yet it has to be said that Frederick took self-harm to a new level when he imposed import dues on goods coming from his own provinces in the west, because he suspected that in reality they were sourced from France and the Low Countries.[168]

If there was one thing Frederick really detested, it was what he called 'the alleged transit trade'. He added 'alleged' because he believed that it was a cover for smuggling goods into Prussia and escaping the excise.[169] So he imposed transit dues so heavy that foreign goods had to be taken round Prussian territory, which proved especially burdensome once Silesia had been conquered.[170] The tariffs he imposed on the Vistula following the first partition of Poland in 1772 achieved modest gains for the Prussian port of Bromberg but at a cost of wrecking the economy of the Polish city of Danzig.[171] Writing in 1792, the distinguished Hamburg economist and statistician Johann Georg Büsch hailed Frederick as great in everything – except anything to do with the commerce between states, adding: 'he hated the transit trade which went through his states and impeded it on every route he had under his control. Unfortunately for his contemporaries, he was, or made himself, master of five of the greatest rivers in the centre of Europe and thus the main means of communication.'[172]

The years after 1763 were gloomy. In the Rhineland, in June 1766, Count Lehndorff recorded in his diary that everyone was outraged at the new customs dues imposed by Frederick on his western territories, predicting that they would lead to the cessation of trade on the river.[173]

---

* See above, pp. 130–31.

Back in Berlin in the autumn he found that there was a dire shortage of ready money and serious deflation. Even those rich in assets were cash poor, unable to raise even 1,000 talers, so precious objects which might have fetched 20,000 talers in the recent past could now be had for 7,000. All classes were complaining bitterly, blaming the new commercial regulations and the bank.[174] Lehndorff was admittedly highly excitable, but he was usually a fervent admirer of Frederick. His indictment was repeated elsewhere, by another enthusiast, Friedrich Nicolai.[175]

A special bone of contention was the *Régie* (or General Administration of Excise and Customs to give its full official title), the new body set up in 1766 to collect indirect taxation.[176] As usual, Frederick was a man in a hurry. By his own account, he knew how close had been his scrape in the Seven Years War and was desperate to rebuild his finances to repair and reinforce his army. At least he understood enough about fiscal policy to realize it was indirect taxation, rather than the inelastic direct taxes on land, that would help him most. He was deeply discontented with the existing personnel. The competent officials had all died, he complained, and the survivors could not even tell him how much coffee was consumed in Prussia.[177] To counter the embezzlement, smuggling and extortion that were rife, a new broom was needed. To wield it, he recruited a team of French experts under the direction of Marc Antoine de la Haye de Launay to supervise Prussian officials.[178] By taking collection away from the existing local authorities and centralizing and standardizing procedures, Frederick counted on a significant increase in revenue.[179] To sweeten the pill and ease it down throats accustomed to cheap comestibles, Frederick ordered that the heaviest weight should fall on the well-to-do. Excise duties on wine, beer, spirits and beef were increased, but the pork favoured by the poor was left unchanged and grain was exempted altogether. This latter concession meant little in practice because the bread tax was simultaneously raised.[180]

The *Régie* was a failure.[181] Revenue grew, but so did the costs of collection, which mushroomed from 300,000 to 800,000 talers per annum.[182] Moreover, it simply cannot be known how much of the increase was due to greater efficiency and how much to the natural recovery of economic activity as the crisis of the 1760s receded. In

1783 the senior minister Friedrich Anton von Heinitz denounced the *Régie* in a lengthy memorandum which he presented to the king despite the latter's well-known support for the organization. In fact, Frederick was in a receptive mood. On 25 May 1781 he had written to de Launay, following the apprehension of a French official called Rougemont for embezzlement: 'you will replace this employee with a trustworthy German, and not with one of these Frenchmen who are professional vagabonds and may well be on the run from their own country'. A year later he added: 'your fellow-countrymen are not worth four horseshoes; they are rascals who steal everything they can lay their hands on, but never do anything to stop smuggling'. He returned to the charge on several other occasions.[183] Heinitz accused the *Régie* officials of obstructing trade, especially between Silesia and Poland, of paying themselves far too much and harassing merchants and manufacturers. Five days after receiving this memorandum, Frederick told de Launay not to employ any more Frenchmen, for they were all 'villains' intent only on extorting as much money as possible before fleeing with their ill-gotten gains.[184]

The *Régie* was even more unpopular among Frederick's subjects. It was felt to be expensive, extortionate, intrusive and foreign. The employment by the French directors of large numbers of ex-NCOs as inspectors served only to emphasize its authoritarian character. According to Heinrich von Beguelin, all classes were united in their hatred of, and opposition to, the new body: 'the citizen sighed, the wit mocked, the soldier cursed'. The peasants divided the officials into two categories: 'great French', who had the right to commandeer six horses to pull their wagons, and 'little French', who were restricted to just two or four.[185] 'Perhaps no idea of Frederick's proved to be so detrimental for his country [than the *Régie*], and the period of its introduction must be regarded as the most miserable of the entire reign,' wrote Christian Wilhelm von Dohm.[186] In 1773 the distinguished French officer Jacques-Antoine-Hippolyte, Comte de Guibert, visited Prussia and noted: 'This new administration [the *Régie*] is cursed – the country ruined, outraged – commerce obstructed, languishing – this French finance the reason for the excessive Francophobia.'[187] Of the domestic critics, the most distinguished was Johann Georg Hamann, 'the Magus of the North', who eked out a living as an excise clerk at Königsberg. His criticism of Frederick's economic policy was so extreme that after 1772 his publisher refused to print his books.[188] Some indication of the violent resistance aroused by the excise men was Frederick's directive of 1784 that the mandatory punishment for killing a member of the *Régie* would be public breaking on the wheel.[189]

As soon as Frederick died, his successor dismissed all French officials and replaced them with natives, although the system remained very much the same.[190] Elsewhere in the economy too, cosmetic changes were the order of the day. The shadow cast by the previous reign could not be dispelled until the shock of defeat in 1806 had cracked the old mercantilist foundations. 'Probably in the world there was never less of a Free-Trader' was Carlyle's verdict on Frederick's economic regime. That was a little strong. On occasions Frederick showed that he appreciated the limitations of his top-down, *dirigiste* state capitalism. Although he never travelled to England, he knew plenty of people who had, and also had first-hand knowledge of the Dutch Republic and its commercial *laissez-faire* capitalism. But he remained adamant that Prussia's geopolitical situation dictated that revenue-raising for the army had to take precedence and that meant strict central control.[191] He was probably wrong. In the Second Hundred Years War of 1688–1815 between Great Britain and France, it was the English economic and fiscal model that proved to have the tougher sinews. From the vantage point of 1786, however, Frederick could congratulate himself on having garnered sufficient resources to take his state from third-rate to first-rate status in Europe. Not only had he conquered Silesia, he had also added the large and potentially prosperous province of West Prussia.

15
At Court and at Home

FREDERICK'S MULTIPLE COURTS

'Frederick has no court,' stated a French visitor to Prussia in 1786.[1] This summed up a belief shared by many contemporaries – by Voltaire, for example, who wrote that Frederick lived '*sans cour, sans conseil, sans culte*'.[2] While he certainly dispensed with a council and a (religious) confession, he could not do without a court. In fact he had several. Although different in many respects from those of other European states, they performed the same essential functions: marriage market, 'foyer of patronage', recreation centre, social interface and diplomatic exchange.[3] What was so special about the Prussian court was the habitual absence of the king. As we have seen, within a few years of coming to the throne Frederick had decided to settle in Potsdam, spending winters in the Town Palace and summers at Sanssouci.* Berlin he visited on a regular basis only for the military inspections in May and August, major family events and during the carnival season in December–January. Moreover, the duration of even these sojourns diminished, as he progressively arrived later and left earlier. As Reinhold Koser put it, Frederick was 'an alien at his own court'.[4]

Frederick's aversion to court etiquette was well advertised at the time and has been much admired by historians since. His public denunciation of his grandfather's extravagance in *Memoirs of the House of Brandenburg* and private assault on ceremonial in the *Political Testament* of 1752 created an attractive image of a ruler too

---

* See above, pp. 160–62.

enlightened to bother with fripperies. He wrote that most European sovereigns had forged ceremonial chains for themselves and now sighed under their weight. Only his father had shown the courage to break them, setting a sterling example which he had followed and taken further. He added that he kept the diplomatic corps as far away as possible, with the happy result that Prussia did not suffer the enervating arguments about protocol and precedence that impeded so many other states.[5] Indeed he did, as the hapless foreign diplomats lamented. They were given a brief royal audience when they arrived and another when they left. In between times, they were very lucky if they even saw Frederick, let alone talked to him.[6] In 1750 the new British envoy, Sir Charles Hanbury Williams, was kept waiting for an hour and was then given an audience of five and a half minutes. Longer experience only confirmed his initial impression: 'a man might as well make his court to a parcel of hogs as to the court of Berlin' was his verdict.[7] On the other hand, Frederick was quick to react if he thought foreign courts were not treating him and his kingdom with the respect they deserved. As another English envoy, Sir Andrew Mitchell, observed: 'Though upon some occasions he laughs at all formalities, yet no man is more tenacious of them in whatever he thinks touches his rank, dignity, and consideration.'[8]

Unfortunately, the need to be attentive to people one finds tiresome is an integral part of public office at every social level. For a sovereign it is essential. Had Frederick brought himself to be agreeable to the foreign diplomatic corps, he might well have reaped political benefits. In an age of very limited information opportunities, it was the diplomats who formed the main conduit to their employers. So when Frederick went out of his way to insult the newly arrived Russian envoy, von Gross, by asking him whether he was related to a journalist of the same name, he was also ensuring that every last piece of malicious gossip would be reported back to St Petersburg.[9] There was plenty of it. Frederick's tongue was as loose as it was sharp. Especially among the female rulers of Europe – the Tsarinas Anna, Elizabeth and Catherine, the Empress Maria Theresa and the French *maîtresses-en-titre* Mesdames de Pompadour and du Barry – he acquired a well-deserved reputation for making malicious and wounding remarks.

If he did not avoid public engagements altogether, he certainly kept them to a minimum. His dislike of Christianity ruled out the church services which at most courts were numerous, regular and lengthy and also played a central role in the representation of power, rank and favour.[10] In Frederick's case, their place was taken by the military inspections and exercises that filled a substantial part of his daily routine at Potsdam. His appearances at court functions in the capital averaged only thirty-four between 1750 and 1767, falling to just seventeen between 1768 and 1785.[11] In his absence, the burden of court duties fell on the two queens: the Queen Mother Sophia Dorothea (until her death in 1757) and Queen Elizabeth Christine. For both women, this surrogate function was welcome. Under her son, the clever, cultured and proud Sophia Dorothea could now rule the roost in Berlin in a way her tyrannical husband Frederick William had never permitted. No longer condemned to spending much of the year at gloomy Wusterhausen, she spent the winter in the royal palace and the summer, from May until September, at her own palace of Monbijou. An indulgent Frederick had the latter modernized and extended by Knobelsdorff and purchased a neighbouring property to extend its gardens. By the time he had finished, he had turned a modest summer residence into a magnificent palace.[12] It was to her that foreign dignitaries and diplomats first went to pay their respects. And it was her soirées, concerts and balls which set the tone of the capital during the first half of the reign.

The actual queen's situation was rather different. Set aside as a wife as soon as Frederick came to the throne,* she also had to play second fiddle to the queen mother. This was made painfully clear even by apparently innocuous newspaper announcements, as in the following from 1749:

> Last Friday Her Majesty the Queen Mother attended a concert at the King's *maison de plaisance* Sanssouci, and after attending another grand banquet there on Saturday, Her Majesty the Queen Mother, attended by Her Royal Highness Princess Amalia, returned to her own Palace of Monbijou. On the same day, Her Majesty the Queen, together with Her Royal Highness the Princess of Prussia, received Holy

---

* See above, pp. 58–60.

Communion at the hands the Very Reverend Pastor Baumgarten, who on this occasion preached a very fine sermon.[13]

On the queen mother's death, she moved to the front rank of the court *faute de mieux*, performing the same indispensable duties. Although she had a large suite of representational rooms at her command in the main Berlin palace, she was not allowed to move to Monbijou, which was kept empty for the rest of the reign as a mute monument of filial devotion to a mother's memory. Elizabeth Christine's devoted service to Frederick in his absence was not, alas, rewarded by any human contact with the beneficiary. In 1764 the royal couple met on only fourteen occasions, even though this was the year in which Frederick visited his capital most often (thirty-nine times). Just to rub in the humiliation, Frederick occasionally invited ladies from his wife's entourage to attend functions at Potsdam, a favour he never extended to their mistress.[14] His aversion was of course noticed and imitated by Prussian high society, so much so that Frederick felt obliged to demand proper respect for the queen.[15] Undeterred, she stuck to her task diligently and without complaint, helped no doubt by the conspicuous piety which made her court a centre for Lutheran clergy and provided a striking contrast with the libertinism of Potsdam.[16]

The official court presided over by the queen was not lively, as the diaries of her chamberlain, Count Lehndorff, make very clear, and the longer the reign lasted, the more tedious it became.[17] Only on rare occasions did Frederick decree that the full panoply of court ceremonial be unfolded. Significantly, these occurred mostly during the first half of the reign. The greatest was the 'Carousel' staged in August 1750 on the *Lustgarten* (pleasure gardens) in front of the royal palace in Berlin.* Nominally a greeting for Frederick's sister Wilhelmine and her husband, the Margrave of Bayreuth, its main purpose was to celebrate the conclusion of the Peace of Aachen in 1748, which had given international recognition to Frederick's conquest of Silesia.[18] Three weeks of operatic and theatrical performances, banquets, masked

---

* A 'carousel' is defined by the *Oxford English Dictionary* as 'a tournament in which knights, divided into companies (quadrilles) distinguished by their liveries and dresses, engaged in various plays and exercises; to this were often added chariot races, and other shows and entertainments.'

balls and firework displays climaxed with the Carousel, a mock tournament-cum-equestrian-ballet between 'Romans' led by Prince August Wilhelm, 'Carthaginians' led by Prince Henry, 'Greeks' led by Prince Ferdinand and 'Persians' led by their kinsman, Margrave Karl of Brandenburg-Schwedt, performed before the whole court seated in grandstands.[19] As a deliberate imitation of Louis XIV's fabled '*Carrousel des cinq nations*' of 1662, it announced to the world the arrival of Prussia as a great power and its king as a mighty military monarch worthy to be ranked with *Louis le Grand*. The extravagance of the costumes of both men and horses proclaimed that this was a court in a different class from the others in the Holy Roman Empire.[20] Held at night and illuminated by 30,000 lanterns, this was representational court culture of the old school.[21] For those unlucky enough not to be in Berlin for the occasion, the event was recorded in word and image.[22] Probably more effective in reaching Frederick's favourite audience – the European intelligentsia – was the account broadcast by Voltaire, who had just arrived for what turned out to be a stay of three years. Indeed, Voltaire himself was a star attraction at the Carousel, as an Italian visitor, Count Alessandro Collini, recorded: 'shortly before the King appeared, there arose an admiring murmur and all around me I heard the name "Voltaire!", "Voltaire!"'[23] The great man duly reciprocated with a poem in praise of the event, which was promptly printed in the official account and in the press. He also spread the word to Paris:

> No words can describe adequately the Carousel I have just witnessed; it combined the Carousel of Louis XIV with a Chinese lantern festival. There was not the slightest disorder, no noise, everyone sat comfortably, attentively and quietly, just as in Paris . . . All this was achieved by one man alone. His five victories and the Peace of Dresden formed a fine ornament for the spectacle.[24]

It was just during these summer months in Berlin that Voltaire finished his *Century of Louis XIV*, which was published there the following year, completing the association with the often-repeated claim 'Frederick is greater than Louis XIV'.[25]

Much of the enormous cost of the Carousel was passed on to the princes and nobles taking part, however extraordinary that may seem.[26] It was not repeated. Indeed, gala occasions of this kind were few and far between. Only once more was the boat pushed out so far: in 1776, when Catherine the Great's son and heir, Grand Duke Paul, was engaged to Sophie Dorothea of Württemberg, whose mother was a Hohenzollern. As Frederick was earnestly seeking a proleptic extension to his alliance with Russia at the time,[27] this was money well spent.* Otherwise the Berlin court was *en fête* only for family visits and marriages, although there were plenty of these. The traditional image of Frederick's Prussia as an austere 'Sparta of the North', to be contrasted with the sybaritic courts of the Catholic world, is mistaken. If the court of Berlin could not compete with Vienna or Versailles in size or splendour, it was well up with the middling courts of the Holy Roman Empire, especially after 1763 when most (devastated Dresden, for example) were forced to retrench.[28]

FAMILY FEUDS AND FRIENDSHIPS

Moreover, the capital boasted a 'pluralist court landscape', for to the courts of the two queens must be added the separate establishments created by Frederick for his numerous siblings. His attachment to the Hohenzollern family, which has already been noted,† was also expressed in a generous provision of palaces for his brothers and sisters. His eldest brother and heir-apparent, August Wilhelm, was given Oranienburg Palace; his youngest brother, Ferdinand, received the Palace of the Order of Saint John on the Wilhelmsplatz as his main residence and Friedrichsfelde Palace as a summer retreat; and unmarried Princess Amalia got the Palais Verzenobre. Best treated of all was Frederick's middle brother, Henry, who was given Rheinsberg in 1744 and a huge town palace on Unter den Linden after the Seven Years War (today the Humboldt University).[29] They also had the run of the New Palace at Potsdam, to which many of them moved every year from April until September. As Frederick's wife was barred from Potsdam, it was Amalia who presided as hostess, even to the extent – so it

---

* See above, p. 289.
† See above, p. 119.

was reported – of attending to her royal brother's laundry.[30] These family gatherings at the New Palace, often also attended by Brunswick, Schwedt and Württemberg relations, were probably designed to show the world that the Hohenzollern dynasty was secure. In reality, it was anything but, for after the death of August Wilhelm in 1758, the only surviving male of the next generation was his son, Frederick William (who eventually succeeded as Frederick William II on Frederick's death). Between 1761 and 1791 the three subsidiary Hohenzollern branches of Bayreuth, Ansbach and Schwedt were all to die out.[31]

Frederick's siblings*

Wilhelmine (1709–58) m. Margrave Friedrich of Bayreuth 1731	Friderike Louise (1714–84) m. Margrave Carl Wilhelm of Ansbach 1729	Philippine Charlotte (1716–1801) m. Duke Karl of Brunswick-Wolfenbüttel 1733	Sophie (1719–65) m. Margrave Friedrich Wilhelm of Brandenburg-Schwedt 1734	Ulrike (1720–82) m. Adolf Friedrich King of Sweden 1744	August Wilhelm (1722–58) m. Louise of Brunswick-Bevern 1742	Amalia (1723–87) Abbess of Quedlinburg unmarried	Henry (1726–1802) m. Wilhelmine of Hessen-Kassel 1752	Augus[t] Ferdina[nd] (1730–18) m. Ann[e] Elizabet[h] Brandenb[urg] Schwe[dt] 1755

* Three other brothers and one sister died in infancy

As Frederick spent most of his time in Potsdam, the junior Hohenzollerns dominated the social scene in Berlin. The diaries of Count Lehndorff reveal a conventional round of balls, dinners, concerts and amateur theatricals, together with the puerile high jinks typical of young royals of every century. In January 1754, for example, the assembled company went to Prince Henry's residence, where they all disguised themselves as Jews. Meanwhile, Prince August Wilhelm had been brought blindfolded, not knowing where he was being taken, and was unveiled in a room decorated to look like a synagogue. Court Marshal von Reisewitz then arrived disguised as a saint and converted them all back to Christianity. After that masks were donned by everyone according to taste and August Wilhelm was dressed up as a woman. 'It was all very funny,' commented Lehndorff.[32] Later the same month, Countess Bentinck also resorted to cross-dressing, in the forlorn hope that her male attire would win her the attention of the exclusively homosexual Prince Henry.[33]

In his personal relations with his brothers and sisters, Frederick did not show himself to advantage. The Marquis de Valori, French envoy to Prussia during the first years of Frederick's reign, reported: 'he is hard and imperious with his brothers, the princes, and he keeps them in a state of dependence which he himself was never able to get used to from his father, who terrified everyone'.[34] Not unreasonably, perhaps, Frederick kept them all well clear of any participation in decision-making. In his *Political Testament* of 1752 he wrote that princes of the blood royal were a menace, judging themselves too grand to take orders. They should be paid the honour appropriate to their rank, he added, but nothing more.[35] In the event, he made an exception for Prince Henry, whose superior qualities as military commander and diplomat he was quick to recognize and make use of. The other two brothers were also made to serve in the army but were discarded when they were found wanting.

Particularly brutal was his treatment of the elder, August Wilhelm, despite his status as heir-apparent. This was a classic case of a victim of bullying being turned into a bully himself.[36] No sooner had his father died than Frederick moved to tyrannize his siblings. If there was no physical violence, there was plenty of coercion. Perhaps because he had been his father's favourite son, August Wilhelm found himself picked on first, being told by his elder brother what to do and when to do it, including what to read, and being tormented with constant criticism of his conduct as an officer.[37] In 1754 he was outraged when Frederick brought in Major General Driesen to be commandant of his regiment of cuirassiers, thus implying that August Wilhelm was incompetent. Worse was to come. Following the retreat back to Silesia after the defeat at Kolin in July 1757,* Frederick not only blamed his brother but in effect accused him of cowardice as well as incompetence: 'it is not my enemies who have sunk me, it is the wretched actions you have taken'.[38] This was most unfair. Lumbered with all the cannons, tents and pontoons Frederick himself did not want to

---

* See above, p. 275.

take with him on his own retreat, August Wilhelm had done as well as could be expected in very difficult circumstances – certainly much better than Frederick had managed during his own, even more cata-strophic retreat from Bohemia in 1744.[39]

Shattered in body and spirit, August Wilhelm left the army and returned to Oranienburg, where he died the following year at the age of thirty-five. Although he probably died of meningitis, many contem-poraries chose to believe that he had died of a broken heart, bullied to death by his brutal brother. Among those who took this view was Prince Henry, whose relationship with Frederick was particularly fraught. Unlike August Wilhelm, Henry was very bright, mercurial and highly strung. He was also a promiscuous homosexual, con-stantly falling in and out of love and surrounded by an entourage of young army officers competing for his favours. His love-life can be followed in some detail through the diaries of Count Lehndorff, who was himself besotted with the prince, as the following sample reveals:

> 1 May 1753 the most miserable day of my life, because Prince Henry is leaving; I go to see him, my heart full of grief. I hurry to my dear prince, what a sorrowful meeting! I leave him without a word, I see tears pour-ing down his face, the dearest in the world, what a man to be worshipped, what a loss for me, I swear eternal devotion. I return to my home in sorrow and cannot sleep, I write my prince a letter.

> 2 May I get a letter from him which makes me burst into tears. I jump on my horse and ride to meet him, but when I see his carriage approach-ing I get off and hide, otherwise my heart would have burst. I did not think that one person could be so devoted to another; in pagan times they would have made him a God.[40]

The sight of Prince Henry in tight riding breeches and looking 'as beautiful as an angel' was enough to send Lehndorff into erotic rap-ture.[41] As this suggests, the hard military masculine world of Prussia had its feminine side too. Unfortunately for fraternal harmony, in 1746 Frederick and Henry found themselves competing for the same catamite, the beautiful page Johann Friedrich von der Marwitz. Fred-erick pulled rank on that occasion, although he told Henry later that the object of their affection had 'a flabby body' and gonorrhoea to boot.[42] At around this time, Frederick sent his brother a number of anguished letters, lamenting the breakdown in relations and protesting his own affection. In the past, he wrote, Henry had shown him warmth only when seeking help with his love-affairs. At other times he displayed 'extreme coldness'.[43]

As with August Wilhelm, Frederick intervened to humiliate Henry militarily as well, by sending Colonel von Rohr to restore order to his regiment. He also took this opportunity to tell Henry that it very much looked as though he did not serve for military reasons but only 'as an excuse for achieving your petty designs', by which Frederick probably meant Henry's sexual conquests.[44] The cruellest stroke he landed came in 1752, when he made Henry get married to the beautiful and charming Wilhelmine of Hessen-Kassel, in the full knowledge that the marriage would not be consummated and that Henry would treat his bride with as much disdain as he himself showed to his own wife. As he told their sister Wilhelmine, what mattered most was to get Henry married, if only in name.[45] This was replicating with a vengeance his own father's abusive treatment.

The result was that Henry loathed Frederick with that special intensity apparently reserved for royal siblings. While the rest of the world acclaimed Frederick's conquest of Silesia, Henry published a pamphlet under the pseudonym of 'Marshal Gessler', criticizing Frederick's strategy and assigning credit for the victories solely to the courage of the Prussian soldiers.[46] His own undoubted military prowess during the campaigns of 1757 prompted an impressed Frederick to write that, if Henry were not his brother, he would praise him even more.[47] This respect was most emphatically not reciprocated. Indicative of Henry's bitterness was the letter he wrote to his sister Amalia in which he greeted the news of Frederick's defeat at Kolin with a gleeful cry: 'At last Phaeton has crashed!', adding that Frederick had taken care to save himself even before the battle had been decided. Alas, this indiscreet document was captured en route for Berlin by Austrian light troops and duly publicized.[48] The cashiering of Prince August Wilhelm in the same year, 1757, sealed the rift. In December, the British envoy Sir Andrew Mitchell, who had followed the Prussian armies in person, wrote: 'Prince Henry is very vain and hates his brother, of whose greatness he is jealous.'[49] Henry went on fighting for Frederick, despite his disapproval of both the way the war had started and the way it was being waged. In December 1759 Frederick sent him a letter from snowbound Freiberg, counselling patience. An enraged Henry wrote underneath:

> I have absolutely no confidence in his information, it is always as contradictory and imprecise as his character. It was he who threw us into this terrible war, and only the courage of his generals and soldiers can get us out of it. From the day he joined my army, he has sowed disorder and misfortune; all my efforts during this campaign and the good fortune that attended them have been lost by Frederick.[50]

Among the abusive epithets levelled at Frederick in the letters Prince Henry addressed to his younger brother Ferdinand were 'cruel', 'heartless', 'bloodthirsty', 'mudslinger', 'liar', 'evil', 'vain', 'jealous', 'stupid', 'incompetent' and 'fantasist'. 'If only our mother had had a still-birth on January 24th 1712!' he exclaimed.[51] Time did not mellow him. In 1781 he told the Emperor Joseph II when he met him at Spa that he wanted nothing more than for Frederick to die.[52] When Frederick's *History of the Seven Years War* appeared posthumously in 1788, Henry scribbled furiously in the margin comments such as 'False!', 'A lie!', 'What an outrage!', 'Fairy-tale!' and against the account of Rossbach he wrote that Frederick had wanted to retreat and that his generals had fought the battle without him.[53]

The sibling with whom Frederick enjoyed the closest relationship was his elder sister, Wilhelmine. Separated by less than three years and united by sharp intelligence and especially a love of music, the two were very close as children. The first surviving letter from Frederick, dated 26 January 1728, is full of effusive declarations of love.[54] Common suffering at the hands of their father tightened the bond further.* After Wilhelmine was married off to the Margrave of Bayreuth in 1731, absence made their hearts grow even fonder. On his own wedding night, it was to Wilhelmine that Frederick wrote 'Thank God, that is over!', adding that he hoped she appreciated that it was she he was thinking of.[55] Even by the standards of mid-eighteenth-century discourse, Frederick's letters were extravagant. When the margrave

---

* See above, pp. 40–41.

came to call at Ruppin in October 1732, Frederick wrote that the two of them had entertained each other for three hours by singing the praises of 'the most incomparable being of our century' and had almost come to blows when disputing who loved her most.[56] Her death from cancer on 14 October 1758 (the same day as the defeat at Hochkirch) caused Frederick intense and prolonged grief, whose sincerity cannot be doubted.[57] Yet it was not an equal partnership. Wilhelmine was never allowed to forget her subordinate status as a woman and the wife of a minor prince. She recorded in her memoirs that when Frederick visited her at Bayreuth in 1734, he derided the provincialism of the 'little courts' of 'princelings' and insisted that even the junior officers of his entourage should be given precedence over the local dignitaries, observing that the lieutenant of a king outranked the minister of a margrave.[58]

Eventually, this imperiousness led to a rift between brother and sister in an episode minor in itself but important in its revelation of just how much Frederick was a chip off the old block. When Wilhelmine moved to Bayreuth, she took with her as a lady-in-waiting Wilhelmine Dorothea von der Marwitz, the daughter of a Prussian general. In April 1744, Frederick learned that the lady was to be married to Count Otto von Burghauss. He told Wilhelmine to put a stop to the match at once, on the grounds that when Miss von der Marwitz left Prussia in 1731 it had been stipulated that she would not be allowed to marry outside the country. This command was reinforced with the threat that not a penny of dowry would be paid. Three days later a further letter told Wilhelmine that General von der Marwitz wanted his daughter back because he had his own bridegroom waiting in the wings and that 'the first and main duty of a child is obedience to its parents'. Not to be intimidated, his sister replied tartly that the promise had died with Frederick William I; that it was wrong to force a woman to marry a man she had never met; and that, in any case, the marriage had taken place the day before Frederick's protest arrived.[59] In this case, as with Prince Henry, it almost seems as though Frederick was determined to make all married couples suffer. The Margrave of Bayreuth's apparent sympathy with Austria during the war completed the alienation, which lasted for a number of years. Frederick's egoism did not allow personal relationships on an equal footing of friendship, not even with his best-loved sibling.[60]

More serious in the long term was Frederick's treatment of his heirs. As we have seen, he ruthlessly broke his brother after the failed Bohemian campaign of 1757. After August Wilhelm's death the following year, his son Frederick William, born in 1744, became the heir-apparent. He grew up to be gigantic in stature and more intelligent than his rough treatment at the hands of subsequent Prussian historians would suggest. Although he shared his royal uncle's liking for music and was also a gifted performer (cello), the two men had little else in common. Easy-going, extravagant, pleasure-seeking and vigorously heterosexual, the 'Prince of Prussia', as he was known officially, was often getting into scrapes over money and women. His first, ill-starred marriage, to his cousin Elizabeth Christine of Brunswick-Lüneburg, ended in divorce after just four years, having produced only one daughter. At least his second, to Friderike Louise of Hessen-Darmstadt, produced eight children at a rate of more than one per annum, including four boys, thus ensuring the dynasty's future.[61] He also maintained a *maîtresse-en-titre* in the attractive shape of Wilhelmine Enke, the daughter of one of the royal musicians.[62]

Though he enjoyed plentiful sex, Frederick William's life was not agreeable. His uncle was determined to make a soldier of him, so attendance at all the military parades and exercises was obligatory, as was a Spartan life-style. Just as Frederick's own father had scorned his taste for 'effeminate' French fashions, so did Frederick now impose the same austere regime on his nephew. Count Lehndorff recorded that on one occasion at Potsdam, when rising from the dinner table Frederick William was surprised to be handed by his page not the fashionably small hat he had brought with him but a larger alternative selected by Frederick, who told him sharply that he should be wearing the same headgear as the other guards officers.[63] Undeterred, the intrepid Frederick William continued to promenade in Berlin dressed in 'a bright red chenille jacket, a blue satin waistcoat decorated with Greek embroidery, and with his hair combed up into a high *toupé*'.[64] It was just as well that Uncle Frederick did not catch sight of him. That was in 1764. His lot did not improve as he waited for his uncle to die. Twenty-one years later, the Marquis de Bouillé reported:

The heir apparent to the throne of Prussia lives in the house of a brewer, one of the poorest in Potsdam, and he is not permitted to spend a night away without royal permission. He is now forty-one years old and has reached only the rank of lieutenant-general. His rooms are small and mean, fitted out with furniture that is dirty and torn, lacking even the decency that might be expected in a simple colonel's household.[65]

At the New Palace, Frederick William was allocated a suite of three apartments much smaller than those enjoyed by other members of the family, a spatial humiliation that will not have gone unnoticed.[66]

This was all very reminiscent of Frederick William's treatment of his son in the years before his marriage. When Frederick sounded forth about his nephew, it might almost be Frederick William I denouncing his son: 'he is the most bovine animal you could imagine . . . Clumsy in everything he does, coarse, obstinate, moody, a roué, degenerate, immoral, a blockhead and a nasty bit of work . . . the scum of the family.'[67] If Frederick was less brutal towards his own heir in a physical sense (apart from anything else, Frederick William was a giant), he was more unrelenting psychologically. Once again, we see an uncanny parallel between the abuse Frederick suffered as crown prince and the treatment he inflicted on his own relations. Frederick William returned the compliment by espousing all the things his uncle disliked – women, German and English literature, religion and mysticism.[68] In 1780 he wrote to his mistress, Wilhelmine Enke, 'that animal [Frederick] is a right scourge of God, spat out of Hell on to earth by God's wrath', adding quickly, 'take care that this letter does not fall into anyone else's hands'.[69]

Other members of the Hohenzollern family were told when and whom to marry. There was nothing unusual about this among the ruling houses of Europe, of course. Caroline of Ansbach's refusal to convert to Catholicism to be able to marry the Habsburg Archduke Charles (who became Emperor Charles VI) was the exception that proved the rule. It has been argued, however, that Frederick deliberately chose brides for his brothers from the lower tier of the imperial nobility to distance himself from the princes of the blood. So at court festivities, his sisters-in-law were demonstratively placed lower in the pecking-order than his sisters.[70] His nieces and nephews were also enlisted in dynastic policy. The marriage of August Wilhelm's daughter Wilhelmina to the Dutch Stadholder William V in 1763 paved the way for an extension of Prussian influence in the Low Countries, although it was not realized until shortly after Frederick's death.[71]

THE *CERCLE INTIME* AND 'CAMP' CULTURE

Frederick had a low opinion of his heir and never allowed him anywhere near decision-making, with the result that Frederick William was ill-prepared when he eventually came to the throne at the age of forty-one.[72] Not to make proper provision for the future government of such a personalized system can only be described as a basic and serious dereliction of monarchical duty. Nor was the crown prince admitted to the *cercle intime* at Potsdam. While Frederick left the heavy lifting of court business to his mother, wife and other relations, he could relax with just a handful of like-minded friends. When Sanssouci was completed, he wrote a verse epistle to d'Argens announcing that at his new home, instead of the tedious and interminable meals of a conventional court, there would be a simple repast enlivened by clever conversation and mockery of the stupid. His model was the kind of Roman country-house party praised by Horace and indeed his verse epistle was modelled on his favourite Latin author.[73] Excluded from this select group was anyone with access to an alternative centre of influence or information at Berlin. Frederick chose as his companions only those who were dependent on him.[74] They had to be clever, knowledgeable across a wide range of subjects, well-read and witty. Absolutely essential was the ability to speak French. When Frederick's new secretary Dieudonné Thiébault arrived, he was asked whether he spoke German. Apologizing, he promised to make good the deficiency as soon as possible. No, no, replied Frederick, I insist that you do *not* learn it, for if you did, Germanisms would soon start polluting the purity of your speech.[75] As Voltaire reported soon after his arrival in August 1750, the language spoken least was German, being used only by soldiers and horses. He added smugly that French language and literature had made more conquests than Charlemagne.[76]

Later that year, Voltaire wrote to Madame Denis from Potsdam: 'I know, my dear child, all the things that are being said across Europe about Potsdam. Women are especially enraged, as they were at Montpellier against M. d'Assoucy;* but all that is none of my business.' He added four lines of verse:

> I have passed that happy age of honest love-affairs,
> And do not have the honour to be a page:
> What is done on Paphos and its neighbourhood,
> Is always a matter of indifference to me.

before concluding, 'I do not meddle in anything here except getting on with my job of patching up the prose and the verses of the head of the household.'[77] As this implies, Frederick's society at Potsdam was exclusively male. Female members of the Hohenzollern family might be invited to grand set pieces and might be allowed to stay in the New Palace in summer, but not even his two favourite sisters, Wilhelmine and Amalia, ever became members of his entourage. This was not only a world without women, it was a world against women. As several of his intimate friends – Fredersdorf, d'Argens, Darget, Catt, for example – discovered, marriage was not welcomed. Any servant found with a woman felt the full force of royal anger. As one of his earliest and most sympathetic biographers, Johann David Erdmann Preuss, observed, Sanssouci was a monastery and Frederick was its abbot.[78]

It was homosocial, but was it also homosexual, as Voltaire implied in his letter to Madame Denis quoted earlier? As we have seen, Frederick in effect came out as a homosexual in 1740 as part of the self-fashioning process that allowed him to come to terms with his father's abuse.† Although there can be no conclusive proof, it seems very likely that his preference was for members of his own sex. Certainly he chose as his close companions men who were homosexual or bisexual, and often went out of his way to promote their careers, as he did with the creepy Abbé Bastiani or Count Philipp Gotthard von

---

* Charles Coypeau d'Assoucy (1605–77), pederastic *libertin* and probable lover of Cyrano de Bergerac.
† See above, pp. 61–70.

Schaffgotsch, whom he made coadjutor to the Prince-Bishop of Breslau and who was described variously as the 'Bishop of Sodom' by Count Lehndorff and as 'the epitome of impiety and depravity, which he takes to disgusting lengths' by the French envoy Lord Tyrconnell.[79] Also suggestive was the swirl of rumours that keep surfacing in contemporary pamphlets and memoirs.[80] At one end of the scale was the obviously scurrilous and politically motivated *Dictionary of all the indecency and boasting that is to be found in the so-called works of Frederick II* written by the prolific Viennese journalist Josef Richter, which accused Frederick of whiling away the time between military operations with sodomy with his pretty pages, his guardsmen and even his greyhounds.[81] More serious, because based allegedly on personal observation, was the account which appeared in Voltaire's *Mémoires*:

> When His Majesty is dressed and booted, for a few moments the Stoic finds time for the sect of Epicurus: he summons two or three favourites, whether lieutenants from his regiment or pages, or lackeys, or young cadets. Coffee is drunk. Whoever is thrown a handkerchief then spends a quarter-of-an-hour in a *tête-à-tête*. Things cannot be taken the whole way because when he was prince his love affairs were punished so brutally by his father that he has suffered irreparable damage. So he can no longer play an active role and has to make do with the passive.[82]

Obviously, Voltaire cannot have been present during these trysts, if they happened, but he did live in close proximity to Frederick for more than two years between 1750 and 1753 and for some of the time was resident at Sanssouci. On the other hand, this memoir dates from 1757–9,[83] or, in other words, after the two men had fallen out spectacularly and Voltaire had left Potsdam in disgrace and vowing vengeance.*

In the absence of the sort of conclusive evidence that is never likely to appear, it is impossible to say whether Frederick was an active – or passive – homosexual. What can be established, however, is that the ambience of his personal court was very distinctive. Moreover, it owed nothing to traditional models and was entirely his own creation. It is

---

* See below, pp. 332–5.

best expressed by the English word 'camp', which has definite homo-erotic or at least sexually ambivalent overtones but denotes much more besides. The best literary expression was provided by Frederick's lengthy verse-satire *Palladium*, composed in 1748–9 and modelled on Voltaire's *The Maid of Orleans*. Based very loosely on an actual episode of the Second Silesian War when Darget, the secretary of the French ambassador Valori, allowed himself to be mistaken for his master and be taken prisoner by Austrian soldiers, it enabled Frederick to attack many of his favourite targets, chief among them the Saxons, Christianity and the Catholic Church. He added a few more, including the Dutch (so slow-witted that it takes them an hour to get out two words), the English (corrupt, suicidal, sport-mad, millionaires down to the beggars, syphilitic), the Portuguese (whose king is so devout that he takes a nun as his mistress), the Russians (who had only been walking upright on two legs since Peter the Great), and so on.[84]

Playful, ironic, anti-clerical, quite witty in places and rather long-winded, *Palladium* encapsulates the atmosphere of Frederick's *cercle intime* at Sanssouci. It is also malicious, even cruel, most notably when it has Darget recount his life. Most offensive to the real Darget were his alleged experiences in a Jesuit college:

> They found in me a little beauty
> And some liveliness of mind.
> One teacher, slobbering with lust,
> Caressing me with wickedness,
> Leading me one day to his room in his quarters,
> Made me a most indecent proposition.

Darget rejects these advances with indignation, but it is not long before another priest tries. This time Darget resists only 'a little' and finally succumbs after being persuaded by the following justification of homosexuality:

> Don't you know your history?
> You will find there glorious heroes,
> Responding both actively and passively
> To their lithe and obliging friends.
> That was what Socrates got from Alcibiades,

Who, by my faith, was not a gloomy Greek;
And just the same were Euryalus and Nisus.*
How many more could I name? A great number,
Julius Caesar, about whom obscene tongues
Told he was the husband of all the Roman women,
When he was the wife of all the husbands.
But just leaf through Suetonius
And see how he deals with the Caesars.
They are all included on this list;
They all served the good god of Lampsacus.†
And if profane examples aren't enough
For you, then let us shift our attack to the sacred:
This good Jesus, how do you think
He got John to sleep in his bed?
Can't you see he was his Ganymede?[85]

As we have seen, Frederick very likely did have a homosexual relationship with Darget, whom he often called 'Lucine', but, not unreasonably, the latter took offence at this public exposure. So shocking were the poem's contents that, although Frederick had it privately printed, only very few copies were distributed and only to close friends. But of course the secret could not be kept, especially not after Voltaire had been given a copy on his arrival in 1750. Frederick tried to make amends with a lengthy verse epistle to Darget on the burdens of kingship, but their relationship could not be restored.[86]

But 'camp' is about a lot more than sex or impudence, it is also about a special kind of milieu involving flamboyant decoration, consumption and self-indulgence. A good example was Frederick's love of very richly decorated snuff-boxes, a taste he inherited from his mother.[87] In the course of his reign he assembled a collection variously estimated at 300 (Friedrich Nicolai) and 1,500 (Dieudonné Thiébault), the most likely total being somewhere between 300 and 400.[88] Encrusted with precious stones, one such box could cost more than

---

* Euryalus and Nisus were shown on one of the four medallions depicting homosexual lovers installed on the columns of the Temple of Friendship at Sanssouci. See above, p. 178.
† Lampsacus, centre of the cult of Priapus.

an old master painting and their total value was estimated to be 1,750,000 talers.[89] Of course, only one could be in use at any one time, but Frederick made sure that a selection of the best pieces was always on display in his rooms and he took his collection with him to Berlin for the carnival season.[90] One of Fredersdorf's many responsibilities was the purchase and maintenance of the collection. It was put to continuous and intensive use, as the British envoy James Harris reported: 'The present King is a great taker of snuff. I could not even get a sight of his snuff-boxes, of which he has a most magnificent collection. That he carries is of an enormous size, and he takes it, not by pinches, but by handfuls. It is difficult to approach him without sneezing.'[91] The same opulence extended to jewellery. When he met Joseph II at Neustadt in Moravia in 1770, for example, Frederick wore on his left hand two valuable rings with solitaire diamonds and on his right a large ring made from chrysoprase, a very rare and beautiful green gemstone whose Silesian origin was also making a political point.[92]

On that occasion he wore a white silk suit richly embroidered with silver, a sight that has to be imagined because it was definitely not recorded visually. The image that contemporaries preferred to foster was that of the austere 'Old Fritz' (*Der alte Fritz*), always in a plain uniform, embellished only with the star of the Order of the Black Eagle. Frederick refused to sit for a portrait after 1740, so we shall never know what clothes he would have selected had he done so. He did however encourage the myth of the shabbily uniformed monarch by appearing as such on the streets of Berlin on one of his famous rides, doffing his tricorn hat to passers-by.* Away from the public eye, he liked to revert to the sort of elaborate French fashions his father had disliked so much. Especially during the first half of the reign, he appeared at court functions in a gala costume lavishly decorated with gold and silver embroidery, diamond buttons and shoe-buckles, and silk stockings. His numerous personal servants were also decked out in splendid livery.[93] He also liked to travel in style, in a magnificent phaeton, decorated with paintings and gilt trimmings, pulled by horses with rich harness and accompanied by footmen.[94]

---

* See above, p. 349.

It was not unusual for a sovereign to live in luxury. What was striking about Frederick was the disjunction between the image of Spartan austerity and the reality of a more Babylonian life-style. In part, this derived from Frederick's daily routine.[95] Up at five in the morning in summer, or six in winter, he attended to political business first before setting forth for military inspections. It was on his return to Sanssouci or the Potsdam Town Palace that the transition to a more self-indulgent regime could begin. An often lengthy luncheon with the *cercle intime* was followed by a rest, more business, a walk, a long period of reading or being read to, a concert and a final supper, also attended by favourite conversation partners.[96] No expense was spared when it came to comestibles.[97] He maintained a very good kitchen, staffed by several top-flight chefs. On a normal day there would be eight courses for the royal table when he had company, rather fewer when he dined alone.[98] The proposed menu was presented to Frederick on the evening before for approval, with the name of the duty chef responsible for each course, for example:[99]

MENU

23 October 1780

Henaut	*Soupe d'écrevisse*	Crawfish soup
Grebendinckel	*Des ailes des perdreaux glacez à l'oseil et laituës*	Partridge wings glazed with sorrel and lettuce
The new chef	*Tendron de mouton à l'Anglaise. Sauce verte.*	Side of lamb in the English manner. Green sauce.
Schilger	*Marktsknedeln & gebratene Fasanen*	Dumplings and roast pheasant
Grebendinckel	*Cardon en petit pois avec cotellettes*	Artichoke with green peas and cutlets
Schilger	*Filets von Zander und Locken à la Palfie au blanc*	Fillets of pike-perch and dogfish
The new chef	*Gratin des Grives à la Viennoise au parmesan, avec garniture gebratene Lerchen*	Thrush gratin in the Viennese style with parmesan topping, trimmed with roast larks

In the event, Frederick put a line straight through these suggestions and substituted in his own hand and in his own idiosyncratic French:

Soupe aux Salssîfie	Salsify soup
Ailes de perdos Glacées	Partridge wings glazed with
au Cardons en petit poix	artichokes and peas
Petit patéz à la Romain	Roman pastry
des allouettes	larks
des clops de Vau à	veal escallops in the English
l'anglaise	manner

To wash it down, there was unlimited Moselle and Pontak, a light red wine, available for his guests, although he himself preferred Bergerac mixed with a little water.[100]

Well ahead of his time in dietary matters at least, Frederick was very fond of fruit and had extensive and expensive greenhouses built in the park at Sanssouci to indulge his taste. In the course of his reign, probably more than half a million talers were spent.[101] Oranges, lemons, melons, figs, apricots, bananas, peaches, cherries, mulberries, pomegranates, greengages, plums, strawberries, pineapples, grapes, pawpaws, walnuts, almonds and many varieties of vegetables, especially asparagus, were all cultivated by an army of gardeners, often in heated greenhouses.[102] Enterprising market gardeners moved to the Potsdam area to take advantage of Frederick's willingness to pay high prices for out-of-season fruit. Although barely credible, the royal accounts show that early cherries were being bought for more than a taler *each*.[103] In 1761 – in the middle of the Seven Years War, in other words – a special glasshouse was built for the cultivation of 'pisang', a banana-like fruit from Malaysia, staffed by a specially trained gardener.[104]

The royal kitchens were also charged with preparing food for Frederick's dogs, who truly lived like kings if not fighting-cocks. It was not odd for a king to like dogs, but it was certainly eccentric to prize them as companions rather than adjuncts for hunting. In this respect, Frederick differed completely from his venatious father.[105] A clear sign that Frederick William had known his end was nigh came in March 1740 when he gave away his hunting dogs to Prince Leopold of

Dessau, sighing that he himself would never be able to hunt again and he feared that Frederick would never take to it.[106] His suspicion would have been confirmed if he had lived long enough to read his son's treatise *Antimachiavel*, for part of that was devoted to an impassioned denunciation of hunting. It was an anti-intellectual, cruel waste of time, Frederick wrote, favoured only by the uncouth and spurned by such great military heroes as Gustavus Adolphus, the Duke of Marlborough and Prince Eugene.[107] Frederick's favourite dogs were not sturdy hunting dogs bred for strength and stamina, but little Italian greyhounds or whippets, combining elegance, delicacy and refinement.[108] Three or four of them were his constant companions, given the free run of the royal apartments and accompanying their master when he went outside for rides or walks. He went to considerable pains to secure the finest specimens from England. The diplomat Thomas Villiers wrote to Algarotti in 1747:

> The Commission for Italian greyhounds is not the less acceptable for being difficult to execute. That sort of dog is very rare and much desired. I will omit no opportunity of obtaining what you want, but I am afraid must wait for the next generation. Few have any but Ladies, & it is not to be expected that they will part with what is fitted to their laps.[109]

Villiers persevered and eventually succeeded. The current favourite sat with Frederick on the sofa, lay under the table at mealtimes, shared his bed at night and was looked after by a dedicated lackey under orders to use the formal *Sie* (rather than the more intimate *Du*) when addressing him or her.[110] According to his physician Dr Zimmermann, while conducting a military review in Silesia in 1785 Frederick had a courier sent each day from Sanssouci to report on the health of a sick dog. Zimmermann added: 'on his return, finding that the little animal was dead and buried, he caused it to be exhumed, that he might have the pleasure of seeing it once more; he shut himself up the whole day, and cried for it like a child'.[111] The ultimate accolade for a favoured dog was to be buried on the terrace of Sanssouci, immediately adjacent to the plot marked out for Frederick's own tomb (although it was not until 1991 that his body was reunited with his canine entourage). Their only rival for Frederick's affections was his favourite horse, the grey gelding bought from England in 1777 and named Condé after Louis XIV's marshal and on whom he lavished the same loving care.[112]

OLD AGE

Frederick had been expecting to join his dogs in their underground tombs for many years – or at least that is what he said. In 1745, at the age of thirty-two, he wrote that he did not expect to live more than twelve years, a prediction that did not seem so foolish when he suffered what contemporaries believed was a mild stroke two years later.[113] On that occasion he wrote: 'once again I have escaped from Pluto's realm, but I was only one station away from the Styx and heard Cerberus howl.'[114] In 1758 he told his secretary, Henri de Catt, that he had only five years left, saying: 'I am getting old. I am getting old.'[115] With gloomy relish, he liked to write to his friends of the inexorable physical decay that had turned him into an old man before his time. The most depressed accounts, not surprisingly, were written at periods of military failure during the Seven Years War. In October 1759, not long after the disaster of Kunersdorf in other words, he told the Marquis d'Argens: 'if you ever see me again, you will find I have aged a great deal: my hair is going grey, my teeth are falling out and no doubt I shall soon be drivelling.'[116] To Countess Camas, his mother's old friend, he added that his face had wrinkles as deep as the folds on a woman's dress, his back was as bent as a bow and he was as sad and depressed as a Trappist monk.[117]

As it turned out, Frederick had more than a quarter of a century left to live, dying at the age of seventy-four, an impressive score by the standards of the day. Like many other long-lived veterans, he was constantly complaining about his health, not unreasonably in his case, for he suffered repeatedly from colic, stomach cramps, migraine, skin rashes, erysipelas, leg ulcers, gout, cramps, asthma, fits of choking, vomiting, constipation, chest pains, fever, dropsy and haemorrhoids, and often simultaneously from a permutation of any of these.[118] They suggest it is likely that he had inherited the porphyria that had made his father's life such a misery.[119] Gout, often accompanied by a high temperature, was a particularly unwelcome visitor, because the pain was often so severe that he had to take to his bed. To Voltaire he wrote at the end of 1775: 'gout held me tied and garrotted for four weeks; gout in both feet, both knees, both hands; and such was its extreme liberality, in both elbows as well. At present the fever and the pain have subsided and I only suffer from very great exhaustion.'[120] Haemorrhoids were another regular affliction, inspiring a playful verse from Voltaire in 1751:

> I wish the haemorrhoidal vein
> Of your royal person
> May cease to trouble your rest.
> When shall I be able to say,
> In a decent way, that my hero's bum
> Is in as good shape as his head?[121]

As Frederick entered his seventh decade, his physical condition naturally deteriorated. That did not stop his inspection journeys, nor did it stop him enjoying himself. A popular image, both contemporary and subsequent, was of 'Old Fritz', prematurely aged, embittered, lonely and misanthropic.[122] It was certainly the case that most of those for whom he felt greatest affection (Keyserlingk, Rothenburg, Fredersdorf, Jordan, his mother, his sister Wilhelmine) had died. He also outlived Johann Joachim Quantz (who died in 1773), Heinrich August de la Motte Fouqué (1774), Charles Théophile Guichard *alias* Quintus Icilius (1775) and Marshal Keith (1778). The loss of the last-named, the Jacobite Earl Marischal, was a particularly bad blow. Lodged by Frederick in a villa on the edge of Sanssouci Park, the bachelor was attended by an exotic entourage known as 'the menagerie', comprising a Tibetan, a Kalmuck and a Moor.[123] He visited his benefactor on a daily basis, at least until he became too infirm, after which Frederick visited him.[124] To these fortuitous losses should be added the friends Frederick drove away by his exploitative behaviour: Algarotti, who left in 1742, returned in 1747 and departed again in 1753; Darget, who left in 1752; and d'Argens, who left in 1765, had to return in 1766 to escape more persecution in France, and left finally in 1768.[125] Frederick's venomous parting shot to d'Argens was: 'you have reinforced the opinion I have always held that princes are only in this world to create ingrates'.[126] To a certain extent, Voltaire has to be added to the list. So any loneliness Frederick may have experienced during his old age was partly of his own making. But in fact the diary of Marchese Girolamo Lucchesini, shows that mealtimes at Sanssouci were still convivial affairs and could last five or six hours. Twenty-eight years old when he arrived in 1779, Lucchesini became Frederick's gentleman-of-the-bedchamber and the person with whom Frederick conversed most, according to the Abbé Denina.[127]

Like most elderly people, Frederick could be demanding, inconsiderate and bad-tempered. As he was also the king, his irritability naturally made life taxing for his immediate entourage. At least he had enough self-knowledge to appreciate that there was nothing he could do about his failing powers. Ten years before his death, he advised d'Alembert to treat his own health problems philosophically: 'our frail bodies decline with age and their decay gradually prepares us for their total disappearance. My gout greets your rheumatism.'[128] Later in 1776, after complaining about an abscess in his ear, he commented: 'nature gives us illnesses and sorrows to disenchant us with this life, which we shall have to leave eventually; I am well aware of this and am resigned to nature's wishes'.[129] So he was determined to make the best of it: 'as I have gout only in my feet and not in my head, my dear d'Alembert, it does not prevent me retaining some traces of my old gaiety'.[130] The best advice for ageing had been provided by the libertine poet Guillaume Amfrye de Chaulieu (1639–1720), he claimed:

> And so, without sorrow and without gloom,
> I feel slow and fateful poison ending my days.
> And yet I spread some flowers
> Along the short path that remains to me.[131]

Ever since he came to the throne, Frederick had pushed his physical resources to the limit. He had preached the virtue of duty and he had practised it. Even if self-inflicted, the rigours of the three Silesian wars had made colossal demands on both his mind and body. Yet he went on pushing them to the limit until almost the very end of his days. On 13 June 1780, for example, he left Küstrin on the river Oder at 3 a.m. after an onerous two-week inspection journey of the eastern provinces. After covering some 100 kilometres in six hours, he was back at his desk in Sanssouci by 9.30 and then spent three and a half hours at table 'as fresh and good-humoured as if he had done nothing that day'.[132] It was not until 1785 that periodic bouts of illness merged into a terminal decline. He went to Silesia as usual for the military exercises, but after spending six hours on horseback in pouring rain on 24 August, he took to his bed with a high temperature. Up again the next day, he was felled by a stroke a month later and was unable to attend the autumn manoeuvres. The winter of 1785–6, spent in the Potsdam Town Palace, was difficult, with symptoms of oedema (dropsy) appearing.[133] On 17 April he returned to Sanssouci, still rising early and working hard, but breathlessness meant he could no longer lie down and had to spend his nights in an armchair. Riding his favourite grey horse, Condé, for forty-five minutes on 4 July left him exhausted. It was around this time that a French brigadier, the Marquis de Toulongeon, paid a visit to Sanssouci. When he saw his '*héros extraordinaire*' on the terrace, he almost fainted with excitement, so imbued was he with '*respect saint*'.[134] Daniel Chodowiecki's image of the dying king in his armchair, looking out over the park, as his dogs frisk around him, was to achieve iconic status.

Conclusion: Death and Transfiguration

The last days of Frederick in the summer of 1786 were described in detail in letters sent by the foreign minister, Count Hertzberg, who arrived at Sanssouci on 8 July, to his colleague Count Finckenstein, who had remained in Berlin. A clear sign that hope had been abandoned came when the medical team was reduced. On 11 July Frederick sent home Dr Zimmermann, whose summons from Hanover the previous month had implied a certain lack of confidence in his regular doctor, Christian Gottlieb Selle. Although Zimmermann's thirty bedside visits cost 2,000 talers, his difficult patient dismissed this last-ditch treatment as 'useless'.[1] In late July there was a sharp deterioration in Frederick's condition, occasioned by digestive problems. By the last day of the month he was in too much pain to cope with the daily session of reading out loud provided by his private secretary, Dantal. Appropriately, what proved to be the last work read to him was by Voltaire.[2] Ten days of semi-remission followed. Frederick regained his appetite, slept better, enjoyed the company of his close circle twice a day and attended to business. But on 12 August, after announcing that he felt 'reborn', he sank into a deep sleep. Although Frederick eventually woke from that, Hertzberg reported: 'he is still transacting all the business, but is doing so with reluctance and in a hurry, and because he is having to force himself, his mind is not fully on what he is reading'.[3] Three days later, he was still working with his secretaries early in the morning, although his shaky signature betrayed growing weakness. His long-standing promise to work until he dropped was very nearly fulfilled. On 16 August he summoned General Rohdich from the antechamber but could not articulate what he wanted to say and fell asleep. He rallied again in the afternoon, and the last order he gave was for a cushion to be found for his dog. His very last words, after a coughing fit had brought some relief, were: 'We have got over the mountain, now our path will be easier.' At 2.19 a.m. on Thursday, 17 August, he expired.[4] It need hardly be added that no clergyman was in attendance.[5] Nor was his wife. Unusually, and for reasons that have never been explained satisfactorily, a death-mask was taken the same day.

For forty-six years, Frederick had tried to rule Prussia single-handed. If he had asked a great deal from himself, he had made just as many demands on his servants and subjects, high and low. How did they all feel when the iron band that held them to their labours finally snapped? According to Mirabeau, the general response was one of overwhelming relief.[6] Whatever else it might prove to be, the next regime was certain to be more relaxed. The new king, who succeeded as Frederick William II, may well have been the most relieved of all. For forty-one years he had been kept on a very tight rein by his disapproving not to say contemptuous uncle. Well into middle age by the standards of the day (he had been born in 1744), he could now make up for lost time by suiting himself.

An early indication that the new king would be his own man came when he overturned Frederick's strict instructions as to how his mortal remains were to be disposed. In his final will and testament dated 8 January 1769, Frederick had stated firmly:

> Gladly and without complaint I return my breath of life to the benevolent nature that was kind enough to grant it to me in the first place, and my body to the elements of which it is composed. I have lived as a philosophe and wish to be buried like one, without any pageantry, pomp or ceremony. I do not wish to be either dissected or embalmed. I am to be interred at Sanssouci on the top terrace, in the vault which I have had built there.[7]

Although Frederick William did not order embalming, he did organize a grandiose set of obsequial ceremonies based on those staged for Frederick William I in 1740. On the evening of the day of his death, Frederick's corpse, clad in the uniform of the First Battalion of Guards, was moved to the Potsdam Town Palace on a hearse drawn by eight horses.[8] After being put on display, it was removed on the following day (18 August) to the vault of the Garrison Church and placed in a simple pewter coffin alongside that of his father.[9] Meanwhile, a hastily assembled team of architects and artists had created a mourning suite of rooms in the Town Palace, the walls covered in purple and black cloth. In the Audience Chamber was placed an empty ceremonial coffin, 'richly ornamented with cloth of silver, laced with gold'.[10] On it were laid Frederick's sword, his sash of the Order of the Black Eagle, gold spurs and marshal's baton. During the next few days around 60,000 members of the public filed by to pay their last respects.[11]

How much more would Frederick have detested the religious element that his successor also imposed. At the end of August it was announced that all memorial services staged across Prussia were to be informed by a verse from the Old Testament: 'And I have been with thee whithersoever thou hast walked, and have cut off all thine enemies from before thee, and have made thee a name like the name of the great men that *are* in the earth' (1 Chronicles 17:8).[12] On 9 September the state funeral was held in the Garrison Church at Potsdam, where Frederick's body was to lie until 1943, when intensifying Allied bombing raids prompted its removal to a place of greater safety. Discovered by American soldiers in a potash mine in Lower Saxony, it was moved first to a church in Marburg and then to the Hohenzollern castle at Sigmaringen on the Upper Danube. It was not until 17 August 1991 that Frederick's wish to be buried at Sanssouci alongside his dogs was eventually fulfilled. Apparently with a straight face, the agent of the Hohenzollern family, Job Ferdinand von Strantz, justified this final chapter in the long odyssey of Frederick's remains on the grounds that he was 'an icon of German unity'.[13] On the day after Frederick's funeral, a memorial service was held in Berlin Cathedral in the presence of the new king and all the royals, including Frederick's widow. The court preacher, Friedrich Samuel Gottfried Sack, delivered a fulsome eulogy but did not try to pretend that the deceased had been distinguished by piety. Rather he emphasized that God had walked with Frederick as his 'protector, helper, guide and saviour', implying that this had been happening whether the beneficiary was aware of it or not.[14]

A Frederick cult got underway at once, as entrepreneurs moved in to satisfy what was clearly a large and growing demand for memorabilia. His image was reproduced on drinking vessels, clocks, bracelets, ribbons, snuff-boxes and vivat ribbons, as well as in books, pamphlets, periodicals and calendars.[15] Perhaps the most enterprising of all were the Pages brothers, who bought Frederick's clothes from the court chamberlain, dressed up a wax figure and then hawked it around Germany, France and the Habsburg Monarchy, making a fortune along the way. So valuable was it that they turned down an offer of 4,000 talers. They were soon flattered sincerely, as imitators hurried to cash in too: by the early nineteenth century, there were sixteen wax figures of Frederick on display in Berlin.[16] In 1796 a leading German periodical, the *Journal of Luxury and Fashion*, reported on a magic-lantern show staged at the theatre in Behrens Street:

> In the distance a bright star appeared; it grew larger and out of it emerged a very good likeness of Frederick the Great in his usual uniform and in his usual stance . . . The impression this vision made on the audience was striking. The clapping and cheering did not stop. When Frederick began to fade back into his star, many shouted 'Oh, stay here with us!' And when he did disappear, the shouts of 'Encore!' were such that he had to come out twice more.[17]

The cult continued to grow. In 1833 the director of the Hohenzollern collection of Frederickian memorabilia wondered at the 'seemingly unquenchable thirst of the multitudes who hurry hither to gain a greater knowledge of the great man ... I am daily witness to the astounding effect that the sight of the precious mementoes of Prussia's Frederick, which are kept here, elicit from beholders of all ages, every class, every nation.'[18] Happily, he had turned out to be wonderfully protean, a man of the Enlightenment to be deployed against the reactionaries, an egalitarian against the aristocrats, a military hero against the civilians, a nationalist against the particularists, a liberal against the conservatives, and so on.

So strong a character had Frederick been that he was to be as divisive in death as he had been in life. His eventful afterlife has been recounted many times and does not need to be repeated here.[19] The contrasting examples of two family members can serve instead to illustrate the extreme reactions he aroused. No relation benefited more from Frederick's generosity than his brother Prince Henry, who was given a princely income, Rheinsberg, a huge palace in Berlin, high command in the army and was entrusted with several important diplomatic missions. Yet this largesse was repaid only with intense hatred, which did not mellow with the passing of time. Four years after Frederick's death, Henry erected a large obelisk at Rheinsberg, so prominently positioned that the attention of anyone looking across the lake from the palace would be drawn to it. Its chief purpose was to serve as a memorial for Prince August Wilhelm, the brother whom Frederick had disgraced after the retreat from Bohemia in 1757.* But it was also intended to be a more general indictment of Frederick as military commander. Twenty-eight medallions commemorated the other heroes whose dedication, skill and courage had made Prussian success possible but whose feats had been ignored by Frederick in his version of the campaigns ('about whom his fucking memoirs say nothing' was how Henry put it in a letter to General Henckel von Donnersmarck[20]). The accompanying inscriptions transferred the credit from commander-in-chief to subordinates. The tribute to Marshal Schwerin, for example, read in part: 'On 10 April 1741 he won the Battle of Mollwitz' and that to General von Möllendorff: 'At Torgau in 1760 he seized the heights of Siptitz and thus wrested victory from the enemy. In 1762 after he had taken the hills above Burkersdorf in the same manner, he forced Marshal Daun to retreat.' General Platen was credited with restoring order after the disaster at Kunersdorf and covering the retreat. More subtle was the commendation awarded to General von Zieten for 'showing contempt to all those who enriched themselves at the expense of conquered civilians'. And so it went on. Although Frederick was never mentioned, he was obviously the target of Prince Henry's bile.[21]

The polar opposite of Prince Henry was Frederick's widow, Elizabeth Christine. If anyone had good reason to celebrate his passing, it was surely she. Ironically, the last time she set eyes on her husband was at Prince Henry's fifty-ninth birthday party on 18 January 1785. Yet when informed of his death, she became 'very deeply distressed' according to Princess Radziwill, who had brought the news: 'She wept

---

* See above, p. 275.

for the King as if she had been loved by him!'[22] During her decade of widowhood (she died on 13 January 1797), she never wavered in her simple devotion to Frederick's memory, always excusing his behaviour towards her by reference to the influence of 'false friends' and his poor health which made travelling from Potsdam to Berlin difficult. She also went on adding to her collection of portraits of Frederick. Back in 1736 she had written to her grandmother that she was very proud to be married to such a great man, the greatest prince of his age thanks to his wisdom, intelligence and sense of justice. That remained her attitude until the end.[23] Always devout, she became conspicuously pious during old age, writing and publishing improving tracts for the times. This would have attracted only the derision of her late husband but it won her the respect and affection of the plain people of Berlin, most of whom probably viewed libertine Potsdam with disdain if not disgust.

'All political lives, unless they are cut off in midstream at a happy juncture, end in failure, because that is the nature of politics and of human affairs,' wrote Enoch Powell in his life of Joseph Chamberlain.[24] He had in mind elected politicians, who never know when to resign and almost invariably hang on too long before sliding back down the greasy pole, but it applies to hereditary sovereigns too, albeit less emphatically. If Louis XIV had died in 1688 or even 1697, he might now bear the sobriquet 'le Grand'. If Napoleon had been killed at Wagram in 1809, he too would qualify for superhuman status. Among the handful of exceptions who died in the nick of time, Elizabeth I of England and Frederick the Great stand out. Almost exactly a year after the latter's death, the Turkish declaration of war on Russia pushed the Eastern Question to the top of the international agenda and began what later developed into the French Revolutionary and Napoleonic Wars. In the short term, this brought the opportunity for massive territorial expansion at the expense of Poland. Indeed, more territory was added to Prussia during the eleven-year reign of Frederick William II, usually depicted as a lazy voluptuary who squandered his inheritance, than during the forty-six-year reign of his predecessor. Of course we know that it all ended in tears at Jena and Auerstedt in 1806. To debate just how much responsibility for that double disaster should be laid at the door of Frederick is not rewarding. However many problems he left unsolved when he died, and, as we have seen, there were plenty of them, his two successors had twenty years in which to address them. Moreover, along with the problems they also inherited many assets, not the least of them being the conviction of most Prussians that, thanks to Frederick's achievements, they lived in a state they could be proud of.

It was Napoleon himself who emphasized the ambivalent nature of Frederick's legacy. On 15 October 1806, the day after his great double victory over Prussia, his Fifth Army Bulletin proclaimed that at last the fifty-year stain of Rossbach had been expunged. On reaching Berlin a week later, he visited both Sanssouci and Frederick's tomb in the vault of the Garrison Church. It was some measure of the importance he attached to his defeat of Prussia that he had a host of Frederickian artefacts, including his sword, statues and paintings, removed to Paris, where they were put on display in the rotunda of the Louvre, renamed the 'Hall of Victory'.[25] Prussia itself was then treated with unprecedented severity, stripped of half its territory at the Peace of Tilsit in 1807, impoverished by massive reparations and bled white by an army of occupation.[26] The revitalization of Prussian institutions and, above all, Prussian attitudes, which then followed, would not have been possible without the participation of numerous 'Prussians by choice', notably Gneisenau, Scharnhorst, Hardenberg and Blücher, attracted from other German states by the ethos fostered by Frederick. It was this transformation which allowed the rump-state to mobilize 279,000 soldiers in 1813–15, a higher proportion (11 per cent) of adult males than was achieved by any other combatant.[27] What is more, the manner in which they fought showed that they had adopted the military methods of the French Revolution but taken them further, an appropriation facilitated by 'the seeds of their innovation being already present in Prussian soil'.[28] To conclude with a continuation of this horticultural metaphor: if the foliage of Prussia in 1786 looked as withered as the old king's body, the tap-root went deep and, when properly cultivated, would again yield the fruits of power and culture.

Notes

ABBREVIATIONS

Œuvres:
Œuvres de Frédéric le Grand, ed. J. D. E. Preuss, 30 vols. (Berlin, 1846–56) http://friedrich.uni-trier.de/de/oeuvres/toc/

P.C.:
Politische Correspondenz Friedrich's des Grossen, ed. Johann Gustav Droysen et al, 46 vols. (Berlin, 1879–1939) http://friedrich.uni-trier.de/de/politKorr/toc/

Carlyle:
Thomas Carlyle, History of Friedrich II. of Prussia, Called Frederick the Great, 6 vols. (London, 1858–65)

Dietrich:
Richard Dietrich (ed.), Die politischen Testamente der Hohenzollern (Cologne, 1986)

Friederisiko, Ausstellung:
Jürgen Luh and Ullrich Sachse (eds.), Friederisiko. Friedrich der Grosse. Die Ausstellung (Munich, 2012)

Friederisiko, Essays:
Jürgen Luh and Ullrich Sachse (eds.), Friederisiko. Friedrich der Grosse. Die Essays (Munich, 2012)

Hintze:
Otto Hintze, Die Hohenzollern und ihr Werk, 8th edn (Berlin, 1916)

Koser:
Reinhold Koser, König Friedrich der Grosse, 2 vols., 3rd edn (Stuttgart and Berlin, 1904)

Lehndorff:
Karl Eduard Schmidt-Lötzen (ed.), Dreissig Jahre am Hofe Friedrichs des Grossen: aus den Tagebüchern des Reichsgrafen Ernst Ahasverus Heinrich von Lehndorff, Kammerherrn der Königin Elisabeth Christine von Preussen, 3 vols. (Gotha, 1907–13)

Sösemann: Bernd Sösemann and Gregor Vogt-Spira (eds.), *Friedrich der Grosse in Europa*, 2 vols. (Stuttgart, 2012)

INTRODUCTION

1. Paul Hartig (ed.), *Henri de Catt, Vorleser Friedrichs des Grossen. Die Tagebücher 1758–60* (Munich and Berlin, 1986), p. 151.
2. Friedrich Nicolai, *Anekdoten von Friedrich dem Grossen und von einigen Personen, die um ihn waren* (Munich, n.d.), pp. 187–90. Nicolai was told all this by Quantz. It certainly has the ring of authenticity.
3. Hartig (ed.), *Henri de Catt*, p. 163.

I. THE INHERITANCE

1. *Œuvres*, vol. 23, p. 412; vol. 9, p. 217.
2. Frederick to d'Alembert, 4 October 1768, ibid., vol. 24, p. 491.
3. Hugo Rachel, 'Der Merkantilismus in Brandenburg-Preussen', in Otto Büsch and Wolfgang Neugebauer (eds.), *Moderne Preussische Geschichte* (Berlin and New York, 1981), vol. 2, p. 954; Joachim Whaley, *Germany and the Holy Roman Empire*, vol. 1: *The Peace of Westphalia to the Dissolution of the Reich 1648–1806* (Oxford, 2011), p. 274.
4. Jürgen Luh, *Kriegskunst in Europa 1650–1800* (Cologne, Weimar and Vienna, 2004), p. 117.
5. Haug von Kuenheim (ed.), *Aus den Tagebüchern des Grafen Ernst Ahasverus Heinrich von Lehndorff* (Berlin, 1982), p. 145.
6. Dietrich, p. 229.
7. Hans Dollinger, *Preussen. Eine Kulturgeschichte in Bildern und Dokumenten* (Munich, 1980), p. 102; Mack Walker, *The Salzburg Transaction. Expulsion and Redemption in Eighteenth-century Germany* (Ithaca and London, 1993), p. 74.
8. Koser, vol. 1, p. 370.
9. There is an excellent and concise account of Brandenburg's history in the early modern period in the first chapter of Karin Friedrich's *Brandenburg-Prussia 1466–1806. The Rise of a Composite State* (Basingstoke, 2012).
10. Koser, vol. 1, p. 364.
11. J. D. E. Preuss, *Friedrichs des Grossen Jugend und Thronbesteigung* (Berlin, 1840), p. 318; Gustavo Corni, *Stato assoluto e società agraria*

in Prussia nell'età di Federico II (Bologna, 1982), p. 79. A slightly lower figure – 3,300,000 – is given by Werner Heegewaldt in 'Friderizianische Domänenpolitik am Beispiel der Kurmark', in Frank Göse (ed.), *Friedrich der Grosse und die Mark Brandenburg. Herrschaftspraxis in der Provinz* (Berlin, 2012), p. 163.

12. Hintze, p. 295; Theodor Schieder, *Friedrich der Grosse. Ein Königtum der Widersprüche* (Frankfurt am Main, Berlin and Vienna, 1983), p. 73.

13. Hans-Heinrich Müller, 'Domänen und Domänenpächter in Brandenburg-Preussen im 18. Jahrhundert', in Büsch and Neugebauer (eds.), *Moderne Preussische Geschichte*, vol. 1, p. 316; Wilhelm Treue, 'Staat, "Untertan" und Gemeinde als Unternehmer in Preussen', in *Preussen – Versuch einer Bilanz* (Hamburg, 1981), vol. 2: *Preussen – Beiträge zu einer politischen Kultur*, ed. Manfred Schlenke, p. 222.

14. Hintze, p. 287.

15. F. L. Carsten, 'Die Entstehung des Junkertums', in Büsch and Neugebauer (eds.), *Moderne Preussische Geschichte*, vol. 1, p. 265.

16. Robert M. Berdahl, *The Politics of the Prussian Nobility. The Development of a Conservative Ideology 1770–1848* (Princeton, 1988), p. 15.

17. Ibid., p. 16.

18. Otto Büsch, *Militärsystem und Sozialleben im alten Preussen* (Berlin, 1962), p. 77.

19. Christopher Clark, *Iron Kingdom. The Rise and Downfall of Prussia 1600–1947* (London, 2006), pp. 162–3.

20. Christof Dipper, *Deutsche Geschichte 1648–1789* (Frankfurt am Main, 1991), pp. 287–8.

21. Whaley, *Germany and the Holy Roman Empire*, vol. 2, p. 216.

22. Peter H. Wilson, 'Prusso-German social militarisation reconsidered', in Jürgen Luh, Vinzenz Czech and Bert Becker (eds.), *Preussen, Deutschland und Europa, 1701–2001* (Groningen, 2003), p. 363.

23. Volker Press, *Kriege und Krisen. Deutschland 1600–1715* (Munich, 1991), p. 363.

24. Walker, *The Salzburg Transaction*, pp. 80–81; Carlyle, vol. 2, pp. 318–19. In some accounts he is referred to as 'Schlabuth'.

25. Dietrich, pp. 228–31.

26. Gustav Schmoller, 'Die Entstehung des preussischen Heeres von 1640 bis 1740', in Büsch and Neugebauer (eds.), *Moderne Preussische Geschichte*, vol. 2, pp. 762–3.

27. Büsch, *Militärsystem und Sozialleben im alten Preussen*, p. 80, n. 8.

28. Schmoller, 'Die Entstehung des preussischen Heeres', p. 763.

29. Edgar Melton, 'The Prussian Junkers, 1600–1786', in H. M. Scott (ed.), *The European Nobilities in the Seventeenth and Eighteenth Centuries* (London, 1995), vol. 2, p. 95.

30. Helga Schultz, *Berlin 1650–1800. Sozialgeschichte einer Residenz* (Berlin, 1987), p. 153; Günter Vogler and Klaus Vetter, *Preussen von den Anfängen bis zur Reichsgründung* (Cologne, 1981), p. 35.

31. Melton, 'The Prussian Junkers', p. 96.

32. Büsch, *Militärsystem und Sozialleben*, pp. 94–5; Christian Graf Krockow, *Warnung vor Preussen* (Berlin, 1982), p. 115.

33. C. B. A. Behrens, *Society, Government, and the Enlightenment: the Experiences of Eighteenth-century France and Prussia* (London, 1985), pp. 143–4.

34. Frank O'Gorman, *The Long Eighteenth Century. British Political and Social History 1688–1832* (London, 1997), p. 136.

35. Hintze, p. 281.

36. Ibid., p. 294.

37. Günter Birtsch, 'Friedrich Wilhelm I. und die Anfänge der Aufklärung in Brandenburg-Preussen', in Oswald Hauser (ed.), *Preussen, Europa und das Reich* (Cologne and Vienna, 1987), p. 88; Gerhard Oestreich, *Friedrich Wilhelm I. Preussischer Absolutismus, Merkantilismus, Militarismus* (Göttingen, 1977), p. 111.

38. Hans Rosenberg, *Bureaucracy, Aristocracy and Autocracy. The Prussian Experience 1660–1815* (Boston, 1966), *passim*. Rosenberg's account of the Prussian bureaucracy is unrelentingly negative.

39. Peter Paret, 'Nationalism and the sense of military obligation', *Military Affairs*, 34, 1 (1970), p. 3.

40. Hintze, p. 171.

41. *Œuvres*, vol. 1, p. 46.

42. See the summary table in Günther Franz, *Der Dreissigjährige Krieg und das deutsche Volk*, 3rd edn (Stuttgart, 1961), p. 15.

43. Quoted in Clark, *Iron Kingdom*, p. 66.

44. Schmoller, 'Die Entstehung des preussischen Heeres von 1640 bis 1740', p. 749.

45. Whaley, *Germany and the Holy Roman Empire*, vol. 2, p. 627.

46. Press, *Kriege und Krisen*, p. 333.

47. Hans Meier-Welcker, *Deutsches Heerwesen im Wandel der Zeit* (Frankfurt am Main, 1956), p. 10.

48. Schmoller, 'Die Entstehung des preussischen Heeres von 1640 bis 1740', p. 749.

49. *Œuvres*, vol. 1, p. 90.

50. Press, *Kriege und Krisen,* p. 360.

51. Dipper, *Deutsche Geschichte 1648–1789,* p. 302.

52. Carl Hinrichs, 'Der grosse Kurfürst', in Gerhard Oestreich (ed.), *Preussen als historisches Problem* (Berlin, 1964), p. 234.

53. Werner Schmidt, *Friedrich I. Kurfürst von Brandenburg, König in Preussen,* 2nd edn (Munich, 1998), p. 181.

54. Heinz Kathe, *Der Soldatenkönig. Friedrich Wilhelm I. 1688–1740. König in Preussen* (Cologne, 1981), p. 23.

55. Schmoller, 'Die Entstehung des preussischen Heeres von 1640 bis 1740', p. 756; Wolfgang Petter, 'Zur Kriegskunst im Zeitalter Friedrichs des Grossen', in Bernhard R. Kroener (ed.), *Europa im Zeitalter Friedrichs des Grossen. Wirtschaft, Gesellschaft, Kriege* (Munich, 1989), p. 254.

56. *Œuvres,* vol. 1, p. 47.

57. Robert Ergang, *The Potsdam Führer: Frederick William I, Father of Prussian Militarism* (New York, 1941), p. 67.

58. Johann Christoph Allmayer-Beck, 'Die friderizianische Armee im Spiegel ihrer österreichischen Gegner', in *Friedrich der Grosse und das Militärwesen seiner Zeit* (Herford and Bonn, 1987) [no editor listed], p. 36.

59. Preuss, *Friedrichs des Grossen Jugend,* p. 348.

60. Gerd Heinrich, *Geschichte Preussens. Staat und Dynastie* (Frankfurt am Main, Berlin and Vienna, 1981), p. 142.

61. Schmoller, 'Die Entstehung des preussischen Heeres von 1640 bis 1740', p. 760; Walther Hubatsch, *Frederick the Great. Absolutism and Administration* (London, 1975), p. 132.

62. Wilson, 'Prusso-German social militarisation reconsidered', p. 364; Clark, *Iron Kingdom,* p. 98.

63. Dietrich, p. 518.

64. Christopher Duffy, *The Army of Maria Theresa. The Armed Forces of Imperial Austria 1740–1780* (London, 1977), p. 52.

65. Dietrich, p. 184.

66. Klaus Deppermann, *Der hallesche Pietismus und der preussische Staat unter Friedrich III. (I.)* (Göttingen, 1961), p. 62.

67. Oestreich, *Friedrich Wilhelm I. Preussischer Absolutismus, Merkantilismus, Militarismus,* p. 84.

68. W. R. Ward, *Christianity under the Ancien Régime 1648–1789* (Cambridge, 1999), p. 80.

69. Deppermann, *Der hallesche Pietismus,* p. 166.

70. Carl Hinrichs, *Preussentum und Pietismus. Der Pietismus in Brandenburg-Preussen als religiös-soziale Reformbewegung* (Göttingen, 1971), p. 128.

71. Ibid., pp. 146–51.

72. Ibid., p. 175. See also Mary Fulbrook, *Piety and Politics. Religion and the Rise of Absolutism in England, Württemberg and Prussia* (Cambridge, 1983), pp. 165–77.

73. Peter H. Wilson, *The Holy Roman Empire 1495–1806*, 2nd edn (Basingstoke, 2011), p. 49.

74. *Mémoires de Charles-Louis Baron de Pöllnitz, contenant les observations qu'il a faites dans ses voyages et le caractère des personnes qui composent les principales cours de l'Europe*, new edn (Liège, 1734), vol. 1, p. 154.

75. The fortunes of the Wettin family can be best followed in word and image in the lavishly illustrated exhibition catalogue edited by Werner Schmidt and Dirk Syndram, *Unter einer Krone. Kunst und Kultur der sächsisch-polnischen Union* (Leipzig, 1997), which contains many excellent scholarly articles. I have discussed the Dresden court in greater detail in my *The Pursuit of Glory: Europe 1648–1815* (London, 2007), ch. 8.

76. Heinz Duchhardt, *Altes Reich und europäische Staatenwelt 1648–1806* (Munich, 1990), p. 27.

77. Ragnhild Hatton, *George I* (London, 1978), p. 46.

78. I have discussed this further in *The Pursuit of Glory*, pp. 275–85. The definitive account of the Holy Roman Empire in the period is now Whaley, *Germany and the Holy Roman Empire*, vol. 2.

79. Thomas Biskup, *Friedrichs Grösse. Inszenierungen des Preussenkönigs in Fest und Zeremoniell 1740–1815* (Frankfurt am Main and New York, 2012), p. 34.

80. Heinrich, *Geschichte Preussens*, p. 130.

81. There is an excellent account of the coronation and its context in Clark, *Iron Kingdom*, pp. 67–77 and see also his article 'When culture meets power: the Prussian coronation of 1701', in Hamish Scott and Brendan Simms (eds.), *Cultures of Power in the Long Eighteenth Century* (Cambridge, 2007). For contemporary accounts of both the coronation and the creation of the Order of the Black Eagle, see Karin Friedrich and Sara Smart (eds.), *The Cultivation of Monarchy and the Rise of Berlin* (Farnham, 2010), chs. 5 and 6.

82. Press, *Kriege und Krisen*, p. 362.

83. Schmidt, *Friedrich I.*, pp. 109–10.

84. *Œuvres*, vol. 1, pp. 112–44.

85. Wolfgang Neugebauer, *Die Hohenzollern* (Stuttgart, 1996), vol. 1, p. 188.

86. Peter Baumgart, 'Der deutsche Hof der Barockzeit als politische Institution', in August Buck, Georg Kauffmann, Blake Lee Spahr and Conrad

Wiedemann (eds.), *Europäische Hofkultur im 16. und 17. Jahrhundert. Vorträge und Referate gehalten anlässlich des Kongresses des Wolfenbütteler Arbeitskreises für Barockliteratur in der Herzog August Bibliothek Wolfenbüttel vom 4. bis 8. September 1979* (Hamburg, 1981), p. 28. A conspicuous absentee from this list of survivors is Frederick I's city palace in Berlin, which was damaged by bombing in 1945 and demolished by the East German regime in 1950.

87. Dietrich, p. 222; Baumgart, 'Der deutsche Hof der Barockzeit als politische Institution', p. 29; Volker Bauer, *Die höfische Gesellschaft in Deutschland von der Mitte des 17. bis zum Ausgang des 18. Jahrhunderts. Versuch einer Typologie* (Tübingen, 1993), p. 68.

88. Gerd Bartoschek, 'Die Malerei im friderizianischen Berlin', in Hans-Joachim Giersberg and Claudia Meckel (eds.), *Friedrich II. und die Kunst* (Potsdam, 1986), vol. 2, p. 169. Some of the musicians found employment with Frederick William's nephew, Margrave Christian Ludwig of Brandenburg-Schwedt, to whom Johann Sebastian Bach in 1721 dedicated the 'Six Concertos for Several Instruments' which later became better known as the 'Brandenburg Concertos'.

89. Dollinger, *Preussen*, p. 103.

90. Schultz, *Berlin 1650–1800*, p. 98.

91. Oestreich, *Friedrich Wilhelm I.*, p. 51; Carsten Kretschmann, 'Präsentation und Repräsentation. Sammlungen und Kabinette als Schnittstellen einer république des lettres', in Sösemann, vol. 1, p. 309.

92. *Œuvres*, vol. 2, p. 1.

93. Thomas Biskup has shown that Frederick William I's frugality has been exaggerated, pointing out that during the second half of the reign, the court expanded once more and that large sums of money were spent on the interior decoration of the royal palace in Berlin – *Friedrichs Grösse*, p. 36 and idem, 'Eines "Grossen" würdig? Hof und Zeremoniell bei Friedrich II.', in Friederisiko, Essays, p. 101. He also initiated a building boom in 1733 which led to the construction of thirty-three new noble residences by the end of the decade – Melanie Mertens, *Berliner Barockpaläste. Die Entstehung eines Bautyps in der Zeit der ersten preussischen Könige* (Berlin, 2003), p. 10. The confident assertion of Gerhard Oestreich in *Friedrich Wilhelm I.*, p. 61 that he spent only 1 per cent of his revenue on the court is unverifiable but certainly too low.

94. *Œuvres*, vol. 2, p. 8. I have used the excellent translation to be found in *Posthumous Works* (London, 1789), vol. 1, p. 12.

2. THE BREAKING OF FREDERICK

1. Ida Macalpine and Richard Hunter, *George III and the Mad-Business* (London, 1969), pp. 196, 214. Although long accepted, recently their findings have been challenged by Timothy J. Peters and D. Wilkinson, in 'King George III and porphyria: a clinical re-examination of the historical evidence', *History of Psychiatry*, 21 (2010), pp. 3–19. They conclude that it is 'very unlikely' that the king was suffering from porphyria and that the cause of his disorder will never be known.

2. Nick Lane, 'Born to the Purple: the story of porphyria', *Scientific American*, 16 December 2002, http://www.scientificamerican.com/article.cfm?id=born-to-the-purple-the-st, accessed 20 March 2012.

3. Claus A. Pierach and Erich Jennewein, 'Friedrich Wilhelm I. und Porphyrie', *Sudhoffs Archiv. Zeitschrift für Wissenschaftsgeschichte*, 83, 1 (1999), p. 52.

4. Ibid., pp. 53–61.

5. Gustav Berthold Volz (ed.), *Friedrich der Grosse und Wilhelmine von Bayreuth* (Leipzig, 1924), vol. 1: *Jugendbriefe 1728–1740*, p. 248.

6. Ibid., p. 54.

7. Crown Prince Frederick to his sister Wilhelmine, Potsdam, 14 October 1734, in Otto Bardong (ed.), *Friedrich der Grosse, Ausgewählte Quellen zur deutschen Geschichte der Neuzeit*. Freiherr vom Stein-Gedächtnisausgabe (Darmstadt, 1982), vol. 22, p. 56.

8. It later went on display in the Hohenzollern Museum – Eva Giloi, *Monarchy, Myth and Material Culture in Germany 1750–1950* (Cambridge, 2012), p. 3.

9. Carl Hinrichs, *Friedrich Wilhelm I. König in Preussen. Eine Biographie* (Hamburg, 1941), pp. 19–20.

10. Ernest Lavisse, *The Youth of Frederick the Great*, trans. Mary Bushnell Coleman (Chicago, 1892), p. 34.

11. Robert Ergang, *The Potsdam Führer: Frederick William I, Father of Prussian Militarism* (New York, 1941), pp. 25, 44.

12. Christian Graf von Krockow, *Die preussischen Brüder. Prinz Heinrich und Friedrich der Grosse. Ein Doppelporträt* (Stuttgart, 1996), p. 16.

13. Theodor Schieder, *Friedrich der Grosse. Ein Königtum der Widersprüche* (Frankfurt am Main, Berlin and Vienna, 1983), p. 19.

14. Gerhard Oestreich, *Friedrich Wilhelm I. Preussischer Absolutismus, Merkantilismus, Militarismus* (Göttingen, 1977), p. 50; Peter Baumgart, 'Friedrich Wilhelm I.', in Frank-Lothar Kroll (ed.), *Preussens Herrscher. Von den ersten Hohenzollern bis Wilhelm II.* (Munich, 2000), p. 142.

15. Krockow, *Die preussischen Brüder*, p. 17.
16. Arnold Berney, *Friedrich der Grosse. Entwicklungsgeschichte eines Staatsmannes* (Tübingen, 1934), p. 3; Baumgart, 'Friedrich Wilhelm I.', p. 142.
17. Volker Hentschel, *Preussens streitbare Geschichte 1494–1945* (Düsseldorf, 1980), p. 54.
18. Peter-Michael Hahn, *Friedrich II. von Preussen* (Stuttgart, 2013), p. 21.
19. Wolfgang Neugebauer, *Die Hohenzollern* (Stuttgart, 1996), vol. 1, p. 198.
20. Krockow, *Die preussischen Brüder*, p. 27. For an illustration and full description, see http://de.wikipedia.org/wiki/Jagdschloss_Stern.
21. Marina thom Suden, *Schlösser in Berlin und Brandenburg und ihre bildliche Ausstattung im 18. Jahrhundert* (Petersberg, 2013), p. 12.
22. Ingeborg Weber-Kellermann (ed.), *Wilhelmine von Bayreuth. Eine preussische Königstochter* (Frankfurt am Main, 1990), p. 103.
23. Seckendorf to Prince Eugene, Altenburg, 22 January 1727, in Friedrich Förster, *Friedrich Wilhelm I. König von Preussen* (Potsdam, 1835), vol. 3, p. 333.
24. A good-quality reproduction can be found at http://de.wikipedia.org/w/index.php?title=Datei:Tabakskollegium-1.jpg&filetimestamp=20111030163456.
25. http://de.wikipedia.org/wiki/Tabakskollegium.
26. Ergang, *The Potsdam Führer*, p. 30.
27. Oestreich, *Friedrich Wilhelm I.*, p. 50.
28. Ergang, *The Potsdam Führer*, p. 28.
29. Hinrichs, *Friedrich Wilhelm I. König in Preussen*, pp. 36–7.
30. Dietrich, p. 243.
31. Ibid., pp. 221–43.
32. Weber-Kellermann (ed.), *Wilhelmine von Bayreuth*, pp. 285–6.
33. Carlyle, vol. 2, p. 55.
34. I have been unable to find a good colour reproduction. The best available is at http://www.google.co.uk/imgres?q=friedrich+wilhelm+i&hl=en&biw=1366&bih=599&gbv=2&tbm=isch&tbnid=pKaQCELNYjIVUM:&imgrefurl=http://www.preussen.de/de/geschichte/1713_friedrich_wilhelm_i./friedrich_wilhelm_i._-_fortsetzung.html&docid=ks-E-FPGts3yPM&imgurl=http://www.preussen.de/Bilder/Geschichte/friedrich_wilhelm_I./friedrich_wilhelm_I_selbstportrait_LDM.jpg&w=210&h=267&ei=svFqT7HvLs7I8gOPl6HKBg&zoom=1&iact=hc&vpx=882&vpy=271&dur=3524&hovh=213&hovw=168&tx=82&ty=173&sig=1037542798
96405635068&page=1&tbnh=121&tbnw=87&start=0&ndsp=30&

ved=1t:429,r:27,s:0. There is a black-and-white reproduction in Krockow, *Die preussischen Brüder*, p. 14.

35. Gerd Bartoschek, 'Die Malerei im friderizianischen Berlin', in Hans-Joachim Giersberg and Claudia Meckel (eds.), *Friedrich II. und die Kunst* (Potsdam, 1986), vol. 2, p. 169; Martina Weinland, 'Friedrich II. Der erste Kronprinz und seine Erziehung durch Friedrich Wilhelm I.', in Martina Weinland (ed.), *Im Dienste Preussens. Wer erzog Prinzen zu Königen?* (Berlin, 2001), p. 76.

36. Hinrichs, *Friedrich Wilhelm I. König in Preussen*, pp. 211–13.

37. Lehndorff, vol. 1, pp. 323–4.

38. Wolfgang Venohr, *Der Soldatenkönig. Revolutionär auf dem Thron* (Frankfurt am Main and Berlin, 1988), pp. 263–5.

39. Weber-Kellermann (ed.), *Wilhelmine von Bayreuth*, p. 63.

40. J. D. E. Preuss, *Friedrichs des Grossen Jugend und Thronbesteigung* (Berlin, 1840), p. 22.

41. Ibid., p. 16.

42. Venohr, *Der Soldatenkönig*, p. 265.

43. Preuss, *Friedrichs des Grossen Jugend*, pp. 23–4.

44. Schieder, *Friedrich der Grosse*, p. 27.

45. Reinhold Koser, *Friedrich der Grosse als Kronprinz* (Stuttgart, 1886), p. 26.

46. Ibid., pp. 10–11.

47. Lavisse, *The Youth of Frederick the Great*, p. 130.

48. Neugebauer, *Die Hohenzollern*, vol. 2, p. 10.

49. Berney, *Friedrich der Grosse*, p. 13.

50. Ibid., p. 8; Preuss, *Friedrichs des Grossen Jugend*, p. 8.

51. Weber-Kellermann (ed.), *Wilhelmine von Bayreuth*, p. 102.

52. Koser, *Friedrich der Grosse als Kronprinz*, p. 8.

53. Schieder, *Friedrich der Grosse*, p. 30.

54. Eugen Paunel, *Die Staatsbibliothek zu Berlin. Ihre Geschichte und Organisation während der ersten zwei Jahrhunderten seit ihrer Eröffnung* (Berlin, 1965), p. 46. The Schlossfreiheit was demolished in 1896 on the orders of Kaiser Wilhelm II to make room for a statue of his grandfather Wilhelm I.

55. Preuss, *Friedrichs des Grossen Jugend*, p. 21; Lavisse, *The Youth of Frederick the Great*, p. 25.

56. Jürgen Luh, *Der Grosse. Friedrich II. von Preussen* (Berlin, 2012), p. 114.

57. Koser, *Friedrich der Grosse als Kronprinz*, p. 21.

58. Heinz Becker, 'Friedrich II.', in *Die Musik in Geschichte und Gegenwart*, ed. Friedrich Blume (Kassel and Basle, 1955), vol. 4, p. 955; Eugene

Helm and Derek McCulloch, 'Frederick II, King of Prussia [Friedrich II; Frederick the Great]', http://www.oxfordmusiconline.com/subscriber/article/grove/music/10176?q=frederick+prussia&search=quick&pos=1&_start=1#firsthit. Accessed 11 April 2012. There is an excellent recording of *Cleofide* by William Christie and Cappella Coloniensis, recently reissued by Capriccio.

59. Weber-Kellermann (ed.), *Wilhelmine von Bayreuth*, pp. 107–8. Carlyle, vol. 2, p. 27, wrote that Frederick enjoyed a sexual relationship with Countess Orzelska too, but this is not at all clear from Wilhelmine's memoirs, which appear to be his only source.

60. Weber-Kellermann (ed.), *Wilhelmine von Bayreuth*, p. 112.

61. Ibid., p. 48.

62. For a recent discussion of their reliability, see Ruth Müller-Lindenberg, *Wilhelmine von Bayreuth: die Hofoper als Bühne des Lebens* (Cologne, 2005), p. 12.

63. Förster, *Friedrich Wilhelm I. König von Preussen*, vol. 3, p. 261.

64. *Œuvres*, vol. 21, p. 96.

65. Ibid., vol. 11, p. 44.

66. Preuss, *Friedrichs des Grossen Jugend*, p. 48, n. 1.

67. The glamour of the Saxon court at this time is brought out very well, in word and image, in Werner Schmidt and Dirk Syndram (eds.), *Unter einer Krone. Kunst und Kultur der sächsisch-polnischen Union* (Leipzig, 1997).

68. Koser, *Friedrich der Grosse als Kronprinz*, p. 10.

69. For example, Carlyle, vol. 2, p. 27; Berney, *Friedrich der Grosse*, p. 13; Johannes Kunisch, *Friedrich der Grosse. Der König und seine Zeit* (Munich, 2004), p. 23.

70. Weber-Kellermann (ed.), *Wilhelmine von Bayreuth*, p. 113.

71. Max Hein (ed.), *Briefe Friedrichs des Grossen* (Berlin, 1914), vol. 1, p. 16.

72. Carlyle, vol. 2, p. 110.

73. Preuss, *Friedrichs des Grossen Jugend*, p. 55.

74. Koser, *Friedrich der Grosse als Kronprinz*, p. 22.

75. Ibid., p. 21.

76. Weber-Kellermann (ed.), *Wilhelmine von Bayreuth*, p. 46.

77. Carlyle, vol. 2, p. 51.

78. Ibid.

79. Andrew C. Thompson, *George II. King and Elector* (New Haven and London, 2011), pp. 82–3.

80. Koser, *Friedrich der Grosse als Kronprinz*, p. 17.

81. Ibid., p. 33.

82. Carlyle, vol. 2, p. 89.

83. Ibid., p. 113.

84. Koser, *Friedrich der Grosse als Kronprinz*, p. 29.

85. Carlyle, vol. 2, p. 114.

86. Koser, *Friedrich der Grosse als Kronprinz*, pp. 29–38.

87. Luh, *Der Grosse*, p. 18.

88. Seckendorf to the Emperor Francis I, Wesel, 14 August 1730, in Förster, *Friedrich Wilhelm I. König von Preussen*, vol. 3, p. 4.

89. Koser, *Friedrich der Grosse als Kronprinz*, p. 51.

90. Weber-Kellermann (ed.), *Wilhelmine von Bayreuth*, pp. 206–7.

91. Hahn, *Friedrich II.*, p. 35.

92. Pierre Gaxotte, *Frederick the Great* (London, 1941), p. 60.

93. Weber-Kellermann (ed.), *Wilhelmine von Bayreuth*, pp. 214–15.

94. Volz (ed.), *Friedrich der Grosse und Wilhelmine von Bayreuth*, vol. 1, p. 68.

95. Paunel, *Die Staatsbibliothek zu Berlin*, p. 47.

96. Förster, *Friedrich Wilhelm I. König von Preussen*, vol. 3, p. 14.

97. Ursula Pia Jauch, 'Annotationen zu den Asylanten, Querdenkern und Avantgardisten in der "Tafelrunde"', in Sösemann, vol. 1, p. 203.

98. Wolfgang Burgdorf, *Friedrich der Grosse. Ein biografisches Porträt* (Freiburg, Basle and Vienna, 2011), p. 83.

99. http://www.erwin-in-het-panhuis.de/online-bibliographie-zur-homosexualit%C3%A4t/bibliographie-1820-bis-heute/.

100. Thomas Stamm-Kuhlmann, 'Vom rebellischen Sohn zum Landesvater. Der Herrscher zwischen Familie und Staat', in Sösemann, vol. 1, p. 14.

101. Burgdorf, *Friedrich der Grosse*, p. 82.

102. Schieder, *Friedrich der Grosse*, p. 40.

103. Förster, *Friedrich Wilhelm I. König von Preussen*, vol. 3, pp. 9, 15.

104. Carlyle, vol. 2, pp. 281, 298.

105. Koser, *Friedrich der Grosse als Kronprinz*, p. 71.

106. Förster, *Friedrich Wilhelm I. König von Preussen*, vol. 3, p. 47.

107. 'Protokoll über die Zusammenkunft Sr. Majestät des Königs mit dem Kronprinzen K.H. in Cüstrin den 15. August 1731', in ibid., p. 50.

108. Hein (ed.), *Briefe Friedrichs des Grossen*, vol. 1, p. 19.

109. Seckendorf to Prince Eugene, 5 September 1730, in ibid., p. 11.

110. There is an excellent genealogical table in Thomas Biskup, 'The hidden queen: Elizabeth Christine of Prussia and Hohenzollern queenship in the eighteenth century', in Clarissa Campbell Orr (ed.), *Queenship in Europe, 1660–1815. The Role of the Consort* (Cambridge, 2004), pp. 310–11.

111. Karin Feuerstein-Prasser, 'Ich bleibe zurück wie eine Gefangene'. Elisabeth Christine und Friedrich der Grosse (Regensburg, 2011), p. 18.
112. Weber-Kellermann (ed.), Wilhelmine von Bayreuth, p. 311.
113. Förster, Friedrich Wilhelm I. König von Preussen, vol. 3, p. 77.
114. Weber-Kellermann (ed.), Wilhelmine von Bayreuth, p. 349.
115. Hein (ed.), Briefe Friedrichs des Grossen, vol. 1, p. 24.
116. Lavisse, The Youth of Frederick the Great, p. 388.
117. Krockow, Die preussischen Brüder, p. 74.

3. THE MAKING OF FREDERICK

1. Johannes Kunisch, Friedrich der Grosse. Der König und seine Zeit (Munich, 2004), pp. 54–5.
2. Reinhold Koser, Friedrich der Grosse als Kronprinz (Stuttgart, 1886), p. 81.
3. Ibid., p. 197.
4. Peter Baumgart, 'Kronprinzenopposition: Friedrich und Friedrich Wilhelm I.', in Oswald Hauser (ed.), Friedrich der Grosse in seiner Zeit (Cologne and Vienna, 1987), p. 12. Baumgart follows G. B. Volz in seeing this as posing an even more serious psychological crisis than the events surrounding the flight of 1730.
5. J. D. E. Preuss, Friedrichs des Grossen Jugend und Thronbesteigung (Berlin, 1840), p. 34.
6. Koser, Friedrich der Grosse als Kronprinz, p. 82.
7. Peter Gay, The Enlightenment: an Interpretation (London, 1967), vol. 1: The Rise of Modern Paganism, pp. 290–95.
8. 'Avertissement de l'Éditeur', Œuvres, vol. 7, p. vi; Pierre-Paul Sagave, 'Preussen und Frankreich', Jahrbücher für die Geschichte Mittel und Ostdeutschlands, 31 (1982), pp. 67–8.
9. The last tribute is in a letter to his brother Prince Henry of 22 April 1764 – Œuvres, vol. 26, p. 343.
10. Werner Langer, Friedrich der Grosse und die geistige Welt Frankreichs, Hamburger Studien zu Volkstum und Kultur der Romanen (Hamburg, 1932), vol. 11, p. 41.
11. Œuvres, vol. 19, p. 282.
12. Horst Steinmetz (ed.), Friedrich II., König von Preussen und die deutsche Literatur des 18. Jahrhunderts. Texte und Dokumente (Stuttgart, 1985), pp. 79–80.
13. Stefan Lorenz, 'Friedrich der Grosse und der Bellerophon der Philosophie. Bemerkungen zum "Roi philosophe" und Pierre Bayle', in Martin

Fontius (ed.), *Friedrich II. und die europäische Aufklärung, Forschungen zur Brandenburgischen und Preussischen Geschichte*, new series (Berlin, 1999), vol. 4, p. 77.

14. Brunhilde Wehinger, 'Introduction', in Brunhilde Wehinger and Günther Lottes (eds.), *Friedrich der Grosse als Leser* (Berlin, 2012), p. 14.

15. Sabine Henze-Döhring, *Friedrich der Grosse – Musiker und Monarch* (Munich, 2012), pp. 12–14. This is one of the shorter books published to mark the tercentenary of Frederick's birth but also one of the most important.

16. Ibid., p. 11. The full passage in French is included in footnote 8 on p. 202.

17. Christoph Henzel, 'Johann Gottlieb Graun' and 'Carl Heinrich Graun', http://www.oxfordmusiconline.com/subscriber/article/grove/music/11653 pg2#S11653.2. Last accessed 1 May 2012.

18. http://www.oxfordmusiconline.com/subscriber/article/grove/music/43903 pg2#S43903.2. Last accessed 1 May 2012.

19. Douglas A. Lee (ed.), *A Musician at Court: an Autobiography of Franz Benda* (Warren, MI, 1998), p. 40.

20. http://www.oxfordmusiconline.com/subscriber/article/grove/music/247 44?q=Schaffrath&search=quick&pos=1&_start=1#firsthit; http://www.oxfordmusiconline.com/subscriber/article/grove/music/14134?q=Janit sch&search=quick&pos=1&_start=1#firsthit. Last accessed 1 May 2012.

21. Christoph Wolff, *Johann Sebastian Bach. The Learned Musician* (Oxford, 2002), p. 195; Daniel Heartz, *Music in European Capitals. The Galant Style, 1720–1780* (New York, 2003), p. 357.

22. Hans-Joachim Kadatz, *Georg Wenzeslaus von Knobelsdorff. Baumeister Friedrichs des Grossen*, 3rd edn (Leipzig, 1998), p. 38.

23. Claudia Sommer, Detlef Fuchs and Michael Rohde, *Schloss Rheinsberg* (Berlin and Munich, 2009).

24. Theodor Fontane, *Wanderungen durch die Mark Brandenburg*, ed. Helmuth Nürnberger (Munich, 2006), vol. 1, p. 274.

25. Kadatz, *Georg Wenzeslaus von Knobelsdorff*, p. 57.

26. Ibid., pp. 60–62.

27. Ernst Posseck, *Die Kronprinzessin. Elisabeth Christine, Gemahlin Friedrichs des Grossen geborene Prinzessin von Braunschweig-Bevern* (Berlin, 1943), p. 355.

28. Peter-Michael Hahn, *Friedrich II. von Preussen* (Stuttgart, 2013), p. 43.

29. Karin Feuerstein-Prasser, *'Ich bleibe zurück wie eine Gefangene'. Elisabeth Christine und Friedrich der Grosse* (Regensburg, 2011), p. 39.

30. Hintze, p. 343.

31. Gerhard Ritter, *Frederick the Great. An Historical Profile*, trans. with an introduction by Peter Paret (London, 1968), p. 26.

32. Theodor Schieder, *Friedrich der Grosse. Ein Königtum der Widersprüche* (Frankfurt am Main, Berlin and Vienna, 1983), p. 56.

33. Kunisch, *Friedrich der Grosse*, p. 79.

34. Ibid. Kunisch cites an article by Ernst Lewy, 'Die Verwandlung Friedrichs des Grossen', *Psyche. Zeitschrift für Psychoanalyse und ihre Anwendungen*, 49, 8 (1995), pp. 758ff. This is a German translation of an article which first appeared in English in *Psychoanalytic Study of Society*, 4 (1967), pp. 252–311. However, in that article Lewy simply repeats Zimmermann's story as if it were proven. In a discussion published in *Der Spiegel Geschichte* in 2011, Kunisch was more emphatic in his denial. Asked about Frederick's alleged homosexuality, Kunisch replied unequivocally: 'Frederick was not homosexual. As a young man he had sex with women, especially peasant girls, and in the process contracted syphilis [*sic*]. An operation left him with a sexual handicap of which he was clearly ashamed. He was no longer sexually active. The king was intensely shy and right into old age prevented his valets from changing his underwear.' In reply to a further question about the statue of Antinous, Kunisch stated: 'Frederick was teasing with this display, it was very much the fashion at that time. There is no indication that he was homosexual that can be taken seriously' – Uwe Klussmann and Norbert F. Pötzl, 'Es gibt das Bedürfnis, ein Heldenbild zu pflegen: Spiegel Gespräch mit Johannes Kunisch', *Der Spiegel Geschichte*, 2 (2011), available online at http://www.spiegel.de/spiegel/spiegelgeschichte/d-77506743.html. It is particularly unfortunate that he has stated this opinion as if it were a proven fact in an interview which appears as part of the *Zweites Deutsches Fernsehen* documentary 'Preussens Friedrich und die Kaiserin' in the series 'Die Deutschen', now available on DVD. The most recent repetition of the Zimmermann story is to be found in H. D. Kittsteiner, *Das Komma von SANS, SOUCI. Ein Forschungsbericht mit Fussnoten* (Heidelberg, 2001).

35. Wolfgang Burgdorf, *Friedrich der Grosse. Ein biografisches Porträt* (Freiburg, Basle and Vienna, 2011), p. 76; Reinhard Alings, '"Don't ask – don't tell" – war Friedrich schwul?', in Friederisiko, Ausstellung, p. 246.

36. Hahn, *Friedrich II.*, pp. 15, 36–7, 61, 157, 167.

37. [Johann Georg] Ritter von Zimmermann, *Fragmente über Friedrich den Grossen zur Geschichte seines Lebens, seiner Regierung und seines Charakters* (Leipzig, 1790), vol. 1, pp. 74–80, 93–4, 100.

38. Anton Friedrich Büsching, *Zuverlässige Beyträge zu der Regierungs-geschichte Königs Friedrich II.* (Hamburg, 1790), pp. 20–21. The information was conveyed to Büsching in a letter from Engel dated Potsdam, 2 April 1790. Zimmermann recorded in his own book on p. 99 that Engel had drained fluid from Frederick's stomach as part of the laying-out process.

39. This is reprinted by Gaston Vorberg in his essay *Der Klatsch über das Geschlechtsleben Friedrichs II. Der Fall Jean-Jacques Rousseau* (Bonn, 1921), p. 14. He adds that Frederick's naked body lay for more than one and a half hours and was seen by at least a dozen people, none of whom noticed any genital deformity.

40. Thomas Lau, 'Wie fälscht man einen König? Johann Georg Zimmermann und der Friedrichmythos', in *Friedrich 300 – Politik und Kulturtransfer im europäischen Kontext*, www.perspectivia.net/content/publikationen/friedrich300-colloquien/friedrich-kulturtransfer/lau_zimmermann. Last accessed 15 May 2012.

41. In the work cited in n. 38, Büsching published a separately paginated 'Historical Appendix' in which *inter alia* he corrected the numerous mistakes in Zimmermann's book.

42. Zimmermann, *Fragmente über Friedrich den Grossen*, pp. 70, 72.

43. *Œuvres*, vol. 16, pp. 9–20.

44. Ibid., p. 13.

45. Friedrich Förster, *Friedrich Wilhelm I. König von Preussen* (Potsdam, 1835), vol. 3, p. 112.

46. Seckendorf to Prince Eugene, Potsdam, 23 February 1732, in ibid., p. 81.

47. Seckendorf to Prince Eugene, Berlin, 29 March 1732, in ibid., p. 91.

48. Gustav Berthold Volz (ed.), *Friedrich der Grosse und Wilhelmine von Bayreuth* (Leipzig, 1924), vol. 1: *Jugendbriefe 1728–1740*, pp. 84, 89. See also Jürgen Luh, *Der Grosse. Friedrich II. von Preussen* (Berlin, 2012), pp. 123–4.

49. Seckendorf to Prince Eugene, Potsdam, 23 February 1732, in Förster, *Friedrich Wilhelm I.*, vol. 3, p. 80.

50. Volz (ed.), *Friedrich der Grosse und Wilhelmine von Bayreuth*, vol. 1, p. 102.

51. Seckendorf to Prince Eugene, Berlin, 29 March 1732, in Förster, *Friedrich Wilhelm I.*, vol. 3, p. 92.

52. Frederick to Grumbkow, Ruppin, 4 September 1732, in ibid., p. 178.

53. Frederick to Grumbkow, Ruppin, 27 January 1733, *Œuvres*, vol. 16, p. 86.

54. Volz (ed.), *Friedrich der Grosse und Wilhelmine von Bayreuth*, vol. 1, p. 140.

55. Ibid., p. 142.

56. Ibid., p. 143. The letter is headed 'Salzdahlum, midnight 12 June 1733'.

57. *Journal secret du Baron Christophe Louis de Seckendorff* (Tübingen, 1811), p. 11.

58. Frederick to Prince August Wilhelm, Pogarell, 8 April 1741, *Œuvres*, vol. 26, p. 99.

59. *Journal secret du Baron Christophe Louis de Seckendorff*, pp. 71–2.

60. Ibid., p. 147.

61. *Œuvres*, vol. 25, p. 538.

62. Ibid., p. 540.

63. Ibid.

64. Rudolf Endres stated this in the discussion which followed the papers given by Peter Baumgart and Volker Press at a symposium held at Bayreuth in 1986 – Manfred Agethen, 'Diskussionsbericht', in Heinz Duchhardt (ed.), *Friedrich der Grosse, Franken und das Reich* (Cologne and Vienna, 1986), p. 196.

65. Hahn, *Friedrich II.*, p. 47.

66. *Œuvres*, vol. 26, pp. 7, 10. In all the letters he wrote to Wilhelmine from Rheinsberg he did not mention his wife once, not even when reporting the comings and goings of guests and the entertainments they had enjoyed – Volz (ed.), *Friedrich der Grosse und Wilhelmine von Bayreuth*, vol. 1, *passim*.

67. *Œuvres*, vol. 26, p. 14.

68. Ibid.

69. Volz (ed.), *Friedrich der Grosse und Wilhelmine von Bayreuth*, vol. 1, p. 80.

70. Carlyle, vol. 2, p. 44; vol. 3, p. 29.

71. 'Gesandtschaftlicher Bericht aus Berlin, über den Regierungsantritt Friedrichs des Grossen', *Neue Berlinische Monatsschrift* (February 1804), p. 99.

72. Thomas Biskup, 'The hidden queen: Elizabeth Christine of Prussia and Hohenzollern queenship in the eighteenth century', in Clarissa Campbell Orr (ed.), *Queenship in Europe, 1660–1815. The Role of the Consort* (Cambridge, 2004), p. 305.

73. Sophie Marie Gräfin von Voss, *Neunundsechszig Jahre am preussischen Hofe* (Leipzig, 1887), p. 10.

74. Quoted in Feuerstein-Prasser, *'Ich bleibe zurück wie eine Gefangene'*, p. 53.

75. Ibid., p. 62.

76. Ibid., pp. 67–8.

77. Lehndorff, vol. 1, p. 359.

78. Alfred P. Hagemann, 'Im Schatten des grossen Königs: Königin Elisabeth Christine und ihr Verhältnis zu Friedrich II.', *Friedrich 300 – Friedrich und die historische Grösse*, p. 1, http://www.perspectivia.net/content/ publikationen/friedrich300-colloquien/friedrich-groesse/hagemann_ schatten. Last accessed on 24 May 2012.

79. Ludwig Geiger, *Berlin 1688–1840. Geschichte des geistigen Lebens der preussischen Hauptstadt* (Berlin, 1893), vol. 1: *1688–1786*, p. 318; Eva Giloi, *Monarchy, Myth and Material Culture in Germany 1750–1950* (Cambridge, 2011), p. 23.

80. Geiger, *Berlin 1688–1840*, vol. 1, p. 316.

81. Lehndorff, vol. 1, pp. 457–8.

82. J. D. E. Preuss, *Friedrich der Grosse – Eine Lebensgeschichte* (Berlin, 1832), vol. 1, p. 152; Hagemann, 'Im Schatten des grossen Königs', p. 3.

83. Bernhard Mundt, 'Fredersdorf, Michael Gabriel, Geheimer Camerier und Obertresorier, Vertrauter Friedrichs d. Gr.,' http://www.ostdeutsche-biographie.de/fredga08.htm. Last accessed 24 May 2012.

84. Johann Friedrich Borchmann, *Briefe zur Erinnerung an merkwürdige Zeiten und ruhmliche Personen, aus dem würdigen Zeitlaufe, von 1740 bis 1778* (Berlin, 1778), p. 29.

85. *Lettres familières et autres de Monsieur le Baron de Bielfeld*, 2 vols. (The Hague, 1763), vol. 1, p. 75.

86. Johannes Richter (ed.), *Briefe Friedrichs des Grossen an seinen vorma-ligen Kammerdiener Fredersdorf* (Mörs, 1979) (unchanged reprint of the 1926 edition), p. 20.

87. Mundt, 'Fredersdorf'.

88. Richter (ed.), *Briefe Friedrichs des Grossen*, p. 21.

89. Koser, vol. 1, pp. 490–91. It is impossible to determine from Koser's notoriously imprecise list of sources where this observation comes from. He does not cite the actual source, which is the scurrilous *Idée de la personne, de la manière de vivre et de la cour du roi de Prusse par M. de ****** juin 1752*, p. 13. According to the French envoy, the Jaco-bite Earl of Tyrconnell, Fredersdorf took money from supplicants seeking royal favours – Reinhold Koser, 'Aus der Korrespondenz der französischen Gesandtschaft zu Berlin 1746–1756', *Forschungen zur Brandenburgischen und Preussischen Geschichte*, 7 (1894), p. 84.

90. Lehndorff, vol. 1, pp. 359–60.

91. Richter (ed.), *Briefe Friedrichs des Grossen*, p. 150. This episode prompted Richter to spend the next nine pages explaining away Frederick's relations with Fredersdorf as just one of those 'intense friendships' that were so common at the time and asserting that Frederick's change of attitude to his wife when he came to the throne was motivated by his determination not to be diverted from the path of duty by sensual appetite – ibid., pp. 151–9.

92. Lehndorff, vol. 1, p. 360.

93. Frederick to his brother August Wilhelm, Pogarell, 8 April 1741, *Œuvres*, vol. 26, p. 99.

94. Hahn, *Friedrich II.*, p. 62.

95. Mundt, 'Fredersdorf'; Richter (ed.), *Briefe Friedrichs des Grossen*, p. 20.

96. Ingrid Mittenzwei, *Friedrich II. von Preussen* (Cologne, 1980), pp. 103–4.

97. Richter (ed.), *Briefe Friedrichs des Grossen*, p. 98.

98. Ibid., pp. 282, 315–16.

99. Mundt, 'Fredersdorf'.

100. Lehndorff, vol. 1, p. 360.

101. Preuss, *Friedrich der Grosse*, vol. 2, p. 34.

102. Lehndorff, vol. 1, p. 210.

103. J. W. von Archenholz, *The History of the Seven Years War in Germany* (Frankfurt am Main, 1843), pp. 32–3.

104. Büsching, *Zuverlässige Beyträge*, appendix, pp. 35–6.

105. Preuss, *Friedrich der Grosse*, vol. 2, p. 402.

106. Walter Bussmann, 'Algarotti, Graf Francesco v.', in *Neue Deutsche Biographie* (Berlin, 1953), vol. 1, pp. 199–200.

107. Reed Browning, 'Hervey, John, second Baron Hervey of Ickworth (1696–1743)', *Oxford Dictionary of National Biography*, Oxford University Press, 2004; online edn, May 2008, http://www.oxforddnb.com/view/article/13116. Last accessed 29 May 2012.

108. Robert Halsband, *Lord Hervey. Eighteenth-century Courtier* (Oxford, 1973), pp. 200, 248.

109. Marc Fumaroli, 'Francesco Algarotti et Frédéric II', in idem, *Quand l'Europe parlait français* (Paris, 2001), p. 150. A recent study of Algarotti and Frederick by Norbert Schmitz blithely ignores all the evidence relating to Algarotti's bisexuality, referring to Hervey only once and then only as a 'friend' of Lady Mary Wortley Montagu. Schmitz also primly observes: 'the voyeuristic looking under the bedcovers of prominent people belongs to the province of the tabloid press' – Norbert

Schmitz, *Der italienische Freund. Francesco Algarotti und Friedrich der Grosse* (Hanover, 2012), pp. 121, 201.

110. Heinrich Menu von Minutoli (ed.), *Correspondance de Frédéric Second Roi de Prusse avec le comte Algarotti* (Berlin, 1837), pp. 5–8. There is no explanation from the editor as to why the two lines of dots have been inserted.

111. *Œuvres*, vol. 21, p. 367.

112. Theodore Besterman (ed.), *Voltaire's Correspondence* (Geneva, 1954), vol. 9, p. 265. As Roger Peyrefitte observed, the correspondence between Voltaire and Frederick reveals 'une sorte d'accord pédérastique entre l'écrivain et le prince' – Roger Peyrefitte, *Voltaire et Frédéric II*. (Paris, 1992), vol. 1, p. 64.

113. Minutoli (ed.), *Correspondance de Frédéric*, p. 16.

114. Rita Unfer Lukoschik and Ivana Miatto (eds.), *Lettere prussiane di Francesco Algarotti (1712–1764)* (Padua, 2011), p. 55.

115. Christopher Clark, *Iron Kingdom. The Rise and Downfall of Prussia 1600–1947* (London, 2006), pp. 67–8.

116. Koser, vol. 1, p. 30.

117. Fumaroli, 'Francesco Algarotti et Frédéric II', p. 150.

118. Lukoschik and Miatto (eds.), *Lettere prussiane*, p. 56.

119. Domenico Michelessi, *Mémoires concernant la vie et les écrits du comte François Algarotti* (Berlin, 1772), p. 133.

120. John Murray Archive, 50 Albemarle Street, London, Algarotti Papers, box 2.

121. Peyrefitte, *Voltaire et Frédéric II*, vol. 1, p. 270.

122. John Murray Archive, box 2.

123. To Voltaire, Charlottenburg, 29 July 1740, *Œuvres*, vol. 22, p. 21.

124. Vanessa de Senarclens, 'Friedrichs Schossgebet', *Die Zeit*, 15 September 2011, p. 21. The poem is reprinted here in the French original and in German translation. In the accompanying commentary Vanessa de Senarclens records that Algarotti was a 'ladies' man' but appears to be unaware that he was a 'gentlemen's man' too.

125. Minutoli (ed.), *Correspondance de Frédéric Second Roi de Prusse avec le comte Algarotti*, p. 26. The love of Medoro and Angelica, an episode from Ludovico Ariosto's *Orlando Furioso*, was depicted by many artists. There is an explicit illustration showing the couple copulating by Agostino Caracci: http://es.wikipedia.org/wiki/Archivo:Carracci_Angelique_et_Medor.jpg.

126. Minutoli (ed.), *Correspondance de Frédéric Second Roi de Prusse avec le comte Algarotti*, p. 18.

127. Christiane Mervaud, *Voltaire et Frédéric II: une dramaturgie des lumières* (Oxford, 1985), p. 121.

128. Minutoli (ed.), *Correspondance de Frédéric Second Roi de Prusse avec le comte Algarotti*, pp. 39–42.

129. Ibid., p. 56.

130. John Murray Archive, box 1.

131. Maria Santifaller, 'Christian Bernhard Rode's painting of Francesco Algarotti's tomb in the Camposanto of Pisa at the beginning of Neo-Classicism', *The Burlington Magazine* (February 1978), vol. 120, no. 899, pp. i–vii.

4. THE MAKING OF FREDERICK (PART TWO)

1. P.C., vol. 1, p. 147.

2. *Journal secret du Baron Christophe Louis de Seckendorff* (Tübingen, 1811), p. 157.

3. *Œuvres*, vol. 25, p. 518.

4. Reinhold Koser, *Friedrich der Grosse als Kronprinz* (Stuttgart, 1886), p. 194.

5. P.C., vol. 1, p. 4.

6. Hintze, p. 322.

7. Peter H. Wilson, 'Prussia's relations with the Holy Roman Empire, 1740–1786', *The Historical Journal*, 51, 2 (2008), p. 353.

8. P.C., vol. 1, pp. 9–10.

9. Ibid., p. 7.

10. Ibid., p. 45.

11. Ibid., pp. 44–5, 57.

12. Koser, vol. 1, p. 36.

13. Hintze, p. 323.

14. Charles W. Ingrao, *The Habsburg Monarchy 1618–1815*, 2nd edn (Cambridge, 2000), p. 129.

15. J. D. E. Preuss, *Friedrichs des Grossen Jugend und Thronbesteigung* (Berlin, 1840), p. 66.

16. Joachim Whaley, *Germany and the Holy Roman Empire* (Oxford, 2012), vol. 2: *The Peace of Westphalia to the Dissolution of the Reich 1648–1806*, p. 160; Wolfgang Neugebauer, *Die Hohenzollern* (Stuttgart, 1996, 2003), vol. 2, p. 9.

17. *Œuvres*, vol. 2, p. 54; I have used here (and subsequently) the excellent translation to be found in *Posthumous Works* (London, 1789); here, vol. 1, p. 83.

18. P.C., vol. 1, p. 50.
19. Gustav Schmoller, 'Historische Betrachtungen über Staatenbildung und Finanzentwicklung', *Schmollers Jahrbuch*, 33 (1909), p. 23; Ingrao, *The Habsburg Monarchy*, p. 150.
20. Koser, vol. 1, p. 70.
21. Ibid., p. 69.
22. Quoted in Brendan Simms, *Europe. The Struggle for Supremacy 1453 to the Present* (London, 2013), p. 94.
23. Alfred Ritter von Arneth, *Geschichte Maria Theresias* (Vienna, 1863–79), vol. 1, pp. 62–70.
24. Hanns Leo Mikoletzky, *Oesterreich – Das grosse Jahrhundert. Von Leopold I. bis Leopold II.* (Vienna, 1967), p. 182.
25. P.C., vol. 1, p. 87.
26. Even by the convoluted standards of eighteenth-century bibliography, the publishing history of *Antimachiavel* is complicated. For an exhaustive account see Charles Fleischauer (ed.), *L'Antimachiavel par Frédéric II, édition critique, Studies on Voltaire and the Eighteenth Century*, vol. 5 (Geneva, 1958), *passim*. There were at least 50 editions published during Frederick's lifetime, 34 in French, 15 in German, 4 in English, and 1 each in Italian, Dutch, Latin, Russian and Swedish – Gerhard Knoll, 'Probleme eines Verzeichnisses der bis ca. 1800 erschienenen Drucke von Friedrichs II.', in Martin Fontius (ed.), *Friedrich II. und die europäische Aufklärung, Forschungen zur Brandenburgischen und Preussischen Geschichte*, new series (Berlin, 1999), vol. 4, p. 91.
27. Frederick to Algarotti, 29 October 1739, *Œuvres*, vol. 18, p. 6.
28. Fleischauer (ed.), *L'Antimachiavel par Frédéric II*, pp. 352–3. I have used the translation in Frederick the Great, *The Refutation of Machiavelli's The Prince or Anti-Machiavel*, ed. Paul Sonnino (Athens, OH, 1981), here at p. 162.
29. Ibid., pp. 159–60.
30. Ibid., p. 163.
31. Arnold Berney, *Friedrich der Grosse. Entwicklungsgeschichte eines Staatsmannes* (Tübingen, 1934), p. 123. That did not prevent later Prussian historians providing Frederick with retrospective justification: see, for example, Leopold von Ranke, *Friedrich der Grosse* (Leipzig, 1878), pp. 9–10.
32. Fleischauer (ed.), *L'Antimachiavel*, p. 50.
33. Peter Gay, *The Enlightenment: an Interpretation* (London, 1967), vol. 1: *The Rise of Modern Paganism*, p. 286.

34. Friedrich Meinecke, *Machiavellism. The Doctrine of Raison d'État and Its Place in Modern History* (London, 1957), pp. 283, 307.

35. Theodor Schieder, *Friedrich der Grosse. Ein Königtum der Widersprüche* (Frankfurt am Main, Berlin and Vienna, 1983), p. 104.

36. It is reprinted in full, in both the original French and in German translation, in Otto Bardong (ed.), *Friedrich der Grosse, Ausgewählte Quellen zur deutschen Geschichte der Neuzeit*. Freiherr vom Stein-Gedächtnisausgabe (Darmstadt, 1982), vol. 22, pp. 29–32.

37. Ibid.

38. Friedrich Förster, *Friedrich Wilhelm I. König von Preussen* (Potsdam, 1835), vol. 3, p. 28.

39. Derek McKay, *Prince Eugene* (London, 1977), pp. 238–9.

40. Förster, *Friedrich Wilhelm I. König von Preussen*, vol. 3, p. 230.

41. McKay, *Prince Eugene*, p. 239.

42. Frederick to Grumbkow, 16 March 1737, *Briefwechsel des Kronprinzen Friedrichs mit Friedrich Wilhelm von Grumbkow*, Publicationen aus den k. preussischen Staatsarchiven (Leipzig, 1898), vol. 72, p. 150.

43. Frederick to Grumbkow, 24 March 1737, ibid., p. 154.

44. Frederick to Grumbkow, 28 January 1737, ibid., p. 147.

45. This can be followed in Förster, *Friedrich Wilhelm I. König von Preussen*, vol. 3. See, for example, pp. 95, 98, 113.

46. Berney, *Friedrich der Grosse*, p. 288, n. 20.

47. Whaley, *Germany and the Holy Roman Empire*, vol. 2, p. 156.

48. Reinhold Koser, *Friedrich der Grosse als Kronprinz* (Stuttgart, 1886), p. 168.

49. Frederick the Great, *The History of My Own Times*, p. 90.

50. Quoted in Tim Blanning, *The Pursuit of Glory: Europe 1648–1815* (London, 2007), p. 543.

51. Michel Antoine, *Louis XV* (Paris, 1989), p. 242.

52. Quoted in Colin Jones, *The Great Nation. France from Louis XV to Napoleon* (London, 2002), p. 52.

53. Pierre Goubert, 'La force du nombre', in Fernand Braudel and Ernest Labrousse (eds.), *Histoire économique et sociale de la France* (Paris, 1970), vol. 2: *Des derniers temps de l'âge seigneurial aux préludes de l'âge industriel (1660–1789)*, pp. 19–21.

54. Blanning, *The Pursuit of Glory*, pp. 207–17; T. C. W. Blanning, *The Culture of Power and the Power of Culture. Old Regime Europe 1660–1789* (Oxford, 2002), pp. 384–92.

55. M. S. Anderson, *Europe in the Eighteenth Century* (London, 1961), p. 173.

56. M. S. Anderson, *Peter the Great* (London, 1978), pp. 78–9.

57. Lucien Bély, *Les Relations internationales en Europe (XVIIᵉ– XVIIIᵉ siècles)*, 3rd edn (Paris, 2001), pp. 481–2.

58. Brendan Simms, *Three Victories and a Defeat. The Rise and Fall of the First British Empire, 1714–1783* (London, 2007), pp. 92–4, 244–6. There is an excellent map on p. xxv.

59. Norman Davies, *Vanished Kingdoms: The History of Half-forgotten Europe* (London, 2011), pp. 351–2.

60. Christopher Clark, *Iron Kingdom. The Rise and Downfall of Prussia 1600–1947* (London, 2006), p. 50.

61. Jochen Vötsch, *Kursachsen, das Reich und der mitteldeutsche Raum zu Beginn des 18. Jahrhunderts* (Frankfurt am Main, 2003), p. 399.

62. *Œuvres*, vol. 2, p. 58.

63. Karl Czok, *Am Hofe Augusts des Starken* (Leipzig, 1989), p. 94.

64. Peter H. Wilson, *German Armies. War and German Politics 1648–1806* (London, 1998), pp. 104, 252.

65. Johannes Ziekursch, *Sachsen und Preussen um die Mitte des achtzehnten Jahrhunderts. Ein Beitrag zur Geschichte des österreich-ischen Erbfolgekriegs* (Breslau, 1904), pp. 13–14.

66. Ibid., pp. 35–6.

67. Georg Schmidt, *Wandel durch Vernunft. Deutsche Geschichte im 18. Jahrhundert* (Munich, 2009), p. 145.

68. Ibid., p. 146.

69. Karl Otmar Freiherr von Aretin, *Das Alte Reich 1648–1806* (Stuttgart, 1997), vol. 2: *Kaisertradition und österreichische Grossmachtpolitik (1684–1745)*, p. 413.

70. Antoine, *Louis XV*, p. 301.

71. G. P. Gooch, *Frederick the Great* (London, 1947), p. 14.

72. Antoine, *Louis XV*, p. 303.

73. As Brendan Simms has pointed out, what became known as the War of the Austrian Succession was really the 'War of the Imperial Succession' – *Europe*, p. 97.

74. Simms, *Three Victories and a Defeat*, pp. 278–9.

75. Ibid.

76. Paul Dukes, *The Making of Russian Absolutism 1613–1801* (London, 1982), p. 108.

77. Koser, vol. 1, p. 92.

78. P.C., vol. 1, p. 127, no. 189, Frederick to Mardefeld at St Petersburg, Berlin, 6 December 1740.

79. *Œuvres*, vol. 2, p. 62.

80. P.C., vol. 1, p. 84, no. 125, to Podewils in Berlin, Rheinsberg, 1 November 1740.

81. Ibid., p. 74, no. 119, 'Dressé et concerté avec son Excellence le Feld-Maréchal Général Comte de Schwerin, à Rheinsberg le 29 d'Octobre 1740, par ordre du roi'.

82. Ibid., p. 90, no. 140, 'Idées sur les projets politiques à former au sujet de la mort de l'empereur'.

83. Koser, vol. 1, p. 44.

84. P.C., vol. 1, pp. 92–3, no. 141, Frederick's marginalia dated Rheinsberg, 7 November 1740.

85. The best readily available narrative is in Koser, vol. 1, pp. 54–9. The best atlas is Holger Tümmler (ed.), *Heimatatlas für die Provinz Schlesien* (Wolfenbüttel, 2007), a reprint of the original edition of 1922.

86. M. S. Anderson, *The War of the Austrian Succession, 1740–1748* (London, 1995), p. 68.

87. *Œuvres*, vol. 18, p. 31.

88. P.C., vol. 1, p. 167.

89. Ibid., p. 173.

90. Koser, vol. 1, p. 54.

91. Ibid., p. 117.

92. *Œuvres*, vol. 22, p. 65.

93. Ibid., vol. 17, p. 97.

94. Ibid., vol. 2, pp. 57, 61.

95. For a recent study which convincingly lays great stress on Frederick's pursuit of glory, see Jürgen Luh, *Der Grosse. Friedrich II. von Preussen* (Berlin, 2012), *passim*.

96. Reinhold Koser, 'Aus der Korrespondenz der französischen Gesandtschaft zu Berlin 1746–1756', *Forschungen zur Brandenburgischen und Preussischen Geschichte*, 7 (1894), p. 88.

97. Dennis Showalter, *The Wars of Frederick the Great* (London, 1996), p. 45.

98. Carl von Clausewitz, *On War*, ed. and trans. Michael Howard and Peter Paret (Princeton, 1976), p. 140.

99. Gottlob Naumann (ed.), *Sammlung ungedruckter Nachrichten, so die Geschichte der Feldzüge der Preussen von 1740 bis 1779 erläutern* (Dresden, 1782), vol. 1, p. 38. The editor of this collection claimed that he had neither added to nor subtracted from this account.

100. Jay Luvaas, 'Student as teacher: Clausewitz on Frederick the Great and Napoleon', *The Journal of Strategic Studies*, 9, 2–3 (1986), pp. 150–51.

101. Koser, vol. 1, p. 112; Arneth, *Geschichte Maria Theresias*, vol. 1, p. 167, states that the retreat did not begin until seven o'clock.
102. Showalter, *The Wars of Frederick the Great*, p. 50.
103. P.C., vol. 1, p. 221.
104. Luh, *Der Grosse*, p. 58.
105. Quoted in Eva Ziebura, *August Wilhelm Prinz von Preussen* (Berlin, 2006), p. 54.
106. Camille Rousset, *Le comte de Gisors 1732–1758* (Paris, 1868), p. 106. Gisors was the son of the Marshal de Belle-Isle. He was killed at the battle of Krefeld in 1758.
107. *The History of My Own Times, Œuvres*, vol. 2, pp. 85–6. For its publishing history, see the *Avertissement de l'éditeur*, p. 1.
108. Carl von Clausewitz, 'Die Feldzüge Friedrichs des Grossen', *Hinterlassene Werke des Generals Carl von Clausewitz über Krieg und Kriegführung*, 2nd edn (Berlin, 1862), vol. 10, p. 28.
109. Berney, *Friedrich der Grosse*, p. 135.
110. Christopher Duffy, *The Fortress in the Age of Vauban and Frederick the Great* (London, 1985), p. 113.
111. *Œuvres*, vol. 2, p. 85.
112. Carlyle, vol. 3, p. 331.
113. H. M. Scott, *The Birth of a Great Power System 1740–1815* (London, 2006), p. 8.
114. Hintze, p. 328.
115. Aretin, *Das Alte Reich 1648–1806*, vol. 2, p. 423.
116. *Œuvres*, vol. 2, p. 105.
117. Koser, vol. 1, p. 129.
118. P.C., vol. 1, p. 258.
119. Quoted in Christopher Duffy, *The Army of Frederick the Great* (Newton Abbot, 1974), p. 161.
120. Koser, vol. 1, p. 139.
121. Duffy, *The Army of Frederick the Great*, p. 161.
122. Ziekursch, *Sachsen und Preussen*, p. 83.
123. Christopher Duffy, *Frederick the Great. A Military Life* (London, 1985), p. 36.
124. Minutes taken by the British minister Lord Hyndford on the agreement reached at Klein-Schnellendorf on 9 October 1741, P.C., vol. 1, p. 371.
125. Anderson, *The War of the Austrian Succession*, p. 87.
126. Arneth, *Geschichte Maria Theresias*, vol. 1, pp. 344–5.
127. Ibid., pp. 345–6.
128. Anderson, *The War of the Austrian Succession*, p. 86.

129. *Œuvres*, vol. 8, p. 281.

130. Arneth, *Geschichte Maria Theresias*, vol. 1, p. 415, n. 58. This is almost too good to be true and one must wonder whether the Austrians invented it. It is not to be found in the *Politische Correspondenz*. However, von Arneth would have had to be complicit, if it were a forgery, which seems improbable.

131. Carlyle, vol. 3, p. 490.

132. The campaign is best followed in Arneth, *Geschichte Maria Theresias*, vol. 2, ch. 1.

133. Carlyle, vol. 3, p. 519.

134. P.C., vol. 2, pp. 108–9.

135. Ibid., p. 63.

136. Olaf Groehler, *Die Kriege Friedrichs II.* (Berlin, 1966), pp. 38–9.

137. *Œuvres*, vol. 2, p. 130. Translation from *Posthumous Works*, vol. 1, pt 1, p. 196.

138. *Œuvres*, vol. 4, p. 8. Translation from *Posthumous Works*, vol. 2, p. 12.

139. Duffy, *Frederick the Great*, pp. 40–45; Koser, vol. 1, pp. 168–71; Arneth, *Geschichte Maria Theresias*, vol. 2, pp. 51–4.

140. P.C., vol. 2, p. 165.

141. *Œuvres*, vol. 17, p. 231.

142. Duffy, *Frederick the Great*, p. 44.

143. Arneth, *Geschichte Maria Theresias*, vol. 2, p. 55.

144. Simms, *Three Victories and a Defeat*, pp. 308–10.

145. P. G. M. Dickson, *Finance and Government under Maria Theresa 1740–1780* (Oxford, 1987), vol. 2, p. 161.

146. Koser, vol. 1, p. 175.

147. P.C., vol. 2, p. 224.

148. The negotiations can be followed in ibid., pp. 225–7.

149. Hintze, p. 333.

150. René Hanke, *Brühl und das Renversement des alliances. Die antipreussische Aussenpolitik des Dresdener Hofes 1744–1756* (Berlin, 2006), p. 53. On the 'extreme hostility' entertained by the Saxons, see Henri Zosime, comte de Valori (ed.), *Mémoires des négociations du marquis de Valori, ambassadeur de France à la Cour de Berlin. Accompagnés d'un recueil de lettres de Frédéric-le-Grand, des princes ses frères, de Voltaire, et des plus illustres personnages du XVIIIe siècle* (Paris, 1820), vol. 1, p. 149.

151. Ziekursch, *Sachsen und Preussen*, p. 82.

152. Whaley, *Germany and the Holy Roman Empire*, vol. 2, pp. 376–8.

153. Koser, vol. 1, p. 214.

154. J. D. E. Preuss, *Friedrich der Grosse – Eine Lebensgeschichte* (Berlin, 1832), vol. 1, p. 207.

155. Koser, vol. 1, p. 220.

156. Ibid., p. 228.

157. *Œuvres*, vol. 3, p. 85. Translation from *Posthumous Works*, vol. 1, pt 2, p. 128.

158. Arneth, *Geschichte Maria Theresias*, vol. 2, pp. 419–21, 434.

159. Duffy, *Frederick the Great*, pp. 53–4.

160. Johann Gustav Droysen, *Geschichte der preussischen Politik*, vols. 1–4 – *Friedrich der Grosse* (Leipzig, 1874–86), vol. 2, p. 366.

161. Groehler, *Die Kriege Friedrichs II.*, p. 26.

162. Ilya Berkovich, *Motivation in the Armies of Old Regime Europe* (unpublished Cambridge Ph.D. dissertation, 2012), p. 59. I am grateful to Dr Berkovich for allowing me to read his dissertation and also for making many helpful bibliographical suggestions.

163. Droysen, *Geschichte der preussischen Politik*, vol. 2, p. 369.

164. Valori (ed.), *Mémoires des négociations du marquis de Valori*, vol. 1, p. 204.

165. *Œuvres*, vol. 3, pp. 67, 84. Translation from *Posthumous Works*, vol. 1, pt 2, pp. 102, 128.

166. Valori (ed.), *Mémoires des négociations du marquis de Valori*, vol. 1, p. 201.

167. Groehler, *Die Kriege Friedrichs II.*, p. 55.

168. Anderson, *The War of the Austrian Succession*, pp. 142–3.

169. Simms, *Three Victories and a Defeat*, p. 337.

170. Quoted in Duffy, *Frederick the Great*, p. 58.

171. Groehler, *Die Kriege Friedrichs II.*, p. 57; Koser, vol. 1, p. 249.

172. Carlyle, vol. 4, p. 128.

173. Johannes Kunisch, *Friedrich der Grosse. Der König und seine Zeit* (Munich, 2004), p. 210.

174. P.C., vol. 4, p. 134. A German translation can be found in Bardong (ed.), *Friedrich der Grosse*, pp. 124–5.

175. Arneth, *Geschichte Maria Theresias*, vol. 3, p. 72.

176. Carlyle, vol. 4, p. 131.

177. Koser, vol. 1, p. 257.

178. Quoted in Duffy, *Frederick the Great*, p. 60.

179. Ibid., p. 64. This contains the best account of the battle, illustrated by many quotations from contemporaries.

180. P.C., vol. 4, pp. 181–3.

181. Arneth, *Geschichte Maria Theresias*, vol. 3, pp. 78–80.

182. Andrew C. Thompson, *George II. King and Elector* (New Haven and London, 2011), p. 164.

183. Duffy, *Frederick the Great*, pp. 69–72.

184. P.C., vol. 4, pp. 290–94.

185. Ibid., p. 296.

186. Alfred P. Hagemann, 'Im Schatten des grossen Königs: Königin Elisabeth Christine und ihr Verhältnis zu Friedrich II.', *Friedrich 300 – Friedrich und die historische Grösse* http://www.perspectivia.net/content/ publikationen/friedrich300-colloquien/friedrich-groesse/hagemann_ schatten. Last accessed 2 August 2012.

187. *Œuvres*, vol. 3, p. 143. Translation from *Posthumous Works*, vol. 1, pt 2, p. 214.

188. Valori (ed.), *Mémoires des négociations du marquis de Valori*, vol. 1, p. 260.

189. Koser, vol. 1, pp. 285–8.

190. Anderson, *The War of the Austrian Succession*, p. 148.

191. *Œuvres*, vol. 3, p. 198.

192. Schieder, *Friedrich der Grosse*, p. 478.

193. Martin Engel, *Das Forum Fridericianum und die monumentalen Res-idenzplätze des 18. Jahrhunderts* (unpublished Free University Berlin dissertation, 2001), p. 115. Available online at http://www.diss. fu-berlin.de/diss/receive/FUDISS_thesis_000000001297. Engel adds that the arch was in fact erected at Frederick's expense and that the inscription was composed by Johann Gottlieb Schmidt, who can be regarded as a court propagandist.

194. Thomas Biskup, *Friedrichs Gröss. Inszenierungen des Preussenkönigs in Fest und Zeremoniell 1740–1815* (Frankfurt am Main and New York, 2012), p. 74.

195. Schieder, *Friedrich der Grosse*, p. 478.

196. Luh, *Der Grosse*, p. 40. The letter in question is in *Œuvres*, vol. 22, p. 114.

197. Luh, *Der Grosse*, p. 60. For a contrary view, see Johann Kunisch's statement that it was Frederick's subjects who invented the sobriquet 'the Great' for him and that he was 'very sceptical' about it – Uwe Klussmann and Norbert F. Pötzl, 'Es gibt das Bedürfnis, ein Heldenbild zu pflegen: Spiegel Gespräch mit Johannes Kunisch', *Der Spiegel Geschichte*, 2 (2011), available online at http://www.spiegel.de/spiegel/ spiegelgeschichte/d-77506743.html.

5. THE MASTERFUL SERVANT OF THE STATE

1. Dietrich, pp. 221–43; Volker Hentschel, *Preussens streitbare Geschichte 1494–1945* (Düsseldorf, 1980), p. 54; Gerhard Oestreich, *Friedrich Wilhelm I. Preussischer Absolutismus, Merkantilismus, Militarismus* (Göttingen, 1977), p. 49.

2. Hintze, p. 281.

3. Fritz Hartung, 'Die politischen Testamente der Hohenzollern', in Otto Büsch and Wolfgang Neugebauer (eds.), *Moderne Preussische Geschichte* (Berlin and New York, 1981), vol. 3, p. 1505.

4. Dietrich, p. 240; Christopher Clark, *Iron Kingdom. The Rise and Downfall of Prussia 1600–1947* (London, 2006), p. 65.

5. Dietrich, p. 239.

6. *Œuvres*, vol. 26, p. 101.

7. Leopold von Ranke, *Memoirs of the House of Brandenburg and History of Prussia during the Seventeenth and Eighteenth Centuries* (London, 1849), vol. 2, p. 45.

8. Carsten Kretschmann, 'Präsentation und Repräsentation. Sammlungen und Kabinette als Schnittstellen einer *république des lettres*', in Sösemann, vol. 1, p. 322. The bust in Sanssouci was actually of Septimus Severus but Frederick did not know that. On Frederick's admiration of Marcus Aurelius, see also Ullrich Sachse, 'Caesar und Cicero sind seine Lehrer', in Friederisiko, Ausstellung, pp. 162–4.

9. Peter Baumgart, 'Kronprinzenopposition. Zum Verhältnis Friedrichs zu seinem Vater Friedrich Wilhelm I.', in Heinz Duchhardt (ed.), *Friedrich der Grosse, Franken und das Reich* (Cologne and Vienna, 1986), p. 9.

10. Voltaire, *La Henriade*, ed. O. R. Taylor, *Studies on Voltaire and the Eighteenth Century* (Oxford, 1965), vol. 39, p. 338.

11. Charles Fleischauer (ed.), *L'Antimachiavel par Frédéric II, édition critique, Studies on Voltaire and the Eighteenth Century* (Geneva, 1958), vol. 5, p. 248.

12. *Œuvres*, vol. 9, p. 208.

13. Ibid.

14. Ewald Graf von Hertzberg, 'Mémoire sur la troisième année du règne de Frédéric Guillaume II, et pour prouver que le gouvernement prussien n'est pas despotique', in *Mémoires de l'Académie Royale des Sciences et des Belles-Lettres. Cl. de belles-lettres. 1786/1787* (Berlin, 1792), pp. 645–6.

15. J. D. E. Preuss, *Friedrichs des Grossen Jugend und Thronbesteigung* (Berlin, 1840), pp. 377–8.

16. Erich Everth, *Die Öffentlichkeit in der Aussenpolitik von Karl V. bis Napoleon* (Jena, 1931), p. 319.

17. H. M. Scott, *The Emergence of the Eastern Powers, 1756–1775* (Cambridge, 2001), p. 149.

18. 'Portrait du Roi de Prusse et réflexions sur le caractère de ce prince', in *Recueil des instructions données aux ambassadeurs et ministres de France depuis les traités de Westphalie jusqu'à la Révolution française* (Paris, 1901), vol. 16: *Prusse*, ed. Albert Waddington, p. lxxxi. This can be found in German translation in Gustav Berthold Volz (ed.), *Friedrich der Grosse im Spiegel seiner Zeit* (Berlin, 1901), vol. 1, p. 154.

19. Quoted in Rolf Straubel, '"Bedienungen vergebe Ich nach Meinem Sinn". Zur Personalpolitik Friedrichs II. im Zivilfach', in Frank Göse (ed.), *Friedrich der Grosse und die Mark Brandenburg. Herrschaftspraxis in der Provinz* (Berlin, 2012), p. 137.

20. Walter L. Dorn, 'The Prussian bureaucracy in the eighteenth century', pt 1, *Political Science Quarterly*, 46 (1931), p. 411.

21. Wilhelm Naudé, 'Denkwürdigkeiten des Ministers Grafen von der Schulenburg', *Forschungen zur Brandenburgischen und Preussischen Geschichte*, 15, 2 (1902), p. 83.

22. Georg Borchardt (ed.), *Die Randbemerkungen Friedrichs des Grossen* (Potsdam, n.d.), vol. 2, p. 78.

23. *Œuvres*, vol. 26, p. 101.

24. Dietrich, p. 326.

25. Ibid., p. 610.

26. *Œuvres*, vol. 11, p. 254. On the other hand, *Palladium* ends with a paean of praise to Locke and the English Deists, who take their place in Heaven instead of the Catholic saints – Thomas Biskup and Peter H. Wilson, 'Grossbritannien, Amerika und die atlantische Welt', in Friederisiko, Ausstellung, p. 147.

27. Friedrich Luckwaldt, 'Friedrichs des Grossen Anschauungen von Staat und Fürstentum', *Historische Aufsätze Aloys Schulte zum 70. Geburtstag gewidmet* (Düsseldorf, 1927), p. 229.

28. Dietrich, pp. 608–12.

29. Peter-Michael Hahn, *Friedrich II. von Preussen* (Stuttgart, 2013), p. 116.

30. J. D. E. Preuss, *Friedrich der Grosse – Eine Lebensgeschichte* (Berlin, 1832), p. 344 and Dorn, 'The Prussian bureaucracy in the eighteenth century', p. 411, which includes an account of Frederick's working day from Mencken, one of the private secretaries.

31. Jürgen Luh, *Der Grosse. Friedrich II. von Preussen* (Berlin, 2012), p. 53.

32. Wolfgang Neugebauer, *Die Hohenzollern* (Stuttgart, 1996, 2003), vol. 2, p. 20.

33. *Recueil des instructions données aux ambassadeurs*, p. 509.

34. Christian Wilhelm von Dohm, *Denkwürdigkeiten meiner Zeit oder Beiträge zur Geschichte vom letzten Viertel des achtzehnten und vom Anfang des neunzehnten Jahrhunderts 1778 bis 1806* (Lemgo and Hanover, 1814–19), vol. 4, pp. 112–21. Von Dohm recorded the general belief that Cocceji could never have secured approval for his judicial reforms, given the fierce opposition they aroused, without Eichel's support in the royal closet.

35. Abbé Denina, *Essai sur le règne de Frédéric II, Roi de Prusse* (Berlin, 1788), p. 419.

36. Lehndorff, vol. 1, p. 242.

37. Von Dohm, *Denkwürdigkeiten*, vol. 4, pp. 115–16; Theodor Schieder, *Friedrich der Grosse. Ein Königtum der Widersprüche* (Frankfurt am Main, Berlin and Vienna, 1983), p. 298.

38. Preuss, *Friedrich der Grosse*, p. 351.

39. Ibid., p. 350; Lehndorff, vol. 2, p. 101. Lehndorff recorded rumours that Eichel had been making money from coinage manipulation. The date of Eichel's death is often given as 1770, but Frederick recorded his death in a letter to Prince Henry dated 5 February 1768, adding ungraciously that Eichel was 'the man who kept the office in order' – *Œuvres*, vol. 26, p. 354.

40. Wolfgang Neugebauer, 'Zur neueren Deutung der preussischen Verwaltung im 17. und 18. Jahrhundert', in Büsch and Neugebauer (eds.), *Moderne Preussische Geschichte*, vol. 2, p. 555.

41. J. R. Seeley, *Life and Times of Stein, or Germany and Prussia in the Napoleonic Age* (Cambridge, 1878), vol. 1, p. 277.

42. Walter L. Dorn, 'The Prussian bureaucracy in the eighteenth century', pt 2, *Political Science Quarterly*, 47 (1932), p. 82.

43. Koser, vol. 1, p. 419. Lenz took advantage of this freedom of action to play divide and rule in the province to tame the fractious town councillors of the main city, Emden.

44. Günter Vogler and Klaus Vetter, *Preussen von den Anfängen bis zur Reichsgründung* (Cologne, 1981), p. 90.

45. Koser, vol. 1, p. 30; Vinzenz Czech, 'Friedrich der Grosse auf Inspektionsreise', in Göse (ed.), *Friedrich der Grosse und die Mark Brandenburg*, p. 234.

46. J. W. L. Gleim (ed.), *Reisegespräch des Königs im Jahre 1779* (Halberstadt, 1784). There is an excellent translation in Peter Paret (ed.), *Frederick the Great: a Profile* (New York, 1972), pp. 79–98. The original can be found online at http://books.google.co.uk/books?id=GeAA AAAAcAAJ&pg=PA1&lpg=PA1&dq=Reisegespräch+des+Königs+im+ Jahre+1779&source=bl&ots=HSOy91IGJO&sig=PmozgK032f09H_x16r-6YL1Hogs&hl=en&sa=X&ei=DGYSUeiKO4600AXK04GwCg&ved= 0CDUQ6AEwAA.

47. Ibid.

48. Ernst Pfeiffer, *Die Revuereisen Friedrichs des Grossen, besonders die schlesischen nach 1763 und der Zustand Schlesiens von 1763–1786* (Berlin, 1904), p. 69.

49. Wolfgang Neugebauer, 'Friedrich als Risiko? Friedrich der Grosse in der Sicht von Untertanen und Geschichtsschreibern', in *Friedrich und die historische Grösse. Beiträge des dritten Colloquiums in der Reihe 'Friedrich300' vom 25./26. September 2009*, Michael Kaiser and Jürgen Luh (eds.), (Friedrich300 – Colloquien, 3), http://www. perspectivia.net/content/publikationen/friedrich300-colloquien/friedrich -groesse/neugebauer_risiko, published on 21 September 2010. Accessed on 6 February 2013.

50. Norbert Conrads, 'Politischer Mentalitätswandel von oben: Friedrichs II. Weg vom Gewinn Schlesiens zur Gewinnung der Schlesier', in Peter Baumgart (ed.), *Kontinuitäten und Wandel. Schlesien zwischen Österreich und Preussen* (Sigmaringen, 1990), pp. 231–2.

51. Dorn, 'The Prussian bureaucracy in the eighteenth century', pt 1, p. 414.

52. Borchardt (ed.), *Die Randbemerkungen Friedrichs des Grossen*, vol. 1, pp. 36, 452.

53. Hubert C. Johnson, *Frederick the Great and his Officials* (New Haven and London, 1975), pp. 44, 48.

54. Quoted in Gerhard Ritter, *Frederick the Great. An Historical Profile*, trans. and with an introduction by Peter Paret (London, 1968), p. 157.

55. P.C., vol. 1, pp. 261–2.

56. Ibid., p. 262, nn. 1–2.

57. For an excellent analysis of Frederick as foreign minister, see H. M. Scott, 'Prussia's royal foreign minister: Frederick the Great and the administration of Prussian diplomacy', in Robert Oresko and Graham Gibbs (eds.), *Royal and Republican Sovereignty: Essays in Memory of Ragnhild Hatton* (Cambridge, 1997), pp. 500–526.

58. Ingrid Mittenzwei, *Preussen nach dem Siebenjährigem Krieg. Ausein-andersetzungen zwischen Bürgertum und Staat um die Wirtschaftspolitik* (Berlin, 1979), pp. 39–43. The Ursinus episode has been recounted many times. Mittenzwei's detailed account is based on a reworking of the Prussian archives.

59. Ibid., p. 43.

60. It was also alleged that Ursinus had taken bribes from merchants with whom he was in cahoots, although the evidence was thin – Rolf Straubel, *Zwischen monarchischer Autokratie und bürgerlichem Emanzipationsstreben. Beamte und Kaufleute als Träger handels- und gewerbepolitischer Veränderungen im friderizianischen Preussen (1740–1806)* (Berlin, 2012), pp. 23–4. Following his release, Ursinus moved to Magdeburg, where he died in 1785. His request for a pension in 1776 on grounds of destitution was denied – Rolf Straubel, *Biographisches Handbuch der preussischen Verwaltungs- und Justizbeamten 1740–1806/15* (Munich, 2009), pp. 1039–40.

61. Reinhold Koser, *Friedrich der Grosse als Kronprinz* (Stuttgart, 1886), p. 95.

62. Lehndorff, vol. 1, pp. 46, 218.

63. Ibid., p. 246.

64. Ibid., pp. 249–52.

65. Dieudonné Thiébault, *Mes Souvenirs de vingt ans de séjour à Berlin; ou Frédéric le Grand, sa famille, sa cour, son gouvernement, son académie, ses écoles, et ses amis littérateurs et philosophes*, 4th edn (Paris, 1813), vol. 2, p. 209.

66. Johann Friedrich Borchmann, *Briefe zur Erinnerung an merkwürdige Zeiten und rühmliche Personen, aus dem wichtigen Zeitlaufe, von 1740 bis 1778* (Berlin, 1778), p. 184.

67. Percy A. Scholes (ed.), *An Eighteenth-century Musical Tour in Central Europe and the Netherlands. Being Dr Charles Burney's Account of his Musical Experiences* (Oxford, 1959), vol. 2, pp. 164, 207.

68. Thomas Bauman, 'Courts and municipalities in North Germany', in Neal Zaslaw (ed.), *The Classical Era. From the 1740s to the End of the Eighteenth Century* (London, 1989), p. 242.

69. Walter Salmen, *Johann Friedrich Reichardt. Komponist, Schriftsteller, Kapellmeister und Verwaltungsbeamter der Goethezeit* (Freiburg im Breisgau and Zürich, 1963), p. 42.

70. L. Schneider, *Geschichte der Oper und des Koeniglichen Opernhauses in Berlin* (Berlin, 1842), p. 17; Ludwig Geiger, *Berlin 1688–1840. Geschichte des geistigen Lebens der preussischen Hauptstadt* (Berlin, 1893), vol. 1: *1688–1786*, p. 609.

71. Ibid.

72. Walter Rösler, '"Die Canaillen bezahlet man zum Pläsier". Die königliche Schaubühne zu Berlin unter Friedrich II. und Friedrich Wilhelm II.', in Georg Quander (ed.), *Apollini et Musis. 250 Jahre Opernhaus Unter den Linden* (Frankfurt am Main and Berlin, 1992), p. 26.

73. Geiger, *Berlin 1688–1840*, vol. 1, p. 610.

74. O. von Riesemann, 'Eine Selbstbiographie der Sängerin Gertrud Elizabeth Mara', *Allgemeine Musikalische Zeitung*, 10 (11 August–29 September 1875), pp. 561, 564, 577.

75. Scholes, *An Eighteenth-century Musical Tour*, vol. 2, p. 167.

76. E. E. Helm, *Music at the Court of Frederick the Great* (Norman, 1960), p. 129.

77. Riesemann, 'Eine Selbstbiographie', p. 533.

78. Sabine Henze-Döhring, *Friedrich der Grosse – Musiker und Monarch* (Munich, 2012), p. 53.

79. Brunhilde Wehinger, 'Introduction', in Brunhilde Wehinger and Günther Lottes (eds.), *Friedrich der Grosse als Leser* (Berlin, 2012), p. 21.

80. http://www.potsdam-wiki.de/index.php/Heinrich_Ludwig_Manger. Last accessed 13 February 2013.

81. Borchardt (ed.), *Die Randbemerkungen Friedrichs des Grossen*, vol. 1, pp. 94–5.

82. Conrads, 'Politischer Mentalitätswandel von oben', p. 228. On the other hand, there was an agreeable anecdote illustrating Frederick's clemency making the rounds during his lifetime: 'Why is that excellent soldier in irons?' 'He was found committing bestiality with his horse.' 'Fool, don't put him in irons, put him in the infantry.' To the soldier: 'I'm sorry you will lose your horse.' – Nancy Mitford, *Frederick the Great* (London, 1970), p. 112.

83. H. W. V. Temperley, *Frederic the Great and Kaiser Joseph. An Episode of War and Diplomacy in the Eighteenth Century* (London, 1915, reprinted 1968), p. 21.

84. H. M. Scott, 'Elliot, Hugh (1752–1830)', *Oxford Dictionary of National Biography* (Oxford, 2004); online edn, Jan. 2008 (http://www.oxforddnb.com/view/article/8664). Accessed 19 February 2013.

85. Heinz Duchhardt, *Freiherr vom Stein. Preussens Reformer und seine Zeit* (Munich, 2010), p. 18.

86. Oswald Hauser, 'Preussen und die Preussenforschung heute', *Jahrbuch der Stiftung Preussischer Kulturbesitz*, 12 (1974), p. 57.

87. Ilsegret Dambacher, *Christian Wilhelm von Dohm. Ein Beitrag zur Geschichte des preussischen aufgeklärten Beamtentums und seiner*

Reformbestrebungen am Ausgang des 18. Jahrhunderts (Bern and Frankfurt am Main, 1974), pp. 12-13.

88. Rudolf Zoeppritz (ed.), *Aus F. H. Jacobis Nachlass. Ungedruckte Briefe von und an Jacobi und Andere* (Leipzig, 1869), vol. 1, p. 49.

89. Horst Möller, 'Wie aufgeklärt war Preussen?', in Hans-Jürgen Puhle and Hans-Ulrich Wehler (eds.), *Preussen im Rückblick* (Göttingen, 1980), p. 200.

90. Von Dohm, *Denkwürdigkeiten meiner Zeit*, vol. 4, p. 615.

6. CULTURE

1. J. D. E. Preuss, *Friedrichs des Grossen Jugend und Thronbesteigung* (Berlin, 1840), p. 348.

2. Christoph Henzel, 'Graun', *Grove Music Online. Oxford Music Online*, Oxford University Press, Web, 19 April 2013, http://www.oxfordmusi conline.com/subscriber/article/grove/music/11653pg3.

3. Carl Mennicke, *Hasse und die Brüder Graun als Symphoniker* (Leipzig, 1906), p. 458.

4. Hans-Joachim Kadatz, *Georg Wenzeslaus von Knobelsdorff. Baumeister Friedrichs des Grossen*, 3rd edn (Leipzig, 1998), p. 340. Thomas Carlyle wrote in vol. 3, p. 129 that Knobelsdorff was sent to Italy in 1740, but may have been confusing this expedition with his earlier Italian journey.

5. Kadatz, *Georg Wenzeslaus von Knobelsdorff*, p. 129.

6. Norbert Schmitz, *Der italienische Freund. Francesco Algarotti und Friedrich der Grosse* (Hanover, 2012), p. 193. In 1751 Algarotti wrote to Burlington to report that he was encouraging Frederick to adopt the architectural style promoted by Burlington in England, but this boast was misplaced, for Frederick and Knobelsdorff had found their way to English-style neo-Palladianism before Algarotti appeared on the scene – James Lees-Milne, *Earls of Creation. Five Great Patrons of Eighteenth-century Art* (London, 1962), p. 138. See also Thomas Biskup and Peter H. Wilson, 'Grossbritannien, Amerika und die atlantische Welt', in Friederisiko, Ausstellung, p. 147.

7. David Watkin and Tilman Mellinghoff, *German Architecture and the Classical Ideal 1740–1840* (London, 1987), p. 18.

8. Hans-Joachim Giersberg, *Friedrich als Bauherr. Studien zur Architektur des 18. Jahrhunderts in Berlin und Potsdam* (Berlin, 1986), p. 30.

9. Reinhard Wegner, 'Friedrich der Grosse und die englische Kunst', *Zeitschrift des Historischen Vereins für Kunstwissenschaft*, 42, 1 (1988), pp. 52–5.

10. Martin Engel, *Das Forum Fridericianum und die monumentalen Residenzplätze des 18. Jahrhunderts* (unpublished Free University Berlin dissertation, 2001), http://www.diss.fu-berlin.de/diss/receive/FUDISS_thesis_000000001297, p. 64.

11. L. Schneider, *Geschichte der Oper und des Koeniglichen Opernhauses in Berlin* (Berlin, 1842), p. 21.

12. Walter Rösler, '"Die Canaillen bezahlet man zum Pläsier". Die königliche Schaubühne zu Berlin unter Friedrich II. und Friedrich Wilhelm II.', in Georg Quander (ed.), *Apollini et Musis. 250 Jahre Opernhaus Unter den Linden* (Frankfurt am Main and Berlin, 1992), p. 14.

13. Carlyle, vol. 3, p. 718.

14. Carl Martin Plümicke, *Entwurf einer Theatergeschichte von Berlin, nebst allgemeinen Bemerkungen über den Geschmack, hiesige Theaterschriftsteller und Behandlung der Kunst, in den verschiedenen Epochen* (Berlin and Stettin, 1781), p. 120, claimed that, at a pinch, between 3,500–4,000 could be crammed in.

15. Ibid., p. 119; J. D. E. Preuss, *Friedrich der Grosse – Eine Lebensgeschichte* (Berlin, 1832), vol. 1, p. 268; Martin Engel, 'Architektur und Bauherrschaft', in Sösemann, vol. 1, pp. 280–81. The best ground-plan of the opera house is to be found in Paul Seidel, *Friedrich der Grosse und die bildende Kunst* (Leipzig and Berlin, 1922), p. 63.

16. Jonas Hanway, *An Historical Account of the British Trade over the Caspian Sea. With a Journal of Travels from London through Russia into Persia and back through Russia, Germany, and Holland* (London, 1753), vol. 2, p. 187.

17. Carlyle, vol. 3, p. 599.

18. Michael Forsyth, *Buildings for Music. The Architect, the Musician, and the Listener from the Seventeenth Century to the Present Day* (Cambridge, MA, 1985), p. 104.

19. His arrivals in the opera house, however, were wholly traditional, being heralded by trumpets and drums. No performance could start until he gave the sign – Johann Friedrich Karl Grimm, *Bemerkungen eines Reisenden durch die königlichen preussischen Staaten in Briefen* (Altenburg, 1779), vol. 2, p. 7.

20. Sibylle Badstuebner-Groeger, 'Aufgeklärter Absolutismus in den Bildprogrammen friderizianischer Architektur?', in Martin Fontius (ed.), *Friedrich II. und die europäische Aufklärung*, *Forschungen zur*

Brandenburgischen und Preussischen Geschichte, new series (Berlin, 1999), vol. 4, pp. 45–7.

21. Quoted in Hans Rosenberg, *Bureaucracy, Aristocracy and Autocracy. The Prussian Experience 1660–1815* (Boston, 1966), p. 42.

22. L. D. Ettlinger, 'Winckelmann', in *The Age of Neo-classicism*, the fourteenth exhibition of the Council of Europe (London, 1972), p. xxxiii.

23. Heinrich Menu von Minutoli (ed.), *Correspondance de Frédéric Second Roi de Prusse avec le comte Algarotti* (Berlin, 1837), p. 39, Chrudim, Bohemia, 18 April 1742.

24. E. E. Helm, *Music at the Court of Frederick the Great* (Norman, 1960), pp. 73–4.

25. Wilhelm Kothe, *Friedrich der Grosse als Musiker, sowie Freund und Förderer der musikalischen Kunst* (Braunsberg, 1869), p. 17: 'Die Franzosen wissen nur Comödie zu spielen und die Italiener zu singen; aber Musik zu schreiben, das verstehen nur die Deutschen.' This is mistranslated by Helm as 'Only the French know how to create comedy, only the Italians can sing, and only the Germans can compose.' Frederick's original remark, if he made it, would have been uttered in French of course. In his footnote, n. 11, on p. 49, Kothe gives no source.

26. Heinz Becker, 'Friedrich II.', in *Die Musik in Geschichte und Gegenwart*, ed. Friedrich Blume (Kassel and Basle, 1955), vol. 4, p. 955.

27. Percy A. Scholes (ed.), *An Eighteenth-century Musical Tour in Central Europe and the Netherlands. Being Dr Charles Burney's Account of his Musical Experiences* (Oxford, 1959), vol. 2, p. 207.

28. Christoph Wolff et al, 'Bach', *Grove Music Online. Oxford Music Online*, Oxford University Press, Web, 22 April 2013, http://www.oxfordmusiconline.com/subscriber/article/grove/music/40023pg12. Bach had already performed for Frederick at Rheinsberg.

29. Sabine Henze-Döhring, *Friedrich der Grosse – Musiker und Monarch* (Munich, 2012), pp. 39–44; E. Eugene Helm and Derek McCulloch, 'Frederick II, King of Prussia', *Grove Music Online. Oxford Music Online*, Oxford University Press, Web, 22 April 2013, http://www.oxfordmusiconline.com/subscriber/article/grove/music/10176.

30. Gustav Berthold Volz (ed.), *Friedrich der Grosse und Wilhelmine von Bayreuth* (Leipzig, 1924), vol. 1: *Jugendbriefe 1728–1740*, p. 287.

31. 'Épitre XIV. À Sweerts. Sur les plaisirs', *Œuvres*, vol. 10, pp. 195–201.

32. Werner Langer, *Friedrich der Grosse und die geistige Welt Frankreichs*, Hamburger Studien zu Volkstum und Kultur der Romanen (Hamburg, 1932), vol. 11, p. vii.

33. Mark Berry, 'The king in Prussia', *Opera*, Annual Festivals Issue (2012), p. 28.

34. Thomas Bauman, 'Montezuma', *The New Grove Dictionary of Opera*, ed. Stanley Sadie, *Grove Music Online*. *Oxford Music Online*, Oxford University Press, Web, 23 April 2013, http://www.oxfordmusiconline. com/subscriber/article/grove/music/O903255.

35. Albert Mayer-Reinach, 'Introduction', in idem and Hans Joachim Mayer (eds.), *Carl Heinrich Graun: Montezuma. Oper in drei Akten* (Wiesbaden and Graz, 1958), p. viii.

36. Berry, 'The king in Prussia', p. 29.

37. Frederick the Great, *Montezuma*. Text accompanying the Capriccio recording, conductor Johannes Goritzki, Deutsche Kammerakademie (Königsdorf, 1992), recording no. 60 032-2, pp. 101-2.

38. 'Gladly and without complaint I return my mortal breath to the beneficient nature which kindly gave it to me and my body to the elements it is made of' – last will and testament, dated 8 January 1769, *Œuvres*, vol. 6, p. 243. For the full quotation, see below, p. 458.

39. Frederick the Great, *Montezuma*, pp. 111, 125, 129, 131, 133-4.

40. Henze-Döhring, *Friedrich der Grosse*, p. 91.

41. Quoted in Daniel Heartz, *Music in European Capitals. The Galant Style, 1720–1780* (New York, 2003), p. 367. The French original is at Minutoli (ed.), *Correspondance de Frédéric Second Roi de Prusse avec le comte Algarotti*, p. 98.

42. Henze-Döhring, *Friedrich der Grosse*, pp. 81-3. There is a full account of the production and performance of *Silla* in Franziska Windt, 'Friedrichs Bühne', in Friederisiko, Ausstellung, pp. 344–59. For a full list of the libretti which Frederick either wrote or contributed to, see Claudia Terne, 'Friedrich II. von Preussen und die Hofoper', in Friederisiko, Essays, pp. 116–29.

43. Henze-Döhring, *Friedrich der Grosse*, p. 125.

44. Ibid., pp. 133-4.

45. Sabine Henze-Döhring, 'Die Musik', in Sösemann, vol. 1, p. 254.

46. Jürgen Luh, *Der Grosse. Friedrich II. von Preussen* (Berlin, 2012), p. 46.

47. Preuss, *Friedrich der Grosse*, vol. 1, p. 347.

48. Ibid.; Koser, vol. 1, p. 512.

49. Peter Schleuning, *Das 18. Jahrhundert. Der Bürger erhebt sich* (Hamburg, 1984), p. 62. Another version of this story had C. P. E. Bach saying that Mrs Quantz's dog was the most terrifying creature in Prussia, if not all Europe, because it terrorized Mrs Quantz, who terrorized

Mr Quantz, who terrorized the king. This was stated in a speech given by Zelter in 1809, which was reprinted by Preuss, *Friedrich der Grosse*, vol. 3, pp. 480–83.

50. Henze-Döhring, *Friedrich der Grosse*, p. 121.
51. Scholes (ed.), *An Eighteenth-century Musical Tour*, vol. 2, p. 181. His verdict was confirmed by another English visitor, James Harris – Earl of Malmesbury (ed.), *Diaries and Correspondence of James Harris, First Earl of Malmesbury* (London, 1844), vol. 1, p. 3.
52. Schleuning, *Das 18. Jahrhundert*, p. 63.
53. Preuss, *Friedrich der Grosse*, vol. 3, p. 481.
54. Helm and McCulloch, 'Frederick II, King of Prussia'.
55. Henze-Döhring, 'Die Musik', in Sösemann, vol. 1, p. 241.
56. For a good guide to recorded music by Frederick, go to http://www.jpc. de/s/friedrich+ii.
57. Helmuth Osthoff, 'Friedrich II. als Musikliebhaber und Komponist', in Erhard Bethke (ed.), *Friedrich der Grosse. Herrscher zwischen Tradition und Fortschritt* (Gütersloh, 1985), p. 179.
58. A good example in all respects is the 'Tribute to Frederick the Great (flute concertos at Sanssouci)' performed by Emmanuel Pahud, Trevor Pinnock and the Kammerakademie Potsdam, available on Blu-Ray and DVD. Despite the subtitle, the concert in fact took place in the theatre of the Neues Palais.
59. Daniel Heartz and Bruce Alan Brown, 'Galant', *Grove Music Online. Oxford Music Online*, Oxford University Press, Web, 24 April 2013, http://www.oxfordmusiconline.com/subscriber/article/grove/music/10512.
60. Ibid.
61. Hans-Günter Ottenberg (ed.), *Der Critische Musicus an der Spree. Berliner Musikschrifttum von 1748 bis 1799* (Leipzig, 1984), pp. 15–16; Daniel Heartz and Bruce Alan Brown, 'Empfindsamkeit', *Grove Music Online. Oxford Music Online*, Oxford University Press, Web, 24 April 2013, http://www.oxfordmusiconline.com/subscriber/article/ grove/music/08774.
62. Volz (ed.), *Friedrich der Grosse und Wilhelmine von Bayreuth*, vol. 1, p. 277.
63. Helm, *Music at the Court of Frederick the Great*, pp. 36–7.
64. Heartz, *Music in European Capitals*, p. 336.
65. Koser, vol. 2, p. 285.
66. Henze-Döhring, *Friedrich der Grosse*, p. 173.
67. Thomas Biskup, 'Das Ceremoniel des grossen Königs: Völkerrecht, Reichsrecht und Friedrichs Rang in der Fürstengesellschaft' (unpublished

paper delivered to the conference *Repräsentation und Selbstinszenierung Friedrichs des Grossen*, Potsdam Museum, 28–29 September 2012).

68. Quoted in Terne, 'Friedrich II. von Preussen und die Hofoper', p. 4.

69. Schneider, *Geschichte der Oper*, p. 21.

70. Dieudonné Thiébault, *Mes Souvenirs de vingt ans de séjour à Berlin; ou Frédéric le Grand, sa famille, sa cour, son gouvernement, son académie, ses écoles, et ses amis littérateurs et philosophes*, 3rd edn (Paris, 1813), vol. 2, p. 310.

71. Terne, 'Friedrich II. von Preussen und die Hofoper', p. 5.

72. Otto von Riesemann, 'Eine Selbstbiographie der Sängerin Gertrud Elizabeth Mara', *Allgemeine Musikalische Zeitung*, 10 (11 August–29 September 1875), p. 546.

73. Ludwig Geiger, *Berlin 1688–1840. Geschichte des geistigen Lebens der preussischen Hauptstadt* (Berlin, 1893), vol. 1: *1688–1786*, p. 603. There is a full discussion of the various rules and regulations of these societies in Heartz, *Music in European Capitals*, pp. 385ff.

74. Christoph Henzel, '"Die Zeit des Augustus in der Musik". Berliner Klassik. Ein Versuch', in Ursula Goldenbaum and Alexander Košenina (eds.), *Berliner Aufklärung: kulturwissenschaftliche Studien* (Berlin, 2003), vol. 2, p. 25.

75. F. W. Marpurg, 'Entwurf einer ausführlichen Nachricht von der Musikübenden Gesellschaft zu Berlin', in *Historisch-kritische Beyträge zur Aufnahme der Musik* (Berlin, 1754–78), vol. 1, 5 (1755), p. 385.

76. Walter Salmen, *Johann Friedrich Reichardt. Komponist, Schriftsteller, Kapellmeister und Verwaltungsbeamter der Goethezeit* (Freiburg im Breisgau and Zürich, 1963), pp. 48–9.

77. Giorgio Pestelli, *The Age of Mozart and Beethoven* (Cambridge, 1984), p. 37.

78. Thomas Bauman, *North German Opera in the Age of Goethe* (Cambridge, 1985), p. 137.

79. Ibid., p. 132.

80. Ibid., p. 174; John Warrack, *German Opera. From the Beginnings to Wagner* (Cambridge, 2001), p. 120.

81. Quoted in Bauman, *North German Opera in the Age of Goethe*, p. 179.

82. Scholes (ed.), *An Eighteenth-century Musical Tour*, vol. 2, pp. 160–61.

83. Henze-Döhring, *Friedrich der Grosse*, pp. 18, 73, 143–4.

84. Friedrich Nicolai, *Beschreibung der Königlichen Residenzstädte Berlin und Potsdam* (Berlin, 1786), vol. 1, p. 210.

85. Thomas Biskup, 'Eines "Grossen" würdig? Hof und Zeremoniell bei Friedrich II.', in Friederisiko, Essays, p. 108.

86. Quoted in Heartz, Music in European Capitals, p. 38.

87. Œuvres, vol. 23, p. 208.

88. Ibid., vol. 24, p. 324; Helm, Music at the Court of Frederick the Great, p. 73, offers a different (and inaccurate) translation.

89. Henze-Döhring, Friedrich der Grosse, pp. 52, 78; Helm, Music at the Court of Frederick the Great, p. 71; Luh, Der Grosse. Friedrich II. von Preussen, p. 46; Mennicke, Hasse und die Brüder Graun als Symphoniker, p. 480. There are several other examples of Frederick's brutally contemptuous treatment of Reichardt in Mennicke's book.

90. Friedrich von Oppeln-Bronikowski and Gustav Berthold Volz (eds.), Das Tagebuch des Marchese Lucchesini (1780–1782). Gespräche mit Friedrich dem Grossen (Munich, 1926), p. 13.

91. Preuss, Friedrich der Grosse, vol. 3, p. 481.

92. Ibid.

93. William S. Newman, 'Emanuel Bach's autobiography', The Musical Quarterly, 51, 2 (1965), p. 363.

94. Henze-Döhring, 'Die Musik', in Sösemann, vol. 1, p. 246; Wolff et al, 'Bach'.

95. Hans-Günter Ottenberg, C.P.E. Bach, trans. Philip J. Whitmore (Oxford, 1987), p. 33.

96. Ibid., p. 86.

97. Ibid., p. 57.

98. Newman, 'Emanuel Bach's autobiography', p. 367. According to one improbable anecdote, he sailed close to the wind at a royal concert at which a member of the audience gushed 'What rhythm!' after Frederick had finished a flute solo, to which Bach added in an audible whisper 'What rhythms!'

99. Thomas Bauman, 'Courts and municipalities in North Germany', in Neal Zaslaw (ed.), The Classical Era. From the 1740s to the End of the Eighteenth Century (London, 1989), p. 250.

100. Henze-Döhring, Friedrich der Grosse, p. 116.

101. Christoph Wolff, Johann Sebastian Bach. The Learned Musician (Oxford, 2002), p. 425. See also James Gaines, Evening in the Palace of Reason (London, 2005), pp. 223–9. Although subtitled Bach Meets Frederick the Great in the Age of Enlightenment, this contains very little about the actual meeting, for the good reason that very little is known. It does, however, have an interesting account and analysis of 'The Musical Offering'.

102. Christoph Wolff (ed.), *The New Bach Reader. A Life of Johann Sebastian Bach in Letters and Documents* (New York and London, 1998), p. 367.

103. Ibid., pp. 226–8.

104. See the ground-plan of the palace in Hans-Joachim Giersberg, *Das Stadtschloss zu Potsdam* (Karwe, 2008), p. 28.

105. Carsten Kretschmann, 'Präsentation und Repräsentation. Sammlungen und Kabinette als Schittstellen einer *république des lettres*', in Sösemann, vol. 1, p. 322. The original, entitled 'Consequences of War' is in the Pitti Palace in Florence.

106. Claudia Sommer, Detlef Fuchs and Michael Rohde, *Schloss Rheinsberg* (Berlin and Munich, 2009), pp. 15–16.

107. Hans-Joachim Giersberg, *Schloss Sanssouci. Die Sommerresidenz Friedrichs des Grossen* (Berlin, 2005), p. 16.

108. Ibid., p. 29.

109. Thomas Biskup, *Friedrichs Grösse. Inszenierungen des Preussenkönigs in Fest und Zeremoniell 1740–1815* (Frankfurt am Main and New York, 2012), p. 38.

110. Karl Heinrich Siegfried Rödenbeck, *Tagebuch oder Geschichtskalender aus Friedrichs des Grossen Regentenleben (1740–1786)* (Berlin, 1840), vol. 1, p. 10.

111. *Œuvres*, vol. 17, p. 188.

112. Ibid., p. 219. An 'astragal' is defined by the *Oxford English Dictionary* as 'a small moulding, of semicircular section, sometimes plain, sometimes carved with leaves or cut into beads, placed round the top or bottom of columns, and used to separate the different parts of the architrave in ornamental entablatures'.

113. Ibid., p. 240.

114. Rödenbeck, *Tagebuch*, vol. 1, p. 71.

115. Kadatz, *Georg Wenzeslaus von Knobelsdorff*, pp. 122–3.

116. Giersberg, *Das Potsdamer Stadtschloss*, pp. 55–6.

117. Peter-Michael Hahn, *Friedrich II. von Preussen* (Stuttgart, 2013), p. 154.

118. Gert Streidt, *Potsdam. Die Schlösser und Gärten der Hohenzollern* (Cologne, 1996), p. 15.

119. Jörg Kirschstein, *Das Potsdamer Stadtschloss. Vom Fürstensitz zum Landtagschloss* (Berlin, 2014), pp. 37–9. This is particularly helpful because it contains many photographs of the interior destroyed by bombing in the Second World War.

120. Lehndorff, vol. 1, p. 129.

121. Kirschstein, *Das Potsdamer Stadtschloss*, pp. 56–7, 62–3.

122. Giersberg, *Schloss Sanssouci*, p. 34. It is on this detailed and scholarly account that most of what follows is based.

123. Ibid., p. 41.

124. Ibid., pp. 38-9.

125. For an examination of just how much of Sanssouci was determined by Frederick, together with good illustrations of his crude sketches, see Seidel, *Friedrich der Grosse und die bildende Kunst*, pp. 96-101.

126. Hahn, *Friedrich II.*, p. 55.

127. Giersberg, *Schloss Sanssouci*, p. 45.

128. Ibid., p. 69.

129. Hahn, *Friedrich II.*, p. 155.

130. Clemens Alexander Wimmer, 'Der Garten – ein Bild. Knobelsdorff und die Gartenkunst', in Ute G. Weickardt, Tilo Eggeling and Gerd Bartoschek (eds.), *'Zum Maler und zum grossen Architekten geboren'. Georg Wenzeslaus von Knobelsdorff 1699-1753. Ausstellung zum 300. Geburtstag* (Berlin, 1999), p. 81.

131. There is a good and well illustrated description of the Sanssouci gardens in their earliest form in Kadatz, *Georg Wenzeslaus Knobelsdorff*, pp. 207-14.

132. Michael Rohde, 'Friedrich II. und die Gartenkunst in Sanssouci', in Friederisiko, Ausstellung, p. 52.

133. Alfred P. Hagemann, 'Zitat und Kopie bei Friedrich II.', in Friederisiko, Ausstellung, p. 179.

134. For those unable to visit Potsdam in person, the lavishly illustrated volume by Giersberg, with 250 pages of photographs by Hillert Ibbeken is a good substitute. There are also excellent illustrations in Marina thom Suden, *Schlösser in Berlin und Brandenburg und ihre bildliche Ausstattung im 18. Jahrhundert* (Petersberg, 2013).

135. Martin Engel, *Das Forum Fridericianum und die monumentalen Residenzplätze des 18. Jahrhunderts* (unpublished Free University Berlin dissertation, 2001), p. 12. It was not latinized as 'Forum Fridericianum' until the twentieth century. It is strange that Engel's important work has not been published, although it can be accessed online at http://www.diss.fu-berlin.de/diss/receive/FUDISS_thesis_000000001297. As Engel points out, previous accounts of the *Forum* have concentrated only on the buildings actually constructed, paying little if any attention to what Frederick originally planned.

136. That was the view of the Saxon ambassador, writing on 16 July 1740. It seems unlikely, for Frederick rebuilt the Town Palace at Potsdam, where he had suffered as much if not more. More influential may well

have been his adored mother, who urged him not to build a new palace – ibid., pp. 91, 94.

137. Ibid., pp. 62, 82.

138. Ibid., p. 84.

139. Klaus Dorst, 'Das Neue Palais von Sanssouci. Architektonischer Schluss-akkord des friderizianischen Zeitalters', in Friederisiko, Ausstellung, p. 280; Streidt, *Potsdam*, p. 88; Frank Göse (ed.), *Friedrich der Grosse und die Mark Brandenburg. Herrschaftspraxis in der Provinz* (Berlin, 2012), p. 31; Manuel Brug, 'Warum Friedrich die Kaiserin im Schrank baden liess', *Die Welt*, 26 April 2012, http://www.welt.de/kultur/history/article106217006/Warum-Friedrich-die-Kaiserin-im-Schrank-baden-liess.html.

140. James Lees-Milne, *Baroque in Italy* (London, 1959), p. 187.

141. Henriette Graf, 'Das Neue Palais – Funktion und Disposition der Appartements', in Friederisiko, Ausstellung, p. 295.

142. Hans-Joachim Giersberg, 'Architektur, Stadtgestaltung und Garten-kunst', in Gert Streidt and Peter Feierabend (eds.), *Preussen. Kunst und Architektur* (Cologne, 1999), p. 203.

143. Streidt, *Potsdam*, pp. 100–101, where a fine illustration is also to be found.

144. Claudia Sommer, 'Edle Gesteine in den Schlössern Friedrichs II. von Preussen', in Friederisiko, Ausstellung, p. 186. It should be added here that Frederick also advertised his riches after 1763 by commissioning a gold dinner service consisting of ninety-six plates and dishes, seven dozen spoons, forks and knives, and sundry other bowls, tureens, warmers and candlesticks – Claudia Meckel, 'Gold und Silber', in Friederisiko, Ausstellung, p. 196. It was all melted down in 1809 to help pay for the reparations extorted by Napoleon.

145. Watkin and Tilman Mellinghoff, *German Architecture and the Classical Ideal*, p. 22.

146. Luh, *Der Grosse. Friedrich II. von Preussen*, p. 107. When Frederick left Saxony in 1763 he took with him seventy-nine crates of porcelain – Michaela Völkel, 'Nicht alle Lust will Ewigkeit. Friedrich und das Porzellan', in Friederisiko, Ausstellung, p. 191.

147. Engel, 'Architektur und Bauherrschaft', in Sösemann, vol. 1, p. 277.

148. Seidel, *Friedrich der Grosse und die bildende Kunst*, p. 121.

149. Volker Thiele, 'Architectura fridericiana – Der König und das Bau-wesen', in Friederisiko, Essays, pp. 187–8.

150. Watkin and Tilman Mellinghoff, *German Architecture and the Classical Ideal*, p. 22.

151. Luh, *Der Grosse. Friedrich II. von Preussen*, p. 162.

152. He had more than forty architectural works in his library to consult – Jutta Götzmann, 'Veduta ideata. Der Alte Mark zu Potsdam als Auftakt und Höhepunkt friderizianischer Stadtgestaltung', in idem (ed.), Friedrich und Potsdam. Die Erfindung seiner Stadt (Munich, 2012), p. 23.

153. Alfred P. Hagemann, 'Das Nauener Tor in Potsdam. Der "Roi philosophe" und das Gothic Revival', in Friederisiko, Essays, pp. 157–8.

154. Kadatz, Georg Wenzeslaus Knobelsdorff, pp. 214–15.

155. Fritz-Eugen Keller, 'Probleme der spätfriderizianischen Architektur', Zeitschrift des Historischen Vereins für Kunstwissenschaft, 42, 1 (1988), pp. 66–7.

156. Engel, Das Forum Fridericianum, pp. 32–3. When the obelisk was restored by the East German regime in 1981, the four Prussian rulers were replaced by stone images of four architects who had played an important role in the development of Potsdam.

157. Hagemann, 'Zitat und Kopie bei Friedrich II.', p. 176.

158. Eugen Paunel, Die Staatsbibliothek zu Berlin. Ihre Geschichte und Organisation während der ersten zwei Jahrhunderten seit ihrer Eröffnung (Berlin, 1965), p. 50.

159. Wegner, 'Friedrich der Grosse und die englische Kunst', pp. 56–7; Hans Kania, Potsdamer Baukunst. Eine Darstellung ihrer geschichtlichen Entwicklung (Berlin, 1926), p. 48.

160. Ibid.

161. Christoph Vogtherr, 'An art collector on the European stage', unpublished paper delivered to 'Frederick the Great and the Republic of Letters', a symposium convened by Thomas Biskup and Katrin Kohl at Jesus College, Oxford, 13–14 July 2012.

162. Ernst Curtius, 'Friedrich II. und die bildenden Künste', in idem, Alterthum und Gegenwart. Gesammelte Reden und Vorträge (Berlin, 1882), vol. 2, p. 203.

163. Kretschmann, 'Präsentation und Repräsentation', p. 311.

164. Gerd Bartoschek, 'Friedrich II. als Sammler von Gemälden', in Hans-Joachim Giersberg and Claudia Meckel (eds.), Friedrich II. und die Kunst (Potsdam, 1986), vol. 1, p. 86.

165. Paul Seidel, 'Friedrich der Grosse als Sammler von Gemälden und Skulpturen', Jahrbuch der Königlich-Preussischen Kunstsammlungen, 13 (1892), p. 192.

166. Helmut Börsch-Supan, 'Friedrich der Grosse und Watteau', in Margaret Morgan Grasselli and Pierre Rosenberg (eds.), Watteau 1684–1721 (Berlin, 1985), p. 553. It is probable that Parisian forgers produced

fake Watteaus expressly to be sold to Frederick – Seidel, *Friedrich der Grosse und die bildende Kunst*, pp. 163–4. In fact only eleven of the 'Watteaus' were genuine, although this is still an impressive total, given the artist's short life – he died in 1721 aged thirty-six.

167. That, at least, is the speculation of Helmut Börsch-Supan in Grasselli and Rosenberg (eds.), *Watteau*, p. 562.

168. Kretschmann, 'Präsentation und Repräsentation', p. 319.

169. Adolf Rosenberg, 'Friedrich der Grosse als Kunstsammler', *Zeitschrift für bildende Kunst*, new series, 4 (1893), p. 210.

170. Helmut Börsch-Supan, 'Brandenburg und Sachsen – die Spannungen im Kunstleben', in Göse (ed.), *Friedrich der Grosse und die Mark Brandenburg*, p. 29.

171. Nina Simone Schepkowski, *Johann Ernst Gotzkowsky. Kunstagent und Gemäldesammler im friderizianischen Berlin* (Berlin, 2009), pp. 77–8.

172. Seidel, 'Friedrich der Grosse als Sammler von Gemälden und Skulpturen', p. 188.

173. Ibid.

174. Kretschmann, 'Präsentation und Repräsentation', p. 317.

175. Tobias Locker, 'Die Bildergalerie von Sanssouci bei Potsdam', in Bénédicte Savoy (ed.), *Tempel der Kunst. Die Geburt des öffentlichen Museums in Deutschland 1701–1815* (Mainz, 2006), p. 219.

176. Schepkowski, *Johann Ernst Gotzkowsky*, pp. 79–80.

177. Saskia Hünecke, 'Introduction', in idem. (ed.), *Die Schönste der Welt. Eine Wiederbegegnung mit der Bildergalerie Friedrichs des Grossen* (Berlin and Munich, 2013), p. 9. This informative and beautifully produced volume contains a detailed description of the collection.

178. Börsch-Supan, 'Brandenburg und Sachsen', p. 30.

179. Helmut Börsch-Supan, 'Friedrichs des Grossen Umgang mit Bildern', *Zeitschrift des Historischen Vereins für Kunstwissenschaft*, 42, 1 (1988), p. 30.

180. James J. Sheehan, *Museums in the German Art World. From the End of the Old Regime to the Rise of Modernism* (New York, 2000), p. 32.

181. Engel, 'Architektur und Bauherrschaft', p. 276.

182. Sheehan, *Museums*, p. 37.

183. Alexandra Nina Bauer, 'Die Gemäldesammlung bis 1786', in Hünecke (ed.), *Die Schönste der Welt*, p. 41.

184. Hünecke, 'Introduction', in ibid., p. 9.

185. Christoph Martin Vogtherr, 'Friedrich II. von Preussen als Sammler von Gemälden und der Marquis d'Argens', in Hans Dickel and Christoph

Martin Vogtherr (eds.), *Preussen. Die Kunst und das Individuum* (Berlin, 2003), p. 43.

186. Börsch-Supan, 'Friedrichs des Grossen Umgang mit Bildern', p. 29; Reinhard Alings, '"Don't ask – don't tell" – war Friedrich schwul?', in *Friederisiko*, Ausstellung, p. 241.

187. Locker, 'Die Bildergalerie von Sanssouci bei Potsdam', p. 225.

188. Vogtherr, 'An art collector on the European stage'.

189. Ibid.

190. Daniel Heartz, *Mozart's Operas* (Berkeley, 1990), p. 3.

191. *Description d'un tableau représentant le sacrifice d'Iphigénie peint par monsieur Carle Vanloo* (Paris, 1757), p. 25. Available online at http://gallica.bnf.fr/ark:/12148/btv1b84430070/f25.image.

192. *Extrait des Observations sur la physique et les arts. Lettre à l'auteur sur l'exposition de cette année* (Paris, 1757), pp. 2–8. Available online at http://gallica.bnf.fr/ark:/12148/btv1b8443009t/f3.image. See also Thomas E. Crow, *Painters and Public Life in Eighteenth-century Paris* (New Haven and London, 1985), pp. 104–5.

193. Friedrich Melchior Grimm, *Correspondance littéraire* (October, 1757), available online at http://artflsrv02.uchicago.edu/cgi-bin/philologic/getobject.pl?c.1:29.grimm.338962.

194. Curtius, 'Friedrich II. und die bildenden Künste', p. 204. The same figure is given by Koser, vol. 1, p. 479.

195. Luh, *Der Grosse*, p. 29.

196. http://ub-dok.uni-trier.de/argens/pic/pers/Stosch.php.

197. Dorothy Mackay Quynn, 'Philipp von Stosch: Collector, Bibliophile, Spy, Thief (1691–1757)', *The Catholic Historical Review* (1941), p. 339. Jonathan Israel has referred to Stosch in *The Radical Enlightenment* (Oxford, 2002), p. 222, as 'the legendary deist, freemason, and open homosexual'.

198. Astrid Dostert, 'Friedrich der Grosse als Sammler antiker Skulptur', in *Friederisiko*, Essays, pp. 230–45.

199. Giersberg, *Das Potsdamer Stadtschloss*, p. 29.

200. Dostert, 'Friedrich der Grosse als Sammler antiker Skulptur', pp. 28–30.

201. Detlev Kreikenbom, 'Die Aufstellung antiker Skulpturen in Potsdam-Sanssouci unter Friedrich II.', in Max Kunze (ed.), *Wilhelmine und Friedrich II. und die Antiken*, Schriften der Winckelmann-Gesellschaft (Stendal, 1998), vol. 15, p. 48. This also includes an illustration. For a good illustration of Mars, see Giersberg, *Schloss Sanssouci*, p. 197.

202. Giersberg, *Schloss Sanssouci*, p. 49.

203. Thomas Blisniewski, 'Mythologie', in ibid., pp. 103–11. See also the illustrations on pp. 181–9.

204. Hahn, *Friedrich II.*, pp. 37–8. Charles XII's main biographer, Ragnhild Hatton, devotes much space to explaining why he never married but does not discuss his sexuality – *Charles XII of Sweden* (London, 1968), *passim*.

205. Hahn, *Friedrich II.*, p. 156.

206. Christoph Martin Vogtherr, 'Absent love in pleasure houses. Frederick II of Prussia as art collector and patron', *Art History*, 24, 2 (2001), p. 237. See also thom Suden, *Schlösser in Berlin und Brandenburg*, p. 206.

207. Hahn, *Friedrich II.*, p. 167; Vogtherr, 'Absent love in pleasure houses', p. 231.

208. Peter-Michael Hahn, *Friedrich der Grosse und die deutsche Nation: Geschichte als politisches Argument* (Stuttgart, 2007), p. 215.

209. *Œuvres*, vol. 2, p. 3. The same scandal was also referred to in Frederick's 'Ode to slander', together with the allegations of homosexuality often levelled at Julius Caesar – ibid., vol. 10, p. 5.

210. *Journal secret du Baron Christophe Louis de Seckendorff* (Tübingen, 1811), p. 12.

211. Thomas Fischbacher, *Des Königs Knabe. Friedrich der Grosse und Antinous* (Weimar, 2011), pp. 47–8.

212. Ibid., p. 80; Emile Michel, 'Frédéric II et les arts à la cour de Prusse', *Revue des deux mondes*, 56 (1883), p. 893.

213. P. C., vol. 5, p. 442.

214. Vogtherr, 'Absent love in pleasure houses', p. 239.

215. Orestes and Pylades, Nisus, and Pirithous all feature in Voltaire's poem 'Le temple de l'amitié', written in 1732 and sent to Crown Prince Frederick in 1738 with an additional verse – Hagemann, 'Zitat und Kopie bei Friedrich II.', p. 183.

216. Franziska Windt, 'Künstlerische Inszenierung von Grösse. Friedrichs Selbstdarstellung im Neuen Palais', in Friederisiko, Essays, pp. 131–49. For the contemporary recognition of Alexander's relationship with Hephaestion having a sexual dimension, see Hannah Smith and Stephen Taylor, 'Hephaestion and Alexander: Lord Hervey, Frederick, Prince of Wales, and the royal favourite in England in the 1730s', *English Historical Review*, 507 (2009), p. 13.

217. Vogtherr, 'An art collector on the European stage'.

218. Sommer, Fuchs and Rohde, *Schloss Rheinsberg*, p. 16; Gustav Berthold Volz (ed.), *Friedrich der Grosse im Spiegel seiner Zeit* (Berlin, 1901), vol. 1, p. 77.

219. Albert Salomon, 'Der Freundschaftskult des 18. Jahrhunderts in Deutschland: Versuch zur Soziologie einer Lebensform', ed. Richard Grathoff, *Zeitschrift für Soziologie*, 8, 3 (1979), p. 290; Jost Hermand, *Freundschaft. Zur Geschichte einer sozialen Bindung* (Cologne, Weimar and Vienna, 2006), p. 11; Wolfdietrich Rasch, *Freundschaftskult und Freundschaftsdichtung im deutschen Schrifttum des 18. Jahrhunderts* (Halle-Saale, 1936), Deutsche Vierteljahrsschrift für Literaturwissenschaft und Geistesgeschichte, vol. 21, p. 83. It has also been argued by British and American scholars in particular that it was in the early eighteenth century that male sexuality was reconceptualized in such a way as to exclude sexual relations between men from the normative experience. Heterosexuality became the predominant, rather than, as previously, the dominant, sexual paradigm, and consequently, rampant heterosexuality became a proof of masculinity – Smith and Taylor, 'Hephaestion and Alexander', p. 14.

220. Helmut Walser Smith, 'The poetry of friendship and the prose of patriotic sacrifice in Prussia during the Seven Years War', in Ursula Goldenbaum and Alexander Košenina (eds.), *Berliner Aufklärung*, p. 10.

7. PEACE AND WAR 1745–1756

1. Alfred Ritter von Arneth, *Geschichte Maria Theresias* (Vienna, 1863–79), vol. 3, pp. 160–66.

2. Jürgen Ziechmann (ed.), *Friedrich der Grosse. Das Palladion* (Bremen, 1985), vol. 2: *Kommentarband*, p. 55.

3. Henri Zosime, Comte de Valori (ed.), *Mémoires des négociations du marquis de Valori, ambassadeur de France à la Cour de Berlin. Accompagnés d'un recueil de lettres de Frédéric-le-Grand, des princes ses frères, de Voltaire, et des plus illustres personnages du XVIIIe siècle* (Paris, 1820), vol. 1, pp. 290–94. It is reprinted in full in English translation in Carlyle, vol. 4, pp. 222–7.

4. Edgar Zevort (ed.), *Le Marquis d'Argenson et le Ministère des Affaires Étrangères de 18 novembre 1744 au 10 janvier 1747* (Paris, 1879), p. 368.

5. Ibid., p. 370.

6. Arneth, *Geschichte Maria Theresias*, vol. 3, pp. 164–8, 445.

7. Karl Heinrich Kaufhold, 'Friderizianische Agrar-, Siedlungs- und Bauernpolitik', in Peter Baumgart (ed.), *Kontinuitäten und Wandel. Schlesien zwischen Österreich und Preussen* (Sigmaringen, 1990), p. 172.

8. Carlyle, vol. 3, p. 165.
9. Herman Freudenberger, 'Industrialisation in Bohemia and Moravia in the 18th century', *Journal of Central European Affairs*, 19 (1960), p. 348.
10. Ibid.; Dietrich, p. 274; Peter-Michael Hahn, *Friedrich II. von Preussen* (Stuttgart, 2013), p. 90.
11. Carlyle, vol. 3, p. 182. There is a good map of the fortresses in Silesia (and other parts of Prussia) on the front inside cover of Bernhard R. Kroener (ed.), *Europa im Zeitalter Friedrichs des Grossen. Wirtschaft, Gesellschaft, Kriege* (Munich, 1989).
12. Johannes Kunisch, *Das Mirakel des Hauses Brandenburg: Studien zum Verhältnis von Kabinettspolitik und Kriegführung im Zeitalter des Siebenjährigen Krieges* (Munich, 1978), p. 95.
13. Wilhelm Treue, 'Schlesiens Eingliederung in das preussische Wirtschaftssystem', in Baumgart (ed.), *Kontinuitäten und Wandel*, pp. 121–3.
14. James Van Horn Melton, *Absolutism and the Eighteenth-century Origins of Compulsory Schooling in Prussia and Austria* (Cambridge, 1988), p. 94.
15. Leopold von Ranke, *Friedrich der Grosse* (Leipzig, 1878), p. 34.
16. J. E. Biester, 'Bemerkungen auf einer Reise in Schlesien; in Briefen', in F. Gedike and J. E. Biester (eds.), *Berlinische Monatsschrift* (Berlin, 1783) (1), p. 242.
17. Norbert Conrads, 'Politischer Mentalitätswandel von oben: Friedrichs II. Weg vom Gewinn Schlesiens zur Gewinnung der Schlesier', in Baumgart (ed.), *Kontinuitäten und Wandel*, p. 222; Ingrid Mittenzwei, *Friedrich II. von Preussen* (Cologne, 1980), p. 51.
18. Kaufhold, 'Friderizianische Agrar-, Siedlungs- und Bauernpolitik', p. 176.
19. Harm Klueting, 'Die politisch-administrative Integration Preussisch-Schlesiens unter Friedrich II.', in Baumgart (ed.), *Kontinuitäten und Wandel*, p. 59.
20. Koser, vol. 1, pp. 392, 395.
21. Ute Frevert, *Gefühlspolitik. Friedrich II. als Herr über die Herzen?* (Göttingen, 2012), p. 61.
22. Ernst Pfeiffer, *Die Revuereisen Friedrichs des Grossen, besonders die schlesischen nach 1763 und der Zustand Schlesiens von 1763–1786* (Berlin, 1904), p. 21.
23. The best concise account of the closing years of the War of the Austrian Succession and the peace is to be found in H. M. Scott, *The Birth of a Great Power System 1740–1815* (London, 2006), pp. 59–67.
24. *Œuvres*, vol. 4, p. 18.

25. Arneth, *Geschichte Maria Theresias*, vol. 4, p. 266.
26. *Œuvres*, vol. 2, pp. 26-7. Translation from Frederick the Great, *The History of My Own Times*, vol. 1, p. 40.
27. 1 June 1743, P.C., vol. 2, p. 370.
28. *Œuvres*, vol. 3, p. 33. Translation from Frederick the Great, *The History of My Own Times*, vol. 1, pp. 49-50.
29. P.C., vol. 2, p. 408.
30. Ibid., vol. 3, p. 169.
31. See the helpful genealogical tables in Simon Dixon, *Catherine the Great* (London, 2009), pp. vi-viii. This distinguished biography also contains an excellent account of the betrothal and marriage of Grand Duke Peter and Catherine.
32. *Œuvres*, vol. 3, p. 32. Translation from Frederick the Great, *The History of My Own Times*, vol. 1, p. 48. The Tsarina Elizabeth had originally thought of Frederick's sister Ulrike as a mate for her son, but Frederick had already picked the Swedish prince, believing he would prove more useful – Agnieszka Pufelska, 'Vom zufälligen Feind zum umworbenen Freund: Friedrich II. und Russland', in Friederisiko, Ausstellung, pp. 122-3.
33. P.C., vol. 3, p. 237.
34. Walther Mediger, *Moskaus Weg nach Europa. Der Aufstieg Russlands zum europäischen Machtstaat im Zeitalter Friedrichs des Grossen* (Brunswick, 1952), p. 249. Unfortunately, this very detailed account of Russian policy is not supported by footnotes.
35. Koser, vol. 1, pp. 466-7.
36. Gaston Zeller, *Histoire des relations internationales. Les temps modernes*, vol. 2: *De Louis XIV à 1789* (Paris, 1955), p. 223.
37. Koser, vol. 1, p. 467; Mediger, *Moskaus Weg nach Europa*, p. 276.
38. R. Nisbet Bain, 'Russia under Anne and Elizabeth', in A. W. Ward, G. W. Prothero and Stanley Leathes (eds.), *The Eighteenth Century*, *The Cambridge Modern History* (Cambridge, 1909), vol. 6, p. 318.
39. Pufelska, 'Vom zufälligen Feind zum umworbenen Freund', p. 124.
40. Klaus Zernack, 'Preussen als Problem der osteuropäischen Geschichte', in Otto Büsch and Wolfgang Neugebauer (eds.), *Moderne Preussische Geschichte* (Berlin and New York, 1981), vol. 3, p. 1608; Klaus Zernack, 'Preussen-Frankreich-Polen. Revolution und Teilung', in Otto Büsch and Monika Neugebauer-Wölk (eds.), *Preussen und die revolutionäre Herausforderung seit 1789. Ergebnisse einer Konferenz*, Veröffentlichungen der Historischen Kommission zu Berlin (Berlin and New York, 1991), vol. 78, p. 22.

41. Norman Davies, *God's Playground. A History of Poland* (Oxford, 1981), vol. 1, p. 500.

42. Robert Howard Lord, *The Second Partition of Poland. A Study in Diplomatic History*, Harvard Historical Studies (Cambridge, MA, 1915), vol. 23, pp. 21, 34.

43. Michael G. Müller, *Die Teilungen Polens 1772 1793 1795* (Munich, 1984), pp. 18–19.

44. F. C. Schlosser, *Geschichte des achtzehnten Jahrhunderts und des neunzehnten bis zum Sturz des französischen Kaiserreichs mit besonderer Rücksicht auf geistige Bildung*, vol. 1 (Heidelberg, 1836), pp. 346–7.

45. Müller, *Die Teilungen Polens*, p. 20.

46. Hintze, p. 314.

47. Michael G. Müller, 'Russland und der Siebenjährige Krieg', *Jahrbücher für die Geschichte Osteuropas*, new series 28 (1980), p. 205.

48. Nisbet Bain, 'Russia under Anne and Elizabeth', p. 314.

49. The fullest account of this episode is to be found in Koser, vol. 1, pp. 465–76. Frederick's response can be followed in detail in P.C., vols. 5–6.

50. William J. McGill, 'The roots of policy: Kaunitz in Italy and the Netherlands 1742–1746', *Central European History*, 1 (1968), p. 137.

51. Ibid., p. 145.

52. Arneth, *Geschichte Maria Theresias*, vol. 4, p. 271.

53. The memorandum is printed in full in Johannes Kunisch (ed.), *Expansion und Gleichgewicht: Studien zur europäischen Mächtepolitik des ancien régime, Zeitschrift für Historische Forschung*, vol. 2 (1986), pp. 168–239. Substantial extracts, including the most important passages, can be found online at http://germanhistorydocs.ghi-dc.org/pdf/deu/9_MilitaryAffairs_Doc.6_German.pdf.

54. The best summary and discussion of this formidable document is still that in Arneth, *Geschichte Maria Theresias*, vol. 4, pp. 271–82.

55. Scott, *The Birth of a Great Power System 1740–1815*, p. 84.

56. Michel Antoine, *Louis XV* (Paris, 1989), p. 400.

57. Colin Jones, *The Great Nation. France from Louis XV to Napoleon* (London, 2002), p. 130.

58. Sven Externbrink, *Friedrich der Grosse, Maria Theresia und das alte Reich: Deutschlandbild und Diplomatie Frankreichs im Siebenjährigen Krieg* (Berlin, 2006), p. 44.

59. Richard Waddington, *Louis XV et le renversement des alliances. Préliminaires de la Guerre de Sept Ans 1754–1756* (Paris, 1896), p. 170.

60. J. D. E. Preuss, *Friedrich der Grosse – Eine Lebensgeschichte* (Berlin, 1832), p. 432.
61. Max Braubach, *Versailles und Wien von Louis XIV. bis Kaunitz* (Bonn, 1952), p. 430.
62. P.C., vol. 1, p. 43.
63. Erich Everth, *Die Öffentlichkeit in der Aussenpolitik von Karl V. bis Napoleon* (Jena, 1931), p. 330.
64. Dietrich, p. 344. Lorraine had been ceded to Louis XV's father-in-law, Stanislas Leszczyński, by the Treaty of Vienna in 1738, with reversion to France on his death, which occurred in 1766.
65. T. R. Clayton, 'The Duke of Newcastle, the Earl of Halifax, and the American origins of the Seven Years' War', *The Historical Journal*, 24, 3 (1981), p. 573.
66. H. M. Scott, 'Hanover in mid-eighteenth-century Franco-British geopolitics', in Brendan Simms and Torsten Riotte (eds.), *The Hanoverian Dimension in British History 1714–1837* (Cambridge, 2007), p. 277.
67. The best concise account is in Andrew C. Thompson, *George II. King and Elector* (New Haven and London, 2011), pp. 192–7.
68. Reed Browning, 'Holles, Thomas Pelham, duke of Newcastle upon Tyne and first duke of Newcastle under Lyme (1693–1768)', *Oxford Dictionary of National Biography*, Oxford University Press, 2004, online edn, May 2011, http://www.oxforddnb.com/view/article/21801. Accessed 25 June 2013.
69. Volker Press, 'Friedrich der Grosse als Reichspolitiker', in Heinz Duchhardt (ed.), *Friedrich der Grosse, Franken and das Reich* (Cologne and Vienna, 1986), p. 42.
70. Arneth, *Geschichte Maria Theresias*, vol. 4, p. 341.
71. Ibid., pp. 343–6.
72. Waddington, *Louis XV et le renversement des alliances*, pp. 148–9. Waddington consistently misspells Starhemberg 'Stahremberg'.
73. This memorandum is quoted and discussed by Johannes Kunisch, 'Der Historikerstreit über den Ausbruch des Siebenjährigen Krieges (1756)', in idem, *Friedrich der Grosse in seiner Zeit. Essays* (Munich, 2008), p. 75.
74. Arneth, *Geschichte Maria Theresias*, vol. 4, p. 390.
75. Ibid., pp. 395–6.
76. Theodor Schieder, *Friedrich der Grosse. Ein Königtum der Widersprüche* (Frankfurt am Main, Berlin and Vienna, 1983), p. 175.
77. Frédéric Masson (ed.), *Mémoires et lettres de François-Joachim cardinal de Bernis* (Paris, 1878), vol. 1, p. 223.

78. D. B. Horn, 'The Diplomatic Revolution', in *The New Cambridge Modern History*, vol. 7: *The Old Regime 1713–1763*, ed. J. O. Lindsay (Cambridge, 1970), p. 445. Bernis wrote in his *Mémoires et lettres* that he had *opposed* such a radical change of the French alliance system because it would be very unpopular inside France, would outrage the German Protestant princes and would lead to a war for which France was not ready. He was writing after the event, of course, and one suspects that his memory would have been different if the Austrian alliance had turned out less disastrously.

79. Eckhard Buddruss, *Die französische Deutschlandpolitik 1756–1789* (Mainz, 1995), p. 42.

80. Antoine, *Louis XV*, p. 675.

81. Waddington, *Louis XV et le renversement des alliances*, p. 182.

82. Horn, 'The Diplomatic Revolution', p. 453.

83. Quoted in Manfred Schlenke, *England und das friderizianische Preussen 1740–1763. Ein Beitrag zum Verhältnis von Politik und öffentlicher Meinung im England des 18. Jahrhunderts* (Munich, 1963), p. 194. Those words had been written in 1753 but they applied *a fortiori* two years later.

84. Nisbet Bain, 'Russia under Anne and Elizabeth', p. 319; Scott, *The Birth of a Great Power System 1740–1815*, p. 89.

85. P.C., vol. 11, pp. 439–41.

86. Reinhold Koser, 'Aus der Korrespondenz der französischen Gesandtschaft zu Berlin 1746–1756', *Forschungen zur Brandenburgischen und Preussischen Geschichte*, 7 (1894), p. 85.

87. Waddington, *Louis XV et le renversement des alliances*, pp. 197–8; Karl Otmar Freiherr von Aretin, *Das Alte Reich 1648–1806* (Stuttgart, 1997), vol. 3: *Das Reich und der österreichisch-preussische Dualismus (1745–1806)*, pp. 79–80.

88. Waddington, *Louis XV et le renversement des alliances*, pp. 199–202.

89. Scott, *The Birth of a Great Power System 1740–1815*, pp. 90–91. Jürgen Luh has argued in 'Frederick the Great and the first "world" war', in Mark H. Danley and Patrick J. Speelman (eds.), *The Seven Years War: Global Views* (Leiden, 2013), p. 13, that Frederick was not motivated by fear but by the belief that the British would be able to use success overseas to gain a favourable settlement for their ally in Europe.

90. Waddington, *Louis XV et le renversement des alliances*, p. 234.

91. P.C., vol. 11, p. 436.

92. Arneth, *Geschichte Maria Theresias*, vol. 4, pp. 418–19.

93. Buddruss, *Die französische Deutschlandpolitik*, pp. 78–9.

94. Ibid., p. 82.

95. Ibid., p. 84.

96. P.C., vol. 12, pp. 322–3.

97. Ibid., p. 327. This reprints Mitchell's despatch to London. Cf. Mediger, *Moskaus Weg nach Europa*, p. 628.

98. P.C., vol. 12, p. 336.

99. Mediger, *Moskaus Weg nach Europa*, p. 633.

100. Schieder, *Friedrich der Grosse*, p. 178.

101. Ibid., p. 179; Hintze, p. 361; Koser, vol. 1, p. 601.

102. Ibid., p. 602.

103. P.C., vol. 13, pp. 206, 280–81.

104. Ibid., p. 309.

105. This paragraph has been based on the account in Buddruss, *Die französische Deutschlandpolitik*, pp. 92–9, which is both the most authoritative and the most judicious.

106. P.C., vol. 2, p. 213.

107. Friedrich Meinecke, *Machiavellism. The Doctrine of raison d'état and its Place in Modern History* (London, 1957), p. 319. Meinecke added in a footnote that the same could be said of the mistake made by Holstein about Great Britain and Russia before 1914.

108. P.C., vol. 12, p. 330.

109. In a letter to Wilhelmine dated 21 September 1755: Gustav Berthold Volz (ed.), *Friedrich der Grosse und Wilhelmine von Bayreuth* (Leipzig, 1924), vol. 1: *Jugendbriefe 1728–1740*, p. 316.

110. Herbert Butterfield, 'The reconstruction of an historical episode: the history of the enquiry into the origins of the Seven Years War', in idem, *Man on his Past* (Cambridge, 1969), pp. 147, 157, 164.

111. P.C., vol. 9, pp. 350–51.

112. Paul Langford, *The Eighteenth Century 1688–1815* (London, 1976), p. 140.

113. P.C., vol. 20, p. 508.

114. There is a full and judicious account of the controversy and examination of the issues in Kunisch, 'Der Historikerstreit über den Ausbruch des Siebenjährigen Krieges', pp. 48–106.

115. Schieder, *Friedrich der Grosse*, pp. 120, 170; Buddruss, *Die französische Deutschlandpolitik*, pp. 90–91 and n. 140.

116. As Peter-Michael Hahn has observed, Frederick's decision to take advantage of Maria Theresa's plight determined the whole course of his reign. He was driven on, a prisoner of his initial success – *Friedrich II. von Preussen* (Stuttgart, 2013), pp. 67, 85.

8. THE SEVEN YEARS WAR: THE FIRST THREE CAMPAIGNS

1. Carl von Clausewitz, *On War*, ed. and trans. Michael Howard and Peter Paret (Princeton, 1976), p. 119.
2. P.C., vol. 13, pp. 296–8.
3. Christopher Duffy, *Frederick the Great. A Military Life* (London, 1985), p. 101. On the lack of military and diplomatic preparations made by the indolent Saxons, see René Hanke, *Brühl und das Renversement des alliances. Die antipreussische Aussenpolitik des Dresdener Hofes 1744–1756* (Berlin, 2006), p. 320.
4. *Œuvres*, vol. 11, pp. 302–3.
5. Alfred Ritter von Arneth, *Geschichte Maria Theresias* (Vienna, 1863–79), vol. 5, pp. 1ff. This remains the fullest and most satisfactory account of the Austrian side of the Seven Years War, despite its obtrusive pro-Austrian bias (albeit no more biased than Prussian accounts of the same period). For an excellent, but of necessity much less expansive, account, see Michael Hochedlinger, *Austria's Wars of Emergence. War, State and Society in the Habsburg Monarchy 1683–1797* (London, 2003), ch. 14.
6. Arneth, *Geschichte Maria Theresias*, vol. 5, p. 15.
7. Duffy, *Frederick the Great*, pp. 102–3. As usual this contains the best detailed account of the battle, supported by a good map on p. 345.
8. P.C., vol. 13, pp. 482, 487.
9. Ibid., p. 482.
10. Quoted in Christopher Duffy, *The Army of Maria Theresa. The Armed Forces of Imperial Austria 1740–1780* (London, 1977), p. 173.
11. Arneth, *Geschichte Maria Theresias*, vol. 5, p. 18.
12. There is a good map in Duffy, *Frederick the Great*, p. 347.
13. Karl Zabeler (ed.), *Militärischer Nachlass des Königlich. Preussischen Generallieutenants, Gouverneurs von Königsberg und General-Inspekteurs der Ostpreussischen Infanterie Viktor Amadäus, Grafen Henckel von Donnersmarck* (Zerbst, 1846), vol. 1, p. 192. Frederick made the same observation to Sir Andrew Mitchell, the British diplomat in attendance – Duffy, *Frederick the Great*, p. 115. The White Mountain was an ironic reference to the great victory won by the Habsburg Emperor Ferdinand II at Prague in 1620.
14. The best account is in Duffy, *Frederick the Great*, pp. 115–21. There is a more concise account in Dennis Showalter, *The Wars of Frederick the*

Great (London, 1996), pp. 152–6, although there is no map and a strange misprint on p. 153 has the battle occurring on 6 June.

15. Ibid., p. 155.

16. Wolfgang Petter, 'Zur Kriegskunst im Zeitalter Friedrichs des Grossen', in Bernhard R. Kroener (ed.), *Europa im Zeitalter Friedrichs des Grossen. Wirtschaft, Gesellschaft, Kriege* (Munich, 1989), p. 253.

17. Koser, vol. 2, p. 86.

18. Franz A. J. Szabo, *The Seven Years War in Europe, 1756–1763* (London, 2008), p. 58.

19. Arneth, *Geschichte Maria Theresias*, vol. 5, p. 179.

20. Reinhold Koser, 'Bemerkungen zur Schlacht von Kolin', *Forschungen zur Brandenburgischen und Preussischen Geschichte*, 11 (1898), p. 198.

21. Ibid., p. 199.

22. Koser, vol. 2, p. 148.

23. Johannes Burkhardt, 'Religious war or imperial war? Views of the Seven Years War from Germany and Rome', in Mark H. Danley and Patrick J. Speelman (eds.), *The Seven Years War: Global Views* (Leiden, 2013), p. 117.

24. Haug von Kuenheim (ed.), *Aus den Tagebüchern des Grafen Ernst Ahasverus Heinrich von Lehndorff* (Berlin, 1982), p. 81.

25. Johann Christoph Allmayer-Beck, 'Die friderizianische Armee im Spiegel ihrer österreichischer Gegner', in *Friedrich der Grosse und das Militärwesen seiner Zeit* (Herford and Bonn, 1987) [no editor listed], p. 43.

26. For example, *Œuvres*, vol. 4, pp. 146–8. See also Jürgen Luh, *Der Grosse. Friedrich II. von Preussen* (Berlin, 2012), p. 19, and his remarks to his personal assistant, de Catt, in Paul Hartig (ed.), *Henri de Catt, Vorleser Friedrichs des Grossen. Die Tagebücher 1758–60* (Munich and Berlin, 1986), p. 70.

27. For example, Koser, 'Bemerkungen zur Schlacht von Kolin', pp. 174–200.

28. Duffy, *Frederick the Great*, pp. 126–30.

29. *Œuvres*, vol. 20, p. 298.

30. Christian Graf von Krockow, *Die preussischen Brüder. Prinz Heinrich und Friedrich der Grosse. Ein Doppelporträt* (Stuttgart, 1996), p. 79.

31. Karl Heinrich Siegfried Rödenbeck, *Lebensbeschreibungen Friedrich Wilhelms I. und Friedrichs des Grossen, Könige von Preussen, nebst einem Anhang, enthaltend ein Tagebuch aus Friedrichs des Grossen Regentenleben von 1740–1786* (Berlin, 1836), vol. 1, p. 309.

32. Matt Schumann and Karl Schweizer, *The Seven Years War: a Trans-atlantic History* (London and New York, 2008), p. 52.

33. Dietrich, p. 558.

34. Theodor Schieder, *Friedrich der Grosse. Ein Königtum der Wider-sprüche* (Frankfurt am Main, Berlin and Vienna, 1983), p. 190.

35. Koser, vol. 2, p. 119. Exemplifying the linguistic confusion of the Habs-burg Monarchy, 'Nádasti' is variously spelt 'Nadasty', 'Nadasky' etc.

36. The events of the summer and autumn of 1757 are best followed in Koser, vol. 2, pp. 106–27.

37. Olaf Groehler, *Die Kriege Friedrichs II.* (Berlin, 1966), p. 105.

38. Chester V. Easum, *Prince Henry of Prussia. Brother of Frederick the Great* (Westport, CT, 1942), p. 59.

39. Gustav Berthold Volz (ed.), *Friedrich der Grosse und Wilhelmine von Bayreuth* (Leipzig, 1924), vol. 1: *Jugendbriefe 1728–1740*, p. 399.

40. *Œuvres*, vol. 19, p. 51.

41. 'Rossbach was a victory almost unexcelled as an example of the super-iority of generalship, training and morale over mere weight of numbers': Christopher Duffy, 'Rossbach', in Cyril Falls (ed.), *Great Military Bat-tles* (London and New York, 1964), p. 65.

42. Koser, vol. 2, p. 96.

43. Claude Louis, Comte de Saint-Germain, *Correspondance particu-lière du comte de Saint-Germain, ministre d'état, avec M. Paris du Verney* (Paris, 1789), p. 157. The letter was written on 11 November 1757.

44. Koser, vol. 2, p. 214.

45. Karl Otmar Freiherr von Aretin, *Das Alte Reich 1648–1806* (Stuttgart, 1997), vol. 3: *Das Reich und der österreichisch-preussische Dualismus (1745–1806)*, p. 97.

46. Koser, vol. 2, p. 87.

47. Quoted in Michael Sikora, *Disziplin und Desertion. Strukturprobleme militärischer Organisation im 18. Jahrhundert* (Berlin, 1996), p. 284.

48. Ibid., p. 219.

49. Aretin, *Das Alte Reich 1648–1806*, vol. 3, p. 97.

50. Volz (ed.), *Friedrich der Grosse und Wilhelmine von Bayreuth*, vol. 1, p. 399.

51. Christopher Duffy, *The Fortress in the Age of Vauban and Frederick the Great* (London, 1985), p. 117.

52. Gunnar Åselius, 'Sweden and the Pomeranian War', in Danley and Speelman (eds.), *The Seven Years War*, pp. 149–52.

53. Arneth, *Geschichte Maria Theresias*, vol. 5, p. 256.

54. *Œuvres*, vol. 4, p. 183. Translation from *The History of the Seven Years War*, in *Posthumous Works* (London, 1789), vol. 2, p. 196.

55. Arneth, *Geschichte Maria Theresias*, vol. 5, p. 263.

56. 'It has never been seriously disputed that Leuthen was the greatest victory of the generation, and perhaps of the century, and that this day alone would have established Frederick's claim to a place among the most celebrated commanders,' Duffy, *Frederick the Great*, p. 153.

57. Quoted in Carlyle, vol. 5, p. 265.

58. As usual, Duffy, *Frederick the Great*, pp. 146–54, gives the most lucid and compelling account of the battle.

59. Ibid., pp. 146–8. Many German historians give an appreciably higher total for the Austrians. One recent account states that there were 80,000 Austrians on the field of battle – Schumann and Schweizer, *The Seven Years War*, p. 96.

60. Duffy, *Frederick the Great*, p. 153; Arneth, *Geschichte Maria Theresias*, vol. 5, p. 266. In a letter to d'Argens dated 19 December 1757 Frederick claimed that in all he was now playing host to 23,000 Austrian prisoners of war, including fifteen generals and 700 officers – *Œuvres*, vol. 19, p. 53.

61. In a letter to the Marquis d'Argens, 19 December 1757 – *Œuvres*, vol. 19, p. 53.

62. Arneth, *Geschichte Maria Theresias*, vol. 5, p. 268.

63. Carlyle, vol. 5, pp. 259–60. Carlyle gives a more literal translation, but I have preferred the version usually sung in English churches.

64. Siegmar Keil, 'Der "Choral von Leuthen" – ein preussisch-deutscher Mythos', *Die Tonkunst*, 4 (2007), pp. 442–9.

65. I have discussed this further in *The Triumph of Music: Composers, Musicians and Their Audiences 1700 to the Present* (London, 2008), pp. 231–3.

66. *Œuvres*, vol. 19, p. 53.

67. Lehndorff, vol. 1, p. 373.

68. Petter, 'Zur Kriegskunst im Zeitalter Friedrichs des Grossen', in Kroener (ed.), *Europa im Zeitalter Friedrichs des Grossen*, p. 245.

69. Klaus-Richard Böhme, 'Schwedens Teilnahme am Siebenjährigen Krieg: innen- und aussenpolitische Voraussetzungen und Rückwirkungen', in ibid., pp. 208–9.

70. *Œuvres*, vol. 4, p. 200. Translation taken from *Posthumous Works*, vol. 2, p. 221.

71. On the siege of Schweidnitz, which was a slow process, see Duffy, *The Fortress in the Age of Vauban and Frederick the Great*, p. 122.
72. Duffy, *Frederick the Great*, p. 158.
73. As usual, the fullest account of events in Vienna is to be found in Arneth, *Geschichte Maria Theresias*, vol. 5, here at pp. 347–55.
74. Johann Wilhelm von Archenholz, *Geschichte des Siebenjährigen Krieges in Deutschland*, ed. August Potthast (Leipzig, 1866), pp. 112–16; Arneth, *Geschichte Maria Theresias*, vol. 5, pp. 371–6. Laudon is often spelt 'Loudon' and Ziskowitz in various ways – 'Siskovics', 'Siskovich', etc.
75. P.C., vol. 17, p. 82.
76. Ibid., p. 85.
77. N. William Wraxall, *Memoirs of the Courts of Berlin, Dresden, Warsaw and Vienna in the Years 1777, 1778 and 1779*, 3rd edn (London, 1806), vol. 1, p. 180. This is also quoted in Duffy, *Frederick the Great*, p. 161.
78. Szabo, *The Seven Years War in Europe*, p. 154.
79. On de Ligne's military career, see Philip Mansel, *Prince of Europe: the Life of Charles Joseph de Ligne (1735–1814)* (London, 2003), ch. 2.
80. Charles Joseph Prince de Ligne, 'Mon journal de la Guerre de Sept Ans', in *Mélanges militaires, littéraires et sentimentaires* (Paris, 1796), vol. 14, p. 114.
81. Dieter Ernst Bangert, *Die russisch-österreichische militärische Zusammenarbeit im Siebenjährigen Krieg in den Jahren 1758–1759* (Boppard, 1971), pp. 46–7.
82. Ibid., p. 42.
83. The best account of the battle is now to be found in Adam Storring, *The Battle of Zorndorf* (forthcoming). I am most grateful to Mr Storring for allowing me to read and cite his account in advance of publication. As yet there is no pagination available. There are good accounts, supported by excellent maps, in Duffy, *Frederick the Great*, pp. 163–72, and also in his *Russia's Military Way to the West. Origins and Nature of Russian Military Power 1700–1800* (London, 1981), pp. 83–90.
84. Arneth, *Geschichte Maria Theresias*, vol. 5, p. 409.
85. Quoted in Duffy, *Russia's Military Way to the West*, p. 89.
86. Petter, 'Zur Kriegskunst im Zeitalter Friedrichs des Grossen', p. 252.
87. 'A truthful description of the bloody Battle of Zorndorf by an old Prussian soldier who served for thirty-four years and is still living now (1793)', first published in German in *Officier-Lesebuch*, ed. C. D.

Kuster (Berlin, 1793), trans. Martin Lange of Toronto. I am grateful to Dr Ilya Berkovich for supplying me with a copy of this piece.

88. Schumann and Schweizer, *The Seven Years War*, p. 97.

89. Storring, *The Battle of Zorndorf*.

90. *Œuvres*, vol. 4, pp. 230–31. Translation here from *Posthumous Works*, vol. 2, p. 265.

91. Bangert, *Die russisch-österreichische militärische Zusammenarbeit im Siebenjährigen Krieg*, p. 106.

92. Arneth, *Geschichte Maria Theresias*, vol. 5, pp. 411–12.

93. Duffy, *Frederick the Great*, p. 176.

94. Wolfgang Burgdorf, *Friedrich der Grosse. Ein biografisches Porträt* (Freiburg, Basle and Vienna, 2011), p. 161.

95. Koser, vol. 2, p. 204.

96. Showalter, *The Wars of Frederick the Great*, p. 233.

97. Easum, *Prince Henry of Prussia*, p. 80.

98. *Racine's Mid-career Tragedies*, trans. into English rhyming verse with introduction by Lacy Lockert (Princeton, 1958); Jörg Ulbert, 'Friedrichs Lektüren während des Siebenjährigen Krieges', in Brunhilde Wehinger and Günther Lottes (eds.), *Friedrich der Grosse als Leser* (Berlin, 2012), p. 76.

99. Willy Schüssler (ed.), *Friedrich der Grosse: Gespräche mit Henri de Catt* (Munich, 1981), pp. 277–8; *Œuvres*, vol. 15, p. ii.

100. Ibid.

101. Schüssler (ed.), *Friedrich der Grosse*, p. 280.

102. Arneth, *Geschichte Maria Theresias*, vol. 5, p. 423.

103. C. D. Küster, *Des Preussischen Staabsfeldpredigers Küster, Bruchstück seines Campagnelebens im Siebenjährigen Kriege*, 2nd expanded edn (Berlin, 1791), p. 93.

104. *Œuvres*, vol. 26, p. 221.

105. Arneth, *Geschichte Maria Theresias*, vol. 5, pp. 435–7.

9. THE SEVEN YEARS WAR: DISASTER AND SURVIVAL

1. Dennis Showalter, *The Wars of Frederick the Great* (London, 1996), p. 232.

2. *Œuvres*, vol. 19, p. 72.

3. There is a good account of the campaign in the west in 1759 in Franz A. J. Szabo, *The Seven Years War in Europe, 1756–1763* (London, 2008), pp. 213–20, 256–64.

4. Ibid., p. 261.

5. Ibid., p. 262.

6. P.C., vol. 18, p. 137.

7. Koser, vol. 2, p. 214.

8. Christopher Duffy, *Russia's Military Way to the West. Origins and Nature of Russian Military Power 1700–1800* (London, 1981), pp. 105–8. There are good maps of the region and also of the battle itself on pp. 106–7.

9. Ibid., p. 111.

10. P.C., vol. 18, p. 481. Translation as in Christopher Duffy, *Frederick the Great. A Military Life* (London, 1985), p. 189, except that I have preferred 'fatherland' to 'country' as a translation of *'patrie'*.

11. *Œuvres*, vol. 5, p. 21. Translation here from *Posthumous Works*, vol. 3, p. 31.

12. *Œuvres*, vol. 19, p. 88 in a letter from Madlitz dated 16 August.

13. Szabo, *The Seven Years War in Europe*, p. 237.

14. P.C., vol. 18, p. 487.

15. Carlyle, vol. 5, p. 480.

16. Duffy, *Frederick the Great*, p. 189.

17. Showalter, *The Wars of Frederick the Great*, p. 249.

18. P.C., vol. 18, p. 510.

19. Ilya Berkovich, *Motivation in the Armies of Old Regime Europe* (unpublished Cambridge Ph.D. dissertation, 2012), p. 15.

20. Duffy, *Russia's Military Way to the West*, p. 112.

21. The complicated comings and goings of the autumn are best followed in Szabo, *The Seven Years War in Europe*, pp. 241–7.

22. Ibid., p. 252.

23. Ibid., p. 253.

24. *Œuvres*, vol. 5, p. 50. Translation here from *Posthumous Works*, vol. 3, p. 71.

25. Koser, vol. 2, p. 233.

26. *Œuvres*, vol. 19, p. 133.

27. Duffy, *Frederick the Great*, p. 197.

28. Szabo, *The Seven Years War in Europe*, p. 279.

29. Ibid., pp. 283–4.

30. Jürgen Luh, '"Der fehlerlose Feldherr" – Der Prinz und die Armee', in Burkhardt Göres (ed.), *Prinz Heinrich von Preussen: ein Europäer in Rheinsberg* (Berlin, 2002), p. 83.

31. Alfred Ritter von Arneth, *Geschichte Maria Theresias* (Vienna, 1863–79), vol. 6, pp. 138–40.

32. The best account of the battle is in Duffy, *Frederick the Great*, pp. 201–6.

33. Koser, vol. 2, p. 265.

34. Antoine Henri, Baron de Jomini, *Histoire critique et militaire des guerres de Frédéric II, comparées au système moderne*, new edn (Brussels, 1842), p. 333.

35. Quoted in Duffy, *Frederick the Great*, p. 206.

36. Carlyle, vol. 6, p. 79.

37. P.C., vol. 19, p. 605.

38. Duffy, *Russia's Military Way to the West*, pp. 114–15.

39. Showalter, *The Wars of Frederick the Great*, p. 283.

40. P.C., vol. 20, p. 5.

41. Ibid., p. 14.

42. Arneth, *Geschichte Maria Theresias*, vol. 6, pp. 173–4.

43. Ibid., p. 179.

44. P.C., vol. 20, p. 46.

45. Duffy, *Frederick the Great*, p. 217.

46. Daniel Hohrath, 'Friedrich, die Armee und der Krieg', in Friederisiko, Ausstellung, pp. 272–3.

47. *Œuvres*, vol. 19, p. 230. The quotation is from Voltaire's *Sémiramis*, Act 1, scene 1.

48. Carl von Clausewitz, *On War*, ed. and trans. Michael Howard and Peter Paret (Princeton, 1976), p. 179.

49. Szabo, *The Seven Years War in Europe*, p. 305. This chapter contains the best account of the war in the west in 1760.

50. Quoted in T. C. W. Blanning, '"That horrid electorate" or "Ma patrie germanique"? George III, Hanover and the *Fürstenbund* of 1785', *The Historical Journal*, 20, 2 (1977), p. 338.

51. Carl William Eldon, *England's Subsidy Policy Towards the Continent during the Seven Years War* (Philadelphia, 1938), p. 136. British subsidies amounted to 27 million talers or about 20 per cent of Frederick's total war expenditure – Thomas Biskup and Peter H. Wilson, 'Grossbritannien, Amerika und die atlantische Welt', in Friederisiko, Ausstellung, p. 154.

52. Duffy, *Frederick the Great*, p. 220.

53. P.C., vol. 20, p. 602.

54. Duffy, *Frederick the Great*, p. 221. See also the excellent map on pp. 376–7.

55. P.C., vol. 20, p. 630.

56. Carlyle, vol. 6, pp. 194–5.

57. To Prince Henry on 3 October, P.C., vol. 21, p. 6.

58. Hintze, p. 375.

59. Duffy, *Frederick the Great*, pp. 225–6.

60. Richard Waddington, *La guerre de sept ans: histoire diplomatique et militaire*, vol. 5: *Pondichéry. Villinghausen. Schweidnitz* (Paris, 1914), pp. 60–61.

61. Szabo, *The Seven Years War in Europe*, p. 353. This chapter – 6 – contains the fullest account of the campaign in the west in 1761.

62. P.C., vol. 21, pp. 165–6.

63. Ibid., pp. 189–90.

64. *Recueil des instructions données aux ambassadeurs et ministres de France depuis les traités de Westphalie jusqu'à la Révolution française* (Paris, 1901), vol. 16: *Prusse*, ed. Albert Waddington, p. 514. Peter has been described by Colin Jones as 'a deranged Fredericophile' – *The Great Nation. France from Louis XV to Napoleon* (London, 2002), p. 244.

65. Agnieszka Pufelska, 'Vom zufälligen Feind zum umworbenen Freund: Friedrich II. und Russland', in Friederisiko, Ausstellung, p. 124.

66. Simon Dixon, *Catherine the Great* (London, 2009), pp. 177–80.

67. Johannes Kunisch, *Das Mirakel des Hauses Brandenburg: Studien zum Verhältnis von Kabinettspolitik und Kriegführung im Zeitalter des Siebenjährigen Krieges* (Munich, 1978), p. 56.

68. Koser, vol. 2, pp. 303–5.

69. *Œuvres*, vol. 5, pp. 185–6. Translation here from *Posthumous Works*, vol. 3, pp. 268–9.

70. *Œuvres*, vol. 5, p. 183.

71. Arneth, *Geschichte Maria Theresias*, vol. 6, p. 253.

72. Ibid., ch. 12 *passim*. See also P. G. M. Dickson, *Finance and Government under Maria Theresia 1740–1780* (Oxford, 1987), vol. 2, pp. 2–3, 37, 282.

73. Jones, *The Great Nation*, p. 241.

74. Dickson, *Finance and Government under Maria Theresia*, vol. 2, p. 186, n. 3.

75. *Œuvres*, vol. 19, p. 332.

76. Duffy, *Frederick the Great*, p. 240.

77. There is a good account of the siege in Christopher Duffy, *The Fortress in the Age of Vauban and Frederick the Great* (London, 1985), pp. 126–30, complete with helpful maps.

78. Jomini, *Histoire critique et militaire des guerres de Frédéric II*, p. 401.

79. Walther Mediger, 'Friedrich der Grosse und Russland', in Oswald Hauser (ed.), *Friedrich der Grosse in seiner Zeit* (Cologne and Vienna, 1987), p. 119.

80. Chester V. Easum, *Prince Henry of Prussia. Brother of Frederick the Great* (Westport, CT, 1942), pp. 210–15; Michael Kaiser, 'Prinz Heinrich im Siebenjährigen Krieg – der Oberbefehl in Sachsen und die Schlacht bei Freiberg', in Göres (ed.), *Prinz Heinrich von Preussen*, pp. 99–100.

81. P.C., vol. 22, p. 303.

82. Ibid., p. 306.

83. Carlyle, vol. 6, p. 325.

84. Arneth, *Geschichte Maria Theresias*, vol. 6, p. 372.

85. Koser, vol. 2, p. 278.

86. Szabo, *The Seven Years War in Europe*, p. 423. On 1 January Frederick had told Prince Henry that all the main points had been agreed in advance and that only the small print had to be dealt with – P.C., vol. 22, p. 429.

87. *Correspondance entre le comte Johan Hartvig Ernst Bernstorff et le duc de Choiseul, 1758–1766* (Copenhagen, 1871), pp. 112–15.

88. P.C., vol. 22, p. 423.

89. Ibid., pp. 534–5. He was probably referring to Aesop's fable of the cat and the mice. There was once a house that was overrun with mice. A cat heard of this, and said to herself, 'That's the place for me,' and off she went and took up her quarters in the house, and caught the mice one by one and ate them. At last the mice could stand it no longer, and they determined to take to their holes and stay there. 'That's awkward,' said the cat to herself; 'the only thing to do is to coax them out by a trick.' So she considered a while, and then climbed up the wall and let herself hang down by her hind legs from a peg, and pretended to be dead. By and by a mouse peeped out and saw the cat hanging there. 'Aha!' it cried. 'You're very clever, madam, no doubt: but you may turn yourself into a bag of meal hanging there, if you like, yet you won't catch us coming anywhere near you.'

90. *Œuvres*, vol. 19, p. 425.

10. THE SEVEN YEARS WAR: WHY FREDERICK WON

1. For an excellent concise account of the Seven Years War in all its aspects, both European and extra-European, see Marian Füssel, *Der Siebenjährige Krieg* (Munich, 2013).

2. Leopold von Ranke, 'The great powers', in idem, *The Theory and Practice of History*, ed. Georg G. Iggers and Konrad von Moltke (Indianapolis and New York, 1973), p. 86.

3. Michael Hochedlinger, *Austria's Wars of Emergence. War, State and Society in the Habsburg Monarchy 1683–1797* (London, 2003), p. 349.

4. Alfred Ritter von Arneth, *Geschichte Maria Theresias* (Vienna, 1863–79), vol. 6, pp. 300, 476.

5. For example, by Paul Langford in his *The Eighteenth Century 1688–1815* (London, 1976), p. 140: 'It was also Frederick, who by his lunatic invasion of Saxony in the summer of 1756, on the slightest evidence of Russian conspiracy, and with scant regard for the susceptibilities of either his allies or European public opinion, pushed France into the Second Treaty of Versailles.'

6. Jürgen Luh, 'Frederick the Great and the first "world" war', in Mark H. Danley and Patrick J. Speelman (eds.), *The Seven Years War: Global Views* (Leiden, 2013), p. 18; Gerd Heinrich, *Geschichte Preussens. Staat und Dynastie* (Frankfurt am Main, Berlin and Vienna, 1981), p. 205.

7. Frank Göse, 'Nachbarn, Partner und Rivalen: die kursächsische Sicht auf Preussen im ausgehenden 17. und 18. Jahrhundert', in Jürgen Luh, Vinzenz Czech and Bert Becker (eds.), *Preussen, Deutschland und Europa, 1701–2001* (Groningen, 2003), pp. 58–9.

8. Henri Zosime, Comte de Valori (ed.), *Mémoires des négociations du marquis de Valori, ambassadeur de France à la Cour de Berlin. Accompagnés d'un recueil de lettres de Frédéric-le-Grand, des princes ses frères, de Voltaire, et des plus illustres personnages du XVIIIe siècle* (Paris, 1820), vol. 1, p. 236.

9. Göse, 'Nachbarn, Partner und Rivalen', p. 57.

10. Dietrich, p. 630.

11. Jürgen Luh, *Kriegskunst in Europa 1650–1800* (Cologne, Weimar and Vienna, 2004), p. 117.

12. Koser, vol. 1, p. 3; Henry Lloyd, *The History of the Late War in Germany between the King of Prussia, and the Empress of Germany and her Allies* (London, 1781), vol. 1, p. xxxv.

13. Luh, *Kriegskunst in Europa 1650–1800*, p. 117; Christopher Duffy, *The Army of Frederick the Great* (Newton Abbot, 1974), p. 128.

14. P.C., vol. 13, pp. 303–4.

15. Hubert C. Johnson, *Frederick the Great and his Officials* (New Haven and London, 1975), p. 170.

16. Günter Vogler and Klaus Vetter, *Preussen von den Anfängen bis zur Reichsgründung* (Cologne, 1981), p. 82.

17. Werner Gembruch, 'Prinz Heinrich von Preussen, Bruder Friedrichs des Grossen', in Johannes Kunisch (ed.), *Persönlichkeiten im Umkreis Friedrichs des Grossen* (Cologne and Vienna, 1988), p. 100.

18. Peter-Michael Hahn, *Friedrich II. von Preussen* (Stuttgart, 2013), pp. 139–40.

19. Johannes Kunisch, 'Die militärische Bedeutung Schlesiens und das Scheitern der österreichischen Rückeroberungspläne im Siebenjährigen Kriege', in Peter Baumgart (ed.), *Kontinuitäten und Wandel. Schlesien zwischen Österreich und Preussen* (Sigmaringen, 1990), p. 32.

20. Luh, *Kriegskunst in Europa*, p. 119.

21. Lloyd, *The History of the Late War in Germany*, vol. 1, pp. xxxii–iv.

22. Dietrich, p. 424.

23. Carlyle, vol. 6, p. 215.

24. Daniel Hohrath, 'Friedrich, die Armee und der Krieg', in Friederisiko, Ausstellung, p. 272.

25. Hahn, *Friedrich II. von Preussen*, p. 141.

26. *Œuvres*, vol. 1, p. 125.

27. The labyrinthine dealings of the Vienna court can be followed in considerable detail in Arneth, *Geschichte Maria Theresias*, vols. 5 and 6, not least in the voluminous – and often illuminating – endnotes.

28. H. M. Scott, *The Birth of a Great Power System 1740–1815* (London, 2006), p. 82.

29. This is a constant theme of Franz A. J. Szabo, *The Seven Years War in Europe, 1756–1763* (London, 2008).

30. Johannes Kunisch, 'Die grosse Allianz der Gegner Preussens im Siebenjährigen Krieg', in Bernhard R. Kroener (ed.), *Europa im Zeitalter Friedrichs des Grossen. Wirtschaft, Gesellschaft, Kriege* (Munich, 1989), p. 95.

31. On Buturlin's shortcomings, see John L. H. Keep, 'Die russische Armee im Siebenjährigen Krieg', in ibid., p. 140, and H. M. Scott, *The Emergence of the Eastern Powers, 1756–1775* (Cambridge, 2001), p. 46.

32. Georg Friedrich von Tempelhoff, *Geschichte des Siebenjährigen Krieges in Deutschland zwischen dem Könige von Preussen und der Kaiserin Königin mit ihren Alliierten, als eine Fortsetzung der Geschichte des General Lloyd* (Berlin, 1783–1801), vol. 4, p. 168; Marian Füssel, 'Friedrich der Grosse und die militärische Grösse', in Friederisiko, Essays, pp. 53–5.

33. Johannes Kunisch, *Das Mirakel des Hauses Brandenburg: Studien zum Verhältnis von Kabinettspolitik und Kriegführung im Zeitalter des Siebenjährigen Krieges* (Munich, 1978), p. 77.

34. Johann Christoph Allmayer-Beck, 'Die friderizianische Armee im Spiegel ihrer österreichischen Gegner', in *Friedrich der Grosse und das Militärwesen seiner Zeit* (Herford and Bonn, 1987) [no editor listed], p. 48.

35. David Chandler, *The Campaigns of Napoleon* (London, 1966), p. 84.

36. *Œuvres*, vol. 19, p. 198.

37. Luh, *Kriegskunst in Europa*, p. 143. For Frederick's insistence on the need for daily practice in fast-loading, see his *Political Testament* of 1768 – Dietrich, p. 532.

38. Allmayer-Beck, 'Die friderizianische Armee im Spiegel ihrer österreichischer Gegner', p. 37.

39. Dietrich, p. 532. In the view of Jürgen Luh, battles were won less by firepower than by sword and bayonet – *Kriegskunst in Europa*, p. 151.

40. Koser, vol. 1, p. 548.

41. Edgar Melton, 'The Prussian Junkers, 1600–1786', in H. M. Scott (ed.), *The European Nobilities in the Seventeenth and Eighteenth Centuries* (London, 1995), vol. 2, p. 96.

42. J. D. E. Preuss, *Friedrich der Grosse – Eine Lebensgeschichte* (Berlin, 1832), vol. 1, p. 378; Carlyle, vol. 5, p. 293.

43. Jörg Muth, *Flucht aus dem militärischen Alltag: Ursachen und individuelle Ausprägung der Desertion in der Armee Friedrichs des Grossen* (Freiburg, 2003), p. 179.

44. Peter Paret, *Yorck and the Era of Prussian Reform, 1807–1815* (Princeton, 1966), pp. 23, 26, 44.

45. Duffy, *The Army of Frederick the Great*, p. 76.

46. Quoted in Frank Wernitz, *Die preussischen Freitruppen im Siebenjährigen Krieg 1756–63* (Wölfersheim-Berstadt, 1994), pp. 8–9.

47. David Parrott, 'Armed forces', in William Doyle (ed.), *The Oxford Handbook of the Ancien Régime* (Oxford, 2012), p. 62.

48. Dietrich, p. 520.

49. Curt Jany, *Geschichte der preussischen Armee vom 15. Jahrhundert bis 1914*, 2nd revised edn (Osnabrück, 1967), vol. 2: *Die Armee Friedrichs des Grossen 1750–1763*, p. 180.

50. Luh, *Kriegskunst in Europa*, pp. 165–73.

51. Ibid., p. 165; Gunther Rothenberg, *The Art of Warfare in the Age of Napoleon* (London, 1977), p. 25.

52. *Œuvres*, vol. 29, p. 47. See also Marcus von Salisch, 'Von Preussen lernen . . . ? Die friderizianische Armee nach dem Siebenjährigen Krieg und die Entwicklungen der Zeit', in Friederisiko, Essays, pp. 68–9.

53. Dietrich, p. 520.

54. Wolfgang Venohr, *Der grosse König. Friedrich II. im Siebenjährigen Krieg* (Bergisch Gladbach, 1995), p. 349.

55. Duffy, *The Army of Frederick the Great*, p. 56.

56. Otto Büsch, *Militärsystem und Sozialleben im alten Preussen* (Berlin, 1962), p. 31.

57. Dietrich, p. 518.

58. Hahn, *Friedrich II.*, p. 98.

59. Horst Steinmetz (ed.), *Friedrich II., König von Preussen und die deutsche Literatur des 18. Jahrhunderts. Texte und Dokumente* (Stuttgart, 1985), p. 214.

60. Quoted in Jay Luvaas (ed.), *Frederick the Great on the Art of War* (New York and London, 1966), p. 12. For further comments on the superiority of the Prussian army, see Jacques-Antoine-Hippolyte, Comte de Guibert, *Journal d'un voyage militaire fait en Prusse dans l'année 1787* (Paris, 1790), p. 135.

61. Dietrich, p. 532.

62. *Œuvres*, vol. 28, pp. 4–6.

63. Jacques-Antoine-Hippolyte, Comte de Guibert, *Observations sur la constitution militaire et politique des armées de S. M. prussienne, avec quelques anecdotes de la vie privée de ce monarque* (Paris, 1777), p. 135.

64. Duffy, *The Army of Frederick the Great*, p. 67.

65. Hans Bleckwenn, 'Bauernfreiheit durch Wehrpflicht – ein neues Bild der altpreussischen Armee', in *Friedrich der Grosse und das Militärwesen seiner Zeit*, p. 66.

66. Ernst Friedrich Rudolf von Barsewisch, *Von Rossbach bis Freiberg 1757–1763. Tagebuchblätter eines friderizianischen Fahnenjunkers und Offiziers*, ed. Jürgen Olmes (Krefeld, 1959), p. 65; translation from Duffy, *The Army of Frederick the Great*, p. 138.

67. Walther Hubatsch, *Frederick the Great. Absolutism and Administration* (London, 1975), p. 129.

68. Guntram Schulze-Wegener, 'Leuthen 1757 – Genesis einer operativen Doktrin', *Historische Mitteilungen*, 18 (2005), p. 11.

69. Ilya Berkovich, *Motivation in the Armies of Old Regime Europe* (unpublished Cambridge Ph.D. dissertation, 2012), p. 15.

70. Ibid., p. 85; Sascha Möbius, *Mehr Angst vor dem Offizier als vor dem Feind? Eine mentalitätsgeschichtliche Studie zur preussischen Taktik*

im Siebenjährigen Krieg (Saarbrücken, 2007), pp. 103, 106, 137; Muth, *Flucht aus dem militärischen Alltag*, pp. 160–61; Peter H. Wilson, 'Prusso-German social militarisation reconsidered', in Luh, Czech and Becker (eds.), *Preussen, Deutschland und Europa, 1701–2001*, p. 367.

71. Duffy, *The Army of Frederick the Great*, p. 64; Büsch, *Militärsystem und Sozialleben im alten Preussen*, p. 30.

72. Preuss, *Friedrich der Grosse – Eine Lebensgeschichte*, vol. 1, p. 208.

73. Hubatsch, *Frederick the Great. Absolutism and Administration*, p. 32; Jules Finot and Roger Galmiche-Bouvier (eds.), *Une mission militaire en Prusse en 1786. Récit d'un voyage en Allemagne et observations sur les manœuvres de Potsdam et de Magdebourg. Publiés après les papiers du marquis de Toulongeon* (Paris, 1881), pp. 285–6.

74. Quoted in Manfred Schlenke, *England und das friderizianische Preussen 1740–1763. Ein Beitrag zum Verhältnis von Politik und öffentlicher Meinung im England des 18. Jahrhunderts* (Munich, 1963), p. 293. Schlenke reprints the 'Observations and Reflections upon the Present Military State of Prussia, Austria and France' in full in an appendix, pp. 371–4.

75. Luvaas (ed.), *Frederick the Great on the Art of War*, p. 118.

76. Büsch, *Militärsystem und Sozialleben im alten Preussen*, p. 35.

77. Luvaas (ed.), *Frederick the Great on the Art of War*, p. 146.

78. Dietrich, p. 414.

79. Finot and Galmiche-Bouvier (eds.), *Une mission militaire en Prusse*, p. 286; Guibert, *Journal d'un voyage militaire fait en Prusse*, p. 130.

80. Haug von Kuenheim (ed.), *Aus den Tagebüchern des Grafen Ernst Ahasverus Heinrich von Lehndorff* (Berlin, 1982), p. 24.

81. Tempelhoff, *Geschichte des Siebenjährigen Krieges in Deutschland*, vol. 4, p. 169; Christian Wilhelm von Dohm, *Denkwürdigkeiten meiner Zeit, oder Beiträge zur Geschichte vom letzten Viertel des achtzehnten und vom Anfang des neunzehnten Jahrhunderts 1778 bis 1806* (Lemgo and Hanover, 1814–19), vol. 4, p. 334.

82. Duffy, *The Army of Frederick the Great*, p. 47.

83. Möbius, *Mehr Angst vor dem Offizier als vor dem Feind?*, p. 107.

84. Ute Frevert, *Gefühlspolitik. Friedrich II. als Herr über die Herzen?* (Göttingen, 2012), p. 59. The text appears in the cantata by J. S. Bach 'Am Abend aber desselbigen Sabbats' (BWV 42). This translation is from Alfred Dürr, *The Cantatas of J. S. Bach,* rev. and trans. by Richard D. P. Jones (Oxford, 2005), p. 295.

85. Berkovich, *Motivation in the Armies of Old Regime Europe*, p. 237.

86. Frevert, *Gefühlspolitik*, p. 80.

87. Finot and Galmiche-Bouvier (eds.), *Une mission militaire en Prusse en 1786*, p. 166.
88. Quoted in Michael Sikora, *Disziplin und Desertion. Strukturprobleme militärischer Organisation im 18. Jahrhundert* (Berlin, 1996), p. 310.
89. Kuenheim (ed.), *Aus den Tagebüchern des Grafen Ernst Ahasverus Heinrich von Lehndorff*, p. 126.
90. Möbius, *Mehr Angst vor dem Offizier als vor dem Feind?*, pp. 118–19.
91. Jacques-Antoine-Hippolyte, Comte de Guibert, *Éloge du roi de Prusse* (Paris, 1787), p. 231.
92. Koser, vol. 2, p. 511.
93. P.C., vol. 15, p. 258.
94. Christopher Duffy, *Frederick the Great. A Military Life* (London, 1985), pp. 199, 204; Möbius, *Mehr Angst vor dem Offizier als vor dem Feind?*, p. 106.
95. Duffy, *Frederick the Great*, p. 205.
96. Allmayer-Beck, 'Die friderizianische Armee im Spiegel ihrer österreichischen Gegner', p. 46.
97. Reinhard Bendix, 'Reflections on charismatic leadership', in Dennis Wrong (ed.), *Max Weber* (Englewood Cliffs, 1970), p. 169.
98. Theodor Schieder, *Friedrich der Grosse. Ein Königtum der Widersprüche* (Frankfurt am Main, Berlin and Vienna, 1983), p. 220. For further discussion of Frederick's charisma in this penetrating biography, see pp. 72, 193, 348, 482.
99. There is more than one version of this speech as recorded by those present. I have preferred that of Friedrich August von Retzow, reprinted in his *Charakteristik der wichtigsten Ereignisse des Siebenjährigen Krieges in Rücksicht auf Ursachen und Wirkungen* (Berlin, 1802), vol. 1, pp. 240–42. There is an abbreviated English translation in Carlyle, vol. 5, pp. 232–4.
100. C. D. Küster, *Des Preussischen Staabsfeldpredigers Küster, Bruchstück seines Campagnelebens im Siebenjährigen Kriege*, 2nd expanded edn (Berlin, 1791), p. 93. For further discussion of this aspect of Frederick's support among the common soldiers, see Sikora, *Disziplin und Desertion*, p. 310.
101. Bernhard R. Kroener, 'Die materiellen Grundlagen österreichischer und preussischer Kriegsanstrengungen 1756–1763', in idem (ed.), *Europa im Zeitalters Friedrichs des Grossen*, p. 47.
102. On the fundamental disunity of French and Russian war aims and war programmes, see Lawrence Jay Oliva, *Misalliance: a Study of French Policy in Russia during the Seven Years War* (New York, 1964), pp. 195–6.
103. Kunisch, 'Die grosse Allianz der Gegner Preussens im Siebenjährigen Krieg', p. 85.

104. John L. H. Keep, 'Die russische Armee im Siebenjährigen Krieg', in Kroener (ed.), *Europa im Zeitalter Friedrichs des Grossen*, p. 136.
105. Christopher Duffy, *Russia's Military Way to the West. Origins and Nature of Russian Military Power 1700–1800*, (London, 1981), pp. 118–22.
106. Gaston Zeller, *Histoire des relations internationales. Les temps modernes* (Paris, 1955), vol. 2: *De Louis XIV à 1789*, p. 244; Keep, 'Die russische Armee im Siebenjährigen Krieg', p. 165.
107. Quoted in Michel Antoine, *Louis XV* (Paris, 1989), p. 743.
108. Eckhard Buddruss, *Die französische Deutschlandpolitik 1756–1789* (Mainz, 1995), p. 289.
109. Ibid., p. 126, n. 39.
110. *Œuvres*, vol. 26, pp. 620–21.
111. Quoted in Luvaas (ed.), *Frederick the Great on the Art of War*, p. 11.
112. Carl von Clausewitz, *On War*, ed. and trans. Michael Howard and Peter Paret (Princeton, 1976), p. 603.
113. For example, by Matt Schumann and Karl Schweizer, *The Seven Years War: a Transatlantic History* (London and New York, 2008), p. 492 or Dominic Lieven, *Russia against Napoleon. The Battle for Europe 1807 to 1814* (London, 2009), p. 19.
114. Carlyle, vol. 4, p. 521.
115. Kunisch, *Das Mirakel des Hauses Brandenburg*, p. 13.
116. Muth, *Flucht aus dem militärischen Alltag*, p. 178.
117. Luh, *Kriegskunst in Europa*, pp. 206–7.
118. Christian Graf von Krockow, *Die preussischen Brüder. Prinz Heinrich und Friedrich der Grosse. Ein Doppelporträt* (Stuttgart, 1996), p. 98.
119. Wolfgang Burgdorf, *Friedrich der Grosse. Ein biografisches Porträt* (Freiburg, Basle and Vienna, 2011), p. 30; Lehndorff, vol. 2, p. 77. See also Gerd Fesser, 'Der König von Rheinsberg', *Die Zeit*, 32 (2002), http://www.zeit.de/2002/32/Der_Koenig_von_Rheinsberg?page=all.
120. Burgdorf, *Friedrich der Grosse*, p. 172; Krockow, *Die preussischen Brüder*, p. 97.

11. A LONG PEACE, A SHORT WAR AND DOUBLE DIPLOMACY

1. Klaus Zernack, 'Negative Polenpolitik als Grundlage deutsch-russischer Diplomatie in der Mächtepolitik des 18. Jahrhunderts', in idem, *Preussen, Deutschland, Polen: Aufsätze zur Geschichte der deutsch-polnischen Beziehungen,* ed. Wolfram Fischer and Michael G. Müller (Berlin, 1991), p. 234.

2. P.C., vol. 4, p. 101.

3. Œuvres, vol. 8, p. 207. See also Wolfgang Stribrny, *Die Russlandpolitik Friedrichs des Grossen 1764-1786* (Würzburg, 1966), p. 9.

4. Œuvres, vol. 26, p. 358.

5. Koser, vol. 2, p. 425.

6. P.C., vol. 23, pp. 141-2.

7. Ibid., p. 167.

8. Isabel de Madariaga, *Russia in the Age of Catherine the Great* (London, 1981), p. 188.

9. Robert Howard Lord, *The Second Partition of Poland. A Study in Diplomatic History*, Harvard Historical Studies (Cambridge, MA, 1915), vol. 23, p. 48. This remains the best English-language account of the Polish dimension of the period. Herbert H. Kaplan's *The First Partition of Poland* (New York and London, 1962) is less impressive. In the view of Michael G. Müller, *Die Teilungen Polens 1772 1793 1795* (Munich, 1984), p. 98, n. 43, it is not so much tendentious, as its Polish critics maintained, as inadequate and wrong.

10. Quoted in Simon Dixon, *Catherine the Great* (London, 2009), p. 186.

11. Franziska Mücke, '"Le mamamouchi est arrivé . . ." Friedrich II. und die erste Gesandtschaft des Osmanischen Reiches in Brandenburg-Preussen', in Friederisiko, Ausstellung, pp. 128-33.

12. P.C., vol. 23, p. 273. The episode is recounted in detail in the excellent article by H. M. Scott, 'Frederick II, the Ottoman Empire and the origins of the Russo-Prussian alliance of April 1764', *European Studies Review*, 7 (1977), pp. 2-22.

13. Koser, vol. 2, p. 437.

14. Norman Davies, *God's Playground. A History of Poland* (Oxford, 1981), vol. 1, p. 517.

15. Ibid., p. 513.

16. Jerzy Lukowski, *The Partitions of Poland 1772, 1793, 1795* (London, 1999), p. 40.

17. Simon Dixon, *Catherine the Great* (London, 2001), p. 162. This excellent analysis of Catherine's regime should not be confused with the more biographical study by the same author listed in footnote 10.

18. P.C., vol. 27, pp. 417-18.

19. Albert Sorel, *La Question d'Orient au XVIIIe siècle* (Paris, 1878), p. 15; Koser, vol. 2, p. 455.

20. The best accessible account of the war is in Madariaga, *Russia in the Age of Catherine the Great*, pp. 205-14, although there are many misprints in the dating.

21. Lukowski, *The Partitions of Poland*, p. 66.

22. Lord, *The Second Partition of Poland*, p. 31.

23. Müller, *Die Teilungen Polens*, p. 13.

24. Lord, *The Second Partition of Poland*, p. 35.

25. Müller, *Die Teilungen Polens*, p. 19.

26. *Œuvres*, vol. 16, p. 3; Hans-Jürgen Bömelburg, *Friedrich II. zwischen Deutschland und Polen. Ereignis- und Erinnerungsgeschichte* (Stuttgart, 2011), p. 16.

27. Dietrich, p. 670.

28. *Œuvres*, vol. 2, pp. 27–8. Translation used is from *Posthumous Works* (London, 1789), vol. 1, pt 1, pp. 41–2. See also Bömelburg, *Friedrich II.*, pp. 84–8.

29. Agnieszka Pufelska, 'Die verpasste Grösse: Friedrich II. und Polen', in *Friederisiko, Ausstellung*, p. 108.

30. *Œuvres*, vol. 23, pp. 235–6.

31. Davies, *God's Playground*, vol. 1, p. 511.

32. *Œuvres*, vol. 14, p. 219.

33. Abbé Denina, *La Prusse littéraire sous Frédéric II, ou histoire abrégée de la plupart des auteurs, des académiciens et des artistes qui sont nés ou qui ont vécu dans les états prussiens depuis MDCCXL jusqu'à MDCCLXXXVI. Par ordre alphabétique. Précédée d'une introduction, ou d'un tableau général des progrès qu'ont faits les arts et les sciences dans les pays qui constituent la Monarchie prussienne* (Berlin, 1790), vol. 2, p. 80.

34. The fullest account of the Austrian side is to be found in Alfred Ritter von Arneth, *Geschichte Maria Theresias* (Vienna, 1863–79), vol. 8, pp. 170ff. See also Derek Beales, *Joseph II* (Cambridge, 1987), vol. 1: *In the Shadow of Maria Theresa 1741–1780*, pp. 282–3.

35. P.C., vol. 28, p. 84.

36. H. M. Scott, *The Emergence of the Eastern Powers, 1756–1775* (Cambridge, 2001), p. 189.

37. P.C., vol. 29, p. 42, n. 1.

38. To Finckenstein, Breslau, 29 August 1769, ibid., p. 53. For the Austrian dimension of this visit, see Beales, *Joseph II*, vol. 1, pp. 284–5.

39. Scott, *The Emergence of the Eastern Powers*, p. 194.

40. Ibid., p. 207. The events of this episode are best followed in this admirably lucid and penetrating account.

41. Ibid., p. 206.

42. Colin Jones, *The Great Nation. France from Louis XV to Napoleon* (London, 2002), p. 278.

43. Lukowski, *The Partitions of Poland*, p. 50.

44. Sorel, *La Question d'Orient au XVIIIe siècle*, pp. 144-5.

45. Kurd von Schlözer, *Friedrich der Grosse und Katharina II.* (Berlin, 1859), p. 230, maintained that the invitation came from Catherine.

46. Quoted in Chester V. Easum, *Prince Henry of Prussia. Brother of Frederick the Great* (Westport, CT, 1942), p. 263.

47. P.C., vol. 30, pp. 406-7; von Schlözer, *Friedrich der Grosse und Katharina II.*, pp. 249-50. Stribrny insisted that it was this approach to Prince Henry which set the ball rolling for Frederick – *Die Russlandpolitik Friedrichs des Grossen*, p. 68.

48. Quoted in Koser, vol. 2, p. 466. See also Frank Göse, 'Prinz Heinrich und die erste Teilung Polens', in Burkhardt Göres (ed.), *Prinz Heinrich von Preussen: ein Europäer in Rheinsberg* (Berlin, 2002), p. 129.

49. P.C., vol. 30, p. 483.

50. Lukowski, *The Partitions of Poland*, p. 100.

51. The negotiations can be followed on a weekly if not daily basis in P.C., vols. 30-31, supplemented by the documents reprinted in Adolf Beer, *Die erste Theilung Polens* (Vienna, 1873), vol. 3. The extracts from Frederick's correspondence with Finckenstein reprinted in vol. 2 can be found in fuller versions in P.C. Most of the documents in Beer deal with the Austrian dimension.

52. Quoted in Beales, *Joseph II*, vol. 1, p. 295.

53. Lukowski, *The Partitions of Poland*, p. 81.

54. H. M. Scott, *The Birth of a Great Power System 1740-1815* (London, 2006), p. 166.

55. Beales, *Joseph II*, vol. 1, pp. 297-8.

56. Davies, *God's Playground*, vol. 1, p. 516. As Paul W. Schroeder has pointed out in *The Transformation of European Politics 1763-1848* (Oxford, 1994), p. 16, this gibe was better evidence of Frederick's cynicism than of Maria Theresa's hypocrisy, for she did have genuine moral scruples and could also see that the partition was against Austria's interests.

57. Lukowski, *The Partitions of Poland*, p. 89.

58. Ibid.

59. P.C., vol. 32, p. 249. Most of this letter is published in German translation in Otto Bardong (ed.), *Friedrich der Grosse, Ausgewählte Quellen zur deutschen Geschichte der Neuzeit*. Freiherr vom Stein-Gedächtnisausgabe (Darmstadt, 1982), vol. 22, p. 473.

60. P.C., vol. 32, p. 267. This has been published in German translation in Bardong (ed.), *Friedrich der Grosse*, pp. 473-4.

61. *Œuvres*, vol. 23, p. 290.

62. Ibid., p. 293. The distance indicated by Frederick was '*vingt milles*'. A German mile in Prussia at that time was about 7.5 km – Fritz Verdenhalven, *Alte Masse, Münzen und Gewichte aus dem deutschen Sprachgebiet* (Neustadt an der Aisch, 1968), p. 36. In this context, the best translation of Frederick's '*quelque police*' is probably 'law and order'.

63. Wolfgang Neugebauer, *Die Hohenzollern* (Stuttgart, 1996, 2003), vol. 2, pp. 41–2.

64. Hans-Jürgen Bömelburg, *Zwischen polnischer Ständegesellschaft und preussischem Obrigkeitsstaat. Vom Königlichen Preussen zu Westpreussen 1756–1806* (Munich, 1995), p. 470.

65. Pierre Rain, *La Diplomatie française d'Henri IV à Vergennes* (Paris, 1945), p. 293; Scott, *The Emergence of the Eastern Powers*, p. 222.

66. Ibid., p. 4.

67. D. B. Horn, *British Public Opinion and the First Partition of Poland* (Edinburgh and London, 1945), p. 11.

68. Christian Friedrich Daniel Schubart (ed.), *Deutsche Chronik auf das Jahr 1774* (reprinted, Heidelberg, 1975), 74 (12 December 1774), p. 586.

69. Lehndorff, vol. 3, p. 242.

70. Heinrich von Treitschke, *Deutsche Geschichte im 19. Jahrhundert* (Leipzig, 1927), vol. 1, p. 63.

71. Davies, *God's Playground*, vol. 1, p. 511.

72. Ibid., p. 525.

73. Schroeder, *The Transformation of European Politics*, p. 19. See also Karl Otmar Freiherr von Aretin, 'Tausch, Teilung und Länderschacher als Folgen des Gleichgewichtssystems der europäischen Grossmächte', in Klaus Zernack (ed.), *Polen und die polnische Frage in der Geschichte der Hohenzollernmonarchie 1701–1871* (Berlin, 1982), pp. 56–9.

74. Quoted in Horn, *British Public Opinion and the First Partition of Poland*, p. 13.

75. Lord Rosebery, *Pitt* (London, 1892), p. 103. This is only one of many arresting metaphors in this brilliant book, a masterpiece of English prose.

76. Beales, *Joseph II*, vol. 1, pp. 301–2.

77. Madariaga, *Russia in the Age of Catherine the Great*, p. 359.

78. P.C., vol. 35, p. 215; vol. 36, pp. 96–7.

79. Beales, *Joseph II*, vol. 1, p. 432.

80. Karl Otmar Freiherr von Aretin, *Heiliges Römisches Reich* (Wiesbaden, 1967), vol. 1, p. 111; Georg Schmidt, *Wandel durch Vernunft. Deutsche Geschichte im 18. Jahrhundert* (Munich, 2009), p. 197.

81. Beales, *Joseph II*, vol. 1, pp. 389–90.

82. P.C., vol. 39, pp. 150–51.

83. Ibid., p. 152.

84. Quoted in T. C. W. Blanning, *Joseph II* (London, 1994), p. 148. The full reference to these remarks is given there in footnote 81 on p. 158.

85. P.C., vol. 1, p. 7.

86. *Œuvres*, vol. 2, p. 32. Translation used is from *Posthumous Works*, vol. 1, pp. 46–7.

87. Barbara Stollberg-Rilinger, *Des Kaisers alte Kleider. Verfassungsgeschichte und Symbolsprache des Alten Reiches* (Munich, 2008), p. 293. For an English-language summary of this important work, see her 'On the function of rituals in the Holy Roman Empire', in R. J. W. Evans, Michael Schaich and Peter H. Wilson (eds.), *The Holy Roman Empire 1495–1806: New Perspectives* (Oxford, 2011), pp. 359–73.

88. Arnold Berney, *Friedrich der Grosse. Entwicklungsgeschichte eines Staatsmannes* (Tübingen, 1934), p. 170.

89. Peter H. Wilson, 'Prussia's relations with the Holy Roman Empire, 1740–1786', *The Historical Journal*, 51, 2 (2008), p. 362.

90. Joachim Whaley, *Germany and the Holy Roman Empire* (Oxford, 2012), vol. 2: *The Peace of Westphalia to the Dissolution of the Reich 1648–1806*, p. 400.

91. Despite contemporary use of the word *Acht* ('outlawry'), this was not what was imposed on Prussia, despite the best efforts of the Austrians. Had they succeeded, they would have gained a legal justification for dismembering Prussia, for Frederick's lands would have been forfeit – Wilson, 'Prussia's relations with the Holy Roman Empire, 1740–1786', p. 350.

92. Aprill's account is reprinted in Carlyle, vol. 5, pp. 184–5.

93. Manfred Schort, *Politik und Propaganda. Der Siebenjährige Krieg in den zeitgenössischen Flugschriften* (Frankfurt am Main, 2006), p. 143.

94. *Goethes Werke* (Weimar, 1890), vol. 26: *Dichtung und Wahrheit*, pp. 288–90.

95. Gustav Berthold Volz, 'Friedrichs des IIten Plan einer Losreissung Preussens von Deutschland', *Historische Zeitschrift*, 122 (1920), p. 276.

96. Gabriele Haug-Moritz, *Württembergischer Ständekonflikt und deutscher Dualismus. Ein Beitrag zur Geschichte des Reichsverbands in der Mitte des 18. Jahrhunderts, Veröffentlichungen der Kommission für geschichtliche Landeskunde in Baden-Württemberg*, series B (Stuttgart, 1992), p. 145; Barbara Stollberg-Rilinger, *Das Heilige Römische Reich Deutscher Nation vom Ende des Mittelalters bis 1806* (Munich, 2006), p. 104.

97. Ibid., p. 169.
98. Peter Baumgart, 'Säkularisierungspläne Friedrichs II.', in Joachim Köhler (ed.), *Säkularisationen in Ostmitteleuropa* (Cologne, 1984), p. 64.
99. Whaley, *Germany and the Holy Roman Empire*, vol. 2, p. 397.
100. Lehndorff, vol. 1, p. 276. In 1757 Crown Prince Ludwig of Hessen-Darmstadt was ordered home by his father.
101. Wilson, 'Prussia's relations with the Holy Roman Empire, 1740–1786', p. 361. Wilson provides a list of all imperial princes and counts serving as Prussian regimental commanders 1713–86 on pp. 366–71.
102. Beales, *Joseph II*, vol. 1, pp. 132–3.
103. P.C., vol. 40, p. 5.
104. *Recueil des instructions données aux ambassadeurs et ministres de France depuis les traités de Westphalie jusqu'à la Révolution française* (Paris, 1901), vol. 16: *Prusse*, ed. Albert Waddington, p. 532.
105. Ibid., p. 9.
106. Koser, vol. 2, p. 523.
107. Beales, *Joseph II*, vol. 1, pp. 392–3.
108. P.C., vol. 40, pp. 55–9.
109. H. W. V. Temperley, *Frederic the Great and Kaiser Joseph. An Episode of War and Diplomacy in the Eighteenth Century* (London, 1915, reprinted 1968), pp. 91–5.
110. P.C., vol. 40, p. 356.
111. Koser, vol. 2, p. 530. Koser provides the best account of the war. There is a good English-language account in David Fraser, *Frederick the Great* (London, 2000), ch. 22.
112. Kurd Wolfgang von Schöning, *Der Bayerische Erbfolge-Krieg* (Berlin and Potsdam, 1854), p. 1. Schmettau also observed of the war 'it was a bad play performed by good actors', ibid., p. 2.
113. Daniel Hohrath, 'Die Rolle des Prinzen Heinrich im Bayerischen Erbfolgekrieg von 1778–1779', in Göres (ed.), *Prinz Heinrich von Preussen*, pp. 113–14.
114. Koser, vol. 2, pp. 531–4.
115. P.C., vol. 41, p. 473.
116. Christopher Duffy, *The Army of Frederick the Great* (Newton Abbot, 1974), pp. 204–5; Christopher Duffy, *The Army of Maria Theresa. The Armed Forces of Imperial Austria 1740–1780* (London, 1977), pp. 210–13.
117. The correspondence is published in *Œuvres*, vol. 6, pp. 205–33.
118. Arneth, *Geschichte Maria Theresias*, vol. 10, pp. 449–69.

119. Beales, *Joseph II*, vol. 1, p. 407.

120. Aretin, *Heiliges Römisches Reich*, vol. 1, p. 119.

121. Arneth, *Geschichte Maria Theresias*, vol. 10, p. 579.

122. Beales, *Joseph II*, vol. 1, pp. 421–2.

123. Theodor Schieder, *Friedrich der Grosse. Ein Königtum der Widersprüche* (Frankfurt am Main, Berlin and Vienna, 1983), p. 257.

124. Alexander Brückner, *Katharina die Zweite* (Berlin, 1883), p. 314; Temperley, *Frederic the Great and Kaiser Joseph*, pp. 186–7.

125. Ibid., p. 202.

126. Karl Otmar Freiherr von Aretin, *Das Alte Reich 1648–1806* (Stuttgart, 1997), vol. 3: *Das Reich und der österreichisch-preussische Dualismus (1745–1806)*, p. 203; Volker Press, 'Friedrich der Grosse als Reichspolitiker', in Heinz Duchhardt (ed.), *Friedrich der Grosse, Franken und das Reich* (Cologne and Vienna, 1986), p. 50.

127. Madariaga, *Russia in the Age of Catherine the Great*, p. 381; Karl Otmar Freiherr von Aretin, 'Russia as a guarantor power of the imperial constitution under Catherine II', *Journal of Modern History*, 58: Supplement, *Politics and Society in the Holy Roman Empire 1500–1806* (1986), pp. 141–60.

128. Koser, vol. 2, p. 534. Cf. Duffy, *The Army of Frederick the Great*, p. 205.

129. Schöning, *Der Bayerische Erbfolge-Krieg*, p. 23.

130. Hans Bleckwenn, 'Bauernfreiheit durch Wehrpflicht – ein neues Bild der altpreussischen Armee', in *Friedrich der Grosse und das Militärwesen seiner Zeit* (Herford and Bonn, 1987) [no editor listed], p. 59.

131. On whether or not Luise really did write these words, see Luise Schorn-Schütte, *Königin Luise. Leben und Legende* (Munich, 2003), p. 74.

132. *Œuvres*, vol. 26, p. 349.

133. Marcus von Salisch, '"Von Preussen lernen … ?" Die friderizianische Armee nach dem Siebenjährigen Krieg und die Entwicklungen der Zeit', in Friederisiko, Essays, p. 72.

134. P.C., vol. 43, p. 70.

135. Ibid., p. 71.

136. Joseph to Count Ludwig Cobenzl, 23 December 1780 – Adolf Beer, *Joseph II., Leopold II. und Kaunitz. Ihr Briefwechsel* (Vienna, 1873), p. 26.

137. The best account of Austrian policy in any language is to be found in the second volume of Derek Beales's biography of Joseph – *Against the World, 1780–1790* (Cambridge, 2009), ch. 11.

138. There is a good account of the negotiations in Karl A. Roider, *Austria's Eastern Question* (Princeton, 1982), pp. 159–62. See also Isabel de Madariaga, 'The secret Austro-Russian treaty of 1781', *The Slavonic and East European Review*, 38 (1959).

139. Stribrny, *Die Russlandpolitik Friedrichs des Grossen*, pp. 77–82, 107.

140. Brückner, *Katharina die Zweite*, p. 334.

141. Beales, *Against the World*, p. 383.

142. Beales, *In the Shadow of Maria Theresa*, p. 436.

143. Isabel de Madariaga, *Britain, Russia and the Armed Neutrality of 1780: Sir James Harris's Mission to St Petersburg during the American Revolution* (London, 1962), pp. 320–21.

144. P.C., vol. 46, p. 15. The *Politische Correspondenz* does not yet go beyond April 1782. For Frederick's continuing belief in the necessary hostility between Austria and Russia, see P. Bailleu, 'Der Ursprung des deutschen Fürstenbundes', *Historische Zeitschrift*, 41 (1879), pp. 415, 425. As Bailleu observed, Frederick was very 'ignorant of and ill-informed about' Catherine's intentions.

145. Bailleu, 'Der Ursprung des deutschen Fürstenbundes', p. 425. See also Robert Salomon, *La Politique orientale de Vergennes (1780–1784)* (Paris, 1935), p. 73.

146. Koser, vol. 2, p. 610.

147. Simon Sebag Montefiore, *Prince of Princes: the life of Potemkin* (London, 2000), p. 158. Even the grand duke and his Württemberg-born wife, Marie, went over to the Austrian side in late 1781 – Stribrny, *Die Russlandpolitik Friedrichs des Grossen*, p. 154.

148. Koser, vol. 1, p. 498; Dietrich, p. 660.

149. *Œuvres*, vol. 26, p. 550.

150. Leopold von Ranke, *Die deutschen Mächte und der Fürstenbund*, (Leipzig, 1871–2), vol. 1, p. 149. Frederick was still maintaining this in 1782 – P.C., vol. 46, p. 427.

151. Bailleu, 'Der Ursprung des deutschen Fürstenbundes', p. 433.

152. Friedrich Karl Wittichen, *Preussen und England in der europäischen Politik 1785–1788* (Heidelberg, 1902), p. 31.

153. T. C. W. Blanning, '"That horrid electorate" or "Ma patrie germanique"? George III, Hanover and the *Fürstenbund* of 1785', *The Historical Journal*, 20, 2 (1977), pp. 314–15.

154. The French reaction is best followed in Alfred Ritter von Arneth and Jules Flammermont (eds.), *Correspondance secrète du comte de Mercy-Argenteau avec l'empereur Joseph II et le prince de Kaunitz* (Paris, 1889–91), vol. 1, pp. 185, n. 2, 188–9.

155. John Hardman and Munro Price (eds.), *Louis XVI and the Comte de Vergennes: Correspondence 1774–1787, Studies on Voltaire and the Eighteenth Century* (Oxford, 1998), vol. 364, p. 134. The substantial introduction (154 pp.) is now the best account of French foreign policy during this period.

156. Karl Gödeke, 'Hannovers Antheil an der Stiftung des deutschen Fürstenbundes', *Archiv des Historischen Vereins für Niedersachsen* (1847), p. 70. Frederick wrote in *Mémoires depuis la paix de Hubertsbourg 1763, jusqu'à la fin du partage de la Pologne* that it was well known that Joseph was aiming at Friuli, Bavaria, Bosnia, Alsace, Lorraine and Silesia – *Œuvres*, vol. 6, p. 78.

157. Quoted in Christof Dipper, *Deutsche Geschichte 1648–1789* (Frankfurt am Main, 1991), p. 225.

158. Quoted in Blanning, *Joseph II*, p. 56.

159. Ibid., pp. 94–5.

160. Ibid., pp. 148–9. See also the literature listed in the footnotes.

161. Blanning, *Joseph II*, p. 144. The fullest account is in Beales, *Against the World*, pp. 393–8.

162. P.C., vol. 43, p. 261.

163. Ibid., vol. 46, p. 427.

164. Alfred Ritter von Arneth (ed.), *Joseph II. und Katharina von Russland. Ihr Briefwechsel* (Vienna, 1869), pp. 224–5, 231.

165. This episode is best followed in Beales, *Against the World*, ch. 11.

166. Ranke, *Die deutschen Mächte und der Fürstenbund*, vol. 1, p. 203.

167. Paul P. Bernard, *Joseph II and Bavaria: Two Eighteenth-century Attempts at German Unification* (The Hague, 1965), p. 203.

168. Beales, *Against the World*, p. 396.

169. Schmidt, *Wandel durch Vernunft*, p. 221.

170. Bailleu, 'Der Ursprung des deutschen Fürstenbundes', p. 411; Ludwig Häusser, *Deutsche Geschichte vom Tode Friedrichs des Grossen bis zur Gründung des deutschen Bundes* (Berlin, 1861), vol. 1, p. 165.

171. On the early stages of this project, see Maiken Umbach, 'The politics of sentimentality and the German *Fürstenbund*', *The Historical Journal*, 41, 3 (1998), pp. 679–704.

172. Schmidt, *Wandel durch Vernunft*, p. 220.

173. Alfred Kohler, 'Das Reich im Spannungsfeld des preussisch-österreichischen Gegensatzes. Die Fürstenbundbestrebungen 1783–1785', in Friedrich Engel-Janosi, Grete Klingenstein and Heinrich Lutz (eds.), *Fürst, Bürger, Mensch. Untersuchungen zu politischen und*

soziokulturellen Wandlungsprozessen im vorrevolutionären Europa (Vienna, 1975), pp. 76–92.

174. Horst Möller, *Fürstenstaat oder Bürgernation. Deutschland 1763–1815* (Berlin, 1989), p. 267.

175. Ranke, *Die deutschen Mächte und der Fürstenbund*, vol. 1, p. 223.

176. Beales, *Against the World*, p. 396.

177. Ibid., p. 397.

178. Kohler, 'Das Reich im Spannungsfeld des preussisch-österreichischen Gegensatzes', p. 92.

179. Wilhelm Adolf Schmidt, *Geschichte der preussisch-deutschen Unionsbestrebungen seit der Zeit Friedrichs des Grossen* (Berlin, 1851), vol. 1, p. 147.

180. Blanning, '"That horrid electorate" or "Ma patrie germanique"?', *passim*.

181. Wolfgang Burgdorf, *Reichskonstitution und Nation. Verfassungsreformprojekte für das Heilige Römische Reich Deutscher Nation im politischen Schrifttum von 1648 bis 1806* (Mainz, 1998), p. 289.

182. Ibid., pp. 347–51; Schmidt, *Wandel durch Vernunft*, pp. 221–5.

183. Schieder, *Friedrich der Grosse*, pp. 281–2.

184. Lord, *The Second Partition of Poland*, p. 71; Dietrich Gerhard, *England und der Aufstieg Russlands* (Munich and Berlin, 1933), p. 182.

185. Aretin, *Das Alte Reich 1648–1806*, vol. 3, p. 315; Peter Baumgart, 'Schlesien im Kalkül Friedrichs II. von Preussen und die europäischen Implikationen der Eroberung des Landes', in idem (ed.), *Kontinuitäten und Wandel. Schlesien zwischen Österreich und Preussen* (Sigmaringen, 1990), p. 11; Press, 'Friedrich der Grosse als Reichspolitiker', p. 26; Whaley, *Germany and the Holy Roman Empire*, vol. 2, p. 382. This remains one area where there is plenty of scope for further research. As Peter Wilson has written, 'the history of Prussian *Reichspolitik*, or political relations with the Empire, remains largely unwritten' – 'Prussia and the Holy Roman Empire 1700–40', *Bulletin of the German Historical Institute*, 36, 1 (2014), p. 6.

12. PUBLIC AND NATION

1. I have discussed this in *The Culture of Power and the Power of Culture. Old Regime Europe 1660–1789* (Oxford, 2002), pt 2. See also James Van Horn Melton, *The Rise of the Public in Enlightenment Europe* (Cambridge, 2001).

2. Franz Etzin, 'Die Freiheit der öffentlichen Meinung unter der Regierung Friedrichs des Grossen', *Forschungen zur Brandenburgischen und Preussischen Geschichte*, 33 (1921), p. 89.

3. Etzin, 'Die Freiheit der öffentlichen Meinung', p. 96.

4. Ibid., pp. 97–8. This is reminiscent of the old joke about the two leading newspapers of the Soviet Union, *Izvestia* (news) and *Pravda* (truth): 'There is no news in the truth and no truth in the news.'

5. Ibid., p. 99.

6. Ernst Consentius, 'Friedrich der Grosse und die Zeitungs-Zensur', *Preussische Jahrbücher*, 115 (1904), p. 220.

7. Ibid., p. 226.

8. *Acta Borussica. Denkmäler der preussischen Staatsverwaltung im 18. Jahrhundert, Behördenorganisation und allegemeine Staatsverwaltung*, vol. 8: *Akten vom 21. Mai 1748 bis 1. August 1750*, ed. G. Schmoller and O. Hintze (Berlin, 1906), p. 317.

9. Ibid., pp. 32–3.

10. Etzin, 'Die Freiheit der öffentlichen Meinung', p. 103.

11. This episode has been recounted many times, most fully in Ludwig Salomon, *Geschichte des deutschen Zeitschriftenwesens von den ersten Anfängen bis zur Wiederaufrichtung des Deutschen Reiches*, 2nd edn (Oldenburg and Leipzig, 1906), vol. 1, pp. 149–50.

12. Etzin, 'Die Freiheit der öffentlichen Meinung', p. 122.

13. Peter Gay, *Voltaire's Politics* (New York, n.d.), p. 35. One account of the incident held that the chevalier, who was watching from a carriage, called out that Voltaire's head should be spared 'as something good might come out of it'.

14. Quoted in Horst Steinmetz (ed.), *Friedrich II., König von Preussen, und die deutsche Literatur des 18. Jahrhunderts. Texte und Dokumente* (Stuttgart, 1985), pp. 50, 290, n. 3.

15. John Moore, *A View of Society and Manners in France, Switzerland and Germany* (4th edn, Dublin, 1789), vol. 2, p. 130.

16. On Moore see H. L. Fulton, 'Moore, John (1729–1802)', *Oxford Dictionary of National Biography*, Oxford University Press, 2004; online edn, January 2008, http://www.oxforddnb.com/view/article/19130. Accessed 11 November 2013.

17. Hans Reiss (ed.), *Kant's Political Writings* (Cambridge, 1970), p. 58.

18. Abbé Denina, *Essai sur le règne de Frédéric II, Roi de Prusse* (Berlin, 1788), pp. 456–7.

19. Dieudonné Thiébault, *Mes Souvenirs de vingt ans de séjour à Berlin; ou Frédéric le Grand, sa famille, sa cour, son gouvernement, son académie,*

ses écoles, et ses amis littérateurs et philosophes, 4th edn (Paris, 1813), vol. 1, p. 60.

20. *Acta Borussica*, vol. 8, p. 785.

21. P.C., vol. 10, pp. 59, 135–6. The pamphlet in question was 'Idée de la personne, de la manière de vivre et de la cour du roi de Prusse'.

22. Charles Henry (ed.), *Œuvres et correspondance inédites de d'Alembert* (Paris, 1887), p. 89.

23. Daniel Jenisch, 'Denkschrift auf Friedrich den Zweiten', in Steinmetz (ed.), *Friedrich II.*, pp. 234–5. See also the tribute paid by Moses Mendelssohn quoted below on p. 383.

24. C. B. A. Behrens, *Society, Government and the Enlightenment: The Experiences of Eighteenth-century France and Prussia* (London, 1985), p. 182.

25. Ann Thomson, *Materialism and Society in the Mid-eighteenth Century: La Mettrie's Discours préliminaire* (Geneva and Paris, 1981), p. 10.

26. H. B. Nisbet, *Gotthold Ephraim Lessing. His Life, Works, and Thought* (Oxford, 2008), p. 88.

27. Denina, *Essai sur le règne de Frédéric II, Roi de Prusse*, p. 98.

28. Robert Darnton, *The Forbidden Best-sellers of Pre-revolutionary France* (London, 1996), p. 95. Darnton includes in this volume a full translation of *Thérèse philosophe*.

29. Hans-Joachim Gehrke, 'Klassische Studien. Paradoxien zwischen Antike und Aufklärung', in Sösemann, vol. 1, p. 112.

30. *Œuvres*, vol. 14, p. 28.

31. Ursula Pia Jauch, 'Frederick's "cercle intime": philosophy at court', in Thomas Biskup and Katrin Kohl, *Frederick the Great and the Republic of Letters: A Symposium Oxford 13–14 July 2012*, forthcoming; Nisbet, *Lessing*, p. 88.

32. *Éloge de M. de La Mettrie, Œuvres*, vol. 7, pp. 26–32. There is an English translation at http://vserver1.cscs.lsa.umich.edu/~crshalizi/La Mettrie/.

33. Nisbet, *Lessing*, p. 126.

34. Gustav Berthold Volz (ed.), *Friedrich der Grosse und Wilhelmine von Bayreuth*, vol. 1: *Jugendbriefe 1728–1740* (Leipzig, 1924), p. 210. See also Werner Langer, *Friedrich der Grosse und die geistige Welt Frankreichs*, Hamburger Studien zu Volkstum und Kultur der Romanen, vol. 11 (Hamburg, 1932), pp. 177–8.

35. Thomson, *Materialism and Society in the Mid-eighteenth Century*, p. 14.

36. David Edmonds and John Eidinow, *Rousseau's Dog. Two Great Thinkers at War in the Age of Enlightenment* (London, 2006), p. 49.

37. Jean-Jacques Rousseau, *The Confessions*, ed. J. M. Cohen (London, 1953), p. 547.

38. Maurice Cranston, *The Solitary Self. Jean-Jacques Rousseau in Exile and Adversity* (Chicago, 1997), p. 15.

39. Ibid., p. 17.

40. Avi Lifschitz, 'Adrastus versus Diogenes: Frederick the Great and Jean-Jacques Rousseau on self-love', in Biskup and Kohl, *Frederick the Great and the Republic of Letters*.

41. *Œuvres*, vol. 19, p. 207.

42. Ibid., vol. 20, p. 321.

43. Ibid., p. 322.

44. Cranston, *The Solitary Self*, p. 38.

45. Ibid., p. 158.

46. Winfried Böhm, 'Bildungsideal, Bildungswesen, Wissenschaft und Akademien', in Erhard Bethke (ed.), *Friedrich der Grosse. Herrscher zwischen Tradition und Fortschritt* (Gütersloh, 1985), p. 186; *Œuvres*, vol. 18, p. 249.

47. Thiébault, *Mes Souvenirs*, vol. 1, p. 7.

48. *Œuvres*, vol. 23, p. 131.

49. Volker Wittenauer, *Im Dienste der Macht. Kultur und Sprache am Hofe der Hohenzollern. Vom Grossen Kurfürst bis zu Wilhelm II.* (Paderborn, Munich, Vienna and Zürich, 2007), pp. 122–5.

50. Roland Vocke, 'Friedrich II. Verhältnis zur Literatur und zur deutschen Sprache', in Bethke (ed.), *Friedrich der Grosse*, p. 175. *Œuvres*, vols. 21–3. Many more letters were found subsequently and published by Reinhold Koser and Hans Droysen (eds.), *Briefwechsel Friedrichs des Grossen mit Voltaire*, Publikationen aus den K. Preussischen Staatsarchiven, vols. 81, 82, 86 (Leipzig, 1908–9, 1911). The most complete edition of Voltaire's correspondence is that edited by Theodore Besterman in 107 volumes, *Voltaire's Correspondence* (Geneva, 1953–65). The volumes covering Voltaire's stay in Prussia 1750–53 are 18–22.

51. Peter Gay, *The Enlightenment: an Interpretation* (New York, 1969), vol. 2: *The Science of Freedom*, pp. 483–4.

52. Uwe Steiner, 'Die Sprache der Gefühle. Der Literaturbegriff Friedrichs des Grossen im historischen Kontext', in Brunhilde Wehinger (ed.), *Geist und Macht: Friedrich der Grosse im Kontext der europäischen Kulturgeschichte* (Berlin, 2005), p. 30.

53. Reinhold Koser, *Friedrich der Grosse als Kronprinz* (Stuttgart, 1886), p. 145.
54. Ullrich Sachse, 'Gross im Tod sein. Friedrichs des Grossen erste Verfügung zur Inszenierung seines Nachlebens', in Michael Kaiser and Jürgen Luh (eds.), *Friedrich und die historische Grösse. Beiträge des dritten Colloquiums in der Reihe 'Friedrich300' vom 25./26. September 2009*, (Friedrich300–Colloquien, 3) http://perspectivia.net/content/publikationen/friedrich300-colloquien/friedrich-groesse/sachse_tod. Last accessed on 14 May 2014.
55. Carlyle, vol. 3, pp. 90, 96.
56. Christopher Clark, '"Le roi historien" zu Füssen von Clio', in Sösemann, vol. 1, p. 162.
57. Koser, vol. 2, p. 120.
58. Theodore Besterman, 'Voltaire's commentary on Frederick's *Art de la guerre*', *Studies on Voltaire and the Eighteenth Century*, 2 (1956), pp. 64–6.
59. Lytton Strachey, 'Voltaire and Frederick the Great', in idem, *Books and Characters, French and English* (London, 1922), pp. 168–70.
60. Peter-Michael Hahn, *Friedrich II. von Preussen* (Stuttgart, 2013), p. 54.
61. Quoted in Gay, *The Science of Freedom*, p. 484.
62. Roger Pearson, *Voltaire Almighty. A Life in the Pursuit of Freedom* (London, 2005), pp. 214–16.
63. Besterman (ed.), *Voltaire's Correspondence*, vol. 18, pp. 43, 104.
64. *Œuvres*, vol. 18, p. 74.
65. Strachey, 'Voltaire and Frederick the Great', p. 168.
66. Besterman (ed.), *Voltaire's Correspondence*, vol. 18, p. 120.
67. Ibid., vol. 20, pp. 38–9. The French seem to have been particularly susceptible to Frederick's big blue eyes – 'the most beautiful I have ever seen' was the verdict of the Marquis de Lafayette, who had looked into quite a few beautiful eyes in his time – quoted in Bernd Klesmann, 'Friedrich II. und Frankreich: Faszination und Skepsis', in Friederisiko, Ausstellung, p. 144.
68. Besterman (ed.), *Voltaire's Correspondence*, vol. 18, p. 515.
69. Pearson, *Voltaire Almighty*, pp. 217–18.
70. Besterman (ed.), *Voltaire's Correspondence*, vol. 18, p. 193.
71. Ibid., p. 197.
72. Ibid., p. 214.
73. A concise account of the issues at stake can be found in appendix 56 of Besterman (ed.), *Voltaire's Correspondence*, vol. 18, p. 263. Although Besterman confessed in his biography *Voltaire* (London, 1969), p. 17,

that 'I have been his lifelong admirer this side of idolatry', he concluded about the Hirschel affair: 'his [Voltaire's] conduct cannot and should not be defended'.

74. Besterman (ed.), *Voltaire's Correspondence*, vol. 19, p. 29.

75. Besterman, *Voltaire*, pp. 315–16.

76. Besterman (ed.), *Voltaire's Correspondence*, vol. 20, p. 43.

77. Ibid., pp. 390–91.

78. Avi Lifschitz, *Language and Enlightenment. The Berlin Debates of the Eighteenth Century* (Oxford, 2012), p. 10; Iwan-Michelangelo D'Aprile, 'Aufklärung, Toleranz und Wissenschaft in Preussen', in Friederisiko, Ausstellung, pp. 101–2.

79. Pearson, *Voltaire Almighty*, p. 226.

80. Ibid., p. 227.

81. Ursula Goldenbaum (ed.), *Appell an das Publikum: die öffentliche Debatte in der deutschen Aufklärung 1687–1796* (Berlin, 2004), vol. 2, pp. 522–9.

82. Lehndorff, vol. 1, p. 62.

83. Ibid., p. 229.

84. Volz (ed.), *Friedrich der Grosse und Wilhelmine von Bayreuth*, vol. 2, pp. 253–7.

85. J. D. E. Preuss, *Friedrich der Grosse – Eine Lebensgeschichte* (Berlin, 1832), vol. 1, p. 248.

86. Besterman, *Voltaire*, pp. 329–30.

87. *Œuvres*, vol. 23, p. 3.

88. Langer, *Friedrich der Grosse und die geistige Welt Frankreichs*, p. 180.

89. *Œuvres*, vol. 25, p. 369; vol. 24, p. 545.

90. Steiner, 'Die Sprache der Gefühle', p. 29.

91. Brunhilde Wehinger, 'Introduction', in Brunhilde Wehinger and Günther Lottes (eds.), *Friedrich der Grosse als Leser* (Berlin, 2012), p. 14.

92. *Œuvres*, vol. 8, pp. 133, 251.

93. Ibid., vol. 1, pp. li, 1.

94. Ibid., vol. 7, p. 9.

95. Ibid., vol. 9, pp. 4, 276.

96. 'Avant-propos sur la Henriade de M. de Voltaire', ibid., vol. 8, p. 62.

97. *Œuvres*, vol. 24, p. 522.

98. Ibid., vol. 9, pp. 107, 161; vol. 12, p. 255; vol. 13, pp. 60, 116; vol. 19, p. 151; vol. 23, p. 290; P.C., vol. 10, p. 135; Jacques Droz, *L'Allemagne et la Révolution française* (Paris, 1949), p. 12.

99. *Œuvres*, vol. 10, p. 164.

100. Ibid., vol. 17, p. 261.

101. Ibid., vol. 23, p. 62.

102. Ibid., vol. 2, p. xx.

103. Helga Schultz, *Berlin 1650–1800. Sozialgeschichte einer Residenz* (Berlin, 1987), p. 33.

104. Ibid., p. 61; Rudolf von Thadden, *Fragen an Preussen. Zur Geschichte eines aufgehobenen Staates* (Munich, 1981), p. 279.

105. Schultz, *Berlin 1650–1800*, p. 66.

106. Ibid., p. 122.

107. Reinhart Koselleck, *Preussen zwischen Reform und Revolution. Allgemeines Landrecht, Verwaltung und soziale Bewegung von 1791 bis 1848*, 3rd edn (Berlin, 1981), p. 125; Horst Möller, *Aufklärung in Preussen. Der Verleger, Publizist und Geschichtsschreiber Friedrich Nicolai* (Berlin, 1974), p. 265. The former lists the garrison with dependants as 60,677, the latter as 33,400. There are rather different figures in Felix Escher, 'Die brandenburgisch-preussische Residenz und Hauptstadt Berlin im 17. und 18. Jahrhundert', in Wolfgang Ribbe (ed.), *Geschichte Berlins*, 2nd edn (Munich, 1988), vol. 1: *Von der Frühgeschichte bis zur Industrialisierung*, p. 383.

108. Schultz, *Berlin 1650–1800*, p. 278.

109. 'Ueber Berlin von einem Fremden', in F. Gedike and J. E. Biester (eds.), *Berlinische Monatsschrift* (Berlin, 1783), p. 337.

110. Iwan-Michelangelo D'Aprile, 'Die königliche Toleranzpolitik in der Wahrnehmung der brandenburgischen Untertanen', in Frank Göse (ed.), *Friedrich der Grosse und die Mark Brandenburg. Herrschaftspraxis in der Provinz* (Berlin, 2012), p. 43. See also the figures conveyed and discussed in my *The Culture of Power and the Power of Culture*, pp. 111–15.

111. Quoted in Lutz Winckler, *Kulturwarenproduktion. Aufsätze zur Literatur und Sprachsoziologie* (Frankfurt am Main, 1973), p. 24, n. 28. For several other examples see my *The Culture of Power and the Power of Culture*, pp. 133–5. The original can be found online at http://www.ub.uni-bielefeld.de/diglib/aufkl/deutschesmuseum/deutschesmuseum.htm.

112. Nisbet, *Lessing*, p. 81.

113. Möller, *Aufklärung in Preussen*. The two periodicals can be read online at http://www.ub.uni-bielefeld.de/diglib/aufkl/brieneulit/index.htm and http://www.ub.uni-bielefeld.de/diglib/aufkl/adb/adb.htm respectively.

114. Hans Dollinger, *Preussen. Eine Kulturgeschichte in Bildern und Dokumenten* (Munich, 1980), p. 125.

115. Möller, *Aufklärung in Preussen*, p. 198.

116. Quoted in Horst Möller, 'Wie aufgeklärt war die Aufklärungs- forschung? Friedrich Nicolai in historiographischer Perspektive', in Rainer Falk and Alexander Košenina (eds.), *Friedrich Nicolai und die Berliner Aufklärung* (Hanover, 2008), p. 7. This relies for its effect on an untranslatable pun on the word '*verdient*': *Hast du auch wenig genug verdient um die Bildung der Deutschen,/ Fritz Nicolai, sehr viel hast du dabei doch verdient.*

117. Andreas Gestrich, *Absolutismus und Öffentlichkeit. Politische Kom- munikation in Deutschland zu Beginn des 18. Jahrhunderts* (Göttingen, 1994), p. 171; Ute Frevert, *Gefühlspolitik. Friedrich II. als Herr über die Herzen?* (Göttingen, 2012), p. 79.

118. Christof Dipper, *Deutsche Geschichte 1648–1789* (Frankfurt am Main, 1991), pp. 174–5.

119. Klaus Gerteis, 'Das "Postkutschenzeitalter". Bedingungen der Kommu- nikation im 18. Jahrhundert', in Karl Eibl, *Entwicklungsschwellen im 18. Jahrhundert, Aufklärung*, 4, 1 (1989), p. 66; Michael Erbe, *Deutsche Geschichte 1713–1790. Dualismus und aufgeklärter Absolutismus* (Stuttgart, 1985), p. 58.

120. Wolfgang Neugebauer, 'Brandenburg im absolutistischen Staat. Das 17. und 18. Jahrhundert', in Ingo Materna and Wolfgang Ribbe (eds.), *Brandenburgische Geschichte* (Berlin, 1995), p. 367.

121. By Horst Möller, in *Aufklärung in Preussen*, p. 251.

122. See, for example, the volume covering the second half of 1784 at http:// www.ub.uni-bielefeld.de/diglib/aufkl/berlmon/berlmon.htm. It included Kant's celebrated essay 'What is Enlightenment?'

123. Rüdiger Hachtmann, 'Friedrich II. von Preussen und die Freimaurerei', *Historische Zeitschrift*, 264, 1 (1997), pp. 21–2.

124. J. D. E. Preuss, *Friedrich der Grosse mit seinen Verwandten und Freun- den: Eine historische Skizze* (Berlin, 1868), p. 36.

125. Horst Möller, *Vernunft und Kritik. Deutsche Aufklärung im 17. und 18. Jahrhundert* (Frankfurt am Main, 1986), p. 217.

126. Hachtmann, 'Friedrich II. von Preussen und die Freimaurerei', p. 37. See also Karlheinz Gerlach, 'Die Berliner Freimaurerei 1783. Eine sozialgeschichtliche Untersuchung', in Helmut Reinalter and Karlheinz Gerlach (eds.), *Staat und Bürgertum im 18. und frühen 19. Jahrhundert* (Frankfurt am Main, 1996), p. 192.

127. Manfred Agethen, 'Diskussionsbericht', in Heinz Duchhardt (ed.), *Fried- rich der Grosse, Franken und das Reich* (Cologne and Vienna, 1986), p. 196.

128. Hachtmann, 'Friedrich II. von Preussen und die Freimaurerei', pp. 46–7; Gerlach, 'Die Berliner Freimaurerei 1783', p. 199.

129. Hachtmann, 'Friedrich II. von Preussen und die Freimaurerei', p. 44.

130. Ibid., p. 48.

131. 'Maurerrede zum Andenken Friedrichs. Berlin den 14. Sept. 1786', in *Berlinische Monatsschrift*, 1786 (2), p. 338.

132. I have discussed this in *The Culture of Power and the Power of Culture*, pt 3.

133. Koser and Droysen (eds.), *Briefwechsel*, vol. 1, pp. 71–2.

134. *Œuvres*, vol. 1, p. 255.

135. K. Biedermann, *Friedrich der Grosse und sein Verhältniss zur Entwicklung des deutschen Geisteslebens* (Brunswick, 1859), p. 5.

136. Koser and Droysen (eds.), *Briefwechsel*, vol. 3, pp. 347–8.

137. The French edition is in *Œuvres*, vol. 7. There is a good German edition in Steinmetz (ed.), *Friedrich II.*, which also includes much other relevant contemporary material. My references are to the latter edition.

138. Steinmetz (ed.), *Friedrich II.*, pp. 61–2, 73, 77. See also Winfried Woesler, 'Die Idee der deutschen Nationalliteratur in der zweiten Hälfte des 18. Jahrhunderts', in Klaus Garber (ed.), *Nation und Literatur im Europa der Frühen Neuzeit* (Tübingen, 1989), p. 722.

139. Steinmetz (ed.), *Friedrich II.*, pp. 81–2. It seems that Frederick read Shakespeare in German translation, which can only have confirmed his prejudice – Wehinger, 'Introduction', in Wehinger and Lottes (eds.), *Friedrich der Grosse als Leser*, p. 12.

140. Several examples can be found in Steinmetz (ed.), *Friedrich II.*

141. Daniel Fulda, '*De la littérature allemande*. Friedrich II. von Preussen, das deutsche Publikum und die Herausbildung des modernen Literaturbegriffs', *Germanisch-Romanische Monatsschrift*, 63, 2 (2013), p. 226.

142. Adolf von Harnack, *Geschichte der königlich preussischen Akademie der Wissenschaften zu Berlin* (Berlin, 1900), vol. 1, pt 1, pp. 266–7, 293–4.

143. Ibid., p. 362.

144. Thiébault, *Mes Souvenirs*, vol. 4, pp. 76–8.

145. Eugen Paunel, *Die Staatsbibliothek zu Berlin. Ihre Geschichte und Organisation während der ersten zwei Jahrhunderten seit ihrer Eröffnung* (Berlin, 1965), p. 74.

146. Harnack, *Geschichte der königlich preussischen Akademie der Wissenschaften zu Berlin*, vol. 1, pt 1, p. 464.

147. Langer, *Friedrich der Grosse*, p. 11.

148. Their relationship is recounted in exhaustive detail by Christiane Mervaud in *Voltaire et Frédéric II: une dramaturgie des lumières*

1736– 1778, Studies on Voltaire and the Eighteenth Century (Oxford, 1985), vol. 234.

149. Johann Friedrich Karl Grimm, *Bemerkungen eines Reisenden durch die königlichen preussischen Staaten in Briefen* (Altenburg, 1779), vol. 2, p. 2; Ruth Freydank, *Theater in Berlin von den Anfängen bis 1945* (Berlin, 1988), pp. 106–7.

150. Ibid., pp. 106–8.

151. Koser and Droysen (eds.), *Briefwechsel*, vol. 3, p. 209. See also his further letter to Voltaire of 19 September 1774, ibid., p. 304.

152. Langer, *Friedrich der Grosse*, pp. 94–5, 185. See also Vocke, 'Friedrich II. Verhältnis zur Literatur und zur deutschen Sprache', in Bethke (ed.), *Friedrich der Grosse*, p. 175.

153. Eckart Klessmann, *Die deutsche Romantik*, 2nd edn (Cologne, 1981), p. 27; Pierre-Paul Sagave, 'Preussen und Frankreich', *Jahrbücher für die Geschichte Mittel und Ostdeutschlands*, 31 (1982), p. 69.

154. Gerd Bartoschek, 'Friedrich II. als Sammler von Gemälden', in Hans-Joachim Giersberg and Claudia Meckel (eds.), *Friedrich II. und die Kunst* (Potsdam, 1986), vol. 2, pp. 86–8; Paul Seidel, 'Friedrich der Grosse als Sammler von Gemälden und Skulpturen', *Jahrbuch der Königlich-Preussischen Kunstsammlungen*, 13 (1892), p. 188; Adolf Rosenberg, 'Friedrich der Grosse als Kunstsammler', *Zeitschrift für bildende Kunst*, new series, 4 (1893), p. 210.

155. Roland Krebs, *L'Idée de 'Théâtre national' dans l'Allemagne des lumières. Théorie et réalisations (Wolfenbütteler Forschungen)*, vol. 28 (Wiesbaden, 1985), p. 529.

156. Quoted in Derek Beales, *Joseph II*, vol. 1: *In the Shadow of Maria Theresa 1741–1780* (Cambridge, 1987), p. 233.

157. Quoted in H. Kiesel and P. Münch, *Gesellschaft und Literatur im 18. Jahrhundert* (Munich, 1977), p. 84.

158. Ruth Freydank, 'Friedrich II. und das Theater', in Giersberg and Meckel (eds.), *Friedrich II. und die Kunst*, vol. 2, p. 149; Freydank, *Theater in Berlin*, pp. 112–13.

159. P.C., vol. 1, p. 58.

160. Margaret C. Jacob, *Radical Enlightenment* (London, 1981), *passim*.

161. Norbert Conrads, 'Politischer Mentalitätswandel von oben: Friedrichs II. Weg vom Gewinn Schlesiens zur Gewinnung der Schlesier', in Peter Baumgart (ed.), *Kontinuitäten und Wandel. Schlesien zwischen Österreich und Preussen* (Sigmaringen, 1990), pp. 229–30.

162. Etzin, 'Die Freiheit der öffentlichen Meinung', p. 111.

163. Andreas Gestrich, 'Kriegsberichterstattung als Propaganda. Das Beispiel des "Wienerischen Diarium" im Siebenjährigen Krieg 1756–1763', in Ute Daniel (ed.), *Augenzeugen. Kriegsberichtserstattung vom 18. zum 21. Jahrhundert* (Göttingen, 2006), p. 24.

164. Manfred Schlenke, *England und das friderizianische Preussen 1740–1763. Ein Beitrag zum Verhältnis von Politik und öffentlicher Meinung im England des 18. Jahrhunderts* (Munich, 1963), p. 235.

165. Ibid., pp. 237–46.

166. Eva Giloi, *Monarchy, Myth and Material Culture in Germany 1750–1950* (Cambridge, 2011), pp. 25–6; Christopher Clark, *Iron Kingdom. The Rise and Downfall of Prussia 1600–1947* (London, 2006), p. 224; Doris Schumacher, 'Der Siebenjährige Krieg in der bildenden Kunst. Von den Anfängen durch Johann Wilhelm Ludwig Gleim und Friedrich II. bis zu den populären Illustrationsfolgen des späten 18. Jahrhunderts', in Wolfgang Adam, Holger Dainat and Ute Pott (eds.), *'Krieg ist mein Lied'. Der Siebenjährige Krieg in den zeitgenössischen Medien* (Göttingen, 2007), p. 242.

167. Gerhild H. M. Komander, *Der Wandel des 'Sehepuncktes': die Geschichte Brandenburg-Preussens in der Graphik von 1648–1810* (Münster, 1995), pp. 166–9.

168. Thomas Weissbrich, 'Inszenierungen im Porträt', in Leonore Koschnick, Arnulf Scriba and Thomas Weissbrich (eds.), *Friedrich der Grosse. Verehrt. Verklärt. Verdammt* (Berlin, 2012), p. 19.

169. Weissbrich, 'Inszenierungen im Porträt', p. 25.

170. Rainer Michaelis, 'Friedrich der Grosse im Spiegel der Werke des Daniel Nikolaus Chodowiecki', in Friederisiko, Essays, p. 264.

171. Eckhart Hellmuth, 'Die "Wiedergeburt" Friedrichs des Grossen und der "Tod fürs Vaterland". Zum patriotischen Selbstverständnis in Preussen in der zweiten Hälfte des 18. Jahrhunderts', *Aufklärung*, 10, 2 (1998), p. 47.

172. Quoted in Thomas Biskup, 'Das Ceremoniel des grossen Königs: Völkerrecht, Reichsrecht und Friedrichs Rang in der Fürstengesellschaft' (unpublished paper delivered to the conference *Repräsentation und Selbstinszenierung Friedrichs des Grossen*, Potsdam Museum, 28–29 September 2012).

173. Frevert, *Gefühlspolitik. Friedrich II. als Herr über die Herzen?*, p. 70.

174. Ibid., p. 72.

175. N. William Wraxall, *Memoirs of the Courts of Berlin, Dresden, Warsaw and Vienna in the Years 1777, 1778 and 1779*, 3rd edn (London, 1806), vol. 1, p. 119. Wraxall was writing about 1777.

176. This point has been well made by Peter-Michael Hahn in *Friedrich II. von Preussen* (Stuttgart, 2013), p. 126.

177. Derek Beales, 'Religion and culture', in T. C. W. Blanning (ed.), *The Short Oxford History of Europe: The Eighteenth Century* (Oxford, 2000), pp. 131–3.

178. Clark, *Iron Kingdom*, p. 218.

179. Hahn, *Friedrich II.*, p. 194.

180. Antje Fuchs, 'Der Siebenjährige Krieg als virtueller Religionskrieg an Beispielen aus Preussen, Österreich, Kurhannover und Grossbritannien', in Franz Brendle and Anton Schindling (eds.), *Religionskriege im Alten Reich und in Alteuropa* (Münster, 2006), pp. 320–21.

181. Ulrich im Hof, 'Friedrich II. und die Schweiz', in Martin Fontius and Helmut Holzhey (eds.), *Schweizer im Berlin des 18. Jahrhunderts* (Berlin, 1996), p. 16.

182. Gay, *The Enlightenment*, vol. 1: *The Rise of Modern Paganism*, p. 100; Böhm, 'Bildungsideal, Bildungswesen, Wissenschaft und Akademien', p. 186.

183. Quoted in Wehinger, 'Introduction', in Wehinger and Lottes (eds.), *Friedrich der Grosse als Leser*, p. 9.

184. Ibid., p. 10.

185. Hannelore Röhm and Sabine Scheidler, 'Die Bibliotheken Friedrichs des Grossen', Friederisiko, Ausstellung, p. 322.

186. Rosenberg, 'Friedrich der Grosse als Kunstsammler', p. 209.

187. Quoted in *Allgemeine Musikalische Zeitung*, 24, 1 (2 January 1822), p. 1.

188. Abbé Denina, *La Prusse littéraire sous Frédéric II, ou histoire abrégée de la plupart des auteurs, des académiciens et des artistes qui sont nés ou qui ont vécu dans les états prussiens depuis MDCCXL jusqu'à MDCCLXXXVI. Par ordre alphabétique. Précédée d'une introduction, ou d'un tableau général des progrès qu'ont faits les arts et les sciences dans les pays qui constituent la Monarchie prussienne* (Berlin, 1790–91), vol. 1, p. 43.

189. *Goethes Werke* (Weimar, 1887–1912), vol. 27, p. 106. See also the similar passage in his *Maximen und Reflexionen*: 'The fact that Frederick the Great wanted to have absolutely nothing to do with them irked the German writers, and so they did their utmost to make themselves seem something in his eyes' – ibid., vol. 42, pt 2, pp. 201–2. This passage is also quoted in Theodor Schieder, 'Friedrich der Grosse – eine Integrationsfigur des deutschen Nationalbewusstseins im 18. Jahrhundert?', in Otto Dann (ed.), *Nationalismus in vorindustrieller*

Zeit (Munich, 1986), p. 127. A similar point was made by Prince August of Gotha in a letter to Herder of 25 December 1780 – Bernhard Suphan, *Friedrichs des Grossen Schrift über die deutsche Literatur* (Berlin, 1888), p. 38.

190. Fulda, '*De la littérature allemande*', p. 227.

191. Langer, *Friedrich der Grosse*, pp. 190–93.

192. Harnack, *Geschichte der königlich preussischen Akademie der Wissenschaften zu Berlin*, vol. 1, pt 1, pp. 397–421. On the importance of the prize competition for Herder, see Robert E. Norton, *Herder's Aesthetics and the European Enlightenment* (Ithaca and London, 1991), p. 105. I am indebted to Professor H. B. Nisbet for this reference.

193. D'Aprile, 'Die königliche Toleranzpolitik in der Wahrnehmung der brandenburgischen Untertanen', pp. 44–5.

194. Lifschitz, 'Adrastus versus Diogenes: Frederick the Great and Jean-Jacques Rousseau on self-love', in Biskup and Kohl (eds.), *Frederick the Great and the Republic of Letters*. This point was made by Thomas Biskup in the discussion which followed Lifschitz's paper.

195. Thomas Bauman, 'Courts and municipalities in North Germany', in Neal Zaslaw (ed.), *The Classical Era. From the 1740s to the End of the Eighteenth Century* (London, 1989), p. 262.

196. Leonard Meister, *Friedrichs des Grossen wolthätige Rucksicht auch auf Verbesserung teutscher Sprache und Litteratur* (Zürich, 1787), p. 21.

197. Ibid., p. 152.

198. Thomas Abbt, 'Einige allgemeine Anmerkungen über das Genie der Deutschen und den Zustand der deutschen Literatur', *Briefe, die Neueste Litteratur betreffend*, 15 (1762), pp. 55–7.

199. Christian Garve, *Fragmente zur Schilderung des Geistes, des Charakters, und der Regierung Friedrichs des Zweyten* (Breslau, 1798), vol. 1, pp. 31, 33, 36, 57, 60, 122.

200. *Goethes Werke*, vol. 27, p. 104.

201. Ibid., p. 105.

202. Christian Wilhelm von Dohm, *Denkwürdigkeiten meiner Zeit, oder Beiträge zur Geschichte vom letzten Viertel des achtzehnten und vom Anfang des neunzehnten Jahrhunderts 1778 bis 1806* (Lemgo and Hanover, 1814–19), vol. 4, p. 615.

203. Rudolf Payer von Thurn (ed.), *Joseph II. als Theaterdirektor. Ungedruckte Briefe und Aktenstücke aus den Kinderjahren des Burgtheaters* (Vienna and Leipzig, 1920), p. 4.

204. Biedermann, *Friedrich der Grosse*, p. 38.

205. Möller, *Vernunft und Kritik*, p. 203. For a similar comment, see Günther Lottes, 'Fürst und Text. Die Leserevolution der Aufklärung als Herausforderung der friderizianischen Selbststilisierung', in Wehinger and Lottes (eds.), *Friedrich der Grosse als Leser*, p. 35.

206. 'Über die neue preussische Justizverfassung', *Berlinische Monatsschrift*, 1784 (1), pp. 521–2, http://www.ub.uni-bielefeld.de/diglib/aufkl/berlmon/berlmon.htm. See also, Möller, *Vernunft und Kritik*, pp. 203–5.

207. Meister, *Friedrichs des Grossen wolthätige Rucksicht auch auf Verbesserung teutscher Sprache und Litteratur*, pp. 154–5.

208. Horst Möller, 'Wie aufgeklärt war Preussen?', in Hans-Jürgen Puhle and Hans-Ulrich Wehler (eds.), *Preussen im Rückblick* (Göttingen, 1980), p. 198.

209. Schieder, 'Friedrich der Grosse – eine Integrationsfigur des deutschen Nationalbewusstseins im 18. Jahrhundert?', in Dann (ed.), *Nationalismus in vorindustrieller Zeit*, p. 115.

210. P.C., vol. 2, p. 280.

211. Letters of 19 April 1753 and 13 August 1766, in Koser and Droysen (eds.), *Briefwechsel*, vol. 3, pp. 3, 127.

212. *Œuvres*, vol. 1, pp. 214–15.

213. Harnack, *Geschichte der königlich preussischen Akademie der Wissenschaften zu Berlin*, vol. 1, pt 1, p. 388.

214. *Œuvres*, vol. 2, p. 41.

215. Thomas Biskup and Peter H. Wilson, 'Grossbritannien, Amerika und die atlantische Welt', in Friederisiko, Ausstellung, p. 147.

216. Koser and Droysen (eds.), *Briefwechsel*, vol. 3, p. 105.

217. Ibid., pp. 130, 135, 148.

218. Ibid., p. 105.

219. Thiébault, *Mes Souvenirs*, vol. 1, p. 9; Langer, *Friedrich der Grosse*, p. 191.

220. *Œuvres*, vol. 14, pp. 290–91.

221. David Watkin and Tilman Mellinghoff, *German Architecture and the Classical Ideal 1740–1840* (London, 1987), pp. 17–18; Biskup and Wilson, 'Grossbritannien, Amerika und die atlantische Welt', p.147. As they rightly observed, to be Francophone did not necessarily require one to be Francophile.

222. Langer, *Friedrich der Grosse*, p. 44.

223. Wilhelm Dilthey, 'Friedrich der Grosse und die deutsche Aufklärung', in idem, *Gesammelte Schriften* (Leipzig and Berlin, 1927), vol. 3, p. 130.

224. *Œuvres*, vol. 1, p. 265.

225. Steinmetz (ed.), *Friedrich II.*, pp. 65–7, 97–9. See also Fulda, '*De la lit-térature allemande*', p. 228. This was a popular image among German sovereigns: Joseph II wrote to his mother from the Silesian frontier in 1766: 'Like Moses, we saw the promised land without being able to enter it' – quoted in Josef Karniel, *Die Toleranzpolitik Kaiser Josephs II.*, Schriftenreihe des Instituts für Deutsche Geschichte Universität Tel-Aviv (Gerlingen, 1986), vol. 9, p. 129.

226. *Œuvres*, vol. 12, pp. 9–16.

227. Ibid., p. 12.

228. Ibid., p. 14. 'Varus' is the Comte de Clermont defeated by Prince Ferdi-nand ('Herman' – or 'Arminius', as Frederick uses the Latin form in his poem) at Krefeld on 23 June 1758.

229. *Œuvres*, vol. 9, p. 141.

230. Gesa von Essen, *Hermannsschlachten. Germanen- und Römerbilder in der Literatur des 18. und 19. Jahrhunderts* (Göttingen, 1998), pp. 57–144; Hans Peter Herrmann, 'Arminius und die Erfindung der Männlichkeit im 18. Jahrhundert', in Hans Peter Herrmann, Hans-Martin Blitz and Susanna Mossmann (eds.), *Machtphantasie Deutschland. Nationalismus, Männlichkeit und Fremdenhass im Vater-landsdiskurs deutscher Schriftsteller des 18. Jahrhunderts* (Frankfurt am Main, 1996), pp. 161–91.

231. *Œuvres*, vol. 12, p. 14. Plutus (properly Ploutos) was the Greek god of wealth; Sardanapalus was the notoriously decadent and self-indulgent last King of Assyria.

232. Bernhard R. Kroener, 'Militärischer Professionalismus und soziale Kar-riere. Der französische Adel in den europäischen Kriegen 1740–1763', in idem (ed.), *Europa im Zeitalter Friedrichs des Grossen. Wirtschaft, Gesellschaft, Kriege* (Munich, 1989), p. 99.

233. *Œuvres*, vol. 12, pp. 84–5. The poem is dated 'Breslau, 20 December 1757'. The belief that Louis XV and his ministers had decided to help the Austrians to destroy him clearly rankled. In both his *History of the Seven Years War* and *Memoirs from the Peace of Hubertusburg to the Completion of the Partition of Poland,* he stated that it had been decided at Versailles to 'crush' him. *Œuvres*, vol. 12, pp. 84–5.

234. Theodor Schieder, *Friedrich der Grosse. Ein Königtum der Wider-sprüche* (Frankfurt am Main, Berlin and Vienna, 1983), p. 455.

235. Ibid., p. 248; Ingrid Mittenzwei, *Friedrich II. von Preussen* (Cologne, 1980), pp. 113–14.

236. Peter Schleuning, *Das 18. Jahrhundert. Der Bürger erhebt sich* (Ham-burg, 1984), p. 553.

237. Clark, *Iron Kingdom*, p. 219.

238. Ibid., p. 221.

239. Ibid., p. 220; Thomas Nicklas, 'Die Schlacht von Rossbach (1757) zwischen Wahrnehmung und Deutung', *Forschungen zur Brandenburgischen und Preussischen Geschichte*, new series, 12 (2002), pp. 35–51. See also the poems reprinted in Franz Muncker (ed.), *Anakreontiker und preussisch-patriotische Lyriker* (Stuttgart, 1895), pp. 243–87, which have a strong religious flavour.

240. Ruth Smith, *Handel's Oratorios and Eighteenth-century Thought* (Cambridge, 1995), p. 220.

241. Ernst Rohmer, '"Der Vater seines Landes [...] ist nicht geringer als der Held". Johann Peter Uz und die Haltung zum Krieg im Markgraftum Brandenburg-Ansbach', in Adam, Dainat and Pott (eds.), *'Krieg ist mein Lied'*, p. 177. There is a good selection of poems by Gleim and others in Gustav Berthold Volz (ed.), *Friedrich der Grosse im Spiegel seiner Zeit* (Berlin, 1901), vol. 2.

242. J. W. L. Gleim, *Preussische Kriegslieder von einem Grenadier*, ed. August Sauer (Heilbronn, 1882), p. 3.

243. Muncker, *Anakreontiker*, p. 183.

244. Gleim, *Preussische Kriegslieder von einem Grenadier*, Sauer's Introduction, p. vii.

245. Ibid., p. 7.

246. Ibid., p. 12.

247. Hans Peter Herrmann, 'Krieg, Medien und Nation. Zum Nationalismus in Kriegsliedern des 16. und 18. Jahrhunderts', in Adam, Dainat and Pott (eds.), *'Krieg ist mein Lied'*, p. 29.

248. Michael Rohrwasser, 'Lessing, Gleim und der nationale Diskurs', in *Lenz-Jahrbuch, Sturm und Drang Studien*, 7 (1997), pp. 137–8; Nisbet, *Lessing*, pp. 232–6.

249. Guido Heinrich, 'Leibhaftige Ästhetisierung und mediale Endverwertung. Die Rezeption der Kriegslyrik Anna Louisa Karschs in Berlin, Halberstadt und Magdeburg', in Adam, Dainat and Pott (eds.), *'Krieg ist mein Lied'*, pp. 137–40.

250. Volker Press, 'Friedrich der Grosse als Reichspolitiker', in Duchhardt (ed.), *Friedrich der Grosse, Franken und das Reich*, p. 42.

251. Herrmann, 'Krieg, Medien und Nation', p. 33; Gonthier-Louis Fink, 'Der deutsche National- und Regionalcharakter in der Sicht der Aufklärung', in Ruth Florack (ed.), *Nation als Stereotyp: Fremdwahrnehmung und Identität in deutscher und französischer Literatur* (Tübingen, 2000), p. 75.

252. Klaus Bohnen, 'Von den Anfängen des "Nationalsinns". Zur literarischen Patriotismus-Debatte im Umfeld des Siebenjährigen Krieges', in Helmut Scheuer (ed.), *Dichter und ihre Nation* (Frankfurt am Main, 1993), p. 123.

253. Christian Friedrich Daniel Schubart, *Leben und Gesinnungen von ihm selbst im Kerker aufgesetzt* (Stuttgart, 1791–3), vol. 1, pp. 33–4. Available online at http://www.zeno.org/Literatur/M/Schubart,+Christian+Friedrich+Daniel/Autobiographisches/Leben+und+Gesinnungen.

254. Christian Friedrich Daniel Schubart (ed.), *Deutsche Chronik auf das Jahr 1774* (reprinted, Heidelberg, 1975), vol. 1, pp. 5–6.

255. Quoted in Schieder, 'Friedrich der Grosse – eine Integrationsfigur des deutschen Nationalbewusstseins im 18 Jahrhundert?', p. 122. The whole poem can be found online at http://www.zeno.org/nid/20005636779.

256. Hans-G. Winter, 'Antiklassizismus: Sturm und Drang', in Viktor Žmegač (ed.), *Geschichte der deutschen Literatur vom 18. Jahrhundert bis zur Gegenwart*, 2nd edn (Königstein im Taunus, 1984), vol 1, pt 1, p. 213.

257. Schubart (ed.), *Deutsche Chronik auf das Jahr 1774*, p. 77.

258. Ibid., p. 133.

259. Ibid., p. 394.

260. Jacques-Antoine-Hippolyte, Comte de Guibert, *Journal d'un voyage militaire fait en Prusse dans l'année 1787* (Paris, 1790), p. 128.

261. R. Köpke, *Ludwig Tieck. Erinnerungen aus dem Leben des Dichters nach dessen mündlichen und schriftlichen Mittheilungen* (Leipzig, 1855), vol. 1, p. 27.

262. Thomas Biskup, *Friedrichs Grösse. Inszenierungen des Preussenkönigs in Fest und Zeremoniell 1740–1815* (Frankfurt am Main and New York, 2012), p. 136.

263. Brigitte Schmitz, 'Christian Daniel Rauchs Denkmal im Berliner Lindenforum', in Giersberg and Meckel (eds.), *Friedrich II. und die Kunst*, vol. 1, p. 57. A full list of the names of all those depicted or listed on the monument can be found in Kurd Wolfgang von Schöning, *Der Siebenjährige Krieg unter allerhöchster königlicher Bewilligung nach der Original-Correspondenz Friedrich des Grossen mit dem Prinzen Heinrich und Seinen Generalen aus den Staats-Archiven bearbeitet* (Potsdam, 1851), vol. 1, pp. x–xiv.

264. There is a good collection of illustrations at http://commons.wikimedia.org/wiki/File:Reiterstandbild_-_Friedrich_der_Gro%C3%9Fe_-_Westansicht. There is also an excellent collection of detailed photographs at http://www.baedicker.de/FriedrichII/index.php?directory=Der%20alte%20Fritz/&page=1.

13. LIGHT AND DARK ON THE HOME FRONT

1. Voltaire, *La Henriade*, ed. O. R. Taylor, *Studies on Voltaire and the Eighteenth Century* (Oxford, 1965), vol. 39, p. 352.

2. Novalis, 'Christendom or Europe', in H. S. Reiss (ed.), *The Political Thought of the German Romantics* (Oxford, 1955), p. 134.

3. Novalis, 'Glauben und Liebe oder Der König und die Königin', in Gerhard Schulz (ed.), *Novalis Werke*, 2nd edn (Munich, 1969), p. 364.

4. Hanns Martin Bachmann, *Die naturrechtliche Staatslehre Christian Wolffs* (Berlin, 1977), p. 40.

5. Ibid., p. 43.

6. Ibid., p. 42.

7. *Œuvres*, vol. 16, p. 288.

8. Ibid., pp. 294–5.

9. Gustav Berthold Volz (ed.), *Friedrich der Grosse und Wilhelmine von Bayreuth* (Leipzig, 1924), vol. 1: *Jugendbriefe 1728–1740*, pp. 314, 318–19, 326, 331–5; Reinhold Koser and Hans Droysen (eds.), *Briefwechsel Friedrichs des Grossen mit Voltaire*, Publikationen aus den K. Preussischen Staatsarchiven (Leipzig, 1908–9, 1911), vol. 81, pp. 1, 13–15, 25.

10. *Œuvres*, vol. 16, p. 195.

11. Ibid., vol. 27, pt 3, p. 207. As usual when addressing a social inferior, Frederick uses the third person.

12. Anton Friedrich Büsching, *Beschreibung seiner Reise von Berlin nach Kyritz in der Prignitz welche er vom 26ten September bis zum 2ten Oktober 1779 verrichtet hat* (Leipzig, 1780), p. 57.

13. Carlyle, vol. 3, p. 203.

14. Nicholas Boyle, *Goethe. The Poet and the Age*, vol. 1: *The Poetry of Desire* (Oxford, 1991), p. 18.

15. J. D. E. Preuss, *Friedrich der Grosse – Eine Lebensgeschichte* (Berlin, 1832), vol. 1, p. 138.

16. Georg Borchardt (ed.), *Die Randbemerkungen Friedrichs des Grossen* (Potsdam, n.d.), vol. 1, p. 79.

17. Ibid., pp. 79–80.

18. Dieudonné Thiébault, *Mes Souvenirs de vingt ans de séjour à Berlin; ou Frédéric le Grand, sa famille, sa cour, son gouvernement, son académie, ses écoles, et ses amis littérateurs et philosophes*, 4th edn (Paris, 1813), vol. 1, p. 59; James Steakley, 'Sodomy in Enlightenment Prussia: from execution to suicide', *Journal of Homosexuality*, 16, 1–2 (1989), p. 166.

19. *Œuvres*, vol. 24, p. 701.

20. Wolfgang Neugebauer, 'Friedrich als Risiko? Friedrich der Grosse in der Sicht von Untertanen und Geschichtsschreibern', in *Friedrich und die historische Grösse. Beiträge des dritten Colloquiums in der Reihe 'Friedrich300' vom 25./26. September 2009*, ed. Michael Kaiser and Jürgen Luh (Friedrich300 – Colloquien, 3), http://www.perspectivia.net/content/publikationen/friedrich300-colloquien/friedrich-groesse/neugebauer_risiko. Last accessed 3 December 2013; Carlyle, vol. 3, p. 17.

21. 'Auszüge gesandschaftlicher Berichte aus Berlin 1740', *Neue Berlinische Monatsschrift* (July 1804), p. 16. The report is dated 16 October 1740.

22. Neugebauer, 'Friedrich als Risiko?', p. 8.

23. Borchardt (ed.), *Die Randbemerkungen Friedrichs des Grossen*, vol. 1, p. 79. On this episode, see Peter Weber, 'Der Berliner Gesangbuchstreit 1781 – Aporiel der Aufklärung "von oben"', in idem, *Literarische und politische Öffentlichkeit: Studien zur Berliner Aufklärung*, ed. Iwan Michelangelo D'Aprile and Winfried Siebers (Berlin, 2006).

24. Dietrich, p. 600.

25. Abbé Denina, *Essai sur le règne de Fréderic II, Roi de Prusse* (Berlin, 1788), p. 404.

26. Borchardt (ed.), *Die Randbemerkungen Friedrichs des Grossen*, vol. 1, p. 84.

27. *Acta Borussica. Denkmäler der preussischen Staatsverwaltung im 18. Jahrhundert, Behördenorganisation und allegemeine Staatsverwaltung* (Berlin, 1907), vol. 9: *Akten von Anfang August 1750 bis Ende 1753*, ed. G. Schmoller and O. Hintze, p. 134.

28. Borchardt (ed.), *Die Randbemerkungen Friedrichs des Grossen*, vol. 1, p. 84.

29. Ibid., p. 87.

30. Ibid.

31. 'Portrait du roi de Prusse', *Œuvres*, vol. 6: *Mélanges de littérature, en vers et en prose* (Paris, 1796). It can be found in German translation in Otto Bardong (ed.), *Friedrich der Grosse, Ausgewählte Quellen zur deutschen Geschichte der Neuzeit*. Freiherr vom Stein-Gedächtnisausgabe (Darmstadt, 1982), vol. 22, pp. 555–62.

32. Nivernais, 'Portrait du roi de Prusse', p. 316.

33. Ibid., p. 322. Even Ursula Goldenbaum, who is at pains to deny Frederick any enlightened characteristics, concedes that he made Prussia stand out as a beacon, made to seem all the brighter by the theological oppression of the surrounding territories – Ursula Goldenbaum, 'Friedrich II. und die Berliner Aufklärung', in Günther Lottes and Iwan

D'Aprile (eds.), *Hofkultur und aufgeklärte Öffentlichkeit: Potsdam im 18. Jahrhundert im europäischen Kontext* (Berlin, 2006), pp. 127–8.

34. Dietrich, p. 316; Voltaire, *La Henriade*, p. 380.

35. Christine Goetz and Victor H. Elbern (eds.), *Die St Hedwigs-Kathedrale zu Berlin* (Regensburg, 2000), p. 21.

36. R. R. Palmer, *The Age of the Democratic Revolution. A Political History of Europe and America, 1760–1800* (Princeton, 1959, 1964), vol. 1, p. 299.

37. Anton Schindling, 'Friedrichs des Grossen Toleranz und seine katholischen Untertanen', in Peter Baumgart (ed.), *Kontinuitäten und Wandel. Schlesien zwischen Österreich und Preussen* (Sigmaringen, 1990), p. 270.

38. Hans-Joachim Giersberg, *Friedrich als Bauherr. Studien zur Architektur des 18. Jahrhunderts in Berlin und Potsdam* (Berlin, 1986), p. 235. According to the Abbé Carlo Denina, he had wanted to build a temple dedicated to Jupiter, Apollo and other pagan gods but had been dissuaded by his friend Jordan – Denina, *Essai sur le règne de Frédéric II, Roi de Prusse*, p. 450.

39. Martin Engel, 'Architektur und Bauherrschaft', in Sösemann, vol. 1, pp. 281–2.

40. Ludwig Geiger, *Berlin 1688–1840. Geschichte des geistigen Lebens der preussischen Hauptstadt*, vol. 1: *1688–1786* (Berlin, 1893), p. 374.

41. Goetz and Elbern (eds.), *Die St Hedwigs-Kathedrale zu Berlin*, p. 15; Iwan-Michelangelo D'Aprile, 'Aufklärung, Toleranz und Wissenschaft in Preussen', in Friederisiko, Ausstellung, p. 81.

42. Geiger, *Berlin 1688–1840*, vol. 1, p. 375.

43. *Geschichte und Beschreibung der neu erbauten catholischen Kirche zu St Hedwig in Berlin nebst einer ausführlichen Erzählung und Erklärung aller Ceremonien welche bey der feyerlichen Einweihung derselben am ersten November 1773 beobachtet worden sind* (Berlin, 1774), p. 3.

44. Ibid., p. 37. On the transfer of the relics from Silesia to Berlin, see the correspondence reprinted in Max Lehmann, *Preussen und die katholische Kirche* (Leipzig, 1878), vol. 4, p. 554.

45. *Geschichte und Beschreibung der neu erbauten catholischen Kirche zu St Hedwig in Berlin*, p. 74.

46. This has been reproduced many times. For a high-quality example see Goetz and Elbern (eds.), *Die St Hedwigs-Kathedrale zu Berlin*, p. 23.

47. Lehmann, *Preussen und die katholische Kirche*, vol. 4, p. 555. Lehmann explains the two '----'s as being indecipherable, but one of them is

probably Vienna, where Joseph II did build a Protestant church ten years later. This document is reprinted in an imperfect German translation in Bardong (ed.), *Friedrich der Grosse*, p. 475.

48. Helga Schultz, *Berlin 1650–1800. Sozialgeschichte einer Residenz* (Berlin, 1987), p. 189.

49. J. D. E. Preuss, *Friedrichs des Grossen Jugend und Thronbesteigung* (Berlin, 1840), p. 337; Preuss, *Friedrich der Grosse*, vol. 1, p. 336.

50. 'Ueber Berlin von einem Fremden', in F. Gedike and J. E. Biester (eds.), *Berlinische Monatsschrift* (Berlin, 1784) (1), pp. 269–70.

51. Johann Friedrich Karl Grimm, *Bemerkungen eines Reisenden durch die königlichen preussischen Staaten in Briefen* (Altenburg, 1779), vol. 1, pp. 548–9, vol. 2, p. 86.

52. Lehndorff, vol. 1, p. 192. Elsewhere in his diaries, Lehndorff makes it clear that he was a firm believer, frequently attending church services, listening to sermons and taking Communion. On August Wilhelm's agnosticism, see Eva Ziebura, *August Wilhelm Prinz von Preussen* (Berlin, 2006), p. 25.

53. *Œuvres*, vol. 1, p. 102. The figure of 400,000 is that given by Frederick but is certainly an exaggeration. The generally accepted figure is 250,000.

54. Ibid., vol. 19, p. 284. When he met Joseph II at Neisse in August 1769 he praised them '*infiniment*' according to the latter, but was probably being mischievous – P.C., vol. 29, p. 43.

55. To Voltaire, 10 December 1773 – *Œuvres*, vol. 23, p. 303.

56. Ibid., vol. 24, p. 700.

57. Ibid., vol. 9, p. 237.

58. Günter Birtsch, 'Religions- und Gewissensfreiheit in Preussen von 1780 bis 1817', *Zeitschrift für historische Forschung*, 11, 2 (1984), p. 184.

59. Carlyle, vol. 3, p. 274.

60. Koser, vol. 1, p. 14.

61. Dietrich, p. 454. I have been unable to verify the remark attributed to him which he made on hearing that an acquaintance had converted to Catholicism: 'I approve: if one has to have a religion, one should have a really stupid one.'

62. J. E. Biester, 'Bemerkungen auf einer Reise in Schlesien; in Briefen', in Gedike and Biester (eds.), *Berlinische Monatsschrift* (1), p. 248.

63. Tobias Schenk, *Wegbereiter der Emanzipation? Studien zur Judenpolitik des 'Aufgeklärten Absolutismus' in Preussen (1763–1812)* (Berlin, 2010), pp. 78–80.

64. Dietrich, pp. 314, 506.

65. Selma Stern, *Der preussische Staat und die Juden: Die Zeit Friedrichs des Grossen* (Tübingen, 1971), vol. 1: *Darstellung*, p. 7.
66. Peter Gay, 'Voltaire's anti-Semitism', in idem, *The Party of Humanity. Studies in the French Enlightenment* (London, 1964), pp. 97–108.
67. *Œuvres*, vol. 15, p. 165.
68. Ibid., p. xv.
69. Joachim Whaley, *Germany and the Holy Roman Empire* (Oxford, 2012), vol. 2: *The Peace of Westphalia to the Dissolution of the Reich 1648–1806*, p. 263.
70. Schultz, *Berlin 1650–1800*, p. 57.
71. *Jewish Encyclopedia*, http://www.jewishencyclopedia.com/articles/308 3-berlin.
72. Schenk, *Wegbereiter der Emanzipation?*, pp. 83–7.
73. Alexander Altmann, *Moses Mendelssohn: a Biographical Study* (London, 1973), p. 17.
74. Christopher M. Clark, *The Politics of Conversion. Missionary Protestantism and the Jews in Prussia 1728–1941* (Oxford, 1995), p. 44.
75. Britta L. Behm, *Moses Mendelssohn und die Transformation der jüdischen Erziehung in Berlin* (New York, Munich and Berlin, 2002), p. 54; Horst Möller, *Aufklärung in Preussen. Der Verleger, Publizist und Geschichtsschreiber Friedrich Nicolai* (Berlin, 1974), p. 265.
76. Gerd Heinrich, *Geschichte Preussens. Staat und Dynastie* (Frankfurt am Main, Berlin and Vienna, 1981), p. 247.
77. Christopher Duffy, *The Army of Frederick the Great* (Newton Abbot, 1974), p. 131. According to Peter Baumgart, 'Absoluter Staat und Judenemanzipation in Brandenburg-Preussen', *Jahrbuch für die Geschichte Mittel- und Ostdeutschlands*, 13/14 (1965), pp. 83–4, the Jewish consortium extracted 50 million talers in gold from Poland, Hungary and Russia.
78. Lehndorff, vol. 2, pp. 295, 354.
79. Koser, vol. 2, p. 311.
80. Anton Balthasar König, *Annalen der Juden in den preussischen Staaten besonders in der Mark Brandenburg* (Berlin, 1790), pp. 290–96.
81. Baumgart, 'Absoluter Staat und Judenemanzipation', p. 84.
82. Altmann, *Moses Mendelssohn*, p. 346; for a list of Mendelssohn's correspondents, see Michael Albrecht, *Moses Mendelssohn 1729–1786. Das Lebenswerk eines jüdischen Denkers der deutschen Aufklärung* (Weinheim, 1986), pp. 124–5.
83. Quoted in Ludwig Geiger, *Die deutsche Literatur und die Juden* (Berlin, 1910), pp. 58–9.

84. David Sorkin, *Moses Mendelssohn and the Religious Enlightenment* (London, 1996), p. 96.

85. Koser, vol. 2, p. 397; H. B. Nisbet, *Gotthold Ephraim Lessing. His Life, Works, and Thought* (Oxford, 2008), p. 64.

86. Brigitte Meier, 'Die königliche Toleranzpolitik in der Wahrnehmung der brandenburgischen Untertanen', in Frank Göse (ed.), *Friedrich der Grosse und die Mark Brandenburg. Herrschaftspraxis in der Provinz* (Berlin, 2012), pp. 52–3.

87. Quoted in Günther Holzboog, 'Mendelssohn – Autor und Verleger im 18. Jahrhundert', in Eva J. Engel and Norbert Hinske (eds.), *Moses Mendelssohn und die Kreise seiner Wirksamkeit* (Tübingen, 1994), p. 242.

88. Bruno Strauss, *Moses Mendelssohn in Potsdam am 30. September 1771* (Berlin, 1994), pp. 19–35.

89. Altmann, *Moses Mendelssohn*, pp. 264–5, 801–2. Also excluded from the Academy was the distinguished Jewish Berlin doctor and zoologist Marcus Elieser Bloch, member of several European academies and the author of *The Natural History of Fish*. Frederick's contemptuous marginal comment on a request for help with the publication of what proved to be a highly successful book was 'We know what fish are and there is no need to write a book about them because no one will buy it' – D'Aprile, 'Aufklärung, Toleranz und Wissenschaft in Preussen', p. 103.

90. 'Tolerante Gesinnung der Regierung', Gedike and Biester (eds.), *Berlinische Monatsschrift*, pp. 159–60.

91. Meier, 'Die königliche Toleranzpolitik in der Wahrnehmung der brandenburgischen Untertanen', pp. 54–5.

92. Goldenbaum, 'Friedrich II. und die Berliner Aufklärung', p. 134.

93. Iwan-Michelangelo D'Aprile, *Friedrich und die Aufklärer* (Berlin, 2012), p. 49; Schenk, *Wegbereiter der Emanzipation?*, pp. 490–96.

94. Tobias Schenk, 'Friedrich und die Juden', in Friederisiko, Essays, p. 171.

95. Behm, *Moses Mendelssohn und die Transformation der jüdischen Erziehung in Berlin*, passim.

96. Steven M. Lowenstein, 'The social dynamics of Jewish responses to Moses Mendelssohn', in Engel and Hinske (eds.), *Moses Mendelssohn und die Kreise seiner Wirksamkeit*, p. 336.

97. Stern, *Der preussische Staat und die Juden*, vol. 2: *Akten*, p. 208. Unfortunately, Stern did not print the full text of this decree.

98. Gotthold Ephraim Lessing, 'Die Juden', *Lessing. Dramen*, ed. Kurt Wölfel (Frankfurt am Main, 1984), p. 122.

99. Ibid., p. 148.

100. Ibid., p. 114. The traveller cannot have been meant to depict Moses Mendelssohn, as is sometimes maintained, as he was only nineteen when the play was written. Spinoza is a more likely candidate – Willi Goetschel, 'Lessing and the Jews', in Barbara Fischer and Thomas C. Fox (eds.), *A Companion to the Works of Gotthold Ephraim Lessing* (Woodbridge, 2005), p. 193. As Ritchie Robertson has pointed out, *The Jews* was not philo-Semitic but anti-anti-Semitic – *The 'Jewish Question' in German Literature 1749–1939. Emancipation and its Discontents* (Oxford, 1999), p. 34.

101. Nisbet, *Lessing*, p. 69.

102. Ibid., p. 65.

103. Goldenbaum, 'Friedrich II. und die Berliner Aufklärung', p. 138.

104. Lessing, 'Die Juden', p. 759. Mendelssohn's letter and Lessing's commentary are published in their entirety in this excellent edition.

105. Stern, *Der preussische Staat und die Juden*, vol. 1: *Darstellung*, p. 7.

106. *Über die bürgerliche Verbesserung der Juden* (Berlin and Stettin, 1781). It was published by Friedrich Nicolai. It has been reprinted many times. The original edition can be read online at http://books.google.co. uk/books?id=lY4vAAAAYAAJ&printsec=frontcover&source=gbs_ge_ summary_r&cad=0#v=onepage&q&f=false.

107. David Sorkin, *The Transformation of German Jewry 1780–1840* (Oxford, 1987), p. 23. On the public debate unleashed by Dohm's treatise, see Gerda Heinrich, '"... man sollte itzt betsändig das Publikum über diese Materie en haleine halten". Die Debatte um "bürgerliche Verbesserung" der Juden 1781–1786', in Ursula Goldenbaum (ed.), *Appell an das Publikum: die öffentliche Debatte in der deutschen Aufklärung 1687–1796* (Berlin, 2004), vol. 2, pp. 813–95. Mirabeau propagated Dohm's views in France through 'Sur Moses Mendelssohn et sur la réforme des juifs', published in 1787 – D'Aprile, 'Aufklärung, Toleranz und Wissenschaft in Preussen', pp. 96–7.

108. Dohm, *Über die bürgerliche Verbesserung der Juden*. Translation from Robert Liberles, 'Dohm's treatise on the Jews: a defence of the Enlightenment', *Leo Baeck Institute Yearbook* (1988), vol. 33, pt 1, p. 34.

109. T. C. W. Blanning, *Joseph II* (London, 1994), p. 72.

110. See the graphic description quoted in Tim Blanning, *The Pursuit of Glory: Europe 1648–1815* (London, 2007), pp. 202–5.

111. *Acta Borussica*, vol. 6, pt 2, p. 8.

112. Theodor Schieder, *Friedrich der Grosse. Ein Königtum der Widersprüche* (Frankfurt am Main, Berlin and Vienna, 1983), p. 291.

113. Werner Ogris, 'Friedrich der Grosse und das Recht', in Oswald Hauser (ed.), *Friedrich der Grosse in seiner Zeit* (Cologne and Vienna, 1987), p. 67.

114. Monika Wienfort, 'Gesetzbücher, Justizreformen und der Müller-Arnold-Fall', in Sösemann, vol. 2, pp. 40, 45.

115. *Acta Borussica*, vol. 6, pt 2, p. 77.

116. Eberhard Schmidt, *Die Kriminalpolitik Preussens unter Friedrich Wilhelm I. und Friedrich II*. Abhandlungen des kriminalistischen Instituts an der Universität Berlin, 3rd series (Berlin, 1914), vol. 1, pt 2, pp. 7, 12–14, 19–20.

117. Quoted in Richard J. Evans, *Rituals of Retribution. Capital Punishment in Germany 1600–1987* (Oxford, 1996), p. 122.

118. Oscar Helmuth Werner, *The Unmarried Mother in German Literature with Special Reference to the Period 1770 to 1800* (New York, 1917), pp. 36–7.

119. Dietrich, p. 506.

120. Schmidt, *Die Kriminalpolitik Preussens*, pp. 64–5.

121. Ibid. See also Frederick's letter to Prince Henry of 7 December 1781 in which he claimed that there were only about twelve executions a year and none at all in Silesia – *Œuvres*, vol. 26, p. 550.

122. V. A. C. Gatrell, *The Hanging Tree. Execution and the English People 1770–1868* (Oxford, 1994), p. 9.

123. Ibid., p. 7; Preuss, *Friedrich der Grosse*, vol. 1, p. 320.

124. Evans, *Rituals of Retribution*, p. 126.

125. Ibid., p. 122.

126. *Acta Borussica*, vol. 6, pt 2, pp. 611–12.

127. Janine Rischke, '"auss Höchster Landes-Herrlicher Macht und Gewalt". Zum Einfluss von Naturrecht und politischem Wertehorizont auf die Rechtspflege Friedrichs II. in Kriminalsachen in den ersten Jahren seiner Regierung', in Göse (ed.), *Friedrich der Grosse und die Mark Brandenburg*, p. 255.

128. Preuss, *Friedrich der Grosse*, vol. 1, p. 321.

129. *Acta Borussica*, vol. 7, p. 441.

130. Albrecht Heinrich Arnim, *Bruchstücke über Verbrechen und Strafen, oder Gedanken über die in den Preussischen Staaten bemerkte Vermehrung der Verbrecher gegen die Sicherheit des Eigenthums: Nebst Vorschlägen, wie derselben durch zweckmässige Einrichtungen der Gefangenanstalten zu steuern seyn dürfte*, vol. 1 (Berlin, 1803), pp. 11–13.

131. For the authorization of torture, see *Acta Borussica*, vol. 9, pp. 309–10.

132. Preuss, *Friedrich der Grosse*, vol. 1, p. 222. The documents in P.C., vol. 5, pp. 203, 205–6 and *Acta Borussica*, vol. 7, pp. 157, 166, indicate that Ferber had composed two scurrilous accounts of Frederick to be used at the Russian court by Bestushev to sow discord between Frederick and the Tsarina Elizabeth. Alas, they do not specify the nature of the libels.

133. Denina, *Essai sur le règne de Frédéric II, Roi de Prusse*, p. 426.

134. Arnim, *Bruchstücke über Verbrechen und Strafen*, vol. 2, pp. 190ff.

135. *Œuvres*, vol. 8, p. 71.

136. Ingrid Mittenzwei, *Friedrich II. von Preussen* (Cologne, 1980), pp. 86–7.

137. Herman Weill, *Frederick the Great and Samuel von Cocceji: a Study in the Reform of the Prussian Judicial Administration 1740–1755* (Madison, 1961), p. 5. On the deterioration of the judicial system under Frederick I, see p. 21.

138. Christopher Clark, *Iron Kingdom. The Rise and Downfall of Prussia 1600–1947* (London, 2006), p. 243.

139. Peter Baumgart, 'Zur Geschichte der kurmärkischen Stände im 17. und 18. Jahrhundert', in Dietrich Gerhard (ed.), *Ständische Vertretungen in Europa im 17. und 18. Jahrhundert* (Göttingen, 1969), p. 159.

140. Gustav Schmoller, *Preussische Verfassungs-, Verwaltungs- und Finanzgeschichte* (Berlin, 1921), p. 162.

141. Koser, vol. 1, p. 328.

142. Hintze, pp. 349–50.

143. Hubert C. Johnson, *Frederick the Great and his Officials* (New Haven and London, 1975), pp. 113–14.

144. *Acta Borussica*, vol. 7, pp. 449–50.

145. Christian Wilhelm von Dohm, *Denkwürdigkeiten meiner Zeit, oder Beiträge zur Geschichte vom letzten Viertel des achtzehnten und vom Anfang des neunzehnten Jahrhunderts 1778 bis 1806* (Lemgo and Hanover, 1814–19), vol. 1, p. 350.

146. C. B. A. Behrens, *Society, Government and the Enlightenment: the Experiences of Eighteenth-century France and Prussia* (London, 1985), p. 108. The fullest account available in English is by David M. Luebke in his article 'Frederick the Great and the celebrated case of the Millers Arnold (1770–1779): A Reappraisal', *Central European History*, 32, 4 (1999), pp. 379–408.

147. This summary is based on the first-person accounts given by two of the protagonists, Friedrich Ludwig Carl Graf Finck von Finckenstein and Georg Karl Friedrich Bandel in, respectively, 'Geschichte des vor der Neumärkischen Regierung geführten Arnold-Gersdorfischen Prozesses

und der Folgen desselben', ed. J. D. E. Preuss, *Zeitschrift für preussische Geschichte und Landeskunde*, 1 (1894), and F. Graner, 'Aus den hinterlassenen Papieren des im Müller Arnoldschen Prozess zur Festungsstrafe verurteilten neumärkischen Regierungsrats Bandel', *Forschungen zur Brandenburgischen und Preussischen Geschichte*, 38 (1926).

148. Luebke, in 'Frederick the Great and the celebrated case of the Millers Arnold', does his best to rehabilitate the Arnolds' case but is not entirely convincing. It has to be said, however, that every single aspect of the case was contested. For an exhaustive, and exhausting, account of all the twists and turns of the legal proceedings, see Malte Diesselhorst, *Die Prozesse des Müllers Arnold und das Eingreifen Friedrichs des Grossen* (Göttingen, 1984), which also reprints many of the documents. On the issue of the water-flow, see p. 41.

149. Finckenstein, 'Geschichte des vor der Neumärkischen Regierung geführten Arnold-Gersdorfischen Prozesses', p. 138.

150. Luebke, 'Frederick the Great and the celebrated case of the Millers Arnold', pp. 402–3.

151. Dohm, *Denkwürdigkeiten meiner Zeit*, vol. 1, p. 268.

152. Koser, vol. 1, p. 543.

153. Graner, 'Aus den hinterlassenen Papieren des im Müller Arnoldschen Prozess zur Festungsstrafe verurteilten neumärkischen Regierungsrats Bandel', p. 94.

154. Ibid., p. 99.

155. Finckenstein, 'Geschichte des vor der Neumärkischen Regierung geführten Arnold-Gersdorfischen Prozesses', p. 150.

156. Peter Baumgart, 'Wie absolut war der preussische Absolutismus?', in *Preussen – Versuch einer Bilanz* (Hamburg, 1981), vol. 2: *Preussen – Beiträge zu einer politischen Kultur*, ed. Manfred Schlenke, p. 103.

157. This has been reprinted many times. A convenient place is Dohm, *Denkwürdigkeiten meiner Zeit*, vol. 1, pp. 534–8, which can be found online.

158. For the favourable response in the Holy Roman Empire outside Prussia, see Iwan-Michelangelo D'Aprile, 'Friedrich und die Aufklärung in Brandenburg-Preussen', in Göse (ed.), *Friedrich der Grosse und die Mark Brandenburg*, p. 41 and Peter Weber, ' "Was jetzt eben zu sagen oder noch zu verschweigen sei, müsst ihr selbst überlegen". Publizistische Strategien der preussischen Justizreformer 1780–1794', in Goldenbaum (ed.), *Appell an das Publikum*, vol. 2, p. 742.

159. Gustav Berthold Volz (ed.), *Friedrich der Grosse im Spiegel seiner Zeit* (Berlin, 1901), vol. 3, pp. 178–81.

160. Diesselhorst, *Die Prozesse des Müllers Arnold*, p. 67.

161. Dohm, *Denkwürdigkeiten meiner Zeit*, vol. 1, p. 274.

162. Daniel Jenisch, 'Denkschrift auf Friedrich den Zweiten' (1801), in Horst Steinmetz (ed.), *Friedrich II., König von Preussen und die deutsche Literatur des 18. Jahrhunderts. Texte und Dokumente* (Stuttgart, 1985), p. 244.

163. Koser, vol. 2, pp. 543–4.

164. Hans Gerhard Hannesen, *Lovis Corinths 'Fridericus Rex'. Der Preussenkönig in Mythos und Geschichte* (Berlin, 1986), pp. 60–62.

165. Diesselhorst, *Die Prozesse des Mülers Arnold*, p. 69.

166. Dietrich, p. 464.

167. Schieder, *Friedrich der Grosse*, p. 292.

168. Peter Weber, 'Das Allgemeine Gesetzbuch – ein Corpus Juris Fridericianum?', in Martin Fontius (ed.), *Friedrich II. und die europäische Aufklärung, Forschungen zur Brandenburgischen und Preussischen Geschichte*, new series (Berlin, 1999), vol. 4, p. 106.

169. Hintze, pp. 396–7.

170. James J. Sheehan, *German History 1770–1866* (Oxford, 1989), p. 70. See also Reinhart Koselleck, 'Staat und Gesellschaft im preussischen Vormärz', in Otto Büsch and Wolfgang Neugebauer (eds.), *Moderne Preussische Geschichte* (Berlin and New York, 1981), vol. 1, pp. 379–81.

171. Hermann Conrad, 'Die geistigen Grundlagen des Allgemeinen Landrechts für die preussischen Staaten von 1794', *Wissenschaftliche Abhandlungen der Arbeitsgemeinschaft für Forschung des Landes Nordrhein-Westfalen*, 77 (1958), p. 17.

172. D'Aprile, 'Friedrich und die Aufklärung in Brandenburg-Preussen', pp. 40–42.

173. Horst Möller, *Vernunft und Kritik. Deutsche Aufklärung im 17. und 18. Jahrhundert* (Frankfurt am Main, 1986), p. 303.

174. Dohm, *Denkwürdigkeiten meiner Zeit*, vol. 1, p. 290.

175. Jenisch, 'Denkschrift auf Friedrich den Zweiten', p. 245.

176. 'Ueber Berlin von einem Fremden', in Gedike and Biester (eds.), *Berlinische Monatsschrift* (1), p. 47.

177. Goethe, *Die Aufgeregten*, act 1, scene 6. Several editions can be accessed online. Originally known as *Breme von Bremenfeld or The Signs of the Times,* the play became better known later as *Die Aufgeregten (Agitation)*. For a summary of the plot and discussion, see Nicholas Boyle, *Goethe. The Poet and the Age*, vol. 2: *Revolution and Renunciation 1790–1803* (Oxford, 2000), pp. 169–71.

178. Vinzenz Czech, 'Friedrich der Grosse auf Inspektionsreise', in Göse (ed.), *Friedrich der Grosse und die Mark Brandenburg*, pp. 51–2.

179. Two helpful collections of essays are: Karl Otmar Freiherr von Aretin, *Der aufgeklärte Absolutismus* (Cologne, 1974) and H. M. Scott (ed.), *Enlightened Absolutism. Reform and Reformers in Later Eighteenth-century Europe* (London, 1990), which contains an article by myself on 'Frederick the Great and enlightened absolutism'. See also Günter Birtsch, 'Der Idealtyp des aufgeklärten Herrschers. Friedrich der Grosse, Karl Friedrich von Baden und Joseph II. im Vergleich', *Aufklärung*, 2, 1 (1987), pp. 9–47.

180. *Œuvres*, vol. 24, p. 46.

181. Ibid., p. 47.

14. COUNTRY AND TOWN

1. Otto Bardong (ed.), *Friedrich der Grosse, Ausgewählte Quellen zur deutschen Geschichte der Neuzeit*. Freiherr vom Stein-Gedächtnisausgabe (Darmstadt, 1982), vol. 22, p. 496.

2. C. B. A. Behrens, *Society, Government and the Enlightenment: the Experiences of Eighteenth-century France and Prussia* (London, 1985), pp. 105–6.

3. William W. Hagen, *Ordinary Prussians: Brandenburg Junkers and Villagers, 1500–1840* (Cambridge, 2002), p. 574.

4. Ibid., p. 590.

5. Dietrich, p. 310.

6. Quoted in Otto Büsch, *Militärsystem und Sozialleben im alten Preussen* (Berlin, 1962), p. 102.

7. Koser, vol. 1, p. 369.

8. Rudolph Stadelmann (ed.), *Preussens Könige in ihrer Thätigkeit für die Landescultur* (Leipzig, 1882), vol. 2, pt 1: *Friedrich der Grosse*, pp. 296–8. The second directive to Cocceji has been reprinted in Bardong (ed.), *Friedrich der Grosse*, p. 163.

9. Ernst Pfeiffer, *Die Revuereisen Friedrichs des Grossen, besonders die schlesischen nach 1763 und der Zustand Schlesiens von 1763–1786* (Berlin, 1904), p. 179. For his attempts to turn back the bourgeois tide, see Peter Baumgart, 'Zur Geschichte der kurmärkischen Stände im 17. und 18. Jahrhundert', in Dietrich Gerhard (ed.), *Ständische Vertretungen in Europa im 17. und 18. Jahrhundert* (Göttingen, 1969), p. 148.

10. Hintze, p. 352; Dietrich, p. 594.

11. Reinhart Koselleck, *Preussen zwischen Reform und Revolution. Allgemeines Landrecht, Verwaltung und soziale Bewegung von 1791 bis 1848*, 3rd edn (Berlin, 1981), p. 83; Horst Möller, *Aufklärung in Preussen. Der Verleger, Publizist und Geschichtsschreiber Friedrich Nicolai* (Berlin, 1974), p. 295.

12. Frank Göse, '"... die Racce davon so guht ist, das sie auf alle art meritiret, conserviret zu werden"', in idem (ed.), *Friedrich der Grosse und die Mark Brandenburg. Herrschaftspraxis in der Provinz* (Berlin, 2012), p. 115.

13. Corina Petersilka, *Die Zweisprachigkeit Friedrichs des Grossen. Ein linguistisches Porträt* (Tübingen, 2005), p. 153.

14. Quoted in Büsch, *Militärsystem und Sozialleben im alten Preussen*, p. 104.

15. Carmen Winkel, *Im Netz des Königs: Netzwerke und Patronage in der preussischen Armee, 1713–1786* (Paderborn, 2013), p. 41.

16. Ibid., p. 93.

17. Paul R. Sweet, *Wilhelm von Humboldt: a Biography* (Columbus, OH, 1978–80), vol. 1, p. 4; Peter Paret, *Yorck and the Era of Prussian Reform, 1807–1815* (Princeton, 1966), p. 8; Behrens, *Society, Government and the Enlightenment*, p. 64; Peter Paret, *Clausewitz and the State* (Oxford, 1976), p. 14.

18. See Büsch, *Militärsystem und Sozialleben im alten Preussen*, pp. 93–4; Koser, vol. 2, p. 507; and Carmen Winkel, 'Ziele und Grenzen der königlichen Personalpolitik im Militär', in Göse (ed.), *Friedrich der Grosse und die Mark Brandenburg*, p. 151.

19. Georg Borchardt (ed.), *Die Randbemerkungen Friedrichs des Grossen* (Potsdam, n.d.), vol. 1, pp. 8, 10.

20. Quoted in Behrens, *Society, Government and the Enlightenment*, p. 64.

21. Koser, vol. 2, p. 506.

22. Borchardt (ed.), *Die Randbemerkungen Friedrichs des Grossen*, vol. 1, pp. 14–16.

23. Robert M. Berdahl, *The Politics of the Prussian Nobility. The Development of a Conservative Ideology 1770–1848* (Princeton, 1988), p. 15.

24. Koselleck, *Preussen zwischen Reform und Revolution*, p. 80.

25. Gerd Heinrich, 'Der Adel in Brandenburg-Preussen', in Hellmuth Rössler (ed.), *Deutscher Adel 1555–1740* (Darmstadt, 1965), p. 307.

26. Koser, vol. 1, p. 530.

27. Winkel, *Im Netz des Königs*, pp. 40–41.

28. Hubert C. Johnson, *Frederick the Great and his Officials* (New Haven and London, 1975), p. 245.

29. Theodor Schieder, *Friedrich der Grosse. Ein Königtum der Widersprüche* (Frankfurt am Main, Berlin and Vienna, 1983), p. 65.

30. Edgar Melton, 'The Prussian Junkers, 1600–1786', in H. M. Scott (ed.), *The European Nobilities in the Seventeenth and Eighteenth Centuries* (London, 1995), vol. 2, p. 98. Melton gives much higher figures for noble casualties than Schieder – seventy-two Wedels and fifty-three Kleists – although these seem barely credible.

31. Friedrich Meinecke, *The Age of German Liberation, 1795–1815*, ed. Peter Paret (Berkeley, Los Angeles and London, 1977), pp. 12–13.

32. Dietrich, p. 310.

33. *Œuvres*, vol. 6, p. 106. Translation used here is from *Posthumous Works* (London, 1789), vol. 4, p. 151.

34. Büsch, *Militärsystem und Sozialleben im alten Preussen*, p. 81.

35. Ibid.; Arnold Berney, *Friedrich der Grosse. Entwicklungsgeschichte eines Staatsmannes* (Tübingen, 1934), p. 241; Gustavo Corni, *Stato assoluto e società agraria in Prussia nell'età di Federico II* (Bologna, 1982), p. 260.

36. Helga Schultz, *Berlin 1650–1800. Sozialgeschichte einer Residenz* (Berlin, 1987), p. 226.

37. Büsch, *Militärsystem und Sozialleben im alten Preussen*, pp. 105, 112; Ingrid Mittenzwei, *Friedrich II. von Preussen* (Cologne, 1980), p. 155; Karl Heinrich Kaufhold, 'Friderizianische Agrar-, Siedlungs- und Bauernpolitik', in Peter Baumgart (ed.), *Kontinuitäten und Wandel. Schlesien zwischen Österreich und Preussen* (Sigmaringen, 1990), p. 182.

38. Kaufhold, 'Friderizianische Agrar-, Siedlungs- und Bauernpolitik', p. 200; Hanna Schissler, 'Die Junker. Zur Sozialgeschichte und historischen Bedeutung der agrarischen Elite in Preussen', in *Preussen in kritischer Perspektive*, ed. Hans-Jürgen Puhle, *Geschichte und Gesellschaft*, special issue 6, 1980, p. 97.

39. Marcus von Salisch, '"Von Preussen lernen . . . ?" Die friderizianische Armee nach dem Siebenjährigen Krieg und die Entwicklungen der Zeit', in Friederisiko, Essays, p. 65.

40. *Œuvres*, vol. 9, p. 235.

41. Klaus Epstein, *The Genesis of German Conservatism* (Princeton, 1966), pp. 212–13.

42. Büsch, *Militärsystem und Sozialleben im alten Preussen*, p. 136.

43. Schieder, *Friedrich der Grosse*, p. 83.

44. See for example his instruction to Minister Michaelis on taking over a department of the General Directory, dated 8 December 1779 and reprinted in Bardong (ed.), *Friedrich der Grosse*, p. 506.

45. Walter L. Dorn, 'The Prussian bureaucracy in the eighteenth century', pt 1, *Political Science Quarterly*, 46 (1931), p. 418.

46. Hans Thieme, 'Die friderizianische Justizreform und Schlesien', in Baumgart (ed.), *Kontinuitäten und Wandel*, p. 20.

47. Büsch, *Militärsystem und Sozialleben im alten Preussen*, p. 22; Koser, vol. 1, pp. 370–72; J. D. E. Preuss, *Friedrich der Grosse – Eine Lebensgeschichte* (Berlin, 1832), pp. 304–5; Pfeiffer, *Die Revuereisen Friedrichs des Grossen*, pp. 121–3.

48. Patrick J. Speelman, 'Conclusion: father of the modern age', in Mark H. Danley and Patrick J. Speelman (eds.), *The Seven Years War: Global Views* (Leiden, 2013), p. 524.

49. Koselleck, *Preussen zwischen Reform und Revolution*, p. 132.

50. Corni, *Stato assoluto e società agraria in Prussia*, p. 415.

51. Ibid.; Büsch, *Militärsystem und Sozialleben im alten Preussen*, pp. 159–60. There were, however, isolated incidents of peasants being sold off the land as if they were true serfs – Schieder, *Friedrich der Grosse*, p. 79.

52. Behrens, *Society, Government and the Enlightenment*, p. 140.

53. S. A. Eddie, *Freedom's Price. Serfdom, Subjection and Reform in Prussia, 1648–1848* (Oxford, 2013), pp. 12, 29.

54. It is reprinted in Bardong (ed.), *Friedrich der Grosse*, pp. 426–41.

55. Koser, vol. 2, p. 590.

56. Wolfgang Neugebauer, *Absolutistischer Staat und Schulwirklichkeit in Brandenburg-Preussen* (Berlin and New York, 1985), p. 180.

57. *Œuvres*, vol. 27, pt 3, p. 281, also reprinted in Bardong (ed.), *Friedrich der Grosse*, p. 505.

58. Ibid.

59. Quoted in Neugebauer, *Absolutistischer Staat und Schulwirklichkeit*, pp. 184–5.

60. Dietrich, p. 504.

61. Koser, vol. 2, p. 591.

62. Anton Friedrich Büsching, *Beschreibung seiner Reise von Berlin über Potsdam nach Rekahn unweit Brandenburg welche er vom dritten bis achten Junius 1775 gethan hat* (Leipzig, 1775), pp. 230–31.

63. Ibid., p. 38.

64. Ibid., p. 322.

65. Ibid., p. 295. On Rochow, see Iwan-Michelangelo D'Aprile, 'Aufklärung, Toleranz und Wissenschaft in Preussen', in Friederisiko, Ausstellung, p. 100.

66. Reinhold Koser and Hans Droysen (eds.), *Briefwechsel Friedrichs des Grossen mit Voltaire*, Publikationen aus den K. Preussischen

Staatsarchiven (Leipzig, 1908–9, 1911), vol. 86, p. 371. Also in *Œuvres*, vol. 23, p. 406.

67. Kaufhold, 'Friderizianische Agrar-, Siedlungs- und Bauernpolitik', p. 190; Koser, vol. 2, p. 370.

68. Kaufhold, 'Friderizianische Agrar-, Siedlungs- und Bauernpolitik', p. 188; Hans-Heinrich Müller, 'Domänen und Domänenpächter in Brandenburg-Preussen im 18. Jahrhundert', in Otto Büsch and Wolfgang Neugebauer (eds.), *Moderne Preussische Geschichte* (Berlin and New York, 1981), vol. 1, pp. 318–20.

69. Ewald Graf von Hertzberg, 'Sur la population des états en général et sur celle des États Prussiens en particulier', in *Dissertations qui ont été lues dans l'assemblée publique de l'Académie des sciences et des belles-lettres à Berlin les années 1784, 1785, & 1786, pour le jour anniversaire du roi*, p. 54; Joachim Whaley, *Germany and the Holy Roman Empire* (Oxford, 2012), vol. 2: *The Peace of Westphalia to the Dissolution of the Reich 1648–1806*, p. 498.

70. For examples of Frederick urging the cultivation of potatoes, see Bardong (ed.), *Friedrich der Grosse*, pp. 381, 444, 453. For a more sceptical comment on the effect of Frederick's policies with regard to potatoes, see Jürgen Luh, *Der Grosse. Friedrich II. von Preussen* (Berlin, 2012), p. 48.

71. B. H. Slicher van Bath, 'Agriculture in the vital revolution', in E. E. Rich and C. H. Wilson (eds.), *The Cambridge Economic History of Europe* (Cambridge, 1977), vol. 5: *The Economic Organization of Early Modern Europe*, p. 78.

72. Georg Schmidt, *Wandel durch Vernunft. Deutsche Geschichte im 18. Jahrhundert* (Munich, 2009), p. 274.

73. Quoted in Tim Blanning, *The Pursuit of Glory: Europe 1648–1815* (London, 2007), p. 148.

74. *Œuvres*, vol. 6, p. 95. Translation used here taken from *Posthumous Works*, vol. 4, p. 136.

75. Behrens, *Society, Government and the Enlightenment*, p. 149; Werner Heegewaldt, 'Friderizianische Domänenpolitik am Beispiel der Kurmark', in Göse (ed.), *Friedrich der Grosse und die Mark Brandenburg*, p. 173.

76. For a discussion of obstacles to agricultural growth, based on Marc Bloch's classic article 'La lutte pour l'individualisme agraire dans la France du XVIIIᵉ siècle', *Annales Économies Sociétés Civilisations*, 2 (1930), see Blanning, *The Pursuit of Glory*, pp. 148–53.

77. H. Kiesel and P. Münch, *Gesellschaft und Literatur im 18. Jahrhundert* (Munich, 1977), p. 34.

78. Müller, 'Domänen und Domänenpächter', p. 320. Cf. Kaufhold, 'Friderizianische Agrar-, Siedlungs- und Bauernpolitik', p. 190.
79. Antonia Humm, 'Friedrich II. und der Kartoffelanbau in Brandenburg-Preussen', in Göse (ed.), *Friedrich der Grosse und die Mark Brandenburg*, pp. 200–202.
80. Dietrich, pp. 264, 494.
81. Hellmuth Rössler, 'Der deutsche Hochadel und der Wiederaufbau nach dem Westfälischen Frieden', *Blätter für deutsche Landesgeschichte*, 101 (1965), p. 132. The counts – now princes – of Castell still reside at Rüdenhausen Castle, owning large estates, forests, vineyards and even a bank.
82. Koser, vol. 1, p. 374.
83. Bernd Ingmar Gutberlet, *Friedrich der Grosse. Eine Reise zu den Orten seines Lebens* (Darmstadt, 2011), pp. 82–9.
84. Corni, *Stato assoluto e società agraria in Prussia*, p. 110; Gustav Schmoller, 'Die ländliche Kolonisation des 17. und 18. Jahrhunderts', in Büsch and Neugebauer (eds.), *Moderne Preussische Geschichte*, vol. 2, p. 935.
85. Günther Franz, *Geschichte des deutschen Bauernstandes vom frühen Mittelalter bis zum 19. Jahrhundert* (Stuttgart, 1970), pp. 200–201.
86. Behrens, *Society, Government and the Enlightenment*, p. 124.
87. Schmoller, 'Die ländliche Kolonisation', pp. 942–5.
88. Ibid., p. 926. The same figures are given by Franz, *Geschichte des deutschen Bauernstandes*, p. 200.
89. Walther Hubatsch, *Frederick the Great. Absolutism and Administration* (London, 1975), p. 110, which gives a break-down by province. These figures are confirmed by Schieder, *Friedrich der Grosse*, p. 339. A much higher figure – 284,487 – is given by Horst Möller, *Fürstenstaat oder Bürgernation. Deutschland 1763–1815* (Berlin, 1989), p. 80.
90. Christian Wilhelm von Dohm, *Denkwürdigkeiten meiner Zeit oder Beiträge zur Geschichte vom letzten Viertel des achtzehnten und vom Anfang des neunzehnten Jahrhunderts 1778 bis 1806* (Lemgo and Hanover, 1814–19), vol. 1, p. 391.
91. Schmoller, 'Die ländliche Kolonisation', p. 925.
92. Johnson, *Frederick the Great and his Officials*, pp. 100–101.
93. Preuss, *Friedrich der Grosse*, vol. 1, p. 279.
94. Schultz, *Berlin 1650–1800*, p. 44.
95. Johnson, *Frederick the Great and his Officials*, p. 102.

96. Hans-Ulrich Wehler, *Deutsche Gesellschaftsgeschichte* (Munich, 1987), vol. 1: *Vom Feudalismus des Alten Reiches bis zur defensiven Modernisierung der Reformära 1700–1815*, p. 120.

97. 'Aus dem Brandenburgischen', in Christian Friedrich Daniel Schubart (ed.), *Deutsche Chronik auf das Jahr 1774* (reprinted, Heidelberg, 1975), 54 (3 October 1774), pp. 427–8.

98. Karl Biedermann, *Deutschland im 18. Jahrhundert*, ed. Wolfgang Emmerich (Frankfurt am Main, 1979), p. 252.

99. Wehler, *Deutsche Gesellschaftsgeschichte*, vol. 1, p. 121.

100. Biedermann, *Deutschland im 18. Jahrhundert*, p. 252.

101. Voltaire to Count and Countess d'Argental, Potsdam, 24 July 1750, in Theodore Besterman (ed.), *Voltaire's Correspondence* (Geneva, 1956), vol. 18, no. 3604, p. 104.

102. Anton Friedrich Büsching, *Beschreibung seiner Reise von Berlin nach Kyritz in der Prignitz welche er vom 26ten September bis zum 2ten Oktober 1779 verrichtet hat* (Leipzig, 1780), pp. 5–7.

103. Felix Escher, 'Die brandenburgisch-preussische Residenz und Hauptstadt Berlin im 17. und 18. Jahrhundert', in Wolfgang Ribbe (ed.), *Geschichte Berlins*, 2nd edn (Munich, 1988), vol. 1: *Von der Frühgeschichte bis zur Industrialisierung*, p. 386.

104. Nikolai Mikhailovich Karamzin, *Letters of a Russian Traveler 1789–1790. An Account of a Young Russian Gentleman's Tour through Germany, Switzerland, France, and England* (New York, 1957), p. 50.

105. Büsching, *Beschreibung seiner Reise von Berlin über Potsdam nach Rekahn*, p. 72.

106. This is one of the epigraphs of John Brewer, *The Sinews of Power: War, Money and the English State 1688–1783* (New York, 1989), p. v.

107. Karl Erich Born, *Wirtschaft und Gesellschaft im Denken Friedrichs des Grossen* (Mainz and Wiesbaden, 1979), p. 13.

108. Volker Hentschel, 'Der Merkantilismus und die wirtschaftlichen Anschauungen Friedrichs II.', in Erhard Bethke (ed.), *Friedrich der Grosse. Herrscher zwischen Tradition und Fortschritt* (Gütersloh, 1985), p. 139.

109. *Œuvres*, vol. 6, p. 86. Translation used here taken from *Posthumous Works*, vol. 4, pp. 119–20.

110. *Œuvres*, vol. 2, p. 1.

111. Quoted in Charles Wilson, *Mercantilism* (London, 1958), p. 24.

112. J. D. E. Preuss, *Friedrichs des Grossen Jugend und Thronbesteigung* (Berlin, 1840), p. 360.

113. Hintze, p. 354; Volker Hentschel, 'Manufaktur- und Handelspolitik des merkantilistischen Wirtschaftssystems', in Bethke (ed.), *Friedrich der Grosse*, p. 148.

114. Thomas Biskup and Peter H. Wilson, 'Grossbritannien, Amerika und die atlantische Welt', in Friederisiko, Ausstellung, pp. 158–9.

115. Hubatsch, *Frederick the Great*, p. 61.

116. Hans Bleckwenn, 'Bauernfreiheit durch Wehrpflicht – ein neues Bild der altpreussischen Armee', in *Friedrich der Grosse und das Militärwesen seiner Zeit* (Herford and Bonn, 1987), p. 56.

117. W. O. Henderson, *Studies in the Economic Policy of Frederick the Great* (London, 1963), p. 144.

118. Dietrich, p. 274.

119. Sheilagh C. Ogilvie, 'The beginnings of industrialisation', in idem (ed.), *Germany: a New Social and Economic History* (London, 1996), vol. 2: *1630–1800*, p. 616.

120. Ibid., p. 597; Henderson, *Studies in the Economic Policy of Frederick the Great*, p. 145.

121. Henderson, *Studies in the Economic Policy of Frederick the Great*, pp. 143–6.

122. Büsching, *Beschreibung seiner Reise von Berlin über Potsdam nach Rekahn*, p. 192.

123. Dietrich, p. 286.

124. *Œuvres*, vol. 23, p. 407.

125. Peter Baumgart, 'Absoluter Staat und Judenemanzipation in Brandenburg-Preussen', *Jahrbuch für die Geschichte Mittel- und Ostdeutschlands*, 13/14 (1965), p. 84.

126. Koser, vol. 2, p. 399.

127. Schultz, *Berlin 1650–1800*, p. 165.

128. Hans Dollinger, *Friedrich II. von Preussen. Sein Bild im Wandel von zwei Jahrhunderten* (Munich, 1986), illustration 147. Karl Christian Wilhelm Baron's handsome picture of the Neues Palais at Potsdam in 1775 shows Frederick on his grey horse riding up an avenue of mulberry trees.

129. Peter-Michael Hahn, *Friedrich II. von Preussen* (Stuttgart, 2013), p. 160.

130. Michaela Völkel, 'Meissen on my mind. Die Königliche Porzellanmanufaktur im internationalen Wettstreit', in Friederisiko, Ausstellung, p. 378.

131. Johanna Lessmann, 'Die Berliner Porzellanmanufakturen im 18. Jahrhundert', in Johanna Lessmann, Michaela Braesel and Katharina

Dück (eds.), *Berliner Porzellan des 18. Jahrhunderts* (Hamburg, 1993), p. ix.

132. Nina Simone Schepkowski, *Johann Ernst Gotzkowsky. Kunstagent und Gemäldesammler im friderizianischen Berlin* (Berlin, 2009), p. 271.

133. Lessmann, 'Die Berliner Porzellanmanufakturen im 18. Jahrhundert', p. x.

134. Michaela Völkel, 'Nicht alle Lust will Ewigkeit. Friedrich und das Porzellan', in Friederisiko, Ausstellung, p. 191.

135. Angelika Lorenz, *Berliner Porzellan 1763–1850* (Münster, 2006), p. 8. This is the catalogue of an exhibition held at the Westfälischen Landesmuseum für Kunst und Kulturgeschichte Münster in 2006–7 and contains many very fine illustrations of porcelain from Frederick's reign.

136. Günter Schade, *Berliner Porzellan. Zur Kunst- und Kulturgeschichte der Berliner Porzellanmanufaktur im 18. und 19. Jahrhundert* (Munich, 1987), p. 64.

137. For a detailed account of the rise and fall of the Gotzkowsky undertaking, see Schepkowski, *Johann Ernst Gotzkowsky*, pp. 274–301.

138. Schade, *Berliner Porzellan*, p. 85.

139. Arnulf Siebeneicker, *Offizianten und Ouvriers: Sozialgeschichte der Königlichen Porzellan-Manufaktur und der Königlichen Gesundheitsgeschirr-Manufaktur in Berlin 1763–1880* (Berlin and New York, 2002), p. 23.

140. Ibid., p. 24.

141. Erich Köllmann, *Berliner Porzellan 1763–1963* (Brunswick, 1966), vol. 1, pp. 35–6; Lessmann, 'Die Berliner Porzellanmanufakturen im 18. Jahrhundert', p. xv.

142. Schade, *Berliner Porzellan*, p. 111.

143. Friedrich Hermann Hofmann, *Das Porzellan der europäischen Manufakturen im XVIII. Jahrhundert: eine Kunst- und Kulturgeschichte* (Berlin, 1932), p. 281.

144. Völkel, 'Meissen on my mind', pp. 378–9. See also Schepkowski, *Johann Ernst Gotzkowsky*, p. 30.

145. Siebeneicker, *Offizianten und Ouvriers*, pp. 25–7.

146. Lorenz, *Berliner Porzellan*, pp. 12–13.

147. Ibid., p. 14.

148. Hofmann, *Das Porzellan der europäischen Manufakturen*, p. 492. For a reproduction of the centrepiece of this extraordinary creation, see Schade, *Berliner Porzellan*, p. 88.

149. Schade, *Berliner Porzellan*, p. 141.

150. Ibid., p. 139.
151. Siebeneicker, *Offizianten und Ouvriers*, p. 28.
152. Schade, *Berliner Porzellan*, p. 112.
153. Lessmann, 'Die Berliner Porzellanmanufakturen im 18. Jahrhundert', p. ix.
154. Siebeneicker, *Offizianten und Ouvriers*, p. 26.
155. Schade, *Berliner Porzellan*, p. 122; Köllmann, *Berliner Porzellan*, p. 31.
156. Thomas Biskup, 'Eines "Grossen" würdig? Hof und Zeremoniell bei Friedrich II.', in Friederisiko, Essays, p. 106.
157. Günter Vogler and Klaus Vetter, *Preussen von den Anfängen bis zur Reichsgründung* (Cologne, 1981), p. 59.
158. Whaley, *Germany and the Holy Roman Empire*, vol. 2, p. 285.
159. Ingrid Mittenzwei, *Preussen nach dem Siebenjährigen Krieg. Auseinandersetzungen zwischen Bürgertum und Staat um die Wirtschaftspolitik* (Berlin, 1979), pp. 21–2.
160. Ogilvie, 'The beginnings of industrialisation', p. 614.
161. Christopher Clark, *Iron Kingdom. The Rise and Downfall of Prussia 1600–1947* (London, 2006), p. 181.
162. Mittenzwei, *Preussen nach dem Siebenjährigen Krieg*, pp. 144–5.
163. Ibid., p. 90.
164. Hahn, *Friedrich II.*, p. 106.
165. Hintze, pp. 380–82.
166. Ibid., p. 382; Mittenzwei, *Preussen nach dem Siebenjährigen Krieg*, p. 19.
167. Ibid., p. 20.
168. Ibid., p. 69.
169. Dietrich, p. 468; Koser, vol. 2, p. 400.
170. Hintze, p. 381.
171. Agnieszka Pufelska, 'Die verpasste Grösse: Friedrich II. und Polen', in Friederisiko, Ausstellung, p. 120.
172. Johann Georg Büsch, *Theoretisch-praktische Darstellung der Handlung in deren mannigfaltigen Geschäften* (Hamburg, 1792), vol. 2, p. 258.
173. Lehndorff, vol. 3, p. 19.
174. Ibid., p. 30.
175. Friedrich Nicolai, *Anecdoten von Friedrich dem Grossen und von einigen Personen die um ihn waren* (Berlin, 1788–92; reprint, Munich, n.d.), pp. 13–14. See also Klaus Schwieger, *Das Bürgertum in Preussen vor der Französischen Revolution* (Kiel, 1972), p. 421.

176. Florian Schui, *Rebellious Prussians. Urban Political Culture under Frederick the Great and his Successors* (Oxford, 2013), ch. 4.

177. Walter L. Dorn, 'The Prussian bureaucracy in the eighteenth century', pt 2, *Political Science Quarterly*, 47 (1932), pp. 79–80.

178. *Œuvres*, vol. 6, p. 85.

179. See his public proclamation of 14 April 1766 and the directive of 21 May 1766, reprinted in Heinrich von Beguelin, *Historisch-kritische Darstellungen der Akzise- und Zollverfassung in den preussischen Staaten* (Berlin, 1797), pp. 114–15 and 123–4.

180. Henderson, *Studies in the Economic Policy of Frederick the Great*, p. 69.

181. Markus A. Denzel, 'Wirtschaftlicher Wandel und institutionelle Erneuerung. Eine merkantilistische Wirtschaftspolitik. Leitgedanken', in Sösemann, vol. 1, p. 375.

182. Henderson, *Studies in the Economic Policy of Frederick the Great*, p. 70.

183. W. Schultze, 'Ein Angriff des Ministers von Heinitz gegen die französische Régie in Preussen', *Forschungen zur Brandenburgischen und Preussischen Geschichte*, 5 (1892), pp. 192–3.

184. Ibid., p. 195.

185. Beguelin, *Historisch-kritische Darstellungen*, pp. 115–17.

186. Dohm, *Denkwürdigkeiten meiner Zeit*, vol. 4, p. 512.

187. Jacques-Antoine-Hippolyte, Comte de Guibert, *Journal d'un voyage en Allemagne, fait en 1773* (Paris, 1803), vol. 1, pp. 222–3.

188. Roy Pascal, *The German Sturm und Drang* (Manchester, 1953), pp. 46–7.

189. Florian Schui, 'Learning from French experience? The Prussian *Régie* tax administration, 1766–86', in Holger Nehring and Florian Schui (eds.), *Global Debates about Taxation* (Basingstoke, 2007), p. 54.

190. Ibid., p. 50.

191. In 1780 he told a delegation led by Ludwig Tieck's father, who called on him at Sanssouci to protest against the chicaneries of the guilds, that he too was opposed to them and would take action. But he never did – Horst Krüger, *Zur Geschichte der Manufakturen und der Manufakturarbeiter in Preussen. Die mittleren Provinzen in der zweiten Hälfte des 18. Jahrhunderts* (Berlin, 1958), p. 76.

15. AT COURT AND AT HOME

1. Jules Finot and Roger Galmiche-Bouvier (eds.), *Une mission militaire en Prusse en 1786. Récit d'un voyage en Allemagne et observations sur*

les manœuvres de Potsdam et de Magdebourg. Publiés après les papiers du marquis de Toulongeon (Paris, 1881), p. 128.

2. Theodor Schieder, *Friedrich der Grosse. Ein Königtum der Widersprüche* (Frankfurt am Main, Berlin and Vienna, 1983), p. 50.

3. John Adamson, 'The making of the ancien-régime court 1500–1700', in idem, *The Princely Courts of Europe. Ritual, Politics and Culture under the Ancien Régime 1500–1750* (London, 1999), pp. 7–41. Revealingly, the chapter on Prussia, by Markus Völkel, ends in 1740, although there are in fact two pages on Frederick – pp. 228–9 – headed 'The military court'.

4. Koser, vol. 1, p. 527.

5. Dietrich, p. 330.

6. Barbara Stollberg-Rilinger, 'Offensive Formlosigkeit? Der Stilwandel des diplomatischen Zeremoniells', in Sösemann, vol. 1, p. 354.

7. H. M. Scott, *The Emergence of the Eastern Powers, 1756–1775* (Cambridge, 2001), pp. 143–5.

8. Quoted in Thomas Biskup, 'Preussischer Pomp. Zeremoniellnutzung und Ruhmbegriff Friedrichs des Grossen im Berliner "Carousel" von 1750', in *Friedrich der Grosse und der Hof. Beiträge des zweiten Colloquiums in der Reihe 'Friedrich300' vom 10./11. Oktober 2008*, ed. Michael Kaiser and Jürgen Luh (Friedrich300 – Colloquien, 2), http://www.perspectivia.net/content/publikationen/friedrich300-colloquien/friedrich-hof/Biskup_Pomp, p. 5.

9. Reinhold Koser, 'Vom Berliner Hof um 1750', *Hohenzollern-Jahrbuch*, 7 (1903), p. 17.

10. Adamson, 'The making of the Ancien Régime court 1500–1700', p. 24.

11. A. P. Hagemann, 'Der König, die Königin und der preussische Hof, in *Friedrich der Grosse und der Hof*, http://www.perspectivia.net/content/publikationen/friedrich300-colloquien/friedrich-hof/Hagemann_Zeitung.

12. Martin Engel, *Das Forum Fridericianum und die monumentalen Residenzplätze des 18. Jahrhunderts* (unpublished Free University Berlin dissertation, 2001), p. 75. Available online at http://www.diss.fu-berlin.de/diss/receive/FUDISS_thesis_000000001297.

13. Hagemann, 'Der König, die Königin und der preussische Hof', p. 31.

14. Ibid., pp. 27, 32.

15. Thomas Biskup, 'Eines "Grossen" würdig? Hof und Zeremoniell bei Friedrich II.', in Friederisiko, Essays, p. 111.

16. Thomas Biskup, 'The hidden queen: Elizabeth Christine of Prussia and Hohenzollern queenship in the eighteenth century', in Clarissa

Campbell Orr (ed.), *Queenship in Europe, 1660–1815. The Role of the Consort* (Cambridge, 2004), pp. 307–8.

17. Lehndorff, *passim*. There is a good selection in Haug von Kuenheim (ed.), *Aus den Tagebüchern des Grafen Ernst Ahasverus Heinrich von Lehndorff* (Berlin, 1982).

18. Biskup, 'Eines "Grossen" würdig? Hof und Zeremoniell bei Friedrich II.', p. 109.

19. J. D. E. Preuss, *Friedrich der Grosse – Eine Lebensgeschichte* (Berlin, 1832), vol. 1, p. 277.

20. Thomas Biskup, *Friedrichs Grösse. Inszenierungen des Preussenkönigs in Fest und Zeremoniell 1740–1815* (Frankfurt am Main and New York, 2012), p. 81.

21. Thomas Biskup, 'Preussischer Pomp'. As Biskup observes, the splendour of the occasion was reminiscent of the 'Asiatic pomp' of Frederick I denounced by his grandson so scathingly in *Memoirs of the House of Brandenburg*. For an account of Louis XIV's carousel, see Peter Burke, *The Fabrication of Louis XIV* (New Haven, 1992), pp. 66–7.

22. *Historische Nachricht von denen Lustbarkeiten, welche der König, bei Gelegenheit der Ankunft Sr. Königlichen Hoheit und des Durchlauchtigsten Markgrafens von Brandenburg-Bayreuth, im Monate August, 1750, zu Potsdam, zu Charlottenburg und zu Berlin angestellet hat* (Berlin, 1750). The event also acquired legendary status, inspiring a depiction by Adolph Menzel of the awarding of the prizes. An equestrian event 'Le Carrousel de Sanssouci' was staged outside the Neues Palais in 2012 as part of the tricentenary celebrations.

23. Quoted in Biskup, 'Preussischer Pomp', p. 27.

24. Ibid., p. 28.

25. Ibid.

26. Thomas Biskup, 'Höfisches Retablissement: Der Hof Friedrichs des Grossen nach 1763', in *Friedrich der Grosse – eine perspektivische Bestandsaufnahme. Beiträge des ersten Colloquiums in der Reihe 'Friedrich300' vom 28./29. September 2007*, ed. Michael Kaiser and Jürgen Luh (Friedrich300 – Colloquien 1), http://www.perspectivia.net/content/publikationen/friedrich300-colloquien/friedrich-bestandsaufnahme/biskup_retablissement, p. 36.

27. Koser, vol. 2, p. 519. On the lavish celebrations staged on this occasion, see the reports of James Harris in Earl of Malmesbury (ed.), *Diaries and Correspondence of James Harris, First Earl of Malmesbury*, vol. 1 (London, 1844), for example that of 27 July 1776 on p. 150, and

Henriette Graf, 'Das Neue Palais – Funktion und Disposition der Appartements', in Friederisiko, Ausstellung, p. 295.

28. Biskup, 'Höfisches Retablissement', especially pp. 12, 18, 22, 26.

29. Biskup, *Friedrichs Grösse*, p. 46.

30. Graf, 'Das Neue Palais – Funktion und Disposition der Appartements', p. 294.

31. Biskup, *Friedrichs Grösse*, pp. 109–10.

32. Lehndorff, vol. 1, pp. 131–2.

33. Ibid., p. 132.

34. Henri Zosime, Comte de Valori (ed.), *Mémoires des négociations du marquis de Valori, ambassadeur de France à la Cour de Berlin. Accompagnés d'un recueil de lettres de Frédéric-le-Grand, des princes ses frères, de Voltaire, et des plus illustres personnages du XVIIIe siècle* (Paris, 1820), vol. 1, p. 266.

35. Dietrich, p. 316.

36. Peter Loewenberg, 'Psychohistorical perspectives on modern German history', *Journal of Modern History*, 47, 2 (June 1975), pp. 234–5.

37. Eva Ziebura, *August Wilhelm Prinz von Preussen* (Berlin, 2006), pp. 8–9.

38. *Œuvres*, vol. 26, p. 162.

39. Jürgen Luh, *Der Grosse. Friedrich II. von Preussen* (Berlin, 2012), p. 67.

40. Lehndorff, vol. 1, p. 70.

41. Ibid., p. 128.

42. Ibid., p. 77. See also, Gerd Fesser, 'Der König von Rheinsberg', *Die Zeit*, 32 (2002), http://www.zeit.de/2002/32/Der_Koenig_von_Rheinsberg?page=all.

43. *Œuvres*, vol. 26, pp. 175–9. These letters are dated only '1746'.

44. Ibid., p. 180.

45. Gustav Berthold Volz (ed.), *Friedrich der Grosse und Wilhelmine von Bayreuth* (Leipzig, 1924), vol. 1: *Jugendbriefe 1728–1740*, p. 209; Christian Graf von Krockow, *Die preussischen Brüder. Prinz Heinrich und Friedrich der Grosse. Ein Doppelporträt* (Stuttgart, 1996), pp. 73–4.

46. Lothar Schilling, *Kaunitz und das Renversement des alliances. Studien zur aussenpolitischen Konzeption Wenzel Antons von Kaunitz* (Berlin 1994), p. 96.

47. Koser, vol. 2, p. 100.

48. Alfred Ritter von Arneth, *Geschichte Maria Theresias* (Vienna, 1863–79), vol. 5, pp. 198 and n. 264 on p. 502.

49. Andrew Bisset (ed.), *Memoirs and Papers of Sir Andrew Mitchell K.B.* (London, 1850), vol. 1, p. 110.

50. P.C., vol. 18, p. 696.

51. Otto Herrmann, 'Friedrich der Grosse im Spiegel seines Bruders Heinrich', *Historische Vierteljahrschrift*, 26 (1931), pp. 365–76.

52. Gustav Berthold Volz, 'Prinz Heinrich als Kritiker Friedrichs des Grossen', *Historische Vierteljahrschrift*, 27 (1932), p. 393.

53. Luh, *Der Grosse. Friedrich II. von Preussen*, p. 84.

54. Volz (ed.), *Friedrich der Grosse und Wilhelmine von Bayreuth*, vol. 1, pp. 63–5.

55. Ibid., p. 143.

56. Ibid., p. 105.

57. See the detailed account by an eye-witness, Frederick's personal assistant Henri de Catt – Willy Schüssler (ed.), *Friedrich der Grosse: Gespräche mit Henri de Catt* (Munich, 1981), pp. 285–91.

58. Ingeborg Weber-Kellermann (ed.), *Wilhelmine von Bayreuth. Eine preussische Königstochter* (Frankfurt am Main, 1990), p. 432.

59. Volz (ed.), *Friedrich der Grosse und Wilhelmine von Bayreuth*, vol. 2, pp. 74–7, 94.

60. Luh, *Der Grosse. Friedrich II. von Preussen*, pp. 169, 207.

61. Daniel Schönpflug, 'Friedrich der Grosse als Ehestifter. Matrimoniale Strategien im Haus Hohenzollern 1740–1786', in Friederisiko, Essays, p. 81.

62. Karin Feuerstein-Prasser, *Die preussischen Königinnen* (Regensburg, 2000), pp. 203–5.

63. Lehndorff, vol. 2, p. 395.

64. Ibid., p. 399.

65. René de Bouillé, *Essai sur la vie du Marquis de Bouillé* (Paris, 1853), p. 138. See also Hardenberg's comment in Thomas Stamm-Kuhlmann, 'Vom rebellischen Sohn zum Landesvater. Der Herrscher zwischen Familie und Staat', in Sösemann, vol. 1, p. 19.

66. Alfred P. Hagemann, 'Friedrich und sein Nachfolger – déjà vu eines Traumas', in Friederisiko, Ausstellung, p. 230.

67. Ibid., p. 232.

68. Ibid., p. 230.

69. Ibid., p. 232.

70. Karoline Zielosko, 'Die Dynastie als Ressource. Friedrich als Oberhaupt der brandenburgischen Hohenzollern', in Friederisiko, Ausstellung, p. 80.

71. I have discussed the successful Prussian invasion of the Dutch Republic in 1787 and its ramifications in *The Origins of the French Revolutionary Wars* (London, 1986), pp. 49–51.

72. Wilhelm Bringmann, *Preussen unter Friedrich Wilhelm II. (1786–1797)* (Frankfurt am Main, 2001), pp. 100–101.

73. Gregor Vogt-Spira, 'Das antike Rom im geistigen Haushalt eines Königs', in Sösemann, vol. 1, pp. 128–9.

74. Biskup, 'Eines "Grossen" würdig? Hof und Zeremoniell bei Friedrich II.', p. 102.

75. Dieudonné Thiébault, *Mes Souvenirs de vingt ans de séjour à Berlin; ou Frédéric le Grand, sa famille, sa cour, son gouvernement, son académie, ses écoles, et ses amis littérateurs et philosophes*, 4th edn (Paris, 1813), vol. 1, pp. 7–8.

76. Theodore Besterman (ed.), *Voltaire's Correspondence* (Geneva, 1956), vol. 18, pp. 131, 188.

77. Ibid., p. 209.

78. Preuss, *Friedrich der Grosse*, vol. 1, p. 424.

79. Lehndorff, vol. 1, p. 129; *The Memoirs of Casanova*, vol. 5 – http://romance-books.classic-literature.co.uk/memoirs-of-jacques-casanova/volume-5e-russia-and-poland/ebook-page-48.asp; Gustav Berthold Volz (ed.), *Friedrich der Grosse im Spiegel seiner Zeit* (Berlin, 1901), vol. 1, p. 271.

80. Peter-Michael Hahn, *Friedrich II. von Preussen* (Stuttgart, 2013), p. 118.

81. Biskup, *Friedrichs Grösse*, p. 128. There is much information about Richter in Leslie Bodi, *Tauwetter in Wien. Zur Prosa der österreichischen Aufklärung 1781–1795* (Frankfurt am Main, 1977), although not, alas, anything about this particular work.

82. Jacqueline Hellegouarc'h (ed.), *Mémoires pour servir à la vie de M. de Voltaire, écrits par lui-même* (Paris, 2011), p. 124. The editor insists that this previously contested work is authentic.

83. Ibid., p. 10.

84. The full text is in *Œuvres*, vol. 11. There is a modern critical edition with commentary – Jürgen Ziechmann (ed.), *Friedrich der Grosse. Das Palladion* (Bremen, 1985). There is a convenient summary in German in E. Cauer, 'Über das Palladion, ein komisches Heldengedicht Friedrichs des Grossen', *Zeitschrift für preussische Geschichte und Landeskunde*, 3 (1866), pp. 484–99.

85. *Œuvres*, vol. 11, pp. 244–5. Perhaps not surprisingly, in this official edition, dated 1849, the words 'Jesus' and 'John' were replaced with '. .'.

See also Fritz J. Raddatz, '". . . die Erde freimütig zu kritisieren". Zum 200. Todestag Friedrichs II. erschien sein frivol-gotteslästerliches *Palladion*', *Die Zeit*, 34 (1986). Also deeply offensive to Christians, especially the Catholics among them, was Frederick's *Dialogue of the Dead between Mme de Pompadour and the Virgin Mary*, in which the former derides the latter as a promiscuous whore whose crucified son was sired either by a carpenter or a Roman soldier – Gerhard Knoll (ed.), *Friedrich II. König von Preussen. Totengespräch zwischen Madame de Pompadour und der Jungfrau Maria* (Berlin, 1999), p. 16. See also Jean Delinière, 'Friedrich II. König von Preussen, Totengespräch zwischen Madame de Pompadour und der Jungfrau Maria', *Annales historiques de la Révolution française*, 323, janvier-mars 2001, online since 6 April 2004, connection on 4 November 2014, http://ahrf.revues.org/1043.

86. Ziechmann (ed.), *Friedrich der Grosse. Das Palladion*, vol. 2, p. 67. The verse epistle can be found in *Œuvres*, vol. 10, pp. 238–49.

87. Winfried Baer, *Prunk-Tabatièren Friedrichs des Grossen* (Munich, 1993), p. 1. I am grateful to Dr Richard Edgcumbe of the Victoria and Albert Museum for drawing my attention to this important work.

88. Nina Simone Schepkowski, *Johann Ernst Gotzkowsky. Kunstagent und Gemäldesammler im friderizianischen Berlin* (Berlin, 2009), p. 22; Carsten Kretschmann, 'Präsentation und Repräsentation. Sammlungen und Kabinette als Schnittstellen einer *république des lettres*', in Sösemann, vol. 1, p. 311; Baer, *Prunk-Tabatièren Friedrichs des Grossen*, p. 2.

89. Hahn, *Friedrich II.*, p. 161. Baer, *Prunk-Tabatièren Friedrichs des Grossen*, p. 2.

90. Carlyle, vol. 4, p. 279; Baer, *Prunk-Tabatièren Friedrichs des Grossen*, p. 12.

91. Earl of Malmesbury (ed.), *Diaries and Correspondence of James Harris, First Earl of Malmesbury*, vol. 1, p. 6.

92. Baer, *Prunk-Tabatièren Friedrichs des Grossen*, p. 6.

93. Preuss, *Friedrich der Grosse*, vol. 1, p. 422.

94. Ibid., p. 427.

95. Frank Althoff, 'Die Arbeit im Kabinett', in Frank Althoff and Eef Overgaauw (eds.), *Homme de lettres. Frédéric. Der König am Schreibtisch* (Berlin, 2012), pp. 23–5.

96. See the description of the Austrian envoy Joseph Heinrich von Ried summarized in Luh, *Der Grosse. Friedrich II. von Preussen*, p. 46. The variations are discussed in Ute Christina Koch, Friederisiko, Ausstellung, pp. 312–21.

97. For a full discussion of Frederick's culinary life, see Bernd Maether, 'Kochen für den König. Der friderizianische Hof im Spiegel der Speisezettel und Hofrechnungen', in *Friedrich der Grosse und der Hof. Beiträge des zweiten Colloquiums in der Reihe 'Friedrich300' vom 10./11. Oktober 2008*, ed. Michael Kaiser and Jürgen Luh (Friedrich300 – Colloquien, 2), http://www.perspectivia.net/content/publikationen/friedrich300-colloquien/friedrich-hof/Maether_Kochen.

98. Abbé Denina, *Essai sur le règne de Fréderic II, Roi de Prusse* (Berlin, 1788), p. 400.

99. Preuss, *Friedrich der Grosse*, vol. 1, pp. 356–7.

100. Ibid.

101. Gerd Schurig, 'Die Blüte der Fruchtkultur im Sanssouci Friedrichs II.', in Friederisiko, Ausstellung, p. 60.

102. Ibid., pp. 56–61. Detlef Karg, 'Die Gärten Friedrichs II. Anmerkungen zur Gartenkunst in der Mark Brandenburg', in Erika Schmidt, Wilfried Hansmann and Jörg Gamer (eds.), *Garten. Kunstkammer. Geschichte. Festschrift für Dieter Hennebo zum 70. Geburtstag* (Worms am Rhein, 1994), pp. 110–11.

103. Schurig, 'Die Blüte der Fruchtkultur im Sanssouci Friedrichs II.', p. 61.

104. Preuss, *Friedrich der Grosse*, vol. 1, p. 355; Denina, *Essai sur le règne de Fréderic II*, p. 400.

105. His only enthusiastic comments about hunting stem from 1732–3 when he was trying to work his way back into his father's good books – Mario Huth, '"[...] denn gegenwärtig siehet es in den hiesigen Heyden etwas lüderlich aus". Forstliche Theorie und Praxis in Brandenburg-Preussen unter Friedrich II. – archivalische Stichproben', in Frank Göse (ed.), *Friedrich der Grosse und die Mark Brandenburg. Herrschaftspraxis in der Provinz* (Berlin, 2012), p. 267.

106. Reinhold Koser, *Friedrich der Grosse als Kronprinz* (Stuttgart, 1886), p. 214.

107. Charles Fleischauer (ed.), *L'Antimachiavel par Frédéric II, édition critique, Studies on Voltaire and the Eighteenth Century*, 5 (Geneva, 1958), pp. 254–9.

108. Ulrich Feldhahn, 'Die stillen Teilhaber der Macht – Friedrich der Grosse und seine Hünde', in Althoff and Overgaauw (eds.), *Homme de lettres. Frédéric*, pp. 129–33. As the breeds were not formally defined until the next century, it is not possible to categorize Frederick's dogs exactly.

109. John Murray Archive, 50 Albemarle Street, London, box. 1.

110. Preuss, *Friedrich der Grosse*, vol. 1, pp. 414–15.

111. *Doctor Zimmermann's Conversations with the Late King of Prussia, when he Attended Him in his Last Illness a Little before his Death* (London, 1791), p. 129.

112. Nadja Geissler, 'Condé', Friederisiko, Ausstellung, p. 337. Frederick William II treated Condé well, allowing him to see out his days at the Berlin Veterinary School, where he died in 1804 at the age of thirty-eight. His skeleton is on display at the Institute for Veterinary Anatomy at the Free University of Berlin.

113. Ingrid Mittenzwei, *Friedrich II. von Preussen* (Cologne, 1980), p. 74. In fact it was probably not a stroke but peripheral neuritis or neuropathy – Ida Macalpine and Richard Hunter, *George III and the Mad-Business* (London, 1969), p. 247.

114. Quoted in ibid., p. 252.

115. Paul Hartig (ed.), *Henri de Catt, Vorleser Friedrichs des Grossen. Die Tagebücher 1758–60* (Munich and Berlin, 1986), p. 74.

116. *Œuvres*, vol. 19, p. 105.

117. Koser, vol. 2, p. 285.

118. Walther Hubatsch, *Frederick the Great. Absolutism and Administration* (London, 1975), p. 124; Eva Ziebura, *August Wilhelm Prinz von Preussen* (Berlin, 2006), p. 90; Hans-Uwe Lammel, 'Philosophen, Leibärzte, Charlatane. Von königlichen Hämorrhoiden und anderen Malaisen', in Sösemann, vol. 1, pp. 52–67.

119. Macalpine and Hunter, *George III and the Mad-Business*, p. 253.

120. *Œuvres*, vol. 23, p. 401. Translation taken from Macalpine and Hunter, *George III and the Mad-Business*, p. 253.

121. *Œuvres*, vol. 22, p. 322.

122. Schieder, *Friedrich der Grosse*, p. 221. For a similar verdict, see Fritz Hartung, 'Die politischen Testamente der Hohenzollern', in Otto Büsch and Wolfgang Neugebauer (eds.), *Moderne Preussische Geschichte* (Berlin and New York, 1981), vol. 3, p. 1513.

123. Thomas Biskup and Peter H. Wilson, 'Grossbritannien, Amerika und die atlantische Welt', in Friederisiko, Ausstellung, p. 153. A Kalmuck was 'a member of a Mongolian people living on the north-west shores of the Caspian Sea'.

124. Koser, vol. 2, p. 347. See also Edward M. Furgol, 'Keith, George, styled tenth Earl Marischal (1692/3?–1778)', *Oxford Dictionary of National Biography*, Oxford University Press, 2004; online edn, May 2006, http://www.oxforddnb.com/view/article/15265. Accessed 13 October 2014.

125. Jürgen Luh, 'Freundschaften? – Verhältnisse. Friedrich und seine Ver-
trauten', in Friederisiko, Ausstellung, pp. 336–8.

126. Luh, *Der Grosse. Friedrich II. von Preussen*, pp. 212–16.

127. Denina, *Essai sur le règne de Fréderic II*, p. 354. See also the diaries of
Count Lehndorff for evidence contradicting the notion that Frederick
was a misanthrope after 1763.

128. *Œuvres*, vol. 25, p. 43.

129. Ibid., p. 62.

130. Ibid., p. 166. This letter is dated 1 May 1780.

131. Ibid., p. 91. The last two lines are quoted in Koser, vol. 2, p. 652.

132. Friedrich von Oppeln-Bronikowski and Gustav Berthold Volz (eds.),
*Das Tagebuch des Marchese Lucchesini (1780–1782). Gespräche mit
Friedrich dem Grossen* (Munich, 1926), p. 22.

133. Koser, vol. 2, p. 653.

134. Finot and Galmiche-Bouvier (eds.), *Une mission militaire en Prusse en
1786*, pp. 130–31.

CONCLUSION: DEATH AND TRANSFIGURATION

1. Hans-Uwe Lammel, 'Philosophen, Leibärzte, Charlatane. Von königlichen Hämorrhoiden und anderen Malaisen', in Sösemann, vol. 1, pp.
33, 54.

2. Koser, vol. 2, p. 654.

3. Ibid.

4. Ibid., pp. 655–6.

5. Present at the end were the chamber lackey Strützky, who had been
holding Frederick upright in the chair, two further servants, Dr Selle,
Hertzberg and General von Görtz – Karl Heinrich Siegfried Rödenbeck, *Tagebuch oder Geschichtskalender aus Friedrichs des Grossen
Regentenleben (1740–1786)* (Berlin, 1842), vol. 3, p. 365.

6. Koser, vol. 2, p. 657.

7. *Œuvres*, vol. 6, p. 243. There is a German translation in Otto Bardong
(ed.), *Friedrich der Grosse, Ausgewählte Quellen zur deutschen
Geschichte der Neuzeit*. Freiherr vom Stein-Gedächtnisausgabe (Darmstadt, 1982), vol. 22, p. 454.

8. Carlyle, vol. 6, p. 697.

9. Friedrich Laske, *Die Trauerfeierlichkeiten für Friedrich den Grossen,
mit Rekonstruktionen des Castrum Doloris im Stadtschloss und der
Auszierung der Hof- und Garnisonskirche zu Potsdam am 9.*

September 1786 (Berlin, 1912), pp. 7–9. This folio volume is lavishly illustrated.

10. Comte de Mirabeau, *The Secret History of the Court of Berlin* (London, 1895), vol. 1, p. 146. See also the report on the mood in Berlin quoted in Johann-Wolfgang Schottländer (ed.), *Carl Friedrich Zelters Darstellungen seines Lebens* (Weimar, 1931), p. 176.

11. Johannes Kunisch, *Friedrich der Grosse. Der König und seine Zeit* (Munich, 2004), p. 537; Eckhart Hellmuth, 'The funerals of the Prussian kings in the eighteenth century', in Michael Schaich (ed.), *Monarchy and Religion. The Transformation of Royal Culture in Eighteenth-century Europe* (Oxford, 2007), pp. 464–6.

12. Kunisch, *Friedrich der Grosse*, pp. 537–8. At least the funeral cantata composed by Reichardt with text by Lucchesini based on an Ode by Horace (*Quem virum aut heroa*) did not mention God, only 'Olympus' – Laske, *Die Trauerfeierlichkeiten* prints the Latin original and the German translation by Ramler.

13. 'Sarg und Asche', *Der Spiegel*, 33 (1991). Available online at http://www.spiegel.de/spiegel/print/d-13488171.html. No author is listed.

14. *Gedächtnisspredigt auf den allerdurchlauchtigsten, grossmächtigsten König und Herrn. Herrn Friederich den Zweyten, König von Preussen etc. etc.* (Berlin, 1786), p. xiv.

15. Eckhart Hellmuth, 'Die "Wiedergeburt" Friedrichs des Grossen und der "Tod fürs Vaterland". Zum patriotischen Selbstverständnis in Preussen in der zweiten Hälfte des 18. Jahrhunderts', *Aufklärung*, 10, 2 (1998), p. 27.

16. Eva Giloi, *Monarchy, Myth and Material Culture in Germany 1750–1950* (Cambridge, 2011), p. 88. This very interesting work contains many other examples.

17. Hellmuth, 'Die "Wiedergeburt" Friedrichs des Grossen und der "Tod fürs Vaterland"', p. 26.

18. Giloi, *Monarchy, Myth and Material Culture in Germany*, p. 109.

19. For a concise overview, see Karl Erich Born, 'Die Wirkungsgeschichte Friedrichs des Grossen', published as an epilogue to Hans Leuschner, *Friedrich der Grosse. Zeit – Person – Wirkung* (Gütersloh, 1986), pp. 205–32. For a fuller treatment, see Peter-Michael Hahn, *Friedrich der Grosse und die deutsche Nation: Geschichte als politisches Argument* (Stuttgart, 2007).

20. Leo Amadeus Graf Henckel Donnersmarck (ed.), *Briefe der Brüder Friedrichs des Grossen an meine Grosseltern* (Berlin, 1877), p. 54. Also quoted in Giles MacDonogh, *Frederick the Great. A Life in Deed and Letters* (New York, 1999), p. 385.

21. A German translation of the inscriptions can be found in Theodor Fontane, *Wanderungen durch die Mark Brandenburg*, ed. Helmuth Nürnberger (Munich, 2006), vol. 1, pp. 283–91. See also, Christian Graf von Krockow, *Die preussischen Brüder. Prinz Heinrich und Friedrich der Grosse. Ein Doppelporträt* (Stuttgart, 1996), p. 173.

22. Karin Feuerstein-Prasser, *'Ich bleibe zurück wie eine Gefangene'. Elisabeth Christine und Friedrich der Grosse* (Regensburg, 2011), p. 106.

23. Alfred P. Hagemann, 'Im Schatten des grossen Königs: Königin Elisabeth Christine und ihr Verhältnis zu Friedrich II.', in *Friedrich und die historische Grösse. Beiträge des dritten Colloquiums in der Reihe 'Friedrich300' vom 25./26. September 2009*, ed. Michael Kaiser and Jürgen Luh (Friedrich300 – Colloquien, 3), http://www.perspectivia.net/content/publikationen/friedrich300-colloquien/friedrich-groesse/hagemann_schatten. Last accessed 6 August 2014.

24. Enoch Powell, *Joseph Chamberlain* (London, 1977), p. 151.

25. Thomas Biskup, 'Das Schwert Friedrichs des Grossen: Universalhistorische "Grösse" und monarchische Genealogie in der napoleonischen Symbolpolitik nach *Iéna*', in Andreas Klinger, Hans-Werner Hahn and Georg Schmidt (eds.), *Das Jahr 1806 im europäischen Kontext. Balance, Hegemonie und politische Kulturen* (Cologne and Weimar, 2008), pp. 185–204.

26. Rudolf Ibbeken, *Preussen 1807–1813. Staat und Volk als Idee und in Wirklichkeit* (Berlin, 1970), pp. 91–4.

27. Ibid., p. 398.

28. Peter Paret, *Yorck and the Era of Prussian Reform, 1807–1815* (Princeton, 1966), p. 242.

Bibliographical Note

The past thirty years or so have witnessed an explosion in publications about Prussian history. Both symptom and cause was the great exhibition about Prussia held in the Berlin Museum of Applied Art (Kunstgewerbemuseum). This proved a colossal success. During the summer and autumn of 1981, more than half a million visitors passed through its thirty-three rooms to view the more than 2,000 artefacts. Their perambulation was assisted by a thick catalogue running to 600 pages, supported by four further volumes of essays on the political, social, cultural and cinematic history of Prussia.[1] Given that West Berlin was still an island in the inhospitable German Democratic Republic, the interest in Prussia's history it revealed was truly arresting. Moreover, the exhibition was only one manifestation of a much wider 'Prussian Wave' which had recently engulfed the public sphere in Germany. Timed to coincide with the exhibition was the appearance of a massive three-volume anthology on Prussian history edited by Otto Büsch and Wolfgang Neugebauer for the Historical Commission of Berlin, consisting of sixty-odd reprinted articles or extracts from books.[2] Two popular histories, Sebastian Haffner's *Prussia Without Legends* and Bernt Engelmann's *Prussia – Land of Unlimited Opportunities,* also proved to be bestsellers, quickly selling tens of thousands of copies in hardback alone.[3]

If the full force of this tsunami was soon spent, every now and again another big wave has rolled in to announce the continuing popularity of Prussian history. The most dramatic has been Christopher Clark's *Iron Kingdom: The Rise and Downfall of Prussia 1600–1947* of 2006, which deservedly achieved the Holy Grail that every professional historian seeks but hardly ever finds: public recognition (prizes galore), critical acclaim (laudatory reviews across the globe) and commercial success (months on the bestseller lists). More recently still, in 2012 the tercentenary of the birth of Prussia's most famous king unleashed a new flood of publications and media events. In the Neues Palais a grand exhibition was staged with the punning title

'Friederisiko' (perhaps best translated as 'Frederick the Risky'), covering every aspect of his long and busy life and reign. The two large-format and lavishly illustrated volumes published to mark the event were signally more entertaining and less didactic than their 1981 equivalents.[4] They also showed that horizons had widened. Sex hardly featured in the earlier exhibition, except rather tangentially in the volume of essays dealing with Prussia's cinematic history. 'Friederisiko' included an essay entitled '"Don't ask – don't tell" – Was Frederick gay?'

As this demonstrates, the austere agenda set by the advocates of 'critical social history' and Germany's allegedly 'special path' (*Sonderweg*), which dominated proceedings in 1981, has been both lightened and fragmented by new cultural perspectives. Topics previously ignored or marginalized have been moved to centre-stage. Among others, self-fashioning, representation, sexuality, music, theatre, collecting and court culture in general have all been plucked from obscurity. In that process, an important role has been played by technology. The proceedings of the eight conferences organized by Michael Kaiser, Jürgen Luh and others between 2007 and 2013 and published online by perspectivia.net have made an enormous contribution, both methodologically and substantively.[5] In this context, it should also be recorded that every historian of this period owes an incalculable debt to all those various agencies which have digitized both primary and secondary material. Pride of place must go to the University of Trier, which has put online the thirty volumes of Frederick's *Œuvres* and forty-six volumes of the still incomplete *Politische Correspondenz* (1740–82), together with other supporting material.[6] Thanks to digitization, all these volumes can be searched by individual word.* To this great resource can be added a huge amount of eighteenth-century printed material, which in the past had to be tracked down in far-flung libraries but can now be accessed from any device with an internet connection. Although the consequent reduction in the need to travel, a need which is also an opportunity, is regrettable in many ways, the rate of research has certainly been accelerated.

Ease of access was an asset enjoyed by the great archivist-historians of the nineteenth century, chief among them being Reinhold Koser, whose massive biography of Frederick remains the first point of reference for any aspiring successor.[7] Working through the 1,200 large pages of small print into which his *c.* 630,000 words are crammed is not a consistently invigorating experience, not to mention the need to grapple periodically with the nightmarish

---

* The search engine can be a false friend, however, for it does not always return every mention.

endnotes. By way of compensation, there is a constant sense of a scholar in full command of his material. Moreover, that material extends a long way beyond Frederick's life. As one of the best of the twentieth-century biographers, Arnold Berney, observed, what Koser offered was really 'a history of Prussia in the age of Frederick the Great'.[8] The same could be said of Koser's Austrian equivalent, the even more prolix Alfred Ritter von Arneth, the Viennese archivist who needed ten fat volumes to recount the life of the Empress Maria Theresa.[9] Also deserving of mention in this heavyweight division is Thomas Carlyle, whose six volumes are more substantial than they sound, for he takes the first five and a half to cover just the first half of the reign before galloping over the last part of the course.[10] His florid, highly idiosyncratic style is not to everyone's taste, and his penchant for what he himself dubbed 'hero-worship' even less so, but his sharp, quirky mind could often throw up insights denied his more stolid colleagues. He is also more entertaining.

Biographies on this scale went out of fashion in the less leisured twentieth century. Single-volume biographies of Frederick the Great, on the other hand, proliferated. The best of them, Arnold Berney's, fell victim to Nazi persecution. Of Jewish origin, Berney emigrated to Palestine after *Kristallnacht* and died at Jerusalem in 1943. If not exactly a bibliographical rarity, his book can be hard to find – it is in only six British libraries, for example. Much more ubiquitous, in both the original German edition of 1936 and the rather belated English translation of 1968, is Gerhard Ritter's short 'historical profile' of Frederick. As might have been expected from a Borussophile national conservative, the tone is also a good deal more friendly towards his subject.[11] By the time the first editions of these two books appeared in the mid-1930s, Frederick and his legacy were enmeshed in what Ritter later called a book: 'The German Problem'.[12] Not surprisingly, the National Socialists had gone to great pains to stress the continuity of Prusso-German history. On 31 March 1933, shortly after their seizure of power, they staged 'The Day of Potsdam' in the Garrison Church there, where Frederick the Great's coffin had been deposited (contrary to his wishes). Hitler's cynical gesture of obeisance to Hindenburg and the latter's reverential descent to Frederick's vault were intended to personify the union of old Prussia with the Third Reich.

The Nazis were not of course the first to politicize Frederick. The *kleindeutsch* German nationalists who sought a unified state without Austria lauded him as the hammer of the Habsburgs and the allegedly moribund Holy Roman Empire. One of the most prolific was J. D. E. Preuss, whose biography of Frederick published in 1832 bore as an epigraph a quotation from Jean Paul: 'The radiance of a genius such as Frederick illuminates the land around his throne just as the blaze of light shining from Correggio's Christ-Child falls on all those in His vicinity. A true prince bestows immortality not just on himself but on all those he governs.'[13] At the other end of the ideological spectrum was the Marxist Franz Mehring, who excoriated Frederick and his regime in *The Lessing Legend*, first published in 1891.[14] Modern-day equivalents have been Walther Hubatsch or Gerd Heinrich in the adulatory category and Rudolf Augstein or Wilhelm Bringmann in the denunciatory.[15] In short, because he has been so divisive, Frederick can claim to be the most controversial figure in German history, much more so than Adolf Hitler, on whom only one verdict is ever pronounced (in public, at least). A more balanced if generally favourable perspective is to be found in the two most substantial biographies of the recent past, by Theodor Schieder and Johannes Kunisch respectively.[16]

Literature on Frederick now exceeds the capacity of even the longest-lived and most industrious scholars. In 1988 Herzeleide and Eckart Henning published a bibliography of works on Frederick which included only titles in the German language but ran to more than 500 pages.[17] Given the extraordinary size and productivity of the German academic community, an updated version would probably be at least double that length. As the endnotes of this present volume reveal, it relies a great deal on the work of other historians, including, among many others, Jürgen Luh, Wolfgang Burgdorf, Thomas Biskup, Franziska Windt, Sabine Henze-Döhring, Christoph Vogtherr, Eckart Hellmuth, Frank Göse, Peter-Michael Hahn, Thomas Stamm-Kuhlmann, Ute Frevert, Ursula Pia Jauch, Andreas Pečar, Martin Engel, Tobias Schenk, Sven Externbrink, Marian Füssel, Bernd Sösemann – the list could be extended almost at will. What follows, in Further Reading, is a short list intended for Anglophone readers.

NOTES

1. *Preussen – Versuch einer Bilanz*, 5 vols. (Hamburg, 1981), 1: *Ausstellungsführer*, ed. Gottfried Korff, with text by Winfried Ranke; 2: *Preussen – Beiträge zu einer politischen Kultur. Aufsätze zur Geschichte Preussens*, ed. Manfred Schlenke; 3: *Preussen – Zur Sozialgeschichte eines Staates. Eine Darstellung in Quellen*, ed. Peter Brandt; 4: *Preussen – Dein Spree-Athen. Beiträge zu Literatur, Theater und Musik in Berlin*, ed. Hellmut Kühn; 5: *Preussen im Film*, ed. Axel Marquardt and Heinz Rathsack. The statistic relating to attendance is taken from Hagen Schulze's very entertaining article 'Preussen – Bilanz eines Versuchs', *Geschichte in Wissenschaft und Unterricht*, 32, 11 (1981), p. 649.

2. Otto Büsch and Wolfgang Neugebauer (eds.), *Moderne Preussische Geschichte 1648–1947*, 3 vols. (Berlin and New York, 1981).

3. Sebastian Haffner, *Preussen ohne Legende* (Hamburg, 1979); Bernt Engelmann, *Preussen. Land der unbegrenzten Möglichkeiten* (Munich, 1979).

4. Jürgen Luh and Ullrich Sachse (eds.), *Friederisiko. Friedrich der Grosse*, 2 vols. (Munich, 2012).

5. http://www.perspectivia.net/content/publikationen/friedrich300-colloq uien. Many of the contributions were republished in the two volumes of *Friederisiko*.

6. http://friedrich.uni-trier.de/de/static/projektbeschreibung/.

7. Reinhold Koser, *König Friedrich der Grosse*, 2 vols., 3rd edn (Stuttgart and Berlin, 1904). The first edition was published in two instalments in 1902 and 1904. As the appearance of a third edition in the same year as the first edition of the second volume suggests, it was a considerable popular success.

8. Arnold Berney, *Friedrich der Grosse. Entwicklungsgeschichte eines Staatsmannes* (Tübingen, 1934), p. iii.

9. Alfred Ritter von Arneth, *Geschichte Maria Theresias*, 10 vols. (Vienna, 1863–79).

10. Thomas Carlyle, *History of Friedrich II. of Prussia, Called Frederick the Great*, 6 vols. (London, 1858–65).

11. Gerhard Ritter, *Friedrich der Grosse. Ein historisches Profil* (Leipzig, 1954); *Frederick the Great. A Historical Profile*, trans. Peter Paret (London, 1968).

12. Gerhard Ritter, *Das deutsche Problem; Grundfragen deutschen Staatslebens, gestern und heute* (Munich, 1962).

13. J. D. E. Preuss, *Friedrich der Grosse. Eine Lebensgeschichte* (Berlin, 1832), vol. 1, title page. Just how Frederick might have reacted to this comparison is a good question.

14. There is a substantial extract in Büsch and Neugebauer (eds.), *Moderne preussische Geschichte 1648–1947*, vol. 1, pp. 142–81.

15. Walther Hubatsch, *Frederick the Great of Prussia. Absolutism and Administration* (London, 1975); Gerd Heinrich, *Friedrich II. von Preussen: Leistung und Leben eines grossen Königs* (Berlin, 2009); Rudolf Augstein, *Preussens Friedrich und die Deutschen* (Nördlingen, 1986); Wilhelm Bringmann, *Friedrich der Grosse. Ein Porträt* (Munich, 2006).

16. Theodor Schieder, *Friedrich der Grosse. Ein Königtum der Widersprüche* (Frankfurt am Main, Berlin and Vienna, 1983). A lightly

abbreviated version was published in an excellent translation by Sabine Berkeley and Hamish Scott in 2000. Johannes Kunisch, *Friedrich der Grosse. Der König und seine Zeit* (Munich, 2004).

17. *Bibliographie Friedrich der Grosse, 1786–1986: das Schrifttum des deutschen Sprachraums und der Übersetzungen aus Fremdsprachen* (Berlin, 1988). It can be supplemented by the selective bibliography compiled by Bernd Sösemann in Sösemann, vol. 2, pp. 479–542.

Further Reading

Adamson, John, 'The making of the Ancien Régime court 1500–1700', in idem (ed.), *The Princely Courts of Europe. Ritual, Politics and Culture under the Ancien Régime 1500–1750* (London, 1999)

Altmann, Alexander, *Moses Mendelssohn: a Biographical Study* (London, 1973)

Anderson, M. S., *The War of the Austrian Succession 1740–1748* (London, 1995)

Bauman, Thomas, 'Courts and municipalities in North Germany', in Neal Zaslaw (ed.), *The Classical Era. From the 1740s to the End of the Eighteenth Century* (London, 1989)

Beales, Derek, *Joseph II*, vol. 1: *In the Shadow of Maria Theresa 1741–1780* (Cambridge, 1987); vol. 2: *Against the World, 1780–1790* (Cambridge, 2009)

Behrens, C. B. A., *Society, Government and the Enlightenment: the Experiences of Eighteenth-century France and Prussia* (London, 1985)

Berdahl, Robert M., *The Politics of the Prussian Nobility. The Development of a Conservative Ideology 1770–1848* (Princeton, 1988)

Bernard, Paul P., *Joseph II and Bavaria: Two Eighteenth-century Attempts at German Unification* (The Hague, 1965)

Besterman, Theodore, 'Voltaire's commentary on Frederick's *Art de la guerre*', *Studies on Voltaire and the Eighteenth Century*, 2 (1956)

Biskup, Thomas, 'The hidden queen: Elizabeth Christine of Prussia and Hohenzollern queenship in the eighteenth century', in Clarissa Campbell Orr (ed.), *Queenship in Europe, 1660–1815. The Role of the Consort* (Cambridge, 2004)

Bisset, Andrew (ed.), *Memoirs and Papers of Sir Andrew Mitchell K.B.*, 2 vols. (London, 1850)

Blanning, Tim, '"That horrid electorate" or "Ma patrie germanique"? George III, Hanover and the *Fürstenbund* of 1785', *The Historical Journal*, 20, 2 (1977)

—, *Joseph II* (London, 1994)

—, *The Culture of Power and the Power of Culture. Old Regime Europe 1660–1789* (Oxford, 2002)

—, *The Pursuit of Glory: Europe 1648–1815* (London, 2007)

Boyle, Nicholas, *Goethe. The Poet and the Age*, vol. 1: *The Poetry of Desire* (Oxford, 1991)

Butterfield, Herbert, 'The reconstruction of an historical episode: the history of the enquiry into the origins of the Seven Years War', in idem, *Man on his Past* (Cambridge, 1969)

Carlyle, Thomas, *History of Friedrich II. of Prussia, Called Frederick the Great*, 6 vols. (London, 1858–65)

Clark, Christopher, *The Politics of Conversion. Missionary Protestantism and the Jews in Prussia 1728–1941* (Oxford, 1995)

—, *Iron Kingdom. The Rise and Downfall of Prussia 1600–1947* (London, 2006)

Clausewitz, Carl von, *On War*, ed. and trans. Michael Howard and Peter Paret (Princeton, 1976)

Craig, Gordon A., *The Politics of the Prussian Army* (Oxford, 1955)

Danley, Mark H., and Patrick J. Speelman (eds.), *The Seven Years War: Global Views* (Leiden, 2013)

Davies, Norman, *God's Playground. A History of Poland*, 2 vols. (Oxford, 1981)

Dixon, Simon, *Catherine the Great* (London, 2001)

—, *Catherine the Great* (London, 2009)

Dorn, Walter L., 'The Prussian bureaucracy in the eighteenth century', *Political Science Quarterly*, 46–7 (1931–2)

Duffy, Christopher, *The Army of Frederick the Great* (Newton Abbot, 1974)

—, *The Army of Maria Theresa* (London, 1977)

—, *Russia's Military Way to the West. Origins and Nature of Russian Military Power 1700–1800* (London, 1981)

—, *Frederick the Great. A Military Life* (London, 1985)

—, *The Fortress in the Age of Vauban and Frederick the Great* (London, 1985)

Dwyer, Philip G. (ed.), *The Rise of Prussia 1700–1830* (Harlow, 2000)

Easum, Chester V., *Prince Henry of Prussia. Brother of Frederick the Great* (Westport, CT, 1942)

Eddie, S. A., *Freedom's Price. Serfdom, Subjection and Reform in Prussia, 1648–1848* (Oxford, 2013)

Eldon, Carl William, *England's Subsidy Policy towards the Continent during the Seven Years War* (Philadelphia, 1938)

Epstein, Klaus, *The Genesis of German Conservatism* (Princeton, 1966)

Ergang, Robert, *The Potsdam Führer: Frederick William I, Father of Prussian Militarism* (New York, 1941)

Evans, R. J. W., Michael Schaich and Peter H. Wilson (eds.), *The Holy Roman Empire 1495–1806: New Perspectives* (Oxford, 2011)

Evans, Richard J., *Rituals of Retribution. Capital Punishment in Germany 1600–1987* (Oxford, 1996)

Forsyth, Michael, *Buildings for Music. The Architect, the Musician, and the Listener from the Seventeenth Century to the Present Day* (Cambridge, MA, 1985)

Fraser, David, *Frederick the Great* (London, 2000)

Frederick the Great, *Posthumous Works*, 13 vols. (London, 1789)

—, *The Refutation of Machiavelli's The Prince or Anti-Machiavel*, ed. Paul Sonnino (Athens, OH, 1981)

Friedrich, Karin, *Brandenburg-Prussia 1466–1806. The Rise of a Composite State* (Basingstoke, 2012)

Gay, Peter, 'Voltaire's anti-Semitism', in idem, *The Party of Humanity. Studies in the French Enlightenment* (London, 1964)

—, *Voltaire's Politics* (New York, n.d.)

Giloi, Eva, *Monarchy, Myth and Material Culture in Germany 1750–1950* (Cambridge, 2011)

Gooch, G. P., *Frederick the Great* (London, 1947)

Hagen, William W., *Ordinary Prussians: Brandenburg Junkers and Villagers, 1500–1840* (Cambridge, 2002)

Hardman, John, and Munro Price (eds.), *Louis XVI and the Comte de Vergennes: Correspondence 1774–1787*, *Studies on Voltaire and the Eighteenth Century*, vol. 364 (Oxford, 1998)

Hellmuth, Eckhart, 'The funerals of the Prussian kings in the eighteenth century', in Michael Schaich (ed.), *Monarchy and Religion. The Transformation of Royal Culture in Eighteenth-century Europe* (Oxford, 2007)

Helm, E. E., *Music at the Court of Frederick the Great* (Norman, 1960)

Henderson, W. O., *Studies in the Economic Policy of Frederick the Great* (London, 1963)

Hochedlinger, Michael, *Austria's Wars of Emergence. War, State and Society in the Habsburg Monarchy 1683–1797* (London, 2003)

Horn, D. B., *British Public Opinion and the First Partition of Poland* (Edinburgh and London, 1945)

—, 'The Diplomatic Revolution', in *The New Cambridge Modern History*, vol. 7: *The Old Regime 1713–63*, ed. J. O. Lindsay (Cambridge, 1970)

Hubatsch, Walther, *Frederick the Great. Absolutism and Administration* (London, 1975)

Ingrao, Charles W., *The Habsburg Monarchy 1618–1815*, 2nd edn (Cambridge, 2000)

Johnson, Hubert C., *Frederick the Great and his Officials* (New Haven and London, 1975)

Jones, Colin, *The Great Nation. France from Louis XV to Napoleon* (London, 2002)

Lavisse, Ernest, *The Youth of Frederick the Great*, trans. Mary Bushnell Coleman (Chicago, 1892)

Lloyd, Henry, *The History of the Late War in Germany between the King of Prussia and the Empress of Germany and her Allies*, 2 vols. (London, 1781)

Lord, Robert Howard, *The Second Partition of Poland. A Study in Diplomatic History*, Harvard Historical Studies, vol. 23 (Cambridge, MA, 1915)

Luebke, David M., 'Frederick the Great and the celebrated case of the Millers Arnold (1770–1779): A Reappraisal', *Central European History*, 32, 4 (1999)

Lukowski, Jerzy, *The Partitions of Poland 1772, 1793, 1795* (London, 1999)

Luvaas, Jay, 'Student as teacher: Clausewitz on Frederick the Great and Napoleon', *The Journal of Strategic Studies*, 9, 2–3 (1986)

— (ed.), *Frederick the Great on the Art of War* (New York and London, 1966)

MacDonogh, Giles, *Frederick the Great. A Life in Deed and Letters* (New York, 1999)

Madariaga, Isabel de, *Russia in the Age of Catherine the Great* (London, 1981)

Mansel, Philip, *Prince of Europe: the Life of Charles Joseph de Ligne (1735–1814)* (London, 2003)

Meinecke, Friedrich, *Machiavellism. The Doctrine of Raison d'État and Its Place in Modern History* (London, 1957)

Melton, Edgar, 'The Prussian Junkers, 1600–1786', in H. M. Scott (ed.), *The European Nobilities in the Seventeenth and Eighteenth Centuries*, 2 vols. (London, 1995)

Melton, James Van Horn, *Absolutism and the Eighteenth-century Origins of Compulsory Schooling in Prussia and Austria* (Cambridge, 1988)

—, *The Rise of the Public in Enlightenment Europe* (Cambridge, 2001)

Mirabeau, Comte de, *The Secret History of the Court of Berlin*, 2 vols. (London, 1895)

Mitford, Nancy, *Frederick the Great* (London, 1970)

Moore, John, *A View of Society and Manners in France, Switzerland and Germany*, 2 vols., 4th edn (Dublin, 1789)

Newman, William S., 'Emanuel Bach's autobiography', *The Musical Quarterly*, 51, 2 (1965)

Nisbet, H. B., *Gotthold Ephraim Lessing. His Life, Works, and Thought* (Oxford, 2008)

Ogilvie, Sheilagh C., 'The beginnings of industrialisation', in idem (ed.), *Germany: a New Social and Economic History*, vol. 2: *1630–1800* (London, 1996)

Oliva, Lawrence Jay, *Misalliance: a Study of French Policy in Russia during the Seven Years War* (New York, 1964)

Paret, Peter, *Yorck and the Era of Prussian Reform, 1807–1815* (Princeton, 1966)

— (ed.), *Frederick the Great: a Profile* (New York, 1972)

Parrott, David, 'Armed forces', in William Doyle (ed.), *The Oxford Handbook of the Ancien Régime* (Oxford, 2012)

Pearson, Roger, *Voltaire Almighty. A Life in the Pursuit of Freedom* (London, 2005)

Reiss, Hans (ed.), *Kant's Political Writings* (Cambridge, 1970)

Ritter, Gerhard, *Frederick the Great. An Historical Profile*, trans. with an introduction by Peter Paret (London, 1968)

Rosenberg, Hans, *Bureaucracy, Aristocracy and Autocracy. The Prussian Experience 1660–1815* (Boston, 1966)

Rothenberg, Gunther, *The Art of Warfare in the Age of Napoleon* (London, 1977)

Schieder, Theodor, *Frederick the Great*, trans. Sabina Berkeley and H. M. Scott (Harlow, 2000)

Scholes, Percy A. (ed.), *An Eighteenth-century Musical Tour in Central Europe and the Netherlands. Being Dr Charles Burney's Account of his Musical Experiences* (London, 1959)

Schroeder, Paul W., *The Transformation of European Politics 1763–1848* (Oxford, 1994)

Schui, Florian, 'Learning from French experience? The Prussian *Régie* tax administration, 1766–86', in Holger Nehring and Florian Schui (eds.), *Global Debates about Taxation* (Basingstoke, 2007)

—, *Rebellious Prussians. Urban Political Culture under Frederick the Great and his Successors* (Oxford, 2013)

Schumann, Matt, and Schweizer, Karl, *The Seven Years War: a Transatlantic History* (London and New York)

Scott, H. M., 'Frederick II, the Ottoman Empire and the origins of the Russo-Prussian alliance of April 1764', *European Studies Review*, 7 (1977)

—, 'Prussia's royal foreign minister: Frederick the Great and the administration of Prussian diplomacy', in Robert Oresko and Graham Gibbs (eds.), *Royal and Republican Sovereignty: Essays in Memory of Ragnhild Hatton* (Cambridge, 1997)

—, *The Emergence of the Eastern Powers, 1756–1775* (Cambridge, 2001)

—, *The Birth of a Great Power System 1740–1815* (London, 2006)

—, (ed.), *Enlightened Absolutism. Reform and Reformers in Later Eighteenth-century Europe* (London, 1990)

Sheehan, James J., *German History 1770–1866* (Oxford, 1989)

—, *Museums in the German Art World. From the End of the Old Regime to the Rise of Modernism* (New York, 2000)

Showalter, Dennis, *The Wars of Frederick the Great* (London, 1996)

Simms, Brendan, *Three Victories and a Defeat. The Rise and Fall of the First British Empire, 1714–1783* (London, 2007)

—, *Europe. The Struggle for supremacy 1453 to the Present* (London, 2013)

Smith, Hannah, and Stephen Taylor, 'Hephaestion and Alexander: Lord Hervey, Frederick, Prince of Wales, and the royal favourite in England in the 1730s', *English Historical Review*, 507 (2009)

Steakley, James, 'Sodomy in Enlightenment Prussia: from execution to suicide', *Journal of Homosexuality*, 16, 1–2 (1989)

Strachey, Lytton, 'Voltaire and Frederick the Great', in idem, *Books and Characters, French and English* (London, 1922)

Szabo, Franz A. J., *The Seven Years War in Europe, 1756–1763* (London, 2008)

Temperley, H. W. V., *Frederic the Great and Kaiser Joseph. An Episode of War and Diplomacy in the Eighteenth Century* (London, 1968)

Thompson, Andrew, *George II. King and Elector* (New Haven and London, 2011)

Umbach, Maiken, 'The politics of sentimentality and the German *Fürstenbund*', *The Historical Journal*, 41, 3 (1998)

Vogtherr, Christoph Martin, 'Absent love in pleasure houses. Frederick II of Prussia as art collector and patron', *Art History*, 24, 2 (2001)

Walser Smith, Helmut, 'The poetry of friendship and the prose of patriotic sacrifice in Prussia during the Seven Years War', *Berliner Aufklärung: kulturwissenschaftliche Studien*, ed. Ursula Goldenbaum and Alexander Košenina (Hanover, 2013)

Warrack, John, *German Opera. From the Beginnings to Wagner* (Cambridge, 2001)

Watkin, David, and Tilman Mellinghoff, *German Architecture and the Classical Ideal 1740–1840* (London, 1987)

Whaley, Joachim, *Germany and the Holy Roman Empire*, 2 vols. (Oxford, 2012)

Wilson, Peter H., *German Armies. War and German Politics 1648–1806* (London, 1998)

—, 'Prussia's relations with the Holy Roman Empire, 1740–1786', *The Historical Journal*, 51, 2 (2008)

—, *The Holy Roman Empire 1495–1806*, 2nd edn (London, 2011)

Wraxall, N. William, *Memoirs of the Courts of Berlin, Dresden, Warsaw and Vienna in the Years 1777, 1778 and 1779*, 2 vols., 3rd edn (London, 1806)

Acknowledgements

In one way or another, I have been reading and writing about Frederick the Great of Prussia for as long as I can remember. German history in general and Prussian history in particular have certainly been a feature of historical scholarship in Cambridge since my student days, beginning with lectures by Sir Herbert Butterfield and Betty Behrens. In the intervening decades, I have incurred many debts, especially to the numerous colleagues who collaborated on a course on German history from 1740 to 1914, including Jonathan Steinberg, Chris Clark, Brendan Simms, Jo Whaley, Niall Ferguson, Barry Nisbet, Nicholas Boyle, Maiken Umbach, Richard Evans and Bernhard Fulda. The first three on that list also read my completed text, making many helpful suggestions and penetrating criticisms. I have also benefited immeasurably from the congenial environment of Sidney Sussex College, which has allowed many questions to be asked and answered over lunch or dinner. In particular, Emma Gilby has helped me to unravel some tricky French language problems. As ever, Derek Beales has been a constant source of encouragement and stimulation. I also record my gratitude to Richard Edgcumbe, Oliver Cox, Virginia Murray, the late (and much lamented) Hagen Schulze, Uwe Puschner, Hamish Scott, Peter Wilson, Heinz Duchhardt, Heinrich Meier, Katrin Kohl, Jürgen Luh, Andreas Pečar, Christoph Vogtherr, James Pullen and Jonathan Jao. I count myself extremely fortunate to have been assisted by an agent, Andrew Wylie, and an editor, Simon Winder, who have been consistently supportive, constructively critical and patient. Of the numerous libraries I have worked in over the years, I am particularly indebted to the Seeley Historical Library and the University Library in Cambridge, the British Library and the Athenaeum in London, the Nationalbibliothek in Vienna, the Staatsbibliothek in Berlin, the Staatsbibliothek in Munich and the Bibliothèque de France in Paris. Although not always aware of it, my family have kept me going by making it all seem worthwhile and it is to them that this book is dedicated.

611

Index

Potsdam 33, 36, 60, 108, 122,
124, 149, 150, 157,
158, 267
French Church 170
Garrison Church 459, 463
Hiller-Brandtsche House 170
hunting lodge 28
leather factory 382
Nauener Gate 170
Neues Palais (New Palace) 141,
163, 165, 166–9, 174,
178, 285, 351, 423, 435,
443, 445
Nikolaikirche 169
Sanssouci Palace 24, 26, 60, 119,
160, 162–9, 172, 175–8, 273,
324, 351, 383–4, 413, 430,
432, 444–53, 457; burial of
dogs at 452; greenhouses 451;
kitchens 450–52; Napoleon's
visit to 463; paintings and
sculpture at 175, 176–8;
Park 454
Town Palace 149, 158, 159, 162,
163, 164, 168, 169, 171, 174,
175, 176, 273, 351, 430, 450,
456, 458, 459, 508–9n
Wilhelmsplatz 421; Palace of the
Order of St John 435
Powell, Enoch 462
'Pragmatic Army' 106
Pragmatic Sanction 74–5, 89, 90
Prague 101, 108–9, 186, 208, 209,
216, 272
Archbishop of 101
battle of 211–16, 224, 232
Praxiteles 69
Premet, Cistercian Abbey 374
Press, Volker 316
Preuss, J. D. E. 36, 445
prisons, Prussian 391
Privy Council 6
Probst, Georg Balthasar 375
Prometheus 329
protectionism 425

Protestantism 4, 8, 11, 18, 37, 93,
109, 136, 186, 200, 220, 284,
348, 350–51, 370–71, 371,
373, 377
Prussia xxiii, 22, 121–2
Academy 121
accused of despotism 121
agriculture in 412–15
army 11–15, 403–7, 427, 429
banking in 425–6
canals and waterways 415–16
cotton industry 424–5
court life in 430–33
crime and punishment in 387–91
education in 410–12
Freemasonry in 341
General Directory 10, 187, 402, 425
General Law Code 397, 398
immigration to 414–15
law and justice in 391–400, 402
linen industry 420
literacy and reading in 338–40
porcelain production 421–4
as *Rechtsstaat* 356
religious toleration in 373
silk industry 420–21, 424
Supreme Court established in 392
taxation 10, 24, 130, 262, 392,
426, 427–8
textile industries 419–21
trade deficit 418–19
trade and manufacturing in 416–29
War and Domains Chambers 10,
129, 397, 418
woollen industry 419–20, 422,
424, 425
Pruth, river 285
Pulteney, William 65
Puttkamer family 405
Puysieux, Marquis de 194

Quadruple Alliance 110
Quantz, Johann Joachim xxii, 34, 49,
149–52, 157, 454
Querelle des Bouffons 148–9